MS

THE ECONOMICS OF ENVIRONMENTAL REGULATION

ECONOMISTS OF THE TWENTIETH CENTURY

General Editors: Mark Perlman, *University Professor of Economics, Emeritus, University of Pittsburgh* and Mark Blaug, *Professor Emeritus, University of London, Professor Emeritus, University of Buckingham* and *Visiting Professor, University of Exeter*

This innovative series comprises specially invited collections of articles and papers by economists whose work has made an important contribution to economics in the late twentieth century.

The proliferation of new journals and the ever-increasing number of new articles make it difficult for even the most assiduous economist to keep track of all the important recent advances. By focusing on those economists whose work is generally recognized to be at the forefront of the discipline, the series will be an essential reference point for the different specialisms included.

A list of published and future titles in this series is printed at the end of this volume.

The Economics of Environmental Regulation

Wallace E. Oates

Professor of Economics, University of Maryland, and University Fellow, Resources for the Future, US

Wallace E. Oates

Professor of Economics, University of Maryland, and University Fellow, Resources for the Future, US

ECONOMISTS OF THE TWENTIETH CENTURY

Edward Elgar
Cheltenham, UK • Brookfield, US

333.7
Olle

ſH

Published by
Edward Elgar Publishing Limited
8 Lansdown Place
Cheltenham
Glos GL50 2HU
UK

Edward Elgar Publishing Company
Old Post Road
Brookfield
Vermont 05036
US

British Library Cataloguing in Publication Data
Oates, Wallace E.
  Economics of Environmental Regulation. –
  (Economists of the Twentieth Century
  Series)
  I. Title II. Series
  333.7

Library of Congress Cataloguing in Publication Data
Oates, Wallace E.
   The economics of environmental regulation / Wallace E. Oates.
   (Economists of the twentieth century)
   Includes bibliographical references and index.
   1. Environmental economics. 2. Environmental impact charges.
3. Environmental policy. 4. Environmental law. I. Title.
II. Series.
HC79.E5025 1996
332.7—dc20   95–39637
                                                                  CIP

ISBN 1 85278 743 0

Printed and bound in Great Britain by
Hartnolls Limited, Bodmin, Cornwall

To Grace Mary

Contents

Acknowledgements

The publishers wish to thank the following who have kindly given permission for the use of copyright material.

Academic Press Inc for articles: 'The Use of Effluent Fees to Regulate Public Sector Sources of Pollution: An Application of the Niskanen Model', *Journal of Environmental Economics and Management*, **5**(3), September 1978, 283–91; 'On Marketable Air-Pollution Permits: The Case for a System of Pollution Offsets', with Alan J. Krupnick and Eric Van de Verg, *Journal of Environmental Economics and Management*, **10**(3), September 1983, 233–47; 'Marketable Permits for the Prevention of Environmental Deterioration', with Albert M. McGartland, *Journal of Environmental Economics and Management*, **12**(3), September 1985, 207–28.

American Economics Association for articles: 'The Net Benefits of Incentive-Based Regulation: A Case Study of Environmental Standard Setting', with Albert M. McGartland and Paul R. Portney, *American Economic Review*, **79**(5), December 1989, 1233–42; 'Environmental Economics: A Survey', with Maureen L. Cropper, *Journal of Economic Literature*, **XXX**, June 1992, 675–740.

Blackwell Publishers for article: 'The Use of Standards and Prices for Protection of the Environment', with William J. Baumol, *Swedish Journal of Economics*, **73**, March 1971, 42–54.

Canadian Economics Association for articles: 'Efficiency in Pollution Control in the Short and Long Runs: A System of Rental Emission Permits', with Robert A. Collinge, *Canadian Journal of Economics*, **XV**(2), May 1982, 346–54; 'Marketable Pollution Permits and Acid Rain Externalities: A Comment and Some Further Evidence', with Albert M. McGartland, *Canadian Journal of Economics*, **XVIII**(3), August 1985, 668–75.

Columbia University Press for article: 'The Instruments for Environmental Policy', with William J. Baumol in *Economic Analysis of Environmental Problems* (ed. Edwin S. Mills), Columbia University Press, 1975, 95–128.

Eastern Economic Association for articles: 'Economics, Economists, and Environmental Policy', **XVI**(4), October–December 1990, 289–96; 'Economic Incentives and the Containment of Global Warming', with Paul R. Portney, *Eastern Economic Journal*, **18**(1), Winter 1992, 85–98.

Elsevier Science Publishers for articles: 'Effluent Fees and Market Structure', with Diana L. Strassman, *Journal of Public Economics*, **24**, 1984, 29–46; 'Economic Competition Among Jurisdictions: Efficiency Enhancing or Distortion Inducing?', with Robert M. Schwab, *Journal of Public Economics*, **35**, 1988, 333–54.

OECD for article: 'Environment and Taxation: The Case of the United States', in *Environment and Taxation: The Case of the Netherlands, Sweden and the United States*, OECD, 1994, 103–43.

Public Finance/Finances Publique for article: 'The Regulation of Externalities: Efficient Behavior by Sources and Victims', *Public Finance*, **XXXVIII**(3), 1983, 362–75.

Routledge for article: 'Market Incentives for Environmental Protection: A Survey of Some Recent Developments', in *Prices, Competition and Equilibrium*, M. Peston and R. Quandt, eds, Philip Allen, 1986, 251–67.

Sage Periodicals Press for article: 'Corrective Taxes and Auctions of Rights in the Control of Externalities: Some Further Thoughts', *Public Finance Quarterly*, **9**(4), October 1981, 471–478.

University of California Press for article: 'The Environment and the Economy: Environmental Policy at the Crossroads', in *American Domestic Priorities: An Economic Appraisal*, J. Quigley and D. Rubinfeld, eds, University of California Press, 1985, 311–45.

University of Pennsylvania Law Review for article: Book Review of '*The Uncertain Search for Environmental Quality*', *University of Pennsylvania Law Review*, **124**(3), January 1976, 864–91.

Introduction

This is an exciting time to be an environmental economist. Environmental issues have come to the fore and are the subject of continuing concern and new legislation. The 'Environmental Revolution' of the 1960s has certainly not lost its steam. On the contrary, as we have learned more about the diverse sorts of environmental threats posed by a wide variety of human activities, the scope and levels of environmental programs have continued to expand. The basic concerns in the early 1970s with problems of domestic air and water quality have extended to broader global issues of transfrontier pollution, acid-rain deposition and potential global warming. A new subfield of 'open economy environmental economics' is coming into being.

Moreover, in recent years policy makers have shown a growing interest in, and receptivity to, incentive-based regulatory instruments for environmental management. In the early days of environmental legislation, the economic aspects of environmental regulation were largely ignored. In the United States, for example, the Clean Air Act Amendments of 1970 and the Clean Water Act Amendments of 1972, the cornerstones of the new Federal legislation emerging from the environmental revolution, were firmly grounded in the traditional Command-And-Control (CAC) approach to regulation. Under these measures, environmental authorities were directed to set standards for environmental quality *without* regard to their cost and then to promulgate source-specific directions to polluters on their required reductions in waste emissions. Likewise, policy makers in Europe eschewed economic incentives for environmental management in favor of direct controls of the sort adopted by their counterparts across the Atlantic.

But there have been dramatic changes. The basic philosophy of regulatory management has undergone a striking transformation: it has become more circumspect towards traditional regulatory measures and more sympathetic to market approaches to our social and economic problems. We hear more about 'regulatory failure' and less about 'market failure'. From this perspective, legislators and environmental administrators have, in many instances, heard the counsel of economists (and others), and this has manifested itself in some exciting new programs for environmental management. In the 1990 Amendments to the Clean Air Act, for example, the U.S. Congress has established a national market for sulfur emissions to address the troubling acid-rain problem. Under these provisions, sources across the nation are enabled to buy and sell entitlements to a limited quantity of sulfur discharges into the atmosphere, leaving sources themselves to determine both the levels of their emissions and the abatement technology. Under this regime, sulfur emissions in the U.S. are scheduled to be cut in half over the next decade. In Europe, the prevailing tendency is not towards systems of marketable rights, but rather toward Green Taxes. Such taxes on polluting activities serve directly to discourage damaging waste emissions and to raise revenues for projects to clean up the environment.

With this growing interest in the economics of environmental management, the community of environmental economists has expanded from a dedicated handful of 'laborers in the vineyard' in the 1960s to a large and energetic body of researchers and policy analysts. Programs of study in 'environmental and natural resource economics' have sprung up in major universities around the world, producing new PhD's with dissertations on pressing issues in the field. In the U.S., the new field was formally recognized in 1981 with the establishment of the Association of Environmental and Resource Economists (AERE). The Association has grown to over 700 members, and has given birth to a sister organization in Europe, which is holding its own conferences and supporting important research.

It has been a fascinating and exciting experience to be part of the evolution of this new field, and Edward Elgar has invited me to take a little space here to reminisce. Following graduate school, my own research focused upon public finance with a particular interest in state and local government finance. But in the late 1960s, I had an opportunity to attend a seminar on environmental policy given by Allen Kneese of Resources for the Future. Kneese, an articulate and engaging speaker, made two things abundantly clear. First, the U.S., with its newly born concern with environmental issues, was headed down a legislative path involving exclusive reliance on traditional command-and-control techniques and with little understanding or consideration of the important economic dimensions of environmental issues. Second, Kneese argued persuasively that economics had much to contribute to the design and implementation of effective policies for environmental protection. Kneese was one of the early voices crying in the wilderness, and I have come to regard him as the 'father' of environmental economics. It came as no surprise in 1990 when the Swedes awarded Kneese, jointly with John Krutilla, the first Volvo Prize in Environmental Science. At any rate, Kneese both convinced and excited me with the potential contribution of economics to environmental policy.

At about this same time, William Baumol, a colleague at Princeton University, was reaching similar conclusions. Will suggested that we join forces on a major project consisting of two components: a book on the pure theory of environmental regulation, and a companion volume addressed to a broader audience of policy makers and interested laymen that would set forth the economist's perspective on environmental issues and policy. The purpose of the first volume was to assemble in a systematic and rigorous way the basic economic theory of environmental regulation and to try to extend it in certain ways. The second volume, which would follow on from the first, would then try to take the economist's message to the wider public. We signed a contract for both volumes with Prentice-Hall and in the subsequent decade completed the two books. *The Theory of Environmental Policy* appeared in 1975, and was later revised (both updated and extended to some new topics) in a second edition (1988) with Cambridge University Press. The second book, *Economics, Environmental Policy, and the Quality of Life*, appeared in 1979; it has been reprinted in the U.K.

In addition to these two books, my research efforts in environmental economics have extended to a series of papers on a variety of topics. I am delighted to have this opportunity to draw the papers together in a systematic way. The collection begins (Part I) with some papers that essentially step back from the field and provide an overall assessment. The first is the text of my 1990 Presidential Address to the

Eastern Economic Association, in which I offered some reflections on the work of economists and its impact on environmental policy.

The next three parts take up a series of issues concerning economic instruments for environmental regulation. Following some general theory and related issues in Part II, the papers in Part III address the use of taxes and effluent charges for environmental management. The paper with Will Baumol sets forth the properties of a system of effluent charges that is used to attain some predetermined set of standards (or targets) for environmental quality. The point here is simply that even if we do not have the full range of information needed to establish the correct Pigouvian taxes on polluting sources, there is still a compelling case for incentive-based policy instruments, in this case taxes, to attain *whatever* standards are deemed socially desirable.

The next two papers, written with Diana Strassmann, explore an issue that has arisen explicitly with the advent of the 1990 Amendments to the Clean Air Act. The economist's theorems on the least-cost properties of economic instruments for environmental regulation depend upon cost-minimizing behavior by polluting agents. But many polluters are not perfectly competitive firms, driven by competitive forces to cost-minimizing behavior in order to survive. There are major polluters that take the form of large corporations with diverse activities, regulated firms including public utilities that produce the bulk of the economy's energy, and agencies in the public sector (including the military) that are, in some instances, major sources of environmental damage. How are such entities likely to behave, and how will this affect the operation of a system of market-based incentives? This question is important in the current context, for the major participants in the new national market for sulfur emissions in the U.S. are public utilities; typically, they are regulated firms subject to a number of restrictions, including rate-of-return limitations. Drawing on a variety of models in which profits are not maximized, Strassmann and I suggest that there are still important forces encouraging cost-saving behavior, giving us good reasons to believe that the deviations from cost-minimizing outcomes may not be of a significant magnitude. This issue, however, requires further study, especially at an empirical level in order to get some estimates of the likely deviations from the least-cost solution.

Part III concludes with an extensive survey that I undertook for the OECD which explores the ways in which the tax system in the United States at Federal, state and local levels affects the environment. This study also addresses the role of environmental taxes as revenue instruments. A central concern here is the potential conflict when a policy instrument is used for two quite different objectives, in this case environmental management and the raising of tax revenues. While it is a straight-forward theoretical problem in 'optimal taxation' to derive the conditions that describe the optimal resolution of this trade-off, it is quite another matter to deal with this tension in the policy arena. Should revenue 'agents' gain control of the rate-setting process, the fear is that we may well find that tax rates are set with an eye primarily to generating large sums of monies and not with much regard to their effect on polluting behavior. My own sense (for a variety of reasons expressed in the paper) is that such tax rates ought to be in the hands of environmental regulators: the rates should be set primarily so as to obtain the desired environmental outcomes with the resulting revenues being regarded largely as a serendipitous augmentation of public monies that can be used to reduce tax rates elsewhere.

In Part IV, I turn to the major alternative market-based instrument to taxes: systems of tradeable emissions permits. The papers in this section explore the properties of such systems, and look at the various ways in which they can be structured. It is interesting that in the United States, in contrast to Europe, environmental policy-makers have, in the main, chosen the tradeable-permit approach over taxes. This can be understood, I believe, in terms of the political economy of instrument choice: tradeable permit systems offer some appealing features to the various interest groups that circumvent some powerful objections to tax regimes.

Part V addresses the interesting and important issue of the locus of environmental authority. The papers in this section address the question of whether (or under what circumstances) a central authority should set uniform standards applicable to all areas of the country – and when such environmental decision-making should be decentralized. The answer to this question revolves largely around the likelihood of distorting economic competition among state and local jurisdictions; the danger is that, in their eagerness to attract new business and jobs, officials will set both excessively lax environmental standards and low tax rates. Robert Schwab and I set out a number of models of local fiscal behavior which suggest that such behavior will typically not be in the interest of local officials; in our basic models, economic competition is efficiency-enhancing, not distortion-inducing.

Part VI contains two papers that deal with the newly emerging subfield of open economy environmental economics. The first tries to provide a fairly general treatment of the issues that arise in an international setting and how they differ from purely domestic environmental policy-making. In the second paper, Paul Portney and I take up a more specific issue: the design of policy instruments in an international economy for the containment of global warming. The debate over the choice between price and quantity instruments takes on some new dimensions in an international context.

The volume concludes in Part VII with an extended survey paper that my colleague Maureen Cropper and I wrote recently on environmental economics. In this paper, we try both to summarize and to assess the work that environmental economists have done on two topics: the regulation of polluting activities and the valuation of environmental amenities. This provides an opportunity to discuss the existing priorities for future research efforts in the field.

As the table of contents reveals, most of the papers in this collection are co-authored. I am most grateful to those in the field with whom I have had the pleasure of working. Effective joint work should have as its outcome findings and insights that go beyond what either party could have done on his own. I know that the co-authored papers in this volume reach beyond what I could have done; I hope that my partners in this enterprise feel the same way. Finally, I want to thank Edward and Sandy Elgar for their encouragement and support. This is the second of my volumes in the series. The first, *Studies in Fiscal Federalism* (1991), pulled together my papers in public finance. I am delighted to add this second volume of papers in environmental economics.

PART I

ECONOMICS AND ENVIRONMENTAL POLICY: AN OVERVIEW

Eastern Economic Journal, Volume XVI, No. 4, October–December 1990

Economics, Economists, and Environmental Policy

Wallace E. Oates*

The evolution of environmental policy and its relation to economics make a curious story. This is one area in the policy arena where we might have expected economics and economists to play an important role. Well before the arrival of the "environmental revolution" in the late 1960's, economists had developed a fairly systematic view of pollution problems in the context of the issue of externalities. The "smoky factory" spewing its fumes over neighboring residents was a frequent image in basic texts. Moreover, economic principles suggested a straightforward and seemingly compelling policy response to this source of "market failure." The imposition of the appropriate Pigouvian tax or effluent fee would internalize the externality and resolve the problem.

As environmental problems moved into the policy spotlight, economists spoke with virtually one voice on this matter. Almost without exception, they enthusiastically championed a central role for economic incentives for pollution control. But regulators proved skeptical. For the most part, they rejected the economist's counsel and turned to the more traditional command-and-control instruments with which they could specify the control techniques that polluters must adopt.

The reasons for the modest impact of economics on environmental policy are varied. In part, it seems that regulators have never come to appreciate the potential of economic incentives for environmental protection—economists have not, apparently, been very effective in their efforts to persuade policy-makers of the advantages of economic approaches to environmental management. At the same time, I think that economists have failed to understand the complexities of the design and implementation of environmental policy. It is a long way from the welfare-maximizing or least-cost theorems on the blackboard to the construction of a workable policy measure. There are many perplexing elements in the actual design of these measures that the economist can assume away (or simply be unaware of) in the classroom.

I will have a bit more to say about all this. But the basic subject of this paper is not itself this constellation of circumstances that has impeded the adoption of economic incentives for pollution control. What is more interesting at this juncture, it seems to me, is a real opportunity for economists to have a significant impact on environmental policy. There is considerable dissatisfaction on a worldwide scale with existing policy—accompanied by a new and more serious interest in the potential of economic incentives or "mixed" policies for the regulation of polluting activities.

What I wish to do here is to share some reflections, based both on certain results from economic theory and from our actual experience with policy, on the potential role of certain forms of economic measures for the regulation of pollution and on the appropriate locus of administrative control. The first substantive section of the paper offers some thoughts on alternative forms of economic incentives—on their strengths and weaknesses as actual policy tools. I then move in the next section to a brief consideration of economic incentives vs. command-and-control (CAC) measures, an area where I think economists (including myself) have drawn some simplistic and sometimes misleading distinctions. The third section addresses the issue of centralization versus decentralization in environmental management and suggests a larger role for "local" authorities in the determination of policy. The paper

*Department of Economics, University of Maryland, College Park, MD 20742 and University Fellow, Resources for the Future. Presidential Address presented before the Eastern Economic Association, March 30, 1990.

concludes with some further reflections on the role of economics and economists in the design of environmental policy.

I want, at the outset, to make one disclaimer. There are a number of economists who have worked long and hard in the determination and analysis of actual policy measures—to them, some of the observations that I offer, particularly in the later sections of the paper, will seem quite obvious and, even perhaps, a bit pretentious. If this be true, I apologize: my only defense is my sense that these matters are often not fully appreciated by those who are one-step (or more) removed from the "firing line." They involve certain oversights that I know I have been guilty of.

1. Economic Instruments for Pollution Control

The standard analysis of problems involving an external cost runs in terms of a corrective tax that serves to internalize the externality. An effluent tax on waste emissions set equal to marginal social damages constitutes the familiar Pigouvian prescription for treating the malady. Effluent fees, however, have not proved altogether popular among policy makers—largely because of the understandable opposition of the often powerful interests that would be the subject of the tax.

It was recognized early on that an alternative policy instrument—namely, a unit subsidy for pollution abatement—shares certain properties with a fee. A subsidy of 10 cents per pound of reductions in sulfur emissions into the atmosphere, for example, creates the same incentive to reduce sulfur emissions as a fee of 10 cents per pound on such discharges. In both cases, the opportunity cost to the polluter of an additional unit of waste emissions is 10 cents so that under either program, a cost-minimizing source will pursue control measures to the point where marginal abatement costs are 10 cents. Subsidies would thus appear to offer an alternative to taxes—and one that would generate much less opposition in a policy setting. Polluters will obviously be far more receptive to measures that assist with the costs of pollution control than to those that place the burden upon themselves.

While there exists this equivalence in terms of first-order conditions for abatement activities, it soon became apparent that there are some fundamental asymmetries between the two policy instruments. Bramhall and Mills (1966), along with some others, pointed out that because they have different effects on the firm's profits, taxes and subsidies have opposite effects on firms' entry and exit decisions. Indeed, it is not hard to show that in a competitive setting, subsidies will lead to an excessively large number of firms and industry output: subsidies shift the industry supply curve out, while taxes shift the curve up and to the left. Although each firm will pollute less than in the absence of the subsidy, there will be more firms—it is even conceivable that aggregate industry emissions could go up (Baumol and Oates, 1988, pp. 218–228)![1]

Subsidies thus are not, in principle at least, a satisfactory alternative to effluent charges. The extent of the distortion is not, however, a matter that has been addressed in the literature. Since abatement costs in most heavily polluting industries appear to run on the order of only 1 to 3 percent of total costs, it is conceivable that the subsidy distortion of entry-exit decisions is not of a large magnitude. But this is a complicated issue. The effects on entry-exit and on long-run industry supply depend in complex ways on the relevant elasticities as well as the magnitude of the cost differential (Mestelman, 1982). This is a matter that probably deserves further study. But until shown otherwise, I think that the subsidy instrument must remain suspect—it should not be regarded as a fully acceptable alternative to taxes on waste emissions.[2]

The other basic alternative to the tax approach is a quantity instrument: marketable emission permits. Instead of setting a charge at the level needed to achieve the requisite reduction in emissions, the environmental authority can simply determine the desired quantity directly by issuing emissions permits and allowing polluters to buy and sell the permits freely among themselves (Dales, 1968). It is a straightforward matter to show that (in a setting of perfect knowledge) a competitive equilibrium in the permit market will lead to an allocatively efficient outcome just as will the tax approach.

In view of the reticence with which regulators had viewed the proposal for effluent fees, I (along with some others) enthusiastically embraced the marketable-permit approach in its early days. In principle, it seemed to have the potential for achieving all the efficiency objectives that characterized a fee system. But in addition, marketable permits appeared to offer some quite compelling advantages in the policy arena. First, the permit approach gives the environmental regulator direct control over quantity: the agency determines the quantity of emissions directly through the issuance of permits, not indirectly through the adjustment of the effluent charge. Since the targets of the regulator are typically specified in quantity terms, this is a very compelling advantage, especially in a setting of inflation and economic growth. Under a fee system, the regulator will have to adjust the fee periodically (typically increase it) to accommodate rising prices and new sources, if pollution levels are to be kept from increasing. But with quantity fixed under a permit system, price will rise to clear the market simply as a result of excess demand. There will be no burden of "affirmative action" on the regulatory authority.

Second, the permit approach offers a way around some of the political opposition that has blocked the introduction of fees. It is true, of course, that the permits could be the subject of an auction so that sources would have to pay for the right to pollute much as they do under a system of effluent charges. But there is another way to set the permit system in motion. The permits can simply be distributed without charge to existing sources who are then free to trade them among themselves or to sell them to new sources. The granting of a valuable asset will obviously encounter much less resistance from polluting firms than the levying of a tax. This is in fact what has been done under Emissions Trading in the United States.

And third, the permit approach promises more ready acceptance simply on the grounds of familiarity. Regulators have experience and are comfortable with the permit instrument—and it seems a much less radical move to make permits transferable than to replace the entire permit system with a scheme of effluent charges.

It thus appeared that tradeable permits offered an alternative that was equivalent in its economic properties to fees but that was likely to be received much more warmly by policy makers and regulators. In the U.S., at least, the latter point received some support from the introduction and proliferation of Emissions Trading for the management of air quality. Under the general rubric outlined by the Environmental Protection Agency, a large number of States established programs that, under some admittedly rather stringent conditions, allowed sources to trade emissions rights.

After more than a decade of experience with Emissions Trading, I find myself much more ambivalent on the matter of fees versus tradeable permits. It has become clear that the permit approach has some serious deficiencies—deficiencies that are peculiar to the permit system and that would not plague a well designed regime of effluent charges.

The major issue concerns the operation of permit markets. It is easy to show formally that a competitive equilibrium in a permit market has the nice economic properties that we wish for our system of pollution control. The difficulty is that, in practice, markets for permits have not exhibited the smooth functioning envisioned in theory. Markets have in fact been quite thin with little participation emerging, in particular, on the supply side of the market. Robert Hahn (1989) contends that this has been largely the result of unfortunate restrictions on trading that have clouded definitions of property rights and raised serious uncertainty about the ability to obtain these rights when needed in the marketplace. Moreover, the number of potential participants in the market is often small with certain large sources in a position to exercise price-setting powers, giving rise to possible monopoly-monopsony distortions (Hahn, 1984). The thinness and infrequency of transactions in the market suggest that polluters will not observe a clear, well defined price signal to indicate the opportunity cost of their waste discharges. This, of course, is the key element in achieving an efficient allocation of emissions among sources—and its absence is a disturbing element in the functioning of a permit market. In contrast, a system of effluent fees presents each source with a well defined price of emissions so that we can presume with more confidence that cost-minimizing behavior on the part of sources will be efficiency-enhancing.

A second matter concerns revenues. A fee system will generate public revenues—and in these days of budgetary deficits and the search for new revenues sources, this has real appeal. It is interesting that the most recent bill for a nationwide system of effluent charges in the United States came not from one of the committees concerned with environmental matters, but from the House Ways and Means Committee. Effluent fees present a very attractive revenue instrument on economic grounds. Conventional forms of taxation typically involve significant "excess burden"—deadweight losses resulting from the distortions in resource allocation that they generate. Fees, in contrast, promise to raise revenue and, at the same time, to improve, not worsen, resource allocation. David Terkla (1984) estimates that revenues from a nationwide tax on stationary sources of sulfur and particulate emissions would generate (in 1982 dollars) revenues ranging from about $2 to $9 billion with efficiency gains on the order of $630 million to $3 billion if substituted for revenues, respectively, from the federal personal income tax or corporation income tax. I don't wish to make too much of this since a permit system could in principle also be a revenue source—if the permits were auctioned off rather than distributed without charge.

There is a third, and somewhat more subtle, point that I see as an important argument in favor of the fee approach. It has its source in the important paper by Martin Weitzman (1974) dealing with the choice of policy instruments in a setting of uncertainty. The Weitzman theorem sets forth the conditions under which price instruments are to be preferred (or not preferred) to quantity instruments. The essence of the argument is that the expected welfare gains from the two instruments depend upon the relative slopes of the marginal damage and cost curves. Where the marginal damage curve is relatively steep (e.g., where there exist significant environmental thresholds that are violated at great damage), it is important to maintain close control over quantity to insure that emissions do not exceed the critical levels. The risk here is that if an effluent fee (because of imperfect information) were set too low, severe damage could result. The Weitzman theorem thus quite sensibly tells us to adopt the quantity instrument in such circumstances.

In contrast, if marginal abatement cost curves are relatively steep with fairly flat marginal damage curves, then the more serious threat is the improper setting of quantity; if permits were set too few in number, for example, it could impose heavy and excessive costs on the economy. An examination of existing circumstances suggests that it is this latter danger that is probably the more serious one. We have come a significant distance now in terms of environmental cleanup—and most studies suggest that we are now operating along rapidly rising segments of marginal abatement cost curves. There is not much evidence that I know of to suggest that we find ourselves on steep portions of marginal damage functions for the major pollutants. I thus suspect that in the setting of environmental policy, we are much more likely to make serious and costly errors if we employ quantity measures than if we adopt price instruments. Polluting firms can always avoid exorbitantly high abatement costs by paying the effluent charge. If they do not have this option because of rigid quantity restrictions, these costs must be borne.

Within the set of policy instruments employing economic incentivies, I thus find that the choice between the price and quantity approach is unclear. Both approaches have the potential to take us a considerable way down the road to the least-cost outcome—but each approach has its own peculiar problems and shortcomings in a realistic policy setting. It remains to consider the class of economic instruments relative to their command-and-control counterparts.

2. *Economic Incentives Versus Command-and-Control*

The literature in environmental economics has frequently drawn a very sharp and all-inclusive distinction between policy instruments that rely on economic incentives and those that do not—with the latter being grouped under the heading of "comand-and-control" (CAC) policies. Although perhaps helpful for rhetorical purposes, I think that this simplistic distinction is, for several reasons, misleading.

First, the CAC category of policies includes a wide variety of measures—some quite crude, indeed, but others relying on cost-sensitive algorithms that can produce reasonably efficient results. In fact, the precise line of demarcation between these two classes of policies is not always clear. Take, for example, a CAC policy under which the environmental authority specifies the control technology to be used by the polluter. This policy leaves the source with little room to maneuver in finding cost-saving techniques for abatement. In contrast, suppose the regulator simply specifies a quota, an overall limit (with no trading of allowances), on the source's emissions. It will then be up to the polluter to seek out the least-cost form of compliance. These are obviously very different kinds of policies—the latter does, in fact, embody some economic incentives in that it encourages the search for the least-cost control technology. And this is an extremely important incentive.

Second, most empirical studies that compare the performance of CAC policies with programs involving economic incentives contain significant built-in biases toward findings that confirm a marked superiority for the latter. These biases are of two sorts. On the cost side, these studies typically calculate a least-cost solution and then (rather cavalierly) associate this least-cost solution with the outcome under the fee or marketable-permit approach. The cost saving under the economic incentive approach is computed by subtracting this least-cost figure from the cost calculated for the CAC program—often a rather crude measure that requires, perhaps, proportional roll-backs in the emissions of all sources. The major problem here is that *realistic* programs of economic incentives (like their CAC counterparts) will *not* be able to realize the least-cost outcome. The compromises that are typically required in these measures, such as uniform tax rates on all sources in an area, will not allow the refinement of tax schedules or restrictions on permit trades that are required to attain the least-cost pattern of control efforts. In short, control costs under realistic programs of economic incentives are bound to exceed those under the least-cost outcome.

In addition, these studies typically overlook the fact that, *for a given set of environmental standards,* the cruder CAC policies typically result in overcontrol of sources so that the resulting environmental quality will tend to be higher under the CAC measures than under a system of taxes or marketable permits designed to achieve the standard at lower cost. One recent study (Oates, Portney, and McGartland, 1990) that explicitly incorporates these "extra benefits" into the calculations finds that the simulated outcome under a fairly sophisticated and cost-sensitive CAC policy (similar to one actually employed in Baltimore for air-quality management) compares reasonably favorably with the outcome under a system of fees or marketable permits.[3]

The moral of all this, it seems to me, is that in comparing alternative policy approaches, we should be careful to look at the specific provisions of individual measures—realistic measures that are feasible in the policy arena and not just ideal prototypes. We should not lump together large classes of programs where there are important distinctions to made within these classes. Most of the programs that will be adopted are likely to be hybrid measures with elements of economic incentives mixed together with more traditional regulatory directives. Economists can, I suspect, make their best contribution by a careful dissection of such programs to point out the desirable and undesirable elements—and thereby suggest a reasonably compatible and effective mixture of policy provisions.

At the same time, it is important not to throw the baby out with the bath water. Economic incentives of various sorts clearly have great potential for the efficient regulation of pollution. Probably even more important than the static cost-saving properties of these measures are the incentives that they provide over the longer haul for research and development of new control technology. I am certainly not suggesting that economists should abandon their strong support for economic incentives for pollution control, but rather that they should see them in a somewhat broader context and appreciate more fully the constraints and compromises that must inevitably be part of incorporating them into actual policy.

3. Environmental Federalism

The other major issue that I wish to consider in this paper is the locus of regulatory authority. This is a matter on which existing policy exhibits a fundamental ambivalence. Under the Clean Air Act Amendments in 1970, for example, the U.S. Congress directed the Environmental Protection Agency to set uniform standards for air quality applicable to all parts of the nation. The EPA responded by establishing national standards, consisting of maximum permissible concentrations of the criteria air pollutants. Yet only two years later, when making amendments to the Clean Water Act, the Congress decided to leave it to the states both to determine their own standards for water quality and to set in place regulatory systems to achieve those standards (although admittedly subject to EPA approval).

The basic issue is whether the setting of standards and the determination of other regulatory parameters should be centralized with the focus on uniform national measures to be satisfied everywhere, or whether a major element of decentralized choice should characterize environmental management. At the first cut, economic principles appear to provide a straightforward answer to this question. It is clear that the benefits and costs of many major pollutants are both highly localized and highly specific to their geography. The emissions of a certain air or water pollutant may be quite damaging in one area and have little effect in another where the assimilative capacity of the environment is much greater. An economic approach that involves balancing control costs against damages at the margin would obviously call for tailoring environmental programs to the particular circumstances of individual localities or regions (Peltzman and Tideman, 1972). An efficient policy for one area may well be quite inefficient elsewhere. There are, of course, pollutants that migrate from one jurisdiction to another (e.g., acid rain) for which more centralized measures are required, but a first-best solution for "localized" pollutants clearly calls for a decentralized approach to environmental regulation.

But as John Cumberland (1981) and others have pointed out, this simple application of principles overlooks much of the political reality of local fiscal and environmental decision-making. Cumberland stresses that local officials, in their concern over jobs, income, and economic development, are likely to engage in "destructive interjurisdictional competition" to attract new business investment. Such competition will take the form of (among other things) the relaxation of environmental standards with excessive environmental degradation the likely outcome. From this perspective, centralized measures are needed to protect local jurisdictions "from themselves."

This is a difficult line of argument to evaluate since, at least until quite recently, we have had little theory to go on and only some anecdotal evidence. In a pair of papers, Robert Schwab and I (Oates and Schwab, 1988 and 1989) have constructed a set of models of local fiscal and environmental choice in which local officials, in the setting of policy parameters, effectively trade-off tax revenues and environmental quality for local jobs and income. For the "basic case," the models produce the salutary result of efficient local choices. It is in the interest of the locality (assuming decisions by simple majority rule) to set the policy parameters such that the cost of improved environmental quality at the margin precisely equals the locals' willingness-to-pay. In short, in our basic models, interjurisdictional competition is efficiency-enhancing—it is not a source of distortions in patterns of resource use.

In the second of the two papers (1989), we extend the analysis to an intertemporal setting to address the troublesome issue of the interests of future generations. An interesting result emerges: in our two-period model, local officials again set fiscal and environmental policy efficiently—in a way that accounts for the well-being of future generations. This happens through the capitalization of both present and future environmental quality into local property values. Present residents are forced to take into account the interests of future residents because future environmental quality is reflected in the present value of land parcels. This is interesting because it suggests a mechanism through which local officials will accommodate the interests of future generations—a mechanism that is *not* available to discipline the choices of centralized decision-makers.

While all this is encouraging in that it supports the case for a first-best environmental federalism, the results are not robust to several sorts of realistic modifications of the models. It is easy to show, for example, that if local officials behave like Niskanen budget-maximizing bureaucrats, they will not only set taxes too high, but will also establish excessively lax environmental standards as a mechanism to bring in more business investment and thereby expand the local tax base (Oates and Schwab, 1988). Alternatively, if the community is fractured into dissident elements—some favoring economic development and others the maintenance of a pristine environment—the outcome will in general not be efficient (although it can involve either too little or too much pollution).

Theory can take us only so far on these matters—and there isn't much by way of systematic empirical work on this matter to provide support one way or the other. The theory provides encouragement, I believe, for decentralized environmental choice—but it is certainly of a highly tentative nature. At this juncture, I think that we must examine the potential losses from adopting the centralized approach. Again, there isn't a whole lot to go on—but there is some. My reading of the evidence at this point suggests that a rigid pursuit of national standards and regulatory policies is likely to be *highly* inefficient. The nature and extent of most of our major environmental problems vary greatly from one geographical setting to another. In the U.S., for example, it is becoming increasingly clear that the costs of requiring Southern California to meet the same standards for air quality as the rest of the nation are exorbitant and unreasonable. Instead of facing up to the issue and establishing a realistic and sensible set of standards tailored to the circumstances of Southern California, we simply keep extending the time for compliance with national standards—and Southern California continues introducing additional measures, unjustifiable on any sort of benefit-cost calculation, and with little prospect of ever attaining the prescribed national standards.

In an ongoing study, Ralph Luken (1990) is examining the effects of regulation of a sizeable sample of paper mills in the United States. Perhaps, the most striking aspect of his results is the marked variation across the sample in the measured level of damages resulting from the operations of the plants. Differences in the size and assimilative capacities of the receiving waters and in the extent of neighboring populations imply that on economic grounds the extent of treatment of wastes should vary dramatically from one plant to the next. From this perspective, some move toward increased local (or regional) discretion in the determination of regulatory parameters could achieve significant welfare gains in environmental management.

The issue of environmental federalism needs to be addressed more carefully and systematically. This isn't a simple matter, for it seems clear that the "optimal degree of decentralization" is likely to exhibit considerable variation across pollutants. But it seems to me that an unexamined adherence to centralized standard setting and control is likely to involve both unnecessarily high costs and the failure to attain some feasible and reasonable goals in areas with their own special environmental problems. The benefits and costs of environmental improvement appear to differ quite significantly across areas—and we need to incorporate this variation more systematically into our approach to environmental management.

4. Concluding Remarks

In concluding this paper, I wish to be sure that the general tone of the observations and remarks has not been misleading. I believe that economics and economists have much to contribute to the design and implementation of environmental policy. In fact, I think it likely that we are at a point in the evolution of environmental policy at which the economics profession is in a very favorable position to influence the course of policy. First, as I mentioned at the outset, the general political and policy setting is one that is receptive to market approaches to solving our social problems. Not only in the United States but in many other countries as well, the prevailing atmosphere is a conservative one with a strong disposition toward the use of market or economic incentives for the realization of social objectives.

Second, we have learned a lot over the last twenty years about the properties of various policy instruments and how they work (or don't work) under different circumstances. As a result, economists know more about environmental policy—and are in a position to offer much improved counsel on the design of economic measures for the control of pollution.

What I have tried to stress is that this knowledge takes us into a more complex world of policy structure than the abstract world of systems of pure fees or tradeable permits. This will require a careful consideration of the properties of individual pollutants to determine which forms of pollution can be regulated most effectively by economic measures. It is a world in which economists must be prepared to come to terms with detailed, but important, matters of implementation: the determination of fee schedules, issues of spatial and temporal variation in fees or allowable emissions under permits, the life of permits and their treatment for tax purposes, rules governing the transfer of pollution rights, procedures for the monitoring and enforcement of emissions limitations, etc. In short, economists must be ready to "get their hands dirty."

But the potential contribution is, I believe, a valuable one. This is especially true, because we have now reached a juncture in environmental management where we can make some enormously costly mistakes. Operating in regions of rapidly ascending marginal abatement costs, we are in a position to make decisions that could place heavy costs on the economy with only a very modest return in terms of improved environmental quality. More than ever, this is a time when sensible decisions will be very important.

NOTES

1. A second problem with the subsidy approach is the need to determine a benchmark level of emissions from which to calculate the quantity of emissions reductions for purposes of determining the subsidy payment. This can itself be an administratively contentious matter (Baumol and Oates, 1988, Ch. 14).
2. There are certain circumstances under which subsidies for abatement will not distort entry-exit decisions. As Martin Bailey (1982) has shown, where benefits and damages are capitalized into property values, appropriately designed subsidies will indeed be equivalent to taxes in their allocative effects. Baumol and Oates (1988, pp. 230–234) provide a brief treatment of the Bailey argument. In a somewhat different vein, Gene Mumy (1980) and John Peezey (1990) have developed an ingenious and provocative scheme that combines charges and subsidies in a way that avoids any distortions in entry-exit decisions.
3. The issue here is that in the control of most air or water pollutants, there will typically be only a few points in the area at which the limit (or standard) is binding. Elsewhere, pollutant concentrations will fall below the allowable limit. At these points where environmental quality exceeds the prescribed minimum, pollution levels will tend to be less under a CAC approach than under the least-cost outcome. This occurs because in its search to reduce control costs, the algorithm for the least-cost solution effectively assigns a shadow price of zero to any "excess" of environmental quality and tries to trade off, wherever possible, such excess quality for further savings in control costs. A cruder CAC approach makes less effective use of "excess" environmental quality—resulting in overcontrol relative to the least-cost solution. See Oates et al. (1989) for a fuller treatment of this matter.

REFERENCES

Bailey, Martin J., "Externalities, Rents, and Optimal Rules," *Sloan Working Paper in Urban Public Economics 16–82,* Economics Dept., University of Maryland, 1982.
Baumol, William J., and Oates, Wallace E., *The Theory of Environmental Policy,* Second Edition (Cambridge: Cambridge University Press, 1988).
Bramhall, D.E., and Mills, E.S., "A Note on the Asymmetry Between Fees and Payments," *Water Resources Research* (No. 3, 1966), *2,* pp. 615–616.
Cumberland, John H., "Efficiency and Equity in Interregional Environmental Management," *Review of Regional Studies* (1981), *10* (2), pp. 1–9.
Dales, J.H., *Pollution, Property, and Prices* (Toronto: University of Toronto Press, 1968).
Hahn, Robert W., "Market Power and Transferable Property Rights," *Quarterly Journal of Economics* (Nov., 1984), *99,* pp. 753–765.
Hahn, Robert W., "Economic Prescriptions for Environmental Problems: How the Patient Followed the Doctor's Orders," *Journal of Economic Perspectives* (Spring, 1989), *3,* pp. 95–114.
Lukens, Ralph, unpublished paper (1990).
Mestelman, Stuart, "Production Externalities and Corrective Subsidies: A General Equilibrium Analysis, *Journal of Environmental Economics and Management* (June, 1982), *9,* pp. 186–193.
Mumy, Gene E., "Long-Run Efficiency and Property Rights Sharing for Pollution Control," *Public Choice* (1980), *35,* pp. 59–74.
Oates, Wallace E., Portney, Paul R., and McGartland, Albert M., "The *Net* Benefits of Incentive-Based Regulation: A Case Study of Environmental Standard Setting," *American Economic Review* (Dec., 1989), *79,* pp. 1233–1242.
Oates, Wallace E., and Schwab, Robert M., "Economic Competition Among Jurisdictions: Efficiency-Enhancing or Distortion-Inducing?" *Journal of Public Economics* (April, 1988), *35,* pp. 333–354.
Oates, Wallace E., and Schwab, Robert M., "The Theory of Regulatory Federalism: The Case of Environmental Management," unpublished paper (1989).
Pezzey, John, "Charges versus Subsidies versus Marketable Permits as Efficient and Acceptable Methods of Effluent Control: A Property Rights Analysis," unpublished paper (1990).
Peltzman, Sam, and Tideman, T. Nicolaus, "Local versus National Pollution Control: Note," *American Economic Review* (Dec., 1972), *62,* pp. 959–963.
Terkla, David, "The Efficiency Value of Effluent Tax Revenues," *Journal of Environmental Economics and Management* (June, 1984), *11,* pp. 107–123.
Weitzman, Martin L., "Prices vs. Quantities," *Review of Economic Studies* (Oct., 1974), *41,* pp. 477–491.

CHAPTER ELEVEN

The Environment and the Economy: Environmental Policy at the Crossroads

Wallace E. Oates

During the past fifteen years, raised environmental consciousness has reacted to growing evidence of environmental damage by generating a flurry of legislation and associated abatement activities to control pollution. Federal, state, and local governments in the United States and public officials abroad have adopted a diverse array of measures to protect the environment. These measures have achieved some success in controlling pollution but, as we shall see, the record is distinctly mixed: levels of certain forms of pollution have fallen discernibly, but other pollutant levels have remained the same or even risen. Pollution control has become costly: during the 1980s the United States is spending over $50 billion a year to control pollution. This has taken a small but measurable toll on the performance of the macroeconomy. Particularly in the context of the general economic slowdown in the past decade both here and abroad, the issue of reconciling our environmental objectives and policies with the goals of continued economic growth and price stability has become a major concern. In June 1984, the O.E.C.D. countries met in Paris to address these issues in a major conference on Environment and Economics.

This moment in the evolution of environmental policy thus appears propitious for a reassessment of our environmental programs to determine their effectiveness and to explore the case for redirection of our policy strategies. This is obviously a tall order for a single observer in one essay, but in spite of the necessarily tentative character of much of the analysis, I undertake here such a reassessment.

A central theme is that polluting activities continue to pose a serious threat to our well-being. Much remains to be done to control a wide range of polluting activities that pose dire risks for society. To achieve this end, we need to employ more sensible procedures for setting environmental-quality standards. In addition, the choice of regulatory instruments for pollution control has resulted in enormous waste: abatement costs far more than is necessary to achieve many of the standards for environmental quality. By redirecting regulatory efforts toward a heavier reliance on economic incentives, we can realize huge cost-savings that will go far to reconcile our environmental objectives with a healthy economy.

BACKGROUND

Concern with environmental degradation has manifested itself in a wide range of legislative measures designed to control various forms of pollution. A brief, highly selective survey of the evolution of some of these measures provides needed background for an assessment of the current state of environmental policy.

Under the Clean Air Act (as amended at various times over the past fifteen years), Congress directed the Environmental Protection Agency (EPA) to set national standards for ambient air quality. The EPA responded in the early 1970s by specifying maximum concentrations for a set of "criteria" air pollutants.[1] The responsibility for attaining these standards was lodged with the individual states. Each state was to design a State Implementation Plan (SIP) for attainment of the primary national ambient-air-quality standards (NAAQS) by 1975. Responding to this charge, the states introduced their own regulatory systems to control waste discharges. These have typically involved estimation of needed reductions in emissions, followed by issuance of individual permits to stationary sources. The states then attempted to develop monitoring and enforcement systems.

To control emissions from mobile sources, the 1970 Amendments to the Clean Air Act mandated a highly restrictive set of auto emission standards involving 90 percent reductions (from 1970–1971 levels) in emissions of three pollutants to be achieved by 1975–1976. It was recognized at the time that these standards were beyond the technical capacity of the auto industry; the premise was that such "technology forcing'" measures would induce the industry to develop the needed control technology within the specified time.

The approach to control of water pollution has been somewhat different. Under the 1972 Water Pollution Amendments, Congress specified two general policy goals: an ultimate objective, eliminating all discharges of pollutants into the navigable waters by 1985; and an interim "fishable-swimmable" goal, protecting waterlife and recreational uses of bodies of water. For obvious reasons, the latter goal has served as the general operational objective. Unlike the Clean Air Act, the states themselves set their own standards for ambient water quality. There is thus an intriguing and important asymmetry in air and water pollution legislation: we have uniform national (minimum) standards for ambient air quality, but self-determined state standards for ambient water quality (more on this issue later).

The general regulatory approach to the control of waste discharges has been similar under the Clean Air and Clean Water acts. It involves specification of technology-based emissions standards for certain classes of polluters and issuance of individual discharge permits to sources. In addition, the federal government has played a major role in funding the construction of municipal waste-treatment plants. Paying up to 75 percent of the cost of these plants, the federal government has spent several billions per year to subsidize construction of new plants.

As the decade of the 1970s progressed, a number of problems and a certain amount of dissatisfaction arose with existing policies. It became clear, for example, that the schedule for meeting mandated objectives was, in many instances, not being met. The auto industry claimed that it was unable to meet standards for auto emissions on schedule; delays and extensions ensued. It also became obvious that many cities would not achieve the NAAQS by the prescribed time. Finally, there was widespread evidence both of long delays in specification of standards and issuance of permits, and of problems of monitoring and noncompliance.

Further amendments to the Clean Air and Clean Water acts were enacted in the late seventies. One provision is of particular interest here. As it became increasingly evident that many cities would be unable to meet the standards for all the criteria air pollutants by the mandated deadline of 1975 (later extended to 1977), an unpleasant confrontation loomed on the horizon. The prospective penalty for "nonattainment areas" was severe: a ban on new sources of emissions or significant expansion of existing sources, implying a virtual cessation to economic growth. Congress and the EPA managed to avoid this confrontation by introducing into the 1977 Amendments to the Clean Air Act a system of "emission offsets." Under the offset provision, new sources could enter nonattainment areas under two conditions: (1) that the new source adopt the most effective abatement technology available; and (2) that existing sources contract emissions sufficiently that a net improvement in air quality would result, i.e., the increment to aggregate emissions from new sources would be more than offset by reduced emissions from existing polluters. As I will discuss later, this admittedly pragmatic response to a potentially serious political confrontation has, somewhat ironically, opened the door to a very promising new approach to the control of pollution: tradable emission permits.

In the early 1970s, the bulk of legislative statutes pertained to the conventional air and water pollutants, but during the decade national attention and legislative activity shifted toward greater concern with "toxic" pollutants. Dramatic and disturbing incidents such as those at Love Canal and Times Beach have increased national awareness of the serious threats posed by such pollutants. New legislative measures were enacted to deal with toxic substances and hazardous wastes: the Safe Drinking Water Act (1974); the Federal Insecticide, Fungicide, and Rodenticide Act (1978); the Toxic Substances Control Act (1976); the Resource Conservation and Recovery Act (1976); and the Comprehensive Environmental Response, Compensation, and Liability Act (1980), which created the Superfund for the cleaning of hazardous waste sites. The basic thrust of these acts is, first, identification and, second, control (or cleanup) of toxic pollutants in the environment.

How successful have these measures been in stemming or reversing ongoing environmental deterioration? Before turning to the trends, a problem of inference requires comment. To evaluate the effectiveness of a policy, we need to know what would have happened in its absence. For example, although one dimension of environmental quality may show no improvement over the past decade, had the policy measure not been introduced the situation might have deteriorated. This issue is particularly relevant here, for the decade of the 1970s was a period of relative economic stagnation encompassing a dramatic increase in fuel prices and changing patterns of fuel consumption that would in themselves have altered levels of emissions of various pollutants. In short, some care is needed in making inferences about the success or failure of policy from environmental trends.

THE STATE OF THE ENVIRONMENT

An examination of the effectiveness of environmental policy as measured by levels and trends in environmental quality reveals a very mixed record.[2] Considerable progress has been made in reducing the levels of urban exposure to several "conventional" air pollutants; in contrast, control of water pollution has been much less effective. Moreover, as noted in the preceding section, the emphasis has to some extent shifted from conventional air and water pollutants to the largely unknown, but potentially insidious, effects of a bewildering array of toxic substances and hazardous wastes.

AIR QUALITY

The effort to improve ambient air quality in the United States has focused on the criteria air pollutants. In 1976, an interagency task force developed a Pollution Standards Index (PSI) that combines the observed concentrations of the criteria pollutants into a single measure. The index is designed so that it will take on a value of 100 or more for a given day if the air pollution level at the site exceeds the primary standard for any of the five criteria pollutants. The PSI thus provides a convenient summary measure by which to examine trends in air quality. The general trend toward reduced air pollution is shown in Figure 11.1, which depicts the average number of days per year that the PSI registered over 100 in a sample of 23 metropolitan areas in the United States. As the figure indicates, this number has fallen from over 90 days in 1974 to about 40 such days in 1981. The extent of improvement has been quite marked in some cities: Chicago, Portland (Oregon), and Philadelphia have recorded reductions since 1974 in the number of "unhealthy" days of 92, 78, and 72 percent, respectively. However, in a few cities, notably Houston, Los Angeles, Sacramento, and San Diego, PSI readings have increased over the past decade.

PSI trends to some extent mask the trends for the individual criteria pollutants. For example, in areas for which consistent monitoring data are available, average concentrations of sulfur dioxide and carbon monoxide have declined by roughly one-third from 1975 to 1982, but measured concentrations of nitrogen dioxide show little change over the period. Total suspended particulates (TSP, thought to be one of the air pollutants most detrimental to health) exhibit a more curious temporal pattern: average concentrations of TSP seem to have remained fairly constant over the 1970s but to have decreased significantly in 1981–1982. It has been suggested that this improvement may represent only a temporary reduction associated with the concomitant decline in industrial production.

FIGURE II.1

Air Quality in 23 Metropolitan Areas, as Measured by the
Pollutant Standards Index (PSI), 1974–1981

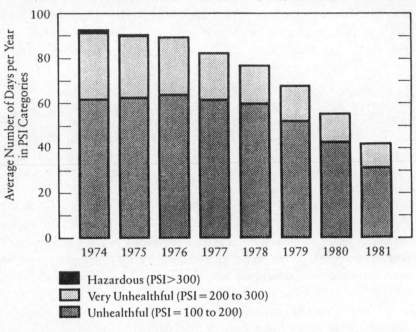

Hazardous (PSI>300)
Very Unhealthful (PSI = 200 to 300)
Unhealthful (PSI = 100 to 200)

SOURCE: Conservation Foundation (1984, p. 88).

The record for air quality, while certainly mixed, does appear on balance to indicate significant improvement in terms of the conventional air
pollutants. Overall, air quality seems to have gotten better in the last
decade in most of our urban areas.[3] However, in many metropolitan areas
the primary standards for air quality still have not been met. Much is yet
to be done, and it is likely that the remaining task will be considerably
more difficult and expensive than in those cases where the initial effort
has already attained the standards.

WATER QUALITY

The trends in water quality in the United States are both less well
documented and less encouraging than for air quality. Some striking
successes in water-quality management have been recorded: the return of
Atlantic salmon to the Connecticut and Penobscot rivers in New England,
for example, and the revival of lakes Erie and Ontario. But existing

evidence of a more general kind suggests little real improvement in surface-water quality over the last decade. Of the conventional pollution indicators (dissolved oxygen, fecal coliform bacteria, suspended sediment, dissolved solids, and phosphorus), the Conservation Foundation reports that "the vast majority of monitoring stations show no significant change in pollutant concentrations between 1974 and 1981, with those showing trends of increase balanced by a comparable number of decreases" (1984, p. 109). These findings, incidentally, are based on reports from the National Ambient Stream Quality Accounting Network (NASQAN) of the U.S. Geological Survey, which provides "the most consistent and comprehensive information available on specific contaminants" (Conservation Foundation 1984, p. 107).

The evidence does suggest considerable progress in the control of "point-source" discharges. According to EPA estimates, industrial discharges have fallen by 70 percent or more from 1972 to 1977, and some progress has also been made in controlling discharges from municipal wastewater plants, the other major point source. The results from a recent nationwide survey indicate that in spite of an increase of 12 percent in oxygen-demanding pollutants entering municipal plants over the period 1972–1982, the quantity of these pollutants emitted from the plants declined by 46 percent. "Pollutants leaving municipal treatment plants would have been almost twice as high as the amount actually discharged in 1982 if there had been no improvement to the facilities that existed in 1972" (Conservation Foundation 1984, p. 119). Periodic difficulties arise with the efficient operation of these plants, however. In particular, since federal subsidies apply to the construction of municipal waste-treatment plants but not to their operation, many newly constructed plants are not operating properly.

Non–point-source pollution—especially agricultural runoff, but also urban runoff—has proved much more difficult to control. State officials, in fact, most often cite these sources as preventing streams from providing desired services. Runoff from agricultural lands contributes most of the sediment, nitrogen, phosphorus, and organic pollutants entering surface waters in the United States, as well as significant amounts of pesticides, bacteria, and dissolved solids. Development of effective programs for the management of non-point sources is essential if we are to realize any substantial improvement in water quality.

Potentially even more troublesome than the control of surface-water quality is the recently recognized spectre of contamination of our ground-water. Underground aquifers are the primary source of water in many parts of the United States. We do not have comprehensive information on the extent of groundwater contamination, but surveys have uncovered hundreds of cases of well closures as a result of contamination from toxic pollutants. Other groundwater sources have been rendered unusable for most purposes due to saltwater contamination, the presence of bacteria and viruses, the intrusion of nitrates, and radioactive contamination. We are just beginning to get some sense of the magnitude of the problem— and it appears to be getting worse.

TOXIC SUBSTANCES AND HAZARDOUS WASTES

So-called toxic pollutants encompass a very diverse range of substances. They include a vast array of toxic metals, organic toxic chemicals such as pesticides and polychlorinated biphenyls (PCBs), and fibrous minerals such as asbestos. Demonstrable progress has been made in reducing exposure to some of these substances. Lead, for example, was identified fairly early on as an insidious pollutant with debilitating health effects. Widely used as a gasoline additive, in automobile batteries, and in pigments and paints, lead found its way into the human environment through several paths. Existing data indicate that lead production and consumption gradually increased over the 1960s and early 1970s. However, between 1977 and 1982, average concentrations of lead as measured at urban monitoring sites have declined by almost two-thirds. There are similar declines over this period in the lead content in samples of human blood. These results are attributable primarily to the growing reliance on unleaded gasolines; moreover, as older, leaded-fuel cars are retired from use, further declines in lead concentrations should take place.[4]

We have also made major progress in reducing levels of exposure to certain other toxic substances: DDT, PCBs, and asbestos are major cases. But against this record must be weighed environmental calamities such as Love Canal and Times Beach, and the frightening prospect of thousands of chemical and other substances with unknown effects being discharged into the human environment. We have learned that many harmful substances are not effectively neutralized when disposed of in landfills; they do not degrade into harmless materials or stay put at the site. Instead they can infect the environment, with sometimes disastrous consequences, long after their disposal. It is estimated that United States industry currently generates over a ton of hazardous wastes per person per year. Many of these wastes find their way into hazardous-waste disposal sites. EPA reports indicate that there are 16,000 to 22,000 inactive or abandoned sites scattered across the United States that are actual or potential sources of contamination. An extensive effort is now underway to identify these sites and to clean them up, in part with federal support from the recently created Superfund.

Yet more perplexing is dealing with the wide range of substances about whose effects we know virtually nothing. The Conservation Foundation (1984, p. 40) notes that although there are over 66,000 chemicals currently in commercial use in the United States, only a tiny fraction of them have been adequately tested for effects on human health. The Foundation Report concludes:

> For the most part, how to determine, or to adequately measure, many of the effects that toxic substances have on people or on the environment remains a mystery. The continuing discovery of previously unsuspected hazards from various chemicals and other substances underscores this point. The environmental and human health effects of even those substances identified for priority consideration, in general, have not been adequately studied. Moreover, until the present decade, testing of suspected toxic substances was confined largely to acute effects. Only in the last few years have the chronic, long-term effects of exposure to many of these substances been understood. Knowledge of environmental effects, how chemicals are transported through the environment, what biological pathways they follow, and where they ultimately end up is still lacking for most suspected toxic materials. A shortage of trained personnel and the absence of a comprehensive system for storing and analyzing information aggravate the scientific bases for government inaction. (pp. 65–66)

The existing evidence on the state of the environment thus indicates that much remains to be done in the control of the conventional air and water pollutants, in the identification of toxic substances and hazardous wastes, and the regulation of their production and disposal. Environmental policy has made a difference over the past decade. As was noted, intensive abatement efforts have resulted in marked improvements in certain dimensions of environmental quality. Moreover, measures of pollutant concentration indicate that levels of several air and water pollutants have at least not increased over the past decade. In the presence of a growing population and economy, this in itself is some evidence of the effectiveness of environmental policies.[5] But the remaining agenda for pollution control is long; it is one that we cannot afford to ignore.

THE COST OF POLLUTION CONTROL

As Table 11.1 indicates, pollution control is not cheap. By 1980, total expenditures on pollution abatement and control in the United States exceeded $50 billion per year, with the business sector undertaking about

TABLE II.I
Expenditures for Pollution Abatement and Control
(billions of dollars)

	1972	1975	1980
Pollution abatement			
Personal consumption	$ 1.5	$ 3.5	$ 7.0
Business	11.0	18.1	34.0
Government	4.7	7.6	11.6
Regulation and monitoring	0.4	0.7	1.3
Research and development	0.8	1.1	1.8
Total	$18.4	$30.9	$55.7

SOURCE: Council on Environmental Quality (1983, table A-80).

two-thirds of this spending and the government sector the remaining third. Such spending in 1980 represented about two percent of the GNP in the United States. As Portney (1981) has stressed, total expenditures are not identical with costs in a full economic sense. Firms, for example, may well employ certain of their own resources for abatement activities that are not reflected in actual expenditures. Probably more important, the regulatory system itself may introduce uncertainties and delays that distort economic decisions and generate costs to the economy that do not show up as spending on pollution control. In all likelihood, expenditures to some extent understate the true costs to the economy of reducing pollution.[6]

The past decade has seen troublesome price inflation and a slowed rate of economic growth. To what extent have the costs of our environmental programs contributed to the relatively poor macroeconomic performance over this period? In answering this question, it is important to emphasize the basic, if obvious, point that standard measurement procedures are, in an important sense, biased against environmental programs. Since the GNP does not include imputations for the services of the environment as a public good, benefits from pollution control do not show up as measured increases in real income.[7] Instead we see the effects expenditures on environmental protection have on the pecuniary cost of economic activities and on the price level.

Several studies have explored the macroeconomic effects of regulatory measures for pollution control. One approach has used some of the large quarterly econometric models to estimate the effect of control expenditures on the rates of price inflation and economic growth (see Portney

1981). For example, Data Resources Incorporated has employed its DRI quarterly model to estimate the macroeconomic effects of environmental regulation in the United States. The DRI results indicate that during the period 1970–1987, environmental regulation will increase the average annual inflation rate by about 0.4 percentage points; for the period 1981–1987, the estimated increase is 0.6 percentage points. DRI projects that the average annual growth rate of the GNP will fall by about 0.1 percentage points per year as a result of environmental programs.

While these are certainly not trivial magnitudes, they are not momentous. In one sense, these results should not be very surprising. The primary determinants of the projections of the macroeconomic models are levels of expenditure. Since spending on pollution control is only a minute fraction of total (and marginal) expenditure in the economy, we would not expect to find this category of spending exerting any major effect on macroeconomic variables. However, with its exclusive reliance on expenditures, this approach neglects the possibly larger adverse effects of environmental regulation, involving delays and other modifications to investment decisions. For example, Quarles (1979) has argued that implementation of the Clean Air Act has in many instances created an atmosphere of such confusion and uncertainty that many firms either delayed or abandoned plans altogether for industrial expansion.

Various other kinds of studies have tried to capture some of these effects contributing to the retardation of productivity growth. Denison (1979) has employed his "growth accounting" framework to estimate the contributions of various determinants to the slowdown in productivity growth. Siegel (1979) has used time-series econometric analysis on macroeconomic variables, and Crandall (1981) has made microeconomic estimates for certain industries that were the subject of heavy environmental regulation. Although these studies do not come to precisely the same conclusions, they reveal the same general picture. The impact of environmental regulation on productivity growth is a measurable but not a dominant one. The effects, for example, of the huge rise in energy prices in the early 1970s seem far more important in retarding growth in productivity than do those of pollution-control regulations. Haveman and Christiansen concluded that "little evidence exists to suggest that as much as 15 percent of the overall slowdown [of productivity growth] can be attributed to these [environmental] regulations. A reasonable estimate—but one resting on a good deal of judgment—is that 8 to 12 percent of the slowdown in productivity is attributable to environmental regulation" (1981, p. 74).

Interestingly, studies in other O.E.C.D. countries suggest roughly similar findings. The estimated effects of environmental measures on the rate of inflation (in terms of percentage points per year) are: Austria 0.1 to 0.3, Netherlands 0.1 to 0.6, Japan 0.4 to 0.6, France and Italy 0.1. Likewise, environmental regulations seem to have had minor effects on productivity growth. A recent O.E.C.D. study concluded: "In sum, then, the evidence makes clear that environmental regulations have contributed only modestly to the last decade's fall-off in measured labor productivity growth, and can in no way be considered the driving force behind this reduction" (1984, p. 37).

Thus, the effects of environmental policy on the performance of the macroeconomy over the past decade have been discernible, but modest. Neither in the United States nor in the other O.E.C.D. countries can environmental programs be seen as the major culprit impeding economic growth and the attainment of stable prices. Nevertheless, pollution control is expensive: the United States will probably spend well over $500 billion on environmental programs during the 1980s. For efforts of this magnitude, it is obviously important to marshall our resources in a sensible and efficient way. Large-scale misuse of these resources will undermine our capacity to achieve both environmental and other pressing social goals.

STANDARDS FOR ENVIRONMENTAL QUALITY

CRITERIA

According to basic economic principles, an activity such as pollution control should be extended to the point where marginal benefits equal marginal costs. From this perspective, the environmental authority should set standards for pollutant concentrations in the environment such that the damages from another increment of pollutant equal marginal abatement costs. Of course, the application of this simple dictum encounters formidable obstacles. For many pollutants, we do not have firm scientific knowledge of how emissions from sources translate into pollutant concentrations in the environment, or of how much harm is caused by exposure to various levels of a pollutant. Moreover, environmental degradation results in many so-called intangible damages—aesthetic insults as well as injury to health. This raises all the knotty problems of trying to assess in money terms a very diverse and uncertain range of effects on individual welfare. Steven Kelman (1981) has introduced a more philosophical objection: the act of placing the pollution problem in a benefit-cost framework itself undermines environmentalist values by making environmental quality just another commodity in the marketplace.

In response to these problems and objections to benefit-cost analysis, Congress has been quite explicit in rejecting this criterion for the determination of environmental standards. In the Clean Air Act, Congress instructed the EPA to set standards for ambient air quality "to protect the public health and welfare." This put the environmental authority in an awkward corner. The scientific evidence for most pollutants suggests a continuum of health damages. Low concentrations typically result in modest health effects; with higher concentrations these damages escalate. The EPA, however, has effectively been directed to find a threshold concentration for each pollutant below which there is *no* impairment to health. A very literal interpretation of the Clean Air Act could require concentrations of zero for certain pollutants. This is, of course, infeasible, since it would imply a complete cessation of fuel combustion and various other forms of economic activity.

The EPA has, in fact, had to make compromises. As Crandall and Portney have pointed out, "Economic and other practical considerations are surely taken into account in setting standards, even if no one is willing to admit it" (1984, p. 53). However, the legislative mandate has led to some very difficult and questionable decisions. Crandall and Portney have cited an interesting case. In 1980, the EPA proposed a tightening of the standard for carbon monoxide, intended for the protection of persons with angina pectoris. The definition of whom to protect is important here, for it was argued by others that even the more stringent standard was inadequate to prevent adverse health effects for hemolytic anemics.

> Despite this definition of the sensitive population, there is evidence that the health protection offered by reduced carbon monoxide had a very high cost indeed. According to the Regulatory Analysis and Review Group of the Executive Office of the President, comparison of the 9 parts per million (ppm) carbon monoxide standard that the EPA was proposing with a less strict alternative, 12 ppm, showed that each sick day prevented by the stricter standard would cost the nation between $6,000 and $250,000. Although the health of those with cardiovascular disease is very important, it is far from obvious that the prevention of one sick day is worth $6,000—much less a quarter of a million dollars. (Crandall and Portney 1984, p. 53)

This is not the only case for which the costs of apparently quite marginal improvements are enormous. The issue here is not that modest increments to health are not worth much—on the contrary, we may as a society be willing to make considerable sacrifices for them. The point is, rather, that the determination of standards for environmental quality inevitably involves difficult and unavoidable trade-offs between economic goals, on the one hand, and such goods as health and aesthetics on the other. The argument, incidentally, is not that environmental decisions should be based in any rigid way on a benefit-cost criterion; the available estimates of benefits and costs are typically far too tentative for that. Rather, benefit-cost estimates can provide a rough sense of orders of magnitude that can be extremely valuable in reaching an informed decision. There appears to be a growing realization of this in the policy arena. The General Accounting Office, for example, has recently issued a report (1984) urging the use of benefit-cost analysis for environmental regulations, and at the recent Paris conference of the O.E.C.D. countries sentiment was widespread that, after acknowledging all its deficiencies, "economic analyses of the costs and benefits of environmental policies can aid this decision-making process by permitting aggregation and comparison of the many heterogeneous impacts frequently associated with environmental policies" (O.E.C.D. 1984, p. 90).

When a particular control activity results in reduced illness and/or loss of life, offensive calculations of the monetary value of health and life can be avoided through a cost-effectiveness approach. This can be quite valuable in rationalizing the use of resources across different kinds of abatement efforts. Cost calculations can suggest, for example, that one form of pollution control is significantly more effective per dollar in reducing the incidence of a certain form of illness than another. Especially where a specific pollutant enters the environment through a number of different avenues, such studies can indicate the least costly way to reduce exposure.

In principle, the level of the standard should depend to some extent on the defensive activities available to those who suffer the effects of pollution.[8] Where, for example, insulation can protect against undesired noise, it is a straightforward matter to show that the marginal social damage curve will lie below that where, ceteris paribus, no such defensive activities exist. Moreover, when the standard is set correctly, it can be shown that individual maximizing behavior will lead to economically efficient levels of these defensive activities (Oates 1983). All this depends, of course, on full information both on the range of effects of the pollutants and on the extent of effectiveness of the defensive measures, information which often is far from complete. But the general point remains valid: the availability (and cost) of ways to avoid the effects of pollutants is one determinant of the optimum standard.

Responding to Kelman's philosophical objection to benefit-cost analysis is more difficult. The basic contention is that environmental resources are, in a sense, different from other goods in the marketplace. Many environmentalists believe that people have a basic right to a clean environment, and that pollution is an infringement of that basic right. Moreover, it is feared that placing environmental concerns in the economist's framework of market value will lead to a depreciation in the perceived value of our environmental resources. The claim here is that tastes for environmental quality are, to a significant degree, endogenous, and subjecting environmental standards to the benefit-cost calculus will, over time, reduce the intensity of preferences in support of environmental objectives. Hence, Kelman sees economists as lobbyists for economic efficiency in a political setting where many environmentalists seek to emphasize other objectives.

While Kelman may well be correct in describing the differing perceptions of the various participants in the environmental debate, I have a basic pragmatic difficulty with his philosophical position. Such a perspective does not provide a sound basis for environmental decisionmaking. Instead, it tends to promote legislative pronouncements like that in the Clean Water Act that specifies as an objective "the elimination of all discharges of pollutants into the navigable water by 1985," and the provision under the Clean Air Act for standards "to protect the public health and welfare." As I have argued, these are not operational objectives, and they have put the environmental authority in the difficult position of paying lip service to existing legislation while proceeding, in reality, to make the compromises inherent in environmental measures. It makes more sense, I think, to make the trade-offs explicit so that they can be assessed in a sensible way.

UNIFORM NATIONAL STANDARDS OR LOCAL VARIATION?

An important issue in standard-setting for environmental quality is whether to allow local diversity. Should the central environmental authority establish a single standard binding in all areas, or should regional or local authorities tailor standards to their own circumstances? Interestingly, as noted above, environmental legislation in the United States is not consistent on this matter. Under the Clean Air Act, Congress instructed the EPA to set national minimum standards for ambient air quality, and the EPA responded by establishing maximum levels of concentration for the criteria air pollutants applicable to all areas in the country. States have

FIGURE 11.2

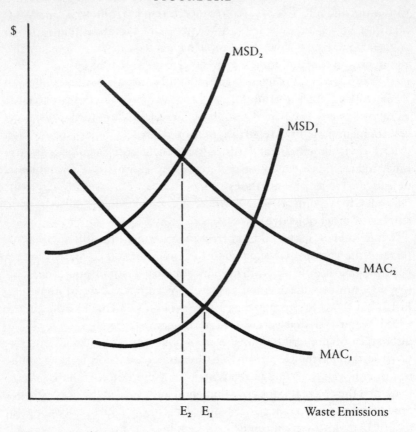

the option of establishing more stringent standards for air quality, but only California has yet chosen to do so. In contrast, under the Clean Water Act, the individual states have the responsibility for setting water-quality standards, although the EPA plays an important role in specifying treatment technology and issuing permits to dischargers. We thus have uniform national standards for air quality but state-specific standards for water quality.

Simple economic analysis again provides a seemingly straightforward resolution of this issue: standards should vary across jurisdictions in accordance with local circumstances. The economically optimal level of environmental quality is that for which the marginal social damages of waste emissions equal marginal abatement cost. Figure 11.2 depicts such an outcome. Suppose that MSD_1 and MAC_1 are, respectively, the marginal-social-damage and the marginal-abatement-cost functions in jurisdiction 1; then the economically optimal level of waste emissions is E_1. Other jurisdictions, however, will typically have different MSD and MAC functions; if, for instance, MSD_2 and MAC_2 are the curves for jurisdiction 2, then local authorities in 2 should set a more stringent standard for environmental quality than in jurisdiction 1 ($E_2 < E_1$).

An interesting question is, would one expect the optimal level of environmental quality to be higher in an urban area or in a less densely populated, rural area? To address this question, we must examine the determinants of the two functions. Since environmental quality is basically a public good, we derive the MSD curve through the vertical summation of individual marginal damage curves. If people's tastes for environmental quality are roughly similar, we would expect a higher MSD curve in a more heavily populated area—reflecting the greater number of people suffering damage from existing pollution. In Figure 11.2, we might associate MSD_1 with the rural area and MSD_2 with the urban area. The MAC curve, in contrast, is a horizontal summation of individual MAC curves. Since a typical urban area will presumably have far more sources of waste emissions than our prototype rural area, we would expect the urban MAC curve to lie to the right of the rural curve. In Figure 11.2, MAC_1 might represent the rural curve, while MAC_2 indicates the comparatively higher level of abatement costs in the urban area for any given level of emissions. We could thus associate MAC_1 and MSD_1 with a representative rural area as compared to MAC_2 and MSD_2 for the urban area. It is now clear that there is no presumption a priori as to whether the optimal level of environmental quality will be higher in urban or rural areas. Both the marginal damages from pollution and the marginal abatement costs are likely to be higher in the urban area, so the outcome depends on the relative magnitudes for a particular case.[9]

The analysis does clearly suggest that the optimal pollution level will vary across jurisdictions. What, then, is the case for uniform national (perhaps minimum) standards? John Cumberland (1979, 1981) has made the case for national minimum ambient standards on two grounds. The first is interregional externalities. Unfortunately, existing political jurisdictions often do not conform at all well to appropriate environmental jurisdictions: pollution generated in one area may well settle elsewhere. This led Cumberland to the conclusion that fully decentralized environmental decisionmaking is likely to result in excessive pollution: "The federal level should set maximum emission or minimum ambient standards to avoid the deliberate or inadvertent tendency of local regions to site detrimental activities on border locations which cause interregional flows to impact inequitably on downstream regions" (1981, p. 8). Second, Cumberland stressed the possibility of "destructive interregional competition." In their eagerness to encourage new business investment and the creation of jobs, state or local authorities may compete with one another in reducing standards for environmental quality so as to reduce costs for prospective business enterprise. The argument here parallels the phenomenon of tax competition among jurisdictions to promote state or local economic development.

Just where all this leaves us is difficult to say. It is really a matter of the comparative magnitude of welfare losses. We know that uniform national standards will entail allocative losses (relative to the first-best outcome), because of the failure to allow local standards to reflect local costs and benefits. But how large are these losses compared to those associated with the likely distortions from interjurisdictional externalities and competition? It is hard to know without careful empirical work to provide a sense of the relevant magnitudes, but let me offer a couple of observations. First, it is not clear that setting minimum national standards is the appropriate response to the problem of interjurisdictional externalities. A national standard for the concentration of a particular pollutant, for example, will not in itself lead one jurisdiction to cease polluting its neighbor. It may simply induce the unfortunate neighbor to reduce its own emissions to offset the unwelcome inflow of the pollutant. What is needed is some mechanism to internalize the externality. This could conceivably take the form of Coasian negotiations between the jurisdictions or, alternatively, of federal intervention to regulate interjurisdictional flows of pollutants (such as restrictions on tall stacks).[10]

The environmental-competition argument is also hard to evaluate. Depreciation of environmental standards will itself impose costs on the local populace, and the extent to which it is in the local authority's interest to promote economic development at the expense of the local environment is unclear. Conceivably, states or localities might choose to compete by offering higher environmental quality. As I noted earlier, no state, save California, presently has ambient-air-quality standards more stringent than the national minima. One might interpret this as an indication that the EPA has set tougher standards than the optimal ones for virtually all states. Alternatively, one could see this outcome as providing support for the interjurisdictional competition argument: states have competed to the fullest extent allowable by holding their standards down to the national minimum.

Although it is admittedly difficult, at this juncture, to reach any firm conclusions on the national/local issue in standard-setting, it is my judgment that some local variation in standards is needed (and, ultimately, inevitable). Several United States cities, for example, are still nonattainment areas for certain of the criteria air pollutants; moreover, it will probably prove infeasible (i.e., too costly) for some of them ever to achieve the standards. I suspect that the optimal level of environmental quality varies widely across jurisdictions and that the welfare losses associated with enforcing a uniform standard are quite large. Greater leeway for tailoring standards to local circumstances is probably in order.

REGULATORY STRATEGIES
FOR CONTROLLING POLLUTION

The second part of the policy problem is the design and implementation of a regulatory mechanism to attain the prescribed standards for environmental quality. Two broad regulatory strategies are available: (1) a command-and-control (CAC) approach under which the environmental authority specifies how polluters are to behave; or (2) a system of economic incentives through which the authority creates economic inducements for abatement activity but leaves polluters free to determine their own responses to these incentives.

Each of the classes of regulatory strategies offers a number of alternative policy instruments (and the distinctions between these policy instruments are important). Under CAC, for example, the environmental agency may prescribe in detail a set of *technology-based standards* that define specific abatement techniques for each source. Alternatively, the agency may simply set *performance standards* consisting of an overall ceiling on emissions for each source, leaving the source to determine the most effective way to meet its emissions limitation. Likewise, economic incentives can take many different forms including effluent charges, marketable emission permits, or various deposit-refund schemes.

COMMAND-AND-CONTROL VERSUS ECONOMIC INCENTIVES

The objective of the regulatory system is to achieve the set of predetermined environmental-quality standards in the least burdensome way. A potential regulatory mechanism thus must be evaluated in terms of its capacity to insure attainment of the standards and to minimize the costs it imposes on society in the course of reaching these standards. In order to minimize aggregate control costs, a regulatory system must satisfy two conditions: (1) each source must meet its own emissions limitation in the least costly way; and (2) the pattern of emissions limitations (or abatement quotas) among polluters must be an efficient one so that savings cannot be realized simply by adjustments to the pattern of waste discharges among sources.

We immediately see a basic difference between the two CAC instruments. Under technology-based standards, the environmental authority must prescribe a specific abatement technology for each source. This makes enormous information demands on the regulatory agency if each source is to employ the least-cost method of pollution control. In contrast, with performance standards the agency need only determine an overall emissions limit for each source; the polluter is left to find for himself the least expensive technique for compliance. Under the performance-standards method, the authority will admittedly not be able to determine the least-cost set of abatement quotas across sources without knowledge of the individual abatement-cost functions, but at least this policy instrument can make use of the cost-minimizing propensity of the individual sources to satisfy the first of the above conditions for minimizing aggregate abatement costs. Moreover, performance standards provide some incentive in a dynamic context for sources to seek new and cheaper technologies to meet their emissions limitation.[11] There is little incentive for such technological change under technology-based standards. Thus a strong case can be made within the CAC framework for the use of performance standards instead of technology-based standards.

However, a properly designed set of economic incentives has the potential to satisfy both of the conditions for cost minimization and to do so with relatively modest informational demands on the regulatory authority. Taking a simple case, suppose that the environmental damages for an increment of emissions are the same across all sources. Then it is easy to show that an effluent charge set so as to restrict aggregate discharges to the level needed to meet the environmental quality standard will generate the least-cost outcome (Baumol and Oates 1975, ch. 10). In this case, the first-order condition for cost minimization is to equate marginal abatement cost (MAC) across all sources. Since cost-minimizing polluters will extend abatement activity to the point at which MAC equals the effluent fee, it follows that the equilibrium outcome will be characterized by the necessary equality of MAC across polluters. Where the marginal damages differ from emissions from various sources as a result of location (or, perhaps, varying chimney heights), the issue becomes somewhat more complicated—a point to which we will return below.

A system of economic incentives can thus promise greater savings in abatement costs than a CAC regime. How large are these potential savings? We now have a substantial body of empirical work that has explored this issue for a considerable variety of air and water pollutants. This work consists mainly of simulation studies that compare the costs of pollution control under different regulatory systems. These studies have two ingredients: a dispersion model of the air shed or waterway that indicates the effect of emissions from each source on pollutant concentrations at the various receptor points, and abatement-cost functions for each source. With these data alternative regulatory "rules" can be simulated to determine the resulting levels of abatement costs and of pollutant concentrations at each receptor point. These simulation outcomes allow us to compare the effects on pollution levels and control costs of a variety of CAC and economic-incentive schemes.

On the whole, these studies suggest very large potential cost savings from properly designed systems of economic incentives as compared to CAC programs. The magnitude of these savings depends on what assumptions are made concerning the form of the economic incentives, and also, of course, on the CAC regime used for purposes of the comparison.

Before turning to the simulation studies, it is worth noting the findings in a survey of the costs of controlling hydrocarbon emissions in a particular metropolitan area. In 1979, a state agency in Maryland collected estimates of abatement costs for a sample of point sources of hydrocarbon emissions in Baltimore. The findings are quite striking. Among the large point sources, for example, unit costs of abatement ranged from $0.06 per pound to $1.55 per pound—a differential in excess of an order of magnitude. The variation in abatement costs among the sources was extremely large, suggesting the potential for large cost-savings from a more efficient allocation of abatement activity among sources.

Some estimates of the magnitude of these potential savings are indicated in Table 11.2, which presents the findings from seven simulation studies of pollution control, five relating to air pollution and two to water quality. The table shows figures for the least-cost solution to the control problem and for a representative CAC system. In some instances the CAC system is modeled on the actual control program (e.g., the state implementation plan, or SIP, for certain of the air pollutants); in other cases the CAC baseline is of a cruder form involving, for example, an assumed equi-proportionate reduction in emissions from all sources. Table 11.2 reveals enormous differentials between aggregate control costs under the CAC system and the least-cost outcome. Aggregate abatement costs un-

TABLE 11.2

Aggregate Abatement Costs: Least-Cost Solution
and CAC Outcome (millions of dollars per year)

Study	Pollutant/Place	Least-Cost	CAC
Seskin et al.	Nitrogen dioxide in		
(1983)	Chicago AQCR	$ 9.0	$66.0
Md. Dept. of Economic	Nitrogen dioxide in	1.7	9.9
Community	Baltimore AQCR	0.4	1.2
Development (1982)		0.07	1.5
McGartland and	Particulates in		
Oates (forthcoming)	Baltimore AQCR	27.0	113.0
Atkinson and Lewis	Particulates in		
(1974)	St. Louis AQCR	0.2	2.7
Palmer et al.	Chlorofluorocarbon		
(1980)	emissions in U.S.	110.0	230.0
Kneese et al.	BOD emissions in	1.6	5.0
(1971)	Delaware River estuary	7.0	20.0
O'Neil et al.	BOD emissions in		
(1983)	Fox River	10.3	16.1

NOTE: The pairs of numbers refer to abatement costs for differing levels of environmental quality.
AQCR = Air Quality Control Region.

der CAC are, in every case save one, at least twice as large as under the least-cost solution—and, in certain instances, more than an order of magnitude larger. The first four simulation studies, which examine nitrogen dioxide and particulate pollutants in the atmosphere, find huge differences in control costs between CAC and the least-cost case. The relative differentials, although still sizable, are somewhat smaller for the water-quality simulations (involving BOD emissions). Because the various studies use different environmental objectives and CAC baselines, their findings are not really comparable, but they do provide some rough sense of the large differences between the least-cost and CAC outcomes.

These findings suggest very large *potential* savings from a more efficient system of regulation. However, the results in a sense stack the deck in favor of economic incentives. The real issue is the extent to which alternative regulatory mechanisms have the capacity to realize these potential savings.

EFFLUENT FEES VERSUS MARKETABLE EMISSION PERMITS

While it is possible in principle to design a system of effluent fees or marketable permits that can generate the least-cost outcome, it is usually not a simple matter. For the special case where the effect of a unit of emissions on pollutant concentrations is independent of the location and other characteristics of the source, the solution is fairly straightforward. The environmental authority can either establish a uniform effluent fee at the requisite level to meet the standard or issue the appropriate number of permits (either through an auction or by direct distribution to sources). The permits would be freely tradable among sources on a one-for-one basis (i.e., a permit for one unit of emission would entitle any source to emit a unit of the pollutant). One interesting case of such a pollutant is chlorofluorocarbons (CFC). The effect of CFCs in depleting the ozone layer in the stratosphere does not appear to depend upon where on the earth's surface the discharge occurs; thus a national (or global) market in emission permits would not have to distinguish among sources.

However, for most air and water pollutants, the location of the source (and certain other characteristics such as chimney height) are quite important determinants of the ultimate effect of a discharge on the pattern of pollutant concentrations in the environment. The effect, for example, of a unit of particulate emission will be very different if it is discharged on the windward side of an air shed than if its source is on the opposite, leeward border of the area. Where spatial (and other) characteristics matter, it can be shown that the first-order conditions for cost minimization require that the "shadow price" for waste discharges for each source reflect the relative contribution of that source's emissions to pollution. If source A's discharges result in twice as much pollution per unit of discharge as source B's, then source A should face a "price" twice as high as B's.

The implication is that a cost-minimizing system of effluent charges (aside from our special case of pollutants such as CFCs) must take the form of a differentiated set of charges among sources. While this may not be a troublesome issue in principle, it is a real liability in the policy arena. The environmental agency is unlikely to have the authority to discriminate among sources in the necessary way; "discriminatory" taxes are often either unconstitutional or very unpopular. Suppose the agency is constrained to a uniform fee system—how seriously is this likely to impair the cost-saving capacity of the system? Simulation studies suggest that uniform fee systems may perform quite badly. For a case in point, we return to the study by Seskin et al. (1983, cited in Table 11.2) on nitrogen dioxide emissions in the Chicago Air Quality Control Region. This study estimated the least-cost outcome to entail annual control costs of about $9 million per annum, while under their CAC system, annual costs are projected to be $66 million. In contrast, a uniform fee sufficiently high to attain the environmental standard would result in abatement costs of $305 million! This astonishing result reflects the high degree of "overcontrol" that many sources must undertake in relatively clean sectors of the air shed in order to get sufficient abatement in the "hot spots." Other studies confirm this general result. The failure to make the necessary spatial (and other) distinctions among sources can seriously undermine the efficiency-enhancing properties of a system of economic incentives.[12]

It is a powerful advantage, I believe, of marketable permit systems that they can incorporate these specific characteristics of the sources in a manner that is less objectionable to policymakers. This is accomplished in the following way: all sales of permits among sources are made subject to the constraint of no violation of the environmental-quality standard at any receptor point. This implies that if, as before, source A's emissions are twice as damaging as source B's, then A will have to purchase from B two units of emission reduction to justify an additional unit of discharge of its own. Note that this is equivalent to charging source A a fee on its emissions that is twice as high as B's fee. Moreover, this condition on trades can be, in principle, and has been, in practice, incorporated into exchanges of emission rights. Thus, systems of marketable permits have, in the policy context, a much greater potential for realizing cost-savings than do effluent charges.

Permit systems have four additional and important advantages over systems of fees. First, from the perspective of a regulator, permits promise more direct control over the level of emissions. The setting of fees puts the regulating agency in the less comfortable position of influencing quantity only indirectly, through price. If the fee is set too low, the resulting emissions will be excessive, with the consequent failure to achieve the mandated level of environmental quality. In a policy setting in which the regulator must insure that specified levels of pollutant concentrations are not exceeded (as under the Clean Air Act in the United States), a preference for control over quantity to control over price is easily understandable.

Second, and closely related to the above issue, are the complications that result from economic growth and price inflation. Under a system of effluent fees, continuing inflation will erode the real value of the fee; similarly, expanding production from both existing and new firms will increase the levels of waste emissions if fee levels are held constant. Both these forces will require the fee to be raised periodically if environmental standards are to be maintained. In short, the burden of initiating action under fees is on environmental officials; the choice will be between unpopular fee increases or nonattainment of standards. Under a system of permits, market forces automatically accommodate inflation and growth with no increase in pollution. The rise in demand for permits translates directly into a higher price.

Third, permits are likely to be more attractive to sources than are fees. Somewhat paradoxically, in spite of the large savings in abatement costs relative to CAC, a system of effluent fees can result in much higher costs for polluters. This results from a new form of costs to sources: the fee bill. Not only must polluters bear their costs of abatement, but they must also pay a fee on their remaining emissions. While such payments represent a transfer from the perspective of society, they are nevertheless a cost to sources. Existing simulation studies suggest some rather staggering estimates for potential fee bills. In the RAND study of chlorofluorocarbon emissions into the atmosphere (Palmer et al., cited in Table 11.2), the control costs under a hypothetical CAC program were estimated to be $230 million. A prospective fee program promised large savings in abatement costs—about 50 percent—with control costs projected at $110 million. But the associated fee payments were estimated by the RAND group at $1400 million! These results suggest that a fee program could impose costs on sources over six times as large as the CAC regime. Another study suggests similar findings. The simulations by Seskin and his colleagues (also cited in Table 11.2) for nitrogen dioxide discharges in the Chicago AQCR reach similarly dramatic conclusions: they estimate that fee payments under a system of uniform effluent fees would total $414 million, as compared to total control costs of $132 million under a representative CAC program.

These are troublesome results. For feasible policy reform, we typically search for proposals that represent a Pareto improvement. Based on existing studies, it is hard to believe that a fee system will typically make sources better off.[13] However, a permit system need not impose additional costs on existing polluters. Instead of auctioning off the permits, the system can be set in motion with an initial distribution of permits to sources. Trading can then proceed from this initial allocation. Some have objected on equity grounds to a distribution to polluters of "property rights" to the environment. However, the equity issue is a complex one. We should recall, for instance, that most sources have already been required to institute extensive control measures to reduce their waste discharges. Starting from the existing CAC equilibrium, the proposal is to allocate entitlements only for the remaining, or residual, discharges.

Fourth, the use of permits offers to both regulators and sources the attraction of familiarity. The introduction of a fee system involves a wholly new form of environmental management with uncertain consequences from the perspectives of the administering agencies and polluters. Permits already exist. It would seem a much less radical move to make permits transferable than to supplant permits altogether by a new system of effluent fees.

In a policy setting, a system of marketable permits thus has some compelling advantages over effluent fees. But I do not want to overstate the case. There surely are circumstances under which fees are the more attractive policy instrument. As Weitzman (1974) has shown, where marginal social damages (MSD) are readily measurable and fairly constant over the relevant range, a fee set equal to MSD can be the more effective means for attaining the efficient level of the polluting activity. Harrison (1983) has suggested that this may well be the case for regulation of airport noise. However, my sense is that the range of application for such a use of fees may be rather limited. Particularly when the spatial dimension of the pollution problem is important so that sources must confront different "prices" (as is true for most major air and water pollutants), the design *and* implementation of the requisite fee system are likely to prove very difficult. For these cases, marketable permits represent the more promising approach. From this perspective, it is not surprising to find the evolution of environmental policy taking the direction of marketable permits instead of fees. Two recent innovative programs in the United States, one for the control of air pollution and one for the management of water quality, represent exciting new experiments with the permit approach to a system of economic incentives for protection of the environment.

EMISSIONS TRADING AND THE WISCONSIN TDP SYSTEM

The Emissions Trading Program has its legislative origins in the 1977 Amendments to the Clean Air Act. As was noted above, Congress and the EPA headed off a political confrontation by introducing a provision for "offsets" in nonattainment areas. Under this provision, new sources could enter such areas if their emissions were more than offset by reductions in existing sources' discharges. This authorization for offsets effectively legalized certain transfers of emissions entitlements among sources. The EPA has extended the offset strategy to encompass a broader set of provisions that will facilitate emissions transfers. This framework, now called emissions trading, has three components: bubbles, offsets, and banking. Under the first, an imaginary bubble is placed over a plant or firm with multiple sources of emissions. Instead of meeting technological standards or permit limits on each source under the bubble, the firm is treated as a single unit subject to an overall emissions limitation. Within this overall limitation, the firm is free to determine its own pattern of abatement activity and emissions. The offset policy amounts, in a sense, to an extension of the bubble to encompass trades between firms. A number of administrative restrictions exist on the use of these procedures, but the basic point is that under the bubble and offset policies, firms can trade emissions both within their own establishments and with other firms.

The most recent component of the emissions trading framework is the banking provision. Introduced in 1979, banking allows firms to receive credits for emissions reductions in excess of those required under existing regulations. These credits can be used later by the firm to increase emissions, or they can be sold for use as an offset by another firm.

In spite of the somewhat exotic terminology, the various components of emissions trading are really no more than routine dimensions of a conventional market. The trades permitted under the bubble and offset provisions and the storing of credits under banking all represent standard forms of economic behavior in the marketplace. From this perspective, emissions trading can be seen as a framework for establishing a market in emissions entitlements. A basic limit to overall emissions is set by the predetermined ambient-air-quality standard, and, subject to this limit, firms can trade emissions. However, the emissions trading program is embedded in a broader body of regulations, some of which prescribe technology-based standards and place obstacles in the way of cost-saving trades. Moreover, each state must implement the general framework for emissions trading with its own state implementation plan (SIP). But emissions trading has made real headway in some regions. Nearly all states now have offset provisions in their SIP, and several hundreds of transactions, many resulting in quite large savings, have taken place.

There have been certain impediments, however, to trading in the air-emissions market. Perhaps the most serious is a general sense of uncertainty concerning the nature and life of this new form of property right. Some sources, fearing changes in regulations (perhaps involving more stringent abatement requirements) have been reluctant to part with their emissions entitlements. It is absolutely essential to the proper functioning of these markets that the participants have firm guarantees and full confidence in the validity of their entitlements. With such guarantees and some further experience with trading institutions and procedures, emissions trades should become more widespread.

The new Wisconsin system of transferable discharge permits (TDP), unlike emissions trading, has its origins in a coordinated effort at the state level. Economists at the University of Wisconsin and officials in the Wisconsin Department of Natural Resources have designed the system to regulate water quality on Wisconsin's most polluted stretches of river, notably the Fox River, with its heavy concentration of paper and pulp mills along with several municipal waste-treatment plants.

The system that emerged is a sophisticated form of transferable discharge permits, designed to achieve a target level of water quality of 5 parts per million of dissolved oxygen (DO)—sufficient to sustain fishlife and allow recreational activities on the river. Along the Fox River there are two stationary "sag points," located behind dams, where the DO content of the water reaches its lowest levels. The problem thus becomes one of insuring that the DO content stays at or above 5 ppm at these locations. A model of the river indicates the effect that a unit of emissions from each source will have on the DO level at the sag points. The permit system begins with an initial allocation of allowable discharges (based on historical levels) among the sources that is consistent with achieving the water-quality target. Sources are then free to trade permits among themselves subject to certain constraints, one of which is that they meet the water-quality standard. Note that, as under emissions trading, this constraint implies that permits typically will not be traded on a simple one-for-one basis. Where the pollution constraint is binding, the source whose emissions have a relatively large effect on water quality at a sag point will have to buy permits from other sources in an amount greater than the increase in its own emissions. The Wisconsin system explicitly incorporates the spatial dimensions of the pollution problem in such a way that it has the potential to realize the least-cost pattern of emissions among sources.

Another interesting feature of the Wisconsin permit system is that allowable emissions vary with the river's capacity to assimilate them. This capacity varies widely over the year with changes in river flow and temperature. During the summer, when water flow is relatively low and temperature comparatively high, emissions tend to be more damaging. Under the Wisconsin plan, the level of emissions allowed per permit is itself variable. Such "flow-temperature" permits require sources to adapt their levels of discharges to river conditions. To help accommodate the needed adjustments, the TDP system can allow short-term leasing of permits among sources.

Like emissions trading, however, the TDP scheme is built on a CAC system that requires certain minimum treatment activities on the part of all sources. Nevertheless, the estimated potential savings compared to a wholly CAC regime are substantial—on the order of 80 percent over a crude CAC system that imposes an equiproportionate cutback on all sources.

SOME FURTHER ISSUES

Marketable permit systems thus appear to offer a promising alternative to an exclusive reliance on the CAC approach to regulation. But there are some potential difficulties that need to be resolved. In their important work in California, Robert Hahn and Roger Noll (1983; F. Cass et al. 1982) have explored the extent of distortions that can arise from market imperfections. In particular, the presence of one large polluter with substantial power in the permit market can result in an inefficient pattern of abatement activity across sources. On another issue, Scott Atkinson and Tom Tietenberg (1982) have voiced their concern that proposed market systems, although meeting the formal standards for ambient air quality, may result in degradation of local air quality in places where, under existing CAC systems, it is currently cleaner than the standards require. However, it has been shown that by introducing a further constraint on trading, such increments to air pollution can, in principle, be avoided. In fact, it is not hard to design a marketable permit system that, starting from an initial CAC equilibrium, can bring both improved environmental quality and reduced abatement costs to polluters (see McGartland and Oates forthcoming). Such a system represents a Pareto improvement from the perspectives both of environmentalists and of sources.

Finally, the response of sources to the opportunities for trading in these markets remains to be seen. This, of course, will be the real test of the ability of systems of marketable emission permits to achieve our environmental objectives at relatively low cost. We have had some experience with emissions trading that suggests certain "start-up" problems including reluctance to engage in trades. However, as all this becomes more familiar, these markets should become more active.

MONITORING AND ENFORCEMENT

Discussions of regulatory systems for the control of pollution inevitably come around to the issue of monitoring waste discharges and enforcing effluent limitations. It is tempting to acknowledge the importance of the matter and then to dismiss it on the grounds that it is not really relevant to the choice of a particular regulatory system; after all, any system will require monitoring and enforcement. However, there are some differences. Market-incentive systems require the actual measurement of the quantity of waste discharges, since the fee bill (or, alternatively, the emissions entitlement under a permit system) is based on the actual level of emissions.[14]

In contrast, the monitoring requirements of a command-and-control system will depend on its characteristics. As was noted earlier, technology-based standards specify the use of particular treatment procedures or equipment. For this kind of system, monitoring need only entail periodic inspections to determine that the mandated procedure is in use—measurement of effluents may not be necessary. Performance standards can be more demanding since, like market-incentive systems, they generally refer to actual levels of discharges. Even these general observations mask the range of subtleties and possibilities in monitoring emissions of particular pollutants. Reasonably satisfactory shortcuts to determining levels of waste emissions (e.g., based on the sulfur content of the fuel used) can exist. Or, as in some instances under emissions trading, transfers may be made contingent on the sources' installation of sophisticated monitoring devices. Monitoring and enforcement are serious issues, but it is not my sense that they constitute anything like insuperable obstacles to the introduction of market-incentive schemes. The potential gains-from-trade typically dwarf the costs of even quite sophisticated techniques for monitoring waste discharges.

THE REAGAN ADMINISTRATION RECORD AND SOME CONCLUSIONS

The Reagan administration inherited an array of environmental policies beset with fundamental problems: widespread delays and noncompliance, inadequate monitoring and data systems, unsatisfactory procedures for standard-setting, a command-and-control regulatory system imposing inordinately and unnecessarily high costs on the economy, and lack of a much-needed analytical and research capability.[15]

While these problems are sources of genuine concern, they represented an opportunity for the incoming administration to give a new direction and impetus to environmental management in this country. The Carter administration had already set in motion one important line of reform, the emissions trading program, which introduced the use of market incentives for pollution control with the potential for large savings. Moreover, the two early cornerstones of environmental legislation, the Clean Air and Clean Water acts, were both scheduled to come before Congress for reconsideration during the Reagan term of office. The time was ripe for some fundamental changes in United States environmental policy.

From this perspective, the overall Reagan record to date is distinctly disappointing (although this last year has seen marked improvement). It began with what proved to be unfortunate appointments of key officials, people with little experience in environmental management and with little confidence in the existing staff. The primary concern of the administration seemed to be cutting the EPA budget (which was accomplished) and easing certain standards, rather than a careful reassessment and restructuring of existing programs. The administration pressed for no fundamental reforms in the Clean Air and Water acts when they came up for renewal; there was a virtual absence of legislative initiatives from the executive branch. What took place instead was unproductive haggling over particular environmental standards. Moreover, until quite recently the administration did little to sustain the momentum established under emissions trading for basic regulatory reform involving the introduction of market incentives for pollution control.

The Reagan administration can point only to a few modest successes in environmental policy: some progress in reducing the regulatory backlog with revised effluent guidelines for water polluters and the processing of SIP modifications, and some recent extensions of emissions trading to encompass, for example, a lead-trading policy. On the whole the record is not impressive: it represents a chronicle of "mistaken priorities and missed opportunities" (Crandall and Portney 1984, p. 61).[16]

In consequence, the agenda for the reform of environmental policy in the United States is much the same as it was when the Reagan presidency began in 1980. In my view, the most pressing issues for reform continue to include:

1. Restructuring regulatory mechanisms for controlling waste discharges to embody more efficient techniques for achieving our environmental quality standards. As I have suggested, measures that incorporate economic incentives, particularly systems of marketable emission permits, provide a very promising alternative to an exclusive reliance on traditional CAC policies. Emissions trading and the Wisconsin TDP system represent innovative and important moves in this direction.

2. Introduction of procedures for setting environmental standards that take account of the relevant benefits and costs. This will require identifying pollutants where scientific knowledge is lacking and undertaking the research needed to provide the requisite information.

3. Reassessment of the roles of the various levels of government in standard-setting and in the design and implementation of regulatory systems. My sense is that the attempt to define and enforce uniform national standards for the criteria air pollutants is ill-advised. Environmental measures will, I suspect, better promote the social welfare if they are tailored to local circumstances.

4. Improvement in systems of monitoring and enforcement. As Crandall and Portney (1984) stress, there exists widespread noncompliance with existing standards—just how wide is not clear, since the monitoring system is at present inadequate to make such a determination. We need to develop an effective nationwide system of monitors for ambient environmental quality, and also more reliable techniques for measuring and testing the discharges of individual sources.

This juncture in the evolution of our environmental policies presents real opportunities for redirection of efforts in ways that can both improve environmental quality and reduce the burden of the regulatory system on the economy.

ACKNOWLEDGMENTS

I am grateful to Paul Portney, John Quigley, Daniel Rubinfeld, and Timothy Sullivan for valuable comments on an earlier draft and to the National Science Foundation for its support of my research into environmental policy.

NOTES

1. The six criteria air pollutants are sulfur dioxide, total suspended particulates, carbon monoxide, nitrogen dioxide, ozone, and lead.

2. This section draws heavily on the Conservation Foundation report (1984) and on the recent annual report by the Council on Environmental Quality (1983).

3. One caveat here is that the nationwide monitoring network is far from adequate. As Crandall and Portney (1984) stress, we cannot have complete confidence in reported readings, because of deficiencies in both the number of monitors and their reliability. Crandall

(1983) is also skeptical of progress as measured in terms of the PSI because, as noted, trends in certain of the air pollutants can pass unnoticed.

4. In a recent move the EPA, reversing an earlier position, has proposed yet more stringent lead standards. This decision is apparently based on a reassessment of the serious health effects of lead (particularly on children in the central cities) and on some evidence suggesting that progress in reducing lead emissions is being undermined by the continued use of older cars, the disconnection of auto emissions-control systems, and illegal use of leaded fuel. The distinction, incidentally, between the criteria air pollutants and toxic substances is not altogether clear; this is illustrated by the inclusion of lead as both a criteria air pollutant and a toxic substance.

5. As was noted earlier, however, not all the improvement can be attributed to policy. Some of the changes in air quality, for example, resulted not from the Clean Air Act but from increases in fuel prices and economic fluctuations that caused reductions in consumption of fuels, and consequently in emissions of certain pollutants.

6. As Portney (1981) has noted, however, in certain instances reported pollution control expenditures may exceed actual spending, for sources may overreport control activities to emphasize how burdensome existing regulatory measures are.

7. It is quite possible for increased environmental degradation to raise the GNP as individuals spend more to defend themselves against damage. See Peskin (1981) for a careful treatment of the relationship between the national income accounts and the quality of the environment.

8. Typically, individuals can mitigate the effects of existing pollution in a number of ways ranging from various sorts of cleansing devices to changes in location or even in occupation to reduce exposure. Such defensive measures obviously vary widely in their cost. Putting it slightly differently, Paul Portney has suggested to me a kind of continuum in the extent of the voluntary character of exposure to pollutants. At one end of the spectrum are activities such as smoking which are wholly by individual choice, while toward the other end is ambient air pollution where exposure is much more difficult to avoid.

9. As Daniel Rubinfeld has pointed out to me, if environmental quality is a normal good and if urban residents have lower incomes on average than rural residents, it is possible that the MSD_1 curve could lie above the MSD_2 curve. The higher willingness-to-pay of rural residents would, in such a case, more than offset their fewer numbers. For some evidence on this relative to clean air, see Harrison and Rubinfeld (1978).

10. Daniel Rubinfeld has suggested to me that existing tort law specifies property rights in such a way that the Coase approach might work under certain circumstances. One possibility within states is nuisance suits across jurisdictions.

11. However, the incentive for innovation in abatement technology under performance standards can easily be eroded if sources have reason to believe that improved abatement techniques will induce the environmental authority to tighten the standards.

12. A feasible compromise might be for the environmental authority to divide the air shed into zones and set a different effluent fee for each zone. Even this is unlikely to be fully satisfactory, however, for the impact of sources within the same zone can differ significantly as a result of source-specific characteristics such as chimney height or the exit velocity of the pollutant.

13. It is possible to design a fee system that is less burdensome to sources by assigning to each source some allowable level of emissions and assessing fees only on discharges in excess of the baseline. For such a proposal see Crandall (1983, ch. 10).

14. In fact, fee systems may demand considerably more refinement in monitoring than marketable-permit systems. Continuous monitoring to determine total discharges over a period will typically be needed to calculate the fee bill. Under a permit system, periodic checks to insure that the emissions entitlement is not being exceeded may be sufficient.

15. The discussion of the Reagan record in this section draws heavily on the excellent paper by Crandall and Portney (1984).

16. But I again note the recent improvement in EPA performance under the direction of its new administrator, William Ruckelshaus. Of particular importance is the effort to initiate cleanup of some of the most serious hazardous-waste sites.

REFERENCES

Atkinson, S., and D. Lewis. 1974. "A Cost Effectiveness Analysis of Alternative Air Quality Control Strategies." *Journal of Environmental Economics and Management* 1: 237–50.

Atkinson, S., and T. Tietenberg. 1982. "The Empirical Properties of Two Classes of Designs for Transferable Discharge Permit Markets," *Journal of Environmental Economics and Management* 9 (June 1982): 101–121.

Baumol, W., and W. Oates. 1975. *The Theory of Environmental Policy.* Englewood Cliffs, N.J.: Prentice-Hall.

Cass, G., R. Hahn, R. Noll, et al. 1982. *Implementing Tradable Permits for Sulfur Oxides Emissions.* Environmental Quality Laboratory Report 22–2. Pasadena: California Institute of Technology.

Conservation Foundation. 1984. *State of the Environment: An Assessment at Mid-Decade.* Washington, D.C.: Conservation Foundation.

Council on Environmental Quality. 1983. *Environmental Quality, 1982.* Washington, D.C.: U.S. Government Printing Office.

Crandall, R. 1981. "Pollution Controls and Productivity Growth in Basic Industries." Pp. 347–68 in T. Cowing and R. Stevenson, eds., *Productivity Measurements in Regulated Industries.* 1981. New York: Academic Press.

———. 1983. *Controlling Industrial Pollution: The Economics and Politics of Clean Air.* Washington, D.C.: Brookings.

Crandall, R., and P. Portney. 1984. "Environmental Policy." Pp. 47–82 in P. Portney, ed., *Natural Resources and the Environment: The Reagan Approach.* Washington, D.C.: Urban Institute.

Cumberland, J. 1979. "Interregional Pollution Spillovers and Consistency of Environmental Policy." Pp. 255–81 in H. Siebert et al., eds., *Regional Environmental Policy: The Economic Issues.* New York: New York University.

———. 1981. "Efficiency and Equity in Interregional Environmental Management." *Review of Regional Studies* 10 (no. 2): 1–9.

Denison, E. 1979. "Pollution Abatement Programs: Estimates of Their Effect upon Output per Unit of Input, 1975–78." *Survey of Current Business* 59 (August 1979): 58–59.

Hahn, R., and R. Noll. 1983. "Barriers to Implementing Tradable Air Pollution Permits: Problems of Regulatory Interactions." *Yale Journal on Regulation* 1, 1: 63–91.

Harrison, D. 1983. "The Regulation of Aircraft Noise." Pp. 41–144 in T. Schelling, ed., *Incentives for Environmental Protection.* Cambridge, Mass.: MIT.

Harrison, D., and D. Rubinfeld. 1978. "Hedonic Housing Prices and the Demand for Clean Air." *Journal of Environmental Economics and Management* 5: 81–102.

Haveman, R., and G. Christiansen. 1981. "Environmental Regulations and Productivity Growth." Pp. 55–75 in H. Peskin et al., eds., *Environmental Regulation and the U.S. Economy.* Baltimore: Johns Hopkins.

Kelman, S. 1981. *What Price Incentives? Economists and the Environment.* Boston: Auburn.

Kneese, A., et al., eds. 1971. *Managing the Environment: International Economic Cooperation for Pollution Control.* New York: Praeger.

Maryland Department of Economic and Community Development. 1982. *Emission Trading to Reduce the Cost of Air Quality in Maryland.* Annapolis: Department of Economic and Community Development.

McGartland, A., and W. Oates. Forthcoming. "Marketable Permits for the Prevention of Environmental Deterioration." *Journal of Environmental Economics and Management.*

Oates, W. 1983. "The Regulation of Externalities: Efficient Behavior by Sources and Victims." *Public Finance* 38, 362–75.

O'Neil, W., et al. 1983. "Transferable Discharge Permits and Economic Efficiency: The Fox River." *Journal of Environmental Economics and Management* 10: 346–55.

Organization for Economic Cooperation and Development (O.E.C.D.). 1984. *Environment and Economics: Issue Papers.* Paris: O.E.C.D.

Palmer, A., et al. 1980. *Economic Implications of Regulating Chlorofluorocarbon Emissions from Nonaerosol Applications.* Santa Monica: RAND.

Peskin, H. 1981. "National Income Accounts and the Environment." Pp. 77–103 in H. Peskin et al., eds., *Environmental Regulation and the U.S. Economy.* Baltimore: Johns Hopkins.

Portney, R. 1981. "The Macroeconomic Impacts of Federal Environmental Regulation." Pp. 25–54 in H. Peskin et al., eds., *Environmental Regulation and the U.S. Economy.* Baltimore: Johns Hopkins.

Quarles, J. 1979. *Federal Regulation of New Industrial Plants.* Environmental Reporter Monograph 28. Washington, D.C.

Seskin, E., et al. 1983. "An Empirical Analysis of Economic Strategies for Controlling Air Pollution." *Journal of Environmental Economics and Management* 10: 112–24.

Siegel, R. 1979. "Why Has Productivity Slowed Down?" *Data Resources Review of the U.S. Economy* 1, 59.

U.S. General Accounting Office. 1984. *Cost-Benefit Analysis Can Be Useful in Assessing Environmental Regulations, Despite Limitations.* Washington, D.C.: U.S. General Accounting Office.

Weitzman, M. 1974. "Prices vs. Quantities." *Review of Economic Studies* 41: 477–91.

BOOK REVIEW

THE UNCERTAIN SEARCH FOR ENVIRONMENTAL QUALITY. By BRUCE A. ACKERMAN, SUSAN ROSE-ACKERMAN, JAMES W. SAWYER, JR., AND DALE W. HENDERSON. New York: The Free Press, 1974. Pp. x, 386. $13.95.

Wallace E. Oates†

The growing concern with environmental protection has manifested itself in both the natural and social sciences in a concerted research effort to extend our understanding of ecological systems and to employ this knowledge in the design of policies for an improved environment. Biologists and chemists have labored, for example, to learn the dynamics of the processes of decay and assimilation of waterborne wastes in streams and rivers; at the same time, economists have turned their tools of applied welfare economics to the evaluation of policy alternatives for the preservation of water quality.

While all this is certainly commendable in itself, the trouble has been that the analyses forthcoming from these efforts have taken a highly technical form. The description of river dynamics (a "materials balance analysis") typically takes the form of a highly complex set of simultaneous differential equations. Likewise, the economist's "cost-benefit analysis" draws on a substantial set of often-implicit assumptions as well as extensive quantitative studies. Simply to understand the character of these analyses *and their limitations* requires considerable expertise.

How, then, can policy-makers, who are not technical experts, evaluate such analyses and incorporate them in an intelligent way into actual policy proposals? This, incidentally, is not simply a matter of following the prescription of an able technical adviser, for there are typically important value judgments and individual interests at stake; technical assistance is obviously important, but it is not the whole of the decision.

In addition to making technical analyses comprehensible, there is the closely related and crucial matter of the actual use of such analyses in the process of debate leading to the formulation

---

† Professor of Economics, Princeton University.

of an environmental program. How, for example, are these studies likely to influence not only the choice of method to achieve the environmental targets but also the selection of the objectives themselves? In short, the issue is how technical analysis itself interacts with the other elements of the decision process.

As a corollary to these problems of technical inputs, how can we design political institutions whose structure will embody the right sorts of incentives for environmental decisions? It is the rule rather than the exception that the natural boundaries for environmental control (water basins and air sheds) do not coincide with existing political jurisdictions. Is it enough simply to ensure that the decisionmaking authority includes representatives from the concerned states and federal agencies?

A recent interdisciplinary study centered at the University of Pennsylvania has produced a profoundly important exploration of these issues in terms of a detailed, thorough examination of the decisionmaking process that resulted in a major and costly program to clean up the Delaware River. The result is, in my view, the most significant book[1] yet written on the determination of environmental policy. The study, under the direction of Bruce Ackerman, is an example of what interdisciplinary research ought to be. Drawing on the technical expertise of natural scientists, economists, and lawyers, the Ackerman group undertook a painstaking three-and-a-half-year effort to understand the roles and interaction of those individuals, both scientists and politicians, whose influence came to bear on the choice of the Delaware program. The book is a fascinating description of this decisionmaking process along with a careful and judicious attempt to ascertain the lessons to be learned from the Delaware experience.

It is this second facet of the Ackerman study that yields something far more then merely an absorbing case study. At appropriate junctures, the authors step back from their analysis of the Delaware decision to consider what of a more generic nature can be gleaned from the proceedings.[2] And it is here that they can generate a series of insights into environmental decisionmaking that transcends the problems of the Delaware Estuary. The reader comes away from the book with a far deeper understanding of the complexities inherent in the application of

---

[1] B. ACKERMAN, S. ROSE-ACKERMAN, J. SAWYER, JR. & D. HENDERSON, THE UNCERTAIN SEARCH FOR ENVIRONMENTAL POLICY (1974) (hereinafter cited as B. ACKERMAN).
[2] *Id.* 67-78, 136-61, 208-20.

cost-benefit analysis and of the limitations of the much heralded "co-operative federalism" in resolving our environmental problems, an understanding greatly enhanced by "seeing" these techniques in action in the Delaware program.

To organize the discussion in this Review, I first describe briefly the institutional structure and proceedings for the Delaware enterprise.[3] With this as background, I subsequently turn to three fundamental issues: the use of formal "modeling" and of cost-benefit analysis to define and evaluate the policy alternatives,[4] the significance of the institutional structure for the choice and implementation of programs,[5] and the selection of a form of regulation of polluters to achieve the designated standards for environmental quality.[6]

I. THE INSTITUTIONAL STRUCTURE
OF THE DELAWARE PROGRAM

The principal actors in the Delaware drama composed two distinct groups. The first was an essentially technical staff supported by the federal Public Health Service to undertake an ambitious scientific analysis: the Delaware Estuary Comprehensive Study (DECS). Greatly intrigued by the appearance of cost-benefit analytical techniques in Washington in the early 1960's, the Public Health Service saw in the Delaware case an opportunity to push these new techniques into the field of water quality. In 1962 the Service launched, at a cost of $1.2 million, the four-year DECS enterprise with the research under the direction of a young sanitary engineer, Robert Thomann, who had recently completed a doctoral thesis involving mathematical modeling of the effects of pollutants on estuaries. The DECS staff was eager to show how such scientific techniques could form the basis for decisions on water quality in an actual estuary.[7]

In contrast to the research-oriented DECS, there existed at the same time a decisionmaking body, the Delaware River Basin Commission (DRBC). Created in 1961, the DRBC was a new "model regional agency" with a constituency from the four interested states (Pennsylvania, New Jersey, New York, and Delaware) and the federal government. The Commission itself took an innovative form of "co-operative federalism": a regional body

---

[3] Text accompanying notes 7-16 *infra*.
[4] Text accompanying notes 17-61 *infra*.
[5] Text accompanying notes 62-83 *infra*.
[6] Text accompanying notes 84-111 *infra*.
[7] B. ACKERMAN, *supra* note 1, at 12-13.

representing the interests of the concerned states and the federal government and endowed with broad decisionmaking powers for the development of the resources of the Delaware River. Moreover, the voting members of the DRBC were not obscure figures; they consisted of the governors of these four states and the Secretary of the Interior.[8]

The origin of both the DECS and the DRBC can be traced to a series of disastrous floods in the Delaware during the 1950's. These pointed up the need for a concerted effort for flood control of the Delaware's waters. This concern, however, soon expanded into a wider undertaking to investigate and control not only water quantity, but also its quality.[9] This enlarged perspective received, moreover, a powerful impetus from the passage of the Federal Water Quality Act of 1965;[10] the Act required the states to submit by June 30, 1967, a set of water quality standards and plans for implementation.[11]

The new federal Act also ushered in a new relationship between the DECS and the DRBC. The Commission faced the difficult task of formulating a set of objectives and programs for water quality in the Delaware, but did not as yet possess an adequate technical staff or research effort to provide a sound and intellectually respectable foundation for such decisions. The DECS staff, however, was well along its way in the development of an operational model of the estuary to be accompanied by estimates of the costs and benefits of alternative water quality objectives.[12] The DECS clearly had what the DRBC needed.

To assist the Commission with its decisions, the DECS staff undertook to produce a preliminary report by mid-1966. This report summarized five potential water quality programs with varying objectives; using a cost-benefit analysis, the staff went on to estimate in dollar terms the benefits and costs associated with each objective set.[13] I have reproduced these estimates as Table I.

What must be emphasized is that it was this set of choices summarized in Table I that came to be the frame of reference for the debate over the Delaware program. When the deliberations began among groups of concerned citizens, polluters, and

---

[8] *Id.* 3-5.
[9] *Id.* 11-12.
[10] 33 U.S.C. § 466 (1970).
[11] *Id.*; B. ACKERMAN, *supra* note 1, at 13.
[12] B. ACKERMAN, *supra* note 1, at 13.
[13] *Id.* 14.

TABLE I

COST-BENEFIT ANALYSIS OF DECS POLLUTION PLANS[14]

Objective Set	Cost	High Estimate-Low Estimate of Benefits
I	$490 million	$355-155 million
II	275 "	320-135 "
III	155 "	310-125 "
IV	110 "	280-115 "
V	30 "	—

the DRBC itself, attention was focused on *which* of the DECS objectives was the most appropriate.[15] In the end, the DRBC adopted a slightly modified version of Objective II[16] (which, incidentially, is considerably more ambitious than Objective IV, which produces the largest expected *net* benefit according to the DECS estimates). Important as the final choice may be, it is of far greater significance that *the technical staff of the DECS effectively defined the alternatives.* Just why this is so critical will become apparent in the next section, where we examine what lies behind the figures in Table I.

II. "MODELING" AND COST-BENEFIT ANALYSIS IN POLICY FORMULATION

The DECS staff had first to confront what is basically a definitional issue: the meaning (in measurable terms) of water quality. Opting for a widely used measure, the staff essentially chose the level of dissolved oxygen (DO) to serve as its "proxy" for water quality. In fact, the objective sets cited in Table I effectively represent differing levels of DO; Table II indicates this correspondence.[17]

The first issue this raises is the adequacy of DO as a measure of water quality. The DO content of a body of water certainly is of some significance: If, for example, the DO level "sags" suffi-

---

[14] *Id.* 15.

[15] *See generally id.* 13-14.

[16] *See id.* 187. *See generally id.* 170-207.

[17] Although the various objective sets did include goals for a number of other pollutants, the DECS staff never considered the costs of reaching any of these "secondary" goals independently of the DO objective. Letter from Susan Rose-Ackerman to Wallace E. Oates, July 20, 1975.

ciently low for an extended period, the waters can no longer support fish life.[18] Moreover, should DO levels approach zero, a noxious process of "anaerobic decomposition" sets in with a vile discoloration of the waters and foul odors.[19] This vitiates any recreational uses (or aesthetic value) of the river or lake.

TABLE II

AVERAGE DO IN PARTS PER MILLION IN MOST POLLUTED AREA
OF THE DELAWARE[20]

Objective Set	Level of DO
I	4.5
II	4.0
III	3.0
IV	2.5
V	1.0

To prevent dissolved oxygen from falling to undesirably low levels, a river authority can undertake a number of measures. Most basic, however, is the control of the quantity and quality of those wastes that utilize oxygen in the process of decomposition; the oxygen consumption made by such wastes is typically measured in terms of its Biochemical Oxygen Demand (BOD).[21] Programs to increase DO levels thus entail both reductions in organic wastes and treatment of such wastes to reduce the BOD emissions into the receiving waters.

While the DO level represents one important dimension of water quality, it is by no means the only significant characteristic. For example, another aspect of pollutants that poses an obvious threat is the toxic properties of certain inorganic wastes which can themselves render the water unsafe for drinking, swimming, or fishlife.[22] In short, a certain DO content may be *necessary* to support fish and for certain recreational uses of the water, but it is not *sufficient*.

---

[18] *Id*. 18.
[19] *Id*. 18-19.
[20] *See id*. 32.
[21] *See id*. 18-22. More precisely, the BOD of a waste discharge is the number of pounds of oxygen that will be consumed in, the biochemical oxidation of the organic impurity present in the emission.
[22] *Id*. 27.

Moreover, the authors point out some particular characteristics of the Delaware estuary that create considerable uncertainty about the gains from a program to increase levels of DO. One problem concerns the high levels of river turbidity, which give the water an opaque brown appearance with adverse aesthetic and recreational consequences.[23] It is not clear that a DO "cleanup" would have much effect on the turbidity; but if it did, the clearer water might well prove far more receptive to the growth of algae so that in the end it "may simply mean that the valley is trading a brown river for a green one."[24]

In addition, the sludge deposits in the bottom of the Delaware support a large population of oxygen-consuming worms ("tubificid"). As DO levels increase, the authorities can expect a rapid multiplication of these worms with the associated rise in the "benthic oxygen demand" on the river's supply of oxygen.[25] The extent of these side effects is uncertain; the point, however, is that the ecology of a river like the Delaware is highly complex, and programs to alter one characteristic of the system are likely to have some additional and unexpected effects on other forms of water life.

Suppose that we push all this aside and accept, for the moment, the adequacy of dissolved oxygen as a measure of water quality for the Delaware. How well does the DECS model describe and predict DO levels in the Delaware estuary? The answer is, only moderately well at best. It must first be recognized that DO content is not a single number. The Delaware Estuary stretches about one hundred miles from Trenton to Liston's Point on the coast,[26] and its DO level exhibits wide variations over different spans of its flow. Rather than one level of DO, the oxygen content of the river is described by a "profile" which exhibits graphically the existing DO concentrations at each point along the river. Such a profile indicates a "sag" in DO immediately below Trenton which becomes even more accentuated downstream from Philadelphia. This, of course, reflects the decomposition of the relatively heavy waste emissions from both industrial sources and municipal waste treatment plants in these two areas of concentrated populations and industrial activity. To analyze DO levels, the DECS staff divided the river below Trenton into thirty sections; the DECS model thus aimed at describ-

---

[23] *Id.* 26.
[24] *Id.* 27.
[25] *Id.* 22, 51-53.
[26] *Cf. id.* 23-24.

ing and predicting DO concentrations in each of these thirty stretches of the river.[27]

This is no easy task. The levels of DO depend not only on the quantities and quality of the wastes emitted at various points along the Delaware, but they are also crucially dependent on the level of the water flows,[28] on water temperatures,[29] and on wind velocities above the river surface.[30] DO is typically at its lowest levels during the hot summer months when the capacity of the river to assimilate waste discharges is at its minimum.[31] Moreover, the water flows are complicated by the fact that the Delaware is an estuary and thus subject to influences from the ocean tides; BOD can flow upstream as well as downstream.[32] Finally, during periods of heavy rain, the sewer systems of Trenton, Camden, Philadelphia, and Wilmington tend to overflow, pouring huge and unpredictable quantities of BOD into the Delaware; these overflows take place about ten days each year.[33]

To keep the problem relatively simple and to reduce data requirements, the DECS staff chose essentially to ignore all these sources of variation over time and to assume a "steady state" condition;[34] that is, they assumed that *"relevant river conditions remained constant over time."*[35] This is obviously a major simplification, but the critical question is the extent to which this assumption impaired the precision of the model's predictions.

Ackerman and his colleagues looked carefully at the performance of the DECS model and found substantial inaccuracies. In about one case out of three, the predicted DO content for a given sector of the Delaware differed from the actual level of DO by more than .5 parts per million.[36] This is not a minor imprecision, as a look at Table II indicates that this can represent the difference between one objective set and another at costs of possibly over one hundred million dollars.[37]

---

[27] See id. 22-25.
[28] Id. 35.
[29] Id. 38.
[30] Id. 49-51.
[31] Id. 38.
[32] Id. 33-34.
[33] Id. 42-45.
[34] Id. 37-39.
[35] Id. 37 (emphasis in original).
[36] See id. 57-58.
[37] If Objective Set I is chosen, for example, the cost will exceed that of Objective Set II by $215 million, see Table I supra; yet with a possible DO error of .5 parts per

Moreover, this appears to understate to some extent the full disparities between "actual" and "predicted" values of DO, for the DECS staff had itself previously adjusted some of the predictions in the light of excessive deviations from actual DO concentrations.[38]

All this is not meant to understate the accomplishments of the DECS. The construction of an operational model of the Delaware represents a substantial achievement. The margins of error in the model's predictions, however, appear quite considerable, and this expected divergence of predicted from actual DO levels is a matter that the decisionmaking body should weigh with care. We shall return to this shortly.[39]

The next step in the DECS analysis was to estimate the potential benefits from increased levels of DO and the costs necessary to achieve these improvements in water quality. At this juncture, the staff turned to the economist's technique of cost-benefit analysis,[40] an approach with a substantial history in the evaluation of water resource projects.

A cost-benefit study involves essentially four steps. The first is simply an enumeration of the various forms of benefits and costs inherent in the undertaking. In the case of the Delaware, the "tangible" benefits from a cleanup of the river were determined to consist primarily of an improved recreational potential: swimming, boating, and fishing.[41] To achieve these benefits, it would be necessary to reduce levels of waste discharges into the river with consequent higher costs to polluters who would have to adopt more expensive alternatives in order to reduce the quantity and/or improve the quality of their waste emissions. The costs of the Delaware program were thus primarily the additional expense in cutting back on wastes and increasing the levels of treatment.

The second step is the assignment of actual dollar values to the various forms of benefits and costs. The DECS staff undertook an extensive questionnaire study of the forty-four major polluters along the Delaware estuary to collect information for the estimation of the costs of reduced BOD emissions.[42] At the

---

million we have no guarantee that the DO level will exceed that available under the rejected Objective Set II, *see* Table II *supra*.

[38] B. ACKERMAN, *supra* note 1, at 59-61.

[39] Text accompanying notes 54-55, 59-60 *infra*.

[40] For a comprehensive treatment of cost-benefit analysis, see E. MISHAN, COST-BENEFIT ANALYSIS: AN INFORMAL INTRODUCTION (2d ed. 1974).

[41] B. ACKERMAN, *supra* note 1, at 102.

[42] *Id*. 85-86.

same time, a range of estimates was made for the benefits from expanded recreational uses.[43]

The third step involves the selection of an appropriate rate of discount for the evaluation of benefits and costs that are expected to accrue in future years. The point is, simply, that 100 dollars in benefits or costs one year hence is worth less than 100 dollars at the present moment; with positive rates of return (interest), 100 dollars today is worth 100 dollars *plus* the accrued interest at some future date. If, for example, we adopt a discount rate of six percent, we are effectively saying that we will assign a "present discounted value" of 100 dollars to a sum of benefits (or costs) of 106 dollars to be realized one year in the future. The final step in the cost-benefit study is simply to take our time profile of dollar benefits and costs along with the chosen rate of discount and then to calculate the present discounted value of the entire expected future stream of benefits and of costs. These are the numbers presented in Table I above, where the DECS staff used a discount rate of three percent.

Although the general cost-benefit approach seems quite straightforward, there are in fact a number of problems or ambiguities, both in principle and in practice. There are effectively two sets of issues at stake. The first is the assumptions inherent in the cost-benefit technique itself, and the second is the particular procedures employed by the DECS staff to reach the estimates of the benefits and costs of the selected set of objectives for the Delaware. I will comment only briefly on these two matters, for the most fascinating dimension of the book goes beyond the content of the DECS cost-benefit study to the *way* in which the study was employed in the decision process.

The authors set out carefully and lucidly for the nonspecialist the nature of cost-benefit analysis.[44] In particular, it is important to recognize just what the cost-benefit test is. In computing the value of the benefits and costs associated with a particular project, the assignment is determined upon the basis of people's "willingness to pay." The cost-benefit test is effectively an attempt to apply market criteria to the evaluation of public projects. When the researcher calculates and compares the present discounted value of the expected future stream of benefits with that of costs, he is asking the question: Does the value of the undertaking, *as measured by what people would be willing to pay,*

---

[43] *Id.* 102-03.
[44] *Id.* 104-09. *See generally* E. MISHAN, *supra* note 40.

exceed (or, alternatively, fall short of) its costs, again measured in terms of actual or imputed market prices? The cost-benefit test is thus an analogue to the profit test in the market place, for it measures whether, in principle, there could be sufficient revenues (if people were to pay for the benefits) to cover costs.

Seen from this perspective, we can determine what a cost-benefit test does *and does not* tell us. It does not, for example, indicate to whom the benefits accrue or who bears the costs; it is an aggregative test in the sense that benefits and costs are summed over all persons. This immediately suggests that although the cost-benefit test may supply some valuable information, it is not in itself the sole criterion on which to base project decisions.

Environmentalists, in particular, have raised a second objection to the application of the cost-benefit approach: its exclusively anthropomorphic perspective.[45] The benefits and costs that enter the calculations are the valuations to human beings. But should not some weight be given to the shad or other wildlife whose well-being is at stake? Does man have the right to destroy animals for his own purposes? This involves some tricky philosophical issues—in the end, for example, men will make the decision and it must, therefore, be men's valuation of the interests of wildlife that is relevant. Nevertheless, one can still argue that man has certain responsibilities or interests regarding the "integrity of nature" that extend beyond the scope of conventional cost-benefit calculations.

In addition to these matters of principle, Ackerman and his colleagues explore carefully the specifics of the DRBC cost-benefit study. Here again they find a number of important anomalies and, in some instances, outright errors. From the outset, the DECS staff carried over all the simplifications in the Delaware model to the cost-benefit calculations; the computations, for example, refer only to the attainment of alternative levels of dissolved oxygen.[46] The valuations of benefits and costs are thus themselves subject to all the reservations cited earlier in this section.

Moreover, the authors find that the DECS estimates of the costs of pollution control were far too low, while (largely because of a conceptual error) the benefits appear somewhat exaggerated. In particular, an underestimate of costs resulted, first from

---

[45] *See* B. ACKERMAN, *supra* note 1, at 138-42.

[46] Thus the benefits are expressed as correlates for DO Objective Sets I-IV, *compare id.* 103, at Table 4 *with id.* 15, at Table 1, *id.* 32, at Table 2, *and id.* 63, at Table 3.

restricting the study to the forty-four major point-source polluters who account for about two-thirds of BOD emissions[47] and,
second, from an inadequate provision for the growth in emissions over time.[48] Some later revised estimates of the costs of
dealing with anticipated increases in wasteloads pushed the price
from 20 million to 140 million dollars; by this time, however,
certain commitments had been made on the basis of earlier estimates, and officials apparently were quick to suppress these new
and potentially embarrassing cost overruns.[49]

On the benefit side, the DECS calculations were based on
existing estimates of the "intrinsic" value (in dollar terms) of a
day of fishing, boating, or swimming, multiplied by a predicted
number of users.[50] This measure of benefits, however, is highly
misleading; the cost-benefit analyst seeks to measure the value of
the new facilities in terms of what consumers would be willing to
pay rather than do without them. This implies that the benefits
from the new recreational opportunities must be evaluated relative to already existing facilities. The proper basis for valuation is
not one of the intrinsic worth of a day of fishing, but rather the
value to fishermen of having the Delaware available in addition
to existing fishing sites.[51] This methodological bungle (for which,
incidentally, there is considerable precedent)[52] probably imparts
a substantial upward bias to the DECS estimates of benefits.

With this as background, we can now turn to the most fascinating part of the Delaware story: the way in which the DECS
cost-benefit study figured in the deliberations on and ultimate
choice of the Delaware program. The preceding paragraphs indicate the substantial degree of imprecision and uncertainty inherent in the DECS estimates of the benefits from and costs of a
cleanup of the Delaware; the sweeping, simplifying assumptions
and the limited availability of critical information suggest that
the findings should be couched in terms of a number of qualifications and warnings. But this is precisely the opposite of what
happened. In their eagerness to impress the outside world with
their accomplishment in constructing an operational model of
the Delaware and using this model to derive actual dollar estimates of the benefits and costs of various programs, the DECS

---

[47] *Id*. 85-86.
[48] *Id*. 86-90.
[49] *Id*. 94-96.
[50] *See generally id*. 124-32.
[51] *See id*. 115-19. *See also id*. 109-15.
[52] Mack & Meyers, *Outdoor Recreation*, in MEASURING BENEFITS OF GOVERNMENT
INVESTMENTS 71-116 (R. Dorfman ed. 1965).

staff produced a report that hardly even hinted at the imprecision inherent in the predictions of the model and the associated
estimates of benefits and costs.

In short, the basic failing of the DECS Report was
not so much that it failed to achieve a degree of com-
prehensiveness and exactitude that is never achieved
outside the most fantastic science fiction; what was seriously defective was the manner in which the DECS Report understood the very idea of "achievement." The
DECS succeeded insofar as it developed a set of equations defining a system that accurately described a small
piece of reality. Thus, in emphasizing its achievement,
the research staff emphasized the accuracy of the numbers its model generated. While this may be fine in a
scientific forum in which the findings will be scrutinized
by other experts concerned with the development of
truth within a single disciplinary speciality, it is nothing
short of disastrous when the same attitude is transposed
into the policy-making arena.[53]

More basic is the effect the DECS study had on the actual
deliberations and the ultimate decision. As noted above,[54] the
DECS findings, summarized in Tables I and II, for all practical
purposes defined the alternatives. The debate among both interested citizens and the DRBC amounted to haggling over the
appropriate objective set from these tables; in short, the DECS
effectively channeled the discussion into a consideration of the
proper level of dissolved oxygen.

This is enormously important, for it means that, from the
outset, public discussion took the narrowest of perspectives. In
the view of the authors, the real questions of strategy for an
environmental program were eclipsed by the DECS report; Ackerman and his colleagues argue quite persuasively that the likely
benefits from the costly Delaware program will be miniscule:

It is easy to imagine that when society decides to
spend almost three quarters of a billion dollars to clean
up a 40-mile stretch of river, something significant will
come of it. The mind rebels at the thought that such
vast sums are spent in vain. Yet in 1978, or 1980 or
1984, when the DRBC announces that it has "suc-

---

[53] B. ACKERMAN, *supra* note 1, at 65-66.
[54] Text accompanying note 15 *supra*.

ceeded" in achieving its DO objectives on the river, the Delaware will be just as cloudy as it ever was; it will be just as difficult to obtain access to the river; boating will be neither better nor worse than it was; the drinking water will taste the same as it always did. *Perhaps* good fishing will be a few minutes closer, and during some years more shad will "survive" their journey up and down the river. Is this what all the talk about improving "the quality of life" amounts to?[55]

The authors contend that primary attention ought to be "focussed on the discharge of exotic chemicals and heavy metals which may pose a real risk to human health when present in drinking water or in seafood";[56] the first priority here is the avoidance of ecological catastrophe. Yet this seemed to have generated little concern among the DECS staff.[57] As to environmental protection generally, Ackerman and his colleagues see little to be gained from extensive and costly efforts to rehabilitate heavily used water systems; instead, they argue that the general strategy should be to preserve those resources as yet relatively unspoiled by twentieth-century life.[58] Rather than attempting at great expense to raise the level of DO in the Delaware around Trenton and Philadelphia, we would do better to preserve the lower estuary from the incursion of sources of pollution.

Whether or not they are correct on this basic issue of environmental strategy, it is striking that in the course of the Delaware deliberations this matter was never even acknowledged![59] The force of the DECS preliminary report was such as to sidetrack the discussion from a consideration of the real alternatives to a relatively trivial controversy over whether the DO level would be brought to 2.5 or 3.0 parts per million. And the ultimate outcome may well be, as the authors suggest,[60] an extremely expensive program with little noticeable effect on the quality of the Delaware's waters.

What are we to conclude from all this? It seems to me that a reader's first reactions may be of two general kinds. One may conclude that the real trouble rests in the DECS analysis; if the technical staff had simply adopted a broader perspective on the

---

[55] B. ACKERMAN, *supra* note 1, at 142 (emphasis in original).
[56] *Id*. 145.
[57] *Cf. id*. (noting DRBC and general national inattention to poisons discharges).
[58] *E.g., id*. 137, 140, 144-45.
[59] *See generally, e.g., id*. 145.
[60] Text accompanying note 55 *supra*.

environmental alternatives and at least made clear the basic qualifications to their findings, we might have expected a far more enlightened public discussion and a more informed choice of a Delaware program. In short, what was needed was a better Delaware model and cost-benefit study. One may, on the other hand, take a more pessimistic stance and reason that such analyses are likely to be more misleading than helpful, that we would do better to give up attempts aimed at "sophisticated" definitions of the problem and at quantification and leave the decision to the judgment of the responsible bureaucrats and elected officials.

Neither of these reactions, however, seems to me the proper inference. It is too easy simply to put all the blame on the DECS study. There were obviously a multitude of serious deficiencies in the analysis *and* in its presentation, and we could certainly look to improved analytical studies to provide a better foundation for public debate. But even if the technical work is of a high quality, there remains the very formidable problem of its transmission in a usable form to decisionmakers. In particular, the nature of analytical studies and the needs of the political decisionmaker seem to verge on incompatibility: Analysis involves simplification which in turn implies important qualifications to any findings, while the political participant is seeking a position or decision he can take without fundamental ambiguities. I do not want to suggest that this is an insurmountable obstacle: We have, for example, benefited greatly from the use of analytical work in determining macro-economic policy. The tension (and the compromises) between the informational needs of the political process and the tentative character of analytical findings and predictions, however, surely exists.

Conversely, it really does not make much sense to abandon analytical studies of policy alternatives. As the authors put it,

> When confronted with this precis, the reader is doubtless tempted to conclude that the DECS exercise, when properly understood, contributed nothing of value to a more precise understanding of the problems confronting the sensitive decision maker. But this would be a mistake; for it is only as a result of our effort to trace the DECS' investigations that it has been possible to obtain a perspective on the probable consequences of the costly program of pollution control which the DRBC has adopted. Our basic complaint does not go to the wisdom of the effort at sustained understanding of

river dynamics but to the way in which the DECS staff chose to *translate their insights into language comprehensible to decision makers.*[61]

Where this discussion leads is not to the abolition of policy analysis but rather to a study of institutional structure. The basic issue is the formation of a set of decision procedures that, first, will pose the proper questions, and, second, will generate and bring to bear the relevant kinds of information and analysis. It is to this matter of institutional structure that we turn next.

III. THE DESIGN OF INSTITUTIONS FOR POLICY DECISIONS

The Delaware experience also represents an innovative venture in "cooperative federalism." Not only was the decisionmaking body, the DRBC, composed of prestigious representatives from both the federal government and the concerned states, but federally supported technical assistance from the DECS staff provided, as we have seen, the basic research capability for the undertaking. How well did this institutional structure fulfill its role?

The authors have grave reservations about the division of the research and decision functions between the DECS (the "thinkers") and the DRBC (the "doers").[62] The problem is best seen by considering the incentives confronting each agency and following through the likely implications. From the standpoint of the federally supported DECS, the basic enterprise was one of implementing *and* selling a highly complex and sophisticated form of environmental analysis. For the staff of the DECS, the Delaware study presented an opportunity to demonstrate the effectiveness of an innovative technique. With this perspective, such a "pure thinking agency may be expected . . . to justify its existence by overselling the accuracy and importance of its preliminary reports by underemphasizing the uncertainties underlying its predictions."[63]

Moreover, the "thinking agency" is unlikely to have a long-term commitment to the program. The DECS staff would realize the bulk of their returns in the short run from the establishment of a basic analytical framework and from the initial results, not from the longer and more mundane efforts to accumulate basic and improved data and to follow up and refine the results.[64]

---

[61] B. ACKERMAN, *supra* note 1, at 64 (emphasis in original).
[62] The authors so label the two agencies, *e.g.*, *id.* 74.
[63] *Id.* 74.
[64] *Id.* 74; *cf.* text accompanying note 7 *supra*.

In contrast, the orientation of the "action agency" is toward the implementation of a program. This agency, in our case the DRBC, typically requires the assistance of a technical body of some sort to help in the formulation of the program and to provide a kind of intellectual respectability.[65] But once the fundamental program is outlined, the action agency, like the thinking agency, is interested in selling the program, not in pointing up existing uncertainties or qualifications;[66] the decisionmakers can thus be expected to reinforce the tendencies of the research group to stress the precision and reliability of the plan. Moreover, once the action agency has implemented the program, its concern will be primarily with the enforcement of the plan, rather than with continuing basic research aimed at future planning efforts.[67] This bifurcation of responsibility appears to discourage follow-through on the basic planning efforts.

The DECS and DRBC seem to have followed this pattern of behavior quite closely. I have already stressed the exaggerated level of precision in the DECS reports.[68] In addition, the research effort apparently lost most of its vitality following the publication of the DECS preliminary report in 1966. The preliminary report promised a definitive "final document" by the end of 1967, a document which has yet to be published.[69] With the completion of the preliminary report, there was a shift of the basic research and planning function from the federally supported staff to the regional level.[70] Although there was much additional work to be done in extending the DECS model and developing a more comprehensive and reliable data base, little seems to have followed on the preliminary report. In fact, the data-collection effort is at present so sporadic and generally inadequate as to preclude further effective research aimed at improving the predictive capability of the model.[71]

From this experience, Ackerman and his colleagues conclude that

> The course of events along the Delaware eloquently warns against placing the federal "thinkers" in one bureaucratic box, then shifting the responsibility for

---

[65] *Cf.* B. ACKERMAN, *supra* note 1, at 74-75.
[66] *Id.* 75.
[67] *Id.*
[68] *Cf.* text accompanying notes 26-38 *supra*.
[69] B. ACKERMAN, *supra* note 1, at 68-69.
[70] *Id.* 69.
[71] *See id.* 69-73.

scientific follow-through to the regional "decision-making" agency, simultaneously consigning the task of data gathering to yet another set of state agencies. In such a structure each component is prone to lose sight of the function it should be performing to enhance the rationality of the pollution control scheme that is the ultimate product of all the sound and fury.[72]

The implication of all this would seem to be that the decisionmaking agency should have within its own organization the basic research capability. This too presents difficulties, however; in particular, the control of the agency's officials over the research personnel may serve to inhibit critical evaluations of existing policies.[73] At least the division of functions in the Delaware provided a certain protection and scope of independence for the DECS staff.

There seems to be no easy resolution of the dilemma. After considering a number of alternatives, the authors propose the creation of a new body: an Environmental Review Board.[74] The Board's function would be to provide an outside, independent assessment of each agency's environmental planning efforts. With a "quasi-judicial independence" from the executive and legislative branches of the government, the Board would scrutinize and evaluate basic environmental plans to ensure that the proper alternatives have in fact been posed *and* that the analysis of the alternatives is sound.[75] In the case of the Delaware, for example, such a Review Board would presumably have required a broadening of the perspective beyond just the DO level of the estuary, as well as the resolution of certain anomalies in the basic model and the cost-benefit analysis. The potential for such a review body is, I think, considerable; our closest relative to the proposed Board has probably been the General Accounting Office (GAO), several of whose reports have been extraordinarily revealing.[76] Simply the existence of such a reviewing agency keeps people on their toes with the knowledge that a shoddy job of analysis may easily be exposed.

---

[72] *Id.* 77.

[73] For an account of the conflict between DECS and DRBC, see *id.* 191-93.

[74] *Id.* 156-61.

[75] *Id.* 156-57.

[76] *See, e.g.*, COMPTROLLER GENERAL OF THE UNITED STATES, EXAMINATION INTO THE EFFECTIVENESS OF THE CONSTRUCTION GRANT PROGRAM FOR ABATING, CONTROLLING, AND PREVENTING WATER POLLUTION (1969) (critical review of federal program for subsidizing construction of municipal waste treatment facilities).

Let us turn next to the decisionmaking process in the DRBC itself. Through a lengthy series of interviews with the actual participants in the DRBC decision and a study of associated written documents, the authors found a number of recurring patterns of behavior which again cast considerable doubt on the efficacy of some of the new forms of cooperative federalism. Without trying to recapitulate the positions and roles of the individual Governors, the Secretary of the Interior, and others with some influence in the decision process, let me simply highlight some of these tendencies.[77] The central difficulty stems from the basic and obvious fact that the primary political commitment of each of the participants is to a constituency other than the regional agency itself. The interviews and proceedings made clear that what was uppermost in the minds of each of the members of the DRBC was how best to further his own interests *in terms of his own political jurisdiction*.[78] This meant, among other things, that these extremely busy political figures were able to devote little effort to an understanding of the distinctly regional dimensions of the Delaware problem. They turned for advice to their own political advisors with the result that a truly regional orientation never developed in the DRBC.[79]

It is not surprising that when it came time to take a position on the Delaware program, each participant consulted his own political calculus. As the Delaware experience makes clear, however, the inevitable compromise that emerges from such an amalgamation of varying interests may bear little resemblance to an effective regional program.

> The technocratic-political decision, whatever its ultimate value, requires tight integration among fact finders, analysts, and politicians. In contrast, federalism is instinct with the demand that power be fractionalized among competing groups and levels of government, and the suspicion that a coherent, tightly organized governing structure will by virtue of that single fact possess too much power and so act irresponsibly. Unfortunately, the federalist effort to eliminate the possibility of the abuse of power can often make it impossible to use power intelligently as well.[80]

---

[77] For a full discussion of the political maneuvers accompanying the DRBC's adoption of the DECS Objective Set II, see B. ACKERMAN, *supra* note 1, at 170-89.

[78] *See id.* 182-87.

[79] *See id.* 193-200.

[80] *Id.* 189 (footnote omitted).

There is, moreover, no obvious way to resolve this fundamental dilemma of American federalism. One potential response would be the creation of a new layer of government: regional political bodies to address explicitly regional issues. But it is difficult to be sanguine about imposing yet another set of bureaucracies and associated political activities on the American system. The authors explore a number of institutional alternatives and offer several provocative proposals. Their approach is essentially to distinguish among various environmental issues according to the sorts of geographical and institutional demands they make on our public institutions. As they see it, the most promising response would involve some national agencies—a Poison Control Board[81] and a Nature Preservation Trust[82]—along with some regional and perhaps metropolitan units to protect and develop recreational facilities.[83] These proposals, however, are an exploration of various responses to an enormously complex set of issues rather than a definitive blueprint for a set of public institutions for the formulation and implementation of environmental policies.

IV. LEGAL-ORDERS VERSUS REGULATION BY MARKET INCENTIVES

In the last section of this Review, I want to examine another set of problems with somewhat more economic content: the method of regulating waste emissions. Once the environmental targets are specified, it becomes necessary to design and implement a program to achieve them. In the case of the Delaware Estuary, we have seen that the designated objective was a certain minimum level of dissolved oxygen.[84] To attain this target, the environmental authority faced the problem of allocating emission quotas among polluters so as to restrict waste discharges to a level consistent with the prescribed level of dissolved oxygen.

The authors' analysis of this issue is most illuminating. In principle, there were two broad options available to the DRBC. The first is "regulation through legal orders." This, in fact, has been the traditional approach: The authority issues orders to each of the polluters specifying a limit to his waste emissions and indicating certain penalties if this limit is exceeded.[85] There is,

---

[81] *See id*. 209-10.
[82] *See id*. 214-15.
[83] *See id*. 210-13.
[84] Text accompanying notes 17-21 *supra*.
[85] *See id*. 225-26.

however, a second general technique for controlling levels of emissions, which the authors call the "market model" of regulation. This approach involves the use of pricing incentives to "ration" the available pollution rights.[86]

Economists have, for many years, been pressing the case for price incentives.[87] And the Delaware experience adds substantial support to this case. The basic appeal of the pricing approach is its potential for achieving the environmental objective at relatively low cost and doing so without making major demands for information or intervention on the part of the regulating authority. In principle, the regulator need only set a price or charge on the BOD content of waste emissions and adjust this charge until polluters cut back waste emissions to the target level.

In addition to its (at least apparent) simplicity, the pricing technique can result in large savings. Suppose, for example, that we have a world of two polluters in which the first can reduce waste emissions at a cost of five cents per pound while the second suffers a cost of twelve cents per pound. To minimize the cost of a reduction in total waste emissions, we would obviously assign the entire cutback to the first polluter, for any cutbacks by polluter number two would involve an "excess" cost of seven cents per pound. Note that this is precisely what would happen under a pricing regime: If, for example, the regulator set a price of six cents per pound, all the reduction in waste emissions would come from the first polluter; the second would pay the charge of six cents per pound and maintain his level of waste discharges.[88] More generally, in a model with many polluters, a single uniform charge will lead to the least-cost pattern of reductions in emissions: Those who can cut back on effluents most cheaply will do so to avoid the charge, while those polluters for whom this is very costly will elect instead to pay the effluent fee.[89]

---

[86] *See id.* 226.

[87] This dates at least to A. Pigou, The Economics of Welfare (1920). For a sampling of more recent literature, see W. Baumol & W. Oates, The Theory of Environmental Policy: Externalities, Public Outlays, and the Quality of Life (1975); A. Kneese & B. Bower, Managing Water Quality: Economics, Technology, Institutions (1968); Freeman & Haveman, *Clean Rhetoric and Dirty Water*, The Public Interest, Summer 1972, at 51.

[88] *See* B. Ackerman, *supra* note 1, at 260-61.

[89] This is a somewhat oversimplified example. In general, the cost per pound of reduction in emissions will depend on the magnitude of the cutback; this, however, does not impair the generality of the argument since each polluter will reduce his waste discharges to the point where the cost of an *additional* pound's reduction (the marginal cost) equals the effluent fee.

One most interesting output of the DECS mathematical model of the Delaware was a set of estimates of the costs of achieving the various objectives by alternative regulatory techniques. The DECS staff found, for example, that a set of legal orders imposing a uniform percentage reduction on the emissions of all polluters sufficient to achieve the DRBC objective (that is, Objective Set II) would entail an estimated treatment cost of 335 million dollars as compared to a cost-minimizing allocation of reductions of 235 million dollars—an "excess" cost of 100 million dollars![90]

This finding becomes of more than hypothetical significance in the light of the actual course of events. The DRBC elected the traditional regulatory approach: a system of legal orders to all polluters.[91] They were well aware, however, of the cost-minimizing potential of varying the quotas among polluters. In particular, the DRBC sought to realize a large portion of these savings by dividing the eighty-six-mile estuary into four zones and assigning different percentage reductions in wastes for each zone, a "zoned-uniform percentage treatment plan." Once the differences in costs implied by the recommended zonal differentials became clear, however, the DRBC was quick to narrow the variation, presumably in the interests of fairness and consensus, until in June, 1968, they promulgated emission reductions for the four zones of 86.0, 89.25, 88.5, and 87.5 percent.[92] The authors conclude that "the DRBC four-zone scheme was nothing more than a public relations triumph, masking a traditional uniform treatment regime. . . . [T]he retreat [of the DRBC] represents a dramatic example of the difficulty of taking even modest steps toward cost minimization when constrained by the traditional version of the legal orders model."[93]

Even these guidelines proved terribly difficult to implement. The appeal of uniform percentage reductions for all polluters is some notion of fairness or equity based on "equal effort." But uniform percentage reduction from what? Surely a refinery that has already instituted extensive and costly treatment procedures should not be required to reduce its emissions by the same proportion as a neighbor who has been emitting untreated wastes into the river. To deal with this issue, the DRBC staff had to undertake the enormously complex task of determining the

---

[90] B. ACKERMAN, *supra* note 1, at 230, Table 7.
[91] *Id.* 231.
[92] *Id.* 234-35.
[93] *Id.* 235-36.

hypothetical "raw waste load" for each major polluter to use as a benchmark for determining its pollution quota.[94] The authors document some of the anomalies that emerged in this case-by-case determination.[95] In particular, their Table 8[96] indicates a range of pollution quotas for different refineries (from 692 to 14,400 pounds of BOD per day) that would probably be difficult to reconcile with any reasonable standard of equity. In short, the legal-orders regime produced an allocation of pollution quotas that appears excessively costly and bears little relation to the "equal effort" principle of fairness.

This experience would seem to make the alternative approach of relying on market incentives all the more attractive. Under this general rubric, however, the environmental authority has two further options. The first is the imposition of effluent charges to induce the necessary reductions in waste emissions.[97] The second is the sale or auctioning of "pollution rights."[98] In principle, both lead to the same outcome: With effluent charges, the regulator raises the fee until the target level of emissions is achieved (he sets the price at the level required to realize the desired quantity); under the pollution-rights scheme, the regulator offers for sale emission rights equal in total to the target level (he sets the desired quantity directly and then lets price adjust to the market-clearing level). This is easily seen in Figure I, where DD^1 is the polluters' demand curve for emission rights and Q_0 is the target level of waste discharges. Under a system of effluent fees, the environmental authority would establish a

FIGURE I

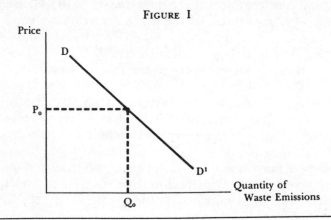

---

[94] *Id.* 248-53.
[95] *Id.* 253-57.
[96] *Id.* 254.
[97] *Id.* 260-61.
[98] *Id.* 261.

price of P_0 to which polluters would respond by emitting wastes of Q_0. Alternatively, the authority could simply sell Q_0 of pollution rights for which the market-clearing price would be P_0.

While these two techniques yield the same result in principle, they have some important differences in practice. In particular, the use of effluent charges involves an element of risk and, perhaps, delay that is not inherent in the pollution-rights method. The difficulty is the imprecision in the authority's knowledge of the demand curve: with only rough estimates of the likely response of polluters to differing levels of charges, the regulator may set a fee other than Figure I's P_0, as a result of which either too much or too little pollution (relative to the target Q_0) will occur.[99] Of course, the environmental authority can make subsequent adjustments to the effluent charge in a process that should converge to the target level of emissions, but this may take time.[100] Moreover, continuing adjustments in charges and levels of emissions are costly to firms and other polluters, as well as politically unpopular.[101] In contrast, if the regulator simply sells the targeted quantity of pollution rights, this source of uncertainty and adjustments is eliminated. Since the objective is a specified level of waste emissions, the authority can set this directly by specifying quantity.[102]

In addition, the authors point to the administrative advantages of the pollution-rights technique in the context of a growing economy. Over time, with the expansion of the economy and industrial activity, we can expect the cost of treatment necessary to maintain a specified level of water quality to grow; new plants

---

[99] *Id.* 262-63, 265-67.

[100] *Id.* 263.

[101] *Id.* 268.

[102] *Id.* 267. By eliminating the uncertainty regarding the *quantity* of emissions, however, the pollution-rights technique necessarily introduces uncertainty concerning the market-clearing price. This may not, incidentally, be a trivial matter. Suppose, for example, that x pounds of BOD emissions have been offered for sale, but that the issue of 1,000 additional pounds of emission licenses would make possible a substantial saving in abatement expenditure (and perhaps release to society resources that could instead be used to build schools and hospitals) with only a very minimal effect on environmental quality. Then the decision to issue only x (rather than $x + 1,000$) pollution rights would have imposed a heavy cost on society, one very likely unforeseen by the environmental authority. The grounds for the choice between the use of fees and the auctioning of pollution rights may then be a matter of which risk constitutes the greater danger. If unanticipated emissions are the most imminent threat to the public welfare, that argues for the auction of rights, which leaves little doubt about the probable volume of pollution. On the other hand, if pressing alternative uses for society's resources mean that excessive outlays on pollution control are a luxury that society can ill afford, then the fees approach, with its firmer control of abatement outlays, may be the preferable procedure.

will appear and the tendency will be toward expanding waste emissions. With a *given* effluent charge, emissions will rise and water quality will deteriorate.

> Of course there is nothing to prevent an aggressive authority from raising the charge whenever this is appropriate. Nevertheless, . . . an effluent fee system will place *the burden of affirmative action* to maintain the agency's original environmental objectives *on nonpolluting river users*. In contrast, under the effluent rights system, the maximum permissible discharge is fixed at the time of the original decision, and the costs of growth will be borne only by polluters who will bid the price of the rights up over time. Thus, the rights system places the *burden of affirmative action on the polluters* to convince the agency that the increasing marginal compliance costs so outweigh the marginal environmental benefits of the status quo that some degradation below current levels should be permitted and additional rights issued.[103]

For these reasons and others, the authors endorse a pollution-rights scheme as the most promising means for controlling waste discharges.[104] While this is by no means a new proposal,[105] it is not (to my knowledge) one that has really been considered very seriously at the policy level, and this is unfortunate. Perhaps this is because the proposal sounds strange: "The auctioning of pollution rights" has an almost otherworldly (Utopian or Satanic) ring.[106] Although unfamiliar, I would suggest that it is quite workable: Once having determined the acceptable level of waste emissions, I see no insuperable barrier to the allocation of quotas by sale rather than by the elaborate, and ultimately unsatisfactory, legal-orders method followed by the DRBC.

For my own tastes, I would be delighted with the introduction of either effluent charges or pollution rights into the pursuit of our environmental objectives. Either technique would represent an enormous improvement over the costly, and often largely ineffective, legal-orders tradition which has dominated

---

[103] *Id.* 269-70 (emphasis in original) (footnotes omitted).
[104] *Id.* 281. *But see id.* 275-81.
[105] *See, e.g.,* J. DALES, POLLUTION, PROPERTY, AND VALUES (1968).
[106] *See generally* B. ACKERMAN, *supra* note 1, at 276-78.

environmental policy in this, and most other,[107] countries. While there is mounting evidence that pricing incentives are an efficient *and* highly effective means for controlling water pollution, air pollution, and the generation of solid wastes,[108] there remains a latent hostility to any technique that explicitly recognizes "pollution rights" or the desirability (in view of the costs) of maintaining positive levels of various polluting activities.[109]

I do not want to leave the impression that the authors (or I) see the "market model" as the sole answer to our environmental problems. In fact, one of the most impressive aspects of this study is its painstaking effort to assess both the advantages *and* *disadvantages* of the various policy alternatives. The market model, if used *alone*, suffers from some serious deficiencies. (For example, there is the problem of coordination: Economies of scale in treatment may dictate the need, in certain instances, for joint planning and use of facilities; but it is not clear that voluntary action on the part of individual polluters will result in the establishment of such facilities in the most advantageous locations.[110] Moreover, some effluents may be so dangerous to human life that their discharge should simply be banned altogether.[111]) The point is rather that a heavy reliance on price incentives should constitute an integral part of an overall environmental strategy. Unfortunately, we have to this point chosen to ignore this potentially powerful instrument for protection of the environment.

V. CONCLUSION

The authors conclude their study on a relatively pessimistic note as regards the formulation and implementation of an effective environmental policy.[112] The Delaware experience not only indicates the deficiencies in a single episode of analysis and decisionmaking, it also reveals a series of extremely complex and troublesome obstacles inherent in the very process of instituting a sensible environmental program. It is clear that we have a

---

[107] COUNCIL ON ENVIRONMENTAL QUALITY, ENVIRONMENTAL QUALITY 348-56 (4th Annual Report 1973).

[108] William Baumol and I are preparing a survey of this evidence to appear as part of our forthcoming book, *Economic Policy for the Quality of Life*.

[109] *See* B. ACKERMAN, *supra* note 1, at 276-78.

[110] *Id*. 282-85.

[111] *See id*. 209-10.

[112] *See id*. 317-30.

great distance yet to travel to our objective of a rational, efficacious policy for the protection of the environment.

What is perhaps most disheartening about this are the recurring lapses in understanding in policy determination in the
most critical places. Not long ago, for example, Congress enacted
the extensive Federal Water Pollution Control Act Amendments
of 1972 with the nonsensical declaration that "it is the national
goal that the discharge of pollutants into the navigable waters be
eliminated by 1985."[113] Such flights of fancy indicate the pervasive character of certain fundamental misconceptions regarding
environmental policy and, in the end, serve to confuse and impede any real progress toward the realization of a reasonable set
of environmental objectives. And on the administrative side, we
witness such things as the agonizing delays and time extensions
to meet emission requirements for new automobiles followed by
recent reports of the ineffectiveness of the new emission-control
devices. All in all, there is much evidence to support the authors'
closing statement:

> What is disappointing, even alarming, is the prospect of
> government, frustrated by the difficulty of structuring a
> coherent response, embarking on an urgent quest to
> achieve a poorly defined goal without institutions pres-
> ent to raise the right questions, and without the reg-
> ulatory tools to achieve objectives either efficiently or
> fairly. The environmental revolution of the 1970's sug-
> gests that we have yet to learn the lessons of the 1960's.
> After all these lessons have been mastered, however, we
> shall only have taken the first step toward a system of
> government that will permit modern men to live in
> harmony with themselves and nature.[114]

Yet the limited perspective of the Delaware hides some real
progress elsewhere. Regarding air pollution, for example, the
last decade has witnessed quite striking reductions in the sulphur
and particulate content of the atmosphere over most of our
major cities (as well as many cities abroad).[115] And new programs, such as Oregon's requiring deposits for beverage containers, are showing encouraging results for the recycling of

---

[113] 33 U.S.C. § 1251(a)(1) (Supp. III, 1973). *See* B. ACKERMAN, *supra* note 1, at
319-25.

[114] B. ACKERMAN, *supra* note 1, at 330.

[115] COUNCIL ON ENVIRONMENTAL QUALITY, *supra* note 107, at 273.

solid wastes.[116] In the water resource field itself there is some evidence of reduced waste discharges in response to municipal waste-treatment fees.[117] Progress, however, is slow and difficult; it is the important contribution of this book to help us to understand why this is so and to face up to the basic dilemmas and tradeoffs inherent in the quest for environmental quality.

---

[116] D. Waggoner, Oregon's Model Bill, Two Years Later (May 1974).

[117] Elliott & Seagraves, *User Charges as a Means for Pollution Control: The Case of Sewer Surcharges*, 3 BELL J. ECON & MGMT. SCI. 346 (1972).

PART II

ECONOMIC INSTRUMENTS FOR ENVIRONMENTAL REGULATION: THEORY AND GENERAL ISSUES

[4]

THE REGULATION OF EXTERNALITIES: EFFICIENT BEHAVIOR BY SOURCES AND VICTIMS*

by

WALLACE E. OATES**

I.

The Pigouvian prescription for the correction of the allocative distortions resulting from an external diseconomy calls for a unit tax on the generator of the externality equal to marginal social damage (MSD). While it is recognized that the Pigouvian measure is not applicable (and can itself be a source of distortions) where costless bargaining takes place among the interested parties (Coase [1960], Turvey [1963]), the Pigouvian tax has been found to retain its desirable properties in an environment of competitive behavior. To be more precise, it has been shown that, in a competitive setting, a tax per unit of the externality levied on its source and equal to MSD *at* the Pareto-efficient level of the externality can sustain an efficient pattern of resource use (see, for example, Baumol and Oates [1975, Ch. 4]).

It is noteworthy that the Pigouvian remedy requires an extra-market inducement solely for the generator of the externality, not for the victim. Yet victims frequently have opportunities to pursue activities that lessen the disutility or "alleviate" the effects of the externality. Improved insulation, for example, can mitigate the annoyance of an external source of noise; alternatively, a victim can relocate to escape the pollution from a nearby factory. The existing literature claims that no supplementary incentives are needed to induce efficient levels of "alleviation activities" by victims; individual maximizing behavior will take care of that (e.g., Baumol and Oates [1975, Ch. 4])[1]

Until recently, however, the literature has not examined very closely the nature of alleviation activities.[2] In two recent and quite interesting papers, Butler and Maher [1981] and Shibata and Winrich [1983] address the issue in terms of models that explicitly incorporate alleviation activities into the victims' set of choice variables with some illuminating results. This paper continues this line of analysis in terms of an alternative model and tries to put the results in perspective.

Public Finance / Finances Publiques   No. 3/1983   Vol. XXXVIII/XXXVIIlième Année

REGULATION OF EXTERNALITIES

I shall make three points:

(1) In a fairly general model similar in spirit to those in the existing externalities' literature, the explicit introduction of alleviation activity does *not* invalidate the Pigouvian prescription. It remains true in this model that a unit tax (or fee) on the generator of the externality equal to MSD can itself sustain efficient levels of both abatement activity by the generator and alleviation activity by the victims.

(2) The presence of alleviation activity does have implications for the level of the Pigouvian tax and for certain matters of interpretation. In particular, the optimal Pigouvian tax will, in general, be lower (and the level of waste emissions higher) in the presence of alleviation activity by victims than in its absence. In addition, the model and its results make clear just where the Coasian argument for taxation of victims goes astray.

(3) The results, however, cannot provide too much comfort at the policy level, for the existence of alleviation activity, as emphasized by Shibata and Winrich, can itself be a source of nonconvexities and multiple local maxima complicating greatly the determination of the efficient pattern of behavior and the appropriate set of fiscal inducements.

II.

The analysis begins with a model typical of the externalities' literature in which the activity of producing certain goods generates an external diseconomy on individuals in the system. The model consists of the following nine equations:[3]

(1) $U_A = U_A(X_A, Y_A, Z_A)$

(2) $U_B = U_B(X_B, Y_B, Z_B)$

(3) $X = X(L_X, S_X)$

(4) $Y = Y(L_Y, S_Y)$

(5) $Z_A = Z_A(S_X + S_Y, L_A)$

(6) $Z_B = Z_B(S_X + S_Y, L_B)$

(7) $L_o = L_X + L_Y + L_A + L_B$

(8) $X = X_A + X_B$

(9) $Y = Y_A + Y_B$

Equations (1) and (2) are the utility functions for individuals A and B; utility is positively related to the individual consumption of two goods, X and Y, and negatively related to the individual's exposure to pollution, Z. The sources of the externality, S_X and S_Y, appear as factor inputs in equations (3) and (4), the production functions for the two goods X and Y. I shall refer to S_X and S_Y as "smoke emissions"; the other factor, a composite factor input, is L. I shall call it "labor". Abatement activity in this model takes the form of reducing smoke emissions $(S_X$ or $S_Y)$ either through the increased use of labor or lower levels of output. The extension of this "typical model" to incorporate alleviation activity is embodied in equations (5) and (6). Although total smoke emissions $(S_X + S_Y)$ have the undepletable property of a pure public good in that their "consumption" by individual A does not reduce their availability to person B, the actual level of pollution (Z) experienced by A and B depends both on the aggregate level of smoke and the amount of L each person chooses to employ to alleviate the effects of the smoke. Note that alleviation activity is private in character: each individual selects the amount of labor input to devote to alleviation so that the final levels of consumption of pollution, Z_A and Z_B, are individual-specific. The remaining three equations, (7) through (9), are "adding-up" constraints that limit labor usage to the given labor supply (L_o) and equate total consumption of X and Y to that produced.

To determine the conditions for Pareto-efficient behavior, we find the stationary values of the Lagrangian:

(10) $M = U_A(X_A, Y_A, Z_A) + \lambda_1[U_B(X_B, Y_B, Z_B) - U_B^0(\cdot)] + \lambda_2[X_A + X_B - X(L_X, S_X)]$

$$+ \lambda_3[Y_A + Y_B - Y(L_Y, S_Y)] + \lambda_4[L_o - L_X - L_Y - L_A - L_B],$$

where $U_B^0(\cdot)$ is B's benchmark level of utility. We obtain among the first-order conditions:

(11) $-\left(\dfrac{\dfrac{\partial U_A}{\partial Z_A}\dfrac{\partial Z_A}{\partial S_X}}{\partial U_A/\partial X_A} + \dfrac{\dfrac{\partial U_B}{\partial Z_B}\dfrac{\partial Z_B}{\partial S_X}}{\partial U_B/\partial X_B}\right) = \dfrac{\partial X}{\partial S_X}$

(12) $-\left(\dfrac{\dfrac{\partial U_A}{\partial Z_A}\dfrac{\partial Z_A}{\partial S_Y}}{\partial U_A/\partial Y_A} + \dfrac{\dfrac{\partial U_B}{\partial Z_B}\dfrac{\partial Z_B}{\partial S_Y}}{\partial U_B/\partial Y_B}\right) = \dfrac{\partial Y}{\partial S_Y}$

(13) $\dfrac{\partial U_A}{\partial Z_A}\dfrac{\partial Z_A}{\partial L_A} = \dfrac{\partial U_A}{\partial X_A}\dfrac{\partial X}{\partial L_X} = \dfrac{\partial U_A}{\partial Y_A}\dfrac{\partial Y}{\partial L_Y}$

(14) $\dfrac{\partial U_B}{\partial Z_B}\dfrac{\partial Z_B}{\partial L_B} = \dfrac{\partial U_B}{\partial X_B}\dfrac{\partial X}{\partial L_X} = \dfrac{\partial U_B}{\partial Y_B}\dfrac{\partial Y}{\partial L_Y}$

Equations (11) and (12) are the familiar results for the efficient level of abatement activity: they indicate that, in the production of goods X and Y respectively, smoke emissions should be at a level such that the marginal social damage of a unit of emissions (equal to the sum of the disutilities of A and B) equals the marginal product of emissions.[4] Of central interest here, equations (13) and (14) indicate that each individual should engage in the alleviation of the pollution he absorbs to the point where the marginal utility from using another unit of labor for alleviation just equals the marginal loss in utility from sacrificing the output which that unit of labor could have produced.

In addition, by solving equations (13) and (14) for $\partial U_A/\partial Z_A$ and $\partial U_B/\partial Z_B$ respectively and substituting into (11), we obtain:

$$(15) \qquad \frac{\partial Z_A/\partial S_X}{\partial Z_A/\partial L_A} + \frac{\partial Z_B/\partial S_X}{\partial Z_B/\partial L_B} = \frac{\partial X/\partial S_X}{\partial X/\partial L_X} \; .$$

Equation (15) says that the marginal cost of reducing pollution by alleviation should equal the marginal cost of reducing pollution through abatement, an instance of Mishan's condition [1974] for the least-cost combination of methods for the control of pollution.

As is well known, competitive behavior by the sources of pollution will not satisfy the efficiency conditions in equations (11) and (12). Since a competitive firm sets the marginal product of smoke emissions equal to the "price" of emissions, the environmental authority must place a unit tax on emissions equal to MSD [the LHS of (11) or (12)] for a competitive equilibrium to satisfy the first-order efficiency conditions (Baumol and Oates [1975, Ch. 4]).

In contrast, it is easy to see that individual-maximizing behavior will satisfy the first-order conditions for efficient levels of alleviation activity. Individual i will maximize utility subject to a budget constraint giving rise to the following Lagrangian:

$$(16) \qquad M = U_i[X_i, \; Y_i, \; Z_i(S_X + S_Y, \; L_i)] + \lambda[P_X X_i + P_Y Y_i + P_L L_i - I_i]$$

where P_X, P_Y, and P_L are the given prices of X, Y, and labor, and I_i is the person's given level of income. Finding the stationary values of (16) yields:

$$(17) \qquad \frac{\partial U_i}{\partial Z_i} \; \frac{\partial Z_i}{\partial L_i} = \frac{\partial U_i}{\partial X_i} \; \frac{P_L}{P_X}$$

Noting that profit maximization by competitive producers implies that $P_L/P_X = \partial X/\partial L_X$, we obtain:

$$(18) \qquad \frac{\partial U_i}{\partial Z_i} \; \frac{\partial Z_i}{\partial L_i} = \frac{\partial U_i}{\partial X_i} \; \frac{\partial X}{\partial L_X}$$

which coincides with conditions (13) and (14) for efficient behavior.

The rationale for these results is quite straightforward. Since abatement activity produces benefits which are external to its source, an inducement in the form of a

Pigouvian tax is required to internalize the benefits. In contrast, alleviation activity in this model is a purely private activity: the benefits accrue solely to the particular victim who undertakes to reduce the amount of pollution he absorbs. Consequently, the utility-maximizing individual will extend alleviation activity to the point where marginal benefits equal marginal cost from society's (as well as the individual's) vantage point. A Pigouvian tax on the generator of the externality is, therefore, all that is required to sustain an efficient pattern of both abatement and alleviation activity.[5]

I should mention, as pointed out by Butler and Maher, that there can surely be instances where alleviation activity has public-good characteristics. A person who picks up trash in a local park benefits other users of the park as well as himself. In cases such as this, alleviation activity will, in general, be suboptimal as a result of the usual public-goods and free-rider problems.

III.

While the introduction of alleviation activity does not alter the basic Pigouvian prescription, it does have some implications for its interpretation. First, as Butler and Maher stress, the concept of marginal social damages requires some further elucidation in the presence of alleviation by victims.[6] Second, a closer examination of the results reveals just why, although it at first seems counterintuitive, that a tax on victims is not needed to internalize the costs that victims' decisions on levels of alleviation activity impose on the sources of waste emissions.

Butler and Maher present a detailed geometric derivation of the "corrected" marginal damage function where alleviation takes place. I summarize their argument in terms of Fig. 1, where MSD_o indicates marginal damages in the absence of any alleviation measures by victims. MSD_o is simply the vertical summation of individual marginal damage curves from smoke emissions. Victims, however, will undertake to alleviate the effects of smoke emissions wherever the marginal cost of alleviation is less than the marginal damages resulting from the emissions. Where alleviation occurs, the resulting cost of smoke emissions to victims will be less than that depicted by MSD_o. Put another way, suppose that victims find it less expensive to alleviate in their entirety the effects of some given level of smoke emissions than to suffer the costs of the associated pollution. In this case, the victims' willingness-to-pay to eliminate the smoke would equal their costs of alleviation (not the damages in the absence of alleviation).

The implication is that the corrected MSD function, MSD_a in Fig. 1, will generally lie below MSD_o, the damage curve in the absence of alleviation.[7] Given the curve indicating the value of the marginal product of emissions, we can determine the Pareto-efficient outcome by the intersection of the MSD_a and VMP

REGULATION OF EXTERNALITIES   367

curves.[8] As Butler and Maher (and also Mishan [1974]) point out and as indicated in Fig. 1, we find that the optimal Pigouvian tax will typically be lower *(Ot_a* instead of *Ot_o)* and the optimal level of smoke emissions will be higher *(OS_a* instead of *OS_o)* in the presence of alleviation. Thus, the introduction of alleviation activity, while it does not alter the principle of Pigouvian taxation, does influence the level of the tax.

Although the analysis indicates clearly that there is no need to tax victims, this matter has been the source of considerable confusion in the externalities' literature. The basic issue, as Coase [1960] has argued, is that decisions concerning the levels of alleviation activity by victims have cost implications for the source of the externality, and these costs do not appear to enter into the victim's decision-making

FIGURE 1

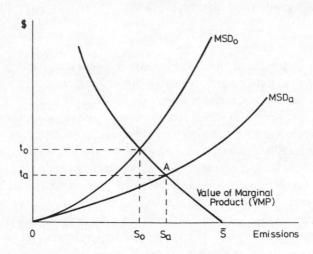

calculus. To make matters more concrete, consider the case where the individual's alleviation activity takes the form of a location decision. An individual works at a nearby factory and suffers during his leisure hours from the pollution emanating from the factory. By locating farther from the factory, he can reduce his disutility from pollution, but this comes at the cost of higher commuting expenses. The individual presumably makes his location decision by equating at the margin the reduction in the smoke damages he absorbs with the increase in his travel costs.

But from a Coasian perspective, this would seem to result in the victim residing excessively near to the factory. The factory owners, subject to an effluent fee equal to MSD, would be willing to pay our individual a sum to move farther away in order to reduce their level of costly abatement activity and/or their effluent fee payments.

Suppose, for example, that by moving one mile farther from the factory, the individual could reduce his disutility from pollution by the same number of utils as would occur if the factory reduced its smoke emissions by one unit. Then the factory owners would be willing to pay this person any sum up to their marginal abatement cost (MAC) to induce him to make this move. However, in a competitive framework and in the absence of Coasian bargaining, this payment will not take place; the individual will consequently not take into account the costs he imposes on the factory owner and will locate too close to the factory. It is for this reason that, in the absence of bargaining, Coase has recommended a tax on victims that induces the additional alleviation activity needed to incorporate the interests of the source of the externality.[9]

We thus seem to have a paradox. Our formal model tells us not to tax victims; however, a compelling line of argument suggests otherwise — that a tax is required to induce victims to internalize the full range of costs relevant to their decisions on alleviation measures. This paradox, however, is only apparent; on closer examination, the analysis makes clear the error in the Coasian line of reasoning. Returning to our example, if we seek out the cost signal that confronts our victim, we find that his incentive to move a mile more distant from the factory is the reduced level of damages that he will absorb. But at the optimal solution, the factory manager has set MSD=MAC so that the individual's incentive to locate farther from the factory is equal precisely to the firm's potential savings in abatement costs (or effluent fees). The victim, it turns out, has exactly the correct incentive to move farther away from the factory, namely the willingness-to-pay of the factory owners to induce him to do so. The more general point, then, is that the marginal costs that the victim imposes on the source by his decision not to undertake the marginal unit of alleviation is apparent to the victim in the form of the marginal damages he must bear from failing to alleviate further.

There is not, incidentally, any double counting involved here. Suppose, for example, that were the victim to relocate a mile farther away from the factory, the owners would choose to maintain abatement at the existing level and thereby reduce their effluent fee payments by the reduction in damages. In this case, the real savings to society from the move are simply the decrease in the damages absorbed by the victim. And individual maximizing behavior will lead the victim to select a level of alleviation activity such that the decrease in damages equals precisely the costs of alleviation at the margin. Alternatively, since MSD=MAC at the optimal solution, the factory owners could equally well decide to reduce their abatement levels by one unit. In this event, the victim, after his move, would find an unchanged level of smoke damages. The savings to society in this case would equal MAC (i.e., the value of the resources released from the marginal unit of abatement activity).

The savings to society thus take the form *either* of reduced abatement costs *or* damage costs (or, perhaps, some weighted average of the two), but not their sum. This second case makes clear a further assumption implicit in the analysis: the victim must take the factory owners' behavior as given. If, for example, the victim knew in advance that smoke emissions would increase following his move, he would not have the proper incentive for relocation.[10]

IV.

While the apparent robustness of the Pigouvian resolution of the externalities' problem may be reassuring, it is at the same time somewhat incomplete and misleading. First, our formal results indicate that the optimal tax will *sustain* an efficient pattern of resource use. This implies that the appropriate Pigouvian tax equals MSD *at* the optimal levels of abatement and alleviation activities (not at existing distorted levels). Thus, the determination of the optimal tax requires extensive information on damages, abatement costs, and costs of alleviation.[11] One might hope that setting a tax equal to *existing* MSD and adjusting it as the economy responds would generate an iterative process that converges on the optimal solution. But we cannot be certain even of this (Baumol and Oates [1975, Ch. 7]; Kraus and Mohring [1975]).

Second, our analysis has examined only the first-order conditions for economic efficiency. But there are reasons for concern over second-order conditions; in particular, the existing literature (Baumol and Bradford [1972], Gould [1977]) shows that externalities may themselves be the source of violations of the second-order conditions for efficient resource allocation. A sufficiently strong externality can, for example, generate nonconvexities in the production set with an associated multiplicity of local maxima.

Moreover, Kraus and Mohring [1975] and more recently Shibata and Winrich [1983] have shown that the introduction of alleviation activities can be a further source of nonconvexities and multiple maxima. Exploring a series of cost functions for alleviation activity, the latter find that quite plausible sorts of interactions between abatement and alleviation cost functions can complicate and, in some instances, undermine some of the standard Pigouvian results. In certain cases, for example, victims' marginal costs of alleviation may depend upon the level of emissions of the polluter. Such an interaction effectively introduces an additional form of externality; as Shibata and Winrich demonstrate, the Pigouvian tax on the polluting firm must, in such instances, incorporate the magnitude of this externality in addition to the usual marginal social damages.

Perhaps more disturbing, however, are the potential implications for violations of second-order conditions. The Shibata and Winrich analysis shows that the interplay of abatement and alleviation activities can effectively multiply the range of possible corner solutions and local maxima making it quite difficult to determine any straightforward rule (like a Pigouvian tax) for the achievement of the global optimum. The consideration of a couple of special cases will illustrate the nature of these problems and correct one misleading conclusion in the Shibata-Winrich paper.

Using an adaptation of Fig. 1, it is easy to depict one of the Shibata-Winrich cases of multiple local maxima. In Fig. 2, MSD_o again indicates the levels of MSD in the absence of any abatement or alleviation activities, and VMP reflects the marginal value of emissions (or marginal abatement cost) to the source. In contrast to Fig. 1,

FIGURE 2

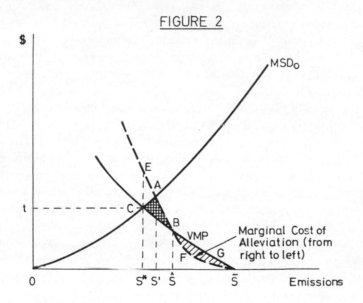

however, the MSD_a curve now has a negative slope over the range indicated by the dashed line $ABF\overline{S}$. This embodies the quite plausible condition that, in some cases, it is less costly to remove a "unit" of pollutant from the environment when the level of pollution is relatively high; as the environment becomes progressively cleaner with reduced concentrations of the pollutant, it becomes continually more difficult to extract yet further units of the pollutant. We see this increasing marginal cost of alleviation by reading from right to left from $\overline{S}$ along the dashed line passing through points F, B, and A. Fig. 2 indicates that in the absence of any abatement activity by the source of the externality, the equilibrium outcome would entail total emissions of $O\overline{S}$ (the uncontrolled level) with $\overline{S}S'$ units "being alleviated" by victims

REGULATION OF EXTERNALITIES

so that the damages absorbed at the margin equal $S'A$.[12] The total cost of alleviation plus residual damages from emissions would equal the area $OABF\overline{S}$.

On further inspection, it would appear that the efficient solution should require a mix of abatement and alleviation activities: if the effects of units $\overline{S}\hat{S}$ were eliminated through alleviation by victims and if units $\hat{S}S^*$ were then controlled through abatement by sources, the total costs of pollution (abatement plus alleviation plus residual damages) would be reduced to $OCBF\overline{S}$. But this outcome is not possible; by the nature of the pollution problem, units of abatement must effectively "precede" units of alleviation. In terms of Fig. 2, the marginal cost of alleviation depends upon the level of emissions (and, hence, upon the extent of abatement activity). Consider, for example, a water-user who is downstream from a polluter and whose alleviation activity consists of removing the damaging impurities from the water. The quantity of the pollutant to be extracted by the victim (and the marginal cost of such extraction) depends on the extent of abatement activities by the source; abatement activity, in this sense, must "precede" alleviation measures.

For such a case in Fig. 2, polluters could abate over the range $\overline{S}\hat{S}$ and then victims could alleviate the effects of units $\hat{S}S^*$, but not vice-versa. However, this latter outcome is obviously not a least-cost solution, as it implies total costs equal to the area $OCEBG\overline{S}$. With such a technological constraint on the relationship between abatement and alleviation activity, it is clear that we have two local optima: the first makes use solely of abatement activity and results in a level of emissions of OS^*, and the second employs only alleviation activity and results in emissions of $O\overline{S}$ (with units $\overline{S}S'$ being "removed" through alleviation measures).[13] Which of these is the efficient outcome cannot be determined *a priori*, since the relative sizes of areas $OCBG\overline{S}$ and $OABF\overline{S}$ depend upon the configuration of the curves for a particular case (i.e., upon whether the shaded or lined area in Fig. 2 is the larger).

This is a disturbing result from a policy perspective. Following the standard Pigouvian prescription, we can set an effluent fee equal to Ot, and this will sustain an outcome with OS^* of emissions, $S^*\overline{S}$ of abatement, and no alleviation activity. This may be the efficient outcome, but we can't be sure since it is only one of the two local optima. The obvious moral to this exercise is that the interaction between abatement and alleviation activities can itself be a source of nonconvexities that may undermine the efficiency properties of the Pigouvian remedy for external effects.

A second case of interest concerns a corner solution. Suppose, as depicted in Fig. 3, that over the entire range of emissions, it is less costly for victims to alleviate the effects of smoke emissions than for sources to control them. The efficient outcome in this instance is clearly for sources to engage in no abatement at all, but for victims

WALLACE E. OATES

to undertake alleviation measures such that the total cost to society equals the area under the MSD_a curve $(O A \overline{S})$. It would appear for this case that there is no need for any action on the part of the environmental authority: sources will emit whatever wastes are consistent with their profit-maximizing levels of output, and victims, as a result of utility-maximizing behavior, will engage in efficient levels of alleviation activity. This would suggest what Shibata and Winrich call a *laissez-faire* solution. In fact, they conclude that "If the solution attainable by the exclusive use of the defensive method were globally optimal, however, a governmental intervention

FIGURE 3

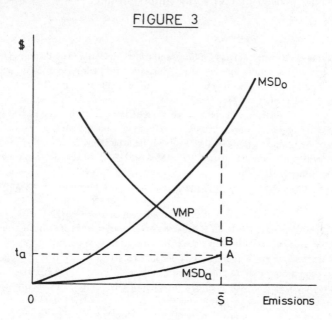

would reduce economic efficiency. In this case, *laissez-faire* would be most efficient..." [1983, p. 435].

On this matter, however, they are not quite correct. The Pigouvian solution would indicate a unit tax on emissions equal to MSD (corrected for alleviation activity) at the optimal level of emissions: a tax of Ot_a. Note that, since the tax is less than marginal abatement cost $(\overline{S}B)$, it will not induce any abatement activity; the fee will not, therefore, create any distortions in abatement decisions. Moreover, the tax is needed to provide the proper longer-run incentives for entry and exit decisions by polluting firms. This issue, incidentally, is one that is frequently overlooked in the externalities literature. The point is that the firm's waste emissions generate an external cost, and, irrespective of the implications for short-run abatement decisions, these costs must enter into the firm's long-run calculations concerning entry and exit. Otherwise, we may have firms entering the industry (or failing to leave) even though the total value of their output to society is less than the total costs (including any external costs) that they impose on society (see Schulze and d'Arge [1974] and Collinge and Oates [1982]).

Aside from this last issue, however, Shibata and Winrich provide an illuminating treatment of the potential pitfalls in a single-minded adherence to the Pigouvian prescription in the presence of alleviation activities by victims. The global optimum may not be readily determined by any simple formula.

NOTES

* I am grateful to Dieter Biehl, Robert Collinge, and Albert McGartland for helpful comments and to the National Science Foundation and the Sloan Foundation for their support of this research.

** The author is Professor of Economics, Department of Economics and Bureau of Business and Economic Research, University of Maryland.

[1] I shall use the term "abatement" to refer to measures undertaken by the source to reduce the level of the externality-generating activity (e.g., to reduce levels of waste emissions). "Alleviation" activities are those undertaken by victims to mitigate the effects of the externality.

[2] For same exceptions, see Browning [1977], Mishan [1974], Kraus and Mohring [1975], and Zeckhauser and Fisher [1976].

[3] This model is easily extended to many individuals, firms, and inputs with no substantive changes in the results.

[4] Alternatively, these conditions state that for an efficient outcome marginal social damages must equal marginal abatement cost. The latter is equal to the marginal product of emissions, since the cost at the margin of reducing emissions is simply the value of the foregone output.

[5] Since most externalities are, in practice, fairly localized in terms of their effects, it would make sense at the policy level for a decentralized public agency to set and administer the Pigouvian tax. As Dieter Biehl has pointed out to me, there is a strong case for observing the "correspondence principle" such that the jurisdiction served by the public agency coincides with the boundaries of the effects of the externality (i.e., a kind of "optimal pollution area" in Biehl's terminology). A centralized agency is less likely to possess the information, motivation, or the flexibility to tailor the tax to local conditions.

[6] See also Browning [1977] on the correct measure of damages.

[7] MSD_a may, as Butler and Maher [1981] show, coincide with MSD_o over certain ranges.

[8] Note that reading from right to left in Fig. 1 from the level of uncontrolled emissions $(\bar{S})$, the ordinate of the VMP curve indicates marginal abatement cost (MAC). Point A thus indicates the level of emissions for which MSD equals MAC.

[9] In the presence of bargaining between sources and victims, an efficient outcome can be realized without taxation of either party. As Coase [1960] has argued, depending on the definition of property rights, either the victim will pay the source to engage in the efficient level of abatement activity or the source will pay the victim to allow the discharge of the efficient level of emissions. The Coasian outcome depends, however, on the absence both of significant transactions costs and of strategic behavior among the parties that could impede a Pareto-improving transaction. As Dieter Biehl pointed out to me, the Pigouvian perspective also involves an assumption concerning transactions costs: it presumes that an

WALLACE E. OATES

institution to tax pollution exists and that its operation is sufficiently "inexpensive" so as not to negate the gains from internalizing the externality. If transactions costs are sufficiently high to prevent voluntary bargains between sources and victims and also to make the operations of a taxing agency uneconomical, the preferred outcome will entail leaving things as they are, with no internalization of the externality. The existence and the cost of mechanisms for internalization are a critical issue in determining the optimal course of action.

[10] This last condition is really implicit in the assumption of a competitive setting in which there are many actors such that the behavior of any one individual has a negligible effect on the equilibrium vector of prices and outputs.

[11] Elsewhere Robert Collinge and I [1982] have described a scheme of marketable emission permits in the Pigouvian spirit that can generate the efficient outcome without requiring any information on abatement costs.

[12] The extension of the curve reflecting marginal costs of alleviation by victims to the left of the MSD_o curve has no relevance, since to the left of point A in Fig. 2 it is less costly for victims simply to absorb the damages from emissions than to undertake to alleviate them. Consequently, the MSD_a curve will, in this case, coincide with MSD_o from the origin to point A and then will change course along the dashed stretch AB from S' to $\bar{S}$.

[13] The efficient outcome would entail a mix of abatement and alleviation activities in Fig. 2, if the VMP curve cut the marginal alleviation cost curve from above rather than from below (reading from left to right).

REFERENCES

Baumol, William, and Bradford, David, "Detrimental Externalities and Non-Convexity of the Production Set," *Economica,* Vol. 39 (May 1972), pp. 160-76.

Baumol, William, and Oates, Wallace, *The Theory of Environmental Policy* (Englewood Cliffs, New Jersey: Prentice-Hall, 1975).

Browning, Edgar, "External Diseconomies, Compensation, and the Measure of Damage," *Southern Economic Journal,* Vol. 43, No. 3 (January 1977), pp. 1279-87.

Butler, Richard, and Maher, Michael, "The Control of Externalities: Abatement Vs. Damage Prevention," Working Draft (November 1981).

Coase, R.H., "The Problem of Social Cost," *Journal of Law and Economics,* Vol. 3 (October 1960), pp. 1-44.

Collinge, Robert, and Oates, Wallace, "Efficiency in Pollution Control in the Short and Long Runs: A System of Rental Emission Permits," *Canadian Journal of Economics,* Vol. 15, No. 2 (May 1982), pp. 346-54.

Gould, J.R., "Total Conditions in the Analysis of External Effects," *Economic Journal,* Vol. 87 (September 1977), pp. 558-64.

Kraus, Marvin, and Mohring, Herbert, "The Role of Pollutee Taxes in Externality Problems," *Economica,* Vol. 42 (May 1975), pp. 171-76.

Mishan, E.J., "What is the Optimal Level of Pollution?," *Journal of Political Economy,* Vol. 82 (November/December 1974), pp. 1278-99.

Schulze, William, and d'Arge, Ralph, "The Coase Proposition, Information Constraints, and Long-Run Equilibrium," *American Economic Review,* Vol. 64 (September 1974), pp. 763-72.

Shibata, Hirofumi, and Winrich, J. Steven, "Control of Pollution When the Offended Defend Themselves," *Economica,* Vol. 50 (November 1983) pp. 425-37.

Turvey, Ralph, "On Divergences Between Social Cost and Private Cost," *Economica,* Vol. 30 (August 1963), pp. 309-13.

Zeckhauser, Richard, and Fisher, Anthony, "Averting Behavior and External Diseconomies," *J.F. Kennedy School Discussion Paper No. 41D* (April 1976).

Summary: *The Regulation of Externalities: Efficient Behavior by Sources and Victims.* — Using a model that explicitly incorporates alleviation activities by victims to reduce the social damages from an externality, this paper demonstrates that the Pigouvian tax on the generator of the externality can still sustain a Pareto-efficient outcome. However, the presence of alleviation activities does have implications for the level of the Pigouvian tax and for certain matters of interpretation. Moreover, policy complications arise because alleviation activities can themselves be a source of nonconvexities and multiple local maxima.

Résumé: *La régulation d'externalités: comportement efficient par des sources et des victimes.* — Nous utilisons un modèle incorporant explicitement les réactions des victimes afin de réduire les dommages sociaux résultant d'une externalité. Ceci pour démontrer que la taxe de Pigou sur le responsable de l'externalité peut toujours entraîner un résultat efficient au sens de Pareto. Toutefois, la présence de ces activités a des implications sur le montant de la taxe de Pigou et sur des problèmes d'interprétation. Des difficultés politiques surgissent par le fait que ces activités peuvent elles-même être source de non-convexité et de maxima locaux multiples.

Zusammenfassung: *Die Regulierung von Externalitäten: effizientes Verhalten von Verursachern und Betroffenen.* — Unter Verwendung eines Models, das explizit Maßnahmen von Betroffenen zur Verringerung des sozialen Schadens durch eine Externalität einbezieht, zeigt der Artikel, daß die Pigou-Steuer auf den Erzeuger einer Externalität trotzdem zu einem Pareto-effizienten Ergebnis führen kann. Jedoch wirken sich Maßnahmen zur Verringerung des Schadens auf die Höhe der Pigou-Steuer und auf gewisse Fragen der Interpretation aus. Darüberhinaus ergeben sich politische Probleme, da die Maßnahmen zur Verringerung des Schadens selbst eine Quelle für Nicht-Konvexitäten und multiple lokale Maxima sein können.

[5]

The Instruments for Environmental Policy

*Wallace E. Oates, Princeton University and
William J. Baumol, New York University
and Princeton University*

In their part of the continuing dialogue on environmental policy, economists have quite naturally stressed the role of policy tools operating through the pricing system. The case for heavy reliance on effluent charges to internalize the social costs of individual decisions is, at least in principle, a very compelling one. However, a cursory survey of potential policy instruments reveals the existence of a wide spectrum of methods for environmental control ranging from outright prohibition of polluting activities to milder forms of moral suasion involving voluntary compliance.

In spite of the economist's predilection for a central role for direct price incentives, we suspect that even he recognizes that a comprehensive and effective (and even the "optimal") environmental policy probably involves a mix of policy tools with the use of something more than only effluent fees. The purpose of this paper is a preliminary exploration of the potential and limitations of the various policy tools available for environmental protection; our concern here is what we can say in a systematic way about the particular circumstances under which one type of policy is more appropriate than another and how various policy tools can interact effectively. We stress the word preliminary, because this paper is, in effect, an interim report on a study of environmental policy.

In the first section, we enumerate and classify the available policy instruments. In the following three sections, we present a simple concep-

NOTE: We are grateful to the National Science Foundation whose support has greatly facilitated our work on environmental policy.

95

tual framework for the analysis of environmental policies and a discussion of what *in principle* would appear to be the appropriate roles for the various policy tools. We turn in the fifth section to an empirical examination of the effectiveness of the different environmental policies. Our work here is in its early stages; we have at this point some admittedly fragmentary and piecemeal evidence on the efficacy of available policy instruments. In some cases, we have had to rely upon evidence that is indirect, occasionally derived from experiences other than environmental programs, to obtain some insight into the likely effectiveness of a particular policy tool.

Policy Tools for Environmental Protection

Before examining the various active policy options available for the control of environmental quality, we want to acknowledge the case for a policy of no public intervention: we could rely wholly on the market mechanism as an instrument for the regulation of externalities, unimpeded by public programs designed to protect the environment. In fact, as Ronald Coase has shown in his classic article, it is actually possible, under certain conditions, to achieve an efficient pattern of resource use through private negotiation that internalizes all social costs or benefits. This can, at least in principle, result from the incentive for parties suffering damage from the activities of others to make payments to induce a reduction in these activities.

The difficulties besetting the Coase solution are well known, particularly the free rider problem and the role of transaction costs. The main point we wish to make here is that the Coase argument is plausible only for the small group case, for only here is the number of participants sufficiently small for each to recognize the importance of his own role in the bargaining process.[1] Note, moreover, that this requires small numbers on *both sides* of the transaction; even if the polluter is a single decisionmaker, a Coase solution is unlikely if the damaged parties constitute a large, diverse group for whom organization and bargaining is costly. A quick survey of our major environmental problems—air pollution in metropolitan areas, the emissions of many industries and municipalities into our waterways—indicates that these typically involve large numbers.

---

1. Even in the small group case, the use of certain bargaining strategies or institutional impediments to side payments may prevent efficient outcomes.

This would suggest that the Coase solution is of limited relevance to the major issues of environmental policy.[2]

Turning to the remaining policy alternatives, we present in the following list a classification of policy tools that is admittedly somewhat arbitrary. We will examine four classes of policy instruments. The first category includes measures that base themselves on economic incentives, either in the form of taxation of environmentally destructive activities or, alternatively, of subsidization of desired actions. Under the second heading, we group programs of direct controls consisting of quotas or limitations on polluting activities, of outright prohibition, and of technical specifications (e.g., required installation of waste treatment devices). Third, we consider social pressure with no legal enforcement powers so that compliance on the part of individual decision makers remains voluntary. Finally, the fourth set of programs consists of an actual transfer of certain activities from the private to the public sector.

Tools for environmental policy:

1. Price Incentives[3]
   a) Taxes
   b) Subsidies
2. Direct Controls
   a) Rationing
   b) Prohibition
   c) Technical Specifications
3. Moral Suasion: Voluntary Compliance
4. Public Production

We stress at the outset that, while the list seems simple enough, it does conceal the vast number of ways in which these policy tools may be employed. Taxes, for example, may vary with time and/or place, may apply to particular inputs, or, alternatively, outputs or byproducts of productive activities, and so forth. Similarly, direct controls on polluting activi-

---

2. In certain instances, no intervention may, of course, be optimal for totally different reasons: not because the market will resolve the externalities itself, but because in that particular case the damage happens to be small while the social cost of regulation is large. Here we fail to intervene not because the disease will cure itself, but because the cure is worse.

3. The auctioning of pollution rights could be added here. However, considering the major environmental problems before us, the practicality of this proposal seems to us rather limited.

ties can take an enormous variety of forms, involving the courts or special regulatory agencies, permitting and sometimes encouraging citizen lawsuits, and so forth. This list is neither exhaustive nor composed of mutually exclusive policy measures. Programs of taxes and regulations, for example, can be combined to control waste emissions; we will, in fact, consider such policy mixes shortly.

Forms of Environmental Damage

In this section, we consider, in general terms, the various forms that insults to the environment may take. More specifically, we are interested in different types of environmental damage functions. As we will argue later, the damage function that characterizes a particular type of polluting activity may be of central importance in determining the policy instrument appropriate for its control.

The first distinction is between the situation in which the current level of environmental quality is a function of the *current* level of the polluting activity and the case where it depends on the history of *past* levels of the activity. The state of purity of the air over a metropolitan area, for example, depends largely on the quantities of pollutants currently being emitted into the atmosphere. This we will call a *flow* damage function.

Alternatively, past levels of activity may build up a stock of pollutant. Therefore, the extent of environmental damage depends on the history of the activity. This we call a *stock* damage function. Such damage functions are typically associated with nondegradable pollutants, such as mercury and DDT. The pollutant accumulates over time and thus constitutes an ever increasing environmental threat. The stock and flow damage functions are pure, polar cases. In reality there is a spectrum of damage functions in which historic levels of polluting activity assume varying degrees of importance in determining the present level of environmental quality.[4] However, the distinction is a useful one for certain policy purposes.

Of equal importance is the particular form of the damage function. Economists are familiar with cost functions which exhibit monotonically increasing marginal costs; a familiar example in the literature is the case

---

4. For an interesting theoretical study using a more general damage function which incorporates both stock and flow elements, see C. G. Plourde.

of crowding on highways. Once costs of congestion set in, the time loss to road users resulting from the presence of an additional vehicle rises rapidly with the number of vehicles. Many environmental phenomena, however, appear to involve more complex damage functions; some exhibit important discontinuities or threshold effects. When, for example, waste loads in a river become sufficiently heavy, the "oxygen sag" may become so pronounced that the assimilative capacity of the stream is exceeded. The dissolved-oxygen content may in such cases fall to zero, giving rise to anaerobic conditions. In such cases, the cost of exceeding the threshold level of the activity may be exceedingly high. There may, moreover, exist a series of thresholds so that the damage function can be exceedingly complex. In addition, the precise form of the damage function itself may be problematic, thus injecting an important element of uncertainty into the situation.

The uncertainty element in the damage function is not a haphazard affair, but arises out of the very nature of the relationship. It is essential to recognize that damage functions are multivariate relationships, functions of a vector of variables many of them entirely outside the control of the policy maker. The effects of a given injection of pollutants into the air depend on atmospheric conditions. The damage caused by a waste emission into a stream is determined largely by the level of the water flow: it may be relatively harmless when poured into a stream that is near its crest, but very dangerous when put into the same stream when depleted by drought. Externalities in urban affairs will be more or less serious depending on the state of racial tension, the level of narcotics use, and a variety of other crucial influences.

Expressed somewhat more formally, the function describing the determination of environmental quality at time s, q_s, may be written

$$q_s = f(m_s, E_s), \tag{1}$$

where m_s is the level of waste emissions and E_s is a vector whose components are environmental conditions, such as the direction and velocity of the wind, the quantity of rainfall, and so forth. The important thing about E_s is that it includes variables over which we have little, if any, control. The exogenous variables describing the vector, E_s, are themselves likely to be random variables, or at least subject to influences which can best be treated as random.

The environmental damage function may be defined as

$$z_s = g(q_s) = h(m_s, E_s). \tag{2}$$

While q_s indicates the state of environmental quality (e.g., the sulfur dioxide content of the atmosphere or the dissolved oxygen level of a waterway), z_s denotes the social cost associated with the value of q_s. For example, higher levels of sulfur dioxide in the air people breath appear to induce a higher incidence of respiratory illnesses and mortality (see Lave and Seskin); the costs associated with these repercussions are represented by z_s.[5]

The introduction of uncontrolled determinants of environmental quality and the associated uncertainty creates some difficult policy problems. For example, environmental control policy may have a combination of several objectives such as (a) the achievement *on average* of a level of environmental quality, q_s, such that the cost of environmental insults is acceptable; and (b) prevention of the attainment of some threshold level of q_s at which there is discontinuity in the damage function, thus causing social costs to soar to unacceptably high levels.

If the values for the components of E_s were known precisely for all future periods, we could set values of m_s for each period s so as to achieve these objectives, and we would look for the least cost methods of holding emissions to these specified levels. Unfortunately, we frequently do not know the values of E_s in advance. Normally however, we can make some predictions about them. In fact, we almost have a kind of probability distribution for variables such as weather conditions. Often the dispersion of the distribution becomes much smaller as the pertinent point in time approaches (e.g., we have a better idea about tomorrow's weather than next week's weather).

Even so, the policy maker cannot control most of the variables in the vector, E, and even his ability to foresee their values remains highly limited. The science of meteorology has not yet reached a stage at which forecasts can be made with a high degree of certainty. Meteorologists are unable to determine the timing of next year's or even next month's atmospheric inversions or rainfall patterns so that plans for the intermittent crises that are likely to result may be made in advance. This phenomenon can be extremely important in the selection of policy tools. It may be that, because of limited attention to this issue in the economics

---

5. More realistically, we can regard q_s and m_s as vectors whose components represent, respectively, various measures of environmental quality and levels of discharges of different types of wastes. This, however, seems to add little to the analysis. Note that z_s is a scalar, not a vector, for it represents the social cost, measured in terms of a numeraire, of the level of environmental deterioration (q_s) generated jointly by m_s and E_s.

literature, we have tended to overlook the merits of policy instruments usually favored outside the profession.

Matching Policy Tools with Environmental Conditions

Before proceeding to a more detailed empirical analysis of policy tools, we want to consider under what circumstances one policy tool is likely to be more appropriate than another. As a frame of reference, let us assume a set of standards or targets for environmental quality with an eye toward devising an effective environmental policy to realize these standards.[6]

In the case of stock damage functions with costs directly related to the accumulated quantity of the pollutant, a positive level of the polluting activity implies that the *level* of environmental damage will increase continually over time. The stock of pollutants will increase over time with the flow of emissions from one period to the next. Environmental quality will thus continue to deteriorate. Any damage thresholds may eventually be exceeded, and clearly the target level of environmental quality will not be achieved. In these cases there would appear to be a strong case for outright prohibition of polluting activities, for simply reducing the level of the activity will serve only to slow the cumulative process of environmental deterioration.[7] Outright prohibition would, therefore, seem to be an appropriate policy measure where damage functions are of the stock form. The recent ban on the use of DDT in the United States is a case in point.

Where, in contrast, environmental quality depends primarily on the current level of polluting activities, prohibition may be excessively costly. Achievement of the target level of environmental quality requires adjustment of the current levels of activities to those consistent with the target.

---

6. We could specify alternative types of objective functions. For example, we could assume standard utility and cost functions and, following the usual maximization procedures, derive our first order optimality conditions requiring that environmental quality be improved (or polluting activities curtailed) to the point where benefits and costs are equal at the margin. The major problem here is the difficulty of measuring benefits and costs. On this issue, see, for example, Baumol and Oates. Most of the discussion in the present paper applies, incidentally, to both of these approaches to environmental policy.

7. It might be desirable to curtail the flow of emissions gradually over time if the costs of rapid adjustment are high. This raises the interesting problem of the optimal path of reduction in the rate of flow, a problem which we note but which goes beyond the scope of this paper.

These required levels, in many cases at least, can be expected to be non-zero. A variety of the policy instruments included in our earlier list may then be appropriate to influence levels of polluting activities.

What *in principle* can we say about the relative effectiveness of these policy instruments? The efficiency-enhancing properties of taxes (effluent charges) are widely recognized and need little discussion here.[8] In terms of our objective, the realization of a set of specified standards of environmental quality, we have shown elsewhere (Baumol and Oates) that, assuming cost-minimizing (not necessarily profit-maximizing) behavior by producers, effluent charges are the least-cost method of attaining the target: the proper effluent fee will generate, through private decisions, the set of activity levels which imposes the lowest costs on society. Any other set of quotas determined by regulatory authorities and consistent with the specified environmental standards will thus involve a higher opportunity cost.

This would appear to establish a presumption at the conceptual level in favor of price incentives over regulatory rationing, and to make a system of fees an ideal standard with which others should be compared and judged as more or less imperfect substitutes. However, the proof of the superiority of the tax instrument involves a number of simplifying assumptions (and typically utilizes a static analytic model); there are several other critical considerations without which it is impossible to understand fully the inclination toward other policy instruments on the part of many noneconomists who are demonstrably well informed and well intentioned.

Once we enumerate these elements, their relevance is obvious. We will show that on economic grounds they may often call for measures other than the tax instruments that receive primary attention in the economic literature. This list includes the following.[9]

---

8. See, for example, Kneese and Bower, and Upton.

9. We might consider adding to this list the "political acceptability" of the program. This is not without an important economic dimension. Suppose we are given two programs *A* and *B* the first of which is shown capable of yielding an allocation of resources slightly better than that which would be produced by the latter. However, suppose that *B* can be "sold" to a legislature with little expenditure of time and effort, while the enactment of *A*, if it can be secured at all, would require a highly costly and time consuming campaign. In such a case, *purely economic considerations* may favor the advocacy of *B* in preference to *A*, if we are willing to take the predisposition of the legislature as a datum in exactly the same way we take the production function for a particular product as given for the problem of determination of outputs.

1. Administrative and enforcement costs (playing a role analogous to transactions costs elsewhere in theoretical analysis).

2. Exclusion or scale problems, which may make it difficult for the private sector to provide activities appropriate for the protection of the environment. (If one wishes, this can be classified as a special case of the problem of high administrative costs, the costs of collecting payment for an environmental service or of assembling the large quantity of capital needed to supply it efficiently.)

3. Time costs. Here we include not only the interval necessary to design a program and put it into effect, but also the period of adjustment of activities to the program.

4. Problems of uncertainty.

Let us now explore how these considerations, in the context of the objective of allocative efficiency, influence the choice among the basic types of policies listed in "Tools for Environmental Policy."

Pollution taxes

Beginning once more with the tax measures we see that, in addition to their desirable allocative properties, effluent charges possess a further major attraction: their enforcement mechanism is relatively automatic. Unlike direct controls, they do not suffer from the uncertainties of detection, of the decision to prosecute, or of the outcome of the judicial hearing including the possibility of penalties that are ludicrously lenient. Like death, taxes have indeed proved reasonably certain. Few are the cases of tax authorities who neglect to send the taxpayer his bill, and that is the essence of the enforcement mechanism implicit in the tax measures. They require no crusading district attorney or regulatory agency for their effectiveness.

However, once we leave this point, we are left with considerations in terms of which tax measures generally score rather poorly. We will defer the issue of time costs to a later point where its role will be more clear. It is true that *enforcement* costs are likely to be relatively low, although like any other taxes we can be confident that they will provide work for a host of tax attorneys employed to seek out possible loopholes. Perhaps more important in many cases are high monitoring or metering costs. One of the major reasons additional local telephone calls are supplied at zero charge to subscribers in small communities is the high cost of devices that record such calls, and the same is apparently true of communities in which water usage is not metered universally. This is particularly to the point when we recognize that allocative efficiency requires tax charges to vary by season of the year, time of day, or with unpredictable changes in environmental conditions (e.g., the charge on smoke emissions should presumably rise sharply during an atmospheric "inversion" that produces a serious deterioration in air quality). Moreover, in many cases there is no one simple variable whose magnitude should be monitored. Waste emissions into waterways should ideally be taxed according to their BOD level, their content of a variety of nondegradable pollutants, their temperature, and perhaps their sheer volume. Obviously, the greater the number of these critical attributes, the more costly will be the monitoring program required by an effective tax policy. This, of course, increases the complexity of other types of regulatory programs as well.[10]

A special problem may arise from the structure of the polluting industry. Under pure competition, fees will, in principle, work ideally; in addition, it is easy to show that they tend to retain their least-cost properties in any industry in which firms minimize cost per unit of output. However, under oligopoly or monopoly, management's interests may conflict with such a goal, and taxes on polluting activities may fail to do their job with full effectiveness. If an industry routinely shifts virtually all of the cost of such fees without attempting to reduce waste emissions in order to lower its tax payments, much of the intended effect of the tax program will be lost.

From all this we do not conclude that economists have been ill-advised in their support of tax measures. On the contrary, we continue to believe strongly that in many applications they will in the long run prove to be the most effective instrument at the disposal of society. However, it is clear that certain environmental and industrial characteristics can impair

---

10. The technology of monitoring industrial waste emissions appears still to be in its infancy; metering devices which provide reliable measures of the composition and quantities of effluents at modest cost are (to our knowledge) not yet available. Environmental officials in New Jersey, for example, rely heavily on periodic samples of emissions which they subject to laboratory tests, which involve costly procedures. However, there is a considerable research effort underway to design effective and inexpensive metering mechanisms. This may well reduce substantially the administrative costs of programs whose effectiveness depends on measurement of individual waste discharges. In this connection, William Vickrey has stressed, in conversation with us, the dependence of the cost of metering on the degree of accuracy we demand of it. In many cases, high standards of accuracy may not be defensible. As Vickrey points out, a ten-hour inspection of an automobile will undoubtedly provide a more reliable and complete description of its exhaust characteristics than a half-hour test, but it is surely plausible that the former exceeds the standard of "optimal imperfection" in information gathering!

their effectiveness. This, as we will suggest shortly, may point to the desirability of a mixed policy of fees and controls.

Subsidies

An obvious alternative to taxes is the use of subsidies to induce reductions in the levels of these activities; what can be accomplished with the stick should also be possible with the carrot. Kneese and Bower, for example, have argued that "Strictly from the point of view of resource allocation, it would make no difference whether an effluent charge was levied on the discharger, or a payment was made to him for not discharging wastes" (p. 57). However, in addition to some extremely important differences at the operational level between taxes and subsidies, Bramhall and Mills have pointed out a fundamental asymmetry between the effects of fees and payments. While it is true that the price of engaging in a polluting activity can be made the same with the use of either a tax or subsidy, the latter involves a payment to the firm while taxes impose a cost on the firm. As a result, the firm's profit levels under the two programs differ by a constant. We have shown formally that, in long-run competitive equilibrium, subsidies (relative to fees) will result in a larger number of firms, a larger output for the industry, and a lower price for the commodity whose production generates pollution. Moreover, it is plausible the net effect will be an *increase* in total industry emissions over what they would be in absence of *any* intervention. Subsidies tend to induce excessive output. Thus, at least at a formal level, taxes are to be preferred.[11]

Direct controls

Direct controls often seem to score poorly on most of our criteria, in spite of their appeal to a curiously heterogeneous group composed largely of activists, lawyers, and businessmen. They are usually costly to administer,

---

11. Subsidies may be desirable if there is reason to suspect that direct controls constitute the only alternative that is feasible politically. Two reasons for this are obvious to the economist: a) direct controls are likely to allocate pollution quotas among polluters in an arbitrary manner while taxes *or* subsidies will do this in a manner that works automatically in the direction of cost minimization; b) a direct control that prohibits a polluter from, say, emitting more than x tons of sulfur dioxide per year, under threat of punishment, offers that polluter absolutely no incentive to reduce his emissions one iota below x even though the private cost of that reduction to him is negligible compared to its social benefits. Thus, subsidies may sometimes be preferable to direct controls even though both of them produce misallocations.

because they involve all the heavy costs of enforcement without avoiding entirely the costs of monitoring in whose complete absence violations simply cannot be detected. We have already noted their tendency to produce a misallocation of resources. Moreover, experience suggests that their enforcement is often apt to be erratic and unreliable, for it depends largely on the vigor and vigilance of the responsible public agency, the severity of the courts, and the unpredictable course of the public's concern with environmental issues.

Yet direct controls do possess one major attraction: *if enforcement is effective,* they can induce, with little uncertainty, the prescribed alterations in polluting activities. We cannot expect controls to achieve environmental objectives at the least cost, but they may be able to *guarantee* substantial reductions in damages to the environment, a consideration that may be of particular importance where threats to environmental quality are grave and time is short. This points up two limitations of effluent charges: first, the response of polluters to a given level of fees is hard to predict accurately, and second, the period of adjustment to new levels of activities may be uncertain. If sufficient time is available to adjust fees until the desired response is obtained, the case for effluent charges becomes a very compelling one. However, environmental conditions may under certain situations alter so swiftly that fees simply may not be able to produce the necessary changes in behavior quickly (or predictably) enough. Where, for example, the air over a metropolitan area becomes highly contaminated because of extremely unfavorable weather conditions, direct controls (perhaps involving the prohibition of incineration or limiting the use of motor vehicles) may be necessary to avoid a real catastrophe.

There *may* be a further role for direct controls in industries dominated by a few large firms whose market power enables them to pass forward taxes on polluting activities without much incentive to undertake major adjustments in production techniques to reduce environmental damage.[12] This is frankly a difficult case to evaluate. Perhaps the best example is the ongoing attempt to impose technical standards for exhaust discharges on new automobiles. Because of the highly concentrated character of the auto industry, it is not clear that taxes on motor vehicles (perhaps graduated according to the level of exhaust emissions) would have much effect

12. Of course, it is normally desirable that some portion of the tax be passed forward in the form of price increases, as a means to discourage demand for the polluting output. The issue is that an oligopoly whose objectives are complex may not always minimize the costs of producing its vector of outputs.

on automobile design or usage.[13] A more promising approach may consist of legislated emission standards that will compel alterations in the design of engines so as to reduce the pollution content of vehicle discharges. However, the use of standards also involves difficult problems: witness the protracted "bargaining" between auto-industry representatives and federal legislators over the level of the standards and the timing of their implementation. Moreover, there is always the danger of adopting standards approaching complete "purity" that impose enormous costs; the reduction of polluting activities typically involves marginal costs that increase rapidly as the required reductions in waste discharges approach 100 per cent. The setting of emission standards without adequate regard for the costs involved may produce some highly inefficient results.

Hybrid programs

Even those policy makers who have come to recognize the merits of a system of charges as an effective instrument of control seem normally unwilling to rely exclusively on this measure. Rather they typically prefer a mixed system of the sort in which each polluter is assigned quotas or ceilings which his emissions are in any event never to be permitted to exceed. Taxes are then to be used to induce polluters to do better than these minimum standards and to do so in a relatively efficient manner.

While this may at first appear to be a strange mongrel, some of the preceding discussion suggests that, under certain circumstances, such a mix of policies may have real merit. If taxes are sufficiently high to cut emissions well below the quota levels, the efficiency properties of the tax measure will be preserved. Moreover, it retains the advantage of the pure fiscal method in forcing recognition of the very rapidly rising cost of further purification as the level of environmental damage is reduced toward zero. It is all too easy to set quotas at irresponsibly demanding levels, paying no attention to the heavy costs they impose. But it is hard not to take notice when tax rates must be raised astronomically to achieve still further improvements in environmental quality.

On the other hand, the quota portion of the program can make two important contributions, safety and increased speed of adjustment and implementation. Suppose, for example, there is a threshold in the damage

13. As Roger Noll points out, the case for effluent fees is the weakest "when regulators must deal with firms with considerable market power, and, at the other extreme, individuals with very little freedom of choice arising either from a lack of economic power, lack of knowledge, or lack of viable technical options" (pp. 34–5).

function so that a form of environmental abuse imposes a serious threat, but only beyond some point that is fairly well known. In this case, a hybrid policy can make considerable sense, since the quotas it utilizes can be employed to make reasonably certain that damages never get beyond the danger point. Taxes can be unreliable for this purpose, since, as noted earlier, the tax elasticities of pollution output are generally not well known and these fees may not induce changes in activity levels with sufficient rapidity. Thus, reliance on tax incentives alone may impose unacceptable risks, which can be prevented by a set of direct controls that set ceilings on levels of polluting activities.

Controls can, moreover, introduce additional flexibility into an environmental program. In terms of our illustrative case, urban air pollution, we noted that authorities may be able to invoke temporary prohibition, or at least limitations, on polluting activities when environmental deterioration suddenly reaches extremely serious levels.

Hybrid programs of taxes and controls thus represent a very attractive policy package. The tax component of the program functions to maintain the desired levels of environmental quality under "normal" conditions at a relatively low cost and also avoids the imposition of uneconomically demanding controls. The controls constitute standby measures to deal with adverse environmental conditions that arise infrequently, but suddenly, and which would result in serious environmental damage with normal levels of waste emissions.[14] Such a mixed program should not involve notably higher administrative costs than a pure tax policy, since much of the monitoring structure used for the latter should also be available for enforcement of the controls. In sum, where threshold problems constitute a serious environmental threat and where levels of polluting activities may require substantial alteration on short notice, which is not a rare set of circumstances, a hybrid program using both fees and controls may be preferable to a pure tax-subsidy program.

Moral suasion: voluntary compliance

We come next to the cases in which it seems appropriate to rely on appeals to conscience and voluntary compliance. As economists, we tend to be somewhat skeptical about the efficacy of long-run programs which

---

14. In this volume, Lave and Seskin report evidence that the mortality danger of air pollution crises may have been exaggerated. Nevertheless, it remains true that, during periods of stagnant air, the social cost of a given emission level will be high, because a great proportion of the polluting element remains over the city for a protracted period.

require costly acts of individuals but offer no compensation aside from a sense of satisfaction or the avoidance of a guilty conscience. In fact, the appeal to conscience can often be a dangerous snare. It can serve to lure public support from programs with real potential for the effective protection of the environment. Later, we will provide some evidence that suggests this to be a real possibility.

There is nevertheless an important role for voluntary programs. In particular, in an unanticipated emergency there simply may be no other recourse: the *time cost* of most other instruments of control may be too high to permit their utilization under such circumstances. A sudden and dangerous deterioration of air quality allows no time for the imposition of a tax or for the drawing up and adoption of other types of regulatory legislation. There may be no time for emergency controls, particularly if they have not previously been instituted in standby form, but there can be an immediate appeal to the general public to avoid the use of automobiles and incinerators until the emergency is passed. Moreover, as we shall indicate in a later section, there is evidence to indicate that the public is likely to respond quickly and effectively to such an appeal. Perhaps social pressures and a sense of urgency lie behind the efficacy of moral suasion in such cases.[15]

Casual observation suggests that the sense of high moral purpose is likely to slip away rather rapidly and thus implies little potential for long-term programs that rest on no firmer base than the public conscience. However, that is no reason to reject this instrument where it can prove effective, particularly since no effective alternative may be available. We suspect that we have not yet experienced the last of the unforeseen emergencies and, in extremis, time cost is likely to swamp all other costs in the choice of policy instruments.

Public provision of environmental services

The direct public "production" of environmental quality may be justified in two types of situations. The first is the case where the current

---

15. There is another precondition for the efficacy of moral suasion, even in an emergency. We can usually expect a few individuals not to respond to a public appeal. Thus, voluntarism cannot be relied upon in a case where universal cooperation is essential, as during a wartime blackout where a single unshielded light can endanger everyone. However, in most environmental emergencies as long as a substantial proportion of the persons in question are willing to comply with a request for cooperation, a voluntary program is likely to be effective. For example if, during a crisis of atmospheric quality, an appeal to the public may lead to a temporary reduction in automotive traffic of some 70 or 80 per cent, that may well be sufficient to achieve the desired result.

quality of the environment is deemed unsatisfactory (i.e., falls below the specified standard) as a result of "natural" causes and where this cannot be corrected through market processes because the particular environmental service is a public good. It is hard to find a perfect illustration, but natural disasters such as periodic droughts or flooding come close. Here the problem is not one of restricting polluting activities on the part of the individual; it is one of providing facilities such as dams and reservoirs to prevent these catastrophies. The private sector of the economy may handle such situations adequately if the commodity needed to avert the disaster is not a public good—that is, if exclusion is possible (or, more accurately, not too costly) and consumption is rival. However, where exclusion is difficult and/or consumption is joint, as in the case of protection from flood damage, the public sector may have to take direct responsibility for the provision of the good.

The second type of situation in which direct public participation *may* be appropriate is that involving large economies of scale and outlays. An example may be the case of a large waste treatment facility used by a multitude of individual decision makers. The reduced cost of treatment of effluents made possible by a jointly used plan may not be realized if left to the private sector.

This example, incidentally, suggests a further type of environmental service that the public sector must provide, namely the planning and direction of systems for the control of environmental quality. The need of reaeration devices, for instance, depends upon water flows (influenced by reservoir facilities), the levels of waste emissions (determined in part by current fees or regulations), and so forth. The point is that the control of water quality in a river basin or atmospheric conditions in an air shed requires systematic planning to integrate effectively the use of quality-control techniques. Kneese and Bower stress the need for river basin authorities to plan and coordinate a program of water-quality management. Urban areas require similar types of authorities to develop integrated air quality programs. Thus, public agencies must not only directly provide certain physical facilities, but must also exercise the management function of coordinating the variety of activities and control techniques that serve jointly to determine environmental quality. Such agencies need not be federal, but must be sufficiently large so that their jurisdiction includes those activities that influence environmental conditions in a given area. This implies jurisdictions sufficiently large to encompass systems of waterways and areas whose atmospheric conditions are dependent on the same activities.

Optimal Mixed Programs: A Simple Model

The logic of the argument in the preceding section for the use of hybrid programs in the presence of random exogenous influences can be more clearly outlined with the aid of a simple illustrative model. Such a model can indicate not only the potential desirability of such a hybrid as against a tax measure or a program using direct controls alone, it can also illustrate conceptually how one might go about selecting the optimal mix of policy instruments.

A relationship apparently used frequently in the engineering literature to describe the time path of environmental quality is (in a much simplified form)[16]

$$q_s = k_s q_{(s-1)} + m_s, \tag{3}$$

where:

q_s is a measure of environmental quality during period s,
k_s is a random exogenous variable (call it "average wind velocity") during time s, and
m_s is the aggregate level of waste emissions in period s.

In the presence of a tax program, the level of waste discharges will presumably be determined in part by the tax. Let us define

m_{is} = waste emissions of firm i in period s,
$c_i(m_{is}, \ldots)$ = the total cost function of firm i, and
t = tax per unit of waste emission.

Then, if the firm minimizes its costs, we will presumably have in equilibrium

$$\frac{\partial c_i}{\partial m_{is}} = -t. \tag{4}$$

That is, the firm will adjust waste discharges to the point where at the

---

16. Other forms of this relationship are obviously possible. For example, k_s and $q_{(s-1)}$ may be additive rather than multiplicative. The facts will presumably vary from case to case, but within wide limits the choice of functional form does not affect the substance of our discussion.

margin the cost increase resulting from a unit reduction of emissions (e.g., the marginal cost of recycling) is equal to the unit emission charge. Using the cost function for the firm and its cost-minimizing emission condition, (4), we can derive a relationship expressing the level of waste discharges of the ith firm as a function of the unit emission tax:

$$m_{is} = h_i(t_s). \tag{5}$$

Aggregating over all i firms, we get an aggregate waste-emission function

$$m_s = h(t_s) = \sum h_i(t_s). \tag{6}$$

From equation (6), we can thus determine the total level of waste discharges into the environment in period s associated with each value of t, the effluent fee.

Next, suppose we know the probability distribution of k_s, our random and exogenous environmental variable ("average wind velocity") in equation (3). For some known value of environmental quality in period $(s-1)$, we can then determine the distribution function of environmental quality in time s associated with each value of the emission tax, t. Figure 1 depicts some probability distributions corresponding to different tax rates.

Figure 1

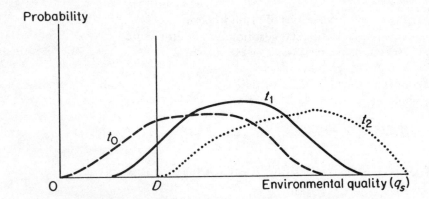

We see that a reduction in the emission tax from t_1 to t_0 shifts the distribution leftward. Once a lower tax rate is instituted, higher levels of waste emissions become profitable, thereby increasing the likelihood of a period of relatively low environmental quality.

Assume, moreover, that the environmental authority cannot readily change t in response to current environmental conditions so that t is essentially fixed for the period under analysis.[17] Let there also be some accepted "danger standard" (i.e., a minimum acceptable level of environmental quality). We designate this danger standard as D in Figure 1 and assume that the environmental authority is committed to maintaining the level of environmental quality above D at *all* points in time.

How can the authority achieve this objective at the least cost to society? One method of guaranteeing that q_s will never fall below D is to set the tax rate so high that waste emissions can never, regardless of exogenous environmental influences, reach a value sufficiently high to induce environmental quality to deteriorate to a level less than D.[18] In terms of Figure 1, this would require an emissions tax of t_2, which shifts the environmental probability distribution rightward until its horizontal intercept coincides with D. However, as we suggested earlier, this method of achieving the objective may be an excessively costly one, because it is likely to require unnecessarily expensive reductions in waste discharges during "normal" periods when the environment is capable of absorbing these emissions without serious difficulty. It may be less costly to set a lower emission tax (less than t_2 in Figure 1) and to supplement this with periodic introductions of controls to achieve additional reductions in waste discharges during times of adverse environmental conditions (periods of "stagnant air").

In Figure 2, we illustrate an approach to the determination of the optimal mix of emission taxes and direct controls. Let the curve TT' measure the *total* net social cost associated with each value of t. There are two components of this social cost. The first is the added costs of production that higher taxes impose by inducing methods of production consistent with reduced levels of waste emissions. This cost naturally tends to rise with tax rates and the associated lower levels of waste discharges. However, we must subtract from this "production" cost a negative cost (or social gain) which indicates the social benefits from a higher level of environmental quality. Over some range of values for t (up to t_0 in Figure 2), we might expect the sum of these costs to be negative, that is, the social benefits from improved environmental quality may well exceed the in-

17. Alternatively, we can assume that the response of waste emissions to changes in t is not sufficiently rapid for the tax adjustments in period s to influence significantly waste discharges during that period.

18. It may, of course, be impossible to achieve such a guarantee with any finite tax rate, no matter how high.

Figure 2

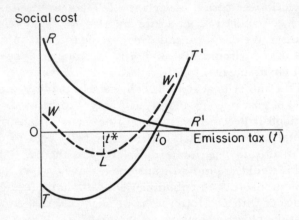

creased costs of production. However, as tax rates rise and waste discharges decline, the *marginal* net social cost will typically rise. The marginal production cost of reductions in waste emissions (equated in value
to t) will obviously increase, while we might expect diminishing social
gain from positive increments in environmental quality.[19] The TT' curve
will, therefore, typically begin to rise at some point and, for values of t in
excess of t_0 in Figure 2, the net social cost of the tax program becomes
positive.

We recall that the environmental authority is committed to the maintenance of a level of environmental quality no lower than the danger
point, D. We will thus assume that, whatever the level of the emission
tax, environmental officials will introduce direct controls whenever necessary to maintain q above D. One relationship is immediately clear: the
higher the emission tax, the less frequently will environmental quality
threaten to fall below D and hence the less often (and less "intensely")
will the use of direct controls be required. Controls, like taxes, impose
increased costs of production by forcing reductions in waste emissions.
Therefore, the more frequent and extensive the use of direct controls,

19. We have drawn TT' with a "smooth" shape (a continuous first derivative), but
there could easily be flat portions of TT' corresponding to ranges of values of t over
which the level of waste emissions remains unchanged. Note, however, that even in this
instance TT' would still exhibit the general shape depicted in Figure 2 and, most important, would still possess a well defined minimum for some value (or continuous
range of values) of t.

the greater the increment in production costs they will generate. We depict this relationship in Figure 2 by the curve RR', which indicates that the higher the tax rate the less the reliance and, hence, the lower the costs associated with the periodic use of direct controls to maintain q above D.[20]

When we sum TT' and RR' vertically, we obtain the net social cost (WW') associated with each level of the emission tax (t) *supplemented* by a program of direct controls which prevents environmental quality from ever falling below the danger point (D). In Figure 2, we see that the lowest point (L) on the WW' curve corresponds to the cost-minimizing or optimal tax rate (t^*) and determines residually the optimal use of direct controls.[21]

We stress that the treatment in this section is purely illustrative. It indicates an approach to the determination of the optimal mix of emission taxes and direct controls. A rigorous solution to this problem requires an explicit recognition of the stochastic element in the curves in Figure 2. The social costs generated by a given tax program depend in part on the values taken by our random exogenous environmental variable ("wind velocity"), so that the curves in this diagram must be regarded in some sense as "averages." More formally, the solution involves the minimization of a stochastic social cost function subject to the constraint that $q \geq D$. Elsewhere we will show how this can be formulated as a nonlinear programming problem, whose solution yields the optimal mix of effluent taxes and direct controls.

Environmental Policy Tools in Practice

In this section, we want to present some preliminary evidence on the effectiveness of the various tools of environmental policy. Since evidence in the form of systematic, quantifiable results is scarce, we have had to resort in some instances to case studies suggesting only in qualitative

---

20. Unlike the tax-cost function (TT'), the social cost of direct controls does not include a *variable* component related to the benefits from varying levels of environmental quality. Direct controls in this model are used solely to maintain q above D. We can treat the social benefits derived from the guarantee that environmental quality never falls below D as a constant (independent of the level of t), and we can, if we wish, add this constant to RR' (or to TT' for that matter). The essential point is that we can expect RR' to be a function that decreases monotonically in relation to t.

21. Note that the curve WW' may possess a number of local minima. It need not increase monotonically to the right of L.

terms the nature of the response to the programs. Many of the findings, however, do seem roughly consistent with the preceding discussion.

Price incentives

While economic theory suggests an important role for price incentives, particularly effluent fees, for environmental control, we really have limited experience with their use. The opposition to proposals for effluent charges has been strong, in some measure, we suspect, because people realize they will be effective and wish to avoid the inevitable costs of environmental protection.[22] Nevertheless, there has been some use of charges, and what evidence is available suggests that effluent fees have in fact been quite successful in reducing polluting activities.

The most striking and important case appears to be the control of water quality in West Germany's Ruhr Valley. The site of one of the world's greatest concentrations of heavy industry, the rivers of the Ruhr Valley could easily have become among the most polluted rivers in Europe. However, since the organization of the first *Genossenschaft* (river authority) in 1904 along the Emscher River, the Germans have been successfully treating wastes in cooperatives financed by effluent charges on their members. There are presently eight *Genossenschaften*. Together they form a closed water-control system which has maintained a remarkably high quality of water. In all but one of the rivers in the system, the waters are suitable for fishlife and swimming. Together, the eight cooperatives collect approximately $60 million a year, mainly from effluent charges levied on their nearly 500 public and private members. The level of charges is based largely on a set of standards for maintaining water quality, although the formulas themselves are rather complicated. As Kneese and Bower point out, the fee formulas do not correspond perfectly to the economist's version of effluent fees ("they violate the principle of marginal cost pricing," p. 251).[23] Nevertheless, the charges, in conjunction with an integrated system of planning and design for the entire river basin, "is a pioneering achievement of the highest order" (Kneese and Bower, p. 253).

There has been a scattered use of effluent fees for environmental protection in North America, and these, to our knowledge, exclusively for

22. For an excellent survey and evaluation of the most frequent arguments directed against programs of effluent fees, see Freeman and Haveman.

23. For a more detailed discussion of the Ruhr experience, see Kneese and Bower, Chapter 12.

the control of water quality. However, this evidence does again point to the effectiveness of fees in curtailing waste emissions. Kneese and Bower cite three instances in which the levying of local sewer charges induced striking reductions in waste discharges.[24] C. E. Fisher reports similar responses to a local sewerage tax in Cincinnati, Ohio. Fees were established in 1953 with the proviso that a rebate would be given to anyone who met a specified set of standards by a certain date. Subsequently, some 23 major companies invested $5 million in pollution control in less than two years to meet these standards.

There also exist three more systematic studies of industrial responsiveness to sewerage fees. Löf and Kneese have estimated the cost function for a hypothetical, but typical, sugar beet processing plant in which cost is treated as a function of BOD removal from waste water. Their results suggest, assuming the firm stays in business, that a very modest effluent charge would induce the elimination of roughly 70 per cent of the BOD contained in the waste water of their typical plant. Likewise, a recent regression study by D. E. Ethridge of poultry processing plants in different cities imposing sewerage fees indicates substantial price responsiveness on the part of these firms. In a total of 27 observations from five plants, Ethridge found that "The surcharge on BOD does significantly affect the total pounds of BOD treated by the city; the elasticity of pounds of BOD discharged per 1,000 birds with respect to the surcharge on BOD is estimated to be −0.5 at the mean surcharge" (p. 352).

The most ambitious and comprehensive study of the effects of municipal surcharges on industrial wastes in U.S. cities is the work of Ralph Elliott and James Seagraves. Elliott and Seagraves have collected time-series data on surcharges, waste emissions, and industrial water usage for 34 U.S. cities. They have put these data to a variety of tests and their findings indicate that industrial BOD emissions and water consumption do indeed appear to respond negatively to the level of surcharges on emissions. In one of their tests, for example, they have pooled their cross-section and time-series observations and, using ordinary least squares, obtained the following estimated equations:

$$T = 13.1 - 14.6S - 120.0G + 36.2P \qquad (7)$$
$$(8.5)\quad\ (79.3)\quad\ (22.6)$$

$$R^2 = .17 \qquad N = 190,$$

---

24. These involved sewerage fees in Otsego, Michigan, in Springfield, Missouri, and in Winnipeg, Canada. See Kneese and Bower, pp. 168–70.

$$W = 2.2 - 5.2S - 36.8N + 8.6P + 75.1F \qquad (8)$$
$$ (2.9) \quad (24.7) \quad (7.2) \quad (26.0)$$

$$R^2 = .32 \qquad N = 179,$$

where;

T = pounds of BOD per \$1,000 of value added in manufacturing;

S = surcharge per pound of BOD in 1970 dollars;

G = price of water (per 1,000 gallons) in 1970 dollars;

P = the real wage rate (per hour) in 1970 dollars;

N = net cost of additional water (per 1,000 gallons) in 1970 dollars;

F = proportion of value added in manufacturing in the city contributed by food and kindred products.

The coefficients on the surcharge variable (S) possess the expected negative sign and are statistically significant using a one-tail test at a .05 level
of confidence. Using typical values for the variables, the authors estimate
the elasticity of industrial BOD emissions with respect to the level of the
surcharge to be -0.8, and the surcharge elasticity of water consumption
at -0.6.[25] We are thus beginning to accumulate some evidence indicating
that effluent fees can in fact be quite effective in reducing levels of industrial waste discharges into waterways.

In contrast, our experience with charges on waste emissions into the
atmosphere is virtually nil. However, there is one recent and impressive
study by James Griffin of the potential welfare gains from the use of
emission fees to curtail discharges of sulfur dioxide into the air. Using
engineering cost data, Griffin has assembled a detailed econometric model
of the electric utility industry.[26] The model allows for desulfurization of
fuel and coal, substitution among fuels, substitution between fuel and
capital (using more capital allows more energy to be derived from a unit
of fuel), and for the substitution away from "electricity-intensive" products by consumers and industry. Griffin then ran a series of nine alternative simulations involving differing effluent fees and other assumptions

25. The explanatory power (R^2) of the Elliott-Seagraves' equations is not extremely
high. Among other things, this reflects the difficulties of accounting for varying industrial composition among cities and for intercity differences in the fraction of waste
emissions that enter the municipal treatment system. Ethridge's equations, which use
observations on only a single industry (poultry-processing), have much higher R^2 (of
about .5).

26. In 1970 "power plants contributed 54% of the nation's sulfur dioxide emissions"
(p. 2).

based on the estimates provided by the Environmental Protection Agency of the social damage generated by emissions of sulfur dioxide. In all the simulations, substantial net welfare gains appeared. The results were somewhat sensitive to assumptions concerning the availability and cost of fuel gas desulfurization processes about which there is some uncertainty. However, with such techniques available at plausible costs, Griffin's average annual welfare gains ranged from $6.5 to $7.7 billion, and these estimates do not allow for possible shifts to nuclear power sources.

The evidence thus does suggest that effluent fees can be an effective tool in reducing levels of waste emissions. This, of course, is hardly surprising. We expect firms and individuals to adjust their patterns of activity in response to changes in relative costs. It has often been observed that in less developed countries, where wages are relatively low, more labor intensive techniques of production are typically adopted than in higher wage countries. Moreover, in a regression study of the capital labor ratios across the states in the U.S. for 16 different manufacturing industries, Matityahu Marcus found that factor proportions did indeed vary systematically in the expected direction with the relative price of capital in terms of labor. There does seem to be sufficient substitutability in relevant production and consumption activities for modest effluent charges to induce pronounced reductions in waste emissions.[27]

What would be even more interesting is some measure of the relative costs of other control techniques (for example, the imposition of uniform percentage reductions in the waste discharges of all polluters). Evidence on this is scarce. However, one such study has been made, a study of the costs of achieving specified levels of dissolved oxygen in the Delaware River Estuary.[28] A programming model was constructed using oxygen balance equations for 30 interconnected segments of the estuary. The next step was to specify five sets of objectives and then to compare the costs of achieving each of these objectives under alternative control policies. Although effluent charges were not included specifically as a policy alternative in the original study, Edwin Johnson headed a subsequent study using the same model and data. This made possible the comparison of four alternative programs for reaching specified levels of dissolved oxygen in the estuary. The results for two D.O. objectives are presented

27. For a useful summary of estimates of price elasticities for polluting activities, see the paper by Robert Kohn.

28. Federal Water Pollution Control Administration, *Delaware Estuary Comprehensive Study: Preliminary Report and Findings* (1966); a useful summary of this study is available in Kneese, Rolfe, and Harned, Appendix C.

in Table 1, where LC is the least-cost programming solution, UT is a program of uniform treatment requiring an equal percentage reduction in discharges by all polluters, SECH is a program consisting of a single effluent charge per unit of waste emission for all dischargers, and ZECH is a zoned charge in which the effluent fee is varied in different areas along the estuary. As indicated by Table 1, the substantial cost savings of a program of effluent fees relative to that of uniform treatment is quite striking. Moreover, it should be noted that the least-cost programming solution involves a great deal more in the way of technical information and detailed controls than do the programs of fees. The reduced costs from the use of fees instead of quotas thus appear to be potentially quite sizable.

TABLE 1
Cost of Treatment Under Alternative Programs

D.O. Objective (ppm)	Program			
	LC	UT	SECH	ZECH
		(million dollars per year)		
2	1.6	5.0	2.4	2.4
3–4	7.0	20.0	12.0	8.6

Source: Kneese, Rolfe, and Harned, p. 272.

As we mentioned in the preceding section, effluent fees are, in theory, a more efficient device for achieving standards of environmental quality than subsidies. Fees appear, moreover, to possess a number of practical advantages as well. The design of an effective and equitable system of subsidies is itself a difficult problem. If a polluter is to be paid for reducing his waste emissions, it then becomes in his interest to establish a high level of waste discharges initially; those who pollute little receive the smallest payments.

In practice, subsidies have been used far more extensively in the United States than fees. The federal government has relied heavily on a program of subsidization of the construction of municipal waste treatment plants and on tax credits to business for the installation of pollution control equipment. The serious deficiencies in the first program are now a matter of record in the 1969 Report of the General Accounting Office. The failure to curtail industrial pollution; the subsidization of plant construction but not operating expenses (resulting in many instances of incredibly ineffective use of the facilities); and the inappropriate location of many plants have resulted in the continued deterioration of many major U.S. waterways despite an expenditure of over $5 billion.[29]

Although we have been unable to find any direct evidence on the tax credit program, there is a simple reason to expect it to have little effect. As Kneese and Bower (pp. 175–78) point out, a firm is unlikely to purchase costly pollution control equipment which adds nothing to its revenues; the absorption of k per cent (where $k < 100$) of the cost by the government cannot turn its acquisition into a profitable undertaking.

Thus both theory and experience point to the superiority of effluent charges over subsidies as a policy tool for environmental protection. Finally, we might also mention that, from the standpoint of the public budget, fees provide a source of revenues, which might be used for public investments for environmental improvements, while subsidies require the expenditure of public funds.

Direct controls

As James Krier points out, "Far and away the most popular response by American governments to problems of pollution—and indeed, to *all* environmental problems—has been regulation . . ." (p. 300). Three general types of regulatory policies for environmental control: quotas, prohibition, and the requirement of specified technical standards are stated in the list of tools for environmental control. However, this classification does not indicate the vast number of ways in which these direct controls may be implemented. The directive for polluters to cease certain activities or to install certain types of treatment equipment may come from an empowered regulatory authority, may result from a court order, or might be forced by the citizenry itself through a referendum. Even this is an oversimplification. There are, for example, several methods by which action through the Courts may be initiated (see Krier). Our category of "direct controls" thus encompasses an extremely broad range of policy options. It is beyond the scope of this paper to examine in detail, for instance, the potential of various forms of litigation for effective environmental policy. We shall rather examine somewhat more generally the success or failure of each of these approaches with particular attention to the circumstances which appear to bear on their effectiveness.

The record of regulatory policies in environmental control is not very impressive. This stems at least as much from administrative deficiencies

29. For further documentation of the ineffectiveness and abuses under this subsidy program, see Marx, and Zwick, and Benstock.

in the application of regulatory provisions as in the establishment of the provisions themselves. A successful regulatory policy generally requires at least three components.

(1) A set of rules that, if practiced, will provide the desired outcome. In this case, satisfactory levels of environmental quality achieved at something reasonably close to the least cost.

(2) An enforcement agency with sufficient resources to monitor behavior.

(3) Sufficient power (the ability to impose penalties) to compel adherence to the regulations.

The design of an efficient set of rules is itself an extremely difficult problem. As mentioned earlier, effluent charges have important efficiency enhancing properties. Moreover, the specification of an efficient set of regulatory provisions will generally require at least as much, and frequently more, technical information than the determination of schedules of fees.[30] In addition, experience suggests that substantial transaction costs in terms of resources devoted to bargaining (as noted earlier in the case of the continuing controversy over auto emission standards) may be involved in the rule selection process.

Even an effective set of regulations can only achieve its objective if it is observed. Unfortunately, the history of environmental regulation in the United States is not encouraging on this count. Regulatory agencies have frequently been understaffed and unable, or unwilling, to enforce antipollution provisions. An interesting historical example is the River and Harbors Act of 1899 which prohibits the discharge of dangerous substances into navigable waterways without a permit from the Army Corps of Engineers. As of 1970, only a handful of the more than 40,000 known dischargers had valid permits. Moreover, the newspapers abound with accounts of huge plants which have paid trivial sums (sometimes a few hundred dollars) for serious violations of pollution regulations. Many of the provisions simply have not given the agencies the power they require for enforcement.

Action through the courts has also not proved very effective. Environmental lawsuits, where a plaintiff can be found, have often stretched over years or even decades without resolution. However, even if judicial proceedings were prompt, it is difficult to envision how suits by individual plaintiffs for damages could lead to an efficient environmental policy.

---

30. In an interesting paper, Karl Göran-Mäler has shown recently that the determination of an efficient set of effluent standards (or quotas) among activities requires at least as much information as that necessary to solve for an optimal set of effluent charges.

Kneese and Bower, while acknowledging the potential of some support from the judicial process, conclude simply that ". . . efficient water quality management cannot be achieved through the courts" (p. 88).

Nevertheless, where enforcment is effective, and it surely has been in a significant number of cases, direct controls can lead to substantial reductions in polluting activities. A variety of regulations in various metropolitan areas have generated large reductions in waste discharges into the atmosphere. The banning of backyard incineration and of the use of sulfur bearing fuels over several months of the year led to significant reductions during the 1950's in smoke, dust, and sulfur oxide discharges into the air shed over the Los Angeles basin. Likewise, tough new regulations in Pittsburgh during the 1940's, requiring the switch from coal fuels to natural gas for heating purposes, resulted in notable improvements in air quality. Strong regulations combined with aggressive enforcement *can* clearly raise the level of environmental quality.[31] The difficulties, of course, are that the improvements may come at an unnecessarily high cost, or, alternatively, may come not at all, if the regulations are themselves inadequate or are ineffectively enforced.

Moral suasion and voluntary compliance

We suggested earlier that, while moral suasion is likely to be an ineffective policy tool over longer periods of time, it may prove quite useful in times of emergency. An interesting illustration of this pattern of response involves voluntary blood donations. In September of 1970, New York City hospitals were facing a blood crisis in which reserves of blood had fallen to a level insufficient for a single day of operation. The response to a citywide plea for donations was described as "fantastic" (*New York Post,* September 4, 1970, p. 3); donors stood in line up to 90 minutes to give blood. The statements by some of the donors were themselves interesting:

"I've never given blood before, but they need it now. That's good enough reason for me."

"I was paying a sort of personal guilt complex."

"It's the least I could do for the city."

31. Direct controls in the form of "technical specifications" for polluting activities may be the only feasible policy instrument, where the monitoring of waste emissions is impractical (or, more accurately, "excessively costly"). For example, if difficulties in metering sulfur dioxide emissions into the atmosphere were to preclude a program of effluent fees (or quotas, for that matter), it might well make sense to place requirements on the quality of fuel used, on the technical characteristics of fuel burners, etc.

And yet within a few months (*New York Times,* January 4, 1971, p. 61), the metropolitan area's blood stocks were again down to less than one day's supply. It was also noted that many donors who promised to give blood had not fulfilled their pledges.[32]

A somewhat similar fate seems to have characterized voluntary recycling programs. Individuals and firms greeted these proposals with substantial enthusiasm and massive public relations efforts. Many manufacturers agreed to recycle waste containers collected and delivered by nonprofit volunteer groups. While the initial response was an energetic one, it seems to have tailed off significantly. "Many (of the groups) disbanded because of a lack of markets or waning volunteer interest" (*New York Times,* May 7, 1972, p. 1 and p. 57). The Glass Manufacturers Institute announced that used bottles and jars returned by the public were being recycled at a rate of 912 million a year, but this represents only 2.6 per cent of the 36 billion glass containers produced each year. Similar reports from the Aluminum Association and the American Iron and Steel Institute indicated recycling rates of 3.7 per cent and 2.7 per cent respectively for metallic containers. The reason for the failure of these programs to achieve greater success is, according to several reports, "that recycling so far is not paying its own way" (*New York Times,* May 7, 1972, p. 1). Experience with recycling programs also points to a danger we mentioned earlier: that these types of programs will be instituted instead of programs with direct individual incentives for compliance. There are a wealth of examples of businesses providing active support for voluntary recycling as parts of campaigns *against* fees or regulations on containers. The *New York Times* (May 7, 1972, p. 57), for instance, cites a recent case in Minneapolis in which the Theodore Hamm Brewing Company and Coca-Cola Midwest, Inc. announced that they would sponsor "the most comprehensive, full-time recycling center in the country." This pledge, however, was directed against a proposed ordinance to prohibit local usage of cans for soft drinks and beer.

A final example of some interest involves a recent attempt by General Motors to market relatively inexpensive auto-emission control kits in Phoenix, Arizona. The GM emission control device could be used on most 1955 to 1967 model cars and could reduce emissions of hydrocarbons, carbon monoxide, and nitrogen oxides by roughly 30 to 50 per cent. The cost of the kits, including installation fees, was about $15 to $20.

32. Other cases we are currently investigating are the formation of car pools both in emergency and "normal" periods to cut down on auto emissions, and the extent of voluntary reductions in usage of electricity during periods of power crises.

Despite an aggressive marketing campaign, only 528 kits were sold. From this experience, GM has concluded that only a mandatory retrofit program for pre-1968 cars, based upon appropriate state or local regulation, can assure the wide participation of car owners that would be necessary to achieve a significant effect on the atmosphere. The Chrysler Corporation has had a similar experience. In 1970 Chrysler built 22,000 used car emission control kits. More than half remain in its current inventory. In fact after 1970 Chrysler had experienced "negative" sales. About 900 more kits were returned than shipped.

The role of moral suasion and voluntary compliance thus appears to promise little as a regular instrument of environmental policy. Its place (in which it may often be quite effective) is in times of crisis where immediate response is essential.

Concluding Remarks

Our intent in this paper has been a preliminary exploration of the potential of available tools for environmental policy. There is, as we have indicated, a wide variety of options at the policy level with differing instruments being appropriate depending upon the characteristics of the particular polluting activity and the associated environmental circumstances. The "optimal" policy package would no doubt include a combination of many approaches including the prohibition of certain activities, technical specifications for others, the imposition of fees, etc. We hope that the analysis has provided some insight into the types of situations in which certain policy instruments promise to be more effective than others.

Our own feeling, like that of most economists, is that environmental policy in the United States has failed to make sufficient use of the pricing system. Policies relying excessively on direct controls have not proved very effective in reversing processes of environmental deterioration and, where they have, we would guess the objective has often been achieved at unnecessarily high cost. Moreover, to the extent that environmental authorities have used price incentives, they have typically adopted subsidies rather than fees. These subsidy programs have often been ill-designed, providing incentives only for the use of certain inputs in waste treatment activities and by absorbing only part of the cost so that investments in pollution reducing equipment continue to be unprofitable. We still have much to learn at the policy level about the proper use of price incentives in environmental policy.

What emerges from all this is the conclusion that there is considerable validity to the standard economic analysis of environmental policy. There is good reason for the economist to continue to emphasize the virtues of automatic fiscal measures whose relative ease of enforcement, efficiency enhancing properties, and other special qualities are too often unrecognized by those who design and administer policy.

On the other hand, we economists have often failed to recognize the legitimate role of direct controls and moral suasion, each of which may have an important part to play in an effective environmental program. These policy tools may have substantial claims in terms of their efficiency, particularly under circumstances in which the course of events is heavily influenced by variables whose values are highly unpredictable and outside the policy-maker's control. In environmental economics we can be quite certain that the unexpected will occur with some frequency. Where the time costs of delay are very high and the dangers of inaction are great, the policy-maker's kit of tools must include some instruments that are very flexible and which can elicit a rapid response. A tightening of emission quotas or an appeal to conscience can produce, and has produced, its effects in periods far more brief than those needed to modify tax rules, and before any such change can lead to noteworthy consequences. Where intermediate targets, such as emission levels, may have to be changed frequently and at unforeseen times, fiscal instruments may often be relatively inefficient and ineffective.

In sum, as in most areas of policy design, there is much to be said for the use of a variety of policy instruments, each with its appropriate function. Obviously this does not mean that just any hybrid policy will do, or that direct controls are always desirable. Indeed, there are many examples in which their use has provided models of mismanagement and inefficiency. Rather, it implies that we must seek to define particular mixes of policy that promise to achieve our environmental objectives at a relatively low cost.

References

1. Baumol, W. and W. Oates. "The Use of Standards and Prices for Protection of the Environment," *The Swedish Journal of Economics* 73 (March 1971), pp. 42–54.
2. Bramhall, D. and E. Mills. "A Note on the Asymmetry Between Fees and Payments," *Water Resources Research* 2 (Third Quarter 1966), pp. 615–616.

3. Coase, R. "The Problem of Social Cost," *Journal of Law and Economics* 3 (October 1960), pp. 1–44.

4. Comptroller General of the United States. *Examination into the Effectiveness of the Construction Grant Program for Abating, Controlling, and Preventing Water Pollution.* Washington, D.C.: Government Printing Office, 1969.

5. Elliott, R. and J. Seagraves. "The Effects of Sewer Surcharges on the Level of Industrial Wastes and the Use of Water by Industry," *Water Resources Research Institute* Report No. 70 (August 1972).

6. Ethridge, D. "User Charges as a Means for Pollution Control: The Case of Sewer Surcharges," *The Bell Journal of Economics and Management Science* 3 (Spring 1972), pp. 346–354.

7. Fisher, C. "Cincinnati Industry Reduces Sewer-Surcharges," *Sewage and Industrial Wastes* 28 (September 1956), pp. 1186–1187.

8. Freeman, A. M. and R. Haveman. "Residual Charges for Pollution Control; A Policy Evaluation," *Science* 177 (July 28, 1972), pp. 322–329.

9. Griffin, J. "An Econometric Evaluation of Sulphur Taxes," *Journal of Political Economy* (forthcoming).

10. Johnson, E. "A Study in the Economics of Water Quality Management," *Water Resources Research* 3, No. 2 (1967).

11. Kneese, A. and B. Bower. *Managing Water Quality: Economics, Technology, Institutions.* Baltimore: Johns Hopkins, 1968.

12. Kneese, A., S. Rolfe, and J. Harned, eds. *Managing the Environment: International Economic Cooperation for Pollution Control.* New York: Praeger, 1971.

13. Kohn, R. "Price Elasticities of Demand and Air Pollution Control," *Review of Economics and Statistics* 54 (November 1972), pp. 392–400.

14. Krier, J. *Environmental Law and Policy.* New York: Bobbs-Merrill, 1971.

15. Lave, L. and E. Seskin. "Acute Relationships Among Daily Mortality, Air Pollution, and Climate," *Economic Analysis of Environmental Problems,* edited by Edwin S. Mills. New York: National Bureau of Economic Research, 1974.

16. Löf, G. and A. Kneese. *The Economics of Water Utilization in the Beet Sugar Industry.* Baltimore: Johns Hopkins, 1968.

17. Mäler, K. G. "Effluent Charges versus Effluent Standards," Working Paper (May 20, 1972).

18. Marcus, M. "Capital-Labor Substitution Among States: Some Empirical Evidence," *Review of Economics and Statistics* 46 (November 1964), pp. 434–438.

19. Marx, W. *Man and His Environment: Waste.* New York: Harper and Row, 1971.

20. Noll, R. "Institutions and Techniques for Managing Environmental Quality," 1970. Mimeographed.

21. Plourde, C. "A Model of Waste Accumulation and Disposal," *Canadian Journal of Economics* 5 (February 1972), pp. 119–125.

22. Upton, C. "Optimal Taxing of Water Pollution," *Water Resources Research* 4 (October 1968), pp. 865–875.
23. Zwick, D. and M. Benstock. *Water Wasteland.* New York: Grossman, 1971.

125 – 41

[1986]

13

Market Incentives for Environmental Protection: A Survey of Some Recent Developments

Wallace E. Oates *

William Baumol's valuable contribution to environmental economics is characteristic of so much of his work: it reflects his innate curiosity and delight with issues in economic theory combined with his concern for economic and social policy. His interest in the general problem of externalities reaches back to his early work on welfare economics (1952). Later, with evidence of mounting environmental damage in the 1960s, he applied this work to the design of environmental policy (1971, 1972, 1975, 1979).

This essay examines the policy side of the matter. I shall explore the evolution of environmental 'policy analysis' over the past twenty years and describe the recent appearance of two exciting and promising experiments in environmental management. Market incentives for pollution control are finally making their bid for a prominent place in the regulator's kit of policy tools. But these market instruments are taking a form somewhat different from that initially envisioned by most economists.

1. Background

As a result of the work of Baumol and others, the Pigouvian prescription for the distortions resulting from external diseconomies is now a familiar element in the lexicon of all economists: a unit tax on such activities equal to

---

* Department of Economics and Bureau of Business and Economic Research, University of Maryland. I am grateful to the National Science Foundation for the support of my research on economic incentives for environmental management.

251

marginal social damage (MSD). And pollution control is the standard text-book illustration of this proposition. It is easy to show that if the environmental authority imposes an effluent fee on emissions of the damaging substance equal to MSD, the response of maximising agents in a competitive setting will lead to the optimal level of such an activity.

However, the Pigouvian dictum has not proved readily translatable into actual policy. In particular, it makes heavy information demands. For most major air and water pollutants we simply do not have reliable measures of damages that can stand up to close scrutiny in the policy arena. It is the case, moreover, that the Pigouvian measure calls for a unit tax equal to MSD *at the optimal level of emissions*, not at the existing level. If marginal damages exhibit significant variation over the relevant range, this introduces another formidable obstacle to the implementation of the Pigouvian fee.[1]

At the policy level, regulators have paid little heed to the economist's proposal for a system of Pigouvian fees. In some instances, policy makers have explicitly rejected the economist's basic analytical framework: under the Clean Air Act, for example, the US Congress ruled out benefit–cost calculations and instructed the Environmental Protection Agency (EPA) to establish maximum allowable concentrations of air pollutants 'to protect the public health'.

Environmental management is typically a two-step process. First, the environmental authority determines a set of standards for environmental quality: ceiling levels of concentrations of various pollutants in the environment. Second, officials introduce a regulatory system to attain these standards. Such systems have been almost exclusively of the command-and-control (CAC) variety under which the authority specifies certain abatement procedures to be followed by sources, or establishes an overall emissions limit source-by-source. Within this more restrictive framework of established environmental quality standards, Baumol (1971) proposed fairly early on that regulators make use of effluent fees to achieve their predetermined environmental targets. Under the 'standards and charges' approach, the environmental authority, after setting the standards, would impose an effluent fee and, where necessary, adjust the fee to the level required to reach the standard. Baumol recognised the potential of pricing instruments in attaining a cost-effective allocation of abatement quotas and in encouraging needed innovation in abatement technology.

However, this proposed 'second-best' role for fees has not made much headway in the policy arena either. Actual legislative proposals for fee systems have surfaced in a few instances, but they have not got very far. Instead, an alternative form of pricing incentives has caught the attention of some policy makers: marketable (or tradeable) emission permits. I shall turn next to this central and intriguing issue of 'prices versus quantities' in policy design, for much of the political economy of environmental management turns on this distinction.

2. Effluent Fees or Marketable Emissions Permits?

There are two strands to the prices-versus-quantities literature. The first is embedded in the full theoretical framework of welfare economics and begins with the seminal paper by Martin Weitzman (1974). Weitzman envisions a policy maker with imperfect knowledge of both the social damage function and abatement cost functions of sources and poses the following question: in the presence of uncertainty (taking the form of stochastic terms in the damage and cost functions), can the environmental authority attain a higher expected level of social welfare by setting an effluent fee or by issuing a limited number of marketable emission permits? The answer to this question turns on the relative slopes of the marginal damage and cost functions. If, for example, marginal damages from emissions are relatively constant while marginal abatement costs rise sharply over the relevant range, the authority does better to set a fee. This would avoid the possibility of incurring exorbitant abatement costs in the event that too few permits are issued. If, instead, the marginal damage function is quite steep, reflecting perhaps some crucial threshold values of pollutant concentrations, then it will be more important to have a firm control over the quantity of emissions. For this case, marketable permits are preferred over fees. Following on Weitzman, Roberts and Spence (1976) show that an appropriate combination of price and quantity instruments can do even better than either alone. The moral of this work is important and straightforward. If an error in the quantity of emissions promises to be relatively costly, then the authority should retain careful control over quantity and issue transferable permits rather than set fees. But if the chief threat is the level of abatement costs, then fees (by effectively setting a ceiling on control costs) will tend to outperform permits.[2]

The second strand of this literature, with its source in J.H. Dales (1968), looks at the prices-versus-quantities issue in the more restricted framework of achieving a predetermined set of environmental standards. Given the standards, the question is whether or not to attain the required reduction in emissions through effluent charges or marketable permits. It is from this more limited perspective that the issue has been considered by policy makers. And from this policy perspective, it has become clear that a marketable-permit system has a number of compelling advantages over a system of fees.

First, the use of marketable permits minimises uncertainty and adjustment costs in attaining mandated levels of environmental quality. Under the fee approach, the environmental authority cannot be completely sure of the response of polluters to a particular level of effluent charges; in particular, if the authority sets the fee too low, environmental standards will not be met. In consequence, the fee may have to be raised and then further altered to generate an iterative path converging on the target level of emissions. This means costly adjustments and readjustments by polluters in their levels of waste discharges and the associated abatement technology. The need for repeated changes in the fee is likewise an unattractive prospect for administrators of the programme. In contrast, under a permit scheme, the environmental agency directly sets the total quantity of emissions at the allowable standard; there is, in principle, no problem in achieving the target.

Second, and closely related to the above issue, are the complications that result over time from economic growth and price inflation. Under a system of effluent fees, continuing inflation will erode the real value of the fee; likewise, expanding production from both existing and new firms will increase the demand for waste emissions. Both of these forces will require the fee to be raised periodically if environmental standards are to be maintained. In short, the burden for initiating action under fees is on environmental officials; the choice will be between unpopular fee increases or nonattainment of standards. Under a system of permits, market forces automatically accommodate inflation and growth with no increase in pollution. The rise in demand for permits simply translates directly into a higher price.

Third, the introduction of a system of effluent fees may involve enormous increases in costs to polluters *relative* to existing regulatory policies. This point may seem somewhat paradoxical in light of the widespread recognition that systems of pricing incentives promise large savings in aggregate abatement costs. But the two are not inconsistent. Although a system of effluent charges will reduce total abatement costs, it will impose a new source of costs, namely a tax bill, on polluting firms. Although the latter form of costs represents a transfer payment from the perspective of society, it is a cost of operation for the firm. Some recent evidence on this issue suggests some rather staggering figures. One such study (Palmer *et al*. 1980) of the use of pricing incentives to restrict emissions of certain halocarbons into the atmosphere estimates that aggregate abatement costs under a realistic programme of mandatory controls would total about $230 million; a system of fees or of marketable permits would reduce these costs to an estimated $110 million (a savings of roughly 50 per cent). However, the cost of the fees or permits to polluters would total about $1,400 million so that, in spite of the substantial savings in abatement costs, a programme of pricing incentives would, in this instance, increase the total cost to polluters by a factor of *six* relative to a programme of direct controls! Some studies of other pollutants also suggest potentially very large fee bills (see, for example, Seskin 1983). While a system of marketable permits *making use of an initial auction* of these rights is subject to these same results, there is an alternative: a permit system can be set in motion with an initial distribution of the permits to existing polluters. This version of the permit scheme would effectively eliminate the added source of costs for existing firms without any necessarily adverse consequences for the efficiency properties of the programme and with some obvious and major advantages for its political acceptability.

Fourth, for several important air and water pollutants, various studies indicate that it is imperative for the environmental authority to differentiate among polluters according to their location if environmental standards are to be realised in a cost-effective way (e.g. Seskin 1983). Sources at a highly polluted location within an air shed cannot be allowed to increase their emissions on a one-to-one basis in exchange for emissions reductions by other sources at a less polluted point. Dealing with the spatial problem can be administratively quite cumbersome under a system of effluent charges, for it will typically require the environmental agency to determine a separate effluent fee for each source depending upon its location in the air shed (or river basin). Such discrimination in fee levels across sources may be either explicitly illegal or, alternatively, politically not feasible. In contrast, a system of marketable permits (as will become clear in the next section) can incorporate these spatial dimensions of the pollution problem in a manner that is less objectionable.

Fifth, marketable permits appear the more feasible approach on grounds of familiarity. The introduction of a system of effluent fees requires the adoption of a wholly new method of controlling pollution, new both to regulators and polluters. Such sharp departures from established practice are hard to sell; moreover, there exist some real questions concerning the legality of charging for pollution. In contrast, permits already exist, and it appears a less radical step to make these permits effectively marketable.

Emerging from this discussion is a case for what we might call the 'standards and marketable permits' approach to environmental management. However, it is a long way from a general decision on policy strategy to the design of an actual system of marketable permits. In the next section, I shall explore the alternative forms of a permits market and then in the final section turn to a description of two new and promising systems of transferable permits in the United States: emissions trading for the control of air pollution and the Wisconsin system of transferable discharge permits (TDP) for water-quality management.

3.   The Design of a System of Marketable Emission Permits[3]

It will facilitate the discussion to provide here a more specific and formal statement of the control problem. Let us consider a specific region consisting of either an air shed or system of waterways in which there are m sources of pollution, each of which is fixed in location. Environmental (air or water) quality is defined in terms of pollutant concentrations at each of n 'receptor points' in the region; this implies that we can describe environmental quality by a vector $Q = (q_1, \ldots, q_n)$ whose elements indicate the concentration of the pollutant at each of the receptors. The dispersion of waste emissions from the m sources is described by an $m \times n$ matrix of unit diffusion (or transfer) coefficients:

$$D = \left[\; \ldots \; d_{ij} \; \ldots \; \right]$$

In this matrix, the element d_{ij} indicates the contribution that one unit of emissions from source i makes to the pollutant concentration at point j.

The environmental objective is to attain some predetermined level(s) of pollutant concentrations within the region; I denote these standards as $Q^* = (q_1^*, \ldots, q_n^*)$. Note that the standard need not be the same at each receptor point; the environmental authority could, for example, prescribe lower concentrations as the target in densely populated areas.

The problem thus becomes one of attaining a set of predetermined levels of pollutant concentrations at the minimum aggregate abatement cost. In other words we are looking for a vector of emissions from our m sources, $E = (e_1, \ldots, e_m)$, which will minimise abatement costs subject to the constraint that the prescribed standards be met at each of the n locations in the region. The abatement costs of the ith source are a function of its level of emissions: $c_i(e_i)$. So our problem, in formal terms, is to:

minimise $\qquad \sum_i c_i(e_i)$

subject to $\qquad ED \leqslant Q^*$
$\qquad\qquad\quad E \geqslant 0$

There are two basic approaches to the design of a marketable permit system to address this control problem (Tietenberg 1980). First, the environmental authority could simply issue q_j^* permits at each receptor point, where these permits are defined in terms of an allowed contribution to the pollutant concentration at j. This would effectively create a separate market corresponding to each receptor point and a source, to justify its emissions, would have to procure a 'portfolio' of permits from the various receptors where its emissions contributed to pollutant levels. More specifically, source i would have to obtain $e_i d_{ij}$ permits from the jth receptor market. This form of permit market is an ambient-permit system (APS) in that the permits have reference not to a source's emissions, but to the effects of these emissions on levels of pollution. Note that this implies that emissions entitlements will not, in general, exchange for one another on a one-for-one basis; a source whose emissions per unit are more damaging at a particular receptor will have to purchase commensurately more emission entitlements from another source whose discharges contribute less per unit to pollutant concentrations at that receptor.

Alternatively, the environmental agency could introduce an emissions-permit system (EPS). The agency would divide the region into zones and, within each zone, sources would trade emissions entitlements on a one-for-one basis. The EPS system has some obvious attractions in terms of simplifying transactions among sources.

We turn next to the properties of the two permit systems. For the APS scheme, Montgomery (1972) has shown in a seminal paper that, if the sources of pollution are cost-minimising agents, the emissions vector and shadow prices that emerge from the above minimisation problem satisfy the same set of conditions as do the vectors of emissions and permit prices for a competitive equilibrium in the permits market. In short, if the environmental authority were simply to issue q_j^* permits (defined in terms of pollutant concentrations) for each of the n receptor points, competitive bidding for these permits would generate an equilibrium solution that satisfies the conditions for the minimisation of total abatement costs.

The APS system thus has the potential for achieving the least-cost outcome. Two properties of this form of permit market are noteworthy. First is the utter simplicity of the system from the perspective of the environmental agency. In particular, officials need have no information whatsoever regarding abatement costs; they simply issue the prescribed number of permits at each receptor point, and competitive bidding takes care of matters from there. Alternatively, the environmental authority could make an initial allocation of these permits to existing polluters. Subsequent transactions in a competitive setting would then establish the cost-minimising solution. As Montgomery proves formally, the least-cost outcome is independent of the initial allocation of the permits. Second, in contrast to the modest burden it places on administrators, this system can be extremely cumbersome for polluters. Note that a firm emitting wastes must assemble a 'portfolio' of permits from *each* of the receptor points that is affected by its emissions: a source at point i will have to acquire permits at each receptor j in the amount $(d_{ij}e_i)$. There will, therefore, exist n different markets for permits, one for each receptor point, and each polluter will participate in the subset of these markets corresponding to the receptor points affected by his emissions. Transactions costs for polluters could be quite high.

The APS system suffers from a second deficiency that is potentially quite troublesome. The analysis here has run in terms of a given and fixed set of receptor points at which predetermined levels of air quality must be attained. However, the Clean Air Act requires that the National Ambient Air Quality Standards (NAAQS) be met at *all* locations. But for pollutants with more localised effects (and this includes most of the major air and water pollutants), it is possible for changing locational patterns of emissions to generate 'hot spots' that do not coincide with designated receptor points. To prevent the occurrence of localised hot spots for such pollutants, a relatively fine mesh of receptor points will be needed implying a large number of receptor markets and comparatively high transactions costs. Further, since each receptor is associated with an individual permit market, receptor points would tend to become 'institutionalised.' Moving a receptor point to account for new pollution patterns would create dislocations: it would alter the structure of permit markets and would probably give rise to difficult administrative and legal problems. And it would not preclude the need for future readjustments. The APS form of the permit market is not without serious problems.

As noted earlier, the emissions permit system (EPS) can greatly simplify life for polluters. Instead of assembling the requisite portfolio of permits from different receptor markets, each source would find itself in a single zone within which emissions entitlements would exchange one-for-one. However, the EPS cannot, in general, achieve the least-cost outcome, and it makes enormous demands on an administering agency that tries to approach the least-cost solution. Since polluters with somewhat varying dispersion coefficients are aggregated into the same zone, one-for-one trades of pollution entitlements will not reflect the differences in the concentrations contributed by their respective emissions. The price of emissions to each polluter will not, in short, reflect accurately the shadow price of the binding pollution constraint. This objection to EPS need not be serious if the dispersion characteristics for emissions within zones are not very different. However, this is often not the case. The ambient effects of emissions do not depend solely on the geographical location of the source; for air pollutants, for example, they depend in important ways on such things as stack height and diameter and on gas temperature and exit velocity. EPS cannot readily incorporate such elements without losing the basic simplicity of one-for-one transfers of emissions entitlements.

A further difficulty with EPS is that, even were there no differences in the dispersion characteristics of emissions within each zone, the environmental authority must still determine an allocation of permits to each zone. And this determination requires *the complete solution* by the administrator of the cost-minimisation problem. To reach this solution, the administering agency must have not only an air-quality model (to provide the d_{ij}) and a complete emissions inventory, but source-specific abatement cost functions and the capacity to solve the programming problem. With less-than-perfect information, the agency's zonal allocation of permits may fail to attain the ambient air-quality targets. If pollution were excessive, the authority would have to re-enter the market (in at least some of the zones, where again the pattern of zonal purchases would require a fairly sophisticated analysis) and purchase or confiscate permits. Such an iterative procedure is not only cumbersome for the administrator of the system, but may create considerable uncertainty for firms as to the future course of permit prices. Note, moreover, that this procedure involves more than just groping once and for all toward an unchanging equilibrium. Altered patterns of emissions resulting from the growth (or contraction) of existing firms, the entry of new firms, and changing abatement technology will generate a continually shifting least-cost pattern of emissions across zones. Under EPS, the environmental authority faces a dynamic problem that will require periodic adjustment to the supplies of permits in each zone.

Both the APS and EPS forms of a marketable permit system are subject to some potentially quite serious objections. However, there is a third alternative that represents a kind of hybrid system capable of meeting these objections: the pollution-offset system (Krupnick *et al.* 1983). Under this approach, permits are defined in terms of emissions (e.g. the permit allows the discharge of X pounds of the pollutant, say, per week). However, sources are not allowed to trade permits on a one-to-one basis. More specifically, transfers of TDPs under the pollution-offset scheme are subject to the restriction that the transfer does not result in a violation of the environmental quality standard at any receptor point. If a proposed transfer encounters a binding pollution constraint at some receptor point, this implies that emissions will be traded at a rate determined by the ratio of the sources' 'transfer coefficients' (d_{ij}).[4] Although permits are defined in terms of emissions like EPS, trades are really governed by the effect on ambient air quality in the spirit of APS.

The pollution-offset system shares with the APS the important property that mutually beneficial trades among sources can lead to the least-cost outcome and that this result is independent of the initial allocation of permits. This coincidence of the 'trading equilibrium' with the least-cost solution can be seen in Figure 13.1. In the figure the horizontal and vertical axes measure, respectively, the levels of emissions of firms 1 and 2 (i.e. e_1 and e_2). The curves C_1 and C_2 are iso-cost curves for pollution abatement costs.[5] Note that higher curves correspond to lower total abatement costs. The line AB indicates the pollution constraint associated with receptor j. Points on AB denote combinations of e_1 and e_2 for which $q_j = q_j^*$; the slope of the line

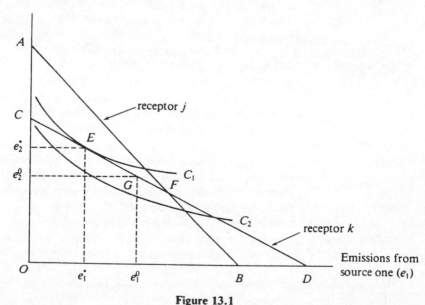

Figure 13.1

equals the ratio of the transfer coefficients (i.e. the rate at which emissions from firm 2 can substitute for emissions from firm 1 with no change in pollution concentrations at receptor j). Similarly, CD depicts the pollution constraint for receptor k. The combinations of emissions from firms 1 and 2 that satisfy the pollution constraint at both receptors are thus the set of points $OCFB$. We see immediately that the least-cost solution occurs at E, at which point the ratio of marginal abatement costs equals the ratio of the transfer coefficients.

Suppose, however, that the environmental authority selected for the initial distribution of permits point G instead of the least-cost outcome E. (Recall that the authority has no knowledge of sources' abatement cost functions and hence is unable to determine e_1^* and e_2^*.) In this instance, source two would find it profitable to purchase permits from source one. The effective rate of exchange of permits would be the slope of the line CD, since receptor k is, in this case, the binding constraint. At this rate of exchange, the transfer of emissions from source one to source two will result in a decrease in aggregate abatement costs. The gains-from-trade would be exhausted at E at which point the ratio of the sources' marginal abatement costs becomes equal to the rate of exchange of permits. We thus find that the 'trading equilibrium' under the pollution-offset system coincides with the least-cost solution.[6]

Like APS (and unlike EPS), the pollution-offset scheme makes modest information demands on the environmental authority. Officials need to know the dispersion characteristics of emissions within the air shed or waterway (i.e. the D-matrix), but need have no information on sources' abatement costs. The authority does not have to solve the cost-minimisation problem to determine the initial allocation of permits: any allocation will do. This, incidentally, is an important property of the system, because it provides the degree of freedom that will probably be needed to reach a 'fair' and politically acceptable distribution of pollution rights.

Unlike APS, however, the pollution-offset system does not require sources to trade in a multitude of separate permit markets. Instead, a firm purchases emissions permits directly from other sources. The pollution-offset scheme thus promises substantial savings in transactions costs to sources relative to APS. In addition, it is not subject (as is APS) to the problem of a fixed and 'institutionalised' set of receptor points. Receptor points can easily be redefined with respect to each trade to coincide with potential hot spots and thus ensure that there are no violations of the environmental standard at any point in the air shed or waterway. Receptor points, incidentally, need not coincide with monitoring locations where air or water quality is actually measured; receptors serve as reference points where pollutant concentrations may be monitored or alternatively inferred from a knowledge of emissions and a dispersion model of the region.

The pollution-offset system captures the major advantages of the ambient- and emissions-permit systems and avoids some of the most serious shortcomings. As such, it offers an attractive approach to the design of a permit market. In the next section, I shall describe two recent and innovative experiments in the United States with systems of marketable permits. It is interesting to find that in both cases the design of these systems is in the spirit of the pollution-offset scheme.

4. Some Recent Experience with Transferable Permits

Emissions Trading for Air Pollutants

The Emissions Trading Programme is, on first glance, a rather curious collection of exotic-sounding provisions ('Bubbles, Banking, and Offsets') that allow the exchange of discharges of air pollutants among sources. The structure and evolution of the programme is best understood in the light of its rather ironical origins. Emissions Trading had its birth not as the result of a rational policy decision to introduce a more effective system of pollution control, but rather as a pragmatic response to a dilemma that emerged under the enforcement of the US Clean Air Act. Under the Clean Air Act of 1970, EPA established standards for ambient air quality for certain 'criteria' pollutants that were to be met in each of the 247 air quality control regions in the United States.[7] As the decade progressed, it became clear that, in many areas, it would not be possible to meet these standards for all the criteria air pollutants by the mandated deadline of 1975 (subsequently extended to 1977). The prospective penalty for such 'nonattainment' areas was severe: no new sources of emissions (or significant expansion of existing sources), implying a virtual cessation of economic growth. An unpleasant confrontation with uncertain consequences was on the horizon as the deadline approached. The EPA managed to circumvent this confrontation through a proposal for 'emission offsets' in nonattainment areas that was enacted as part of the 1977 Amendments to the Clean Air Act. Under the Offsets provision, nonattainment areas were enabled to accommodate new sources through a procedure that involves (1) the adoption by any new source of the most effective abatement technology available, and (2) the contraction of emissions by existing sources with a resulting net improvement in air quality. The increment to aggregate emissions from new sources would thus be more than 'offset' by reduced emissions from existing polluters. In this way the door was opened for the transfer of emission entitlements among sources, and a handful of widely publicised offset transactions occurred in various parts of the country.

EPA has subsequently extended the offset strategy to encompass a broader set of provisions to facilitate emissions transfers. This framework, now called Emissions Trading, has three components: Bubbles, Banking, and Offsets. Under the Bubble provision, an imaginary 'bubble' is placed over a plant or firm with multiple sources of emissions. Instead of meeting technological standards or permit limits on each source under the bubble, the firm is treated as a single unit subject to an overall emissions limitation. Within this overall limitation, the firm is free to determine its own pattern of abatement activity and emissions. The Offset policy amounts; in a sense, to an extension of the Bubble to encompass 'interfirm trades'. There are a number of administrative restrictions on the use of these procedures, but the basic point is that under the Bubble and Offset policies, firms can effect emissions trades both within their own establishment and with other firms.[8] Some proposed and actual implementations of these procedures promise quite large savings in abatement costs.

The most recent component of the Emissions Trading framework is the Banking provision. Introduced in 1979, Banking allows firms to receive 'credits' for emissions reductions in excess of those required under existing regulations. These credits can be used later by the firm for a subsequent expansion of emissions or, alternatively, sold for use as an offset by another firm.

In understanding and assessing the Emissions Trading Programme, it is important to recognise that the various components of the programme are really no more than routine dimensions of a conventional market. The trades permitted under the Bubble and Offset provisions and the storing of credits under Banking all represent standard forms of economic behaviour in the marketplace. From this perspective, Emissions Trading can be seen as a framework for establishing a market in emission entitlements. There exists a basic limitation on overall emissions established by the predetermined ambient air-quality standard and, subject to this limit, firms can trade emissions entitlements. Emissions Trading is thus in the spirit of the pollution-offset system described in the preceding section.

Unfortunately, Emissions Trading is still embedded in a broader body of regulation that places obstacles in the way of attaining the least-cost solution. New sources, for example, must meet technological abatement requirements under the provisions for New Source Performance Standards; these standards serve to interfere with cost-saving trades in emission entitlements.

At any rate, Emissions Trading can be seen as an important step in the direction of a system of marketable emission permits. The experience with Emissions Trading has varied across the country. It is important to understand that the actual design and implementation of programmes to manage air quality take place in the individual states under a State Implementation Plan (SIP). Emissions Trading defines only a legal framework, not a fully specified system. Moreover, each state has the discretion under its SIP to introduce its own variant of the Emissions Trading framework, or alternatively to rely on a more traditional command-and-control type of regulatory structure. Several states have, in fact, introduced their forms of Emissions Trading. A recent report by the General Accounting Office (GAO

1982) surveys and assesses this experience. The GAO study found numerous obstacles to getting these systems started. In some instances, as in the Bay Area in California, existing uncertainty concerning regulatory procedures (including the possibility of more stringent abatement requirements in the future) appears to have made existing sources reluctant to part with their emissions entitlements so that frequent trading has not taken place. To some extent, the sheer novelty of these new systems for pollution control has made potential participants cautious in engaging in transactions. GAO found 'no evidence that prospective buyers offered to pay a price which covered more than the direct pollution abatement costs of offsets, even though there are good reasons to expect a higher minimum price asked by the seller' (p. 96). GAO concludes that these impediments to the 'eventual emergence of a full-scale market in air-pollution entitlements do not seem unresolvable' (p. v). Once trading procedures and institutions become better understood and a sufficient number of trades take place to generate some sense of the market-clearing price of emissions entitlements, participation in the emissions market will, in all likelihood, become more widespread.

Emissions Trading has made real headway in certain regions (see Palmisano 1982 and EPA 1981, 1982). As of November 1982, EPA had approved (or proposed to approve) 31 bubbles with estimated cost savings of $120 million *and* with greater emissions reductions than under existing regulatory requirements. Over 100 additional bubble applications averaging about $2 million each in projected cost savings were under review at the state or federal level. Moreover, nearly all states had incorporated offset provisions into their SIPs; EPA indicates that about 1,900 offset transactions have taken place. As of the end of 1982, there were three areas (Louisville, San Francisco and Puget Sound) with formal banking systems in operation. Each has several hundred tons of banked emission 'deposits' and in each case interfirm trades have taken place using some of these deposits. At least seven other areas are in the process of proposing or drafting banking provisions. This experience suggests that, while the obstacles to establishing Emissions Trading systems and getting them functioning are surely real, they do not appear insurmountable.

A System of Transferable Discharge Permits (TDP) in Wisconsin

The history of the new TDP system for the management of water quality is very different from that of Emissions Trading. Unlike the latter, the TDP system has been designed and introduced virtually wholly through the efforts of an innovative and imaginative group in the state of Wisconsin. Although the enabling national legislation for the control of water pollution does not prohibit systems of fees or marketable permits, it does not encourage them. In particular, the 1972 Water Pollution Amendments introduced a system of technology-based effluent standards to be determined by the EPA for various classes and categories of industries. Until very recently the EPA has itself undertaken no initiatives for the introduction of pricing incentives for the management of water quality.

Under a coordinated effort involving a group of economists and engineers at the University of Wisconsin and officials in the Wisconsin Department of Natural Resources, a plan was devised to regulate water quality on the state's more heavily polluted rivers. One of them, the Fox River, flows about 45 miles from Lake Winnebago to Green Bay, and has along its banks the heaviest concentration of paper mills in the world including 15 paper and pulp plants along with 6 municipal waste-treatment plants. The Wisconsin River has a similar number and mix of dischargers spread over 130 miles. Even after complying with EPA's technology-based standards, officials found that they could not achieve the desired level of water quality at all times of the year. Further abatement efforts were needed.

The target level of water quality (a level sufficient to sustain fish life and allow recreational activities on the river) was established at five ppm of dissolved oxygen. The system was designed to achieve this water-quality objective for all but the most unfavourable constellations of circumstances. It should be emphasised that from the very early stages of development of the plan for attaining water-quality standards, the sources of the emissions were active participants in the design of the overall programme (David and Joeres 1983). The polluters themselves thus played a role in the evolution of the ultimate proposal.

The structure of the TDP system is itself of interest. Along the Fox River, for example, there are two stationary 'sag points' located behind the dams on the river. The dissolved-oxygen (DO) content of the waters reaches its lowest levels at these two sag points. The problem thus becomes one of ensuring that the DO content of the water stays at or above five ppm at these two points on the river. A model of the river indicates the impact of a unit of BOD emissions from each source on the level of dissolved oxygen at the sag points. The permit system begins with an initial allocation of allowable discharges (based on historical levels) among the sources that is consistent with the achievement of the water-quality target. Sources are then free to trade permits among themselves subject to certain constraints, one of which is the absence of any violations of the water-quality standard. Note that this constraint implies (as under Emissions Trading) that permit trades typically will not take place on a one-for-one basis. Where the pollution constraint is binding, the source whose emissions have a relatively large impact on water quality at the receptor (sag) point will have to purchase emission permits from other sources totalling an amount greater than the increase in its own emissions. The Wisconsin system is, in this respect, a form of the pollution-offset scheme discussed earlier.[9]

Another interesting feature of the Wisconsin permit system is the variability of allowable emissions with the assimilative capacity of the river. The capacity of the rivers to absorb BOD discharges varies widely over the year with river flow and temperature. During the summer periods, for example, when water flow is relatively low and temperature comparatively high, BOD emissions tend to be more damaging as the waters are less able to assimilate the wastes. Under the Wisconsin plan, the emissions allowable per permit are themselves variable and depend upon both water flow and temperature. Such 'flow-temperature' permits require sources to adapt their levels of BOD discharges to river conditions. To help accommodate the needed temporal adjustments in levels of discharges, the TDP system can allow for short-term leasing of permits among sources.

The combination of flexible flow-temperature permits and the offset condition on trades can result in considerable cost savings. Building on the work of O'Neil (1980), David and David (1983) have estimated that the Wisconsin system of variable and transferable permits can reduce aggregate abatement costs by about 80 per cent as compared to a representative CAC regime that imposed an equiproportional cutback on all sources. It is too early to learn just how much of the potential savings from transfers of permits will be realised through actual trades, for the system was only introduced in the spring of 1981. Negotiations have reportedly begun for two transfers of permits among sources.

Although the introduction of Emissions Trading and the Wisconsin TDP system are fascinating and important events in the evolution of US environmental policy, it is premature to characterise them as heralding the arrival of a broad movement for the adoption of pricing incentives for pollution control. It would be more accurate to regard them as two intriguing 'experiments' with an innovative regulatory structure. Their future and their ultimate impact on the development of environmental policy are, at this juncture, uncertain. However, there are a number of encouraging signs: not only certain policy makers, but a number of environmentalists have recently indicated a genuine interest in, and receptiveness to, the marketable-permit proposal. There is even interest abroad: several European countries are following closely the US experience with transferable emissions entitlements. At long last, Pigou may be making his appearance in the policy arena, but it is in rather different garb than in the original script.

Notes

1. The iterative procedure of setting the unit tax equal to *existing* MSD and adjusting it in response to alterations in emissions and levels of damages may, but need not, generate a path converging on the optimal outcome. See Baumol and Oates (1975, Ch. 7).
2. For some interesting case studies of pollution control drawing on the Weitzman perspective, see Schelling (1983).
3. This section draws heavily on Krupnick *et al.* (1983).
4. The ratio of the transfer coefficients indicates the rate at which emissions from one source can substitute for emissions from the other with no change in pollutant concentrations at the relevant receptor.
5. A sufficient (but not necessary) condition for the iso-cost curves to have the

desired curvature in Figure 13.1 is that both firms face a schedule of rising marginal abatement costs.

6. I refer to this as a 'trading' equilibrium rather than a 'market' equilibrium, since we have not shown formally that there exists a specific set of prices that will sustain an equilibrium among buyers and sellers corresponding to the efficient allocation of permits among polluters. The discussion suggests that the only allocation of permits for which there exist no potential gains-from-trade (the definition here of a 'trading equilibrium') corresponds to the least-cost allocation of emission entitlements.

7. The criteria air pollutants include particulate matter, sulfur oxides, carbon monoxides, nitrogen dioxide, ozone, hydrocarbons, and lead.

8. Under some recent extensions of these policies, there are now instances where the Bubble can be used for interfirm transfers of entitlements among *existing* firms, and where offsets can be employed within firms for *new* sources in nonattainment areas.

9. The Wisconsin scheme is not quite a pure pollution-offset system because, as noted in the text, EPA under the 1972 Water Pollution Amendments imposed technology-based standards on *all* sources in the United States. Consequently, each source on the Fox River must undertake some minimum level of abatement activity to comply with the national legislation. It is the abatement increment above this minimum that is available for trading under the Wisconsin TDP programme.

References

Baumol, William J. (1952) *Welfare Economics and the Theory of the State*, Harvard University Press.

Baumol, William J. (1972) 'On taxation and the control of externalities', *American Economic Review*, vol. 62, June, pp. 307–322.

Baumol, William J. and Oates, Wallace E. (1971) 'The use of standards and prices for protection of the environment', *Swedish Journal of Economics*, vol. 73, March, pp. 42–54.

Baumol, William J. and Oates, Wallace E. (1975) *The Theory of Environmental Policy*, Prentice-Hall.

Baumol, William J. and Oates, Wallace E. (1979) *Economics, Environmental Policy, and the Quality of Life*, Prentice-Hall.

Dales, J.H. (1968) *Pollution, Property, and Prices*, University of Toronto Press.

David, Martin and David, Elizabeth (1983) 'Cost-effective regulatory options for water quality limited streams', *Water Resources Bulletin*, vol. 19, June, pp. 421–428.

David, Martin and Joeres, Erhard (1983) 'Is a viable implementation of TDPs transferable?', in E. Joeres and M. David (eds) (1983) *Buying a Better Environment*, University of Wisconsin Press, pp. 233–248.

Krupnick, Alan J., Oates, Wallace E. and Van De Verg, Eric (1983) 'On marketable air pollution permits: the case for a system of pollution offsets', *Journal of Environmental Economics and Management*, vol. 10, September, pp. 233–247.

Montgomery, W. David (1972) 'Markets in licenses and efficient pollution control programs', *Journal of Economic Theory*, vol. 5, December, pp. 495–518.

O'Neil, William (1980) *Pollution Permits and Markets for Water Quality*, Ph.D. Dissertation, University of Wisconsin.

Palmer, Adele *et al.* (1980) *Economic Implications of Regulating Chlorofluorocarbon Emissions from Nonaerosol Applications*, The Rand Corporation, Santa Monica, California.

Palmisano, John (1982) 'Have markets for trading emission reduction credits failed or succeeded?', unpublished paper, July.

Roberts, Marc J. and Spence, Michael (1976) 'Effluent charges and licenses under uncertainty', *Journal of Public Economics*, vol. 5, April–May, pp. 193–208.

Schelling, Thomas C. (ed.) (1983) *Incentives for Environmental Protection*, MIT Press.

Seskin, Eugene P., Anderson, Jr., Robert J. and Reid, Robert O. (1983) 'An empirical analysis of economic strategies for controlling air pollution', *Journal of Environmental Economics and Management*, vol. 10, June, pp. 112–124.

Tietenberg, Thomas H. (1980) 'Transferable discharge permits and the control of stationary source air pollution: a survey and synthesis', *Land Economics*, vol. 56, November, pp. 391–416.

US Environmental Protection Agency (1981) *The Controlled Trader*, vol. 1, no. 3, November.

US Environmental Protection Agency (1982) *Emissions Trading Status Report*, November 19.

US General Accounting Office (1982) *A Market Approach to Air Pollution Control Could Reduce Compliance Costs Without Jeopardizing Clean Air Goals*, March 23.

Weitzman, Martin (1974) 'Prices vs. quantities', *Review of Economic Studies*, vol. 41, October, pp. 477–491.

[7]

The *Net* Benefits of Incentive-Based Regulation:
A Case Study of Environmental Standard Setting

By WALLACE E. OATES, PAUL R. PORTNEY, AND ALBERT M. McGARTLAND*

Economists interested in environmental, safety, and health regulation have long argued that decentralized, incentive-based (or IB) policies are more efficient than centralized, command-and-control (or CAC) approaches (see Charles Schultze, 1977, for instance). These arguments generally have been based on the assumption that IB policies will accomplish the same goals as their CAC counterparts, but at less cost to society.

However, some of those touting IB policies have overlooked an important point: environmental, workplace, or even product-safety standards typically take the form of maximum permissible concentrations of harmful substances, so that compliance only requires that all monitoring points or samples register readings below these critical levels. For this reason, IB policies typically assign a shadow price of zero to improvements that exceed the standard(s), while more crude CAC policies generally result in "overcontrol" beyond the standards. If there is no value to this overcontrol, CAC policies will not improve at all on IB approaches and will indeed be more expensive. If, however, reduced concentrations below the level of the standards bring with them further im-

provements in health or the environment, CAC approaches will produce greater benefits than IB approaches. Thus, a fair comparison between the two necessitates that any additional benefits associated with CAC policies be offset against the cost advantages enjoyed by their IB counterparts.

Although this possibility has been recognized by others (Scott Atkinson and T. H. Tietenberg, 1982, for instance), it is little appreciated and its empirical significance has never been ascertained. That is our purpose here. We do so by developing data on the costs and benefits of controlling a common air pollutant, total suspended particulates (or TSP), in Baltimore. By comparing the TSP levels likely under both IB and CAC approaches, we are able to estimate the marginal costs and benefits associated with a variety of alternative air quality standards which take the form of maximum permissible concentrations. This in turn allows us to determine the *net* benefits arising from the two kinds of regimes.

In the next section we present a simple conceptual framework for our analysis. Section II describes the estimation of the costs and benefits of our hypothesized air pollution controls in Baltimore. Section III presents our somewhat surprising findings, and Section IV discusses those findings and their potential significance for regulation in the "real world."

*The authors' affiliations are, respectively, Department of Economics and Bureau of Business and Economic Research, University of Maryland, and University Fellow, Resources for the Future; vice president, Resources for the Future; and Economist, Abt Associates. The views in this paper are those of the authors and do not necessarily reflect those of the organizations with which they are affiliated. We are very grateful to Karen Clay, Julie Kurland, and especially Stephen McGonegal for their invaluable assistance with the empirical work. In addition, we wish to thank Ann Fisher, Kerry Smith, our colleagues at Resources for the Future, and two referees for their most helpful comments on earlier drafts of this paper. Finally, we are indebted to the National Science Foundation and the Andrew W. Mellon Foundation for their support of this research.

I. The Conceptual Framework

Before turning to our Baltimore data, it will be helpful to set the problem in a more general framework. Suppose that we have a specific "region"—it could be an air shed, a system of waterways, or even the ambient environment in a large factory—in which there are m sources of pollution, each of which is fixed in location. Environmental quality is defined in terms of pollutant concentrations at each of n "receptor points" in the region. We can thus measure environmental quality by a vector $Q = (q_1, q_2, \ldots, q_n)$ whose elements indicate the concentration of the pollutant at each of the receptors. This, incidentally, makes one important, if obvious, point: the "level" of environmental quality is actually a set of pollutant concentrations at different points in the region—it is not (for most pollutants) simply a single level of pollution.

The dispersion of emissions from the m sources in the region is described by an $m \times n$ matrix of unit diffusion (or transfer) coefficients:

$$D = \ldots d_{ij} \ldots,$$

where d_{ij} indicates the increase in pollutant concentration at receptor j from an additional unit of emissions of the pollutant by source i. If we denote by e_i the level of emissions by source i, we can then describe the pattern of waste emissions in the region by the vector $E = (e_1, e_2, \ldots, e_m)$. The levels of pollution at the various receptor points can then be determined by mapping the vector of emissions through the diffusion matrix:

$$ED = Q.$$

Finally, we introduce the abatement cost function: $C_i(e_i)$ is the cost to source i of holding its emissions to e_i.

Let us suppose that some standard for environmental (or workplace) quality has been set—we take it for now as predetermined. The standard takes the form of a maximum permissible level of pollutant concentration at any receptor point in the region. There are various regulatory strategies that an environmental agency might pursue to comply with the standard. Following a "command-and-control" (CAC) approach, the agency might specify abatement technologies for the sources. Suppose, as is common practice, that it required all similar sources to adopt the same control proce-

dures and tightened up these procedures until the standard was everywhere satisfied. Such a control program would result in a specific vector of emissions from sources —call it E_c. And this vector would map through the diffusion matrix into a vector Q_c of pollutant concentrations.

Note that in virtually all cases the standard will be binding at only one or a few receptors. Most receptors will have pollutant concentrations below that required by the standard so that environmental quality at most points in the air shed, waterway, or workplace will exceed that prescribed by the standards. *It is also clear that the resulting vector of environmental quality (and the associated levels of damages and control costs) depends on the specific regulatory program adopted by the agency.*

Suppose instead that the environmental agency pursues an IB strategy. By this we mean that it seeks that vector of emissions (E_1) that can attain the standard at the minimum aggregate abatement cost:

$$\text{Min } \Sigma C(e_i)$$

$$\text{s.t. } ED \leq Q^*$$

$$E \geq 0,$$

where Q^* is the upper bound on allowable pollutant concentrations. There are various ways this might be done, including the use of effluent fees or transferable discharge permits. Such a program will, by definition, achieve the standard at a cost less than (or equal to) our CAC program. And this will involve a different vector of emissions. In general (as existing studies show), the IB vector will entail higher levels of emissions and higher levels of pollutant concentrations at nonbinding receptor points than will the CAC solution. This is not surprising, since the cost-minimization procedure assigns a zero shadow price to any additions to pollutant concentrations so long as the standard is not exceeded. In its search to reduce abatement costs, the IB approach effectively makes use of any "excess" environmental capacity to allow increased emissions. *Thus, for any given Q^*, we expect in general to find* *levels of emissions, concentrations, and damages that are higher under the IB solution than under the CAC outcome.*

The levels of both benefits and control costs associated with a particular standard will, in consequence, tend to be higher under a CAC than under an IB regime. Just how the levels of *net* benefits and the optimal standard will compare under these approaches is not something we can determine a priori; it is an empirical matter. To get a sense of the magnitudes involved, we investigate in the succeeding sections the benefit and cost functions for a specific air pollutant in the Baltimore region.

II. Estimating Benefits and Costs

To estimate the marginal costs of TSP control under the two regimes, we used a model developed by McGartland (1983, 1984) which reflects the technological control possibilities, associated particulate reduction efficiencies, and costs for about 400 actual sources in Baltimore. The marginal abatement cost function under the IB approach reflects, for each possible standard considered, the least-cost combination of control options across all particulate sources that ensures attainment at all receptors. To estimate marginal costs for the CAC regime, we adopted the basic spirit of the regulatory strategy used in Baltimore. First, all sources were categorized and similar sources grouped together—for instance, industrial coal-fired boilers, grain shipping facilities, etc. Then, marginal costs for additional control were estimated for each source *category*. Finally, when additional controls were required to reduce particulate levels, the source *category* with the lowest cost-per-ton was targeted for further regulation; all sources within that category were required to adopt the same technology regardless of their individual costs or location.

To estimate the marginal benefits associated with alternative standards, we first assigned the 1980 population of the Baltimore metropolitan area to one of the 23 receptors in the area using the geographic coordinates of each census tract and each receptor. This gave us an "exposed population" by receptor

ranging from as few as 3,800 people assigned to one receptor to more than 180,000 at another.

Given these exposures, we calculated marginal benefits from successively tighter TSP standards for four different categories: reduced premature mortality, reduced morbidity, reduced soiling damages to households, and improved visibility. For each category, the changes in TSP levels that would accompany successively tighter standards were first translated into physical improvements (fewer sick days, fewer "statistical" lives lost, reduced soiling, and increased visibility). To do so, we relied primarily on the peer-reviewed dose-response studies actually used by the EPA in setting the national air quality standard for particulates. We then monetized these physical improvements using recent studies on the valuation of premature mortality, morbidity, soiling, and visibility.[1] While we have made what we feel are the best estimates possible for marginal benefits and costs, the real value of the analysis lies in the comparisons between the IB and CAC approaches. Such comparisons are more important and more legitimate than inferences about the actual levels of benefits and costs.

To summarize, given a hypothetical change in the TSP standard for Baltimore, the cost model is used to determine how that change will be accomplished technologically under both the CAC and IB approaches. The model not only determines the pattern of controls, emissions reductions, and associated costs under each regime, but also produces a vector of ambient TSP levels at each of the 23 receptors. By comparing this vector with the preexisting one, we can determine the change in air quality at each receptor. Using the mortality, morbidity, soiling, and visibility

---

[1] We will provide upon request a detailed description of the methods used to calculate the benefit functions. Briefly, the mortality and morbidity benefit estimates are based on cross-section and time-series epidemiological studies of the effects of particulate matter on health coupled with valuations of $2 million per life "saved," $100 per lost work day, and $25 for each restricted activity day. Soiling and visibility benefits are estimated in an analogous way.

"dose-response" functions, we translate the physical changes in air quality into welfare improvements and, simultaneously, value them to arrive at estimates of marginal benefits. That is the process behind the empirical results presented below.

III. The Findings

We report in Table 1 and depict in Figures 1 and 2 our basic results. As we move from left to right along the horizontal axes in the figures, we encounter successively more stringent *standards* as indicated by lower permissible maximum concentrations of TSP. Consider, for example, a TSP standard of $100 \mu g/m^3$ under the IB case. We see from Table 1 that the marginal control costs of moving from a standard of $105 \mu g/m^3$ to the more stringent standard of $100 \mu g/m^3$ are $1.82 million, while the associated marginal benefits are $8.53 million. These values appear in Figure 1 as points on the MC and MB curves at a TSP standard of 100.[2]

A cursory examination of the table and the accompanying figures suggests, first, that were we to select an "optimum" standard

under each system by equating marginal benefits and costs, the IB approach would give us a more stringent standard than the CAC regime. From Table 1, we see that the "optimum" standard under the IB case is 90 $\mu g/m^3$, while for the CAC case this standard is only 100 $\mu g/m^3$.[3] This result appears to confirm a point that environmental economists have long argued: the adoption of less costly control techniques should make it possible to attain higher levels of environmental quality.

This inference, however, is misleading. The source of the confusion is the natural inclination to associate air quality *standards* with air quality *levels*. But as we have seen, these are not the same thing. We cannot emphasize this distinction enough: an air quality standard maps into a vector of pollutant concentrations and the mapping itself depends, as we have seen, upon the regulatory regime. While it is true for our Baltimore case that the IB "optimum" would lead us to select the more stringent *standard* for air quality, it does not necessarily follow that this would actually result in better air quality throughout the area. Standards do not provide an unambiguous measure of air quality; they are ceilings on permissible levels of pollutant concentrations—most receptors will have concentrations well below the standard. *Thus, the same standard on the horizontal axis in our figures will produce a different vector of air quality under our two regulatory systems.*

To provide a better sense of these differences, we present in Table 2 estimated TSP concentrations for the various standards for a representative sample of our 23 Baltimore

[2] The marginal benefit and abatement cost curves are reasonably well behaved for the least-cost case in Figure 1. Marginal benefits remain roughly constant over most of the relevant range with some tendency to tail off after a standard of $85 \mu g/m^3$ is achieved. The relative constancy of marginal benefits results primarily from the fact that the dose-response functions that we use (based on EPA documents) are linear over the range of air quality standards that we consider. The occasional "ups and downs" in the MB curve reflect the differing degree to which individual receptors are controlled as we move to successively more stringent standards.

Marginal abatement costs remain low and well below marginal benefits for less stringent standards, but begin to rise rapidly after a standard of $90 \mu g/m^3$ is reached. The functions are not so well behaved for the CAC case in Figure 2. In particular, the marginal cost curve exhibits a large "hump" around a standard of $90 \mu g/m^3$. This hump has its source partly in our rule for regulatory behavior. It turns out that to go from a standard of $95 \mu g/m^3$ to $90 \mu g/m^3$ requires the adoption of some additional and rather costly control measures by a large number of sources; our CAC rule necessitates that these measures be applied to a whole class of polluting sources (irrespective of location), resulting in a sharp increase in control costs.

[3] It is interesting that the "optimum" standard for Baltimore for the IB case is quite close to the EPA primary standard for TSP concentrations of about 85 $\mu g/m^3$. (With a standard deviation of roughly 1.5, the EPA primary standard of 75 $\mu g/m^3$ expressed as a geometric mean translates roughly into a standard of 85 $\mu g/m^3$ as an arithmetic mean). As we indicated earlier, we should not make too much of this, for there is considerable uncertainty surrounding the estimates we have used for the benefit and cost functions. What is of more interest is the comparison between the IB and CAC cases.

TABLE 1—MARGINAL CONTROL COSTS (MC) AND MARGINAL BENEFITS
(MB) UNDER THE INCENTIVE-BASED AND CAC SYSTEMS
(IN MILLIONS OF 1980 DOLLARS)

| Standard | Incentive-Based Case | | |
	MC	MB	(MB-MC)
115	1.36	7.25	5.89
110	1.90	12.94	11.04
105	2.63	9.09	6.46
100	1.82	8.53	6.71
95	4.60	13.22	8.62
90	8.66	15.14	6.48
85	20.98	16.37	−4.61
83	35.23	3.88	−31.35
Standard	Command & Control Case		
	MC	MB	(MB-MC)
115	0.50	2.18	1.68
110	2.45	10.52	8.07
105	3.32	9.69	6.37
100	9.14	11.48	2.34
95	15.06	7.51	−7.55
90	54.67	10.00	−44.67
85	16.00	6.49	−9.51
83	9.95	1.19	−8.76

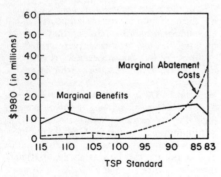

FIGURE 1. LEAST-COST CASE

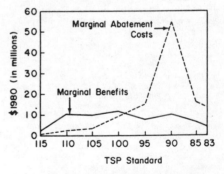

FIGURE 2. COMMAND AND CONTROL CASE

receptors under the IB and CAC regimes. Consider, for example, the TSP levels at receptor 1 under each system. We find that for receptor 1 the TSP level under CAC for a standard of 100 $\mu g/m^3$ is 61.4 $\mu g/m^3$; under the IB "optimum" of 90 $\mu g/m^3$, the TSP level at receptor 1 is 61.6 $\mu g/m^3$. For this particular receptor, then, the less stringent standard under CAC actually results in a higher level of air quality than does the more stringent standard under the least-cost outcome. This is not the case for all the receptors. For example, the binding receptors will obviously have higher TSP concentrations where the standard is less stringent (compare, for example, the TSP levels at receptor 5). Table 2 also makes clear the wide variation in air quality among the various recep-

TABLE 2—TSP CONCENTRATION BY RECEPTOR

Receptor	120	115	110	105	100	95	90	85	83
				Incentive-Based Case					
1.	67.8	67.4	66.2	66.0	65.3	63.7	61.6	59.3	58.6
2.	64.6	63.7	62.2	61.8	60.9	58.7	55.5	51.7	50.9
3.	56.2	56.0	55.5	55.5	55.3	54.6	53.7	52.5	52.2
4.	116.3	113.8	107.8	104.3	100.0	95.5	90.0	85.0	84.0[a]
5.	119.7	115.3	110.4	105.5	100.0	95.2	89.5	84.7	83.5
6.	52.4	51.6	49.1	47.5	46.0	43.4	40.9	38.2	37.6
7.	120.0	114.9	110.4	101.0	99.6	93.0	79.5	53.3	45.4
8.	105.3	102.8	98.9	97.7	95.1	90.4	83.8	74.1	70.1
				Command & Control Case					
1.	65.1	65.0	64.0	62.9	61.4	60.6	59.3	58.4	58.3
2.	60.7	60.4	58.9	57.2	54.9	53.6	52.0	50.7	50.5
3.	54.5	54.4	54.1	53.8	53.2	52.9	52.5	52.1	52.1
4.	109.9	108.7	103.1	99.5	95.2	92.0	87.8	85.0	84.0[a]
5.	120.8	115.5	109.8	104.7	99.6	95.0	89.3	84.2	83.4
6.	45.8	45.5	44.0	42.7	41.0	39.9	38.5	37.6	37.4
7.	106.0	105.8	102.9	94.7	71.9	64.9	58.1	43.9	42.7
8.	97.0	96.5	92.8	88.8	82.5	78.1	73.9	69.8	69.2
			Population-Weighted Averages of Receptor TSP Levels						
IB	77.4	75.7	72.9	70.9	69.0	66.2	62.9	59.3	58.5
CAC	71.1	60.6	68.3	66.2	63.7	62.0	59.9	58.5	58.2

[a]Although the standard is 83 $\mu g/m^3$, there are no controls in the model capable of reducing air pollution at this receptor.

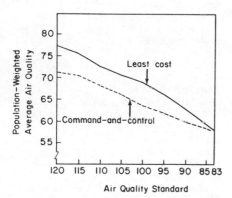

FIGURE 3. POPULATION-WEIGHTED AVERAGE AIR QUALITY UNDER THE LEAST COST AND COMMAND AND CONTROL SYSTEMS

tors; the TSP concentrations at receptors 1, 2, 3, and 6, for example, are far below the standard—in some instances the concentrations are less than one-half of the standard.

In the bottom rows of the table and in Figure 3, we present a summary measure of air quality: a population-weighted average of TSP levels at all 23 receptor points. A comparison of these weighted averages for the "optima" under the two systems reveals that the IB outcome yields a weighted average TSP level of 62.9 $\mu g/m^3$ as compared to the weighted average of 63.7 $\mu g/m^3$ under CAC. Thus, average air quality is only very slightly (probably negligibly) higher under the IB "optimum" than under the CAC "optimum." This is in sharp contrast to the large difference under the two systems in the "optimal" *standard*.

Our first result then is that although the IB regime results in a more stringent "optimal" standard, there is really little difference in overall air quality under the "optima" of our two systems.

The second issue concerns the *total net benefits* of pollution control under the two systems. This calculation is more problematic. The data in Table 1 only allow us to compute the *marginal* net benefits for successively tighter air quality standards beginning with a standard of 120 $\mu g/m^3$. Ideally, we should compare the net benefits of going

TABLE 3—A COMPARISON OF THE CUMULATIVE NET BENEFITS
UNDER THE TWO SYSTEMS (MILLIONS OF 1980 DOLLARS)

1. *Incentive-Based Case: Net Benefits from Moving from a Standard of 120 $\mu g/m^3$ to the "Optimal" Standard of 90 $\mu g/m^3$*

	Cumulative MB	$66.17
	Cumulative MC	20.97
	Cumulative Net Benefits	$45.20

2. *Command & Control Case: Net Benefits from Moving from a Standard of 120 $\mu g/m^3$ to the "Optimal" Standard of 100 $\mu g/m^3$*

	Cumulative MB	$33.86
	Cumulative MC	15.41
	Cumulative Net Benefits	$18.45

3. *Adjustment of Net Benefits Under the CAC System*

Cumulative Net Benefits Under CAC	$18.45
Less: Baseline Control Costs in Excess of IB Case	7.81
Plus: Baseline Benefits in Excess of IB Case	28.67
Adjusted Cumulative Net Benefits	$39.31

from a baseline of the totally uncontrolled level of emissions to the optimal standard under each system. (The uncontrolled outcome involves very high levels of TSP concentrations of around 500 $\mu g/m^3$).

We feel that the benefit functions cannot legitimately be extended to value changes in air quality over such extreme levels of TSP concentrations. Consequently, we chose as a baseline the vector of air quality that results from a standard of 120 $\mu g/m^3$. For the IB system, when we sum the differences between the MB and MC curves from this baseline to the "optimal" level of 90 $\mu g/m^3$, we find that the net benefits (from our arbitrary baseline) are roughly $45 million.

Two adjustments must be made to calculate a comparable net benefit estimate for the CAC regime. Recall that, for any given standard (including our baseline), the resulting vector of air quality under the CAC outcome indicates cleaner air than under the IB result. Therefore, we cannot sum the differences between the MB and MC curves from 120 $\mu g/m^3$ to the "optimal" standard of 100 $\mu g/m^3$ and compare this estimate to the IB net benefit calculation. The two calculations have different starting points.

To make the CAC "starting point" comparable to that under the IB system, we must

make both a cost and a benefit adjustment. Turning first to the cost adjustment, we find that to go from the uncontrolled level of about 500 $\mu g/m^3$ to our baseline of 120 $\mu g/m^3$, it costs an estimated $7.81 million more under the CAC approach than under the IB system. So for purposes of comparison, we must add to the cumulative costs of the CAC system this additional sum of $7.81 million.

Second, we must make a benefit adjustment. Although we do not attempt to measure the benefits from moving from the uncontrolled state to the baseline for reasons discussed earlier, we must account for the cleaner air (and correspondingly higher benefits) that the CAC outcome provides at the baseline standard. Our benefit functions yield an estimate of $28.67 million for the value of the differentially higher level of air quality produced by the CAC relative to the IB outcome at our baseline standard of 120 $\mu g/m^3$. After making these two adjustments so that the CAC starting point is equivalent to that under the IB regime, we find that the *net* benefits of the CAC scheme are roughly $39 million.

Table 3 summarizes these net benefit calculations including the adjustments needed to permit comparisons between the IB and

CAC outcomes. It is important to interpret these numbers properly. We emphasize that they do *not* provide estimates of the cumulative net benefits under each system; in fact, they greatly underestimate these net benefits because they omit any valuation of the benefits provided by the improvement in air quality from the uncontrolled state to the baseline. And these benefits are no doubt very large. We omit them because (as mentioned earlier) we are not comfortable using our benefit functions to value changes over such extreme levels of pollution. But these benefit figures have been omitted from the estimates for both systems so that cumulative benefits are understated by the same sum for the IB and CAC cases. The figures can thus be used legitimately to compare the net benefits under the two systems.

When we do this, we find that the difference between the cumulative net benefits under the two systems is quite small. As Table 3 shows, the cumulative net benefits under the IB outcome exceed those under the CAC case by only about $6 million when evaluated at their respective "optima."

It is interesting to contrast this comparison with one in which no consideration is given to the differentials in benefits under the two systems. Suppose, for example, that we were to choose a standard of 100 μg/m^3 and were simply to compare the costs under the two systems of achieving that standard (under the implicit and mistaken assumption that air quality is the same in both cases). Our computations indicate that the attainment of this standard would cost $32.7 million under the IB system as compared to $48.1 million under the CAC regime. We would thus conclude that the CAC approach costs about half again as much to attain the same outcome. But, as we have seen, the outcomes are far from the same.[4]

Finally, we stress once again that while we believe that our findings provide a legitimate basis for comparison between our two prototypical systems, the absolute levels of benefits and costs associated with the various standards must not be taken very seriously. Some sensitivity analysis using upper and lower bounds for our benefits estimates suggests that the "optimal" standard under both systems is quite sensitive to our choice of benefits measures.

IV. Concluding Remarks

The theme of this paper is that IB policies designed to achieve prescribed regulatory standards at least cost may not be so obviously superior to CAC approaches as has been supposed. This will be the case when CAC policies are designed with at least one eye on cost savings—as they sometimes are —and when reductions below the level of the relevant environmental, workplace, or product standards result in beneficial effects. In these cases, the "overcontrol" that makes CAC policies more expensive also makes them more efficacious.

---

[4]Although there are considerable differences in the outcomes under our two systems over most of the range of alternative standards for air quality, the outcomes converge as air quality approaches relatively high levels. When we reach a TSP concentration of 83 μg/m^3, the highest of the standards indicated in our figures and tables, the outcomes under the IB and CAC systems are virtually the same (as is evident in the population-weighted air quality in Figure 3). This occurs because we have now reached the point at which virtually all sources are controlling their emissions to the maximum degree possible under existing control technologies. This manifests itself in the IB case by very rapidly increasing marginal control costs, which are the result of having to introduce control measures in suburban areas in an attempt to reduce pollutant concentrations at the binding receptors which are located in the center city.

These rapidly increasing marginal control costs under the least-cost system have an interesting implication for the design of a regulatory system for pollution control. Following Martin Weitzman's seminal paper (1974) on the choice between quantity and price instruments, our results suggest a strong preference for an effluent fee system over a system of marketable emission permits. In a setting of uncertainty regarding the true benefit and cost functions, a mistake in setting the environmental standard is likely to result in a more costly error when the marginal cost curve is steep relative to the marginal benefit curve in the relevant region. A look at Figure 1 indicates that this is indeed the case for our pollutant at the least-cost outcome. This suggests that the environmental authority should employ the fee approach where errors are likely to be less costly.

One problem with this conclusion, of course, is that neither approach results in the economically optimal outcome in the full sense. We have been careful to describe the standard for which marginal benefits equal marginal costs under either system as the "optimal" outcome, using quotation marks to emphasize that the standard is optimal only with respect to that system. But it is clear that there is an economically superior outcome, namely the Pareto-efficient solution.

One may legitimately ask why we do not reject both of the suboptimal regimes we examine in favor of the first-best outcome. After all, we would seem to have all the information needed to determine the first-best solution. Our response to this question is twofold. First, while it is admittedly an easy matter, in principle, to characterize the first-best outcome, calculating it is a more complicated matter. The characterization is straightforward: the first-order conditions for the economic optimum would have us determine an emissions vector such that *for each source* the marginal benefits from an additional unit of abatement equal marginal cost. This would involve a very complicated general-equilibrium calculation, one that could easily entail a multiplicity of local optima. Nevertheless, with sufficient ingenuity and patience, one might determine this outcome. This solution, incidentally, would typically involve assigning abatement techniques on a polluter-by-polluter basis. Alternatively, one might design some differentiated set of effluent fees to induce the requisite pattern of abatement behavior.

While this may be conceivable in principle, we find it very difficult to see how an environmental agency could implement such procedures. And this is our second, and more basic, point. As the spirit of this paper suggests, we have sought to consider those alternatives that appear feasible in an actual policy setting. The achievement of some selected standards for environmental quality either through a command-and-control approach or through a general incentive-based approach represent alternatives *with precedent* in the policy arena. While the former is certainly the more common, there are now programs (such as EPA's Controlled Trading Program) that make some use of economic incentives to attain the specified environmental standards.

In the choice between the two approaches, we have argued that the case in the literature has been biased in favor of IB measures. However, it is important to put this contention in the proper perspective. One reason that the CAC outcome fares so well in our analysis is that Baltimore air quality authorities employed a somewhat sophisticated and relatively cost-effective procedure for TSP control. Under a less enlightened regulatory regime, control costs could be much higher for equivalent air quality levels.[5]

This brings us to what we see as the basic implication of our findings. They suggest that a carefully designed and implemented CAC system may stack up reasonably well relative to a feasible IB counterpart. However, where CAC standards and implementation procedures are motivated primarily by political considerations (for example, the avoidance of plant closings or of unpopular increases in the cost of local power), CAC policies will get bad marks in comparison to the IB alternatives. Badly designed CAC measures, in short, will yield bad outcomes.

Where, in contrast, economic analysis plays a larger role in CAC standard setting and program design—as it did in Baltimore and does for certain programs at EPA—one may have to take a harder look at such

---

[5]As one referee pointed out, our results are also sensitive to the choice of pollutant. To take the extreme case, if there were "perfect mixing" such that an emission of the pollutant at any place contributed equally to pollutant concentrations at all receptor points, then air quality would everywhere be the same. The standard would be binding at all receptors, and there would be no overcontrol under the CAC system to provide differential benefits relative to the IB counterpart. However, where the effects of the pollutant become more highly localized, overcontrol at some receptors will tend to be more pronounced. Our sense is that the pollutant we have used in this study is somewhere to the middle of the "localization spectrum." While volatile organic compounds, for example, exhibit somewhat greater mixing propensities than TSP, many other pollutants including carbon monoxide, "air toxics" (like lead and various chemicals), and certain workplace agents have far more localized effects than TSP.

approaches. Efforts by economists to make CAC measures more effective may, for particular programs, produce outcomes that compare quite well with IB alternatives. Particularly when we take into account real-world regulatory institutions that require uniformity of fees (or in other ways reduce the flexibility needed to achieve the full advantages of the IB approach), incentive-based programs may not clearly dominate well-designed CAC measures.[6]

---

[6]We should also note that the argument in this paper relates solely to the *static* efficiency properties of the alternative approaches. Over the longer haul, it is of great importance that we have a system that embodies the appropriate incentives for research and development of new abatement technologies. IB approaches, as economists have long argued, have compelling advantages over typical CAC regimes on this count. Even here, however, there is some scope for designing CAC programs in a way that encourages, rather than impedes, R&D efforts.

REFERENCES

Atkinson, Scott and Tietenberg, T. H., "The Empirical Properties of Two Classes of Designs for Transferable Discharge Permit Markets," *Journal of Environmental Economics and Management*, June 1982, *9*, 101–21.

McGartland, Albert M., "The Cost Structure of the Total Suspended Particulate Emission Reduction Credit Market," *Baltimore Region Emission Report, Vol. V.*, Regional Planning Council, Baltimore, MD, 1983.

_____, *Marketable Permit Systems for Air Pollution Control: An Empirical Study*, unpublished doctoral dissertation, University of Maryland, College Park, 1984.

Schultze, Charles L., *The Public Use of Private Interest*, Washington: The Brookings Institution, 1977.

Weitzman, Martin L., "Prices vs. Quantities," *Review of Economic Studies*, October 1974, *41*, 477–91.

PART III

TAXES AND FEES FOR ENVIRONMENTAL MANAGEMENT

[8]

THE USE OF STANDARDS AND PRICES FOR PROTECTION OF THE ENVIRONMENT

*William J. Baumol and Wallace E. Oates**

Princeton University, Princeton, N.J., USA

Summary

In the Pigouvian tradition, economists have frequently proposed the adoption of a system of unit taxes (or subsidies) to control externalities, where the tax on a particular activity is equal to the marginal social damage it generates. In practice, however, such an approach has rarely proved feasible because of our inability to measure marginal social damage.

This paper proposes that we establish a set of admittedly somewhat arbitrary standards of environmental quality (e.g., the dissolved oxygen content of a waterway will be above x per cent at least 99 per cent of the time) and then impose a set of charges on waste emissions sufficient to attain these standards. While such *resource-use prices* clearly will not in general produce a Pareto-efficient allocation of resources, it is shown that they nevertheless do possess some important optimality properties and other practical advantages. In particular, it is proved that, for any given vector of final outputs such prices can achieve a specified reduction in pollution levels at minimum cost to the economy, even in the presence of firms with objectives other than that of simple profit maximization.

In the technicalities of the theoretical discussion of the tax-subsidy approach to the regulation of externalities, one of the issues most critical for its application tends to get the short end of the discussion. Virtually every author points out that we do not know how to calculate the ideal Pigouvian tax or subsidy levels in practice, but because the point is rather obvious rarely is much made of it.

This paper reviews the nature of the difficulties and then proposes a substitute approach to the externalities problem. This alternative, which we shall call the environmental pricing and standards procedure, represents what we consider to be as close an approximation as one can generally achieve in practice to the spirit of the Pigouvian tradition. Moreover, while this method does not aspire to anything like an optimal allocation of resources, it will be shown to possess some important optimality properties.

---

* The authors are members of the faculty at Princeton University. They are grateful to the Ford Foundation whose support greatly facilitated the completion of this paper.

Swed. J. of Economics 1971

1. Difficulties in Determining the Optimal Structure of Taxes and Subsidies

The proper level of the Pigouvian tax (subsidy) upon the activities of the generator of an externality is equal to the marginal net damage (benefit) produced by that activity.[1] The difficulty is that it is usually not easy to obtain a reasonable estimate of the money value of this marginal damage. Kneese & Bower report some extremely promising work constituting a first step toward the estimation of the damage caused by pollution of waterways including even some quantitative evaluation of the loss in recreational benefits. However, it is hard to be sanguine about the availability in the foreseeable future of a comprehensive body of statistics reporting the marginal net damage of the various externality-generating activities in the economy. The number of activities involved and the number of persons affected by them are so great that on this score alone the task assumes Herculean proportions. Add to this the intangible nature of many of the most important consequences—the damage to health, the aesthetic costs—and the difficulty of determining a money equivalent for marginal net damage becomes even more apparent.

This, however, is not the end of the story. The optimal tax level on an externality generating activity is not equal to the marginal net damage it generates *initially*, but rather to the damage it would cause if the level of the activity had been adjusted to its *optimal* level. To make the point more specifically, suppose that each additional unit of output of a factory now causes 50 cents worth of damage, but that after the installation of the appropriate smoke-control devices and other optimal adjustments, the marginal social damage would be reduced to 20 cents. Then a little thought will confirm what the appropriate mathematics show: the correct value of the Pigouvian tax is 20 cents per unit of output, that is, the marginal cost of the smoke damage *corresponding to an optimal situation*. A tax of 50 cents per unit of output corresponding to the current smoke damage cost would lead to an excessive reduction in the smoke-producing activity, a reduction beyond the range over which the marginal benefit of decreasing smoke emission exceeds its marginal cost.

The relevance of this point for our present discussion is that it compounds enormously the difficulty of determining the optimal tax and benefit levels. If there is little hope of estimating the damage that is currently generated, how much less likely it is that we can evaluate the damage that would occur in an optimal world which we have never experienced or even described in quantitative terms.

There is an alternative possibility. Instead of trying to go directly to the optimal tax policy, one could instead, as a first approximation, base a set of

---

[1] We will use the term marginal *net* damage to mean the difference between marginal social and private damage (or cost).

taxes and subsidies on the current net damage (benefit) levels. Then as outputs and damage levels were modified in response to the present level of taxes, the taxes themselves would in turn be readjusted to correspond to the new damage levels. It can be hoped that this will constitute a convergent, iterative process with tax levels affecting outputs and damages, these in turn leading to modifications in taxes, and so on. It is not clear, however, even in theory, whether this sequence will in fact converge toward the optimal taxes and resource allocation patterns. An extension of the argument underlying some of Coase's illustrations can be used to show that convergence cannot always be expected. But even if the iterative process were stable and were in principle capable of yielding an optimal result, its practicality is clearly limited. The notion that tax and subsidy rates can be readjusted quickly and easily on the basis of a fairly esoteric marginal net damage calculation does not seem very plausible. The difficulty of these calculations has already been suggested, and it is not easy to look forward with equanimity to their periodic revision, as an iterative process would require.

In sum, the basic trouble with the Pigouvian cure for the externalities problem does not lie primarily in the technicalities that have been raised against it in the theoretical literature but in the fact that we do not know how to determine the dosages that it calls for. Though there may be some special cases in which one will be able to form reasonable estimates of the social damages, in general we simply do not know how to set the required levels of taxes and subsidies.

2. The Environmental Pricing and Standards Approach

The economist's predilection for the use of the price mechanism makes him reluctant to give up the Pigouvian solution without a struggle. The inefficiencies of a system of direct controls, including the high real enforcement costs that generally accompany it, have been discussed often enough; they require no repetition here.

There is a fairly obvious way, however, in which one can avoid recourse to direct controls and retain the use of the price system as a means to control externalities. Simply speaking, it involves the selection of a set of somewhat arbitrary standards for an acceptable environment. On the basis of evidence concerning the effects of unclean air on health or of polluted water on fish life, one may, for example, decide that the sulfur-dioxide content of the atmosphere in the city should not exceed x percent, or that the oxygen demand of the foreign matter contained in a waterway should not exceed level y, or that the decibel (noise) level in residential neighborhoods should not exceed z at least 99 % of the time. These acceptability standards, x, y and z, then amount to a set of constraints that society places on its activities. They represent the decision-maker's subjective evaluation of the minimum standards that must be met in order to achieve what may be described in persuasive terms as "a reasonable quality of life". The defects of the concept will immediately be clear to the reader, and, since we do not want to minimize them, we shall examine this problem explicitly in a later section of the paper.

For the moment, however, we want to emphasize the role of the price system in the implementation of these standards. The point here is simply that the public authority can levy a uniform set of taxes which would in effect constitute a set of prices for the private use of social resources such as air and water. The taxes (or prices) would be selected so as to achieve specific acceptability standards rather than attempting to base them on the unknown value of marginal net damages. Thus, one might tax all installations emitting wastes into a river at a rate of $t(b)$ cents per gallon, where the tax rate, t, paid by a particular polluter, would, for example, depend on b, the BOD value of the effluent, according to some fixed schedule.[1] Each polluter would then be given a financial incentive to reduce the amount of effluent he discharges and to improve the quality of the discharge (i.e., reduce its BOD value). By setting the tax rates sufficiently high, the community would presumably be able to achieve whatever level of purification of the river it desired. It might even be able to eliminate at least some types of industrial pollution altogether.[2]

Here, if necessary, the information needed for iterative adjustments in tax rates would be easy to obtain: if the initial taxes did not reduce the pollution of the river sufficiently to satisfy the preset acceptability standards, one would simply raise the tax rates. Experience would soon permit the authorities to estimate the tax levels appropriate for the achievement of a target reduction in pollution.

One might even be able to extend such adjustments beyond the setting of the tax rates to the determination of the acceptability standards themselves. If, for example, attainment of the initial targets were to prove unexpectedly inexpensive, the community might well wish to consider making the standards stricter.[3] Of course, such an iterative process is not costless. It means that at least some of the polluting firms and municipalities will have to adapt their

---

[1] BOD, biochemical oxygen demand, is a measure of the organic waste load of an emission. It measures the amount of oxygen used during decomposition of the waste materials. BOD is used widely as an index of the quality of effluents. However, it is only an approximation at best. Discharges whose BOD value is low may nevertheless be considered serious pollutants because they contain inorganic chemical poisons whose oxygen requirement is nil because the poisons do not decompose. See Kneese and Bower on this matter.

[2] Here it is appropriate to recall the words of Chief Justice Marshall, when he wrote that "The power to tax involves the power to destroy" (McCulloch vs. Maryland, 1819). In terms of reversing the process of environmental decay, we can see, however, that the power to tax can also be the power to restore.

[3] In this way the pricing and standards approach might be adapted to approximate the Pigouvian ideal. If the standards were revised upward whenever there was reason to believe that the marginal benefits exceeded the marginal costs, and if these judgments were reasonably accurate, the two would arrive at the same end product, at least if the optimal solution were unique.

operations as tax rates are readjusted. At the very least they should be warned in advance of the likelihood of such changes so that they can build flexibility into their plant design, something which is not costless (See Hart). But, at any rate, it is clear that, through the adjustment of tax rates, the public authority can realize whatever standards of environmental quality it has selected.

3. Optimality Properties of the Pricing and Standards Technique

While the pricing and standards procedure will not, in general, lead to Pareto-efficient levels of the relevant activities, it is nevertheless true that the use of unit taxes (or subsidies) to achieve the specified quality standards does possess one important optimality property: it is the least-cost method to realize these targets.[1] A simple example may serve to clarify this point. Suppose that it is decided in some metropolitan area that the sulfur-dioxide content of the atmosphere should be reduced by 50 %. An obvious approach to this matter, and the one that often recommends itself to the regulator, is to require each smoke-producer in the area to reduce his emissions of sulfur dioxide by the same 50 %. However, a moment's thought suggests that this may constitute a very expensive way to achieve the desired result. If, at existing levels of output, the marginal cost of reducing sulfur-dioxide emissions for Factory A is only one-tenth of the marginal cost for Factory B, we would expect that it would be much cheaper for the economy as a whole to assign A a much greater decrease in smoke emissions than B. Just how the least-cost set of relative quotas could be arrived at in practice by the regulator is not clear, since this obviously would require calculations involving simultaneous relationships and extensive information on each polluter's marginal-cost function.

It is easy to see, however, that the unit-tax approach can *automatically* produce the least-cost assignment of smoke-reduction quotas without the need for any complicated calculations by the enforcement authority. In terms of our preceding example, suppose that the public authority placed a unit tax on smoke emissions and raised the level of the tax until sulfur-dioxide emissions were in fact reduced by 50 %. In response to a tax on its smoke emissions, a cost-minimizing firm will cut back on such emissions until the marginal cost of further reductions in smoke output is equal to the tax. But, since all economic units in the area are subject to the same tax, it follows that the marginal cost of reducing smoke output will be equalized across all activities. This implies that it is impossible to reduce the aggregate cost of the specified decrease in smoke emissions by re-arranging smoke-reduction quotas: any alteration in this pattern of smoke emissions would involve an increase in

---

[1] This proposition is not new. While we have been unable to find an explicit statement of this result anywhere in the literature, it or a very similar proposition has been suggested in a number of places. See, for example, Kneese & Bower, Chapter 6, and Ruff, p. 79.

smoke output by one firm the value of which to the firm would be less than the cost of the corresponding reduction in smoke emissions by some other firm. For the interested reader, a formal proof of this least-cost property of unit taxes for the realization of a specified target level of environmental quality is provided in an appendix to this paper. We might point out that the validity of this least-cost theorem does not require the assumption that firms are profit-maximizers. All that is necessary is that they minimize costs for whatever output levels they should select, as would be done, for example, by a firm that seeks to maximize its growth or its sales.

The cost saving that can be achieved through the use of taxes and subsidies in the attainment of acceptability standards may by no means be negligible. In one case for which comparable cost figures have been calculated, Kneese & Bower (p. 162) report that, with a system of uniform unit taxes, the cost of achieving a specified level of water quality would have been only about half as high as that resulting from a system of direct controls. If these figures are at all representative, then the potential waste of resources in the choice between tax measures and direct controls may obviously be of a large order. Unit taxes thus appear to represent a very attractive method for the realization of specified standards of environmental quality. Not only do they require relatively little in the way of detailed information on the cost structures of different industries, but they lead automatically to the least-cost pattern of modification of externality-generating activities.

4. Where the Pricing and Standards Approach is Appropriate

As we have emphasized, the most disturbing aspect of the pricing and standards procedure is the somewhat arbitrary character of the criteria selected. There does presumably exist some optimal level of pollution (i.e., quality of the air or a waterway), but in the absence of a pricing mechanism to indicate the value of the damages generated by polluting activities, one knows no way to determine accurately the set of taxes necessary to induce the optimal activity levels.

While this difficulty certainly should not be minimized, it is important at the outset to recognize that the problem is by no means unique to the selection of acceptability standards. In fact, as is well known, it is a difficulty common to the provision of nearly all public goods. In general, the market will not generate appropriate levels of outputs where market prices fail to reflect the social damages (or benefits) associated with particular activities. As a result, in the absence of the proper set of signals from the market, it is typically necessary to utilize a political process (i.e., a method of collective choice) to determine the level of the activity.[1] From this perspective, the selec-

---

[1] As Coase and others have argued, voluntary bargains struck among the interested parties may in some instances yield an efficient set of activity levels in the presence of externalities. However, such coordinated, voluntary action is typically possible only in small groups. One can hardly imagine, for example, a voluntary bargaining process involving all the persons in a metropolitan area and resulting in a set of payments that would generate efficient levels of activities affecting the smog content of the atmosphere.

48   *W. J. Baumol and W. E. Oates*

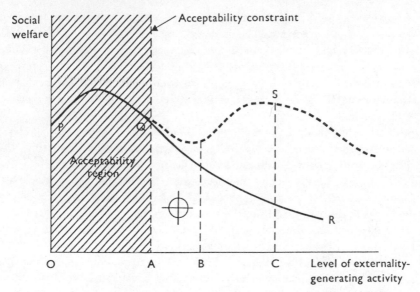

Fig. 1

tion of environmental standards can be viewed as a particular device utilized in a process of collective decision-making to determine the appropriate level of an activity involving external effects.

Since methods of collective choice, such as simple-majority rule or decisions by an elected representative, can at best be expected to provide only very rough approximations to optimal results, the general problem becomes one of deciding whether or not the malfunction of the market in a certain case is sufficiently serious to warrant public intervention. In particular, it would seem to us that such a blunt instrument as acceptability standards should be used only sparingly, because the very ignorance that serves as the rationale for the adoption of such standards implies that we can hardly be sure of their consequences.

In general, it would seem that intervention in the form of acceptability standards can be utilized with any degree of confidence only where there is clear reason to believe that the existing situation imposes a high level of social costs *and* that these costs can be significantly reduced by feasible decreases in the levels of certain externality-generating activities. If, for example, we were to examine the functional relationship between the level of social welfare and the levels of particular activities which impose marginal net damages, the argument would be that the use of acceptability standards is justified only in those cases where the curve, over the bulk of the relevant range, is both decreasing and steep. Such a case is illustrated in Fig. 1 by the curve *PQR*. In a case of this kind, although we obviously will not have an accurate knowledge of the relevant position of the curve, we can at least have some assurance that the selection of an acceptability standard and the imposition of a unit tax sufficient to realize that standard will lead to an increase in social welfare. For example, in terms of the curve PQR in Fig. 1, the levying of a tax sufficient to reduce smoke outputs from level OC to OA to ensure that the quality of the air meets the specified environmental standards would obviously increase social welfare.[1]

On the other hand, if the relationship between social welfare and the level of the externality-generating activity is not monotonically decreasing, the changes resulting from the imposition of an acceptability standard (e.g., a move from S to Q in Fig. 1) clearly may lead to a reduction in welfare. Moreover, even if the function were monotonic but fairly flat, the benefits achieved might not be worth the cost of additional intervention machinery that new legislation requires, and it would almost certainly not be worth the risk of acting with highly imperfect, inconclusive information.

In some cases, notably in the field of public utility regulation, some economists have criticized the employment of acceptability standards on both these grounds; they have asserted that the social costs of monopolistic misallocation of resources are probably not very high (i.e., the relevant portion of the social-welfare curve in Fig. 1 is not steep) and that the regulation can itself introduce inefficiencies in the operations of the regulated industries.

Advocacy of environmental pricing and standards procedures for the control of externalities must therefore rest on the belief that in this area we do have a clear notion of the general shape of the social welfare curve. This will presumably hold true where the evidence indicates, first that a particular externality really does have a substantial and unambiguous effect on the quality of life, if, for example, it makes existence very unpleasant for everyone or constitutes a serious hazard to health; and second that reductions in the levels of these activities do not themselves entail huge resource costs. On the first point, there

---

[1] The relationship depicted in Fig. 1 is to be regarded as an intuitive device employed for pedagogical purposes, not in any sense as a rigorous analysis. However, some further explanation may be helpful. The curve itself is not a social-welfare function in the usual sense; rather it measures in terms of a numeraire (kronor or dollars) the value, summed over all individuals, of the benefits from the output of the activity minus the private *and* net social costs. Thus, for each level of the activity, the height of the curve indicates the *net* benefits (possibly negative) that the activity confers on society. The acceptability constraint indicates that level of the activity which is consistent with the specified minimum standard of environmental quality (e.g., that level of smoke emissions from factories which is sufficiently low to maintain the quality of the air in a particular metropolitan area). There is an ambiguity here in that the levels of several different activities may jointly determine a particular dimension of environmental quality, e.g., the smoke emissions of a number of different industries will determine the quality of the air. In this case, the acceptable level of pollutive emissions for the firm or industry will clearly depend on the levels of emissions of others. If, as we discussed earlier, unit taxes are used to realize the acceptability standards, there will result a least-cost pattern of levels of the relevant externality-generating activities. If we understand the constraint in Fig. 1 to refer to the activity level indicated by this particular solution, then this ambiguity disappears.

is growing evidence that various types of pollutants do in fact have such un-fortunate consequences, particularly in areas where they are highly concen-trated. [On this see, for instance, Lave & Seskin]. Second, what experience we have had with, for example, the reduction of waste discharges into water-ways suggests that processes involving the recycling and reuse of waste mate-rials can frequently be achieved at surprisingly modest cost.[1] In such cases the rationale for the imposition of environmental standards is clear, and it seems to us that the rejection of such crude measures on the grounds that they will probably violate the requirements of optimality may well be considered a kind of perverse perfectionism.

It is interesting in this connection that the pricing and standards approach is not too different in spirit from a number of economic policy measures that are already in operation in other areas. This is significant for our discussion, because it suggests that regulators know how to work with this sort of approach and have managed to live with it elsewhere. Probably the most noteworthy example is the use of fiscal and monetary policy for the realization of macro-economic objectives. Here, the regulation of the stock of money and the availability of credit along with adjustments in public expenditures and tax rates are often aimed at the achievement of a selected target level of employ-ment or rate of inflation. Wherever prices rise too rapidly or unemployment exceeds an "acceptable" level, monetary and fiscal variables are readjusted in an attempt to "correct" the difficulty. It is noteworthy that this procedure is also similar to the pricing and standards approach in its avoidance of direct controls.

Other examples of this general approach to policy are not hard to find. Policies for the regulation of public-utilities, for instance, typically utilize a variety of standards such as profit-rate ceilings (i.e., "fair rates of return") to judge the acceptability of the behavior of the regulated firm. In the area of public education, one frequently encounters state-imposed standards (e.g., subjects to be taught) for local school districts which are often accompanied by grants of funds to the localities to help insure that public-school programs meet the designated standards. What this suggests is that public administrators are familiar with this general approach to policy and that the implementation of the pricing and standards technique should not involve insurmountable administrative difficulties. For these reasons, the achievement of specified environmental standards through the use of unit taxes (or subsidies) seems to us to possess great promise as a workable method for the control of the quality of the environment.

---

[1] Some interesting discussions of the feasibility of the control of waste emissions into waterways often at low cost are contained in Kneese & Bower. In particular, see their description of the control of water quality in the Ruhr River in Germany.

5. Concluding Remarks

It may be useful in concluding our discussion simply to review the ways in which the pricing and standards approach differs from the standard Pigouvian-prescription for the control of externalities.

(1) Under the Pigouvian technique, unit taxes (or subsidies) are placed on externality-generating activities, with the level of the tax on a particular activity being set equal to the marginal net damage it generates. Such taxes (if they could be determined) would, it is presumed, lead to Pareto-efficient levels of the activities.

(2) In contrast, the pricing and standards approach begins with a predetermined set of standards for environmental quality and then imposes unit taxes (or subsidies) sufficient to achieve these standards. This will not, in general, result in an optimal allocation of resources, but (as is proved formally in the appendix) the procedure does at least represent the least-cost method of realizing the specified standards.

(3) The basic appeal of the pricing and standards approach relative to the Pigouvian prescription lies in its workability. We simply do not, in general, have the information needed to determine the appropriate set of Pigouvian taxes and subsidies. Such information is not, however, necessary for our suggested procedure.

(4) While it makes no pretense of promising anything like an optimal allocation of resources, the pricing and standards technique can, in cases where external effects impose high costs (or benefits), at least offer some assurance of reducing the level of these damages. Moreover, the administrative procedures—the selection of standards and the use of fiscal incentives to realize these standards—implied by this approach are in many ways quite similar to those used in a number of current public programs. This, we think, offers some grounds for optimism as to the practicality of the pricing and standards technique for the control of the quality of the environment.

References

1. Bohm, P.: Pollution, Purification, and the Theory of External Effects. *Swedish Journal of Economics 72*, no. 2, 153–66, 1970.
2. Coase, R.: The Problem of Social Cost. *Journal of Law and Economics 3*, 1–44, 1960.
3. Hart, A.: Anticipations, Business Planning, and the Cycle. *Quarterly Journal of Economics 51*, 273–97, Feb. 1937.
4. Kneese, A. & Bower, B.: *Managing Water Quality: Economics, Technology, In-*stitutions. Baltimore, 1968.
5. Lave, L. & Seskin, E.: Air Pollution and Human Health. *Science 21*, 723–33 Aug. 1970.
6. Portes, R.: The Search for Efficiency in the Precence of Externalities. *Unfashionable Economics: Essays in Honor of Lord Balogh* (ed. P. Streeten), pp. 348–61. London, 1970.
7. Ruff. L.: The Economic Common Sense of Pollution. *The Public Interest*, Spring 1970, 69–85.

APPENDIX

In the text, we argued on a somewhat intuitive level that the appropriate use of unit taxes and subsidies represents the least-cost method of achieving a set of specified standards for environmental quality. In the case of smoke-abatement, for instance, the tax-subsidy approach will automatically generate the cost-minimizing assignment of "reduction quotas" without recourse to involved calculations or enforcement.

The purpose of this appendix is to provide a formal proof of this proposition. More precisely, we will show that, to achieve *any* given vector of final outputs along with the attainment of the specified quality of the environment, the use of unit taxes (or, where appropriate, subsidies) to induce the necessary modification in the market-determined pattern of output will permit the realization of the specified output vector at minimum cost to society.

While this theorem may seem rather obvious (as the intuitive discussion in the text suggests), its proof does point up several interesting properties which are noteworthy. In particular, unlike many of the propositions about prices in welfare analysis, the theorem does not require a world of perfect competition. It applies to pure competitors, monopolists, or oligopolists alike so long as each of the firms involved seeks to minimize the private cost of producing whatever vector of outputs it selects and has no monopsony power (i.e., no influence on the prices of inputs). The firms need not be simple profit-maximizers; they may choose to maximize growth, sales (total revenues), their share of the market, or any combination of these goals (or a variety of other objectives). Since the effective pursuit of these goals typically entails minimizing the cost of whatever outputs are produced, the theorem is still applicable. Finally, we want simply to emphasize that the theorem applies to whatever set of final outputs society should select (either by direction or through the operation of the market). It does not judge the desirability of that particular vector of outputs; it only tells us how to make the necessary adjustments at minimum cost.

We shall proceed initially to derive the first-order conditions for the minimization of the cost of a specified overall reduction in the emission of wastes. We will then show that the independent decisions of cost-minimizing firms subject to the appropriate unit tax on waste emissions will, in fact, satisfy the first-order conditions for overall cost minimization.

Let

x_{iv} represent the quantity of input i used by plant v $(i=1, ..., n)$, $(v=1, ..., m)$,
z_v be the quantities of waste it discharges,
y_v be its output level,
$f_v(x_{1v}, ..., x_{nv}, z_v, y_v) = 0$ be its production function,
p_i be the price of input i, and
k the desired level of $\sum z_v$, the maximum permitted daily discharge of waste.

In this formulation, the value of k is determined by the administrative authority in a manner designed to hold waste emissions in the aggregate to a level consistent with the specified environmental standard (e.g., the sulphuric content of the atmosphere). Note that the level of the firm's waste emissions is treated here as an argument in its production function; to reduce waste discharges while maintaining its level of output, the firm will presumably require the use of additional units of some other inputs (e.g., more labor or capital to recycle the wastes or to dispose of them in an alternative manner).

The problem now becomes that of determining the value of the x's and z's that minimize input cost

$$c = \sum_i \sum_v p_i(x_{iv})$$

subject to the output constraints

$$y_v = y_v^* = \text{constant} \qquad (v = 1, ..., m)$$

and the constraint on the total output of pollutants

$$\sum_v z_v = k.$$

It may appear odd to include as a constraint a vector of given outputs of the firms, since the firms will presumably adjust output levels as well as the pattern of inputs in response to taxes or other restrictions on waste discharges. This vector, however, can be *any* vector of outputs (including that which emerges as a result of independent decisions by the firms). What we determine are first-order conditions for cost-minimization which apply to *any* given vector of outputs no matter how they are arrived at. Using $\lambda_v(v = 1, ..., m)$ and λ as our $(m+1)$ Lagrange multipliers, we obtain the first-order conditions:

$$\left.\begin{array}{ll} \lambda_v f_{vz} + \lambda = 0 & (v = 1, ..., m) \\ p_i + \lambda_v f_{vi} = 0 & (v = 1, ..., m)\,(i = 1, ..., n) \\ y_v = y_v^* & (v = 1, ..., m) \end{array}\right\} \qquad (1)$$

where we use the notation $f_{vz} = \partial f_v / \partial z_v$, $f_{vi} = \partial f_v / \partial x_{iv}$.

Now let us see what will happen if the m plants are run by independent managements whose objective is to minimize the cost of whatever outputs their firm produces, and if, instead of the imposition of a fixed ceiling on the emission of pollutants, this emission is taxed at a fixed rate per unit, t. So long as its input prices are fixed, firm v will wish to minimize

$$c = tz_v + \sum_i p_i x_{iv}$$

subject to

$$y_v = y_v^*.$$

54   *W. J. Baumol and W. E. Oates*

Direct differentiation of the m Lagrangian functions for our m firms immediately yields the first-order conditions (1)—the same conditions as before, provided t is set equal to λ. Thus, if we impose a tax rate that achieves the desired reduction in the total emission of pollutants, we have proved that this reduction will satisfy the necessary conditions for the minimization of the program's cost to society.[1]

------

[1] In this case, λ (and hence t) is the shadow price of the pollution constraint. In addition to satisfying these necessary first-order conditions, cost-minimization requires that the production functions possess the usual second-order properties. An interesting treatment of this issue is available in Portes. We should also point out that our proof assumes that the firm takes t as given and beyond its control. Bohm discusses some of the problems that can arise where the firm takes into account the effects of its behavior on the value of t.

JOURNAL OF ENVIRONMENTAL ECONOMICS AND MANAGEMENT 5, 283–291 (1978)

The Use of Effluent Fees to Regulate Public Sector Sources of Pollution

An Application of the Niskanen Model

WALLACE E. OATES

Department of Economics, Princeton University, Princeton, New Jersey 08540

AND

DIANA L. STRASSMANN [1]

Department of Economics, Harvard University, Cambridge, Massachusetts

Received September 9, 1977; revised February 8, 1978

The economics literature on environmental policy makes a compelling case for the use of effluent fees to control polluting activities. This analysis, however, proceeds from the assumption of profit maximizing behavior by polluters. Since (non-profit-maximizing) public agencies are a major source of environmental damage, this paper investigates the likely response of bureaucrats to effluent fees in terms of some extended versions of the Niskanen model of bureaucratic behavior. We find that, at least for a range of plausible cases, such fees can induce significant reduction in polluting activities. The results are sufficiently encouraging to make the extension of fees to public agencies worthy of serious consideration.

Economists have long argued the case for a heavy reliance on pricing incentives for protection of the environment. By requiring polluters to pay for the costs they impose on society, effluent fees can induce individuals and firms to undertake socially desirable abatement activities. Moreover, such a system of fees possesses some compelling advantages over alterative means of controlling pollution. Baumol and Oates [4], for example, have shown that, whatever the standard of environmental quality the public authority selects, effluent charges can realize that standard at the least cost to society. But even aside from such claims for optimality, the economist prefers altering the structure of prices to make pollution abatement activities directly profitable to the individual rather than adopting and trying to enforce a system of regulations that polluters will try to circumvent.[2]

This approach, however, is based on the premise of profit maximizing (or, at least, cost minimizing) behavior on the part of polluters. But even a cursory study of the sources of environmental damage indicates that agencies in the

---

[1] We are grateful to William Baumol, Lee Erickson, Roger Gordon, and Harvey Rosen for helpful comments on an earlier draft. Financial support to do this research was provided from a grant to the Princeton University Economics Department from the Sloan Foundation.

[2] A survey of the evidence suggests that fees (to the limited extent they have been employed) have been extremely effective in curtailing waste emissions and other forms of polluting activities. For such a survey, see Baumol and Oates [2].

public sector are a major contributor to the problem. Waste emissions generated in the government sector range from sewage dumped into our rivers by municipal waste-treatment plants and sulfur released into the atmosphere by publicly operated power plants to the disposal of dangerous by-products of the modern weapons systems employed by the Department of Defense. Since profit maximization is presumably not the primary objective of public agencies, the question arises as to whether it makes any sense to apply effluent charges to public sector sources of pollution. Must we not abandon the fee approach and seek to regulate them by direct controls?

The evidence we have been able to assemble on public sector sources of pollution indicates that this is a most troublesome matter on two distinct counts. First, the quantity of waste emissions emanating from government agencies is very large. The 1975 National Residual Discharge Inventory conducted by the National Academy of Sciences reports that municipal discharges into U.S. waterways in 1973 amounted to 5.6 billion pounds of BOD (biochemical oxygen demand) and 5.9 billion pounds of TSS (total suspended solids); these discharges accounted for approximately 57% of BOD and 5% of TSS discharges from point sources in the United States for that year [6, p. 257]. Public transportation systems, though less noxious per head than the automobile, constitute another significant source of pollution from state and local facilities. Federal public installations also release huge quantities of effluents into the nation's waterways and atmosphere. One study found that in 1968 "the U.S. Department of Defense alone discharged more than 335 million gallons of human waste each day . . . over 25 to 30% of which was given less than secondary treatment" [14, p. 340]. Another federal agency, the Tennessee Valley Authority (TVA), is the nation's number one sulfur dioxide polluter; its coal fired power generating plants emit over 2 million tons of sulfur oxides yearly, which make up 38% of the total sulfur emissions in the whole of the Southeast and 16% of all such emissions in the United States [9].

Second, in addition to being major sources of pollution, public agencies (somewhat paradoxically) have proved extremely difficult to regulate. Environmental authorities have, in numerous instances, had considerably more success in curtailing emissions from private sources than those from government facilities. The TVA is a prime example. Despite pressures and legal suits from environmentalists, "TVA has demonstrated massive resistance to compliance, being only 16% in compliance with the law, as against 74% compliance by all utilities nationally" [9, p. 20]. The problem is that federal agencies (TVA among them) have claimed that they are exempt from state environmental regulation, and various Supreme Court decisions have provided some support for this position.[3] Likewise, local environmental agencies have encountered obstacles in regulating the activities of other local public units. In New York City, for example, when the Department of Air Pollution Control attempted to upgrade incinerators in apartment buildings under "Local Law 14," the New York Public Housing Authority, in May 1969, refused to comply (for lack of available funds).

[3] For example, in *Hancock v. Train* and *EPA v. California* the U.S. Supreme Court held that, although states may define the "substantive" pollution requirements applicable to federal installations, the states may not legally enforce pollution standards on federal facilities through "procedural" requirements. The enforcement of such requirements, the Court decided, rests with the EPA. This decision constitutes a serious obstacle to the development of state permit systems to regulate levels of effluents. On all this, see Watson [13].

EFFLUENT FEES AND PUBLIC SECTOR POLLUTION   285

The public sector is thus itself both a major source of pollution and one which has proven surprisingly resistant to its own regulatory activities.[4] Could the extension of effluent fees to public agencies prove more effective than direct controls in inducing pollution abatement efforts? This paper seeks to provide some insights into this issue by using some of the recent models of bureaucratic behavior to predict the likely response of bureaucrats to a system of effluent fees. In Section I of the paper, we use the original, simple version of the Niskanen model [11] to obtain a predicted response. The results in this case are ambiguous: under one set of circumstances, effluent fees induce reductions in levels of waste emissions, while in a second case, this need not be true.

In Section II, we develop a somewhat more realistic variant of the Niskanen model (which incorporates some of the criticism of the original model and Niskanen's own subsequent revision); here we find that we can predict unambiguously a reduction in the bureau's effluents. Somewhat more surprising (at least in terms of our initial expectations when we began work on the problem), we have found that we can extend the Baumol–Oates cost minimization theorem [4] to a system composed both of cost minimizing firms and public agencies. We will argue that, in an economy in which pollution emanates from both firms and public bureaus, effluent fees on waste emissions lead (at least theoretically) to the least-cost solution for the attainment of any specified standard of environmental quality. We conclude in Section III with some observations on the robustness of this result in the light of actual budgetary procedures. While there are some important reservations, we believe that the results are sufficiently encouraging to make the extension of effluent fees to public agencies worthy of serious consideration.

I

The original Niskanen model [11] is founded on two basic premises. The first is that the objective of the bureaucrat is simply to maximize the size of his budget.[5] And the second is that the bureau exchanges a specified level of output for a budget that equals the total value of this output to the public. The implication of this second assumption is that the bureau is effectively a perfectly discriminating monopolist: for whatever level of output it provides, the bureau appropriates all the consumers' surplus.

From these two postulates, Niskanen deduces a series of propositions concerning bureaucratic behavior. The first is that bureaus will always provide excessive levels of output. This is easily seen diagrammatically. In Fig. 1, let DD' represent the (income compensated) demand for the bureau's output, while MC_1 is the marginal cost of providing that output. In this case, the bureau will extend output to OD'; it will extract the entire area under the demand curve as

---

[4] The experience, incidentally, in centrally planned economies is not entirely dissimilar to that in the United States. The Soviet Union, for example, has encountered great difficulty in inducing (state-owned) industrial enterprises to reduce environmental abuse. On this, see Goldman's excellent book [8].

[5] This is not meant to imply that bureaucrats maximize "profits" or even salaries. Rather, Niskanen intends the size of the bureau's budget to serve as a proxy variable for the prestige, power, perquisites, etc., of the bureau. These latter elements are the true arguments in the bureaucrat's objective function; budget maximization is simply a manifestation of these other variables.

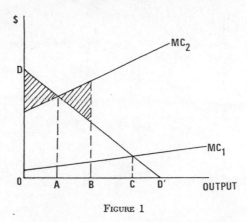

FIGURE 1

its budget. This obviously exceeds the socially optimal output of OC where marginal valuation equals marginal cost.

A second property of this outcome is noteworthy. With a marginal cost function of MC_1 (which represents the *minimum* cost of providing an additional unit of output), the bureau's budget (the area ODD') exceeds the total minimum cost of providing output OD' (i.e., the area under MC_1 out to OD'). This indicates the presence of "fat" in the bureau's budget; not only does the bureau produce an excessive output, but it does so inefficiently. The bureaucrat is thus in a position to hire a larger staff, pay higher salaries, or perhaps obtain more office perquisites than are required to provide the actual level of output. The bureau in this case is said to be demand constrained.

Suppose, however, that the bureau's cost function is MC_2. In this case, the cost of providing output OD' exceeds the budget that the bureaucrat can obtain. The highest level of output for which costs can be covered is OB. The bureaucrat effectively trades the excess of valuation over cost of earlier units (the shaded triangle to the left) for losses on units above OA (the shaded triangle to the right) until the budget attains the maximum level at which the bureau can still cover its costs of production. In this case, the bureau is said to be budget constrained. In contrast to the demand constrained case, the bureaucrat is, in this instance, a cost minimizer; the budget constrained bureau produces at minimum cost in order to reach the largest possible output and budget.

With this as background, consider the response of a Niskanen bureaucrat to an effluent charge. Suppose that the production activities of the bureau involve a negative externality (e.g., its plants spew smoke into the atmosphere) and that a unit fee is imposed upon such spillover costs.

If the bureau is budget constrained, the outcome is unambiguous: the bureaucrat will reduce the level of output and pollution. We see in Fig. 2 that the fee shifts the bureau's marginal cost curve from MC_2 to MC_3, and this induces a fall in the bureau's output from OB to OC. If, however, there exists a less polluting technology such that abatement costs are less than the effluent charge (illustrated in Fig. 2 by MC_4), the bureaucrat will shift to the alternative technology, for the savings in the bill for effluents will permit an expansion in output from OC to OE. Since the budget constrained bureaucrat is a cost minimizer, the

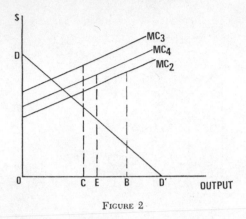

FIGURE 2

bureau can save on fees by adopting less polluting methods of production (as would a cost minimizing firm).

The response of the demand constrained bureaucrat to an effluent fee is less clear. The Niskanen model implies that the bureau will simply absorb the fees with some of its "fat." [6] If this is the case, an effluent fee will be unable to induce a demand constrained bureaucrat to reduce waste emissions. If, however, we relax Niskanen's implicit assumption that bureaucrats treat all costs equally, then bureaucrats may have some incentives to economize on fees (lost dollars, in effect) so as to put the fat to uses that provide some measure of additional utility. This is a theme to which we will return in Section II. But at this juncture, we note that the logic of the simple Niskanen model does not permit an unambiguous prediction regarding the impact of effluent charges on pollution abatement activities of demand constrained bureaucrats.

II

Critics of the original Niskanen model have questioned both of its fundamental postulates. Thompson [12] and Breton and Wintrobe [5] have argued that the bureaucrat's position in the process of budget determination is not so powerful as that of a perfectly discriminating monopolist. Rather they liken the situation to one of bilateral monopoly between the bureau and the legislature. This line of criticism does not, however, bear directly on the proposition that we will establish here so we merely note it in passing.

More to the point is the issue of the bureaucrat's objective function. Migué and Bélanger [10] show that utility maximization by bureaucrats need not imply budget maximization. If, as Niskanen claims, bureaucrats derive utility from such things as salary, perquisites of the office, power, ease of managing the agency, etc., then the use of budget size as the single variable in the objective function overlooks the fact that an increased budget comes at the expense of some of those variables. The budget constrained bureau, for example, will trade any fat in its budget for extra units of output, even if marginal cost exceeds marginal valuation of the output. This prediction, moreover, does not appear to square with the

---

[6] This assumes that the fees are not sufficiently high to push the bureau from a demand constrained to a budget constrained situation.

facts: as Thompson points out, inefficiency in bureaus is a widely observed phenomenon and frequently occurs where the marginal value of output is obviously not zero.

The evidence suggests that bureaus face a trade-off between budget size and the fat in the budget. Migué and Bélanger, who refer to this "fat" as the bureau's "discretionary budget," argue that bureaus actually maximize a utility function which contains as arguments both output and the size of the discretionary budget.[7]

In the spirit of the Migué and Bélanger formulation, we will employ a utility function that includes both the bureau's output (Q) and the level of perquisites (P):[8]

$$U = U(Q, P). \tag{1}$$

Perquisites here are intended to include the whole range of "extras" (higher salaries, additional facilities, expanded staff, and perhaps reduced effort) derived from the fat in the bureau's budget. Suppose, for simplicity, that the bureau has a production function with two inputs, labor (L) and waste emissions (E):

$$Q = Q(L, E). \tag{2}$$

Consequently, if output is held at some fixed level, then emissions can only be reduced if more labor is employed (e.g., additional workers to recycle wastes).[9] We finally assume that the bureau operates subject to a budget constraint:

$$B = wL + fE + cP, \tag{3}$$

where B is the bureau's budget, w is the competitive wage rate (a given to the bureau), f is the effluent charge per unit of waste emissions, and c is the cost of a "unit" of perquisites.

The bureaucrat (or, perhaps, a committee of bureaucrats) seeks to maximize the utility function (1) subject to the constraints implicit in (2) and (3). However, there is a bit more to the problem: the budget determination process. This can complicate matters. We shall assume initially that, through some type of budgetary (or bargaining) process, the bureau strikes an agreement with the legislature which specifies the services (output) it will provide and the funds it will receive. This implies that, at least over the short run, Q and B are fixed in the budgetary process at some specified levels: Q_0 and B_0.

With Q_0 a predetermined variable, the bureaucrat's maximization problem is simplified to that of maximizing perquisites (P) subject to the production and budget constraints. To solve this decision problem, form the Lagrangian:

$$M = P + \lambda_1[Q_0 - Q(L,E)] + \lambda_2[B_0 - wL - fE - cP], \tag{4}$$

where λ_1 and λ_2 are the Lagrangian multipliers. Taking the requisite partial

---

[7] This is not dissimilar to some formulations of the objective function of the private firm. Baumol [1], for example, has contended that the firm's objectives include increased sales as well as profits.

[8] For the use of an alternative objective function with arguments representing productive efficiency and staff size, and an analysis of the pursuit of these objectives under alternative programs to curtail polluting activities, see Dole [7].

[9] We assume that the utility and production functions are continuous, twice differentiable, and satisfy the usual second-order conditions.

derivatives and solving for the first-order condition yield a familiar result:

$$MP_E/MP_L = f/w. \tag{5}$$

Utility maximizing bureaucrats satisfy the same first-order condition as a cost-minimizing firm: they use a combination of factor inputs such that the ratio of the marginal products is equal to the ratio of factor prices.

This result for the bureau must be interpreted with some care, for we know that, with fat in the budget, the bureau is not providing its output at the least cost to society. However, in an important sense the bureaucrat is a "cost minimizer." It may be helpful to conceptualize the decision process as follows. Once the budget and output have been determined by the legislature, the bureaucrat seeks to maximize his perquisites by finding the least-cost method of producing Q_0. This first step of determining the least-cost technique for providing Q_0 is embodied in Eq. (5).

After satisfying this condition, the bureaucrat then uses the excess budget for extras such as higher-than-competitive salaries, an expanded staff, improved facilities, etc. Note that wL in the budget constraint is not necessarily the bureau's wage bill: it is the wages that must be paid for the cost minimizing method of output. To get the actual wage bill, we must add any extra staff or excessive salaries that are classified here as perquisites.

What is important here for our purposes is that *the bureaucrat is a cost minimizer with respect to pollution abatement activities.* In order to maximize perquisites, the bureaucrat will reduce waste emissions to the point where the (rising) marginal cost of pollution abatement equals the effluent fee. The point is really a rather obvious one: effluent charges represent a drain on the budget which provides no perquisites in return. The bureaucrat thus wants to reduce these payments as long as the marginal cost of doing so is less than the fee.

The utility maximizing bureaucrat behaves precisely as does the cost minimizing firm with respect to pollution abatement. Thus, it is clear that we can extend the cost minimization theorem to a world composed both of bureaus and of firms, for the theorem depends only on the condition that all polluters are cost minimizers as regards the reduction of waste emissions. In particular, we assert the following proposition: *In an economy consisting of cost minimizing firms and utility maximizing bureaus, the selection of the appropriate unit tax on waste emissions applicable both to firms and bureaus will lead to the achievement of the designated standard of environmental quality (necessary reduction in aggregate waste emissions) at the least cost to society.*[10] Since the formal proof of the theorem is essentially the same as that which appears in Baumol and Oates [3, pp. 140–144], it is unnecessary to reiterate it here.[11]

III

The notion that the cost minimizing properties of effluent fees apply to a world in which polluters include public agencies as well as private firms may strike

[10] This theorem is subject to some further qualifications concerning, for example, differential damages from pollution emanating from different locations. On this see Baumol and Oates [3, Chap. 10].

[11] All that is needed is to consider some of the m plants in the formulation to be public bureaus; the assumption of cost minimization (to maximize profits for the firm or perquisites in the case of the bureau) assures the validity of the theorem.

some as a tenuous and rather suspect proposition. Is this notion in fact consistent with what we know of actual processes of budget determination? In our formalization of the problem, we assumed that the bureau first negotiated its budget and output with the legislature and then took both its budget and output as given in determining the composition of inputs (including perquisites).

However, if we relax this assumption, we could envision a short-run response in which, after the imposition of the effluent fee, the bureau went back to the legislature for a budgetary supplement to cover its new tax bill. Conceivably, the bureau could maintain its existing level of waste emissions and simply meet the effluent charges from this addition to its budget. While such a response is certainly conceivable, there are reasons to question its general applicability. First, if the bureau had already appropriated the entire consumer surplus (à la Niskanen), then the bureau is (by definition) already getting the largest possible budget for its specified level of services, and the legislature will simply refuse to grant the supplement.[12] If the bureau were able to obtain a larger budget by claiming higher costs, then the Niskanen bureaucrat should already have exploited this opportunity.

Nevertheless, suppose that the legislature does agree to the budgetary supplement. The bureaucrat may still have an incentive to shift to a less polluting technique of production. Particularly if the legislature has little knowledge of the bureau's options and only loose budget controls, then the bureau may still be able to increase perquisites by a cost minimizing strategy for pollution abatement.

A second issue is somewhat more troublesome. Our conceptualization of the bureaucrat's decision procedure involved the minimization of pollution abatement costs (including fees) in order to maximize perquisites. If, however, an important perquisite is "ease of management" resulting in laxity in production controls, then our conceptual distinction between decisions on pollution control activities and those on perquisites may be suspect. In particular, the bureaucrat may use some of the fat in the budget to avoid the effort and possible complications associated with introducing new techniques to reduce waste emissions. The importance of this qualification to our theorem is hard to determine. In many instances, the cost minimizing response to changes in the relative prices of inputs is quite apparent and relatively easy. A tax, for example, on the sulfur content of fuels may make it quite obviously cheaper for a power generating plant to cease using low-grade, high-sulfur coal. Utilities are, in fact, quite responsive to changes in the relative prices of fuels in terms of substituting one fuel for another. Where, however, the cost minimizing response involves the identification of sophisticated abatement techniques and the introduction of major modifications in production processes, the bureaucrat may be somewhat more lax than his or her counterpart in the private sector.[13]

---

[12] One minor qualification is that, if the legislature is also the recipient of the effluent fees, it might not view the supplement as a *net* increase in the bureau's budget.

[13] A reviewer has pointed out quite correctly that a more general caveat is in order. In particular, in light of the above qualification to the theorem, we cannot conclude with certainty that an effluent fee is a more efficient method to achieve a designated standard of environmental quality than a regulatory technique in an economy with bureaucratic waste. It is conceivable, for example, that a regulatory policy *could* induce bureaucrats to assign more "fat" to pollution abatement than an effluent fee. Our sense of the implications of the analysis is not that they establish the superiority of fees beyond doubt, but rather that the findings are sufficiently encouraging to warrant serious consideration of the application of fees to public agencies.

On balance, it seems to us that we can probably expect effluent charges to provide a powerful inducement to reduce pollution in public sector agencies, as well as among private firms. At any rate, it seems well worth at least some limited experimentation, for our experience with direct controls has surely left much to be desired.[14]

REFERENCES

1. W. Baumol, "Business Behavior, Value and Growth," rev. ed., Harcourt Brace and World, New York, 1967.
2. W. Baumol and W. Oates, "Economics, Environmental Policy, and the Quality of Life," Prentice-Hall, Englewood Cliffs, N.J., 1978.
3. W. Baumol and W. Oates, "The Theory of Environmental Policy," Prentice–Hall, Englewood Cliffs, N.J., 1975.
4. W. Baumol and W. Oates, The use of standards and prices for protection of the environment, *Swedish J. Econ.* 73, 42–54 (1971).
5. A. Breton and R. Wintrobe, The equilibrium size of a budget-maximizing bureau, *J. Political Econ.* 83, 195–207 (1975).
6. Council on Environmental Quality, "Environmental Quality, The Seventh Annual Report of the Council on Environmental Quality," U.S.G.P.O., Washington, D.C. (1976).
7. M. Dole, "An Economic Theory of Bureaucracy," Ph.D. Dissertation, University of California, Los Angeles, 1974.
8. M. Goldman, "The Spoils of Progress: Environmental Pollution in the Soviet Union," MIT Press, Cambridge, Mass. (1972).
9. W. King, T. V. A., a major polluter, faces suit to cut sulfur dioxide fumes, *New York Times* 76, 1, 20 (July 4, 1977).
10. J. Migué and G. Bélanger, Toward a general theory of managerial discretion, *Public Choice* 17, 27–43 (1974).
11. W. Niskanen, "Bureaucracy and Representative Government," Aldine–Atherton, Chicago, 1971.
12. E. Thompson, Book Review, *J. Econ. Lit.* 11, 950–953 (1973).
13. R. Watson, State control of federal pollution: Taking the stick away from the states, *Ecology Law Quarterly* 6, 429–454 (1977).
14. D. Zwick and M. Benstock, "Water Wasteland," Grossman, New York, 1971.

[14] Lee Erickson has suggested to us that, since public utilities are a major source of waste emissions in the United States, it would be useful to employ some of the models of the regulated firm to study the likely response to alternative policies to curtail waste emissions. This we hope to do in a subsequent paper.

[10]

Journal of Public Economics 24 (1984), 29–46. North-Holland

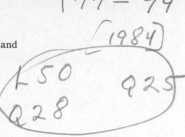

EFFLUENT FEES AND MARKET STRUCTURE

Wallace E. OATES

Bureau of Business and Economic Research, University of Maryland, College Park, MD 20742, USA

Diana L. STRASSMANN*

Rice University, Houston, TX 77001, USA

Received May 1982, revised version received May 1983

This paper explores the efficiency properties of a system of effluent fees in a mixed economy in which polluting agents take a variety of organizational forms: private monopoly, the managerial firm, regulated firms, and public bureaus. The analysis, including some crude empirical estimates, suggests that the welfare gains from pollution control are likely to dwarf in magnitude the potential losses from the various imperfections in the economy. The tentative conclusion is that the case for a system of fees that is invariant with respect to organizational form is not seriously compromised by likely deviations from competitive behavior.

1. Introduction

The formal analysis of a Pigouvian tax on polluting activities typically proceeds in terms of perfectly competitive firms whose productive pursuits impose external costs on other agents in the economy. Moreover, the optimality properties of the Pigouvian measure depend upon this assumption of perfect competition. A cursory inspection of the real world, however, reveals that the major sources of pollution encompass a wide variety of institutional structure. The public sector, for example, is itself a major polluter [see Oates and Strassmann (1978)]. Municipal waste-treatment plants dump enormous quantities of wastes into our waterways, and publicly-owned power plants are heavy contributors to air pollution. The largest single sulfur polluter in the United States is the Tennessee Valley Authority (TVA), which accounts for 16 percent of sulfur emissions in the nation [see King (1977)]. In addition, private but publicly-regulated firms (including utilities that provide electrical power) are among the very largest of polluters. Finally, many of the large factories that emit massive quantities of wastes are owned and operated by huge firms in highly concentrated

*We are grateful for many helpful comments on earlier drafts of this paper to Peter Altroggen, William Baumol, Richard Caves, Robert Dorfman, Joseph Kalt, Margaret Lewis, Robert Mackay, Albert McGartland, Lee Preston, Eugene Seskin, Jeffery Smisek, and anonymous referees. We are also indebted for the support of parts of this work to the National Science Foundation and the Sloan Foundation.

0047-2727/84/$03.00 © 1984, Elsevier Science Publishers B.V. (North-Holland)

J.P.E.— B

industries like steel, chemicals, and automobile manufacturing. The application of the competitive model with its myriad of small firms acting as price-takers is thus suspect for many classes of polluters.

The economic analysis of market incentives for pollution control must, therefore, push beyond the simple competitive model. We must ask how polluters with widely varying sets of objectives are likely to respond to these incentives. In this paper, we seek to determine what some standard models of organizational behavior tell us about how decision-makers in different institutions would respond to the introduction of a set of effluent charges.[1] We then use these results to evaluate the implications of these responses for efficient resource allocation, taking explicit account of the distortions that market imperfections, bureaucratic behavior, and public regulation of private firms themselves introduce.

2. The problem of 'allocative efficiency'

2.1. The conceptual issue

We begin the analysis with the standard monopoly model under which a profit-maximizing firm has some discretion over the price it charges for its output. We assume that the firm has a production function of the form:

$$Q = Q(L, E), \tag{1}$$

where L (which we shall call 'labor') represents a vector of all inputs other than E, the firm's level of waste emissions. We thus treat the source of pollution, namely waste emissions, as a productive input from the perspective of the firm. If factor markets are perfectly competitive and if the environmental authority confronts the firm with a Pigouvian charge on its emissions equal to marginal social damage (MSD), it follows that the firm, in the process of minimizing its costs, will select what from society's point of view is the cost-minimizing combination of factor inputs for whatever level of output it chooses. In short, cost-minimizing behavior ensures 'technical efficiency' in the use of all inputs including the services of the environment. A corollary is that, for the case where units of emissions from all sources are equally damaging, a uniform effluent fee will lead cost-minimizing polluters to equate their marginal abatement costs and hence to achieve the desired level of environmental quality at the minimum aggregate abatement cost (our 'least-cost theorem').

---

[1]The analysis also has relevance for systems of marketable pollution permits. However, it would need to be extended to account for any imperfections in the permit market itself [Hahn (1981)]. The assumption here is that, under a system of effluent fees, individual polluters take the fee structure as given.

The problem in this case concerns allocative distortions in the pattern of final outputs. As Buchanan (1969) has pointed out, the monopolist's sub-optimal level of output is the source of a basic dilemma for the formulation of policy to regulate externalities. An effluent fee provides an incentive for needed pollution abatement, but, at the same time, raises the firm's marginal cost and thereby induces a reduction in output. The result is some gain in efficient resource allocation from reduced waste emissions, but some loss in efficiency from the contraction in output; the *net* effect on social welfare is uncertain. In short, an effluent fee (Pigouvian or otherwise) may represent too much of a good thing.

The analysis must, therefore, take explicit account of Buchanan's tradeoff between pollution abatement and monopolistic output restriction. Following Baumol and Oates (1975, ch. 6), we depict the nature of this tradeoff in fig. 1. Let DD' represent the industry demand curve confronting a monopolist, with DMR being the corresponding marginal-revenue curve. We assume that the monopoly can produce at constant cost (PMC=private marginal cost), but that its production activities impose costs on others. In particular, in the absence of any fees, the monopolist's (private) cost-minimizing technique of production generates pollution costs per unit equal to AB so that the SMC_0 (social marginal cost) curve indicates the true cost to society of each unit of output. To maximize profits, the monopolist would produce OQ_m.

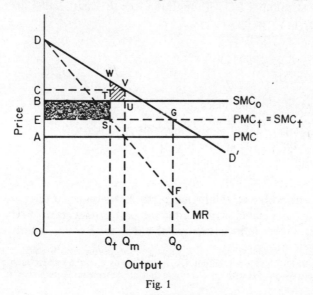

Fig. 1

Suppose next that we subject the monopolist to a pollution tax, a fee per unit of waste emissions. This will provide an incentive to alter the production process in a way that yields lower emissions per unit of output. In fig. 1 this would have two effects: it would raise the PMC curve and, over some range, would tend to lower SMC. This second effect results from the choice of what, from society's standpoint, is a lower-cost method of production (taking into account the costs of pollution). The minimum social cost of production will be reached when the pollution costs are wholly internalized so that $PMC_t = SMC_t$ (where the subscript t refers to costs in the presence of a Pigouvian tax). At this point, the firm's selection of a production process will be based upon a set of input prices (including a price of waste emissions) that reflects true social opportunity costs.

Since there exist two distinct sources of allocative distortions, a full resolution of the problem will, in general, require two policy actions: a Pigouvian tax on waste emissions equal to MSD *and* a subsidy per unit of output equal to GF (the difference between marginal cost and marginal revenue at the Pareto-efficient level of output). A typical environmental agency, however, will have neither the authority nor the inclination to offer subsidies to monopolists.

In this constrained setting, the problem of the environmental authority takes on a second-best character: the determination of the effluent fee which balances, at the margin, the social gain from increased abatement against the social loss from reduced output from the monopolist. Lee (1975), and more recently Barnett (1980), have derived formally the first-order conditions for this second-best optimal fee. Although the Lee–Barnett results take a slightly different form, they can be expressed as:

$$t_j = t^* - \frac{C_j}{|\eta_j|}, \tag{2}$$

where

t_j = optimal tax per unit of waste emissions for the jth polluter,
t^* = Pigouvian tax on the competitive firm,
C_j = marginal abatement cost, and
η_j = price elasticity of demand.

The second term on the RHS of eq. (2) reflects the marginal welfare loss from reduced output associated with a unit increase in the tax.[2] For a perfectly competitive firm, this term is zero so that $t_j = t^*$. But for a firm with some

---

[2]It is easy to see, incidentally, that in accord with intuition this term is equal to the marginal welfare loss per unit of reduced output (i.e. price minus marginal cost) multiplied by the reduction in output associated with an additional unit of abatement. More formally:

$$\frac{C_j}{|\eta_j|} = \frac{P_j}{|\eta_j|} \cdot \frac{\partial Q_j}{\partial a_j} = (P_j - MR_j)\frac{\partial Q_j}{\partial a_j} = (P_j - MC_j)\frac{\partial Q_j}{\partial a_j},$$

where a_j is the level of abatement activity and where profit maximization implies that $MR_j = MC_j$. The marginal cost of abatement, $P_j(\partial Q_j / \partial a_j)$ is expressed in terms of the value of forgone output.

control over market price, the optimal unit tax on emissions will vary inversely with marginal abatement cost and directly with the price elasticity of demand for the firm's output.

In principle, therefore, we can determine the optimal set of effluent fees on all polluters, be they competitive firms or monopolists. However, this is not, in fact, very comforting. First, such a determination would require an enormous amount of information encompassing both the price elasticities of demand *and* the abatement costs for each polluter. And second, even if the environmental authority were able to assemble all these data, it is difficult to envision a legal and political setting in which such a discriminatory set of fees would be acceptable.

At the policy level, the real choice may well be that between a single fee applicable both to perfect and imperfect competitors or the abandonment of a system of pricing incentives for environmental protection. From this perspective, the important issue is the *extent* of the welfare loss associated with the pattern of reductions in output induced by the charge on waste emissions. There is a substantial empirical literature suggesting that the magnitude of the overall allocative losses in the economy attributable to monopolistic distortions is quite small.[3] Since the large estimated welfare gains from pollution abatement would seem to dwarf the apparently small welfare losses from effects on the pattern of industry outputs, it is tempting simply to conclude that concern over monopolistic distortions represents, in this case, a theoretical nicety that we can safely ignore in the design of environmental policy.

This, however, will not quite do. The proper question is: *Given the existing pattern of monopolistic distortions* (i.e. existing divergences between price and marginal cost), do the *additional* reductions in monopoly outputs generate efficiency losses of a substantial magnitude?

2.2. A rough estimate

In order to get some feel for just how damaging the existence of monopolistic elements in the economy is to the case for an effluent fee that is invariant with respect to industry structure, we have undertaken some admittedly quite crude, partial-equilibrium calculations making use of a representative polluter.[4] Our procedure involves a comparison of two

---

[3]The seminal paper presenting this result is Harberger (1954). Several later studies support Harberger's general finding [e.g. Schwartzman (1960)]. However, for a dissenting view, see Cowling and Mueller (1978) who have criticized the earlier work on methodological grounds and have calculated their own estimates of allocative losses from monopoly for both the United States and the United Kingdom. Their estimates for these losses are much more sizable.

[4]The shortcoming of a partial-equilibrium approach is clear. A full, general-equilibrium treatment of the problem would take into account the interaction between markets; the outcome in this setting would depend not only on the magnitude of the initial distortion and the own price elasticity of demand, but also on cross elasticities.

equilibrium positions: the first involves no control over the externality (and hence no abatement), and the second is the outcome under a system of effluent fees where the fee does not vary with industry structure. In moving from the former to the latter, we compare the welfare gains from reduced pollution *net* of abatement costs to the *increment* of new allocative losses associated with monopoly elements in the existing market structure. We use existing environmental programs in the United States as a (rough) benchmark for overall abatement efforts.

Proceeding in terms of a 'representative polluter', we assume that the social marginal cost of production associated with each level of abatement activity is approximately constant over the relevant range. We can then approximate the welfare gain from reduced pollution net of abatement costs by:

$$W_g = Q[SMC_0 - SMC_t], \tag{3}$$

where SMC_0 and SMC_t are, respectively, social marginal cost before and after the introduction of a set of Pigouvian taxes. The welfare gain is simply the reduced cost (private plus external) per unit times the level of output (area $EBTS$ in fig. 1). Likewise, we can approximate the welfare loss from reduced output by:

$$W_l = \Delta Q(P - SMC_0). \tag{4}$$

Welfare loss is the loss per unit (equal to the difference between price and *social* marginal cost) times the change in output (an approximation to area $TWVU$ in fig. 1). To determine the relative sizes of these two effects, we divide (4) by (3) to obtain:

$$W_r = \frac{\Delta Q}{Q} \frac{[P - SMC_0]}{[SMC_0 - SMC_t]}. \tag{5}$$

It will facilitate the numerical comparisons to divide both numerator and denominator by P:

$$W_r = \frac{\Delta Q}{Q} \frac{[P - SMC_0]/P}{[SMC_0 - SMC_t]/P}. \tag{6}$$

The next step is to try to make some educated guesses as to the orders of magnitude of the various terms in eq. (6). To do this, we construct a profile of a representative polluter that incorporates reasonable estimates of the parameters. In each instance we lean in the direction of magnitudes that are favorable to the finding of a relatively large welfare loss associated with monopolistic distortions.

The first term in eq. (6) is the percentage change in quantity, which we can express as the percentage change in price times the price elasticity of demand (η). There are available for the United States fairly detailed data on abatement expenditures by sector, and we make use of a careful ongoing study by H. David Robison (1983) in which he uses these data and a large input–output model to estimate existing abatement costs per dollar of output for 78 sectors in the U.S. economy. Using 1977 data, Robison finds, for example, the following percentage increases in costs attributable to abatement expenditures: 2.0 for the paper industry, 2.1 for ferrous metals, 2.3 for copper, and 3.3 for electric utilities. He assumes that these costs are passed forward in terms of higher prices. Deriving a 'representative' increase in prices under a fee system from these estimates is problematic, since the effect of a set of fees on costs would differ in two important respects from the existing command-and-control system. First, as existing studies indicate, a fee system would tend to reduce abatement costs significantly through more cost-efficient patterns of abatement and technology, but, second, such savings in abatement costs must be balanced against the effluent fees that sources would have to pay. We take as a 'typical' increase in price for our representative polluter a figure of 5 percent, where we assume that this cost increase to our polluter (and the consequent rise in price) is constituted in equal parts of control costs (2.5 percent) and effluent fees (2.5 percent).[5] A best estimate for a representative price elasticity of demand is also uncertain, but for the major industries of concern, including power generation, chemicals, pulp and paper, etc., a typical value of two is probably a generous assumption. This gives us a value of $\Delta Q/Q$ for our representative polluter of:

$$\frac{\Delta Q}{Q} = |\eta| \frac{\Delta P}{P} = 2(0.05) = 0.1. \tag{7}$$

We thus assume a 10 percent reduction in output for our representative polluter attributable to the adoption of the fee program.

Turning next to the numerator of the second term in (6), we note that $[P - SMC_0]$ is equal to that portion of the difference between price and private marginal cost that is not offset by the marginal social damage of waste emissions; that is:

$$\frac{[P - SMC_0]}{P} = \frac{[P - (PMC + MSD)]}{P}, \tag{8}$$

where MSD is the marginal external cost associated with polluting emissions. Finding appropriate magnitudes for these variables is somewhat

[5]This distinction is important, because control costs represent actual social costs, while fee payments are, from the perspective of society, a transfer payment.

more conjectural. However, we can make a very rough guess by noting that existing estimates of the benefits from air pollution control in the United States are about twice the level of abatement costs; Lave and Seskin (1977, p. 230), for example, offer a conservative estimate of health benefits alone from meeting standards for ambient air quality of about \$16 billion as compared to EPA's estimate of \$9.5 billion for abatement costs.[6] If we double our representative estimate for abatement costs of 2.5 percent and add on another 2.5 percent for residual damages, we reach a figure of 7.5 percent of marginal cost for our estimate of marginal social damages in the absence of any control program.[7]

Next we need a figure for monopolistic markup over marginal cost. There exists an empirical literature that has estimated the relationship between price–cost margins and industry concentration [e.g. Shepard (1972)]; these studies find that the margin of price over cost rises by about one percentage point for every increase of ten percentage points in the four-firm industry concentration ratio (C_4). If we assume that 'competition' involves a C_4 of about 20 and that 'monopolistic' industries have a typical C_4 of 70, we would have a level of monopolistic prices that exceeds competitive prices by about 5 percent. Leaning in the direction of a more generous estimate, we take 10 percent as our representative monopolistic markup over private marginal cost. This leaves us with an estimate of 2.5 for the difference between price and social marginal cost as a percentage of price.[8]

The denominator of the second term in eq. (6) follows directly from the preceding profile of our representative polluter. The representative reduction in marginal social damages from the control program is 5 percent of price (since we assume benefits equal to twice the level of abatement costs); from this, we subtract 2.5 percent of price for abatement costs leaving us with a net reduction in social marginal cost of 2.5 percent of price.

Pulling together our results for the various terms in (6), we arrive at:

$$W_r = (0.1)\frac{0.025}{0.025} = 0.1. \tag{9}$$

[6]These figures admittedly refer to total, rather than marginal, benefits and costs. However, since we are considering the entire increment from the introduction of a program of effluent fees, we take them as a reasonable approximation.

[7]Our estimate thus implies that the fee program reduces the representative marginal damages from pollution by about two-thirds. This seems to us a relatively conservative figure, since abatement efforts have typically led sources to reduce emissions by well over 50 percent (in excess of 90 percent in several cases); such reductions in the presence of increasing marginal damages (the typical case) would suggest reductions in damages from pollution far in excess of one-half.

[8]Note that if the markup were only 5 percent, then social marginal cost for our representative polluter would actually exceed the monopoly price so that a contraction in output would raise, rather than lower, social welfare. Such may well be the case in some instances.

We thus estimate the monopolistic welfare loss from a program of effluent fees to be roughly an order of magnitude smaller than the welfare gain from reduced pollution (net of abatement costs). While this estimate obviously depends on our choice of values for the various parameters, we believe that the 'representative calculation' is relatively generous to the magnitude of the potential welfare loss from reduced monopoly outputs and that 'reasonable' parameter values are unlikely to suggest that this loss can rival in size the gains from improved environmental quality. In view of the range of policy options available to the environmental authority, our conclusion is that it is probably safe to ignore the issue of incremental output distortions associated with a system of effluent fees.

3. The problem of technical efficiency

In the preceding section, the assumption of simple profit-maximizing behavior with its corollary of cost minimization allowed us to ignore the issue of technical efficiency: faced with a Pigouvian fee, cost-minimizing agents will select the socially least-cost combination of inputs and will operate along their minimum cost curves. In this section of the paper we drop this assumption and explore the implications of technical inefficiencies for the efficacy of a system of effluent fees. We examine a series of models in which the failure to minimize costs comes from either of two sources: a more complex objective function that incorporates variables other than (or in addition to) the level of profits, or some type of regulatory constraint that provides the decision-maker with an incentive to choose something other than the cost-minimizing pattern of factor inputs.

3.1. Managerial models of maximizing firms

For our purposes, the Williamson (1963) model captures the spirit of the results that emerge when a firm's managers maximize an objective function that contains variables other than simply short-run profits. In particular, Williamson formulates a managerial utility function that incorporates 'expense preferences' for expenditures on staff (S), managerial emoluments (M) (extra salary and perquisites), and 'discretionary profits' consisting of the difference between actual profits and the minimum profits demanded. The firm thus maximizes:

$$U = U[S, M, \pi_R - \pi_0 - T] \quad \text{subject to} \quad \pi_R > \pi_0 + T \tag{10}$$

or

$$U = U\{S, M, (1-t)[R(X) - C(X) - S - M] - \pi_0\}, \tag{11}$$

where

$$R = \text{revenue} = P \cdot X; \; \partial^2 R/\partial X \partial S \geq 0,$$
$$P = \text{price} = P(X, S; \varepsilon); \; \partial P/\partial X < 0; \; \partial P/\partial S \geq 0; \; \partial P/\partial \varepsilon > 0,$$
$$X = \text{output},$$
$$S = \text{staff (in money terms) or (approximately) general}$$
$$\text{administrative and selling expense};$$
$$\varepsilon = \text{a demand shift parameter},$$
$$C = \text{costs of production} = C(X),$$
$$M = \text{managerial emoluments},$$
$$\pi = \text{actual profits} = R - C - S,$$
$$\pi_R = \text{reported profits} = \pi - M,$$
$$\pi_0 = \text{minimum (after-tax) profits demanded},$$
$$T = \text{taxes, where } t = \text{tax rate, and}$$
$$\pi_R - \pi_0 - T = \text{discretionary profits}.$$

To treat waste emissions and the effluent fee explicitly, we amend the Williamson model to distinguish between these emissions (E) and all other inputs (L). Eq. (11) thus becomes:

$$U = U\{S, M, (1-t)[R(g(L, E)) - P_l L - fE - S - M] - \pi_0\}, \tag{12}$$

where P_l is the price of other inputs and f denotes the effluent fee. Maximization of this utility function yields as one of the first-order conditions the familiar result:

$$\frac{P_l}{f} = \frac{\partial X/\partial L}{\partial X/\partial E}. \tag{13}$$

This is the usual condition for the cost-minimizing combination of factor inputs: marginal products proportional to factor prices. It may seem surprising at first glance to find that firms that are technically inefficient (i.e. do not produce at minimum cost *overall*) are effectively cost-minimizers with regard to pollution abatement. However, the rationale is quite straightforward: since abatement activities contribute nothing to staff or emoluments and reduce discretionary profits, the firm's managers have an incentive to minimize the expenditure on abatement (consisting of effluent fees plus pollution-control costs) by extending abatement activity to the point where marginal abatement cost equals the effluent fee. We can thus extend our cost-minimization theorem to encompass certain managerial models of maximizing firms: a world of such firms subject to an effluent fee can, in principle, achieve the desired standard of environmental quality at the minimum aggregate abatement cost.[9]

[9]As one potential qualification to this result, we note that abatement activities could, under certain circumstances, enter directly into the managerial utility function. The firm's managers might perceive, for example, that activities to curtail pollution produce some valuable 'good-will' for the firm. In such instances, the firm might well extend abatement activities beyond the point at which marginal abatement cost equals the effluent fee.

3.2. Organizational models of firm behavior

Organizational models of firm behavior treat managerial decisions in the context of the firm's internal structure and environment. Firm behavior in these models cannot be characterized by an explicit objective function. These models include both the Carnegie Tech type that emphasizes internal coalitions, information costs, limited time, and bounded rationality [e.g. Cohen and Cyert (1962)] and the Harvard Business School variety that focus on the internal dynamics and structure of the firm [e.g. Chandler (1962) and Bower (1970)]. Without probing in detail into these alternative views of managerial decision-making, we wish to note in passing that both of these approaches imply the possible presence of a degree of 'managerial slack'.

Such slack may well have some implications for the effectiveness of a system of effluent fees. In particular, the case for effluent fees rests on the presumption that an increase in the price of effluents will induce firms to use less effluents relative to other inputs; over the longer haul, fees will induce firms to engage in R&D that will allow them to develop cheaper abatement technologies. However, the incentives to change production policies quickly in response to relative price changes may be quite weak in a managerial context. Changes in production methods (particularly to less pollution-intensive methods) may involve major changes in equipment. If an important perquisite is 'ease of management', the firm might conceivably employ some of the fat in its budget to avoid the effort and possible complications associated with the adoption and development of new abatement techniques. There are, in fact, some investigations of the diffusion of knowledge and new technologies that have found that firms in concentrated industries do not respond as quickly to price changes and the availability of new innovations as do firms in more competitive industries [see Kamien and Schwartz (1975)]. The evidence on this issue, however, is not conclusive; yet the lack of consensus certainly provides some justification for skepticism about the belief that effluent fees will work as well in highly concentrated industries as they might in more competitive cases.

We shall return to this issue again in our discussion of bureaucratic leanings toward 'ease of management'. What we can say is that all of the models of imperfectly competitive firm behavior that we have discussed establish some presumption that effluent fees will induce firms to pollute less; how closely the outcomes approach a cost-minimizing solution is less clear.

3.3. Public bureaus

Since models of bureaucratic behavior typically posit neither profit maximization nor cost minimization, the response of public agencies to pricing incentives is problematic [see Oates and Strassmann (1978)]. To explore the impact of effluent fees on public decision-makers, we first examine a variant of the Niskanen (1977) model of bureaucratic behavior. As we shall see, the model and its implications for abatement activities bear a strong resemblance to our analysis in the Williamson framework of private managerial maximization. We then discuss the implications of Wilson et al.'s (1980) richer study of public agencies.

In our varient of the Niskanen model, we postulate that the bureau's decision-makers seek to maximize an objective function that contains as arguments the bureau's output (Q) and its level of perquisites (P):

$$U = U(Q, P). \tag{14}$$

Bureaucrats desire an increased output (or 'size'), for this enhances the bureau's power and prestige and with these its capacity to influence the course of events. Migue and Belanger (1974) have contended that agency officials also place a premium on the bureau's 'discretionary budget', the excess of the bureau's funding above its necessary costs. This 'fat' in the budget can be employed for a variety of perquisites ranging from higher salaries and expanded staff to additional facilities or, perhaps, reduced effort.

As earlier, we assume that the production function for the bureau's output depends on waste emissions, E, and a vector of other outputs, L:

$$Q = Q(L, E). \tag{15}$$

Moreover, the bureau is subject to a budget constraint:

$$B = wL + fE + cP, \tag{16}$$

where B is the bureau's budget, w is the price of 'other' inputs (given to the bureau), f is the effluent fee per unit of waste emissions, and c is the (constant) marginal cost of perquisites. Note that L is defined to include only the minimally necessary quantity of other inputs such as labor to provide a given output; likewise, w can be thought of as the lowest wage that will keep employees. Extra salary and labor are viewed as perquisites.

The budget-determination process is the remaining issue. Here we follow Niskanen and assume that the bureau possesses a kind of monopoly power in its dealings with the legislative agency that provides its funding. In particular, the bureau submits (and obtains) a budget of an all-or-nothing character that extracts the entire area under the legislature's demand curve up to the bureau's proposed level of output. In short, the bureau behaves much like a perfectly discriminating monopolist; for whatever level of output it selects, say $\hat{Q}$, the bureau's budget equals:

$$B = \int_0^{\hat{Q}} D(Q) \, dQ, \tag{17}$$

where $D(Q)$ is the legislature's inverse demand function for the bureau's output.[10]

In this framework the bureaucrat's problem becomes that of maximizing the utility function in eq. (14) subject to its budget constraint:

$$M = U[Q(L, E), P] + \left[wL + fE + cP - \int_0^Q D(Q)\,dQ \right].$$

(18)

Solving for the stationary values of (18) yields (among other results):

$$\frac{\partial Q/\partial E}{\partial Q/\partial L} = \frac{f}{w}.$$

(19)

This result is essentially the same as that obtained from our analysis of the Williamson model. Eq. (19), like that for the managerial model of the maximizing firm, implies cost minimization in only a limited sense: the bureau minimizes pollution abatement and other costs that do not generate perquisites. Effluent fees are effectively lost dollars; they provide no utility to the bureaucrat. By minimizing pollution-abatement costs, the bureau maximizes the remaining budget for the procurement of perquisites. Like cost-minimizing firms, a bureau behaving according to this model has an incentive to extend pollution-abatement activities to the point where marginal abatement cost equals the effluent fee.

An important qualification to this result introduces an indeterminacy similar to that in the satisficing models of firm behavior. Bureaucrats, like the employees of firms, are likely to have some preferences for the perquisite 'ease of management'. Just how pervasive such behavior is in public agencies is unclear; however, it could introduce some inefficiencies in the allocation of abatement quotas among polluters. Although, as the analysis suggests, bureaucrats are likely to have some incentive to economize on abatement costs, the discussion in the previous section on diffusion of innovations is also likely to apply to bureaus. Bureaus, like firms protected by managerial slack, do not need to respond as quickly to price changes and to the availability of new technologies as do competitive firms, since the survival of a bureau does not, in general, depend on an aggressively tight management.

The model is admittedly a very simplistic one that cannot begin to encompass the diversity in circumstances and particular objectives of different public agencies. In a recent series of case studies of bureaucratic behavior, Wilson et al. (1980) criticize such simplistic approaches to the characterization of public agencies. Their studies find that the behavior of these agencies is 'complex and changing' (p. 373); it is not subject, for

[10]Alternatively, we might simply assume that the budget is, for our purposes, some predetermined sum [see Oates and Strassmann (1978)]. This would not alter the results.

example, to the broad generalization of the 'captive theory', that, as a rule, 'Regulation is acquired by the industry and is designed and operated primarily for its benefit' [Stigler (1971, p. 3)]. Instead, Wilson et al. suggest that 'We view these agencies as coalitions of diverse participants who have somewhat different motives' (p. 373). Wilson et al. find that the studies reveal public agencies to '...prefer security to rapid growth, autonomy to competition, stability to change... Government agencies are more risk averse than imperialistic' (p. 376). This serves to underline our earlier observations on the potential for public agencies to respond sluggishly to incentives for change.

We note of particular interest the general similarity of the findings and qualifications of the behavior of managers of public and (imperfectly competitive) private enterprises. In a set of case studies of several electric utilities, Roberts and Bluhm (1981) can likewise find no systematic differences in behavior between publicly and privately owned concerns; they conclude that 'The mere fact of public or private ownership by itself does not tell us very much about the kind of behavior to expect' (p. 335).

In summary, although the formal model in this section predicts minimization of abatement costs by public agencies, the interpretation of this result and the broadening of our perspective on bureaucratic behavior suggest some basic reservations. We surely cannot, in a simplistic way, extend the umbrella of our cost-minimization theorem to encompass public agencies. At the same time, the analysis does suggest that an explicit price on pollution activities will present managers (public or private) with a real incentive for abatement. Managers are obviously not entirely oblivious to the costs of alternatives; Roberts and Bluhm, for example, in describing the history of the huge publicly-owned utility, TVA, found that 'Despite the agency's broad responsibility for conservation and regional development, most of its engineering decisions have reflected a continuing attempt to minimize the cost of power' (p. 63).

3.4. Regulated firms

The presence of regulated firms introduces, in principle, another source of technical inefficiency: a regulatory constraint that effectively distorts the relative prices of inputs to the firm. By setting some maximum 'fair' rate of return to capital inputs, the regulatory authority creates an incentive for the firm to extend its use of capital, for by using more capital, the firm is able to enlarge the base upon which its profit constraint is determined. All this is well known and has been described in terms of the Averch and Johnson (1962) (A–J) model; the distortion in factor inputs involving an excessive use of capital is the A–J effect.[11]

---

[11]For excellent, comprehensive treatments of the analytics of the A–J model, see Baumol and Klevorick (1970) and Bailey (1973).

It is fairly straightforward exercise to take the standard version of the A–J model (in which the regulated firm maximizes profits subject to a rate-of-return constraint), to introduce waste emissions into the production function as earlier, and then to examine the first-order conditions for profit maximization in the presence of an effluent fee. We shall not go through the mechanics here, but wish simply to note that the results of this exercise indicate that the regulated firm will not, in general, be a cost minimizer with respect to abatement activity.[12] It would be quite plausible, for example, for such a firm to extend abatement activity beyond the level at which marginal abatement cost equals the effluent fee, if by doing so the firm could expand its capital stock through the use of pollution-control equipment. The rationale from the perspective of the firm is the higher level of absolute profits that the expanded capital stock would allow. But from society's vantage point, this represents, of course, an excessive level of abatement. Under these circumstances, a system of effluent fees could not be expected to generate the least-cost set of pollution-abatement quotas among sources.

More generally, we cannot even conclude that an increase in the effluent fee will lead to a reduction in the waste emissions of the regulated firm. Bailey (1973, pp. 135–137) shows that for the two-factor case, a rise in the wage rate need not lead to reduced labor input; although there must surely be a strong presumption of this result, the outcome is formally indeterminate. Likewise, in his two-factor formulation of the A–J model, Cowing (1976) finds that the sign of the derivative of waste emissions with respect to the effluent fee is ambiguous.

While these results are, in principle, disturbing, there remains the important practical question of the actual magnitude of the A–J effect. The literature has not produced any compelling evidence of a widespread A–J effect [e.g. Baron and Taggart (1977), Spann (1974)]. Not only is there an absence of empirical support for 'over-capitalization' by regulated firms, but there is evidence that the rate-of-return constraint may often not even be binding.

In addition to the empirical studies, recent theoretical work casts further doubt on the applicability of the A–J theorem. Peles and Stein (1976) show that the theorem is 'highly sensitive' to the treatment of uncertainty; if uncertainty is multiplicative in form, the A–J effect is reversed! Perhaps even more basic is the issue of the interaction between the regulated firm and the regulating authority [e.g. Stigler (1971), Peltzman (1976), Joskow (1972, 1973)]. In the A–J model, the firm simply takes the rate-of-return constraint as exogenous. In the real world, however, the regulated firm must typically make application for any price changes, and, as Joskow (1972) shows, the determination of the allowed rate of return appears to involve a fairly complicated process of interaction between the regulator and the regulated firm.

---

[12]We would be happy to provide the formal analysis to any interested readers.

The industrial-organization literature thus establishes some compelling reasons for being quite skeptical about the A–J description of the behavior of the regulated firm. However, it does not, at this juncture, provide a straightforward alternative framework for our analysis of the regulated firm's response to an effluent fee. Some of the literature notes (as does our treatment of managerial models of the firm and of public agencies) the presence of other variables in the objective function in addition to profit maximization; for example, Roberts and Bluhm (1981) conclude that 'Our studies have shown that regulated firms are not pure incentive-oriented profit maximizers. To varying extents, managers are sensitive — albeit within financial limits — to not harming the public and to doing "the right thing"' (p. 384). Moreover, to the extent that the costs associated with effluent charges can be passed along through viable requests for higher prices to the regulatory authority, there may be grounds for questioning a highly 'cost-conscious' response to a system of fees.

We emerge with the sense that our expectations for the regulated firm are much in the spirit of those for the 'managerial' firm and the public bureau. In all these cases, we envision a managerial utility function which contains a multiplicity of objectives as a consequence of which cost-minimization plays an important, but not a singular, role in the determination of behavior.

4. Conclusion

While the analysis in this paper cannot yield any firmly grounded conclusions about the effectiveness of a system of effluent fees in a mixed economy, it does, we think, suggest some tentative results. First, our admittedly crude calculations in section 2 suggest that any distortions in the vector of final outputs resulting from a system of effluent fees (or probably from other forms of pollution control) are unlikely to be the source of substantial welfare loss. The 'allocative' issue that has troubled Buchanan and others in the design of systems to regulate externalities appears to be relatively unimportant in terms of its magnitude.

Second, although it is more difficult to get a sense of the extent of the 'technical inefficiencies' associated with deviations from cost minimization, the analysis does indicate that even where profit maximization is not the sole or dominant objective of the source, there are other considerations that can make it in the interest of polluters to engage in (relatively) efficient levels of abatement activities in response to effluent charges. We found, for example, that in our versions of both the Williamson model of utility-maximizing managers of private firms and the Niskanen model of bureaucracy, there exist incentives promoting cost-minimizing behavior with respect to abatement activities. While these incentives are no doubt blunted somewhat by a certain amount of 'managerial slack', there is at least a real rationale for managers and bureaucrats to seek out cost-saving abatement techniques.

More generally, the central point is that the case for relying on pricing incentives for pollution control in a mixed economy is really little different from that for using prices to guide the allocation of other inputs. While there obviously exists some degree of technical inefficiency in the economy associated with departures from cost-minimizing behavior, there is little reason to believe that the extent of such inefficiencies in pollution control under a system of effluent fees (or marketable emission permits) will be any greater (or any less) than in the use of labor, capital, and other factor inputs.

The importance of introducing pricing incentives for pollution control is underscored by an emerging empirical literature that indicates that existing programs of direct controls are generating enormous waste: abatement costs on the order of two to ten times as large as needed to attain the designated standards of environmental quality [see, for example, Atkinson and Lewis (1974), Palmer et al. (1980), Seskin et al. (1983), and Kneese et al. (1971, appendix C)]. These estimates, moreover, refer only to savings based upon existing abatement technology; they do not address the important long-run issues of the stimulus such pricing incentives would provide for research and development of new techniques for the curtailment of emissions. Our judgement is that a least-cost solution over time to the achievment of our objectives for cleaner air and water would probably involve aggregate costs no larger than 20–25 percent of those under the command-and-control programs that have been adopted in the United States.

Even in the presence of a substantial amount of 'slippage' in the form of technical inefficiencies, it is our view that the likely gains from a system of pricing incentives are quite large. We doubt that the complications arising from the existence of a mixed economy compromise significantly the case for a system of pricing incentives for environmental management.

References

Atkinson, S. and D. Lewis, 1974, A cost-effectiveness analysis of alternative air quality control strategies, Journal of Environmental Economics and Management 1, 237–250.

Averch, H. and L. Johnson, 1962, Behavior of the firm under regulatory constraint, American Economic Review 52, 1052–1069.

Bailey, E., 1973, Economic theory of regulatory constraint (Heath, Lexington, Mass.).

Barnett, A., 1980, The Pigouvian tax rule under monopoly, American Economic Review 70, 1037–1041.

Baron, D. and R. Taggart, Jr., 1977, A model of regulation under uncertainty and a test of regulatory bias, Bell Journal of Economics 8, 151–167.

Baumol, W. and A. Klevorick, 1970, Input choices and rate of return regulation: An overview of the discussion, Bell Journal of Economics and Management 1, 162–190.

Baumol, W. and W. Oates, 1975, The theory of environmental policy (Prentice-Hall, Englewood Cliffs, N.J.).

Bower, J., 1970, Managing the resource allocation process (Harvard Business School, Cambridge, Mass.).

Buchanan, J., 1969, External diseconomies, corrective taxes, and market structure, American Economic Review 59, 174–177.

Chandler, Jr., A., 1962, Strategy and structure (MIT Press, Cambridge, Mass.).

Cohen, K. and R. Cyert, 1962, Theory of the firm: Resource allocation in a market economy (Prentice-Hall, Englewood Cliffs, N.J.).

Cowing, T., 1976, The environmental implications of monopoly regulation: A process analysis approach, Journal of Environmental Economics and Management 2, 207–223.

Cowling, K. and D. Mueller, 1978, The social costs of monopoly power, Economic Journal 88, 727–748.

Hahn, R., 1981, Market power and transferable property rights, unpublished paper.

Harberger, A., 1954, Monopoly and resource allocation, American Economic Review 44, 77–87.

Joskow, P., 1972, The determination of the allowed rate of return in a formal regulatory hearing, Bell Journal of Economics and Management Science 3, 632–644.

Joskow, P., 1973, Pricing decisions of regulated firms: A behavioral approach, Bell Journal of Economics and Management Science 4, 118–140.

Kamien, M. and N. Schwartz, 1975, Market structure and innovation: A survey, Journal of Economic Literature 13, 1–37.

King, W., 1977, T.V.A., a major polluter, faces suit to cut sulfur dioxide fumes, New York Times 76 (July 4).

Kneese, A., S. Rolfe and J. Harned, eds., 1971, Managing the environment (Praeger, New York).

Lave, L. and E. Seskin, 1977, Air pollution and human health (Johns Hopkins Press, Baltimore).

Lee, D., 1975, Efficiency of pollution taxation and market structure, Journal of Environmental Economics and Management 2, 69–72.

Migue, J. and G. Belanger, 1974, Toward a general theory of managerial discretion, Public Choice 17, 27–43.

Niskanen, Jr., W., 1977, Bureaucracy and representative government (Aldine, Chicago).

Oates, W. and D. Strassmann, 1978, The use of effluent fees to regulate public-sector sources of pollution: An application of the Niskanen model, Journal of Environmental Economics and Management 5, 283–291.

Palmer, A., et al., 1980, Economic implications of regulating chlorofluorocarbon emissions from nonaerosol applications (Rand, Santa Monica, California).

Peles, Y. and J. Stein, 1976, The effect of rate of return regulation is highly sensitive to the nature of uncertainty, American Economic Review 66, 278–289.

Peltzman, S., 1976, Toward a more general theory of regulation, Journal of Law and Economics 19, 211–240.

Roberts, M. and J. Bluhm, 1981, The choices of power: Utilities face the environmental challenge (Harvard University Press, Cambridge, Mass.).

Robison, H.D., 1983, Three essays on input–output analysis, unpublished Ph.D. dissertation, University of Maryland, College Park, Md.

Schwartzman, D., 1960, The burden of monopoly, Journal of Political Economy 68, 627–630.

Seskin, E., R. Anderson, Jr. and R. Reid, 1983, An empirical analysis of economic strategies for controlling air pollution, Journal of Environmental Economics and Management 10, 112–124.

Shepard, W., 1972, Elements of market structure: An inter-industry analysis, Southern Economic Journal 38, 531–537.

Spann, R., 1974, Rate of return regulation and efficiency in production: An empirical test of the Averch–Johnson thesis, Bell Journal of Economics and Management Science 5, 38–52.

Stigler, G., 1971, The theory of economic regulation, Bell Journal of Economics and Management Science 2, 3–21.

Williamson, O., 1963, Managerial discretion and business behavior, American Economic Review 53, 1032–1057.

Wilson, J., et al., 1980, The politics of regulation (Basic Books, New York).

[11]

ENVIRONMENT AND TAXATION:

THE CASE OF THE UNITED STATES

(W. E. OATES, Department of Economics, University of Maryland and
University Fellow, Resources for the Future)

Table of Contents

INTRODUCTION

The impact of taxation on the environment in the United States has consisted primarily of the side effects of taxes that were designed and introduced with other objectives in mind. This does not mean, however, that the subject of "pollution taxes" has been entirely ignored. As early as 1971 a bill was introduced in the U.S. Congress for a nationwide tax on sulfur emissions into the atmosphere. And again, more recently in 1987, a bill in the House Ways and Means Committee proposed national taxes on sulfur and nitrogen oxide emissions.[1] While such bills have not come close to enactment, they do indicate the presence of some interest in such measures.

Moreover, the current policy "atmosphere" is, in certain important ways, more receptive to proposals for pollution taxes than in past periods. First, the prevailing sentiment is strongly oriented toward market measures for the solution of social problems. There is a widespread sense that coercive public regulations of the CAC variety have not proved fully effective in achieving our economic, social, and environmental objectives. The current emphasis is on "incentive-based" measures that provide market signals to individuals to behave in socially beneficent ways (Hahn and Stavins, 1991). And this represents a major departure from earlier policy stances. President Bush has made this quite explicit. In discussing potential policies for addressing the problem of global climate change, the President asserted that "Wherever possible, we believe that market mechanisms should be applied and that our policies must be consistent with economic growth and free-market principles in all countries" (Hahn and Stavins, p. 3). Second, these are times in the U.S. of extreme budgetary stringency. The huge deficits in the federal budget have sent policy makers searching for new sources of revenues. Indeeed, the proposed pollution tax legislation in 1987 had, as much of its motivating force, its potential as a revenue source. In the current setting, proposals for environmental taxes are likely to receive a more sympathetic hearing than in the past. There is, for example, serious ongoing discussion of systems of taxes to discourage carbon emissions into the atmosphere as a means of addressing the threat of global warming.[2]

The purpose of this report is to provide both a description and assessment of the impact of the system of taxation in the United States on the environment. I begin in the first section with an overview that provides a conceptual framework for thinking about the role of taxes and the environment. My purpose here is to review briefly the theory of pollution taxes both as instruments for environmental management and as potential sources of revenue--and the potential conflicts that such dual objectives can pose in the policy arena. Section II then turns explicitly to the structure of taxes in the United States and explores the way in which various tax instruments impinge (positively or negatively) on environmental quality. Section III proceeds to the current policy debate on tax measures for environmental protection. And the concluding section provides an assessment of the potential of tax policies for addressing our environmental problems and some thoughts on their design and implementation.

Chapter 1

OVERVIEW

1.1   Some theoretical background

The economic theory of environmental regulation sets forth in rigorous terms an explicit role for taxes on polluting activities. Pollution, from this perspective, is seen as a side effect of production and consumption in the economy: this side effect (or "externality") is a form of social cost that is not borne by the agent who is its source. The theoretical analysis leads to a straightforward prescription to correct the misallocation of resources that results from these side effects on the environment: a unit tax on the polluting activity that is equal to the marginal social damage of the pollution. Such a Pigouvian tax has the potential to "internalize" the external cost and can lead to socially efficient levels of environmental protection. The nature and properties of such taxes on pollution have been worked out carefully in the literature in environmental economics (see, for example, Baumol and Oates, 1988).

Such taxes will also, of course, be the source of public revenues. And this has received somewhat less attention in the literature. However, it is a straightforward matter in principle to extend the analysis of pollution taxes to take account of their role as a source of public revenues as well as an instrument of environmental management (Lee and Misiolek, 1986; Oates, forthcoming). We turn to this issue now.

From the revenue perspective, pollution taxes are seen as a subset of potential revenue instruments. In an optimal-taxation framework, the basic objective is to design a system of taxation that generates the requisite revenues at the least cost to society. The problem here is that most conventional taxes have distorting side effects on the functioning of the economy: in the course of producing revenues, they introduce distorting incentives for individual economic behavior such that the full cost of the taxes to society exceeds the level of the tax revenues that they produce. An efficient tax system will minimize these additional costs (the so-called "excess burden") from taxation. This requires, in principle, that the rates on the various tax bases be set such that the excess burden from an additional dollar of revenue is equated across all revenue sources (e.g., Rosen, 1988, Chs. 14-15).

The intriguing and appealing property of taxes on pollution is that, over some range at least, they have negative excess burden: they improve rather than distort the functioning of the market economy. By the proper substitution of environmental taxes for more conventional levies, we can design a more efficent overall system of public revenues. An efficent tax system, therefore, will, in principle, encompass taxes on activities that impose external costs on the environment.

David Terkla (1984), in a study in the United States, has actually developed some measures of the potential efficiency gains from taxes on pollution. Examining a hypothetical set of nationwide taxes on particulate and sulfur oxide emissions from stationary sources in the U.S., Terkla estimates the efficiency gains that would result from using the revenues from these taxes to replace partially those from either the federal income tax (on labor income) or the corporation income tax. He finds that the potential gains from a more efficient overall tax system range from $630 million to over $3 billion in 1982 dollars. These estimates depend, of course, on the specific assumptions concerning the scope and rates of these taxes. A broader set of taxes, including perhaps Green Taxes on carbon emissions, could generate much higher levels of efficiency gains.

The analysis implies that from the expanded perspective of an efficient revenue system, the determination of the optimal level of pollution taxes must take account not only of their role as instruments of environmental management but also their potential for reducing distortions from other taxes. This raises an interesting question. Does this imply that we should set rates on pollution taxes that are higher or lower than the rates that would be set on purely environmental grounds?

Dwight Lee and Walter Misiolek (1986) have provided the answer to this question. We know from the literature on environmental economics that the tax rate, for purely environmental purposes, should be set such that the marginal gains from a cleaner environment equal marginal abatement cost. Lee and Misiolek show that, from the broader optimal tax perspective, this condition must be amended to take account of the reduction in excess burden from other taxes that accompanies the reduced rates on these other sources of revenue. More specifically, the condition for an efficient pollution tax in this expanded framework is that the marginal benefits from a cleaner environment plus the marginal reduction in excess burden on other taxes should equal marginal abatement cost. In short, we must, in setting the levels of pollution taxes, take into account both the value of the improved environmental quality and the gains from a less distorting overall tax system.

This implies that we should generate more revenues from pollution taxes than would be indicated by purely environmental considerations. But what does this imply for the levels of tax rates on polluting activities? As Lee and Misiolek demonstrate, optimal-tax considerations may require either a higher or lower level of pollution tax rates relative to the purely Pigouvian rate that equates marginal environmental gains with marginal abatement costs. The answer depends on tax elasticity. If tax elasticity is greater than unity, then a lower tax rate will generate a higher level of tax revenues--hence, the optimal tax rate on polluting activities will be lower than the purely "environmental rate." Conversely, if tax elasticity falls short of unity, then a higher tax rate will generate more revenues--and the optimal-tax solution will call for a rate higher than the Pigouvian level. For the special case of unitary tax elasticity, the rates will be the same.

Lee and Misiolek turn to the existing empirical literature in environmental economics to see which of these cases is the typical one. The elasticity estimates in this literature do not provide a general answer to the question. The estimates, covering a wide variety of air and water pollutants, exhibit wide variation: some are well below unity, while the upper range for most reaches well above unity. Their interval estimate, for example, of the tax elasticity for the emissions of particualte matter from U.S. electric utilities is 0.99-1.34, suggesting that the rate on this source of emissions would, under an optimal-tax regime, likely be less than the purely environmental charge. It thus appears that there is no general prescription here: an optimal-tax approach is likely, in some instances, to require higher taxes than a purely environmental regime--and, in other cases, lower tax rates. The implication of optimal-tax considerations for the level of environmental quality is unclear.

110

1.2 Some public choice issues

The optimal-taxation approach to environmental taxation provides a precise theoretical result that involves balancing the gains in environmental quality and reduced excess burden against costs of abatement at the margin. While this result may be unimpeachable in principle, it is somewhat less compelling in a policy setting. To implement the optimal-tax prescription, we would need a very well informed public decision-maker whose interests transcend competing environmental and revenue pressures--an enlightened agent in a position to weigh environmental concerns against revenue needs.

This is a formidable institutional requirement. Environmental management and revenue-raising responsibilities are typically lodged in different agencies within the public sector. In such a setting, it seems unlikely that we will get the systematic weighing of environmental concerns against revenue needs that is envisioned in the optimal-tax theorem. It seems more likely that the responsibility for designing and administering pollution taxes will be lodged either with the environmental authority or with the taxing agency. In the first case, we might expect to see environmental objectives dictate the form and level of the tax, while in the latter case, revenue needs would be more likely to be foremost in the minds of the administering authority.

This suggests some potential for a public-choice approach to this issue. Suppose, for example, that the design and management of pollution taxes were the responsibility of the public revenue authority--the Treasury or a Legislative Tax Committee. To take an extreme case, Brennan and Buchanan (1980) have suggested that we might expect such an agency to behave as a revenue maximizer, a Leviathan seeking to extract the maximum level of revenues. What would such revenue-maximizing behavior imply for the level of tax rates on pollution? The answer (much like earlier) is unclear: it depends on the elasticity of the tax base. If tax elasticity exceeds unity, then a revenue-maximizer will lower the tax rate; if, in contrast, the tax base is inelastic, revenues will be increased by raising the rate.[3] Leviathan, in short, could prove to be either a friend or foe of the environment!

Revenue maximization is admittedly an extreme assumption. We might expect that even a revenue authority would give some consideration to environmental concerns--in response perhaps to the lobbying efforts of concerned groups. It is interesting in this regard that the recent adoption of "eco-taxes" in Sweden took place in an explicitly revenue-neutral setting: existing taxes were, in fact, reduced with the introduction of pollution charges (Barde, 1991, p. 7). Likewise, attempts (although not successful) to introduce environmental taxes in Austria involved the packaging of the proposed levies with proposed cuts in other taxes. In the United States, there is the potential for such coordination in the U.S. Congress where "interested" committees sometimes have joint jurisdiction over certain regulatory programs; the interaction between the Congress and the President on most tax matters provides a further opportunity for an integration of environmental and tax objectives.[4] While such coordination may occur, there remains a potential policy problem here. Pollution taxes, in an optimal-tax framework, serve two ends: an environmental objective and a revenue-raising objective. And it seems quite possible that, in the policy arena, one or the other of them will get the upper hand in the design and management of this policy instrument. I shall return to this issue in the concluding section.

1.3   The linkage issue

The discussion to this point has run in terms of environmental taxes that are designed and attached explicitly to polluting activities. The environmental economics literature is quite specific about the nature of such taxes: they must be per-unit levies applied directly to the waste emissions or other vehicles of environmental damage. Such taxes must be directly <u>linked</u> to the source of the pollution.

In some cases, such a direct linkage may be a relatively easy matter. However, in other circumstances, it may be both difficult and costly to measure and monitor waste emissions. In such cases, the best we can do may involve taxing an input or other activity that is associated with the polluting activity. Such indirect linkages are admittedly not fully satisfactory. A tax, for example, on the sulfur content of coal purchased provides an incentive to use higher grade coal, but it does not encourage the use of scrubbers to treat the emissions as they pass through enter the stack. The tax should, in principle, be attached directly to the emissions that enter the atmosphere.

There is a second reason why such linkages may be indirect. Some taxes may have been enacted for other than environmental purposes. Taxes on gasoline, for example, were originally intended in the U.S. as a source of funds for the construction of highways and other roads. Yet such taxes may well have unintended side effects on the environment. Thus, indirect linkages may come into being unintentionally.

This is an important issue, for, as the next section makes clear, most of the taxes in the United States that have an impact on environmental quality are of the latter variety: their linkage to the environment is indirect in character. This means that in assessing their role as instruments in environmental policy, we must look carefully at the channels through which they impact on the environment and the likely magnitude of their effect.

Chapter 2

EXISTING TAXES AND THE ENVIRONMENT

Simply describing the structure of "environmentally relevant" taxes in the United States is not an easy task. The U.S. has a federal system of government with a central government, 50 states, and many thousands of local governments (including counties, cities, municipalities, townships, and special districts). Moreover, the fiscal system in the U.S. is a relatively decentralized one in which lower levels of government play an important role both in the raising and disbursement of revenues. And there is a bewildering variety of tax structures: each state has its own fiscal system with its distinctive forms and mix of taxes. Even where they rely on the same general forms of taxation, state and local governments introduce their specific provisions and rate structures. This makes it difficult (and sometimes misleading) to try to summarize the fiscal structure of the nation in terms of a simple set of summary numbers.

All this variety in fiscal structure, while perhaps somewhat confusing, has an interesting and potentially valuable dimension. The U.S. federal system has been characterized as a "laboratory" in which a multiplicity of experiments are going on at any moment in time. From the results of these various experiments, we may be in a position to learn something about what works and what doesn't work, lessons that may then drawn upon by the other members of the union. With this in mind, I turn to the existing tax structure in the U.S. as it relates to environmental concerns.

2.1   The excise tax on ozone-depleting chemicals

At the central government level, there is one tax that has been designed and introduced for ostensibly environmental reasons (although, as I will suggest, there is some ambiguity here). This is the ozone-depleting chemical tax introduced in conjunction with the Montreal Protocol to phase out emissions of chlorofluorocarbons (CFCs) and halons into the atmosphere. The Montreal Protocol established a schedule under which emissions of these ozone-depleting chemicals will systematically be phased out over the coming decade. More specifically, under the amended Protocol, all but one of these chemicals will be phased out by the year 2,000; the remaining chemical, methyl chloroform, will go out of use by the year 2005. In 1990, the U.S. accelerated this schedule somewhat as part of the Amendments to the Clean Air Act. And, more recently in 1992, President Bush announced that the U.S. will further accelerate the phaseout of ozone-depleting substances well ahead of earlier timetables; the President has urged other countries to join the U.S. in this effort.

The ozone-depleting chemical tax, introduced on January 1, 1990, and extended effective January 1, 1991, is an excise tax imposed on each pound of ozone-depleting chemicals. The exact tax for a specific chemical is determined by taking a <u>base amount</u> for the tax and multiplying it by an <u>ozone-depleting factor</u> applicable to the particular chemical. The base amount rises over time with an initial value of $1.37 per pound in 1990, increasing to $3.10 in 1995 and an additional $0.45 per year thereafter. The chemical-specific multiplication factors range from 0.1 to 10.0 so that the taxes applicable to particular chemicals vary widely in accordance with their presumed contribution to ozone depletion. A complete schedule of these base amounts and ozone-depleting factors appears in Appendix A. The tax is projected to produce revenues of $890 million in 1991, rising to $1,380 million by 1996.

The tax has thus been designed properly from the standpoint of applying a uniform penalty per unit of ozone-depleting potential across all chemicals and uses. But what is interesting, and in a way puzzling, about the tax is that it has been applied on top of a set of quantitative restrictions for the phase-out of these chemicals. From the persepctive of regulating emissions, this will create a redundancy: one of the policy instruments, either the quantity restriction or the tax, will be binding and the other will not. If, for example, the quantity restriction is the binding constraint, then the tax will have no effect on levels of emissions. It will serve solely to raise revenues. This will, incidentally, serve an equity objective: it can capture some of the excess profits that accrue to those in control of the limited supplies of these chemicals. And this is one of the objectives of the tax.

There is apparently some evidence to suggest that the tax may be binding on some uses of these chemicals. One report (OECD 1991) notes that the tax seems to have reduced substantially the demand for CFCs in the manufacture of soft foams and is likely to reduce the use of CFCs in "rigid foam insulation" when the partial exemption for chemicals used in their manufacture expires in 1994. The demand for certain uses of halons, in contrast, appears quite price inelastic because of the absence of good substitutes, and is hence unlikely to be affected by the tax.

2.2   Taxes on gasoline

Gasoline taxes are levied in the United States both by the federal and by state governments, although, even in combination, the total level of tax rates is low by most European standards. The federal tax is currently $.14 per gallon ($.20 per gallon for diesel fuel), while, as Table 2.1 indicates, as of December 1990, state gasoline taxes ranged from a high of $.22 in the states of Connecticut and Washington to a low of $.04 in Florida. The median state tax rate was $.16, suggesting a "typical" federal plus state tax rate of about $.30 per gallon.[5]

Several states have introduced incremental increases in their rates over the last year: fifteen states increased motor fuel or motor vehicle taxes and only one lowered them for fiscal year 1992. These taxes produce sizeable revenues. In fiscal year 1989, the federal excise tax on gasoline and gasohol generated $9.96 billion, while state government revenues from this source were $18.0 billion.

The tax on gasoline was one of the first widely used taxes on commodities by the states in this country (the other is the tax on tobacco products). Oregon first introduced the tax in 1919, and by 1929 it was used by every state in the union. During the 1930s and 1940s, it became the most important single source of tax revenues for state governments, producing over one-quarter of state tax revenues. The federal government introduced a gasoline tax in 1932 (despite vigorous protests from the states) and later expanded the tax as part of the new Highway Trust Fund in 1956.

114

The primary objective of gasoline taxes has historically not been an environmental one. These taxes have in large part been seen as an equitable way for financing the construction and maintenance of roads and highways; from this perspective, they are sometimes viewed as "user taxes," although taxes paid by a particular driver are surely far from a perfect measure of benefits received.[6] Most of the revenues from these taxes are, in fact, earmarked for transportation programs. The federal government has used the great bulk of the revenues from the Highway Trust Fund for grants-in-aid to state and local governments for the construction of a national system of interstate highways. About 98 percent of the actual spending on highway facilities and services is done by state and local governments.

While the tax is not primarily an instrument for environmental management, it clearly has some side effects on environmental, especially air, quality. As we learned in the 1970s, the price elasticity of demand for gasoline is certainly not zero. With gasoline prices in the United States running at somewhat above $1 per gallon, excise taxes are probably raising the "typical" price of motor fuels in the U.S. by around 25 percent. This has some discernible impact in terms of encouraging the use of more fuel-efficient cars, reducing commuting distances, and increasing the use of mass-transit forms of transportation.

Such changes in behavior reduce auto emissions and contribute to some extent to improved air quality, especially in urban areas. If we take -0.7 as a representative estimate of the long run price elasticity of the demand for gasoline, this suggests that gasoline taxes in the U.S. reduce auto emissions by something on the order of 15 percent. While this is not a huge fraction, it is nevertheless of real importance, since auto emissions are such a major source of urban air pollution. The U.S. could clearly go much farther in this direction (as many OECD countries have done), but there doesn't appear to be much political impetus, at this juncture at least, for such moves (with one exception to be mentioned later).

2.3   Other taxes and charges related to motor vehicle use

In addition to excise taxes on gasoline, federal, state, and local governments impose a variety of other taxes and fees that are related to motor vehicle usage. The federal government levies a 12 percent manufacturers excise tax on trucks and trailers, an annual use tax on "heavy vehicles" (trucks), and an excise tax on tires that weigh in excess of 40 pounds. In addition, there is a federal government "Gas Guzzler" tax on automobiles with unsatisfactory fuel economy ratings. State and local governments (primarily the former) levy a variety of auto taxes and fees. The major items here include annual registration fees for automobiles (ranging from $8 in Arizona and Georgia to $52 in New Jersey), operator's license fees, auto inspection fees, and sales taxes on the purchaes of automobiles.[7] State motor vehicle and license fees raised revenues of $10.15 billion in 1989.

Table 2.1

State Gasoline Taxes: Rates per Gallon, Selected Years, 1978-1991

Region and State	1991	1990	1989	1988	1987	1986	1985	1984	1982	1980	1978
Exhibit: Federal Tax	$.14	$.09	$.09	$.09	$.09	$.09	$.09	$.09	$.04	$.04	$.04
Median	0.18	.16	.16	.145	.145	.13	.12	.12	.10	.09	.08
Alabama+°	0.11	.11	.11	.11	.11	.11	.11	.11	.11	.07	.07
Alaska+°	0.08	.08	.08	.08	.08	.08	.08	.08	.08	.08	.08
Arizona	0.18	.18	.17	.16	.16	.16	.13	.13	.10	.08	.08
Arkansas	0.185	.135	.135	.135	.135	.135	.135	.095	.095	.095	.085
California+o°	0.15	.14	.09	.09	.09	.09	.09	.09	.07	.07	.07
Colorado	0.22	.20	.20	.18	.18	.18	.12	.13	.09	.07	.07
Connecticut°	0.25	.22	.20	.20	.19	.17	.16	.15	.11	.11	.11
Delaware°	0.19	.16	.16	.16	.16	.11	.11	.11	.11	.09	.11
District of Columbia	0.18	.18	.18	.155	.155	.155	.155	.155	.14	.10	.10
Florida+°	0.04	.04	.04	.04	.04	.04	.04	.04	.08	.08	.08
Georgia o°	0.075	.075	.075	.075	.075	.075	.075	.075	.075	.075	.075[b]
Hawaii+o°	0.16	.11	.11	.11	.11	.11	.11	.085	.085	.085	.085
Idaho°	0.22	.19	.18	.18	.145	.145	.145	.145	.125	.095	.095
Illinois+o°	0.19	.13	.13	.13	.13	.13	.13	.12	.075	.075	.075
Indiana o	0.15	.15	.15	.15	.14	.14	.14	.111	.111	.085	.08
Iowa	0.20	.20	.20	.18	.16	.16	.15	.13	.13	.10	.085
Kansas°	0.17	.16	.15	.11	.11	.11	.11	.11	.08	.08	.08
Kentucky°	0.15	.15	.15	.15	.15	.15	.10	.10	.098	.09	.09
Louisiana o	0.20	.20	.20	.16	.16	.16	.16	.16	.08	.08	.08
Maine°	0.19	.17	.17	.16	.14	.14	.14	.14	.09	.09	.09
Maryland	0.185	.185	.185	.185	.185	.135	.135	.135	.11	.09	.09
Massachusetts°	0.21	.17	.11	.11	.11	.11	.11	.11	.104	.085	.085
Michigan	0.15	.15	.15	.15	.15	.15	.15	.15	.11	.11	.09
Minnesota	0.20	.20	.20	.20	.17	.17	.17	.17	.13	.11	.09
Mississippi+°	0.18	.18	.18	.17	.15	.09	.09	.09	.09	.09	.09
Missouri	0.11	.11	.11	.11	.11	.07	.07	.07	.07	.07	.07
Montana+	0.205	.20	.20	.20	.20	.15	.15	.15	.09	.09	.08
Nebraska°	0.234	.214	.22	.182	.176	.19	.164	.149	.137	.105	.095
Nevada+°	0.18	.1625	.1625	.1625	.1425	.1125	.1125	.1025	.1025	.06	.06
New Hampshire	0.18	.16	.14	.14	.14	.14	.14	.14	.14	.11	.10
New Jersey°	0.105	.105	.105	.105	.08	.08	.08	.08	.08	.08	.08
New Mexico+	0.162	.162	.162	.142	.14	.11	.11	.11	.10	.08	.07
New York+o°	0.08	.08	.08	.08	.08	.08	.08	.08	.08	.08	.08
North Carolina°	0.226	.215	.209	.14	.155	.12	.12	.12	.12	.09	.09
North Dakota	0.17	.17	.17	.17	.17	.13	.13	.13	.08	.08	.08
Ohio°	0.21	.20	.18	.148	.147	.12	.12	.12	.117	.07	.07
Oklahoma°	0.16	.16	.17	.16	.16	.10	.10	.09	.0658	.0658	.0658
Oregon+°	0.20	.18	.16	.14	.12	.11	.10	.09	.08	.07	.07
Pennsylvania	0.12	.12	.12	.12	.12	.12	.12	.12	.11	.11	.09
Rhode Island°	0.26	.20	.20	.15	.13	.13	.13	.13	.10	.10	.10
South Carolina	0.16	.16	.16	.15	.15	.13	.13	.13	.13	.10	.09
South Dakota+	0.18	.18	.18	.18	.13	.13	.13	.13	.13	.12	.08
Tennessee+°	0.20	.21	.21	.17	.17	.17	.12	.09	.09	.07	.07
Texas	0.20	.15	.15	.15	.15	.10	.10	.05	.05	.05	.05
Utah°	0.19	.19	.19	.19	.19	.14	.14	.14	.11	.09	.09
Vermont o	0.15	.15	.15	.13	.13	.13	.13	.13	.11	.09	.09
Virginia+o°	0.175	.175	.175	.175	.175	.15	.11	.11	.11	.11	.09
Washington+o°	0.23	.22	.18	.18	.18	.18	.18	.18	.12	.12	.11
West Virginia	0.155	.155	.155	.105	.105	.105	.105	.105	.105	.105	.105
Wisconsin°	0.222	.215	.208	.209	.20	.175	.165	.16	.13	.09	.07
Wyoming	0.09	.09	.09	.08	.08	.08	.08	.08	.08	.08	.08

Note: For 1978-1987, rates are as of July 1; for 1988, October 1; for 1989-1991, December 1.

+ Local taxes may be additional.

o State sales taxes are additional.

Source: Advisory Commission on Intergovernmental Relations, *Significant Features of Fiscal Federalism*, 1992 Edition Vol. I (Washington, D.C.: ACIR, 1992), Table 34, p. 102.

Various states have introduced other vehicle- (or fuel-) related taxes (State Tax Notes, Nov. 11, 1991). Arkansas, for example, recently imposed fees on tires and batteries; likewise, Tennessee has, in fiscal year 1992, imposed a tax on new tire sales. Texas has, this year, introduced a coastal protection fee of 2 cents per barrel on crude oil. There is not available, at this juncture, a systematic inventory of such taxes or fees (more on this later), but many such charges exist (and are being introduced) at state and local levels.

2.4   Severance taxes

Severance taxes are excise taxes levied on the extraction of mineral resources (notably petroleum). These taxes are employed primarily at the state level in the United States. Although 38 states levy severance taxes, they are not a major source of revenue for the states as a whole, accounting for only between 1 and 2 percent of total state general revenues. They are, however, a significant revenue source for a few states, notably Alaska, Louisiana, Texas, and Wyoming. Meiszkowski and Toder (1983) estimate that in 1981 the seven major energy producing states collected about $500 per capita, a sizeable sum, in natural resource revenues. Both the level of rates and the definition of the tax base vary widely among the states.

Severance taxes can affect the environment through the impact that they have on the rates and timing of extraction of mineral resources. Economic theory suggests that these taxes will have two kinds of effects (Deacon, 1990). First, they will discourage both exploration and extraction activities at the margin. The issue here is simply that taxation will render unprofitable those exploration and extraction operations that were barely profitable in the absence of the tax. This effect is called "high-grading" to indicate that "lower-grade" deposits will, under taxation, be ignored. Second, severance taxes alter the time profile of the profit-maximizing pattern of extraction: they "tilt" it toward the future. Relative to the untaxed path, such taxes reduce drilling and output in all periods, but to a greater extent in early, than in more distant, periods. In addition, drilling activity ceases prematurely.

How large are these effects in the United States? Robert Deacon (1990) has undertaken an interesting and suggestive simulation study of the petroleum industry in the U.S. in an attempt to answer this question. The issue is somewhat more complicated because exhaustible resources in this country are subject to three forms of taxation: corporation income taxes, severance taxes, and local property taxes. Deacon finds that corporation income taxes have little effect on extraction rates. In contrast, local property taxes have a real impact. Like severance taxes, they discourage exploration and extraction, but (unlike severance taxes) they encourage earlier extraction. Since under property taxation, the value of the minerals under ground is subject to tax, it pays to get them out of the ground earlier. Deacon's simulations suggest that, overall, the effects of this set of taxes in the U.S. is to reduce levels of exploration and extraction and to tilt the time profile to some extent toward the future. The estimated reduction in total oil production resulting from these taxes is 10 to 15 percent.

It is difficult to translate these findings into a set of clear effects on the environment. About all that can be said is that the lower levels of exploration, development, and extraction activities occasioned by these taxes should result in somewhat less environmental disruption. To say more than this would require a careful study.

117

2.5   User fees for local solid waste disposal services[8]

There is growing concern in the United States with the problem of disposal of municipal solid wastes. Not only have the quantities of such wastes risen dramatically, but the costs of their disposal have also increased as the capacity of existing landfills has been exhausted, as stricter environmental regulations governing landfills and incinerators have been introduced, and as public aversion to disposal sites has grown. In most communities in the U.S., residential waste services are financed through general revenues (typically through local property taxation) or by flat fees such that the marginal cost of additional refuse to the household is zero.

There is now some interest in, and a limited use of, fees for municipal waste services that vary with the level of refuse discarded. Such fees will, in principle, provide a direct incentive to reduce the household's quantity of solid wastes. A limited number of communities in the U.S. have been experimenting with such fee systems. These systems typically take one of two forms. The first requires households to specify a number of waste containers of a given size per week. Households are then charged for their subscribed number of containers irrespective of how full or heavy the containers are. The second form of these systems requires that all waste containers for pickup be specially marked plastic bags or self-provided containers marked with a sticker or tag. Under this variant, the household is charged a price for the bags (or the stickers or tags) which reflects collection and disposal costs. Both types of fee systems provide some incentive to the household to reduce its level of refuse. One fear, however, is that such a system also encourages illegal dumping of refuse to avoid the fee.

Marginal cost pricing is quite common for commercial solid wastes, but, as noted, relatively rare for residential wastes. The important issue here is the price responsiveness of quantities of refuse. In one recent study, Robin Jenkins (1991) was able to collect data for a sample of communities experimenting with user-pricing schemes and a set of control communities with general-fund financing of waste disposal services. With these data, Jenkins estimated the price elasticity of demand for waste disposal services separately for residential and commercial sources of refuse. Her findings consist of a statistically significant, but modest, response of quantities of refuse to user prices: the estimated price elasticities are -0.12 for residential demand and -0.29 for commercial demand. These findings thus suggest that user fees for solid waste disposal will generate some response in terms of reduced wastes, although not an enormous one. The response may become somewhat larger over time as households become more accustomed, and adjust, to such pricing regimes.

2.6   State fiscal incentives for solid waste disposal

Closely related to local efforts to charge for residential waste pickups are a number of state measures designed to facilitate waste disposal efforts. These measures take a wide variety of forms including tax incentives for recycling, deposit-refund schemes for beverage containers, and state packaging and materials taxes. I shall try to summarize here the nature and extent of these programs in the U.S.

The first class of programs consists of tax incentives for recycling. According to one recent source (American Legislative Exchange Council, 1991), 23 states had such measures as of January,

1991. These incentives include tax credits or deductions for investment in recycling equipment, sales tax exemptions for purchases of recycling machinery, and various loans or grants for related activities.

The second group of programs are the so-called "Bottle Bills," or beverage container deposit laws. These measures provide for deposits upon the purchase of beverages that are refundable upon the return of the empty containers. Although such measures have a long history in the U.S., they were "re-introduced" by the State of Oregon in October, 1972. There are now nine states that have such deposit-refund laws. There has been considerable interest in national legislation to provide a nationwide beverage container deposit law. But there exists substantial opposition to such a measure. A recent General Accounting Office report (U.S. GAO, 1990) has examined the "Trade-offs in Beverage Container Deposit Legislation."

The benefits from such deposit programs are largely environmental in character: they reduce litter, conserve energy and natural resources, and reduce the quantites of solid waste going into landfills. Studies of these programs indicate that they have reduced the volume of beverage container litter between 79 and 83 percent and the overall amount of solid waste by as much as 6 percent by weight and up to 8 percent by volume. However, the programs also entail costs. These include additional capital and operating costs to the beverage industry. In addition, there is some concern that deposit programs divert potential revenues away from curbside recycling programs, making the latter economically infeasible.

There have been several studies of the costs and benefits of container deposit legislation, but the studies produce conflicting results on the relative magnitude of benefits and costs. Interestingly, there seems to be widespread national support among the populace for a national beverage container deposit law. The GAO conducted a telephone survey which (along with other surveys) found that the vast majority of Americans would support such legislation. Moreover, the GAO study found that most states with deposit laws also had local curbside recycling programs, suggesting that such deposit measures and curbside recycling can coexist.

Nevertheless, it is hard, on purely economic grounds, to make an airtight case for deposit laws. The GAO concludes that "Although nine states currently have deposit laws and various studies on the effects of these laws have been conducted, we do not believe that the effects of deposit legislation have been quantified to the extent that it can be conclusively determined whether a mandatory national deposit system would be advantageous from a strict cost/benefit standpoint...Given this situation, we believe that the desirability of national beverage container deposit legislation is essentially a public policy decision in which value judgments must be made about the trade-offs between costs and environmental benefits and the desirability of federal involvement in solid waste management, an area that has generally been a local responsibility" (p. 5).

Third, eight states have a variety of packaging and materials taxes. These range from taxes on specific items such as newsprint and beverages to more general taxes on manufacturers, wholesalers, distributors, and retailers.

2.7   Other state environmentally related taxes and fees

There are a host of other, quite diverse taxes and fees that are in various ways, directly or indirectly, related to the environment. A number of states, for example, employ environmental permit fees. In most instances, these are flat fees that entitle the permit recipient to engage in a particular activity (e.g., wastewater discharge). Because of their fixed-sum character, they do not vary with the level of the activity and, hence, do not provide an incentive to reduce levels of waste emissions. They serve rather to deter entry into the activity.

There are a few instances, however, where fees are related to the levels of discharges. The State of New Jersey, for example, has introduced a set of fees for discharges into waterways, where the fees are determined by the Department of Environmental Protection and based on the quantity of the contaminants and their relative risk to public health. Likewise, California levies a water waste discharge permit fee based on type and volume of discharged pollutants. Many of the fee programs are designed to provide revenues for funding environmental programs.

2.8   Other federal excise taxes[9]

There are a few additional federal excise taxes that relate to environmental matters. To finance the Superfund program, which provides for cleaning up abandoned toxic waste sites, the Congress established a trust fund with which the EPA can finance public cleanups. The monies for the trust fund come from a variety of sources, among them some federal excise taxes. The major source is a "feedstock tax" on the petroleum and chemical industries. The feedstock tax is a varying, per-unit levy on a wide range of primary inputs to the production of chemical and petroleum derivatives. This tax was never thought of in terms of its incentive effects; rather, it has been viewed solely as a source of funds for Superfund cleanup operations. The feedstock tax has been supplemented by an "environmental tax," consisting of an assessment on every domestic corporation of 0.12 percent of the corporation's minimum taxable income over $2 million.

In addition, there is a federal excise tax on coal sales of $1.10 per ton for underground mines and $0.55 per ton for surface mines, a tax on crude oil of $0.082 per barrel of domestically produced oil and of $0.117 per barrel of imported crude, a tax on the use of harbors and ports, and a set of excise taxes on sport-fishing equipment, bows and arrows, and firearms. The revenues from most of these excise taxes flow into trust funds for the support of programs related to the taxed activity.

Finally, the federal fiscal system provides "tax-subsidies" for certain environmentally related activities. There are depletion allowances that are taken against tax liabilities for oil and gas production, coal and other hard minerals, and for timber. The tax law also allows energy tax credits for solar, geothermal, and ocean thermal properties and a production credit for alternative fuels.

2.9   A concluding note

As this section has indicated, most of the major tax and other fiscal programs with effects on the environment are state and local programs in the United States. In addition, they are a mixed bag: they vary widely in character and from state to state. This makes it difficult in a report like this to pull together in a systematic and comprehensive way an inventory and assessment of these fiscal programs and their incentive effects. As I have learned in the process of writing this report, such an inventory simply does not exist for state and local programs of "environmental taxes and fees." I have, however, worked closely with the Chief Economist of the National Conference of State Legislatures and others concerned with state and local taxation. In view of the wide and growing interest in this topic of environmental taxes, I hope that this report will provide some stimulus to a new effort in the U.S. to provide a comprehensive and systematic collection of information on state and local environmental taxes and fees.

Chapter 3

THE POLICY DEBATE

This section of the paper explores the central issues figuring in the debate over the use of tax instruments for environmental protection. As noted earlier, the atmosphere for this discussion has shifted in important ways in the United States--it is now much more sympathetic to the use of incentive-based measures for environmental management. The first part of this section examines this new "receptiveness" to market-oriented policy instruments and describes some of its manifestations in the U.S. policy arena. I then take up a series of issues that are central to the ongoing policy debate: quantity versus price instruments, international competitiveness, regulatory federalism (i.e., centralized versus decentralized regulatory management), and equity issues.

3.1   The current policy atmosphere

We have come a long way from the days in which economic incentive approaches to environmental regulation were denounced as "licenses to pollute" or summarily dismissed as "impractical." There is widespread interest in, and considerable support for, incentive-based measures as potential alternatives or supplements to the more traditional command-and-control (CAC) policies. This interest has manifested itself both in the Administration, where (as noted earlier) President Bush has explicitly supported the use of market incentives for environmental protection, and in the U.S. Congress where numerous proposals and bills have been introduced for the use of incentive-based policy instruments. As Hahn and Stavins (1991, p. 20) have put it recently, there are "winds of change from Washington."

In the Administration, this support has taken the form, not only of general statements, but of some concrete proposals including the newly enacted system of tradeable permits to address the acid rain problem under the 1990 Amendments to the Clean Air Act. In the EPA itself, Administrator William Reilly has appointed an Economics Incentives Task Force to seek out new ways to implement market-incentive approaches to environmental regulation. There are at the EPA ongoing studies, for example, of the potential use of incentive-based measures for the control of global warming.

This interest is shared in certain quarters in the U.S. Congress and has manifested itself in the passage by both the House and Senate of the new Amendmendments to the Clean Air Act in which both bodies supported the Administration's proposal for a system of tradeable permits to reduce sulfur dioxide emissions. Under this legislation, sulfur dioxide emissions will be cut by 10 million tons (about 50 percent) over the next decade, and this reduction will be allocated among sources through a market in emissions permits.

A more general interest in economic incentive approaches is evident in a bipartisan study, initiated and sponsored in 1988 by U.S. Senators Timothy Wirth of Colorado and John Heinz of Pennsylvania. This study resulted in an imaginative report ("Harnessing Market Forces to Protect Our Environment: Initiatives for the New President," also known as "Project 88") that suggested a broad range of specific incentive-based measures for environmental management (see Stavins, 1988). More recently, bills have been introduced in the Congress for deposit-refund systems for the recycling of batteries and for the use of tradeable permit systems for dealing with municipal waste-treatment problems.

Interestingly, many of these measures have had some support from a formerly hostile source: environmental advocacy groups. Such groups, in the earlier days of the environmental movement, were virtually unanimous in their outspoken opposition to systems that "put the environment up for sale." But many environmentalists have come to understand and appreciate the potential of pricing incentives for protection of the environment. The Environmental Defense Fund, for example, was an active participant in Project 88 and worked closely with White House Staff in the design of the Administration's Clean Air Act proposal. Several other important national organizations, including the National Audubon Society, the Sierra Club, and the National Resources Defense Council, now support at least certain uses of incentive-based policies. Private industry likewise is showing widespread interest in such measures as a way to reduce the costs of pollution control (Hahn and Stavins, 1991, pp. 25-6).

The sources of this new receptivity to economic incentives are, in part, associated with the "market-oriented" era on which we have entered. With the collapse of many centrally planned economies and their embracing of market principles, there is a widespread sense of the potential efficacy of market approaches to dealing with a wide class of social problems. Incentive-based strategies are in vogue.

Moreover, the more traditional CAC policies have not, in the view of many, been highly successful in resolving our environmental problems. Especially as we attempt to introduce yet more stringent controls in a setting of rising marginal control costs, there is a real concern with finding more efficient ways of achieving our environmental objectives. And economic incentive approaches offer just such a promise. At any rate, the setting is a much more sympathetic one. Nevertheless, many observers still harbor serious reservations. And the policy arena is the site of the debate of many difficult issues concerning the design and implementation of these policy measures. We turn now to some of these issues.

3.2   Quantity versus price instruments

While the general atmosphere in the policy arena has become much more receptive to the use of market-based incentives for environmental protection, the specific form of these instruments has itself been the subject of some interesting and intense debate. As noted earlier, the tendency in the United States has been to opt for the use of so-called quantity instruments (systems of tradeable emissions permits) rather price instruments (fees or taxes).

The rationale for this preference among incentive-based policy instruments is of some interest. Although, in principle, we can achieve the requisite reductions in polluting activities with either systems of tradeable permits or effluent taxes, these two approaches have some important differences in a policy setting. First, the quantity approach gives the environmental authority direct control over the levels of waste discharges. Under the tax approach, the regulator must determine the level of the tax, and if, for example, the tax turns out to be too low, then emissions will exceed the targeted levels. Since environmental objectives or standards are often stated in quantity terms, an agency will find itself in a better position to achieve its regulatory objectives if it has direct control over the quantities of waste emissions rather than indirect control through a price instrument.

This consideration assumes even more significance in an intertemporal setting. In a world of growth and inflation, a specific nominal tax that restricts emissions adequately at one time will fail to do so later in the presence of economic growth and rising prices. The environmental authority will have to enact periodic (and unpopular) increases in tax rates. In contrast, a system of tradeable permits automatically accomodates itself to growth and inflation. Since there is no change in the aggregate supply of emissions permits without explicit action by the environmental regulator, the increased demand for waste emissions will simply translate itself into a higher market-clearing price for permits with no effect on the overall level of discharges.

A second issue has probably been of even greater importance in the United States. New taxes of any sort have been fiercely opposed in the U.S. The proposal (mentioned earlier) for a nationwide system of taxes on sulfur and nitrogen dioxide emissions in 1987 induced an immediate and hostile response from industry (especially public power utilities) and representatives of labor, who made much over the cost increases and lost jobs that they claimed would result from the new taxes. This opposition ultimately doomed the bill. A system of tradeable permits, in contrast, can avoid this source of opposition. If the permits are auctioned off to sources, then, of course, they result in new costs to polluters--just like taxes. But rather than allocating the permits by auction, the environmental authority can choose to distribute these permits freely among existing sources. Some form of "grandfathering" can be used to allocate the permits based on historical performance. Existing firms thus receive a marketable asset, which they can then use either to validate their own emissions or sell to another polluter. Sources are naturally much more receptive to a system that provides them with a valuable asset than to one that imposes a new cost on them. This kind of distribution of permits has, in fact, been employed in the quantity approach in the United States.

And, third, permits have the importance advantage of familiarity. Environmental regulators have had long experience with permits--and it is a much less radical step to make such permits effectively tradeable than to replace the whole system with a set of taxes for environmental management (with which there is virtually no experience). For these three reasons, policy makers in the U.S. have, to this juncture, preferred to adopt quantity rather than price instruments for environmental regulation. There is some reason to believe that taxes are becoming a somewhat more appealing alternative in the current setting--and I will return to this issue in the concluding section of the paper.

3.3   International competitiveness

The issue of international competitiveness has come to the fore in the U.S. in the debate over environmental policy. In particular, the charge is that environmental measures in the United States have burdened domestic industries with additional costs and put them at a competitive disadvantage relative to their counterparts in certain other countries that have a more relaxed environmental posture. Especially in the current period of recession with unemployment running at high rates, U.S. policy makers have become very sensitive to this issue. It has reached the point where actual legislation has been introduced in the U.S. Congress. On April 25, 1991, Senator David Boren of Oklahoma introduced a bill entitled "The International Pollution Deterrence Act of 1991." This bill calls for "countervailing duties" (tariffs) on goods coming into the United States from countries with environmental standards that are less strict than those in the U.S. The amount of the tariff would be equal to the per-unit difference in environmental compliance costs. In introducing the bill, Senator Boren stated that "We are upholding our responsibilities to the world environment but many of our trading partners are not...This means fewer jobs in America as cheaper foreign goods compete with our products and it means more environmental problems for everybody because pollution knows no national boundaries."

These international issues, interestingly, have been the subject of some attention in the environmental economics literature.[10] It is clear, for example, that the introduction of costly abatement measures in some countries can alter the international structure of relative costs with potential effects on patterns of specialization and world trade (e.g., Baumol and Oates, 1988, ch. 16). This general point has taken a more specific form. The concern has become that the less developed countries, with their efforts directed toward economic development rather than environmental protection, will tend to develop a comparative advantage in pollution-intensive industries. The world's dirty industries, according to this view, will find it less costly to locate in the developing countries than in the industrialized nations where they are subject to substantial pollution-control costs. In consequence, the fear is that the developing countries will become "havens" for the world's heavy polluters: this contention is the so-called "pollution-haven hypothesis."

Some early studies, using simulation techniques, tried to estimate the extent of this effect. But we are now in a position to examine what has happened historically, at least to this juncture. Two recent studies, quite different in character, have addressed this issue directly. Jeffrey Leonard (1988), in what is largely a case study of international trade and investment flows for several key industries and countries, finds little evidence that pollution-control measures have exerted a systematic effect on international trade and investment. After examining some aggregate figures, the policy stances in several industrialized and developing countries, and the operations of multinational corporations, Leonard concludes that "the differentials in the costs of complying with environmental regulations and in the levels of environmental concern in industrialized and industrializing countries have not been strong enough to offset larger political and economic forces in shaping aggregate international comparative advantage" (p. 231).

James Tobey (1989, 1990) has studied the same issue in a large econometric study of international trade patterns in "pollution-intensive" goods. After controlling for the effects of relative factor abundance and other trade determinants, Tobey cannot find any effects of the various measures he uses of the stringency of domestic environmental policies. Tobey estimates two sets of equations that explain, respectively, patterns of trade in pollution-intensive goods and changes in trade patterns from 1970 to 1984. In neither set of equations do the variables measuring the stringency of domestic environmental policy have the predicted effect on trade patterns.

Why have domestic environmental measures not induced "industrial flight" and the development of "pollution havens"? The primary reason seems to be that the costs of pollution control have not, in fact, loomed very large, even in heavily polluting industries. Existing estimates suggest that control costs in the U.S. have run on the order of only 1 to 2-1/2 percent of total costs in most pollution-intensive industries; H. David Robison (1985, p. 704), for example, reports that total abatement costs per dollar of output in the United States were well under 3 percent in all industries with the sole exception of electric utilities where they were 5.4 percent. Such small increments to costs are likely to be swamped in their impact on international trade by the much larger effects of changing differentials in labor costs, swings in exchange rates, etc. Moreover, nearly all the industrialized nations have introduced environmental measures--and at roughly the same time--so that such measures have not been the source of significant cost differentials among major competitors. There seems not to have been a discernible movement in investment in these industries to the developing countries because major political and economic uncertainties have apparently loomed much larger in location decisions than have the modest savings from less stringent environmental controls.

In short, domestic environmental policies, at least to this point in time, do not appear to have had significant effects on patterns of international trade. This is a comforting finding in one respect. It suggests that too much is being made of this issue in the policy arena. Especially in difficult economic times, it is easy to see why politicians may find such issues an attractive way to deflect concern and blame away from more fundamental domestic ills. But the evidence does not appear to support their claims.

3.4   Regulatory federalism

In the context of a federal system of government with a substantial degree of fiscal and regulatory decentralization, there is considerable concern and interest in the United States in the respective roles of federal, state, and local government in environmental management. For issues that clearly transcend local and state boundaries (such as acid-rain problems), a major role for centralized management is clearly in order. But many environmental problems are of a local character: the emissions of certain air and water pollutants, for example, result in environmental damages that are limited mainly to the area at or around the site of their discharge. For such forms of pollution, there is a real case for decentralized environmental regulation.

This issue has manifested itself in terms of an intriguing anomoly in U.S. environmental legislation. Under the Clean Air Act in 1970, the U.S. Congress instructed the Environmental Protection Agency to set uniform national standards for air quality: maximum permissible concentrations of key air pollutants applicable to all areas in the nation. But two years later under the Clean Water Act, the Congress decided to let the individual states determine their own standards (subject to EPA approval) for water quality. This poses the important question of the locus of regulatory authority: Should environmental decision-making be centralized or left to state and local government?

Basic economic principles appear to suggest a straightforward answer to the question. For those environmental phenomena which are essentially localized in terms of their effects, the optimal standards for environmental quality are likely to vary among jurisdictions in accordance with local preferences and cost conditions. An optimal outcome will thus involve differentiated environmental standards across jurisdictions that reflect these basic cost and taste differences. From this perspective, uniform national standards cannot achieve an optimal outcome. What is needed is a system of "regulatory federalism" that places the responsibility and authority for environmental management at the appropriate level for each form of polluting activity.

Some environmental economists, such as John Cumberland (1981), have objected to this general proposition on the grounds of political naivete. Their claim is that in their eagerness to attract new business investment and jobs, state or local officials will tend to set excessively lax environmental standards: they will set tax rates on polluting levels of activities that are too low or quantities of tradeable permits that are too high. The fear, in short, is that economic competition among states and localities will undermine efforts for environmental protection.

This issue has been the subject of some recent attention in the environmental economics literature.[11]   Oates and Schwab (1988a, 1988b), for example, have constructed a series of prototypical models of economic competition among decentralized jurisdictions that involve both fiscal and environmental policy variables. The basic outcomes in these models do not exhibit the kinds of distortions that Cumberland and others fear: decision-makers in these models choose standards for environmental quality for which marginal benefits equal marginal cost. However, these results are not especially robust: it is easy to introduce plausible modifications that can result in excessive environmental degradation.

At the policy level, there is continuing concern with this issue. State and local governments continue to play a major role in the management of U.S. environmental programs, but there is a real tension in the balance between centralized and decentralized authority. To cite one case, it has become increasingly clear that the costs of requiring Southern California to meet the same standards for air quality as the rest of the nation are exhorbitant and unreasonable. The geography and economy there combine in ways to make clean air <u>far</u> more expensive than elsewhere. But, instead of recognizing the special circumstances of the Southern California basin, U.S. officials have responded by extending the time schedule for compliance, and Southern California continues adopting new measures, unjustifiable on any sort of benefit-cost calculation, and with no prospect of ever attaining the national standards. The cost, in such cases, of ignoring the need for environmental federalism is likely to be very high.

3.5   Equity issues

In the debate over the the 1987 House Bill for a national tax on sulfur and nitrogen oxide emissions, the opposition raised as one objection to the tax its potential regressivity. They contended that it would substantially drive up the utility bills of individual households and that this would fall much more heavily on lower, than on higher, income households. Such arguments are frequently voiced in the debate over new environmental measures, expecially tax measures. And this raises two important questions. Are environmental regulations, and especially taxes on polluting activities, likely to be regressive in their pattern of incidence? In short, is this claim true? And, second, if it is true, what sorts of alternatives, if any, are available to soften the adverse redistributive impact of these policies?

The redistributive implications of environmental programs can raise some very complicated and tricky issues.[12]   But there is some evidence to suggest that the costs of the major existing programs for the control of air and water pollution in the United States have, in fact, had a regressive pattern of incidence. To take one careful study, H. David Robison (1985) examined the distribution of the costs of industrial pollution abatement in a full general-equilibrium framework. Using a highly disaggregated input-output model, Robison assumed that the control costs in each industry were passed forward in the form of higher prices. He was then able to trace these price increases through a general-equilibrium system to determine their effect on the prices of various consumer goods. Robison's model divides individuals into twenty income classes, and, for each class, he had data describing the pattern of consumption in considerable detail. With this information, he was able to estimate for each of his income classes the increase in the prices of the items that they purchase. He finds that the pattern of incidence of control costs is quite regressive. Costs as a fraction of income fall over the whole range of income classes: they range from 0.76 percent of income for his lowest income class to 0.16 percent of income for the highest income classes. Other studies have obtained similar findings, thus giving some substance to the claim that pollution-control measures (including taxes) are likely to be regressive in their incidence.

There are certainly some ways to address the issue of the undesirable distribution of the costs of environmental programs. Some programs have "transitional effects" that hit certain groups much harder than others. Programs, for example, to reduce airborne sulfur emissions may put substantial numbers of coal miners out of work. Such shifting patterns of employment with transitional job losses can be very painful indeed. These transitional costs suggest the need for some form of "adjustment assistance," including unemployment compensation, retraining programs, and perhaps relocation assistance to help those who suffer from altered patterns of output and employment. Such programs are familiar accompanyments to legislation for the reduction of tariffs and other trade restrictions.

More generally, the regressive pattern of price changes (of the sort indicated by the Robison study) will require companion measures if their redistributive impact is to be neutralized. To take an example from the earlier discussion, a proposed system of pollution taxes can be accompanied by cuts in other taxes to make the overall measure revenue neutral. There is an opportunity here to make these cuts in other taxes so as to provide the most generous relief to lower income groups. The pollution taxes might, for example, be packaged with tax credits to low income groups or reductions in the lowest income tax rates.

While such supplementary measures can offset the undesired redistributive impact of pollution taxes, it is critical that such amendments do not compromise the basic incentives provided by the environmental measures themselves. It is important to remember that the basic objectives of taxes on pollution (or other environmental programs) are allocative in nature: their purpose is to achieve important targets for environmental quality. Such measures are often not well suited to achieving redistributional goals. Where their adverse redistributional impact can be easily addressed, it is surely important to do so, but environmental measures should not, in general, be side-tracked on redistributional grounds. We have other policy tools for dealing with the distribution of income.

Chapter 4

TAXES AND THE ENVIRONMENT: AN ASSESSMENT

To conclude this report, I will return to a number of issues in the design and introduction of tax measures that seem to me important if we are to make better use of the tax system for environmental protection. There are, I believe, some real opportunities on the horizon to make some useful steps in this direction. I shall begin with a further exmination of the choice among incentive-based policy instruments and will then proceed to some other important matters in the actual design of environmentally "sensitive" tax policies.

4.1   Quantity versus price instruments again

In the preceding section, I indicated why, it seems to me, regulators in the United States have opted for systems of tradeable permits rather than taxes for environmental management. However, based on this experience and on some further considerations, I think that taxes now stand in a somewhat more favorable light. I see three significant reasons for this. First, the U.S. experience with Emissions Trading has encountered a troublesome obstacle in the actual operation of permit markets. These markets have frequently failed to operate as smoothly as envisioned in theory. In particular, permit markets have often been very thin, especially on the supply side. Robert Hahn (1989) contends that this has been largely the result of unfortunate restrictions on trading that have clouded definitions of property rights and raised serious uncertainties about the ability to obtain these rights in the marketplace when needed. In addition, the number of potential participants in some of these relatively localized markets has often been small with certain large sources in a position to exercise monopolistic influence on permit prices. The thinness of these markets and infrequency of transactions suggests that sources may not observe a clear, well defined price signal to indicate the opportunity costs of their emissions. The absence of such a clear price can impair the effective functioning of the permit system. A regime of effluent taxes, in contrast, encounters no such problems: the tax itself provides a clear, unambiguous measure of the cost of emissions. There is no need to worry about the way the market "works."

A second issue that seems to favor taxes over permits concerns the use of these policy instruments in a setting of uncertainty.[13] Use of a quantity instrument like permits gives the environmental authority a firm control over the aggregate level of polluting emissions. However, in a setting of imperfect information and uncertainty about the costs and benefits of pollution control, the regulator may not have a very good idea about the costs that such a quantity approach will impose on sources. In contrast, under tax regime, there is a well defined limit on the costs that will be imposed on sources, for polluters can always elect to pay the tax and not reduce emissions further. The tax constitutes an upper limit to the costs to polluters; there is no such upper limit under a

131

permit system. Conversely, however, the limit on costs under the tax approach introduces uncertainty as to the quantity of emissions, since the regulator is unsure as to the precise way in which sources will respond to the tax. The regulator does not know the exact proportions by which sources will choose to reduce emissions or pay taxes.

The issue here is which form of uncertainty, uncertainty over costs or uncertainty over the level of emissions, is likely to be the more threatening?[14] The answer to this question depends on the particular character of the environmental damages and of the control costs associated with the form of pollution. Suppose, for example, that the nature of the damages is such that important environmental threshold effects exist. If pollutant concentrations exceed some critical value, then an environmental disaster occurs. In such a setting, it is obviously crucial to have careful control over the quantity of waste emissions. The use of environmental taxes could be very dangerous, for if the tax were set too low, emissions could exceed the critical level with catastrophic results. In such instances, it is best to employ a quantity system under which the regulator has direct control over the level of emissions and can avoid the uncertainty over quantity that accompanies the use of a price instrument (such as an effluent charge).

In contrast, in other settings, the damages from additional emissions may be relatively stable over the relevant range; the potential damage from being off a bit on the quantity of emissions will, in such cases, be modest. However, it may be that the marginal costs of pollution control vary dramatically. There exist, in fact, many estimates of the marginal costs of emissions control which indicate that, after a relatively constant range, marginal costs begin to increase sharply. In this setting, the more pressing danger from a mistake in policy is one of excessive costs. If the regulator sets too tough a standard for emissions reductions, he may impose enormous costs on sources. The danger, in this case, is greater with the quantity instrument, for if the supply of permits is set too low, then excessive control costs will be forced upon polluting firms. Under a fee regime, this danger is avoided, since sources can always opt to pay the fee and avoid the more costly controls.

Which of these two dangers is the more prevalent? It is impossible to be completely general on this, but there is, I think, a strong presumption that for many cases of pollution, the larger threat is from excessive costs. Few environmental phenomena seem to be characterized by critical threshold levels over the relevant range of pollution; if we are off by a bit from our environmental targets, the consequences are typically not too serious. In contrast, there is considerable evidence suggesting that existing environmental programs have already induced extensive abatement efforts and that these efforts have pushed us onto the rapidly rising portions of marginal abatement cost curves. Decisions that involve excessively stringent control measures (e.g., too few permits) have the potential to be inordinately costly. And this makes a strong case for a reliance on price, rather than quantity, instruments. In a policy setting characterized by uncertainty, pollution taxes probably provide us with greater protection from serious error than do systems of tradeable permits.

Third, taxes provide public revenues. Although there is strong opposition to new taxes, there is also an almost desperate need for new revenue sources to reduce the budgetary deficit in the United States. Their revenue potential thus gives environmental taxes some real appeal in the current policy setting. For all these reasons, I think that the tax approach is likely to get a more sympathetic hearing in the U.S. than it has in the past. Current policy discussion and analysis is certainly including taxes among the important candidates for incentive-based approaches to environmental protection.

4.2   On the design of environmental tax measures

I introduced in the initial section the issue of the locus of management of environmental taxes. Ideally, in the spirit of the optimal tax approach to this issue, the design and administration of the tax should reflect both environmental and taxation objectives. The tax rate should be set so as realize the joint gains from pollution control and a reduced reliance on distorting taxes. In practice, however, such an integrated approach to tax policy may not always be possible. Where a choice must be made on the locus of the authority for pollution taxation, I think that there are compelling reasons for giving environmental regulators a dominant role in the design and administering of such taxes, rather than assigning responsibility to a taxing agency.

Pollution taxes are a potentially powerful and effective tool for environmental management. There is now a large theoretical and empirical literature that makes a persuasive case for an extensive reliance on economic incentives for pollution control.[15] To remove pollution taxes from the sphere of the environmental authority is effectively to place one of the primary determinants of levels of waste emissions +under the management of another public agency. This is likely to constrain quite severely the policy options for environmental management; it will force environmental regulators to turn to less effective command-and-control instruments for pollution control.

Tax authorities, in contrast, have a substantial range of tax bases from which to choose. Revenues from environmental taxes can ultimately finance only a modest portion of the public budget. This suggests, in my view, that it makes sense for the tax authority to leave tax rates on pollution to the discretion of environmental regulators. The tax authority would view the revenues from such pollution taxes as an exogenous (but welcome) revenue source--and would then determine rates on other tax bases so as to produce the requisite overall level of revenues. I stress here that pollution taxes, effectively employed for purposes of environmental management, can be the source of sizeable revenues. And the "side benefits" in terms of a less distorting tax system can be quite substantial.

Another potentially complex and delicate issue that arises in the design of environmental taxes is the matter of earmarking of funds. As Robert Hahn (1989) and others note, where pollution taxes have been employed in such countries as France, Germany, and the Netherlands for water quality management, the revenue aspect of these taxes has been of central importance. Environmental authorities have typically set tax rates in such a way as to generate the revenues needed for various pollution-control programs. They have looked on these taxes as a source of monies to fund projects for water-quality management, not primarily as instruments for the regulation of waste flows.[16] This earmarking (or creation of "trust funds") for the revenues from environmental taxes is a typical element in legislation for such taxes. In the 1987 U.S. Bill mentioned earlier for a national tax on sulfur and nitrogen oxide emissions, there was a provision to direct the revenues collected from the tax into a special "Sulfur and Nitrogen Emissions Trust Fund" which would be used to assist polluters in meeting their control costs.

Such provisions have a certain appeal in the policy arena. To the extent that the funds are used for financing environmental "cleanup" projects, they are consistent with the OECD "Polluter Pays Principle." Moreover, as Jean-Philippe Barde has suggested to me, such trust funds may serve as a kind of second-best measure where the heavy costs of taxes makes their introduction infeasible without some form of earmarking assistance.

At the same time, earmarking has some very troubling aspects. One of the arguments for environmental taxes is the potential improvement in the overall tax system that results from the substitution of revenues from these sources for the funds from other distorting taxes. If the revenues from pollution taxes are siphoned off into increased spending for environmental projects, then they will obviously make no contribution to the enhancement of the overall tax system by reducing the reliance on distorting taxes. The revenues may (as some public-choice writers fear) simply serve to expand the public budget.

Such trust funds may have other perverse allocative effects. In the proposed U.S. bill, a primary use of the revenues would have been to assist polluters in covering their control costs. From the perspective of economic efficiency, this is misplaced assistance. The tax is itself to serve as a signal to polluters to guide their decisions on levels of control activities. Rebates on control costs would distort this signal. Morever, over the longer haul, it is important that polluters bear the full cost of their abatement activities and pollution taxes so that profits (net of costs) will provide the right incentives for entry and exit into the industry (Baumol and Oates, 1988, pp. 52-4).

This is, of course, not to be taken to mean that important environmental projects should not be undertaken. But they should have to meet the same budgetary and economic tests as other public projects. They should not be undertaken simply by virtue of the availability of some earmarked funds.

My own sense then is that, as a rule, earmarking (or the creation of trust funds) should probably be discouraged in the design of environmental taxes. It is better that the revenues be directed into the "general fund" and used as a means to reduce reliance on other distorting forms of taxation.

4.3   Environmental taxes: some specifics

In this part of the paper, I shall suggest a few areas where, it seems to me, that environmental taxation has some potential in the United States. The treatment is neither comprehensive nor in depth; my intent is simply to point to a few uses of environmental taxes that appear promising and that merit further study.

i)   Heavier taxation of gasoline and other fuels. Both the federal and state governments in the U.S. tax gasoline and other fuels for motor vehicles and aircraft, but the taxes rates are low relative to their counterparts in most Europe countries. Although the demand for gasoline appears to be price inelastic, it is far from perfectly inelastic. The price response over the longer haul to higher gasoline prices is substantial and can have a marked impact on the fuel efficiency of vehicles, commuting patterns, and location decisions. In short, such taxes reduce fuel use and thereby reduce air pollution and other congestion and noise problems associated with automobiles. There doesn't appear to be a strong impetus in the U.S. to move in this direction, with the exception, perhaps, of a general carbon tax to be discussed shortly.

ii)   Taxes to increase the fuel efficiency of motor vehicles. There is presently a federal Gas Guzzler excise tax on cars that do not meet specified fuel efficiency standards. There is no tax, however, on cars that meet the standard. A schedule of taxes with rates that decline as fuel efficiency rises could provide a continuing incentive for improving the fuel efficiency of the whole fleet of motor vehicles.

iii)   Taxes on various fertilizers and pesticides that result in polluting runoff into rivers, lakes, and bays. The control of various forms of non-point source pollution, notably agricultural runoff, is a serious problem. It is difficult to tax such runoff directly, but a second-best approach involves the taxation of agricultural inputs that have the potential for contributing to such runoff. Such taxes can provide an incentive to seek other forms of farming and pest management.

iv)   A wider use of deposit-refund systems to encourage the proper disposal of environmentally damaging wastes. Interesting candidates include lead batteries, tires, and autos themselves (as in Sweden). In addition, the Project 88 report (see Stavins, 1988) recommends such a system for "containerizable hazardous wastes."

v)   Waste-end taxes. In addition to (or in place of) "front-end" taxes on inputs into waste generating activities (like the Superfund "feedstock taxes"), there may be a useful place for taxes levied after the generation of wastes at the disposal stage. Such taxes can influence both the level of generation of wastes and disposal practices. A central problem to be addressed here is the incentive that such a tax can create for illegal dumping.

vi)   Tax credits for the introduction of less polluting agricultural techniques. Again, because of the difficulty in taxing runoff directly, second-best methods are needed to address the problem. The use of tax credits for investments in agricultural technology that reduce the runoff of pollutants has real potential.

vii)   Effluent taxes on discharges of major air and water pollutants. Although the U.S. has opted for systems of tradeable permits for the regulation of certain air and water pollutants, I don't think that we should take this as a closed issue. There remains a case for effluent taxes, and it deserves further study and discussion.

4.4   International issues

It seems suitable to conclude this report with a brief discussion of the international dimensions of U.S. tax policy for the environment. There is a growing concern with global issues that is manifesting itself in a move towards an "open-economy environmental economics" (Oates, 1991). The concern with ozone depletion, leading to the Montreal Protocol, and now the threat of global warming point to the need for international cooperation in addressing the future of the planet.

This has set off a lively policy debate in the United States, as in the rest of the world. Of central interest here, it has led to the study of proposals for a carbon tax, of a national or, perhaps, international scope (Poterba, 1991). For example, the U.S. Congressional Budget Office (1990) has published the results of an extensive study of the taxation of fossil fuels in the U.S. Similar studies are underway in other government agencies, notably the EPA, and also in research institutes and academia. Again, a major issue in the debate is the choice between policy instruments: taxes versus systems of tradeable permits.

Should policy makers opt for the tax approach to regulate carbon emissions, they will acquire a tax base with massive potential for tax revenues. Many of the issues treated in this paper will have to be addressed: Who administers the tax? How is the rate determined? What is to be done with the revenues?

Tax policy over the coming decades has the potential to exert a powerful influence on the course of the environment, both at the national and global levels.

Notes

1. H.R. 2497, the "Sulfur and Nitrogen Emissions Tax Act of 1987," introduced on May 21, 1987.

2. President Bush has expressed his strong opposition to <u>any</u> new taxes at this juncture. But this obviously doesn't rule out new non-tax incentive-based measures, or <u>perhaps</u> some revenue-neutral tax reforms of the sort to be discussed later in the paper.

3. For a more thorough discussion of this case, see Oates (forthcoming).

4. Agency interaction, for example, is evident in the case of Superfund taxes where the EPA has played a major role in the design of the taxes, although they are administered by the Internal Revenue Service.

5. In addition, there are a few states in which local governments also levy excise taxes on gasoline. These taxes are typically at a relatively low rate with the exception of Hawaii where local taxes range from from $.088 to $.165 per gallon.

6. According to the Department of Transportation, in 1985 about 75 percent of the funding for highway expenditures came from highway user taxes and tolls (largely taxes on gasoline), income from invested funds, and proceeds of transportation bond sales. Motor fuel taxes cover a little more than half of total highway expenditures. See Ronald Fisher (1988, ch. 19).

7. In some states, motor vehicles are also subject to state and/or local property taxation. See Appendix B.

8. The material in this section is based on a recent Ph. D. dissertation at the University of Maryland by Robin R. Jenkins (1991).

9. For a useful summary and description of federal environmental tax policy, see U.S. Joint Committee on Taxation (1990).

10. See the survey paper by Cropper and Oates (1992) for a summary of this work.

11. See Cropper and Oates (1992) for a survey of this literature.

137

12. See Baumol and Oates (1988, ch. 15) for a systematic consideration of these issues.

13. See Martin Weitzman (1974) for the formal genesis of this point.

14. As Weitzman (1974) has shown, the formal answer to this question depends on the relative slopes of the marginal benefit and marginal abatement cost functions. I present the intuition underlying the Weitzman theorem in the text.

15. See Cropper and Oates (1992) for a recent survey of this literature.

16. There are a few instances in which incentive effects have figured importantly in environmental taxes: fees on discharges into Dutch river basins and some of the new "eco taxes" in Sweden on carbon and other airborne emissions. But these appear to be the exception rather than the rule.

Annex 1[1]

The tax per pound of each ozone-depleting chemical is determined by multiplying the base tax amount for the applicable year times the ozone-depleting factor specific to the chemical. The base amounts per pound (in U.S. dollars per pound) rise over time according to the following schedule:

	1990	1991	1992	1993	1994	1995
Chemicals Restricted by the Original Protocol	1.37	1.37	1.67	2.65	2.65	3.10
Chemicals Restricted by the Amended Protocol	-	1.37	1.37	1.67	3.00	3.10

where the base amounts increase by $0.45 per year after calendar 1995.

The ozone-depleting factors are normalized on CFC-11 and are as follows:

Chemicals Restricted by the Original Protocol	Ozone Depleting Factor
CFC-11	1.0
CFC-12	1.0
CFC-113	0.8
CFC-114	1.0
CFC-115	0.6
Halon-1211	3.0
Halon-1301	10.0
Halon-2402	6.0

Chemicals Restricted by the Amended Protocol	Ozone Depleting Factor
CFC-13	1.0
CFC-111	1.0
CFC-112	1.0
CFC-211, 212, 213, 214, 215,	1.0
216, 217	1.0
Carbon Tetrachloride	1.1
Methyl Chloroform	0.1

---

[1]   The data and information presented in this appendix and in the text on the excise tax on ozone-depleting chemicals comes from OECD (1991).

The ozone-depleting factor for a particular chemical (for example, 0.8 for CFC-113) is multiplied times the base amount to determine the tax for the chemical in a specific year (e.g., the tax per pound on CFC-113 in 1992 would be 0.8 times 1.67 or 1.336).

A different set of base amounts and ozone-depleting factors has been determined for halons and chemicals used in rigid foam insulation. For the years 1991-93, the tax on these chemicals is approximately $0.25 per pound.

The taxes are projected to generate substantial revenues. The estimates of these revenues by fiscal year:

1991	$ 890 million
1992	1,000 "
1993	1,430 "
1994	1,640 "
1995	1,530 "
1996	1,380 "

Bibliography

American Legislative Exchange Council, *Legislative Update: State Solid Waste Policy: January, 1991*, Washington, D.C., 1991.

BARDE, Jean-Philippe, The Use of Economic Instruments for Environmental Protection in OECD Countries, unpublished paper (1991).

BAUMOL, William J., and Oates, Wallace E., *The Theory of Environmental Policy*, Second Edition (Cambridge: Cambridge University Press, 1988).

BRENNAN, Geoffrey, and Buchanan, James, *The Power to Tax: Analytical Foundations of a Fiscal Constitution* (Cambridge: Cambridge University Press, 1980).

CROPPER, Maureen L., and Oates, Wallace E., "Environmental Economics: A Survey," *Journal of Economic Literature*, 30, June, 1992), pp. 675-740.

CUMBERLAND, John H., "Efficiency and Equity in Interregional Environmental Management," *Review of Regional Studies*, No. 2 (1981), pp. 1-9.

DEACON, Robert T., Taxation, Depletion, and Welfare: A Simulation Study of the U.S. Petroleum Resource, Working Paper No. ENR 90-10, Resources for the Future, Washington, D.C. (June 1990).

FISHER, Ronald C., *State and Local Public Finance* (Glenview, Illinois: Scott, Foresman, and Co., 1988).

HAHN, Robert W. "Economic Prescriptions for Environmental Problems: How the Patient Followed the Doctor's Orders," *Journal of Economic Perspectives*, 3 (Spring, 1989), pp. 95-114.

HAHN, Robert W., and Stavins, Robert N., "Incentive-Based Environmental Regulation: A New Era from an Old Idea?" *Ecology Law Quarterly* 18, No. 1 (1991), pp. 1-42.

JENKINS, Robin R., Municipal Demand for Solid Waste Disposal Services: The Impact of User Fees, Ph.D. Dissertation, University of Maryland (1991).

LEE, Dwight R., and Misiolek, Walter S., "Substituting Pollution Taxation for General Taxation: Some Implications for Efficiency in Pollution Taxation," *Journal of Environmental Economics and Management 13* (Dec., 1986), pp. 338-347.

LEONARD, H. Jeffrey, *Pollution and the Struggle for the World Product* (Cambridge: Cambridge University Press, 1988).

MIESZKOWSKI, Peter, and Toder, E., "Taxation of Energy Resources," in C. McLure and P. Mieszkowski, eds., *Fiscal Federalism and the Taxation of Natural Resources* (Lexington, Mass.: Heath-Lexington, 1983).

OATES, Wallace E., Global Environmental Management: Towards An Open Economy Environmental Economics, University of Maryland, Dept. of Economics Working Paper No. 91-17 (1991).

OATES, Wallace E., "Pollution Charges as a Source of Public Revenues," in H. Giersch, ed., *Economic Evolution and Environmental Concerns* (forthcoming).

OATES, Wallace E., and Schwab, Robert M., Economic Competition Among Jurisdictions: Efficiency Enhancing or Distortion Inducing?" Journal of Public Economics 35 (April 1988a), pp. 333-354.

OATES, Wallace E., and Schwab, Robert M., The Theory of Regulatory Federalism: The Case of Environmental Management, University of Maryland, Dept. of Economics Working Paper No. 88- 26 (1988b).

POTERBA, James M., "Tax Policy to Combat Global Warming: On Designing a Carbon Tax," in R. Dornbusch and J. Poterba, eds., *Global Warming: Economic Policy Responses* (Cambridge, Mass.: M.I.T. Press, 1991), pp. 71-98.

ROBISON, H. David, "Who Pays for Industrial Pollution Abatement?" *Review of Economics and Statistics 67* (Nov., 1985), pp. 702-6.

ROSEN, Harvey S., *Public Finance*, Second Edition (Homewood, Illinois: Irwin, 1988).

State Tax Notes (Nov. 11, 1991) (Arlington, Va.: Tax Analysts).

STAVINS, Robert H., ed., Project 88--Harnessing Market Forces to Protect Our Environment: Initiatives for the New President. A Public Policy Study Sponsored by Senator Timothy E. Wirth, Colorado, and Senator John Heinz, Pennsylvania (Washington, D.C., Dec., 1988).

TERKLA, David, "The Efficiency Value of Effluent Tax Revenues," *Journal of Environmental Economics and Management 11* (June, 1984), pp. 107-23.

TOBEY, James A., The Impact of Domestic Environmental Policies on International Trade, Ph.D. Dissertation, University of Maryland, 1989.

TOBEY, James A., "The Effects of Domestic Environmental Policies on Patterns of World Trade: An Empirical Test," *Kyklos 43* (No. 2), pp. 191-209.

WEITZMAN, Martin L., "Price vs. Quantities," *Review of Economic Studies* 41 (Oct., 1974), pp. 477-91.

U.S. Congressional Budget Office, Carbon Charges as a Response to Global Warming: The Effects of Taxing Fossil Fuels (Washington, D.C.: U.S. GPO, 1990).

142

U.S. General Accounting Office, <u>Trade-offs in Beverage Container Deposit Legislation</u> (Washington, D.C., Nov. 14, 1990).

U.S. Joint Committee on Taxation, <u>Present Law and Background Relating to Federal Environmental Tax Policy</u> (Washington, D.C.: U.S. Government Printing Office, March 1, 1990).

PART IV

THE DESIGN OF SYSTEMS OF TRADEABLE EMISSIONS PERMITS

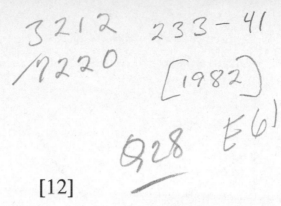

[12]

Efficiency in pollution control in the short and long runs: a system of rental emission permits

ROBERT A. COLLINGE / *University of Maryland*
WALLACE E. OATES / *Bureau of Business and Economic Research and University of Maryland*

While a Pigouvian tax on waste emissions equal to marginal social damage (MSD) can sustain an efficient pattern of emissions among existing polluters in the short run, the recent literature on externalities stresses that this is not, in general, sufficient to ensure efficiency in the long run (see Rose-Ackerman, 1973; Gould, 1977; and Burrows, 1979). Economic efficiency over both the short and long runs makes two demands on polluting firms (Schulze and d'Arge, 1974): (1) the marginal value of the firm's output must equal marginal cost (including any external, as well as private, costs); (2) the total value of the firm's output must not be less than total cost (where again costs include both private and external costs).

The Pigouvian tax ensures the satisfaction of the first (short-run) condition for economic efficiency. Assuming that the prices of other inputs reflect accurately their social opportunity costs and that firms are price takers, a tax on waste emissions equal to MSD 'internalizes' the social cost of waste emissions and leads the profit-maximizing firm to produce where price equals (social) marginal cost. All this is well understood.

However, the recent literature points out that policy measures to correct the allocative distortions associated with externalities must also satisfy a 'total' or 'exit-entry' condition: the firm's net contribution to social welfare

We are grateful to Martin J. Bailey, William Baumol, Michelle White, and anonymous referees for comments on an earlier draft of this paper, and to the National Science Foundation and the Sloan Foundation for their support of this work.

Canadian Journal of Economics / Revue canadienne d'Economique, XV, No. 2
May / mai 1982. Printed in Canada / Imprimé au Canada

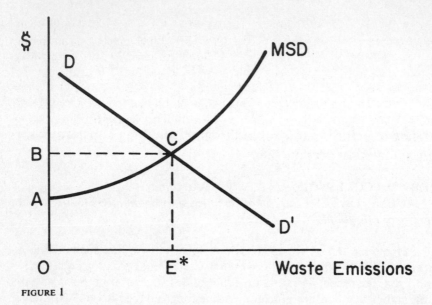

FIGURE 1

must be non-negative.[1] The Pigouvian tax will not satisfy this condition in instances where marginal social damages are not constant over the relevant range.[2] This discovery has led to some pessimistic judgments: "Thus we have the interesting conclusion that none of the 'practicable' instruments moves the system to a Pareto optimum when the marginal damage cost curves slope upwards" (Burrows, 1979, 500).

Our purpose in this paper is to describe a system of marketable emission permits that can, in quite a straightforward way, rectify matters. As we show in the second section, a system of rental emission permits (REP) can satisfy both the short-run and entry-exit conditions, even where marginal social damages vary with the polluting firm's level of emissions. In the first section we briefly review the nature of the problem.

THE ENTRY-EXIT ISSUE

The nature of the entry-exit problem is easily seen in terms of figure 1. Suppose that we have a region in which there is a single polluter. The MSD curve depicts the marginal social damages associated with the polluting firm's

---

1 This condition also applies to the short run; the firm should engage in production only if the value of its output exceeds total variable costs.
2 Carlton and Loury (1980) contend that the Pigouvian tax fails even where MSD are constant. We have shown elsewhere (Oates and Collinge, 1981), however, that their treatment involves a misspecification of the Pigouvian tax. Properly understood, we contend that the Pigouvian tax is not subject to their objection.

emissions, while DD' is the firm's demand curve for waste emissions.[3] The optimal level of emissions is E^*. A Pigouvian levy consisting of a unit tax on emissions equal to OB will induce the firm to emit the socially desired quantity of wastes. The difficulty is that the firm's total tax bill, $OBCE^*$, will exceed the total damages that its emissions impose on society ($OACE^*$) by the amount ABC. The total levy is thus excessive and in the long run may force the firm to leave the industry, even though its output has a net positive value to society. In the case where the MSD curve is downward-sloping, the opposite is obviously the case: the firm's total tax bill will understate the damages of its emissions and therefore may induce entry (or discourage exit) where the firm's total costs to society exceed the value of its output.

We thus find that where the MSD curve is not horizontal, a Pigouvian tax equal to MSD will not, in general, satisfy our long-run, entry-exit condition for efficient resource allocation. The tax itself will induce a distortion in the vector of final outputs with too little output in industries confronting upward-sloping MSD curves and excessive outputs in those with downward-sloping marginal damage functions. What is needed is a schedule of taxes reflecting the changing level of MSD with successive units of emission.[4] This last point, incidentally, suggests that we could regard this particular objection to Pigouvian taxation as largely a semantic one. As Burrows points out, the problem arises if we interpret the Pigouvian tax "as a *fixed-rate* charge per unit of effluent emission equal to the marginal damage at the Pareto optimum" (1979, 495). One could easily argue, however, that in the context of a rising or falling MSD curve, the spirit of the Pigouvian prescription of a unit tax equal to MSD implies a schedule of taxes.

However one is inclined on the semantic issue, the point remains that a non-horizontal MSD curve complicates greatly the administrative feasibility of a Pigouvian fee. The problem may not appear to be too serious in terms of the case we have examined in this section; we could envision, for example, the environmental agency confronting our single polluter with a schedule of effluent fees, where the marginal fee varies over successive units of emissions. But what about cases of more than one source of pollution? As Rose-Ackerman notes, 'With a large number of dischargers this solution is not possible since there is no unambiguous way of allocating total damage among polluters' (1973, 515). Some type of determination would seem to be necessary as to which polluter is entitled to which 'stretch' of the tax

3 We treat waste emissions as a factor input so that DD' is the value of the marginal product of emissions. Note that for any point on the horizontal axis the vertical distance to DD' is also the firm's marginal abatement cost.
4 Alternatively, the environmental authority could supplement the Pigouvian tax on emissions with a fixed-sum subsidy (or levy) on entry. In terms of figure 1. the unit tax on emissions of OB would be accompanied by a subsidy to the firm of ABC so that the total tax bill (net of the subsidy) would equal total damages. Were the MSD curve downward-sloping, the supplementary measure would be a fixed-sum tax. We doubt, however, that this alternative approach has much appeal at the policy level.

schedule. We describe in the next section a system of rental emission permits that can resolve this problem; the system satisfies both the short-run and entry-exit conditions for economic efficiency in cases of one, several, or many polluters.

A SYSTEM OF RENTAL EMISSION PERMITS (REP)

Our basic problem is to design a system that confronts each polluter with a charge at the margin equal to MSD and with a total payment equal to the total damages that its emissions impose. We begin by describing the mechanics of a system of rental emission permits (REP) and then explore how it achieves these two objectives. We assume throughout that the pollution damage function is convex.

Implementation of the REP system proceeds as follows.

Step 1. Print permits, each allowing emission of some designated quantity of pollutant over some interval of time (e.g., one ton of sulfur per month).

Step 2. Number these permits and order them sequentially ($i = 1, \ldots , I$).

Step 3. Attach a rental price (R_i) to each permit, i, equal to the marginal social damage that would be caused by the quantity of emissions specified (E_i) on the permit, given that all permits with smaller numbers were being fully utilized. The rental payment per emission right would thus vary directly with the permit number; for a permit numbered 'θ,' the rental price would be:

$$R_\theta = C \left(\sum_{i=1}^{\theta} E_i \right) - C \left(\sum_{i=1}^{\theta-1} E_i \right),$$

where $C(\cdot)$ is the total damage (or social cost) function.

Step 4. Distribute these permits (by any of several methods to be discussed later), subject to a rental payment of R_i to be paid each time period until the permit is returned. Following the initial distribution of permits, any unclaimed permits would be available without an *initial* charge to anyone willing to make the rental payment associated with the particular permit.

Step 5. Allow firms to buy and sell these permits, with each transaction registered with the environmental authority.

This procedure effectively generates a supply curve of emission rights approximately equal to MSD (labelled S_{REP} in figure 2).

We turn next to the properties of the REP system for our three cases of one, many, or a 'few' sources of pollution. If there is only a single polluter, that polluter will face a marginal cost of pollution that approximates the true marginal social damage function. This occurs because the polluter (a

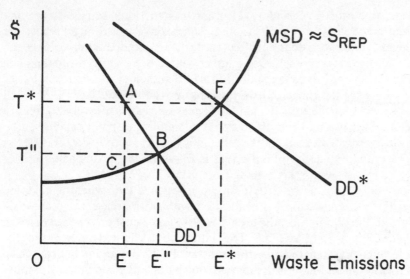

FIGURE 2

monopsonist in this case) will select permits with the lowest possible rental price (R_t) per unit of emission. Our first-order condition is thus satisfied, since the monopsonist will equate the marginal cost of permits (the supply schedule) with the value of his marginal product. Likewise, this procedure satisfies the entry-exit condition: the total cost of the permits to the polluter is equal to the sum of the incremental damages (i.e., the total damages) he imposes on society.

The REP system works equally well for the case of many 'small' polluters where the marginal social damages are (approximately) constant over the range of emissions of any single source. In this case the unit cost of holding emission rights should equal the Pigouvian tax rate. This is just what occurs, since a resale market for permits would develop. A competitive market would generate a single, market-clearing price for emission rights equal to the Pigouvian tax rate (T^*). The price of any particular REP, θ, would be:

$$P_\theta = (T^* \cdot E_\theta) - R_\theta.$$

Although not necessary for the efficiency of our proposal, the life of permits could (and presumably would) extend over many (N) periods. In this case, the market price of a permit θ in the current period would become:

$$P_\theta = \sum_{t=1}^{N} [(T_t^* \cdot E_{\theta t}) - R_{\theta t}]/(1 + r)^t,$$

where r is the market rate of discount and T^* is the expected value of the

Pigouvian tax rate in period *t*. The REP system thus satisfies both the first-order and entry-exit conditions in a 'competitive world' (i.e., where the firm's level of emissions does not affect the level of marginal social damages).[5]

The third case is one of a 'few' polluters: where there exists more than one source but where at least one polluting firm is of sufficient size that MSD varies significantly over the range of its emissions. We depict this case in figure 2. Let DD^* represent the total demand for emission rights from all *j* sources in the region. Suppose that the *j*th source is a 'significant' polluter. The curve DD' is the aggregate demand of the remaining $(j - 1)$ sources: $DD' = DD^* - DD^j$. The optimal quantity of emissions is E^* with OE' having as its source firms $1, \ldots, j - 1$, and $E'E^*$ coming from firm *j*.

It is evident from figure 2 that source *j* imposes two types of costs on society: the external damages associated with an increase in total waste emissions in the region (i.e., the area $E''BFE^*$) and a cost on other sources in the region equal to $E'ABE''$.[6] The latter cost element represents the opportunity cost associated with the transfer of emission rights to firm *j* from other firms in the region; it is the increase in abatement costs that these other firms are forced to bear in order to accommodate the emissions of the *j*th source.[7] Both these cost elements should enter the calculations of polluter *j*, and under the REP system they will. This is easiest to see in the case where source *j* is a new entrant into the region. Before the advent of *j*, the equilibrium level of waste emissions is E'' with marginal abatement costs equal to T''. The new equilibrium following the entry of source *j* will find *j* laying claim to the rental permits corresponding to the emissions over the range E'' to E^* and purchasing permits for $E'E''$ from existing sources. The area $E'CFE^*$ (equal to MSD) indicates the rental payment that source *j* must make for its emissions, and the area ABC is the payment that *j* must make to other firms to induce them to part with the permits for emissions $E'E''$. Since area ABC is also the social opportunity cost of transferring emissions from sources $1, 2, \ldots, j - 1$ to any other source, we find that a 'significant' polluter will both equate marginal abatement cost to MSD and make a total payment equal to the sum of the damages its emissions impose on society and the opportunity cost of the emissions to other sources.[8] In this way both the short- and long-run efficiency conditions are met.

---

5 The many-period formulation of the REP system allows some room for speculative activity that may be the source of inefficiency. A slightly more complex formulation of the system can avoid this. See Collinge (1981, 3).

6 Since any particular polluter under consideration is, in a sense, 'marginal,' we associate the damages from its emissions with the stretch of the MSD curve to the right of the total emissions of other sources.

7 This particular cost element seems to have escaped notice in earlier studies (e.g., Burrows, 1979).

8 Source *j* may, of course, hold or purchase permits other than those corresponding to the range $E'E^*$. However, as noted in the text, the price of any permit will equal $(T^* \cdot E_\theta - R_\theta)$ so that the effective cost of all permits is, in equilibrium, the same.

352 / Robert A. Collinge and Wallace E. Oates

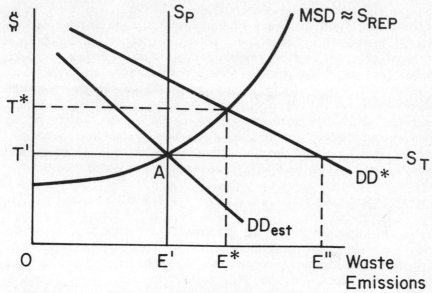

FIGURE 3

ON INFORMATIONAL ECONOMIES

The REP system thus satisfies both conditions for the efficient control of externalities for the cases of one, many, or a few polluters. We would stress, in addition, that REP achieves these objectives while making *relatively* modest informational demands on the environmental authority. In particular, the administering agency need have no knowledge whatsoever of firms' demands for emission rights (i.e., of marginal abatement costs). The REP system effectively confronts polluting firms with a schedule of prices for emissions that reflects the true social cost; the decentralized decisions of cost-minimizing polluters take matters from there with a resulting Pareto-efficient outcome. This is a very attractive property of a scheme to regulate pollution in a world where information is costly.

The standard alternative systems, a Pigouvian tax or a system of (undifferentiated) marketable permits, make much stronger informational demands. Suppose, for example, that the administering agency knows the MSD schedule but is uncertain about the levels of firms' demands for emission permits. In terms of figure 3, suppose that DD^* is the true demand for permits, while DD_{est} is the estimated demand on the part of the environmental authority. Under the Pigouvian approach the agency will set a unit tax on emissions of OT', resulting in a level of emissions of E'' (in excess of the efficient level E^*). Alternatively, under a system of marketable permits, the agency would establish a supply of E', resulting in a subefficient level of emissions.

The source of the problem is the failure of the 'supply schedule' of emission rights to correspond to marginal social damages. A Pigouvian tax effectively results in a supply schedule which is infinitely elastic at the tax rate (see S_T in figure 3). In contrast, a system of marketable permits errs in the opposite direction: it generates a perfectly inelastic supply of emission rights (see S_P in figure 3). There is only one point (A) on either of these schedules corresponding to marginal social damage. This means that if the environmental authority, as a result of imperfect information concerning firms' abatement costs, sets the tax rate incorrectly (or alternatively, introduces the wrong number of permits), the resulting level of pollution diverges from the socially efficient level. In contrast, the REP system replicates the MSD schedule and thereby circumvents the need for any information on abatement costs.

EQUITY AND THE INITIAL ALLOCATION OF PERMITS

Step 4 of the implementation of the REP system is the initial allocation of the permits. We stress here that there are many possible ways initially to distribute the permits that are consistent with the efficiency properties of the system. Certain types of auctions of the permits, for instance, would provide an efficient source of revenue in addition to the rental payments. Alternatively, initial ownership of the permits could be conferred by lottery, perhaps on the basis of levels of emissions in some base year. The essential point is that the probability of receiving permits must not be influenced by current emission levels; otherwise, strategic behaviour by polluters can introduce inefficiencies in both short and long runs.

The initial allocation of permits certainly does have distributive implications. In particular, an initial auction of the permits to polluters places the burden upon them, not only of the costs of abatement and the rental charges associated with the permits, but also of a further one-time payment for the right to discharge emissions into the environment. Some existing studies (of non-rental permit schemes) suggest that these payments may be quite large. A RAND study (Palmer et al., 1980) of a system of undifferentiated marketable permits for the emission of certain halocarbons into the atmosphere estimates that abatement costs under the system would total about $110 million (a savings of roughly 50 per cent compared to a realistic program of mandatory controls). However, the study estimates that the cost to polluters of purchasing the permits would come to about $1,400 million – nearly seven times the level of costs of abatement![9] While these payments for the purchase of permits are simply a transfer from the perspective of society as a whole, they could represent a very sizeable cost to polluting firms.

In one sense the auctioning of permits under the REP system might appear

9 Under the REP system, the purchase price of permits under an auction would be considerably less than under a system of marketable permits with no rental payments, since polluters' willingness-to-pay for rental permits would be reduced by the current value of the future stream of rental payments. However, if the RAND study is any guide, our sense is that even after making this adjustment, the cost to polluters of the initial purchase of the permits under an auction scheme would be quite high.

354 / Robert A. Collinge and Wallace E. Oates

to be unfair to polluters. Since in the aggregate polluters pay a sum of rents that equals the pollution damages that their emissions impose on society, the fairness of extracting further payments through an auction of the permits is questionable. Moreover, the additional cost burden to polluters of an auction could easily prove fatal to the political feasibility of such a program (see Zeckhauser, 1981). As an alternative, the environmental authority simply could allocate the permits initially among polluters free of charge. One allocation method with some appeal is a lottery. Under the lottery approach a 'fair' assignment of probabilities achieves equity in an ex ante sense. Moreover, in a sufficiently developed market, ex post equity also obtains, since each potential recipient could ensure his fair share by selling his ex ante probability for its expected cash value (or gamble, if that is his preference). Note that no moral hazard or adverse selection would exist in this insurance market.[10]

While it goes beyond the scope of this paper to explore in detail the range of possible distributive outcomes of the REP system, we conclude with the observation that the basic REP proposal allows considerable leeway in the determination of a pattern of incidence of the costs among polluters and the rest of society. The selection of a particular form of the system that is regarded as both equitable and at the same time consistent with the political feasibility of the program requires an explicit judgment from the political arena.

REFERENCES

Burrows, P. (1979) 'Pigouvian taxes, polluter subsidies, regulation, and the size of a polluting industry.' This JOURNAL 12, 494–501
Carlton, D. and G. Loury (1980) 'The limitations of Pigouvian taxes as a long-run remedy for externalities.' *Quarterly Journal of Economics* 45, 559–66
Collinge, R.A. (1981) 'Efficiency in an uncertain world: a policy approach.' Working Paper no. 1981–3. University of Maryland, Department of Economics
Gould, J.R. (1977) 'Total conditions in the analysis of external effects.' *Economic Journal* 87, 558–63
Oates, W.E. and R.A. Collinge (1981) 'The limitation of Pigouvian taxes as a long-run remedy for externalities: a comment and extension.' Unpublished paper
Palmer, A.R. et al. (1980) *Economic implications of regulating chlorofluorocarbon emissions from nonaerosol applications* (Santa Monica: Rand)
Rose-Ackerman, S. (1973) 'Effluent charges: a critique.' This JOURNAL 6, 512–27
—— (1977) 'Market models for water pollution control: their strengths and weaknesses.' *Public Policy* 25, 383–406
Schulze, W. and R. d'Arge (1974) 'The Coase proposition, information constraints, and long-run equilibrium.' *American Economic Review* 64, 763–72
Zeckhauser, Richard (1981) 'Preferred policies where there is a concern for the probability of adoption.' *Journal of Environmental Economics and Management* 8, 215–37

10 As Rose-Ackerman (1977) points out, an initial distribution of permits to polluters without requiring their purchase provides some relief to *existing* sources; new sources, however, will have to purchase permits (or, under REP, acquire previously unissued permits with relatively high rental rates).

7220

242-56

[1983]

[13]

JOURNAL OF ENVIRONMENTAL ECONOMICS AND MANAGEMENT **10**, 233–247 (1983)

Q28

On Marketable Air-Pollution Permits: The Case for a System of Pollution Offsets

ALAN J. KRUPNICK

Resources for the Future 1755 Massachusetts Avenue, N. W., Washington, D.C. 20036

WALLACE E. OATES

Department of Economics and Bureau of Business and Economic Research, University of Maryland, College Park, Maryland 20742

AND

ERIC VAN DE VERG

Department of Economic and Community Development, 2525 Riva Road, Maryland 21401

Received October 26, 1981; revised November 1982

After examining the properties of several alternative forms of marketable permit systems for the control of air pollution, this paper proposes a system of pollution offsets as the most promising approach. Under the pollution-offset scheme, sources of emissions are free to trade emissions permits subject to the constraint of no violations of the predetermined air-quality standard at any receptor point. The paper shows that the pollution-offset system has the capacity to achieve the predetermined standards of air quality at the minimum aggregate abatement cost, while making comparatively modest demands both on the sources and on the administering agency.

For most air and water pollutants, the extent and spatial pattern of the damages to the environment depend not only upon the level of emissions, but upon the locations and the dispersion characteristics of the sources. This implies that there is an inherently spatial problem in the design of a system to control these pollutants. A regulatory system that ignores the spatial problem can pass up cost savings that are potentially quite large in the achievement of our objectives for environmental quality.

The purpose of this paper is to explore alternative techniques for incorporating spatial elements into a system of marketable air-pollution permits. There exist several such alternatives, and they have fundamentally different implications for the structure and functioning of a permits market. We shall contend that, among the alternatives, a system of "pollution offsets" offers the most promising approach to the design of an effective market in pollution permits. Moreover, we find that the Environmental Protection Agency (EPA) through its Emissions Trading policy has provided a framework for the introduction of such a system.

The seminal paper on this issue is that of Montgomery [8]. The Montgomery paper analyzes two systems of marketable pollution permits: a system of "pollution licenses" that defines allowable emissions in terms of pollutant concentrations at a set of receptor points, and a system of "emission licenses" that confer directly the right to emit pollutants up to a specified rate. Montgomery demonstrates that the

233

former system satisfies the important condition that a market equilibrium coincides with the least-cost solution for attaining any predetermined level of environmental quality and does so for *any* initial allocation of licenses among polluters.

However, as we shall discuss, the transactions costs for polluting firms associated with Montgomery's system of pollution licenses are likely to be quite high. His alternative system of emissions licenses promises considerable savings in transactions costs. Unfortunately, however, the Montgomery paper also demonstrates that an extremely restrictive (and sometimes unattainable) condition is required for an initial allocation of permits to ensure that the market equilibrium is the least-cost solution. This finding is particularly disturbing on two counts. First, the environmental authority may not be able to find an initial allocation of permits that ensures an efficient outcome. And, second, even should such an allocation exist, a substantial degree of flexibility in the choice of this initial allocation may be lost; such flexibility can be extremely important in designing a system that is politically feasible (as well as efficient).

We show in this paper that this shortcoming of Montgomery's system of emission licenses is the result of an unnecessarily restrictive condition that he imposes on the trading of the licenses. By suitable (and quite straightforward) modifications of this condition, we find that an efficiency property similar to the one that characterizes his system of pollution licenses also characterizes our modified scheme of "pollution offsets": a "trading equilibrium" exists that coincides with the least-cost pattern of emissions for *any* initial allocation of emissions permits. We show also that the pollution-offsets approach offers some important advantages over other techniques in terms of minimizing the total abatement and transactions costs.

In the early part of the paper, we shall go back over some familiar terrain to put the problem and Montgomery's analysis in its proper perspective.[1] We shall then proceed to an analysis and assessment of the alternative approaches to the design of a system of marketable pollution permits.

I. A FORMAL STATEMENT OF THE PROBLEM: A BENCHMARK CASE

It will clarify the analysis and allow us to establish a baseline case if we set forth, at this point, a more formal statement of the spatial problem.[2] Let us assume that we have a specific region, an air shed, in which there are m sources of pollution, each of which is fixed in location. Air quality in terms of a particular pollutant is defined by concentrations at n "receptor points" in the region; we thus describe air quality by a vector $Q = (q_1, \ldots, q_n)$ where q_j is the concentration of the pollutant at point (receptor) j.[3] The dispersion characteristics of the problem are described in terms of

---

[1] Such a restatement is needed in part to clear up some confusion in the literature. Tietenberg [10], for example, has misinterpreted the Montgomery proposal for "emission licenses" to refer to a system of zones within which permits trade on a one-for-one basis (pp. 405–406). Montgomery's system of emission licenses is, however, quite different from a system of permit zones.

[2] Here we follow Montgomery [8] closely. Although we have framed the discussion in terms of air pollution, the analysis has obvious relevance to the regulation of water pollution as well.

[3] By receptor points, we are not referring to the location of monitors. Consider a concentration gradient for an area that is constructed, for example, from monitoring data in conjunction with an air-diffusion model. The environmental agency would select points on that gradient (e.g., the locations of relatively high concentrations of the pollutant) to be receptor points. There need not be any actual monitors at these locations.

a diffusion model which we represent by an $m \times n$ matrix of unit diffusion or transfer coefficients

$$D = \begin{bmatrix} & \vdots & \\ \cdots & d_{ij} & \cdots \\ & \vdots & \end{bmatrix}$$

In this matrix, the element d_{ij} indicates the contribution that one unit of emissions from source i makes to the pollution concentration at point j.[4]

The environmental objective is to attain some predetermined level(s) of pollutant concentrations within the region; we denote these standards as $Q^* = (q_1^*, \ldots, q_n^*)$. Note that the standard need not be the same at each point; the environmental authority could, for example, prescribe lower concentrations as the target in densely populated areas.

The problem thus becomes one of attaining a set of predetermined levels of pollutant concentrations at the minimum aggregate abatement cost. Or, in other words, we are looking for a vector of emissions from our m sources, $E = (e_1, \ldots, e_m)$, that will minimize abatement costs subject to the constraint that the prescribed standards are met at each of the n locations in the region. The abatement costs of the ith source are a function of its level of emissions: $c_i(e_i)$. So our problem, in formal terms, is to

$$\text{Minimize} \quad \sum_i c_i(e_i)$$

$$\text{s.t.} \quad ED \leqslant Q^*$$

$$E \geqslant 0.$$

Montgomery [8] has shown that such a vector of emissions exists and, moreover, that, if the sources of pollution are cost-minimizing agents, the emission vector and shadow prices that emerge from the minimization problem satisfy the same set of conditions as do the vectors of emissions and permit prices for a competitive equilibrium in an air-permits market. In short, if the environmental authority were simply to issue q_j^* permits (defined in terms of pollutant concentrations) for each of the n receptor points, competitive bidding for these permits would generate an equilibrium solution that satisfies the conditions for the minimization of total abatement costs.

These results establish a benchmark case for a control system that minimizes abatement costs. Two properties of this outcome are noteworthy. First is the utter simplicity of the system from the perspective of the environmental agency. In particular, officials need have no information whatsoever regarding abatement costs; they simply issue the prescribed number of permits at each receptor point, and competitive bidding takes care of matters from there. Alternatively, the environmental authority could make an initial allocation of these permits to existing polluters. Subsequent transactions in a competitive setting would then establish the cost-mini-

---

[4]We should note that the d_{ij} are, in fact, dependent on stack height and diameter, gas temperature, and exit velocities, as well as on a host of meteorological conditions; we will consider some of these complications later.

mizing solution. As Montgomery [8] proves formally, the least-cost outcome is independent of the initial allocation of the permits. Second, in contrast to the modest burden it places on administrators, this system can be extremely cumbersome for polluters. Note that a firm emitting wastes must assemble a "portfolio" of permits from *each* of the receptor points that is affected by its emissions: a source at point i will have to acquire permits at each receptor j in the amount $(d_{ij}e_i)$. There will, therefore, exist n different markets for permits, one for each receptor point, and each polluter will participate in the subset of these markets corresponding to the receptor points affected by his emissions. It would appear that the transactions costs for polluters are likely to be substantial under our benchmark system, although this expense may be justified, under certain circumstances, by the savings in abatement costs.

II. THE DESIGN OF A MARKETABLE PERMIT SYSTEM: AN ALTERNATIVE APPROACH

The scheme examined in the preceding section is a prototype for an *ambient-based* system (APS) of pollution permits: the permits are defined in terms of pollutant concentrations at the receptor points. An alternative approach in the literature is an *emission-based* system (EPS) under which the permits are defined in terms of levels of emissions rather than in terms of the effects of these emissions on ambient air quality.[5] This latter approach often makes use of a set of emission zones within which emissions of a particular pollutant are treated as equivalent. The environmental authority determines an allocation of permits to each zone, and polluters within a zone trade permits on a one-to-one basis. There are no trades across zones: each zone is a self-contained market with its own price for permits determined by the polluters' demand for permits and the supply as determined by the authority.[6]

From this perspective, we can envision at one extreme for EPS (following Tietenberg [10]) a system in which the entire region is a single market. The environmental authority issues a fixed number of permits for the region as a whole, and the subsequent bids and offers of participants generate a single market-clearing price. As we move away from this special case, we encounter continually more finely divided systems of zones designed to take into account the spatial character of the air shed. However, regardless of the total number of zones, each pollution source will lie only in a single zone and will consequently operate in only one permit market for a given pollutant.

It is this last feature of EPS that constitutes its basic appeal. Recall that under APS the polluter must operate in a number of markets for each pollutant (in the benchmark case, one for each receptor site that his emissions affect) and is subject to a different "weighting parameter" (i.e., diffusion coefficient) in each market. The assembling of the requisite portfolio of permits could become quite complicated for

---

[5]For reasons that will become clear, our choice of terminology to describe alternative systems of marketable permits differs from that of Montgomery. Our ambient-based approach (APS) is in the spirit of his system of "pollution licenses." However, we shall distinguish among several types of emission-based systems that are quite different from Montgomery's system of emission licenses.

[6]Under a variant of this approach, trading may take place across zones at "exchange rates" set by the administering agency to reflect the damage attributable to emissions from the various zones. More will be said on this later.

firms; they might even find themselves, in some instances, buying in one market while selling in another (Russell [9]). It is not altogether clear just how large these "transactions costs" are likely to be (more on this shortly); some well-organized brokerage operations could conceivably facilitate greatly the transfer of permits. But it would appear, nonetheless, that, from the perspective of the polluter, EPS offers a major attraction by requiring polluters to buy and sell permits within a single market and with no system of source-specific weights attached to individual firms.

However, while the EPS approach may simplify life for polluters, it is a potential nightmare for the administrators of the system. Recall that under APS the environmental authority need only establish the number of permits to be offered for sale at each receptor site (so as to meet the prescribed air-quality standard) and specify the diffusion or transfer coefficients for each source of pollution. Market forces take over from there and, under competitive conditions, generate the least-cost pattern of waste emissions.[7]

In contrast, EPS will not, in general, achieve the least-cost outcome, and it makes enormous demands on an administering agency that tries to approach the least-cost solution. To do so, the agency must have knowledge of the source-specific abatement costs in addition to the air-modeling data required for APS. Moreover, EPS requires continuing readjustments among zonal stocks of permits. The reason the least-cost solution is unlikely to be achieved is straightforward; since polluters with somewhat varying dispersion coefficients are aggregated into the same zone, one-for-one trades of pollution rights will not reflect the differences in the concentrations contributed by their respective emissions. The price of emissions to each polluter will not, in short, reflect accurately the shadow price of the binding pollution constraint. Further, the system of zones may prevent one source from making beneficial trades with another source which happens to be located in a different zone.

These objections to EPS need not be serious, if the dispersion characteristics for emissions within zones are not very different (Hahn and Noll [5]). This suggests that an increase in the number of zones can reduce the "excess abatement costs" associated with EPS. However, increasing the number of zones will tend to reduce the number of participants in each market with the undesirable repercussions from the decrease in competitiveness of markets for permits and increased uncertainty of permit prices.

A more troublesome issue is that, even were there no differences in the dispersion characteristics of emissions within each zone, the environmental authority must still determine an allocation of permits to each zone. And this determination requires *the complete solution* by the administrator of the cost-minimization problem. To reach this solution, the administering agency must have not only an air-quality model (to provide the d_{ij}) and a complete emissions inventory, but source-specific abatement cost functions and the capacity to solve the programming problem.[8] With less-than-

---

[7]This may be something of an oversimplification for the reason that changes in emission levels can be associated with changes in dispersion coefficients. A polluter may reduce his emissions by the installation of new equipment, of bag houses, precipitators or scrubbers, or by the addition of after burners to stacks in such ways as to alter the source's emission parameters. Trades involving such changes may thus require a recalculation of dispersion coefficients.

[8]Of course, with all this information, a market would hardly be necessary. After solving the cost-minimization problem, the environmental authority could simply distribute the optimal number of permits to each polluter.

perfect information, the agency's zonal allocation of permits may fail to attain the ambient air-quality targets. If pollution were excessive, the authority would have to reenter the market (in at least some of the zones, where again the pattern of zonal purchases would require a fairly sophisticated analysis) and purchase or confiscate permits. Such an iterative procedure is not only cumbersome for the administrator of the system, but may create considerable uncertainty for firms as to the future course of permit prices.

We stress, moreover, that this procedure involves more than just groping once and for all toward an unchanging equilibrium. Altered patterns of emissions resulting from the growth (or contraction) of existing firms, the entry of new firms, and changing abatement technology will generate a continually shifting least-cost pattern of emissions across zones. Under EPS, the environmental authority faces a dynamic problem that will require periodic adjustments to the supplies of permits in each zone. We conclude that the zone approach suffers both from its inability to realize the least-cost pattern of emissions and from the formidable burden it places on the administering agency.

III. A HYBRID APPROACH: A MARKET FOR POLLUTION OFFSETS

From Sections I and II, we find that both the ambient-based and emission-based systems for pollution control have some troublesome properties. There is an alternative, however, that combines certain characteristics of both the APS and EPS approaches and possesses some quite attractive properties. The basic idea is to define permits in terms of emissions and to allow their sale among polluters, but not on a one-to-one basis. More specifically, transfers of emission permits are subject to the restriction that the transfer does not result in a violation of the air-quality standard at any receptor point. The source of new emissions (or of expanded emissions) must purchase a sufficient number of emission permits from existing sources to "offset" the effects of the new emissions on pollutant concentrations in such a way that the pollution constraint is everywhere satisfied. For this reason, we prefer to call this general approach to a system of marketable permits one of "pollution offsets."

The hybrid character of the offset approach is apparent. Like EPS, it involves the purchase and sale of emission permits; the permits are not associated explicitly with a particular receptor market as under APS. At the same time, however, it captures the spirit of the ambient-based system in that the ratio at which permits exchange for one another depends on the relative effects of the associated emissions on ambient air quality at the receptor points.

The Montgomery system of "emission licenses" is, in fact, a special case of the offset approach. Montgomery places as a constraint on the transfer of emission permits a "nondegradation condition": he effectively requires that any transactions among polluters result in no increase in pollutant concentrations at any receptor point. As we shall see shortly, this condition is unnecessarily restrictive. Moreover, it generates an outcome that, for many initial allocations of permits, will not coincide with the least-cost solution.

By relaxing Montgomery's overly stringent constraint on the trading of emissions permits, we can show that an equilibrium outcome under an appropriately designed system of pollution offsets coincides with the least-cost solution irrespective of the initial allocation of emission permits. We develop the argument in terms of Fig. 1 in

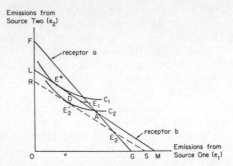

FIG. 1. Spatially differentiated permit systems.

which the horizontal and vertical axes measure, respectively, the levels of emissions of firms 1 and 2 (i.e., e_1 and e_2).[9] The curves C_1 and C_2 are isocost curves for pollution abatement costs.[10] Note that higher curves correspond to lower total abatement costs ($C_1 < C_2$). The line *FG* indicates the pollution constraint associated with receptor *a*. Points on *FG* denote combinations of e_1 and e_2 for which $q_a = q_a^*$; the slope of the line equals the ratio of the transfer coefficients (i.e., the rate at which emissions from firm 2 can substitute for emissions from firm 1 with no change in pollution concentrations at receptor *a*). Similarly *LM* depicts the pollution constraint for receptor *b*. The combinations of emissions from firms 1 and 2 that satisfy the pollution constraint at both receptors are thus the set of points *OLAG*. We see immediately that the least-cost solution occurs at E^*, at which point the ratio of marginal abatement costs equals the ratio of the transfer coefficients.

E^* is therefore the optimum; our problem is to determine the circumstances under which E^* will also be the market equilibrium. Under Montgomery's system of "emission licenses", the environmental authority makes an initial allocation of permits to polluting firms, after which firms are free to buy and sell the permits subject to a "nondegradation" condition. More formally, each firm faces the constraints

$$d_{ij}e_i \leqslant \sum_k d_{kj}l_{ik} \qquad j = 1,\ldots,m$$

where l_{ik} is the emission permits that firm i purchases from firm k. This restriction implies that a transfer of emission permits from one polluter to another must take place in such a way that there is no increase in the level of pollution at *any* receptor point.

Returning to Fig. 1, suppose that the environmental authority established an initial allocation of emission permits indicated by E_1. Firm 2 would then find it profitable to purchase permits from firm 1.[11] The effective rate of exchange of

[9] This diagram is a modification of Fig. 2 in Montgomery [7, p. 30].

[10] A sufficient (but not necessary) condition for the isocost curves to have the desired curvature in Fig. 1 is that both firms face a schedule of rising marginal abatement costs.

[11] The potential gains-from-trade from sales of emission rights by firm 1 to firm 2 follow from the fact that the linear pollution constraint at E_1 is steeper than the isocost curve passing through that point. In the case, for example, where the slope of the constraint *LM* is minus one (indicating that emissions from

permits would be the slope of the line LM, since the constraint at receptor b is, in this instance, the binding constraint. The gains from trade would be exhausted at E^*. For the initial allocation of rights indicated by E_1, we thus find that the market equilibrium coincides with the optimum.

Suppose, however, that instead of E_1, the environmental authority had selected E_2 as the initial allocation of permits. Once again firm 2 would find it profitable to purchase permits from firm 1, but Montgomery's nondegradation constraint would now limit the feasible set of outcomes to ORE_2G. Trading would now take place along the dotted line RS (which is parallel to LM since the ratio of the sources' diffusion coefficients is unchanged). The market equilibrium would, in this instance, be E_2', which does not coincide with the optimal outcome. The solution at E_2' entails an excessive level of expenditure on abatement resulting in a sense from an "excessive" level of environmental quality. The nondegradation constraint prevents a movement from E_2' to E^*. We thus find that attainment of the least-cost solution is not independent of the initial allocation of emission permits.

The problem confronting the environmental authority in our example is that it must know which segment of the frontier contains E^* before it can determine an initial allocation of permits that makes the market solution coincide with E^*. There is one qualification: if the initial allocation is that represented by point A, market transactions will move the outcome to E^* irrespective of whether E^* happens to lie on line segment LA or segment AG. This is Montgomery's restriction on the initial allocation of permits: the initial allocation must be such that the pollution constraint is binding at all receptor points to ensure that the market equilibrium coincides with the least-cost solution.[12]

While this condition seems reasonable enough in terms of our example in Fig. 1 with only two receptor points, the severity of the problem becomes clear when we introduce additional receptors. A third line in Fig. 1 indicating the pollution constraint for yet another receptor point would pass through point A only by coincidence. This implies that, for the two-source case, with three or more receptor points there will not, in general, exist a vector of emissions for which all the pollution constraints are binding! In such instances, the environmental authority typically will not be able to find an initial allocation of permits that will ensure the least-cost outcome without a complete solution of the programming problem. In these cases, Montgomery's system requires the agency to determine E^* (which requires knowledge of firms' abatement cost functions as well as the transfer coefficients) before it can specify an initial allocation of permits that will ensure that E^* is the market equilibrium. Even if this can be done, it removes most of the

---

firms 1 and 2 have equivalent effects on pollutant concentrations at receptor b), firm 2 has a higher marginal abatement cost at E_1 than does firm 1 so that transfers of permits from 1 to 2 can be mutually profitable.

[12] The intuitive explanation of this condition is clear in terms of our discussion of the initial allocation of permits, E_2, in Fig. 1. More generally, suppose that the least-cost solution entails a binding constraint at some particular receptor point j (i.e., the least-cost solution implies that $q_j = q_j^*$). Assume, however, that the initial allocation of emission rights selected by the environmental authority results in pollutant concentrations at receptor j that are less than the allowable level so that the constraint at j is not binding. Under Montgomery's nondegradation restriction on subsequent trades of permits, it is clear that these trades cannot generate the least-cost outcome, because the restriction implies that ambient air quality at j cannot be less than that under the initial allocation. Thus, the constraint at j can never become binding. One way to circumvent this problem is to establish an initial allocation of permits such that $q_j = q_j^*$ for all j. However, as we note in the text, such an allocation may not even exist.

flexibility in setting the initial permit allocation, a flexibility that may be extremely important for rendering such a system politically feasible.[13]

However, as the analysis suggests, Montgomery's constraint on the market behavior of polluters is unnecessarily restrictive. Returning to our case in Fig. 1 where the initial allocation of permits was E_2, we saw that trades took place along the dotted line RS instead of the actual constraint LM implied by our predetermined standards of air quality. Montgomery's restriction on market trades of permits is sufficient to ensure that $q \leqslant q^*$ for all receptors, but it is not necessary. By relaxing this restriction, we can describe a modification of Montgomery's system for which the only point representing an equilibrium is the least-cost outcome.

Suppose that we supplement Montgomery's nondegradation condition on trades of permits with the following provision: *firms can always obtain from the environmental authority additional permits so long as the air-quality standard is not violated at any receptor point.* We note immediately in Fig. 1 that this disqualifies E_2' as a point of market equilibrium; since the pollution constraint is not binding at either receptor point, firms will obtain additional permits from the environmental agency.[14] Suppose, for example, that firm 2 obtained LR of additional permits thereby moving the vector of emissions from E_2' to point D. At D, there exists the potential for mutually profitable sales of emission permits by firm 1 to firm 2 until E^* is attained. In short, E^* would be a "trading equilibrium" (and the only such equilibrium).[15]

More generally, we can see that our amendment to Montgomery's condition on the issue and trading of permits gives the modified system two important properties:

(1) No point inside the frontier of feasible points established by the air-quality standards can be an equilibrium (since polluters will seek and obtain additional permits);

(2) No point on this frontier other than the least-cost solution can be an equilibrium (since at any other point mutually profitable transfers of permits exist).

Our amended version of the pollution-offset system is, however, a bit artificial or contrived. It may be useful, for expository purposes, to envision firms making trades along the line representing Montgomery's nondegradation constraint and then obtaining additional permits where there are no resulting pollutant concentrations in excess of the predetermined standards. However, there is a much more direct and less cumbersome method that can attain the same outcome. We can dispense altogether with the nondegradation condition and simply require the source of new emissions to induce existing polluters to reduce their emissions by amounts sufficient to prevent violations at any receptor point. Suppose, for example, that in Fig. 2 our

---

[13]More generally, in the case where the number of receptors exceeds the number of sources (where $m < n$), the system will typically be overdetermined so that there will not exist a vector of emissions such that the air-quality constraint binds at every receptor. If $m \geqslant n$, vectors (typically more than one) will exist that can be determined without knowledge of abatement costs and that allow the attainment of the least-cost solution under Montgomery's system of emission licenses. The vectors represent points where all *binding* receptor constraints intersect.

[14]This requires that, over the relevant range, the marginal product of waste emissions for polluting firms is strictly positive.

[15]We refer to our equilibrium under the offset approach as a "trading" equilibrium rather than a "market" equilibrium, since we have not shown formally that there exists a specific set of prices that will sustain an equilibrium among buyers and sellers corresponding to the efficient allocation of permits among polluters. We show instead that the only allocation of permits for which there exists no potential gains from trade (our definition of a "trading equilibrium") is the efficient one.

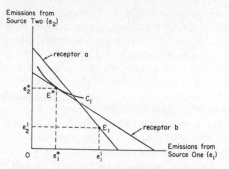

FIG. 2.   An alternative pollution-offset system.

initial point were E_1, where $E_1 = (e_1^1, e_2^1)$ and $E^* = (e_1^*, e_2^*)$ are the emissions vectors corresponding to E_1 and E^*, respectively. Firm 2 would pay firm 1 to reduce its emissions from e_1^1 to e_1^*, which would enable firm 2 to increase its emissions from e_2^1 to e_2^*. This transaction would, at the same time, move the system directly from E_1 to E^* and exhaust the potential gains from trade. When we refer to our basic case of the pollution-offset system throughout the rest of this paper, it is this last case that we have in mind: firms are free to buy and sell emission permits subject only to the constraint that there result no violations of the standards for air quality at any receptor point.

We conclude that the trading equilibrium under our offset system coincides with the least-cost solution irrespective of the initial allocation of emission permits; like APS, a suitably designed offset system can achieve the predetermined standards for air quality at the least cost for any initial allocation of emission permits.

Moreover, as we discuss in detail in the next section, the offset system should typically require fewer transactions than APS. Instead of purchasing ambient permits in each of the receptor markets affected by its emissions, a polluting firm need only purchase emission permits from other firms sufficient to prevent any violations of the air-quality standards.[16]

IV. THE CHOICE AMONG ALTERNATIVE SYSTEMS: SOME FURTHER THOUGHTS

Our search is for the system that promises to minimize the sum of abatement and transactions costs for the attainment of predetermined levels of ambient air quality.[17] As we noted earlier, the object of our quest depends in fundamental ways on the characteristics of the particular pollutant and the geographical setting. Consider, for

---

[16] This determination, incidentally, would involve a fairly straightforward procedure making use of an air-quality model. One would simply enter a new emissions vector (incorporating the proposed addition to emissions and deleting the offsetting reductions) and examine through a simulation exercise the projected effects on pollutant concentrations at each of the receptor points. The proposed transaction would be approved so long as there were no violation of standards at any receptor point.

[17] We define transactions costs broadly to include both the costs to polluters and the costs to the environmental authority of managing the system.

example, a polar case of perfect mixing where a unit of emissions from a point within the air shed has the same effect on concentrations at all points in the area. For this special case, all three of our systems essentially degenerate into one. Since there is a need only for a single receptor point and the dispersion coefficients of all sources are identical, the APS system will involve only a single market in which permits trade on a one-for-one basis. This is obviously identical to an EPS system with a single zone encompassing the entire air shed or to an offset system in which sources will find that, to increase emissions by one unit, they must induce another source (any source in the air shed) to reduce its emissions by one unit.

The simplicity of this special case is a great attraction; it implies substantial savings in transactions costs for both polluters and administrators. Under APS, for example, polluting firms need operate in only a single permit market. Under EPS, the single, large zone means more potential buyers and sellers along with a much simplified planning problem for the environmental agency. Likewise, under the offset approach, the increased scope for trades at a single "rate of exchange" should facilitate the functioning of the permit market.

An interesting case of (at least virtually) perfect mixing involves the emission of chlorofluorocarbons (CFCs) which are thought to affect adversely the stratospheric ozone layer. The location of emissions is, as we understand it, irrelevant; CFCs and the ozone problem seem to involve a truly global public good so that there is no need to differentiate the incentives for abatement by the location of the source. For cases like CFCs, the permit market can take on a very simple structure, and, other things equal, should work quite well. The EPA is, in fact, considering a national permit market for CFC emissions.

The potential savings in transactions costs suggest that, even for cases that deviate somewhat from perfect mixing, it may, on balance, be beneficial to maintain the fiction of our polar case. Existing EPA procedures for modeling the effects of hydrocarbon emissions are an important example; these procedures allow one-for-one trades over a wide area. In such circumstances, the savings in transactions costs may exceed the "excess" abatement costs from the failure to make finer spatial distinctions. In an intriguing study of water pollution involving BOD emissions into the Willamette River, Eheart [3] has found that only a very small increase in total abatement costs results from simply allowing all sources to trade permits on a one-for-one basis. Hahn and Noll [5] suggest a similar result for sulfate pollution of the atmosphere in Southern California. For such cases (and even where the abatement cost differential is somewhat larger), the optimal system is likely to be our polar case.

The more general point is that the attempt to introduce finer spatial differentiation, while reducing total abatement cost, results in increased transactions costs for both polluters and administrators. There is, in short, a tradeoff between the savings in abatement costs and the higher transactions costs associated with finer spatial distinctions. As we move farther away from our case of perfect mixing, the excess abatement costs from ignoring spatial differences tend to grow. For air pollutants like particulate matter and nitrogen dioxide, for example, the spatial pattern of emissions is typically quite important.[18] For such cases, our problem becomes that of

[18]See, for example, the Atkinson and Lewis study [2] of particulate emissions in the St. Louis AQCR and the studies of nitrous oxide emissions by Anderson *et al.* [1] and EPA [11] in the Chicago AQCR and by Krupnick [6] for the Baltimore AQCR. All these studies produce large estimates of the potential cost-savings from a spatially sensitive policy.

choosing among our three general approaches to the design of a system of marketable permits.

Our treatment establishes a strong presumption in favor of our modified system of pollution offsets, especially where the number of receptor points is large. The APS approach has the attractive property of minimization of aggregate abatement costs. But, as we have shown, so does the offset approach. Moreover, the offset system should entail large savings in transactions costs relative to APS, since under the latter a polluter will typically have to operate in a multiplicity of different permit markets.[19]

While promising some savings in transactions costs for sources, the EPS approach with a system of emission zones cannot, in general, attain the least-cost pattern of emissions. And, as we discussed earlier, the planning problem for the environmental agency wishing to approach the least-cost solution is a very formidable one for which the solution is continually changing over time. In addition, the assumption under EPS that a unit of emissions from one source in a zone is precisely equivalent in its effects on air quality to a unit of emissions from any other source in the zone *may*, under certain circumstances, do serious violence to reality. The ambient effects of emissions do not depend solely on the geographical location of the source; they depend in important ways on such things as stack height and diameter, and on gas temperature and exit velocity. Variations in these parameters across polluters can be accommodated under the offset system through their effects on the source's vector of transfer coefficients. In contrast, EPS cannot readily incorporate such elements without losing the basic simplicity of one-for-one transfers of emission rights. EPS has some problems that are potentially quite troublesome and that do not plague the pollution-offset scheme.

Finally, there is an extremely important issue that goes beyond the confines of the formal problem as set out at the beginning of the paper. The analysis has run in terms of a given and fixed set of receptor points at which predetermined levels of air quality must be attained. However, the Clean Air Act requires that the National Ambient Air Quality Standards (NAAQS) be met at *all* locations. But for pollutants with more localized effects (and this includes most of the criteria air pollutants), it is possible for changing locational patterns of emissions to generate "hot spots" that do not coincide with designated receptor points. To prevent the occurrence of localized hot spots for such pollutants, a relatively fine mesh of receptor points will be needed implying comparatively high transactions costs under an APS system or small zones (and thin markets) under EPS.

Further, since under the APS system each receptor is associated with an individual permit market, receptor points would tend to become "institutionalized." Moving a receptor point to account for new pollution patterns would create dislocations: it would alter the structure of permit markets and would probably give rise to difficult administrative and legal problems. Moreover, it would not preclude the need for future readjustments. This problem, however, is easily resolved under the offset system, since there is no need to institutionalize the receptor points.

Under the offset approach, the environmental agency can adopt air-modeling procedures that effectively identify the location of the worst air quality, no matter

---

[19]Based on a given set of dispersion coefficients, the APS approach also encounters problems where (as noted earlier) trades entail changes in dispersion coefficients. The offset approach accommodates such changes more routinely by incorporating them into the calculations of the net effects on air quality of a proposed trade.

where it is, for each individual transaction. The agency would maintain a current record of the emissions and emission characteristics of each source and the currently applicable air model for the pollutant being traded. Proposed emissions trades would be "modeled" to ensure that the resulting pattern of pollutant concentrations meets the air-quality standard everywhere in the air shed. This procedure would, in principle, produce the same abatement costs and pattern of emissions as an APS system with a receptor at every location (i.e., an infinite number of receptors). Unlike APS, however, the transactions costs under the offset system would be essentially unchanged as the number of receptor points under consideration increases to infinity.

In comparing the APS and the offset systems, it is important to recognize that since the market (or trading) equilibrium under both systems coincides with the least-cost solution, the two schemes imply the same transfer of emissions entitlements among sources from any initial allocation of permits to the equilibrium. The number of sources that must take part in trading to achieve the least-cost pattern of emissions is consequently the same under both systems. The difference is in the number of individual transactions that are needed to reach the equilibrium solution. Under APS, one source can find itself purchasing (and, conceivably, at the same time selling) ambient permits from (to) another source such that the number of separate transactions between the two sources can be as many as the number of different receptor points for which their transfer coefficients are both nonzero. Note that each transaction will involve the transfer of ambient permits designated in terms of a particular receptor and will have its own price per permit. In contrast, under the pollution-offset system, all these separate transactions can, in principle, be effected through a single transfer of emissions permits between the two sources.[20]

The pollution-offset system thus offers compelling advantages both to sources and to the administering agency for regulating air quality where the spatial element is important. In particular, the offset system meets practical criteria that enable an environmental agency to use it in all circumstances including those in which the APS system becomes unworkable because it requires the environmental agency to monitor sources' impacts on pollution at a specific set of locations and either to ignore pollution levels at other locations or to institutionalize a very large number of receptors. In contrast, the offset system allows the environmental agency the flexibility to consider pollution levels at any and all locations when evaluating an emissions trade. At the same time, it promises significant savings in transactions costs for sources.

---

[20]More specifically, consider a proposed increase in emissions from one source in the air shed. Suppose that relative to the initial emissions vector, the new equilibrium (least-cost) outcome entails changes in emissions levels for m_k sources (where m_k is a subset of the m sources in the air shed). Then under the pollution-offset system, the maximum number of transactions (two-party trades) required to attain the new equilibrium is $\binom{m_k}{2} = (m_k(m_k - 1))/2$. Under APS, the required number of transactions could be as many as n times this quantity: $n\binom{m_k}{2}$, where n is the number of receptor markets where trades are necessary.

In a dynamic framework with imperfect knowledge, things can admittedly become more complicated. Initial trades among some parties may generate opportunities for further profitable trades among others. There would result some kind of iterative process until the potential gains-from-trade were exhausted. This, incidentally, would be the case both for the APS and pollution-offset systems.

V. TOWARD IMPLEMENTATION

We have described in a fairly general way a model of a pollution-offset system under which polluting firms trade emission permits subject to the constraint of no violations of the ambient air-quality standards at any receptor point. And we have demonstrated the efficiency properties of this system: we found that potential gains-from-trade exist for any vector of emissions other than the least-cost one.[21]

We have not, however, been very specific about the market structure or institutions under which such trading of permits would take place. In fact, over the past several years the Environmental Protection Agency (EPA) has been in the process of introducing regulatory reforms that bear a close resemblance to our pollution-offset scheme [12]. Under the rubric of Emissions Trading, the EPA has assembled a set of provisions to facilitate the trading of emission permits: the "Bubble, Offset, and Banking" provisions. With the Bubble, existing firms were initially permitted to make intraplant "swaps" of emissions of a particular pollutant to effect savings in abatement costs; the Bubble provision has subsequently been extended to encompass emission swaps across existing plants and even across existing firms so long as air pollution is not made worse. In a similar spirit, the EPA Offset provision requires that new sources of emissions in nonattainment areas obtain offsets from existing sources for their "net" emissions (i.e., those remaining after the installation of required technologies). In addition, under Banking, firms can accumulate credit for emissions reductions beyond those required in the State Implementation Plan.

We emphasize, however, that while the framework created under the Emissions Trading policy establishes the potential for creating systems that could realize much of the cost savings, each state must specify the exact form of its Emissions Trading system. Emissions Trading defines only a legal framework, not a fully specified system.[22] And it is on the details of the design and implementation of these systems by the states that the success of the program will largely depend. In addition, certain statutory provisions under the Clean Air Act and additional regulatory requirements prevent the realization of all the potential cost savings, even if the states were to resolve fully any problems of implementation. For example, the New Source Performance Standards that require new sources to adopt specific abatement technologies, or the regulatory stipulation that "reasonable further progress" be measured by reductions in emissions rather than in pollutant concentrations, are serious impediments to the efforts to achieve our environmental standards at lower costs.

Although formidable obstacles remain to the ultimate introduction of efficient systems of marketable permits, it is reassuring to find that EPA has adopted, in principle, what we see as the most promising approach to the design of such systems. To cite one specific case, a proposed system of this type is currently under consideration in the State of Maryland. Under the Maryland version of Emissions Trading, a polluting firm would propose a package of emissions reductions by

[21]Allan Gruchy [4] has recently proposed yet another conceptual alternative to Montgomery's system of "emission licenses." Gruchy's scheme effectively makes the initial allocation of rights endogenous; each polluter, in a sense, defines his own rights in the course of determining his level of emissions. Gruchy shows that his version of the emission-license system, in contrast to Montgomery's, generates the least-cost solution. While the Gruchy system is thus of considerable interest at a conceptual level, we have been unable to translate it into a workable proposal for a system of marketable pollution rights.

[22]Van De Verg and Frucht [13] examine some of the pitfalls which states may encounter as they prepare Emission Trading regulations.

existing polluters (for which it presumably makes payment to the latter) and an increase in its own emissions subject to the restriction that the resulting pattern of pollutant concentrations does not violate the air-quality standards at any receptor point. Such a system promises to encourage an efficient pattern of emissions consistent with the attainment of air quality standards and to do so with relatively modest transactions costs.

VI. CONCLUDING REMARKS

The preceding sections have explored a wide range of issues concerning the design and administration of systems of tradeable emission permits. From this discussion, we emerge with a proposed design for a system of pollution offsets for which we have been able to demonstrate its capacity for realizing the least-cost pattern of abatement activity; at the same time, the system promises to make relatively modest transaction demands on both sources and the administering agency. We have found, moreover, that the EPA has established the framework for introducing such systems under its Emission Trading strategy for the control of air pollution. However, as we have noted, a number of changes need to be made in the Clean Air Act and in existing regulatory procedures before the potential cost savings from a market-oriented approach to the management of air quality can be fully realized.

ACKNOWLEDGMENTS

We are grateful to William Baumol, Charles Bausell, Martin David, Matthew Gelfand, Allan Gruchy, Jr., Albert McGartland, and Henry Peskin for their helpful comments; to Padraic Frucht, former Director of the Division of Research of the Maryland Department of Economics and Community Development, for his direction of a program of research on economic incentives to control air pollution in the State of Maryland; and to the National Science Foundation, the Appalachian Regional Commission, and the Sloan Foundation for their support of parts of this work.

REFERENCES

1. R. Anderson *et al.*, "An Analysis of Alternative Policies for Attaining and Maintaining a Short-Term NO_2 Standard," Math–Tech, Inc., Princeton, N.J. (Sept. 17, 1979).
2. S. Atkinson and D. Lewis, A cost-effectiveness analysis of alternative air quality control strategies, *J. Environ. Econ. Manag.* **1**, 237–250 (1974).
3. J. W. Eheart, Cost-effectiveness of transferable discharge permits for the control of BOD discharges, unpublished paper (1980).
4. A. Gruchy, Market systems for pollution control—Another view, unpublished paper (1980).
5. R. Hahn and R. Noll, Designing a market for tradable emissions permits, unpublished paper (April 1981).
6. A. Krupnick, "Simulating Alternative Policies for Controlling NO_x Emissions," draft report for the Department of Economic and Community Development, State of Maryland (July 1981).
7. W. D. Montgomery, Artificial markets and the theory of games, *Public Choice* **18**, 25–40 (1974).
8. W. D. Montgomery, Markets in licenses and efficient pollution control programs, *J. Econ. Theory* **5**, 395–418 (1972).
9. C. Russell, The Delaware model in the Sloan project: Alternative instruments and model structure, unpublished paper (March 1980).
10. T. Tietenberg, Transferable discharge permits and the control of stationary source air pollution: A survey and synthesis, *Land Econ.* **56**, 391–416 (1980).
11. U.S. Environmental Protection Agency, An analysis of market incentives to control stationary source NO_x emissions, unpublished paper (October 1980).
12. U.S. Environmental Protection Agency, Emission trading policy statement, *Fed. Regis.* **47** (67), 15076–15086 (April 7, 1982).
13. E. Van De Verg and P. Frucht, On trying to be first: Maryland's efforts to implement EPA's "Controlled Trading" policy, unpublished paper (June 1981).

[14]

JOURNAL OF ENVIRONMENTAL ECONOMICS AND MANAGEMENT **12**, 207–228 (1985)

Marketable Permits for the Prevention of Environmental Deterioration[1]

ALBERT M. MCGARTLAND

Environmental Protection Agency

AND

WALLACE E. OATES

*Department of Economics and Bureau of Business and Economic Research,
University of Maryland, College Park, Maryland 20742*

Received June 9, 1983; revised November 11, 1983

This paper develops a modified system of marketable emission permits that promises both savings in abatement costs to sources and improved environmental quality relative to an initial command-and-control (CAC) outcome. Using a model of TSP emissions for the Baltimore Air Quality Control Region (AQCR), a series of simulation exercises indicates that such a permit system could generate large cost savings while inducing significant reductions in TSP concentrations as compared to the existing CAC regime in Baltimore. © 1985 Academic Press, Inc.

1. INTRODUCTION

A typical approach to environmental management calls for the regulatory authority to determine a set of minimum standards for environmental quality. Under the Clean Air Act Amendments of 1970, for example, the Environmental Protection Agency (EPA) in the United States was directed to establish standards for maximum concentrations of certain "criteria" air pollutants. The attainment of these standards then becomes the objective of some kind of system to regulate the emissions of polluting entities. In the economics literature, there is now a substantial list of studies that explore the design of systems that can achieve such a set of predetermined standards at the least cost (e.g., [11, 3, 12, 5]).

A difficulty with this approach is that such standards, under one interpretation at least, imply a troublesome fiction about the nature of environmental damages: they suggest a kind of "threshold" below which damages are negligible and above which the damages suddenly become unacceptably large [4, pp. 30–43].[2] This "threshold

---

[1] The authors are associated with, respectively, the Environmental Protection Agency, and the Department of Economics and the Bureau of Business and Economic Research, University of Maryland. They are grateful to Alan Krupnick, Eric Van De Verg, and two anonymous referees for helpful comments and to the National Science Foundation and Sloan Foundation for support of this research.

[2] Alternatively, from an economic perspective, the standard could be interpreted as the "optimal" level of environmental quality for which the marginal social damages from another unit of emissions equal marginal abatement cost. However, this is not the interpretation that is typically evident at the policy level. In the Clean Air Act, for example, the U.S. Congress has explicitly rejected such an economic tradeoff in the determination of standards; legislators have instead instructed the EPA to set standards for air quality at a level "to protect the public health" (see [4, p. 31]).

207

myth" when translated into policy prescriptions yields some disturbing consequences. Since it implies that the damages from environmental degradation are
effectively zero until the threshold or standard is reached, it follows that there is
little cost associated with introducing polluting activities into previously clean areas
so long as pollution levels do not exceed the standard. Or, put more formally, it
suggests that our policy problem can be formulated as one in which we attempt to
minimize the aggregate cost of pollution abatement subject to the constraint of the
attainment of the predetermined levels of air or water quality [11, 5]. When a
particular pollution constraint is not binding, the implied cost of additional environmental degradation is zero.

However, such a formulation is unacceptable both in principle and at the policy
level. There is little evidence of the existence of such thresholds for most air and
water pollutants: some pollution typically yields some damages and somewhat more
pollution results in somewhat more damages. At the policy level, the implicit
recognition of a continuous damage function is embodied in a variety of measures to
maintain or even to improve air and water quality in cases where it is already better
than the current standards. As one example, the U.S. Congress has introduced a set
of provisions in the 1977 Amendments to the Clean Air Act for the "prevention of
significant deterioration" (PSD) in various types of areas where air quality already
exceeds the standards. Moreover, under existing command-and-control (CAC) systems, state regulators have imposed relatively strict abatement requirements on
sources whose emissions would not otherwise imperil the achievement of existing air
or water quality standards.

The purpose of this paper is to describe a system of marketable or transferable
discharge permits (TDP) that can effectively both attain the predetermined standards for environmental quality and, at the same time, prevent any deterioration in
areas which are already cleaner than the standards. The system is, in fact, dis-
armingly simple. It calls for redefining the environmental quality standards: the new
standard at each point in the region is equal to the predetermined standard
established by the environmental authority or the initial level of environmental
quality, whichever is the higher. Free trading of permits is then allowed provided
that no violation of these *new* air or water quality standards takes place.

Drawing on previous results in the literature [11, 5], we will show that the
competitive equilibrium of this new permit system exists and that it satisfies the
first-order conditions for the least-cost solution for the attainment of the resulting
level of environmental quality. Moreover, we shall find that compared to the initial
equilibrium under a command-and-control system, the new competitive equilibrium
represents a Pareto improvement for all parties involved, including both environmentalists and polluters. Under this system, not only will sources typically have
reduced costs, but environmental quality will, in general, improve (at a minimum, it
can never get worse). Even areas that are already clean will tend to become cleaner.
In short, the proposed system has the attraction at the policy level of promising
benefits both in terms of a cleaner environment and reduced abatement costs.

We also present some empirical estimates of the potential cost savings and air
quality improvements based upon a model of particulate emissions (TSP) for the
Baltimore Air Quality Control Region (AQCR). We find that potential gains from
implementing this system are quite large: air quality improves while aggregate
abatement costs are significantly reduced.

We acknowledge at the outset an obvious deficiency of the proposed system: the outcome will not, in general, be Pareto optimal, since the resulting level of environmental quality will not be such that marginal damages equal marginal abatement costs at each location. But this deficiency, of course, characterizes virtually any approach in the absence of explicit damage functions. The system thus promises a Pareto improvement over the initial state (at least in attainment areas), but not a fully Pareto-optimal outcome.

2. A MORE FORMAL STATEMENT OF THE PROBLEM

Let us consider a specific region consisting either of an air shed or system of waterways in which there are m sources of pollution, each of which is fixed in location. Environmental (air or water) quality is defined in terms of pollutant concentrations at each of n "receptor points" in the region; this implies that we can describe environmental quality by a vector $Q = (q_1, q_2, \ldots, q_n)$ whose elements indicate the concentration of the pollutant at each of the receptors. The dispersion of waste emissions from the m sources is described by an $m \times n$ matrix of unit diffusion (or transfer) coefficients:

$$D = \begin{bmatrix} & \vdots & \\ \ldots & d_{ij} & \ldots \\ & \vdots & \end{bmatrix}$$

where d_{ij} indicates the increase in pollutant concentration at receptor j from one unit of emissions of the pollutant by source i.

The environmental authority determines a set of standards that specifies the maximum allowable concentrations at each receptor point: $Q^* = (q_1^*, q_2^*, \ldots, q_n^*)$. For expositional convenience, we shall refer to the Q^* as the "national standards." We note that although the q^* are typically the same for all i, they need not be so. For example, under the Clean Air Act Amendments, EPA has defined a *uniform* minimum air quality standard for certain "criteria" pollutants, but states are free to impose more stringent standards in any region they desire. Under the system we present in this paper, the state environmental authority would do precisely that: redefine more stringent standards for some parts of the region thereby preventing any deterioration of environmental quality once a permit system is implemented. After the standards are redefined, no new emissions or transfers of emissions among sources would be allowed if they result in a violation of the *new* standards at any receptor point.

The policy problem is, therefore, that of attaining the predetermined, "national" set of standards at a minimum of aggregate abatement costs subject to the constraint that air (or water) quality may not deteriorate in areas where the pollutant concentration is already below that allowed by the standard. Suppose that $Q^0 = (q_1^0, q_2^0, \ldots, q_n^0)$ describes the levels of pollutant concentration under the current CAC approach. Then, if e_i is the level of emissions from source i and if $C_i(e_i)$ is its abatement cost function, we are searching for a vector of emissions, $E = (e_1, \ldots, e_m)$, that represents the solution of the following problem:

$$\text{Minimize} \sum_i C_i(e_i)$$

$$\text{s.t.} \quad ED \leq \min(Q^*, Q^0), \quad E \geq 0.$$

The novelty of this formulation of the problem is the inclusion of the Q^0 term in the first constraint. Several papers have explored the solution to the problem where $ED \leq Q^*$ (see, for example, [11, 5]). But, as we have already indicated, the disturbing property of previously proposed TDP systems is that they treat increases in pollutant concentrations as costless to society so long as there are no violations of the national standard. Many empirical studies indicate enormous potential savings in aggregate abatement costs for systems of economic incentives that can approach the least-cost solution as compared to existing command-and-control systems. It is not clear, however, what portion of these cost savings are achieved by allowing increased emissions (and their associated increased pollutant concentrations) at receptor points where the standard is not a binding constraint. In two studies that have addressed this matter, Atkinson and Tietenberg [2] and Atkinson [1], have found that a substantial fraction of the savings in abatement costs resulted from projected increases in emissions in those parts of the region where air quality was better than the national standard. It may thus be that much of the cost savings promised by these systems of transferable permits cannot be realized if the control system no longer regards any existing "shortfall" in pollutant concentrations as a form of "excess capacity" to be exploited at zero cost in the search for abatement cost savings to sources.

From a strictly economic perspective, the introduction of the constraint that air quality not deteriorate beyond current levels is obviously not the appropriate way to address the problem: the decision of whether or not to allow increased emissions should be based on a comparison of marginal damages with marginal abatement costs. However, not only are such calculations extremely difficult, they may not (as in the case of the Clean Air Act in the United States) even be legally admissible. In the absence of these calculations, we shall describe an admittedly second-best approach using economic incentives that promises gains (potentially quite large) in terms both of reduced abatement costs and improved environmental quality.

The system of transferable discharge permits to be considered here is a modification of what elsewhere has been called the "pollution-offset" system [5]. Under this general approach, permits are defined in terms of emissions (e.g., the permit allows the discharge of X pounds of the pollutant, say, per week). However, sources are not allowed to trade permits on a one-to-one basis. More specifically, transfers of TDPs under the pollution-offset scheme are subject to the restriction that the transfer does not result in a violation of the national environmental quality standard at any receptor point. If a proposed transfer encounters a binding pollution constraint at some receptor point, this implies that emissions will be traded at a rate determined by the ratio of the sources' "transfer coefficients" (the d_{ij}'s).[3] For purposes of the analysis here, we will modify the pollution-offset system in two respects:

(1) Free trading of permits will be allowed provided no violation in the *redefined* standards [$\min(Q^*, Q^0)$] occurs as a result of the trade.

---

[3] This ratio indicates the rate at which emissions from one source can be substituted for emissions from the other source with no change in pollutant concentrations at the applicable receptor point.

(2) For attainment areas (areas where the national standards have been met), there will be an initial distribution of TDPs such that each source will receive the number of permits needed to validate its current level of emissions.

We shall describe the *modified* system simply as the "offset system" (or modified offset system) in the remainder of the paper; the term "pollution-offset" system will refer to the system summarized above and presented in detail in [5].

3. PROPERTIES OF THE OFFSET SYSTEM

In this section, we explore the static properties of the offset system in terms of a convenient diagrammatic framework [10]. First, the analysis develops the least-cost properties of the system: it indicates that the "trading equilibrium" (the outcome at which there are no further gains from exchanges of permits) coincides with the least-cost allocation of permits for the resulting level of environmental quality. Second, we find that for the case where the initial CAC equilibrium has attained the national standards, the equilibrium under the offset system typically results in both an improvement in environmental quality and a reduction in costs to all sources. For the nonattainment case, in contrast, some sources *may* experience an increase in control costs.

For a more rigorous treatment of these matters, we refer the reader to the Appendix where, following Montgomery's seminal paper [11], we appeal to the Montgomery proof to demonstrate the existence of a competitive equilibrium for the offset system and to show that this equilibrium satisfies the conditions for the least-cost solution to the control problem. In addition, we explore further the relationship of the offset system to Montgomery's system of emissions licenses; the discussion serves to clarify and, on one point, to correct Montgomery's treatment.

3.1. The Attainment Case

Figure 1 depicts the case of two sources and two receptor points where the horizontal and vertical axes measure, respectively, the levels of emissions of sources 1 and 2 (i.e., e_1 and e_2). The curves C_1 and C_2 are iso-cost curves for total pollution abatement costs, where a higher curve indicates lower aggregate abatement costs

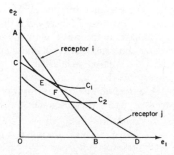

Fig. 1. Pollution-offset system.

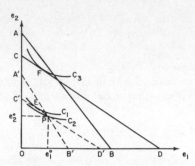

FIG. 2. Modified-offset system: Case I.

$(C_1 < C_2)$. The line AB represents the pollution constraint associated with receptor i. Points on AB depict combinations of e_1 and e_2 for which $q_i = q^*$; the slope of the line equals the ratio of the transfer coefficients and hence indicates the rate at which emissions from source 2 can substitute for emissions from source 1 with no change in pollutant concentrations at receptor i. Likewise, line CD embodies the pollution constraint for receptor j. The combinations of emissions from the two sources that satisfy the national standards at both receptor points are thus the set of points $OCFB$. We find that the least-cost solution occurs at E, at which point the ratio of the sources' marginal abatement costs equals the ratio of their transfer coefficients. Note further that under the pollution-offset system where sources are free to discharge wastes (if the pollution standard is not a binding constraint) or to trade TDPs (if it does bind), E will also represent the "trading equilibrium" [5]. At any other point in the feasible set, there will be potential gains either from reducing abatement efforts and/or from trading emissions entitlements. The trading equilibrium thus coincides with the least-cost solution under the pollution-offset system.

Suppose, however, that under the prevailing CAC system, the environmental authority has held pollutant concentrations below the national standard at both receptor points, i and j. Point P in Fig. 2 indicates such an outcome. If we now introduce the modified-offset system, sources 1 and 2 will receive transferable discharge permits in the amounts of e_1^0 and e_2^0, respectively. Since the redefined environmental quality standard is now set equal to the prevailing environmental quality, the new constraints on emissions are indicated by the lines $A'B'$ and $C'D'$.[4] The least-cost solution, given these constraints, is E. Moreover, since E can be achieved at lower total abatement cost than P, there exists the potential for mutually profitable trading: source 2 will have an incentive to purchase permits from source 1 in an amount sufficient to move the combination of emissions from P to E. At E, all potential gains-from-trade will have been exhausted.

Further examination of E reveals that, not only have cost savings been achieved by the move from P, but environmental quality has improved. Pollutant concentrations at receptor i are now lower than they were under the CAC equilibrium, while

---

[4] The lines representing the new constraints have the same slopes as those indicating the standard (equal to the ratio of the transfer coefficients). Their position, however, refers to the initial level of environmental quality which is in excess of the national standard.

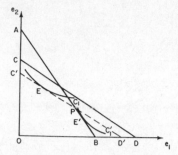

FIG. 3. Modified-offset system: Case II.

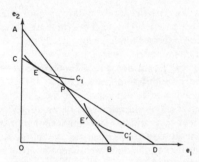

FIG. 4. Modified-offset system: Case III.

concentrations at receptor j are unchanged. Such cost reductions *and* improvements in environmental quality will obviously take place in all cases except that where the tangency with the highest iso-cost curve occurs at P; for this special case, the outcomes under the CAC and offset systems will coincide.[5] We note in passing that under the pollution-offset system, the trading equilibrium in Fig. 2 would be at F; this would allow further savings in abatement costs (relative to E), but at the price of a deterioration in environmental quality up to the national standard.

Figures 3 and 4 depict the other two possible cases for an attainment area and indicate the same general properties of the trading equilibrium as in Fig. 2. In Fig. 3, the initial state, P, under the CAC regime is such that the national standard is itself a binding constraint at one of the receptors. For this case, trading subject to the redefined environmental quality standard implies the constraint $C'PB$, where the segment $C'P$ reflects the redefined portion of the constraint. In Fig. 4, we have the special case in which the initial state occurs precisely at the national standard for

---

[5] This result depends on the assumption that the initial state under the CAC regime represents a least-cost solution for each source *given* its assigned level of emissions. If, however, the environmental authority had specified a particular abatement technology that was not the least-cost one, the sources typically would not be operating on the iso-cost curves. In this case, some cost savings could be realized under the offset system without any changes in emission levels by simply moving to the least-cost technology.

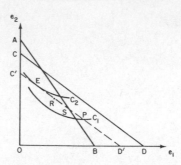

FIG. 5. Nonattainment area: Case I.

both receptor points; in this instance, the standards would require no redefinition, since $q^0 = q^*$ at both receptors. We note that, for both cases (as in Fig. 2), the trading equilibria at E or E' (corresponding respectively to C_1 or C_1') represent both a reduction in abatement costs and an improvement in air or water quality at one of the receptor points.[6] For Fig. 4, incidentally, the outcome under our offset system coincides with that under the pollution-offset scheme.

We thus find that for all three configurations of the initial state under the CAC regime in an attainment area, the introduction of an offset system will typically result in reduced abatement costs and a cleaner environment. For the special case in which the tangency of the iso-cost curve occurs at the initial state, there will be no change: the CAC initial state and the outcome under the offset system will coincide. But in no instances under the offset system can there be a deterioration in environmental quality at any receptor point or an increase in costs for any polluter.

3.2. The Problem of Nonattainment Areas

We found in Section 3.1 that if under the CAC regime the environmental authority has achieved the predetermined national standards for air or water quality, then the introduction of the offset system promises a Pareto improvement that will typically improve environmental quality and reduce abatement costs. However, if the initial state is one of nonattainment where the national standards have not yet been everywhere achieved, this dual result can no longer be guaranteed. The offset system still promises to promote attainment of the standards at least cost, but some sources *may* experience increased control costs. Typically, the environmental authority's problem in the nonattainment case is that some parts of the region are in violation of the standard (say, the central business district for air quality), while the environmental quality in the remaining parts of the region is better than the predetermined standard (e.g., the suburbs).

The nature of the problem is apparent in Figs. 5 and 6. Suppose that the initial state under the CAC system is again represented by point P. However, in this

---

[6] In the multidimensional case involving more than one, say, n, receptor points, there can be improved air or water quality at as many as $(n - 1)$ receptors. If, for example, the binding constraint at the trading equilibrium involves a single receptor, then environmental quality may have improved at all the other receptor points in the region.

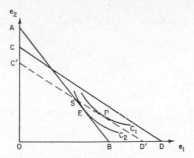

Fig. 6. Nonattainment area: Case II.

instance P is outside the acceptable set of outcomes, for the pollutant concentration at receptor i exceeds the standard indicated by line AB. The pollutant concentration at receptor j, in contrast, is below the maximum permitted level (i.e., P lies inside line CD). The introduction of the offset system implies a new set of environmental standards: to preserve current environmental quality, the standard at receptor j will be tightened as indicated by the line $C'D'$. Line AB will still represent the relevant standard for receptor i, since the pollutant concentration at i is higher than the national standard.

The introduction of the offset system (or any other attempt to reach the standards) will require some contraction in emissions by at least one source to meet the standards. The problem for the environmental authority is to choose some allocation of permits among the sources which will sustain attainment. Unlike the attainment case, these allocations obviously cannot equal current levels of discharges. Instead the authority must select some combination of permits on (or inside) the frontier $C'SB$ to meet the newly defined standards.

Suppose this point is represented by R. There would then exist an incentive for source two to purchase permits from source one until the least-cost solution is reached, at which point all the gains-from-trade would be exhausted (at point E in Fig. 5). Note, moreover, that for this case, total abatement costs actually decline relative to the initial nonattainment point P. For such a case, a Pareto improvement for all sources can be achieved with an appropriate initial allocation of permits. In Fig. 6, in contrast, the trading equilibrium at E entails an increase in total abatement costs relative to P. For cases such as this, some sources (at least one) will necessarily experience higher control costs.

4. SOME EMPIRICAL FINDINGS

To explore the potential differences among a typical CAC regime, a pollution-offset system, and our modified-offset system, we have made use of a computer-based model constructed for an earlier analysis of particulate emissions (TSP) in the Baltimore Air Quality Control Region [9]. The model incorporates control-cost estimates, associated collection efficiencies, and dispersion characteristics for over 400 sources. The control-cost estimates take the form of integer step functions and were estimated using the costing algorithm explained in a series of articles by [13]. In

TABLE I
Annualized Costs to Achieve Air Quality of 98 $\mu g/m^3$ under Three Systems[a]

		Control systems	
	CAC	Modified offset	Pollution offset
Annualized cost	112.9	46.3	27.1

[a]All costs in millions of 1980 dollars.

addition, a careful listing of all CAC requirements was assembled which allowed a simulation of the CAC system presently employed in Baltimore.

The simulation of the existing CAC system produced annualized cost estimates and a vector of air quality readings indicating pollutant concentrations at each receptor throughout the area. Although Baltimore is a nonattainment area for the primary air quality standard for TSP established by the EPA, most of the region had air quality far better than the standard. In general, the central business district (CBD) is the troublesome area (or "hot spot") because of the large number of sources whose emissions contribute to the pollutant concentrations there.

For purposes of comparison with the CAC simulation, the solutions to the following problems (representing the outcomes of the pollution-offset system and the modified-offset system respectively) were estimated

$$\text{Minimize} \sum_i C_i(e_i) \tag{1}$$

$$\text{s.t.} \quad ED \leq Q^*, \quad E \geq 0,$$

$$\text{Minimize} \sum_i C_i(e_i) \tag{2}$$

$$\text{s.t.} \quad ED \leq \min[Q^*, Q^0], \quad E \geq 0,$$

where Q^0 is the air quality vector resulting from the CAC simulation and Q^* is the existing air quality in the central business district (CBD). Note that for this first set of simulation exercises, we assume (contrary to fact) that the existing CAC system has achieved the national standard; we thus equate Q^* with the existing TSP concentration in the CBD of 98 $\mu g/m^3$.

Table I presents the cost estimates associated with each of the three control systems, while Fig. 7 depicts the air quality vector for each case. As Table I indicates, either permit system promises quite large potential cost savings relative to the existing CAC regime: in excess of 50%.[7] From these figures, we get some sense of how much of the cost savings relative to the CAC case come from a more efficient allocation of abatement quotas and how much from the increase in pollution allowed at above-standard sites under the pollution-offset system. For this case, we see that the modified-offset system (which allows no deterioration at any site relative to the CAC outcome) achieves roughly two-thirds of the cost savings under the pollution-offset system. We thus conclude that for this simulation, a more efficient pattern of

[7]For a detailed analysis of the sources of these cost differences, see McGartland [8].

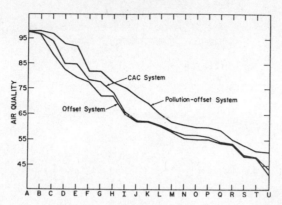

FIG. 7. Air quality under three control systems (receptors ranked in order of pollutant concentrations).

abatement activity accounts for about three-fourths of the cost savings with the remaining quarter attributable to reduced controls and the consequent increase in pollutant concentrations at receptors where the air is cleaner than the national standard under the CAC regime.

As Fig. 7 indicates, however, the further increment in cost savings under the pollution-offset system comes at a discernible "price" in terms of deterioration of air quality at various sites in the Baltimore region. The figure shows the projected TSP concentrations under each of the three systems for 20 representative receptors that were designated as "strategically located" by the Maryland Air Management Administration. Interestingly, the ranking of the receptors is not very sensitive to the choice of regime: the receptor with the worst air quality (A) is the same for all systems, and in all but four instances the ranking of the other receptors is unchanged across the three systems. Examination of Fig. 7 indicates that TSP concentrations at all the receptors (except A for which $q^0 = q^*$) increase significantly under the pollution-offset system from their CAC levels, in some instances by as much as 10 $\mu g/m^3$. In contrast, concentrations under the modified-offset system are less than CAC levels with the largest improvements in air quality occurring at receptors with relatively high levels of pollution. At those same receptors, the differences in air quality between the pollution-offset and modified-offset systems are the most pronounced reaching 10 to 12 $\mu g/m^3$. These results would thus seem to provide some support for the concern over the deterioration in environmental quality that can occur with the adoption of the pollution-offset system.

We previously pointed out that two other studies, Atkinson and Tietenberg [2] and Atkinson [1], have found that a substantial portion of the abatement cost savings from achieving a least-cost solution resulted from projected increases in aggregate emissions. The total emissions associated with each of our three control systems in the first simulation is reported in Table II. As indicated, emissions under the pollution-offset system do increase dramatically relative to the existing CAC system. However, under the modified-offset system, total emissions are not much higher than the emissions associated with the CAC approach—roughly 4%. The reader may be puzzled as to how total emissions can increase yet air quality remain the same or improve at every receptor. Closer inspection of the source-by-source final allocation

TABLE II

Emissions under Three Systems Achieving a Minimum Air Quality of 98 $\mu g/m^3$

	Control system		
	CAC	Modified offset	Pollution offset
Emissions (tons/year)	23,358	24,325	49,392

TABLE III

Annualized Costs Necessary to Achieve the Primary Standard under the Pollution Offset and Modified Offset Systems[a]

	Modified offset	Pollution offset
Annualized cost	76.6	61.4

[a]All figures in millions of 1980 dollars.

of emissions can provide an answer to the question. Some sources' emissions travel relatively far. In fact, a large percentage of these emissions traveling long distances settle on the Chesapeake Bay or Atlantic Ocean. When these emissions increase, the effects on air quality can easily be offset by strategically reducing the emissions of others at a less than one-to-one ratio. Both improved air quality and reduced control costs are thus achieved under the modified-offset system by essentially altering the *pattern* of emissions in such a way as to reduce pollutant concentrations in the region.

In the second set of simulations, we took as the standard for TSP concentrations the EPA-determined primary standard of 85 $\mu g/m^3$.[8] With $Q^* = 85$, there are three receptors in violation of the standard so that the initial CAC regime implies that the Baltimore AQCR is a nonattainment area. Table III and Fig. 8 present the results. For this second case, we find that the differences in costs and in air quality between the pollution-offset and our modified-offset systems are not very large. Closer examination of the resulting distribution of emissions tells us why. As the air quality standard becomes more stringent, sources whose emissions have a relatively large impact on the "problem area" (the CBD) quickly control as much as possible. When the stricter standard is still not reached, sources farther away must adopt tighter controls to help reduce the pollutant concentration at the CBD. When the standard was 98 $\mu g/m^3$, these more distant sources did not have to adopt such strict (and expensive) abatement techniques. As these suburban sources adopt more stringent controls, the surrounding air quality improves even though it already exceeds the standard. In other words, as sources farther away from the problem area adopt stricter controls in an attempt to reduce pollution within the CBD, other areas also experience improved air quality. Therefore, as the predetermined standard is

[8]EPA standards for TSP are generally stated in geometric means. With a standard deviation of roughly 1.5, a primary standard of 75$\mu g/m^3$ expressed as a geometric mean, translates roughly to a standard of 85 $\mu g/m^3$ as an arithmetic mean. See Larsen [6].

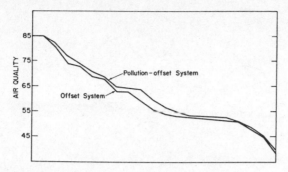

FIG. 8. Air quality under two permit systems.

tightened, the difference between the two systems goes to zero, since they face similar binding constraints. In the limit, if the systems were asked to achieve the lowest pollutant concentration possible, both systems would generate the same outcome: every source would control as much as technically feasible.

Table III indicates that the projected annualized costs are $76.6 million for the modified-offset system versus $61.4 million for the pollution-offset regime. The difference is attributable to two receptors with relatively low pollutant concentrations for which q^0 is a binding constraint under the modified system. We thus find that where the standard requires high levels of control throughout the region, the differences between our two versions of the offset system are much less in terms both of control costs and air quality. In contrast, the potential savings under either system relative to the CAC regime are large: a comparison of Table I and III, for example, indicates that either permit system can achieve the EPA primary standard for TSP concentrations at an aggregate cost far less than that under the *existing* CAC system (which, as yet, has been unsuccessful in achieving the standard.)

5. ON THE DYNAMICS OF PERMIT TRADING

The analysis to this juncture has been wholly in terms of statics; we have compared the equilibrium outcomes under a variety of regulatory systems with respect to certain definitions of allowable pollutant concentrations. We have not, however, explored dynamic issues such as the sequence of trades that leads to the equilibrium. The dynamic properties of most markets are not well understood, but there are some features of the permit market that are of particular note.

We introduce the discussion in terms of a constraint on trades, a "nondegradation condition," that has received some attention in the literature [5]. Recall that under the modified-offset system, trades among sources are subject to the constraint of no violation of the redefined standard (equal to the predetermined, national standard or the initial level of environmental quality, whichever implies less pollution). The nondegradation constraint is a far more stringent condition that applies to *each trade*: it requires that for each trade, environmental quality must not deteriorate at *any* receptor point. (In contrast, the modified-offset system allows increased pollutant concentrations at a receptor so long as the redefined standard is not violated.)

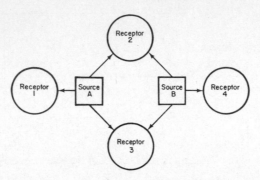

FIG. 9. Trading under a nondegradation constraint.

We wish to emphasize that the nondegradation condition is an extremely restrictive constraint on trades—so restrictive, in fact, that it is likely to paralyze the functioning of the permit market. It is easy to see that a nondegradation condition on individual trades of permits effectively limits trading between two sources solely to cases in which the buyer's emissions affect receptors which are a subset of the receptors affected by the emissions of the seller. Consider, for example, the operation of the modified-offset system in the context of the spatial patterns depicted in Fig. 9. Assume that the air quality at receptor one is better than the redefined standard [i.e., pollutant concentrations are less than $\min(q^0, q^*)$], while these concentrations at the other receptors are equal to the standard. If source A affects receptors 1, 2, and 3 and B affects 2, 3, and 4, A could buy emissions permits from B. Source A would simply buy enough permits to "offset" the effects of his emissions on pollutant concentrations at receptors 2 and 3. Since the pollutant concentration at receptor one is already below the redefined standard, A does not have to acquire any offsets there.

Under a nondegradation condition, however, A and B could not trade. Since air quality deteriorates at receptor one as a result of the trade, the nondegradation constraint would be violated. The nondegradation condition effectively redefines the standard after *every trade*, so that the standard at each receptor is always binding. Thus, if any "excess capacity" is generated by previous trades, it is instantly taken away. As a result, two-party trades are impossible unless it happens that the emissions of the buyer affect only a subset of the receptors that are affected by the seller's discharges.

The moral of this discussion is that it is generally desirable to avoid a nondegradation constraint on trades of permits, for such a constraint is likely to prevent many cost-saving trades. The reader may, however, have noticed that we were careful in the above example to assume that the pollutant concentration at receptor one was below the redefined standard. But that need not be true in which case the non-degradation constraint would effectively apply to the trade in our example. Source A would, in this instance, have to purchase permits from a third source whose emissions affect receptor one, in addition to his purchases from source B. More generally, it is clear that under the modified-offset system, the nondegradation constraint effectively applies to the initial trade. This follows from the introduction of the redefined standard that makes $\min(q^0, q^*)$ a binding constraint at all receptors.

This is admittedly troubling, for it restricts the range of allowable trades at the outset. It is our conjecture, however, that this need not, in general, constitute a serious obstacle to the initiation of permit trading. At the original CAC equilibrium there will typically exist (as in our case of particulate emissions in Baltimore) large potential gains-from-trade, involving a substantial number of sources. The number of permutations among these sources for mutually profitable trades will tend to be relatively large so that it should not be difficult to find buyers whose emissions impinge on only a subset of the receptors affected by the seller (or, alternatively, perhaps two sellers whose discharges encompass all the receptors of relevance to the buyer).[9]

As a few trades are made, excess capacity will quickly be generated so that only a few receptors will remain as binding constraints. For instance, in our Baltimore simulation, we find that at the final equilibria for the standards of 98 and 85 $\mu g/m^3$, there are, respectively, only four and three binding receptors. Were there to be any further trades, some increment to pollutant concentrations would be allowable at all the other (nonbinding) receptors. In contrast, the presence of a nondegradation constraint on every purchase and sale of permits will tend to become a more formidable obstacle to trading as the system moves closer to the least-cost outcome. As the trading process progresses, fewer and fewer potentially profitable exchanges of permits will remain so that it will become increasingly difficult to find combinations of interested buyers and sellers such that a transaction will not result in higher pollutant concentrations at *any* receptor.

Thus, we surmise that the modified-offset system is not likely to encounter the kind of paralysis that will tend to characterize a permit market with a nondegradation constraint in place. More generally, it is difficult to reach specific results on the dynamic properties of the offset system. McGartland [8] offers some discussion of the trading process under the pollution-offset and modified-offset systems. It is clear, for example, that there are cases where the least-cost outcome can involve a fairly complicated transfer of permits among several parties. Whether the multilateral trades implied by such conditions are likely to be realized in the marketplace is not fully clear. As McGartland shows, there can be opportunities for free-rider behavior that will impede the attainment of the desired outcome. It may be that a sequence of bilateral trades can sometimes approach the least-cost solution fairly closely. These issues are hard to analyze in the abstract; they require an explicitly dynamic analysis, preferably using some actual configurations of sources and air sheds and incorporating some reasonable conditions concerning the (for practical purposes) irreversible nature of many types of investment in abatement technology. Important research remains to be done to clarify the dynamic properties of the various forms of permit systems. We must, therefore, conclude on an admittedly

[9]A hypothetical case may help to suggest how trading could get underway. With the existence of substantial gains-from-trade, two sources relatively close to one another could initiate a trade by asking the environmental authority to "simulate" (with an air dispersion model) the effects of possible trades between the two parties. The simulations would identify any areas that would experience violations of the redefined standard along with nearby small area or point sources whose effects on air quality are relatively localized. An area source (e.g., a dirt or gravel road) could be incorporated as a second seller in the trade making a small but important contribution by reducing pollutant concentrations in the area that the buyer affects but the primary seller does not.

cautious note: the modified-offset system has a number of attractive static properties that invite further attention to its potential for improving environmental quality while simultaneously reducing control costs to sources.

6. CONCLUDING REMARKS

The offset system of transferable discharge permits described in this paper has the property that it can attain the predetermined standards for environmental quality and, at the same time, ensure that there is no deterioration in any areas that are cleaner than the standard. And the equilibrium outcome under this system satisfies the first-order conditions for the minimization of aggregate abatement costs for the resulting level of environmental quality (whatever it may be). Moreover, for regions in which the initial state under a command-and-control system already satisfies the standards, the offset equilibrium will typically imply both reduced costs to polluters and further cleanup of the environment. If, instead, the initial state is one of nonattainment of the standards, the reduction in costs to all sources cannot be assured.

Our empirical results suggest that the potential gains-from-trade under a system of pricing incentives are quite large. Although systems that allow increased emissions in those parts of the region where the air or water is cleaner than the standard promise the largest cost savings, substantial savings can still be had while at the same time preventing any deterioration in environmental quality. This feature makes the modified-offset system attractive on both economic and political grounds.

At the same time, we are reluctant to make a completely unqualified case for the modified-offset over the pollution-offset system. Even aside from certain troublesome dynamic issues, the cost in the full economic sense of an absolute ban on any environmental deterioration at any location may be undesirably high. In an area, for example, which has no pollution at present, the adoption of the modified-offset system could amount to a virtual ban on any sort of economic development. Such a ban may be desirable under certain circumstances, but not under others. It may make sense, for instance, to draw some distinctions like those made in the 1977 Amendments of the Clean Air Act between certain areas where no deterioration in air quality is to be allowed and others where some limited increment to pollutant concentrations (still, in total, less than the EPA primary standard) is permissible. In short, one might wish to "modify" our modified-offset system a bit further to allow, in certain circumstances, for the redefinition of the standard to be a little less stringent than the existing level of environmental quality.

APPENDIX

In 1972, Montgomery published a seminal paper [11] on the properties of two alternative forms of marketable permit systems. The Montgomery results have been widely cited in the subsequent literature, but as Krupnick *et al.* [5] show, they have been the subject of some basic misinterpretation. Our purposes in this Appendix are twofold: first, we present a further discussion of Montgomery's emission-license system that serves both to clarify Montgomery's treatment and to correct it on one important point, and second, we then use the Montgomery framework to demonstrate that for our modified-offset system, a competitive equilibrium exists and that this equilibrium satisfies the conditions for the least-cost solution to our control problem.

1. On Montgomery's System of Emission Licenses

Montgomery's emission-license system begins with a distribution of emission permits to each of M sources such that the environmental quality standard is not violated at any receptor point when all permits are fully utilized. Sources are then free to trade permits, but unlike the pollution-offset system where the permits are defined in terms of emissions (properly "weighted" by transfer coefficients), Montgomery's permits confer the right to pollute certain groups of receptors. This distinction is illustrated in Fig. 10.

Consider a transaction where source A buys rights from source B. Further assume that A's emissions influence pollutant concentrations at receptors 1 and 2, while B's emissions affect receptors 1, 2, and 3. Under Montgomery's system, when the transaction is completed, A acquires the right to pollute at receptors 1, 2, *and* 3, even though A's emissions do not affect the pollutant concentration at receptor 3. Montgomery accomplishes this by permanently indexing permits by the dispersion characteristics of the initial holder of permits (in this case B); A thus acquires the right to pollute *all* the areas that B would have polluted if it had continued to hold the permits.

It is easy to show that this property of Montgomery's permits makes the existence of a least-cost equilibrium unlikely under reasonable assumptions. Because his emission-license system does not allow polluters to "break-up" permits so that A would not have to buy the implicit right to pollute at receptor 3, two conditions must be satisfied for the competitive equilibrium to satisfy the least-cost conditions. Montgomery correctly states the first condition: the initial allocation of permits must be such that if all permits are utilized, the pollutant concentrations at every receptor must just equal the standard:

$$E^0 D = Q^*,$$

where E^0 is the vector of emissions implied by the initial allocation of permits. This is, incidentally, a very stringent condition that will not, in general, hold, since for any semipositive D and Q^*, there will not, in general, be a nonnegative solution to E^0.

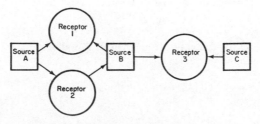

FIG. 10. Trading of emissions licenses.

There is a second constraint that must be satisfied which Montgomery does not treat satisfactorily. Because permits cannot be "broken-up," the final distribution of permits must also satisfy a basic condition. Some notation will help explain the problem. Let X_{ik} be the number of emission licenses originally distributed to source k but now held by source i (in the final equilibrium). With this alternative notation, we can formulate Montgomery's initial condition as

$$\sum_{k=1}^{M} \sum_{i=1}^{M} X_{ik} d_{kj} = q_j^* \qquad j = 1, \ldots, N.$$

In other words, the total amount of pollution at each receptor implied by the initial distribution of permits must be equal to the predetermined standard. (Note that the subscript on the dispersion coefficient denotes the initial holder of the permit.) But, not only must there exist an initial distribution of permits which allows for full utilization of the assimilative capacity of the atmosphere, but also a *final* distribution which allows each polluter to emit the optimal amount of emissions:

$$e_i^* d_{ij} \leq \sum_{k=1}^{M} X_{ik} d_{kj} \qquad j = 1, \ldots, N \qquad i = 1, \ldots, M,$$

where e_i^* is the amount of emissions implied by the joint cost-minimization problem.

Although Montgomery attempts to prove that this latter set of conditions is automatically satisfied, there is no guarantee that it will be. Montgomery's Proposition 1 states that X_{ik} will exist such that $\sum_k d_{kj} X_{ik} \geq d_{ij} e_i^*$. But Montgomery's proof of this proposition is faulty, since it is easy to show a counterexample where Proposition 1 does not hold. Consider the case of three polluters, A, B, and C, and the two receptors, 1 and 2. Let

$$\begin{aligned} d_{A1} &= 20 & d_{A2} &= 0 \\ d_{B1} &= 20 & d_{B2} &= 20 \\ d_{C1} &= 0 & d_{C2} &= 20 \end{aligned}$$

with

$$\begin{aligned} q_1^* &= 400 & q_2^* &= 400 \\ 1_A^0 &= 10 \\ 1_B^0 &= 10 \\ 1_C^0 &= 10 \end{aligned}$$

where 1_i^0 is i's initial allocation of permits. Under this allocation, the constraint on the initial distribution of permits is satisfied:

$$d_{A1} 1_A^0 + d_{B1} 1_B^0 + d_{C1} 1_C^0 = q_1^*$$

by substitution

$$20 \cdot 10 + 20 \cdot 10 + 0 \cdot 10 = 400$$

and

$$d_{A2}1_A^0 + d_{B2}1_B^0 + d_{C2}1_C^0 = q_2^*$$

by substitution

$$0 \cdot 10 + 20 \cdot 10 + 20 \cdot 10 = 400.$$

Further assume that the solution to the cost-minimization problem is

$$e_A^{**} = 20 \qquad e_B^{**} = 0 \qquad e_C^{**} = 20.$$

Trading would thus require that A and C buy permits from B. However, in Montgomery's system there is no way to distribute B's *fixed* group of pollution rights. If A buys B's permits to increase its pollution at receptor 1, then A also acquires the right to pollute at receptor 2, even though it is of no use to A.

The nature of the latter set of constraints is straightforward. Again, since these rights cannot be "broken-up," each polluter must collect a portfolio of permits, each of which carries the right to pollute at a number of receptors. For example, one emission permit obtained *from* source k is, in reality, a right to pollute at n receptors equal to $d_{k1}, d_{k2}, \ldots d_{kn}$, respectively. Each source must accumulate a portfolio of these permits from different sources to minimize costs, and at the same time satisfy the above constraints.

Thus, for the existence of an equilibrium which satisfies the first-order conditions of the two joint cost-minimization problems, a semipositive matrix, X, of dimension $M \times M$ must exist which satisfies $N(M + 1)$ constraints: Montgomery's N constraints on the initial distribution of permits plus $M \cdot N$ additional constraints on the *final* distribution when the market is in equilibrium. Presumably Montgomery assumes that these latter conditions will hold, but they are not necessarily satisfied. Note that it is quite possible for Montgomery's initial condition to have a solution, but for the latter constraints to be violated.

Permits under the modified offset and pollution-offset systems effectively allow the breaking-up of rights to pollute at different receptors and, as a consequence, need not satisfy the above conditions on the final distribution of permits. Referring back to the proposed transaction where polluter A buys permits from polluter B, recall that A's emissions do not affect the pollutant concentration at receptor 2 while B's do. Under the offset systems, B is free to include polluter C (who only affects receptor 2) in the bargaining process. Then when B reduces his emissions, A and C can simultaneously increase theirs. The greater degree of flexibility is obvious. In addition, as we demonstrate in the next section, the competitive equilibrium under the modified-offset system exists and satisfies the first-order conditions for the solution to the cost-minimization problem. The constraint to be satisfied under the modified-offset system is similar to Montgomery's; permits must be distributed so that:

$$E^0 D = Q^*.$$

Our modified offset system is able to guarantee that this constraint is satisfied, since Q^* is redefined such that the standard at each receptor exactly equals the concentrations allowed under the initial allocation of permits.

2. The Competitive Properties of the Offset System

In this section, we use Montgomery's [11] formal proof to demonstrate that the competitive equilibrium of the offset system exists and that it satisfies the first-order conditions of the joint cost-minimization problem.

Recall that our problem is

$$\text{Minimize} \sum_i C_i(e_i) \tag{A.1}$$

$$\text{s.t.} \quad ED \le \min[Q^*, Q^0], \quad E \ge 0.$$

Montgomery [11] has constructed a simple proof that the solution to this problem exists, and we will not repeat it here. We will, however, characterize the polluter's problem. The source wishes to minimize

$$C_i(e_i) + P_i(1_i^* - 1_i^0) \tag{A.2}$$

$$\text{s.t.} \quad e_i \le 1_i^*$$

where 1_i^* is the quantity of permits held in equilibrium and 1_i^0 is the quantity initially distributed to source i.

In a truly competitive market, the value of an emission license, P_i, can be represented as the sum of the values of the right to increase the pollutant concentration at each receptor j. For example, when polluter B in Fig. 10 in the Appendix wishes to sell his emission permits, polluter A will pay the value of increasing pollutant concentrations at receptors 1 and 2, and polluter C will pay the competitive price of increasing the pollutant concentration at receptor 3. Therefore, we may write

$$P_i = \sum_j d_{ij} p_j \tag{A.3}$$

where p_j is the value of the right to increase the pollutant concentrations at receptor j by one unit and d_{ij} is the coefficient that translates a unit of emissions from source i into the incremental pollutant concentration at receptor j. Rewriting (A.2) restates the polluter's minimization problem as

$$\text{Minimize} \; C_i(e_i) + \left[\sum_j d_{ij} p_j (1_i^* - 1_i^0) \right] \tag{A.4}$$

$$\text{s.t.} \quad e_i \le 1_i^*.$$

Noting that the term $e_i d_{ij}$ is equal to increased pollutant concentration at receptor j and the fact that an emission right can be "broken-up," we can represent 1_i^* and 1_i^0 as l_{ij}^*/d_{ij} and l_{ij}^0/d_{ij}, $j = 1, 2, \ldots, n$, respectively. Here, l_{ij} refers to the right to increase the pollutant concentration at receptor j by one unit. Therefore, l_{ij} divided by d_{ij} denotes the implied emission right for source i holding 1_{ij}, $j = 1, 2, \ldots, n$.

Rewriting (A.4) restates the polluter's problem as

$$\text{Minimize } C_i(e_i) + \sum_j d_{ij} p_j \left[\left(l_{ij}^*/d_{ij} - l_{ij}^0/d_{ij} \right) \right] \qquad (\text{A.5})$$

$$\text{s.t.} \qquad e_i \le l_{ij}^*/d_{ij} \qquad j = 1, \ldots, n.$$

The d_{ij}'s in the objective function cancel and (A.5) becomes

$$\text{Minimize } C_i(e_i) + \sum_j p_j \left[l_{ij}^* - l_{ij}^0 \right]$$

$$\text{s.t.} \qquad d_{ij} e_i \le l_{ij}^* \qquad j = 1, \ldots, n.$$

This polluter's problem is identical to the one associated with Montgomery's ambient permit system. Further, the joint cost-minimization problem of the regulator is also the same under each system provided that permits can be initially distributed so that the air quality constraint is binding at every receptor point. Under Montgomery's ambient permit system, we can easily distribute permits so that, if all permits are fully utilized, the pollutant concentrations at every receptor point are just equal to the standard. But as Montgomery and this Appendix show, when emission rights are distributed this is a much more difficult task.

But one of the basic properties of our modified-offset system is that the standards are redefined so that every receptor constitutes a binding constraint if all permits are utilized under the initial allocation. Therefore, our regulator's problem and polluter's problem are identical to those associated with Montgomery's ambient permit system.[10] For this system, he was able to show formally that the equilibrium exists and satisfies the first-order conditions of the joint cost-minimization problem. Since our system is mathematically identical, we can appeal to his proofs to show that the same results hold for the modified-offset system.

REFERENCES

1 S. Atkinson, Nonoptimal solutions using transferable discharge permits: The implications of acid rain deposition, in "Buying a Better Environment" (Joeres and David, Eds.), Univ. of Wisconsin Press, Madison (1983).

2. S. Atkinson and T. Tietenberg, The empirical properties of two classes of designs for transferable discharge permit markets, J. Environ. Econ. Manag. 9, 101–121 (1982).

3. W. Baumol and W. Oates, "The Theory of Environmental Policy," Chap. 10, Prentice–Hall, Englewood Cliffs, N.J. (1975).

4. A. M. Freeman III, Air and water pollution policy, in "Current Issues in U.S. Environmental Policy" (Portney, Ed.), Johns Hopkins Press, Baltimore, Md. (1978).

[10] One reviewer noted that the formal equivalence of the regulator's and polluter's problems under the ambient permit and modified offset systems should lead to the conclusion that the implementation of the latter will be fully as difficult as implementing an ambient permit system. This is only partially true. As we show in this Appendix and as in discussed in Krupnick et al. [5], within a purely competitive framework with perfect information and zero transactions costs, there are no real barriers to the implementation of either system. However, when we introduce positive transactions and search costs, some very important distinctions arise. As McGartland [7] shows, the offset system may allow buyers and sellers to concentrate on a very few receptor markets, while the ambient permit system requires each polluter to trade many permits simultaneously.

5. A. Krupnick, W. Oates, and E. Van De Verg, On marketable air pollution permits: The case for a system of pollution offsets, *J. Environ. Econ. Manag.* **10**, 233–247 (1983).

6. R. Larsen, "A Mathematical Model for Relating Air Quality Measurements to Air Quality Standards," U.S. Environmental Protection Agency, Office of Air Programs, Publication AP-89 (1971).

7. A. McGartland, "A Comparison of Two Marketable Discharge Permit Systems," Economic Analysis Division, Environmental Protection Agency Working Paper (1984).

8. A. McGartland, "The Cost Structure of the Total Suspended Particulate Emission Reduction Credit Market," Baltimore Region Emission Report, Vol. V, Regional Planning Council, Baltimore, Md. (1983).

9. A. McGartland, "Marketable Permit Systems for Air Pollution Control: An Empirical Study," unpublished Ph.D. dissertation, University of Maryland, College Park (1984).

10. W. D. Montgomery, Artificial markets and the theory of games, *Public Choice* **18**, 25–40 (1974).

11. W. D. Montgomery, Markets in licenses and efficient pollution control programs, *J. Econ. Theory* **5**, 395–418 (1972).

12. T. Tietenberg, Transferable discharge permits and the control of stationary source air pollution: A survey and synthesis, *Land Econ.* **56**, 391–416 (1980).

13. W. Vatavuk and R. Neveril, Estimating costs of air pollution control systems, Parts I to VIII, *Chem. Eng.* Oct. 1980–June 1981.

[15]

Marketable pollution permits and acid rain externalities: a comment and some further evidence

WALLACE E. OATES University of Maryland
ALBERT M. McGARTLAND U.S. Environmental Protection Agency

In a recent paper, Scott Atkinson (1983) has provided some important insights into the design of systems of marketable permits for the control of air pollution. Atkinson reaches two major conclusions:

1. A system of marketable permits that minimizes the control costs for the attainment of *local* ambient air-quality standards for SO_2 is likely to increase significantly the extent of long-range sulfate depositions (acid rain) as compared to a traditional command-and-control (CAC) strategy.
2. Solely from the perspective of local air quality, the cost-minimizing system of marketable permits *must* imply higher levels of local pollution relative to an alternative system of emissions permits or to a prototype CAC system.

We have no quibbles with the first point. Moreover, Atkinson's simulation results suggest that the trade-off between local air pollution and the long-range transport of sulfur is a serious issue. This is largely a matter of stack height. Higher chimneys allow sulfur emissions to escape the local environment only to result in increased sulfate pollution at more distant locations. This suggests that stack height must be treated as a critical variable in the design of systems to control jointly local and 'global' pollution.

Our concern in this note is with Atkinson's second point. We shall show, first, that the Atkinson theorem is formally incorrect: the cost-minimizing permit system need *not* result in increased local pollution. However, as a practical matter, Atkinson may well be right. We shall supplement his simulation results with some findings from another set of simulations for a different air pollutant, particulate matter, in the Baltimore Air Quality Control

The authors are grateful to the National Science Foundation for support of their research into market incentives for pollution control.

Canadian Journal of Economics Revue canadienne d'Economique, XVIII, No. 3
August août 1985. Printed in Canada Imprimé au Canada

Region (AQCR). The latter results confirm Atkinson's findings that the cost-minimizing permit system produces more local pollution than an emissions permit system. However, there are ways to adapt the cost-minimizing approach to prevent deterioration in local air quality, while still realizing large cost-savings compared with either an emissions permit or a CAC system. We briefly describe the design of such a system and present some simulation results indicating the rough magnitude of the potential cost-savings.

THE ATKINSON THEOREM

Atkinson purports to prove the following proposition: 'Measured at local receptors, the ambient degradation of the local ADP strategy will equal or exceed that of the local EDP and SIP strategies and, consequently, the cost of the local ADP strategy will be less than or equal to that of the local EDP and SIP strategies' (711). Briefly, the three strategies (or systems) under comparison here are

1. Ambient discharge permits (ADP): a system under which the allowable pollutant concentration at each receptor point is available for sale in the form of permits. A source that contributes to pollutant concentrations at a particular receptor must purchase sufficient permits to validate its contribution to pollution at each receptor. Montgomery (1972) has shown that the competitive market equilibrium under an ADP system satisfies the conditions for the minimization of total control costs subject to the constraint of attaining the predetermined air-quality standard at each receptor.

2. Emissions discharge permits (EDP): a system under which the environmental authority issues a limited number of emissions permits that can be bought and sold among sources. The authority limits the total number of permits sufficiently to attain the air-quality standard at each receptor. Except under some extremely restrictive conditions, EDP will not generate the least-cost outcome.

3. State implementation plan (SIP): In Atkinson's terms, this is a CAC system under which all sources undertake an equiproportional cut-back in emissions (from a defined baseline) sufficient to attain the standards.

Atkinson's claim is that the least-cost system (ADP) will necessarily result in higher levels of local pollution than either EDP or SIP. We shall reject this claim by means of a simple counter-example that provides some insight and intuition into the working of the three systems.

Consider the local air-shed depicted in figure 1, where S_1 and S_2 are the two sources of pollution and R_1 and R_2 are the two receptor points. The a_{ij} are 'transfer coefficients'; they indicate the increase in pollutant concentration at receptor i that results from another unit of emissions from source j. For example, if source 2 increases its emissions by one unit, pollutant concentrations rise by one unit at receptor 1 and by 0.25 units at receptor 2. Both sources

670   Wallace E. Oates and Albert M. McGartland

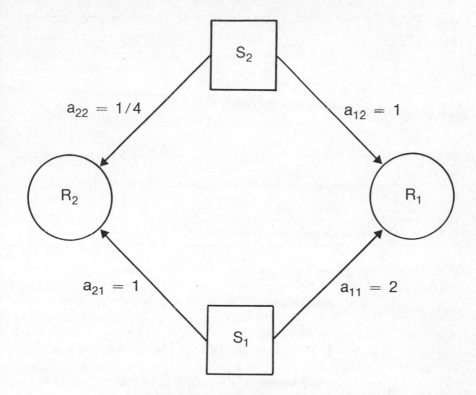

Total abatement cost (TAC) = $(1/2)r^2$
Marginal abatement cost (MAC) = r
Uncontrolled level of emissions ($\bar{e}$) = 20
Uncontrolled levels of air quality:
    $\bar{Q}_1$ = 60
    $\bar{Q}_2$ = 25

FIGURE 1

are assumed to have the same abatement cost function:

Total abatement cost (TAC) = $(1/2)\, r^2$

Marginal abatement cost (MAC) = $d(\text{TAC})/dr = r$,

where r is the reduction in emissions from a baseline, or uncontrolled, level of emissions, $\bar{e}$, of 20 units. If r equals 5, then emissions, e, are 15. The abatement cost function exhibits rising marginal control costs.

The outcome under each of the three systems is described in table 1. Consider, first, the Emission Discharge Permit (EDP) system. In a permit market cost-minimizing behaviour will lead each source to purchase permits to the point at which MAC equals the price of a permit. This implies under EDP

TABLE 1

Outcomes under three control systems

EDP	SIP	ADP
$r_1 = r_2 = 14$	Same as	$r_1 = 16.8, r_2 = 8.4$
$e_1 = e_2 = 6$	EDP	$e_1 = 3.2, e_2 = 11.6$
$\text{TAC}_1 = \text{TAC}_2 = 1/2 \, (14)^2 = 98$		$\text{TAC}_1 = 0.5 \, (16.8)^2 = 141.1$
$\text{TAC} = 98 + 98 = 196$		$\text{TAC}_2 = 0.5 \, (8.4)^2 = 35.3$
$Q_1 = 2 \, (6) + 6 = 18$		$Q_1 = 2 \, (3.2) + 11.6 = 18$
$Q_2 = 6 + 0.25 \, (6) = 7.5$		$Q_2 = 3.2 + 0.25 \, (11.6) = 6.1$

where

r_j = reduction in emissions for uncontrolled level by source j
e_j = level of emissions of source j
TAC_j = total abatement cost of source j
MAC_j = marginal abatement cost of source j
Q_i = pollutant concentration (air quality) at receptor i.

---

that MAC will be equalized across sources. Since, in our example, both sources have the same abatement cost function, it follows that they will adopt identical levels of control and, hence, emissions. We thus have, for the EDP outcome, that $r_1 = r_2$ (or $e_1 = e_2$). The air-management authority must limit the total number of permits sufficiently to attain the standard of $Q^* = 18$.[1] This implies a total quantity of permits of $Q = 12$; in equilibrium, each source will thus purchase 6 permits, and we shall have $e_1 = e_2 = 6$ (and $r_1 = r_2 = 14$). The contributions of sources 1 and 2 to the pollutant concentration at receptor 1 are 12 and 6, respectively, summing to the predetermined limit of $Q = 18$. Note that the pollution level at receptor 2 is only 7.5 – well below the limit so that the concentration at receptor 2 is not a binding constraint. Finally, the control costs for each source are 98, giving an aggregate abatement cost of 196.

For our example the outcome under the SIP system is identical to that under EDP. Since the air-management authority must impose an equi-proportionate reduction in emissions on both sources sufficient to attain the standard ($Q^* = 18$), it follows that the agency will require a cutback of $r_1 = r_2 = 14$. Each source will thus end up with emissions of 6; the resulting level of abatement costs and pollutant concentrations at receptors 1 and 2 will be the same as under EDP.

Under ADP, however, the response of the two sources will differ. With receptor 1 as the binding constraint, source 1 will have to purchase two permits (from receptor 1) to validate each unit of emissions, while source 2 need purchase only one permit per unit of emissions. Cost-minimizing behaviour thus implies that $\text{MAC}_1 = 2(\text{MAC}_2)$, or, given our abatement cost functions, that

---

1 The contribution of source j to the pollutant concentration at receptor i is determined by multiplying the source's level of emissions, e_j, times the relevant transfer coefficient, a_{ij}. In our case, for example, the effect of source 1's emissions on receptor 1 is found by multiplying $e_1 = 6$ times $a_{11} = 2$, yielding a contribution of 12 to the pollutant concentration at receptor 1.

672   Wallace E. Oates and Albert M. McGartland

$r_1 = 2r_2$. The market equilibrium now implies that $r_1 = 16.8$, $r_2 = 8.4$, or, in terms of emissions, that $e_1 = 3.2$, $e_2 = 11.6$.[2] Note that under the ADP outcome, source 1, whose emissions are the more damaging at receptor 1, will undertake the larger share of the abatement effort − which is as it should be for an efficient outcome. We find that total abatement costs (corresponding to the least-cost solution) are 176.4, less than the total control costs of 196 under EDP and SIP. But of central interest here, not only are control costs less, but air quality is *better* under ADP than under the other systems. We find that the pollutant concentration at receptor 2 is only 6.1 under ADP, compared with 7.5 under EDP or SIP. For this case ADP results in *both* cost-savings and cleaner air relative to the alternatives.

The rationale for this result is straightforward. Since the emissions from source 1 are the more damaging at the binding receptor, R_1, the least-cost solution for attaining the ambient air-quality standard implies that source 1 should undertake the larger share of the abatement effort. But source 1's emissions are also the more damaging at the other, non-binding receptor, R_2; source 2's emissions result in comparatively little damage at R_2. As a result, the substitution of emissions by source 2 for those of source 1 produces less pollution at R_2 as well as R_1.[3] In contrast, if $a_{22} > a_{21}$, then air quality under ADP would be worse than under EDP or SIP. But the general point here is that because of the inefficiencies inherent in the EDP and SIP systems, it is possible for the least-cost system, ADP, to result in both reduced costs and improved air quality.

SOME FURTHER EVIDENCE ON CONTROL COSTS AND AIR QUALITY

While the trade-off between abatement costs and local air quality among our three control systems is not logically necessary, it may well represent the typical case. In his simulations, Atkinson finds that the ADP system 'leads to the greatest local environmental loading with SO_2. Under the local ADP strategy, air quality is degraded to the level of the ambient standard at four of eight receptors. However, under both the SIP and EDP strategies, this occurs at only

---

2   We determine the market-equilibrium outcome by the simultaneous solution of the following two equations: $r_1 = 2r_2$; and $2(20 - r_1) + (20 - r_2) = 18$. The second of these equations describes the air-quality constraint at the binding receptor, R_1.

3   Since $a_{11} > a_{21}$ and $a_{12} > a_{22}$, R_2 will always be cleaner than the air-quality standard whenever the pollutant concentration at R_1 is at (or below) the target level. Thus, for this configuration of polluters, R_2 is never binding. Our general result, however, does not depend upon this characteristic of one non-binding receptor. Consider, for example, the case where

$$a_{11} = 1.33 \qquad a_{12} = .667$$
$$a_{21} = 1.3 \qquad a_{22} = .7$$

For this case, each receptor can be binding. When ADP is substituted for EDP, both total control costs and the pollution concentration at receptor one fall, while the pollution level at receptor two remains at the standard of 18.

TABLE 2

Costs and emissions under four control systems to achieve a TSP standard of 98 $\mu g/m^3$ in the Baltimore AQCR

	SIP	EDP	ADP	MOS
Annualized costs (in millions of 1980 dollars)	112.9	46.1	27.1	46.3
Total emissions (in tons per year)	23,358	21,420	49,352	24,325

---

one receptor' (717). For the Atkinson case of sulfur pollution in the Cleveland region the least-cost system does appear to imply more local air pollution.

We find a similar result for another air pollutant, particulate matter (TSP), in the Baltimore Air Quality Control Region (AQCR). These results, presented in table 2, are derived from a computer-based model constructed for the analysis of particulate emissions in the Baltimore region (McGartland, 1984). The model incorporates control-cost estimates, associated collection efficiencies, and dispersion characteristics for over 400 sources. The control-cost estimates take the form of integer step functions and were estimated using the costing algorithm developed in a series of articles by Vatavuk and Neveril (1980-1). In addition, a careful listing of all CAC requirements was assembled which allowed a simulation of the SIP system currently employed in Baltimore. Our version of the SIP system is thus based on actual, required treatment procedures for each source.

Table 2 indicates the total control costs and aggregate emissions under the various systems where the predetermined TSP standard not to be violated at any receptor point is taken to be 98 $\mu g/m^3$.[4] We find that ADP promises very large cost savings compared with SIP and EDP outcomes. However, as Atkinson suggests, these cost savings come at the expense of local air quality. Total emissions under ADP are about twice the level of those under SIP and EDP. Moreover, our simulations show that the higher level of emissions under ADP translates into substantially higher TSP concentrations at virtually every receptor point in the region. Our results thus confirm Atkinson's concern: the least-cost permit system, in both our case studies, implies higher levels of local air pollution.

---

4 The assumed TSP standard of 98 $\mu g/m^3$ (annual arithmetic mean) is not, incidentally, the EPA-determined primary standard for TSP concentrations. It is, instead, the existing TSP concentration in the central business district, which is in excess of the primary standard. We use the existing concentration to permit comparisons with the current SIP system. We note that annual standards for TSP are generally stated as geometric means. With a standard deviation of roughly 1.5, the EPA primary standard of 75 $\mu g/m^3$ expressed as a geometric mean translates into a standard of 85 $\mu g/m^3$ as an arithmetic mean.

674   Wallace E. Oates and Albert M. McGartland

AN ALTERNATIVE PERMIT SYSTEM: THE MODIFIED OFFSET SYSTEM (MOS)

However, there must be (and is) a better way. Both SIP and EDP are inherently inefficient: whatever level of environmental quality they achieve, they do so with excessive control costs. There thus exists a less costly allocation of abatement effort among sources that can achieve the same level of air quality.

We have elsewhere (McGartland and Oates, forthcoming) described a system of marketable permits that can, in principle, accomplish this. More precisely, this system, which we call the 'Modified Offset System' (MOS), will, in general, sustain an outcome that involves *both* cleaner air and lower control costs than SIP. In brief, MOS takes the existing SIP outcome as its point of departure. Sources are then free to buy and sell emissions entitlements subject to the constraint that a trade does not increase pollutant concentrations at any receptor point above the level under the initial SIP state. Trading, then, can only improve – it cannot degrade – air quality. Moreover, we show that the market equilibrium under MOS satisfies the first-order conditions for the solution to the following problem:

$$\text{Minimize} \sum_{j} C_j(e_j)$$

$$\text{s.t. } EA \leq \min (Q^*, Q_0)$$

$$E \geq 0,$$

where $C_j(e_j)$ is the abatement cost function of source j, E is the vector of emissions of the j sources, A is a matrix of transfer coefficients, Q^* is the predetermined air-quality standard (in terms of pollutant concentration), and Q^0 is the initial pollutant concentration under the existing SIP system. A MOS equilibrium thus represents the least-cost solution for the resulting level of environmental quality. As we indicate in the fourth column of table 2, the potential cost savings of MOS relative to SIP and EDP are very large - over 50 per cent for our TSP case in Baltimore. Moreover, the pollutant concentration at every receptor point under MOS is, by design, equal to, or less than, the TSP level under SIP.[5] Finally, we note that compared with the initial SIP state, the equilibrium under MOS represents a Pareto-improvement for all parties involved, including both environmentalists and polluters. Sources realize reduced control costs, while consumers enjoy a cleaner environment. In sum,

---

5 If we return to our illustrative case in figure 1, we find that MOS, in that particular instance, coincides with the ADP outcome. Using SIP as the initial state, sources 1 and 2 would find it mutually profitable for two to purchase emissions entitlements from one. These transfers of entitlements would continue until $MAC_1 = 2 (MAC_2)$. Note that since source 2's emissions are less damaging at receptor 2 (as well as at receptor 1), this transfer of emissions would not violate the MOS constraint preventing degradation of air quality at *any* receptor point.

the inefficiencies under existing CAC systems provide us with an opportunity to design more efficient systems of marketable permits that promise *both* large cost-savings and reduced pollution.[6]

REFERENCES

Atkinson, Scott E. (1983) 'Marketable pollution permits and acid rain externalities.' This JOURNAL 16, 704-22
McGartland, Albert M. (1984) 'Marketable permit systems for air pollution control: an empirical study.' Unpublished Ph D dissertation, University of Maryland
McGartland, Albert M. and Wallace E. Oates (forthcoming) 'Marketable permits for the prevention of environmental deterioration.' *Journal of Environmental Economics and Management*
Montgomery, W. David (1972) 'Markets in licenses and efficient pollution control programs.' *Journal of Economic Theory* 5, 395-418
Vatavuk, W. and R. Neveril (1980-1) 'Estimating costs of air pollution control systems.' Parts I to VIII. *Chemical Engineering* (appears in issues from October 1980 to June 1981)

6 As we indicated at the outset of this note, our treatment of pollution control addresses only the 'local' issues. Our Baltimore simulations involve a pollutant, TSP, for which long-range transport and deposition are not a real problem. Obviously, our claim that the modified-offset system results in a Pareto-improvement for both polluters and environmentalists will not generally be true for something like SO_2 emissions unless we introduce a further constraint requiring no increase in the long-range transport of the pollutant.

Abstract Taking as its point of departure the Holcombe-Meiners contention that a system of marketable pollution rights is susceptible to the monopolization of these rights as a means to forestall the entry of competitors, this article explores more broadly the relative merits of systems of effluent fees and of marketable rights for the control of pollution. The article suggests, first, that the Holcombe-Meiners problem concerning the use of pollution rights as a barrier to entry is likely to be inconsequential, and, second, that from a wider perspective, a system of marketable pollution rights under which the rights are initially distributed to existing polluters has some quite compelling advantages in practice over the economist's more traditional proposal for a system of effluent fees. It is, moreover, the direction in which environmental policy appears to be moving in the United States.

CORRECTIVE TAXES AND AUCTIONS OF RIGHTS IN THE CONTROL OF EXTERNALITIES: SOME FURTHER THOUGHTS

6243
3212
3230

WALLACE E. OATES
University of Maryland

#23 828 D44

In a recent issue of this journal, Randall Holcombe and Roger Meiners (1980) contend that there exists an important difference between a system of Pigouvian taxes and one of marketable pollution rights in which the environmental authority auctions the rights to polluters. Specifically, they argue that under the marketable rights scheme, there is the danger that a single polluting firm may purchase all the rights to pollute and use its monopolistic control of these rights to exclude potential competitors. In short, the control of pollution rights could constitute a major barrier to entry. Note that a system of Pigouvian

AUTHOR'S NOTE: The author is grateful to the National Science Foundation for its support of his research on a system of marketable air pollution rights.

PUBLIC FINANCE QUARTERLY, Vol. 9 No. 4, October 1981 471-478
© 1981 Sage Publications, Inc.

471

taxes is not subject to this objection, since any firm is free to pollute so long as it pays the effluent fee.[1]

This issue is a particularly important one in light of recent developments in the design and implementation of environmental policy. There is a growing sense that the economist's traditional policy tool for the control of externalities, the Pigouvian tax, has some serious shortcomings relative to a system of marketable pollution rights. The Holcombe-Meiners concern (which has been voiced by others as well) would seem to cast some doubt on this alleged superiority of a system of marketable rights over one of fees. My purpose here is to consider the Holcombe-Meiners contention a bit further, and to place it in the context of the debate over the relative merits of the two approaches with respect to the regulation of externalities.

At the most formal level in a world of perfect certainty, the two are obviously equivalent: the environmental agency can either set price (the Pigouvian tax) and allow polluters to establish the optimal quantity of waste emissions or, alternatively, set the optimal quantity of emissions directly and let the bids of polluters establish the market-clearing price. The outcome under the two approaches is formally equivalent.[2] In particular, either system will achieve the desired level of environmental quality at minimum aggregate abatement cost.

From the perspective of the practical concerns of policymakers, however, some quite important distinctions emerge between these two policy measures that on balance seem to favor a system of marketable rights. In this context, I shall assume that the policymaker's problem is to find the most effective means for achieving a set of predetermined standards for environmental quality (see Baumol and Oates, 1975: ch. 10). From this vantage point, I see marketable rights as possessing four significant advantages relative to the more traditional system of effluent fees:

(1) The use of marketable permits minimizes uncertainty and adjustment costs in attaining mandated levels of environmental quality. Under the fee approach, the environmental authority cannot be completely sure of the response of polluters to a particular level of effluent charges: in particular, if the authority

sets the fee too low, environmental standards will not be met. In consequence, the fee may have to be raised and then further altered to generate an iterative path converging on the target level of emissions. This means costly adjustments and readjustments by polluters in their levels of waste discharges and the associated abatement technology. The need for repeated changes in the fee is likewise an unattractive prospect for administrators of the program. In contrast, under a permit scheme, the environmental agency directly sets the aggregate quantity of emissions at the allowable standard; there is, in principle, no problem in achieving the target.

(2) Closely related to the above issue are the complications that result over time from, first, economic growth and, second, price inflation. Under a system of effluent fees, continuing inflation will erode the real value of the fee; likewise, expanding production from both existing and new firms will increase the demand for waste emissions. Both of these forces will tend to raise pollution levels over time *unless the nominal fee is increased.* This means that the environmental authority will find it necessary to raise the fee periodically if environmental standards are to be met. In short, the burden for affirmative action under fees is on environmental officials; the choice will be between unpopular fee increases or nonattainment of standards. Under a system of permits, market forces automatically accommodate inflation and growth with no increase in pollution. The rise in demand for permits simply translates directly into a higher price.

(3) The introduction of a system of effluent fees may involve enormous increases in costs to polluters relative to existing regulatory policies. This point may seem somewhat paradoxical in light of the widespread recognition that systems of pricing incentives promise large savings in aggregate abatements costs. But the two are not inconsistent. Although a system of effluent charges will reduce total abatement costs, it will impose a new source of costs, namely a tax bill, on polluting firms. Although the latter form of costs represents a transfer payment from the perspective of society, it is a cost of operation for the firm. Moreover, some recent evidence on this issue suggests some rather

staggering figures. One such study (Palmer et al., 1980) of the use of pricing incentives to restrict emissions of certain halocarbons into the atmosphere estimates that aggregate abatement costs under a realistic program of mandatory controls would total $230 million; a system of fees or of marketable permits would reduce these costs to an estimated $110 million (a savings of roughly 50%). However, the cost of the fees or permits to polluters would total about $1,400 million, so that in spite of the substantial savings in abatement costs, a program of pricing incentives would, in this instance, increase the total cost to polluters by a factor of six relative to a program of direct controls! While a system of marketable rights making use of an initial auction of these rights is subject to these results, there is an alternative: a system of marketable rights can be set in motion with an initial distribution of these rights to existing polluters. This version of the marketable-rights scheme would effectively eliminate the added source of costs for existing firms without any necessarily adverse consequences for the efficiency properties of the program, and with some obvious and major advantages for its political acceptability.[3]

(4) Finally, marketable permits appear the more feasible approach on grounds of familiarity. The introduction of a system of effluent fees requires the adoption of a wholly new method of controlling pollution, new both to regulators and polluters. Such sharp departures from established practice are hard to sell; moreover, there exist some real questions concerning the legality of charging for pollution. In contrast, permits already exist, and it appears a less radical step to make them effectively marketable.

Although the case for a system of marketable pollution rights over one of fees seems a formidable one, there are grounds for some reservations:

(1) While a permit scheme minimizes uncertainty in achieving the target level of environmental quality, a corollary is that fees reduce the danger of excessive abatement costs from overly stringent standards. There exists the threat under a system of marketable rights that an overly zealous environmental authority might set extremely high standards for environmental quality

which impose huge and unjustified abatement costs on society. Fees, in contrast, establish a ceiling on abatement costs, since firms always have the option of continuing their emissions and paying the fee. One suggested modification to the marketable-permit proposal to mitigate this shortcoming is the inclusion of a high fee or penalty to serve as an "escape valve" in the event that prices of pollution permits threaten to reach exorbitant levels.[4]

(2) Under the version of the marketable-rights proposal that makes an initial distribution of the rights without charge to existing polluters, there is a potential objection on equity grounds. The scheme effectively vests the right to pollute with existing polluters; as such, it represents a wealth transfer to them. This is a difficult and rather complicated issue. One might argue that clean air belongs to the general public and, in consequence, that polluting firms should pay from the very outset of the program for the clean air that they "employ." This line of argument, however, is far from conclusive. In most instances, firms have historically had de facto rights to emit at least certain levels of waste emissions into the environment; they have made location and other costly decisions on this basis, and to make them now purchase the rights that they have used without charge in the past might seem inequitable. Moreover, under existing regulatory programs, most major polluters have already engaged in extensive abatement activity: to give them the (transferable) right to emit their remaining discharges may, in fact, represent a reasonable compromise.

(3) Finally, we come to the Holcombe-Meiners concern over the monopolistic control of pollution rights as a means to thwart competition. On closer examination, it is my belief that this concern is largely misplaced. First, firms in a particular area compete with one another for other factors of production including labor, raw materials, and land. Why might one expect the supply of the newly marketable input, namely waste emissions, to be more susceptible to monopolization for purposes of forestalling competition than the supplies of other inputs? One answer might be that the supply of emission rights is fixed in total. But then the supplies of others factors, such as land, may also be highly

inelastic. Second, and perhaps more compelling, is the recognition that competition in output markets need not come from local production. Even were a firm to monopolize the entire stock of pollution rights in a specific locale (e.g., an air shed), this would not prevent competitors from locating in neighboring (or distant) jurisdictions; only in the case where production in the particular locale confers substantial cost-savings could monopolization of emission rights constitute any sort of barrier to entry. And third, note that under the system where emission rights are distributed initially to existing polluters, there is no way to force existing firms to leave their respective industries; firms need not sell their emission rights unless they find it desirable to do so. Entry of new firms might conceivably be discouraged, but it would be difficult for a firm to eliminate competition from existing local producers. Finally, one might want to give the environmental agency the authority to take action against firms where the monopolization of pollution rights is employed as an exclusionary device. In short, it really seems quite unlikely that the monopolization of pollution rights could prove to be an effective means for the establishment of monopoly positions in output markets.

My conclusion, at this juncture in the development of our thinking, is that the case for a system of marketable rights relative to the fee approach is quite a compelling one. And this is, in fact, the direction in which we are moving. At the national level, the Environmental Protection Agency has strongly endorsed this effort in the form of its own proposed system of Controlled Trading consisting of Bubbles, Banking, and Offsets for the control of air pollution. In spite of the rather exotic language, what all this amounts to is a set of machinery to facilitate the transfer of pollution rights to points where they will generate the largest savings in abatement costs. Likewise, moves are afoot in several states to establish systems of transferable pollution rights. In my own state of Maryland, we are well along the way toward the introduction of a system for the regulation of air pollution under which firms (and perhaps others) will engage in the purchase and sale of the right to emit pollutants. The efforts of economists to enlist the use of pricing incentives for protection of the environment seem finally to be coming to fruition, although the specific means is, in the end, taking a form somewhat different from that envisioned by Pigou.

NOTES

1. There is one minor qualification to this. Although it would seem extremely unlikely, there is at least the possibility in principle that under a system of Pigouvian charges a firm might increase emissions above the level for which its marginal abatement cost equals the fee, in order to induce an increase in the fee that in turn would serve to keep out competitors.

2. In contrast, in a world of uncertaintly, some intriguing differences arise between systems of fees amd marketable pollution rights. See, for example, Weitzman (1974) and Roberts and Spence (1976).

3. To avoid allocative distortions, it is essential that the distribution of rights to polluters be lump sum in character. It must be based only upon historical behavior—not on any current or future decision variables, or else firms will have an incentive to expand emissions in order to increase their entitlements (see Oates and Collinge, 1980).

4. For an interesting proposal of a mixed system (fees and marketable licenses) which incorporates the strengths of both approaches, see Roberts and Spence (1976).

REFERENCES

BAUMOL, W. J. and W. E. OATES (1975) The Theory of Environmental Policy. Englewood Cliffs, NJ: Prentice-Hall.

HOLCOMBE, R. G. and R. E. MEINERS (1980) "Corrective taxes and auctions of rights in the control of externalities." Public Finance Q. 8(July): 345-349.

OATES, W. E. and R. A. COLLINGE (1980) Efficiency in the Presence of Externalities: An Issue of Entry and Exit, College Park, MD: University of Maryland, Department of Economics Working Paper 1980-38.

PALMER, A. R. et al. (1980) Economic Implications of Regulating Chlorofluorocarbon Emissions from Nonaerosol Applications. Santa Monica. CA: The Rand Corporation.

ROBERTS, M and M. SPENCE (1976) "Effluent charges and licenses under uncertainty." J. of Public Economics 5(April-May): 193-208.

WEITZMAN, M. L. (1974) "Price vs. quantites." Rev. of Econ. Studies 41(Oct.): 477-491.

Wallace E. Oates is Professor of Economics at the University of Maryland. He has had, over the last decade, a continuing research interest in the economics of environmental policy, and has a current interest in the design and implementation of a market for pollution rights. This has resulted in a series of journal articles and two books co-authored with William Baumol: The Theory of Environmental Policy *(Prentice-Hall, 1975) and* Economics, Environmental Policy, and the Quality of Life *(Prentice-Hall, 1979). He is currently supporting the efforts of the Department of Economic and Community Development in the State of Maryland to introduce a system of marketable rights for the control of air pollution.*

PART V

ENVIRONMENTAL FEDERALISM

[17]

Journal of Public Economics 35 (1988) 333–354. North-Holland

297–318
[1988]
H77 H2 1
R53 H7 3

ECONOMIC COMPETITION AMONG JURISDICTIONS: EFFICIENCY ENHANCING OR DISTORTION INDUCING?

Wallace E. OATES and Robert M. SCHWAB*

University of Maryland, College Park, MD 20742, USA

Received March 1987, revised version received February 1988

This paper explores the normative implications of competition among 'local' jurisdictions to attract new industry and income. Within a neoclassical framework, we examine how local officials set two policy variables, a tax (or subsidy) rate on mobile capital and a standard for local environmental quality, to induce more capital to enter the jurisdiction in order to raise wages. The analysis suggests that, for jurisdictions homogeneous in workers, local choices under simple-majority rule will be socially optimal; such jurisdictions select a zero tax rate on capital and set a standard for local environmental quality such that marginal willingness-to-pay equals the marginal social costs of a cleaner environment. However, in cases where jurisdictions are not homogeneous or where, for various reasons, they set a positive tax rate on capital, distortions arise not only in local fiscal decisions, but also in local environmental choices.

1. Introduction

The literature on local public finance contains two sharply contrasting themes. The first views interjurisdictional competition as a beneficent force that, similar to its role in the private sector, compels public agents to make efficient decisions. The cornerstone of this position is the famous Tiebout model (1956) in which individual households choose among jurisdictions in much the same way that they choose among sellers of private goods: an efficient provision of local public goods results from this process of 'voting with one's feet'. Likewise, in the more recent Leviathan literature that views government as a revenue-maximizing entity, competition among jurisdictions is seen as a powerful constraint on the undesirable expansionary tendencies of the public sector. Brennan and Buchanan (1980), for example, argue that

*Oates is also a member of the Bureau of Business and Economic Research, University of Maryland. Both authors were visiting scholars at Resources for the Future while much of this research was done. We are grateful to the National Science Foundation, the Sloan Foundation, and Resources for the Future for their support of this research. For helpful comments on an earlier draft, we thank William Baumol, Paul Courant, William Fischel, Marvin Frankel, Edward Gramlich, Bruce Hamilton, Robert Lee, Michael Luger, Therese McGuire, Peter Mieszkowski, Peter Murrell, Arvind Panigariya, Paul Portney, John Quigley, Daniel Rubinfeld, John Wilson, George Zodrow, the participants in the Sloan Workshop in Urban Public Economics at the University of Maryland and two anonymous referees.

0047-2727/88/$3.50 © 1988, Elsevier Science Publishers B.V. (North-Holland)

competition among governments in the context of the 'interjurisdictional mobility of persons in pursuit of "fiscal gains" can offer partial or possibly complete substitutes for explicit fiscal constraints on the taxing power' (p. 184). Competition, by these arguments, can serve its welfare-enhancing 'disciplinary' function in the public, as well as the private, sector.

However, a second body of literature contends that interjurisdictional competition is a source of distortion in public choices. The general theme here is that in their pursuit of new industry and jobs, state and local officials will hold down taxes and other sources of costs to households and particularly to business enterprise to such an extent that public outputs will be provided at suboptimal levels. There are several strands to this line of argument. One focuses on 'tax competition' and contends that incentives to attract business investment will keep tax rates below levels needed to finance efficient levels of public services [Oates (1972, pp. 142–143)]. As Break (1967) has put it,

> The trouble is that state and local governments have been engaged for some time in an increasingly active competition among themselves for new business.... In such an environment government officials do not lightly propose increases in their own tax rates that go much beyond those prevailing in nearby states or in any area with similar natural attractions for industry.... Active tax competition, in short, tends to produce either a generally low level of state-local tax effort or a state-local tax structure with strong regressive features. (pp. 23–24).

Such 'cut-throat competition', as the ACIR (1981, p. 10) observes, has given rise to proposals for federal intervention to 'save the states from themselves'.

Cumberland (1979, 1981) has developed a second strand of the competition argument; it is his contention that local setting of standards for environmental quality would be subject to 'destructive interregional competition'. In their eagerness to attract new business and create jobs, state and local authorities, Cumberland argues, are likely to compete with one another by relaxing standards for environmental quality so as to reduce costs for prospective business firms. Cumberland concludes that national (minimum) standards for environmental quality are needed to prevent the excessive degradation of the environment that would result from state or local standard setting.

The distortion arguments are not, however, fully convincing. If existing residents care about public outputs (including environmental quality), and presumably they do, then tax or standard competition to attract economic activity imposes real costs on the citizenry. It is not at all clear that such competition is likely to extend to levels that ultimately result in suboptimal public outputs. Stigler (1957), for example, has contended that 'Competition of communities offers not obstacles but opportunities to various communities to choose the type and scale of government functions they wish' (p. 216). Nevertheless, the possibility of 'destructive competition' surely seems plausible and, in consequence, makes observers (like Cumberland) justifiably reticent to vest responsibility for setting environmental standards at state or local levels.

Part of the difficulty is that there exists little systematic analysis of these distortionary forms of interjurisdictional competition from which we can reach normative conclusions about local policy decisions.[1] The discussion is typically informal, often times anecdotal, and does not establish any soundly grounded results. Consequently, one may be geniunely disturbed by the possibly detrimental effects of tax and standard competition, but have little sense as to their likely importance.

It is our purpose in this paper to develop a simple model of interjurisdictional competition that can provide some insights into the basic normative issue. Using a standard kind of neoclassical model of production in tandem with a median-voter procedure for making local public decisions, we construct a model in which individual communities select both a tax rate on capital and a level of local environmental quality. We begin with a basic model of homogeneous 'worker' jurisdictions in which we find that simple-majority rule generates socially optimal decisions as regards both the taxation of capital and the setting of environmental standards. We then extend the model in two different ways. We introduce first a positive tax rate on capital that can have its source either in various realistic constraints on the choice of tax instruments or in a Niskanen-type of local government behavior; here we find outcomes involving not only fiscal distortions but also excessive degradation of the local environment. The second extension entails the introduction of mixed communities with both wage-earners and non-wage-earners. In this setting, the interests of the two groups within the community diverge, and the median-voter outcome is no longer socially optimal (unless some rather unlikely sorts of cooperation take place).

As this Introduction suggests, one of the interesting features of the model is that it incorporates into the decision process two distinct sources of interjurisdictional competition: local taxation and the choice of environmental standards. As the analysis will show, the joint determination of these two policy variables within a community can involve some intriguing interrelationships between revenue and environmental considerations.

2. The basic model

In this section we set forth a simple model that we believe captures the

---

[1]There is some recent theoretical work on tax competition. See, in particular, Mintz and Tulkens (1986), Wilson (1985, 1986), and Zodrow and Mieszkowski (1983, 1986).

spirit of interjurisdictional competition. In the model, jurisdictions compete for a mobile stock of capital by lowering taxes and relaxing environmental standards that would otherwise deflect capital elsewhere. In return for an increased capital stock, residents receive higher incomes in the form of higher wages. The community must, however, weigh the benefits of higher wages against the cost of forgone tax revenues and lower environmental quality.

We envision with a large number (say *n*) of local jurisdications, where the jurisdictions are sufficiently large that:

(i) individuals live and work in the same jurisdiction, and

(ii) pollution generated in one jurisdiction does not spill-over into another.

Suppose that each of these *n* jurisdictions produces a private good, Q, that is sold in a national market. Production requires capital, K, labor, L, and polluting waste emissions, E, where we treat E as a non-purchased input. We posit further than the production function exhibits constant returns to scale and possesses all of the nice curvature properties of a standard neo-classical production function.

An important part of the model is the specification of local environmental policy and the way in which it impinges on local productive activity. We shall assume that the local government sets a standard for local environmental quality: it specifies, for example, that the concentration of pollutants in the environment shall not exceed some physical quantity. This standard then translates into a limitation on the aggregate level of waste emissions in the locality. The local environmental authority thus effectively determines $\sum E$ for the jurisdiction. We will assume further that this aggregate is allocated among firms according to some measure of their level of productive activity. More precisely, we posit that a firm's allowable emissions are directly proportional to its labor force. Environmental policy thus determines the emissions–labor ratio, α, in the jurisdiction.[2] If we define k to be the capital–labor ratio, we can write the production function for a particular jurisdiction as:[3]

$$Q = F(K, L, E)$$
$$= Lf(k, \alpha). \tag{1}$$

[2] There are obviously other ways in which one could specify the form of local environmental policy. The form we have chosen, in addition to seeming reasonable, facilitates the analysis. As will become evident, it allows us to capture the effects of environmental policy both on environmental quality and on the production of output in terms of a single parameter, α, that enters both the production and utility functions. It is not inconsistent, incidentally, for α to correspond both to a particular level of aggregate emissions and to a specific emissions–labor ratio, for (as we will note shortly) the labor input in a jurisdiction is taken to be fixed. Finally, we stress that none of the basic results of the paper changes if communities use certain other policy tools such as Pigouvian taxes on emissions rather than the command and control strategy we have assumed here. See Oates and Schwab (1987) for a discussion of this point.

[3] For notational simplicity, we shall not employ a superscript to denote a particular jurisdiction, although the functions are understood to be jurisdiction-specific.

While the production function exhibits constant returns to scale in all inputs, the nature of environmental policy allows firms to act as though there were constant returns to scale in just the purchased inputs, capital and labor. If a firm doubles its input of labor, it is allowed to double emissions; therefore, a doubling of capital and labor implies a doubling of all inputs and, hence, output. In equilibrium, we will then observe firms that are of finite (though indeterminate) size earning zero profits.

Throughout the paper we use subscripts to denote partial derivatives, and we therefore write the marginal products of capital, emissions, and labor as f_k, f_α, and $(f - kf_k - \alpha f_\alpha)$. We assume that marginal products are diminishing and that increases in α raise the marginal product of capital; f_{kk} and $f_{\alpha\alpha}$ are therefore negative and $f_{k\alpha}$ is positive.

We also assume that there is a fixed stock of capital in this society which is perfectly mobile (at least in the long run) across jurisdictions. This capital is distributed so as to maximize its earnings, which implies that the return to capital, net of any local taxes, will be equated across jurisdictions.[4] All of the communities are small in the sense that they treat this rate of return as a parameter. This is analogous to an assumption of perfect competition in product markets; just as perfectly competitive firms believe they have no influence on price and therefore behave as price-takers, these competitive communities take the rate of return on capital as given.[5] The community raises tax revenues by levying a tax of t dollars on each unit of capital; per capita tax revenue T is then tk.[6] Capital receives its marginal product f_k, and therefore given some rate of return r available in other jurisdictions, the local stock of capital will adjust so that

$$f_k - t = r. \tag{2}$$

Labor, in contrast, is perfectly immobile.[7] We assume initially that each

[4]We assume that the ownership of capital in this society has been determined exogenously. There is no requirement in the model that people necessarily own capital in their community; capital is traded in a national market.

[5]For a model more in the spirit of 'imperfect competition' in which there is explicit interaction between the policy decisions of two competing jurisdictions, see Mintz and Tulkens (1986).

[6]We can extend the model by introducing local public goods that provide services to capital such as roads and police and fire protection. Suppose that each unit of capital requires services which cost s dollars. If the tax rate on capital is t', then we can think of t as the difference between t' and s (i.e. as the tax on capital in excess of the cost of services consumed by capital). t, incidentally, can be negative in which case it would indicate a unit subsidy to capital.

[7]We assume labor to be immobile for two reasons. First (and most obvious), it greatly simplifies the analysis. And, second, it seems an appropriate assumption in view of the policy problem under study. More specifically, we are considering the decisions of a given population as they relate to the inflow and outflow of business investments that generate 'local' income. The analysis thus focuses on how existing residents view the effect of their collective choices on interjurisdictional movements of capital. However, as we have shown in Oates and Schwab (1987), all of the basic results in this paper emerge from a model in which labor is perfectly mobile and the size of each community is fixed. We thank Robert Lee for raising the mobility issue with us.

community consists of individuals identical in both tastes and productive capacity and whose pattern of residence across jurisdictions is 'historically determined'. Each individual puts in a fixed period of work (e.g. a 40-hour week). The labor market is perfectly competitive, and the real wage w equals the gains from hiring an additional worker. w is then the sum of (i) the marginal product of labor, and (ii) the additional output stemming from the increase in permitted emissions, αf_α; under constant returns to scale, w then equals $(f - kf_k)$.

Each of the identical residents receives utility from consumption c and from the local level of environmental quality. Since environmental quality depends on the local choice of α, we can write

$$u = u(c, \alpha), \tag{3}$$

where u is a quasi-concave function that is increasing in c, but decreasing in α (i.e. α is a 'bad', and therefore u_α is negative).

Each resident's income consists of an exogenous component y, wages w, and tax revenues T collected from capital.[8] The budget constraint for any representative individual then requires:

$$c = y + w + T$$

$$= y + (f - kf_k) + tk. \tag{4}$$

Note that an individual has two roles here. First, he is a consumer, seeking in the usual way to maximize utility over a bundle of goods and services that includes a local public good, environmental quality.[9] And, second, he supplies labor for productive purposes in return for his income. From the latter perspective, residents have a clear incentive to encourage the entry of more capital as a means to increasing their wages. But this jurisdiction must compete against other jurisdictions. To attract capital, the community must reduce taxes on capital (which lowers income and, therefore, indirectly lowers utility) and/or relax environmental standards (which lowers utility directly). These are the tradeoffs inherent in interjurisdictional competition.

---

[8]It is easiest to think of the tax revenues from capital simply being distributed on an equal per-capita basis to the residents of the community; this is how we shall treat these revenues. Alternatively (and equivalently), we could envision these revenues as being employed to finance outputs of various local public goods with a corresponding reduction in local tax payments by residents.

[9]For simplicity, we have not, at this juncture, incorporated into the model the rest of the public sector. Instead, we simply assume that, behind the scenes, the local government provides efficient quantities of the various local public goods which it finances through the imposition of lump-sum taxes. We return to this matter later.

2.1. The median-voter outcome

The interesting normative issue here is whether there is any systematic tendency for residents to choose other than optimal values for α and t. To address this issue, we must specify a collective-choice rule for the determination of these two policy parameters and then compare the outcome under this rule to the socially optimal outcome. For this purpose, we adopt in this section the widely used median-voter model as the mechanism for determining α and t. Since all individuals within a jurisdiction are in every respect identical, we can determine the median-voter outcome by maximizing the utility of any representative consumer.[10] Formally, the median-voter model requires the maximization of the utility function in eq. (3) subject to the budget constraint in (4) and the constraint on the rate of return in (2).

The first-order conditions for the solution to this problem are:

$$u_c = \lambda_1, \tag{5a}$$

$$u_\alpha = \lambda_1 f_\alpha - (\lambda_2 - \lambda_1 k) f_{k\alpha}, \tag{5b}$$

$$\lambda_1 t = (\lambda_1 k - \lambda_2) f_{kk}, \tag{5c}$$

$$\lambda_2 = \lambda_1 k, \tag{5d}$$

where λ_1 is the Lagrange multiplier associated with the budget constraint and λ_2 is the Lagrange multiplier associated with the constraint on the rate of return. From these conditions, we find that maximization requires:

$$t = 0, \tag{6a}$$

$$-u_\alpha/u_c = f_\alpha. \tag{6b}$$

Eq. (6a) indicates that the community should set the tax rate on capital exactly equal to zero. It should neither try to attract capital by offering a subsidy $(t < 0)$, nor try to raise any revenue by taxing capital $(t > 0)$.[11] Eq. (6b) says that the community should choose a combination of consumption and environmental standards such that its marginal rate of substitution between the two is equal to f_α, the 'marginal product of the environment'.

[10] With identical persons, we could just as well invoke a beneficent local official who chooses the parameters of public policy so as to maximize the welfare of the residents of the jurisdiction.

[11] If capital requires local public services (see footnote 6), then (6a) would indicate that the community should set a tax on capital which exactly covers the cost of those services. Where head taxes are available, Zodrow and Mieszkowski (1983) also find that a tax rate of zero on capital is optimal.

We offer the following interpretation of these results. The rate of return constraint implies that we can write the community's budget constraint:

$$c = y + (f - kf_k) + (f_k - r)k$$

$$= y + (f - rk). \tag{4'}$$

Wage and tax income are thus always equal to the surplus which remains after output has been sold and capital receives its market-determined rate of return. The community is much like a perfectly competitive firm that has a fixed quantity of labor but can vary its capital. Like such a firm, the community maximizes its net income by choosing a capital stock such that the marginal product of capital, f_k, equals its price, r. But if f_k equals r, then the tax rate, t, must be zero; the community thus takes all its surplus in the form of wages and none as tax revenues.

We can gain further insight into the setting of environmental policy as described in eq. (6b) by considering the impact of a small change in α on consumption. From the budget constraint, the change in consumption is the sum of the change in the wage and the change in tax revenues. We thus see that environmental policy has two distinct effects on consumption: a 'wage effect' and a 'fiscal effect'.

Consider first the wage effect. Differentiation of the wage equation shows that a tightening of environmental policy taking the form of a decrease in α of $d\alpha$ would reduce wages by $(f_\alpha - kf_{k\alpha})\,d\alpha$ if the capital stock remained constant. This is the direct effect. Tightening environmental policy, however, must cause the capital stock to fall in order to maintain the rate of return r, and therefore the wage rate falls further. If the change in the capital stock is dk, then this additional change in w must be $-(kf_{kk})\,dk$; total differentiation of eq. (2) shows that dk must equal $-(f_{k\alpha}/f_{kk})\,d\alpha$, and therefore the indirect effect of tightening environmental standards is a fall in the wage of $kf_{k\alpha}\,d\alpha$. The sum of the indirect and direct effects of a decrease in α on the wage is thus $f_\alpha\,d\alpha$. This is the wage effect of environmental policy.

Now consider the fiscal effect. The change in tax revenue, dT, is $t\,dk$. From the discussion above, dk is $-(f_{k\alpha}/f_{kk})\,d\alpha$, and therefore the fiscal effect of environmental policy must be $-t(f_{k\alpha}/f_{kk})\,d\alpha$.

The total effect of a decrease in α on consumption is then:

$$dc = dw + dT$$

$$= f_\alpha\,d\alpha - t(f_{k\alpha}/f_{kk})\,d\alpha. \tag{7}$$

However, if the tax rate has been set equal to zero, the fiscal effect vanishes; the change in consumption, in this case, is simply equal to the change in the wage, $f_\alpha\, d\alpha$. Maximizing behavior thus implies that the community will set α so that the change in wage income equals the marginal willingness-to-pay for environmental quality, $-u_\alpha/u_c$. But the change in wage income, as we see from (7) with $t=0$, is precisely equal to the increment in output associated with a marginal change in environmental policy. Since the wage effect equals the 'output effect' of a marginal change in α, we find in (6b) that local environmental decisions are such that the marginal willingness-to-pay for environmental quality equals the 'marginal product' of the environment.

It is important to stress that the determination of the environmental standard and the tax rate on capital are closely intertwined. In particular, if the tax rate (for whatever reason) is non-zero, then the marginal rate of substitution will no longer equal the marginal product of the environment, since in that case the fiscal effect will not vanish. We return to this issue in section 3 of the paper.

2.2. Efficiency in the basic model

We know that perfect competition among firms leads to efficiency; we wish to know if competition among communities also fosters efficiency. Efficiency requires that we maximize the utility of a representative consumer in one community subject to three constraints: (i) we allow a representative consumer in every other community to reach a specified level of utility (which may vary across communities), (ii) aggregate production in the society equals aggregate consumption, and (iii) we allocate society's stock of capital among the n communities. The necessary conditions for the solution to this problem require:

$$-u_\alpha^i/u_c^i = f_\alpha^i, \quad i=1,2,\ldots,n, \tag{8a}$$

$$f_k^i = f_k^j, \quad i,j=1,2,\ldots,n. \tag{8b}$$

where the superscripts refer to communities.

As we argued above, if eq. (8a) did not hold in some community, then it would be possible to change α and consumption in that community so as to increase welfare; if (8b) did not hold, it would be possible to increase aggregate output by moving capital from a community where the marginal product of capital is low to a community where it is high.[12]

It is clear that these conditions will be satisfied under the basic model we have described. The aggregate demand for capital at some rate of return r is the horizontal summation of the communities' demand curves. The market will clear at a rate of return r^* which equates aggregate demand and

---

[12]Note that since environmental quality is a non-traded good, it is not necessary that the marginal product of the environment or the marginal rate of substitution between consumption and the environment be equal across communities.

society's fixed stock of capital. We showed that all communities would set a tax rate of zero, and therefore the marginal product of capital in all communities will be r^*, satisfying (8b). We also showed that if each community maximizes the utility of a representative consumer, then it will equate the marginal rate of substitution between c and α and the slope of the consumption possibility curve, thereby satisfying (8a). In our basic model, competition among jurisdictions is thus conducive to efficient outcomes.

We can offer the following interpretation of these results. We showed above that the marginal private cost of improving environmental quality (measured in terms of forgone consumption) must be f_α, inasmuch as f_α is the change in the wage and there is no fiscal effect of environmental policy when the tax rate is set at its optimal level of zero. We also showed that the community maximizes utility by equating the marginal private cost of improving environmental quality and marginal private benefit. But clearly, f_α is also the marginal social cost of tightening standards, since f_α represents society's forgone consumption. Thus, utility-maximizing behavior promotes efficiency in this model because society's and the community's evaluation of the costs and benefits of environmental policy are identical.[13]

3. The interaction between tax and environmental policies

We showed above that if communities set the optimal tax on capital of zero, then competition would lead jurisdictions to establish efficient standards for environmental quality. As we discuss below, however, communities may choose to tax or subsidize capital for a variety of reasons. In this section of the paper we examine the choice of environmental policy when tax policy has not been set optimally.

3.1. Capital taxation as a 'second-best' tax

Communities may be forced to tax capital if they are unable to finance local public goods by imposing a non-distorting tax such as a head tax; fiscal constraints may thus result in the adoption of a levy on capital as a 'second-best' tax. Recently, Wilson (1986), Zodrow and Mieszkowski (1986), and Wildasin (1986) have shown that communities will underprovide local public goods if they must rely on a tax on capital. The argument is basically as follows. Communities realize that as they raise the tax rate to finance the

---

[13]Given our assumption that jurisdictions are sufficiently large that pollution created in one jurisdiction does not spill-over into another, there is no divergence between the marginal private benefit and marginal social benefit of reducing pollution. If there exist any interjurisdictional externalities occasioned by the transport of pollution from one community to another, then (for the usual sorts of reasons) local choice will not generate a socially optimal outcome. For an excellent general treatment of a variety of interjurisdictional externalities, see Gordon (1983).

local public good, they will drive out capital. Thus, they raise the tax rate only to the point at which the cost of the public good, including the negative effects of a smaller capital stock, equals the benefits. But as Wildasin (1986) explains, the social cost of local public goods is less than the private cost, since capital that leaves one community will be deflected to another. Thus, underprovision of local public goods arises, because communities fail to take into account the beneficial externalities they confer on other communities.

Our purpose in this section is to show that the taxation of capital also distorts the choice of environmental standards. One way to establish this point is to introduce a local public good explicitly into the median-voter model developed in section 2 of the paper; in the presence of such a good, tax revenues must be positive. We present such an expanded model in the appendix. But we can also make our basic point somewhat more simply.

Suppose the community has chosen some positive tax rate t. We might then ask what level of environmental policy α the community should choose in order to maximize $u(c, \alpha)$ subject to the rate of return constraint in (2) and the budget constraint in (4). The analog to eq. (6b) for this problem is

$$-u_\alpha/u_c = f_\alpha - t(f_{k\alpha}/f_{kk}).\tag{9}$$

It is clear in (9) that the social benefit from improving the environment, $-u_\alpha/u_c$, will exceed social cost, f_α, inasmuch as all of the terms on the right-hand side are positive except f_{kk}; therefore, environmental quality is set at an inefficiently low level. This contrasts with our earlier result where we found that social costs and benefits would be equal if the community chose the optimal tax rate of zero.

The interpretation is straightforward. From the discussion of eq. (7), it is clear that the first term on the right-hand side of (9) is the wage effect of environmental policy and that the second term is the fiscal effect. Thus, (9) shows that the community will continue to tighten environmental standards to the point that willingness to sacrifice the composite good equals the *sum* of lost wages and forgone tax revenues. The lost wages, as shown above, are equal to lost output (i.e. the wage effect equals the output effect); the forgone tax revenues (the fiscal effect) thus represent a wedge between the private and social cost of improving the environment.

3.2. An alternative model of public choice

We can get a result similar to that in the preceding section without actually constraining the community to tax capital. Instead, we can invoke the spirit of some of the recent public-choice literature which posits that government agencies have their own set of concerns in the political arena that typically are not in complete harmony with the interests of their constituents. One common hypothesis [with Niskanen (1977) as its source] is that bureaucrats seek to maximize their budgets. Salary, perquisites of office, reputation, power, and the capacity to award patronage typically rise as the agency's budget expands.

In the Niskanen spirit, we thus specify a government objective function, g, which has two arguments: revenues from the taxation of capital T (which are equal to tk) and the utility of a representative voter:

$$g = g[T, u(c, \alpha)], \tag{10}$$

where we would expect the partial derivatives of g with respect to T and u to be positive. We include the utility of voters since government, even if its central concern is to maximize its own welfare, cannot entirely ignore the well-being of its constituents. We thus envision a government which must balance its desire to realize the benefits of higher taxes today against the possibility that the voters will 'turn the rascals out' tomorrow.

It is not difficult to show that the maximization of this objective function subject to the community's budget constraint and the constraint on the rate of return on capital implies that government will set a positive tax rate on capital and that the marginal social benefit of further improving the environment will exceed marginal social cost, i.e. environmental quality will be set at an inefficiently low level. The intuition behind these results is straightforward. The Niskanen public agent derives utility from increased tax revenues. This provides an incentive to entice capital into the jurisdiction with lax environmental standards so as to increase the tax base. Thus environmental policy again has a fiscal effect as it provides a further means by which the bureaucrat can generate additional tax revenue, and this fiscal effect leads to excessive local pollution.

3.3. Efficiency under distorting taxes on capital

Our analysis of the interaction between tax and environmental policies suggests that it is important to pay close attention to the notion of efficiency. We argued above that if an omnipotent planner faced only the three constraints we described, then, as shown in (8a), this planner would choose an environmental standard for each community such that $-u_\alpha^i/u_c^i$ equals f_α^i. It is not true, however, that (8a) is the efficiency condition for the choice of an environmental standard in the presence of distorting local taxes on capital.[14]

To see this point, consider the special case where the society consists of

[14] We thank an anonymous referee for bringing this issue to our attention and working out its implications.

only two communities. Suppose we wish to maximize the utility of community 1 residents subject to the constraints that we allow community 2 residents to reach some given level of utility, that consumption equal production, and that we allocate society's fixed stock of capital between the two communities; a fourth constraint requires that there be a wedge between the marginal product of capital in the two communities of $(t^1 - t^2)$. The solution to this probem requires:

$$-u_\alpha^1/u_c^1 = f_\alpha^1 - (t^1 - t^2)[f_{k\alpha}^1/(f_{kk}^1 + \mu f_{kk}^2)], \tag{11}$$

where μ is the ratio of the number of workers in the two communities, L^1/L^2.

Clearly, if $(t^1 - t^2)$ were zero, then (11) reduces to (8a). If this wedge is positive, however, then efficiency requires the marginal social benefit from reducing pollution in community 1, $-u_\alpha^1/u_c^1$, to exceed the marginal product of the environment in 1, f_α^1. The explanation is as follows. If the environmental standard in 1 were relxed, capital would flow from 2 to 1 in order to maintain the wedge between the marginal product of capital in the two communities. Aggregate output would rise by the product of the difference in marginal products and the flow of capital. Efficiency requires us to loosen the standard in 1 to the point that the marginal social loss from increased pollution equals the gain in output. Thus, communities that set high tax rates should set relatively lax environmental standards to offset the distortions introduced by fiscal policy.

4. Another extension of the basic model: Environmentalists vs. advocates of economic growth

While we believe that our simple model captures the spirit of interjurisdictional competition, there is an important intrajurisdictional dimension to such behavior that cannot be addressed in a model with a homogeneous population. In particular, several empirical studies stress that the 'environmental–jobs' tradeoff often involves an intense conflict of interest among different constituencies within the local community. There are frequently conservationist groups whose opposition to economic development and the associated environmental degradation runs directly counter to the interests of those whose employment and income depend on the entry of new industry. Deacon and Shapiro (1975), for example, in a study of voting behavior on a conservationist measure in California, found a significant propensity for 'laborers and construction craftsmen' to oppose the conservation act, reflecting presumably their preference for economic development and new jobs. Likewise, in a study of a pulp-mill referendum in New Hampshire, Fischel (1979) found systematic tendencies for 'laborers' to favor the mill and for 'professionals' to oppose it. This suggests that we extend the model to encompass individuals with different circumstances and interests, and observe how this affects local decisions on public outputs and taxes.

To put the results in the sharpest perspective, we return to our basic model and introduce one new element. We assume that the community now contains two types of people. The first type are, like before, wage-earners; for them, the presence of more capital implies a higher wage rate, and, hence, an increase in income. In contrast, the other subset consists of individuals who have no wage income. Members of this second group have an exogenous component of income supplemented by their share of revenues from the taxation of capital. There thus arises a potential conflict of interest between the two groups in the community: workers, L, have an incentive to encourage the influx of capital as a source of higher wage income, while non-wage-earners, N, without this incentive are likely to be more concerned with the environmental deterioration that can accompany an increased stock of capital. The two groups are unlikely to see eye-to-eye on the tradeoff between environmental quality and jobs. We shall characterize outcomes in such a divided community for two distinct cases: a worker majority and a non-worker majority.

4.1. Worker-majority outcome

Let us assume first that the group of workers constitutes the majority (i.e. $L > N$) and that, under median-voter rule, this group enforces its will on the community as a whole. Assuming (as before) that workers are homogeneous in every way, we need simply maximize the utility of a representative worker subject to the relevant constraints. On first inspection, this would seem to pose an identical problem to that in our initial model. However, this is not quite so; there is an important difference with significant implications for the outcome. In particular, the presence of non-wage-earners introduces an asymmetry affecting wage income, but not the division of tax revenues. Instead of eq. (4), the budget constraint for the representative worker becomes:

$$c = y^l + w + T$$

$$= y^l + f - kf_k + \theta tk, \tag{4''}$$

where $\theta = L/(N + L)$ and y^l is per-capita exogenous income for wage-earners. In the last term on the RHS of (4''), we now have the parameter θ, reflecting the (equal) division of tax revenues among non-wage-earners as well as workers. The presence of θ results in certain changes in the first-order conditions; in place of (5a) through (5d), we now find that

$$u_c^l = \lambda_1, \tag{5a'}$$

$$u_\alpha^l = -\lambda_1 f_\alpha - (\lambda_2 - \lambda_1 k) f_{k\alpha}, \tag{5b'}$$

$$\lambda_1 t = \frac{1}{\theta}(\lambda_1 k - \lambda_2) f_{kk}, \tag{5c'}$$

$$\lambda_2 = \lambda_1 \theta k, \tag{5d'}$$

with the parameter θ entering into (5c') and (5d').

By suitable rearrangement, we find that utility maximization of the subset of workers requires [instead of (6a) and (6b) as earlier] that

$$t = \left(\frac{1-\theta}{\theta}\right) k f_{kk}, \tag{6a'}$$

$$\frac{-u_\alpha^l}{u_c^l} = f_\alpha - \theta t \frac{f_{k\alpha}}{f_{kk}}. \tag{6b'}$$

In contrast to our earlier results, workers no longer desire a zero tax rate on capital; in fact, (6a') is unambiguously negative, indicating that the worker-determined outcome implies a subsidy to capital. The rationale for this result is clear. Workers reap all the gains from the increased wage income associated with a larger capital stock, but they no not bear the full cost of the subsidy to capital – some of the cost of the subsidy falls on non-wage-earners. Thus, a small change, dt, from zero in a negative direction yields an increase in wages (that although equal to the subsidy to capital) exceeds the part of the subsidy subscribed by the group of workers.

Similarly, we find a change in moving from (6b) to (6b'); workers, in a sense, now prefer a somewhat higher level of environmental quality as their marginal rate of substitution is now less than f_α. This result reflects the fiscal effect of environmental policy; since t is negative, workers must take into account their share of higher subsidy payments if they choose to increase α. Workers therefore find it in their interest to raise wages by subsidizing capital directly rather than by relaxing environmental standards.

4.2. Non-wage-earners in the majority

Our second case involving a majority of non-wage-earners (i.e. $N > L$) is more straightforward, since the tradeoff for these individuals is simply between environmental quality and revenues from the taxation of capital. Here we maximize the utility of a representative non-wage-earner subject to the relevant constraints – that is, we maximize (3) subject to (2) and the applicable budget constraint:

$$c = y^n + \theta t k, \tag{4'''}$$

where y^n is an exogenously-determined component of income. By suitable manipulation of the first-order conditions, we obtain:

$$t = -k f_{kk}, \tag{6a''}$$

$$\frac{-u_\alpha^n}{u_c^n} = \frac{-\theta t f_{k\alpha}}{f_{kk}}. \tag{6b''}$$

In contrast to (6a') for the workers, (6a'') is unambiguously positive: non-wage-earners desire a positive tax on capital. Eq. (6b'') embodies a pure 'fiscal effect' in the choice of environmental standards; it indicates that the MRS of non-wage-earners for environmental quality should be set equal to the marginal fiscal gains per capita from the taxation of capital. These two conditions, incidentally, imply a kind of Laffer-curve effect: if we hold α constant, we see that the derived tax rate on capital is such that the change in revenues from the tax is zero. To see this, let $T = \theta k t =$ per-capita revenues from the taxation of capital. Then,

$$dT = \theta(k\,dt + t\,dk). \tag{12}$$

From our return-on-capital constraint, $(f_k - t) = r$, we obtain $f_{kk}\,dk = dt$. Substituting this and (6a'') into eq. (12), we find that:

$$dT = \theta(k f_{kk}\,dk - k f_{kk}\,dk) = 0. \tag{13}$$

The results for our two special cases of worker-majority rule and a non-wage-earner majority make two basic points. First, the desired policies of the two groups clearly differ. Workers wish to subsidize capital in order to augment their wage income, while non-wage-earners, in contrast, want to tax capital as a source of revenues. Likewise, the two groups will prefer different levels of local environmental quality; there is some presumption that wage-earners will opt for a lower level of environmental quality (i.e. a higher value of α) than will non-wage-earners, although we have not been able to demonstrate this as a general result.[15]

---

[15] Eqs. (6a') and (6b') together imply that the wage-earner's marginal rate of substitution of consumption for environmental quality will be $(f_\alpha - k f_{k\alpha}) + \theta k f_{k\alpha}$; similarly, (6a'') and (6b'') imply that non-wage-earner's MRS will be $\theta k f_{k\alpha}$. $(f_\alpha - k f_{k\alpha})$ is the derivative of the wage rate with respect to α and is presumably positive. It does not seem possible, however, to determine whether the term common to both will take on a larger value in the wage-earner or non-wage-earner equation; we can establish that θ (by definition) is larger in the wage-earner case, but there seems to be no such general claim concerning the relative value of k and $f_{k\alpha}$. The terms that we can sign thus point to a higher MRS for wage-earners and suggest that wage-earners will choose a lower level of environmental quality. But this result is clearly not general; this would require a number of further assumptions regarding the preference functions and levels of relative income.

Second, it is evident that the outcome under a majority of either group is not socially optimal. The conditions for the maximization of social welfare are, as we saw earlier, satisfied by the median-voter outcome for a system of homogeneous jurisdictions of wage-earners. But if the jurisdictions are divided between workers and non-wage-earners, not only will there be a divergence of desired policies within each community, but the median-voter outcome will not, in either case, be an economically efficient one.[16]

In concluding this section, we would note that although we have framed the conflict of interests as involving environmentalists versus growth advocates, we have not assumed that there are any systematic differences in preferences between the two groups. One might, for example, postulate that certain groups possess utility functions that place a greater weight on environmental amenities than do those of others. However, it is not necessary to make such a distinction to provide a source for such conflicts of interest. In this section, the divergence of interests has its source solely in differing economic circumstances: the income of one group depends on the local stock of capital, while that of the other does not. The tension between the two groups thus represents a special case of a more general phenomenon under which one group attempts to use the fiscal system in order to 'exploit' the other. Workers attempt to saddle non-wage-earners with subsidies to capital that raises wages, while the latter group seeks to tax capital so as to enhance local revenues at the expense of wages. This model may, incidentally, have some explanatory power. As we have seen, the subsidization of capital makes little sense in our basic model with a homogeneous population. Yet we know that states and localities often engage in vigorous efforts to attract new business capital. Perhaps this is best understood as an effort of certain interest groups to further their ends at the expense of the remainder of the populace.

5. Summary and concluding remarks

To summarize our results, we present in table 1 the outcomes for our basic model of homogeneous jurisdictions of workers $[\theta = L/(L+N) = 1]$, for our

---

[16]The inefficiencies that characterize either outcome indicate that there are potential 'gains-from-trade' between the two groups in the setting of policy, since both of our majority-rule outcomes lie inside the utility-possibilities frontier. If there were some mechanism to reach a 'cooperative' solution, welfare gains would be possible. It is a straightforward matter to describe such a cooperative outcome by solving for the Pareto-efficiency conditions for the community as a whole. Such an exercise demonstrates that the cooperative solution involves zero taxation of capital and a Samuelsonian condition for the level of environmental quality. These conditions (like those for our basic model) satisfy the social optimality conditions for the system as a whole. It is not easy, however, to envision a mechanism to facilitate such cooperative action. There may in some instances exist other issues so that some kind of log-rolling maneuver may permit an approximation to the cooperative outcome. But, more generally, there do not seem to exist institutions to accommodate the necessary bargains.

Table 1

Summary of results.

Case	Tax rate	Marginal rate of substitution
$\theta = 1$	$t = 0$	$-\dfrac{u_a}{u_c} = f_a$
Tax-constrained	$t > 0$	$-\dfrac{u_a}{u_c} = f_a - t\dfrac{f_{ka}}{f_{kk}}$
Niskanen	$t > 0$	$-\dfrac{u_a}{u_c} = f_a + kf_{ka}\dfrac{g_T}{g_u u_c}$
$1/2 < \theta < 1$	$t = \left(\dfrac{1-\theta}{\theta}\right)kf_{kk} < 0$	$-\dfrac{u_a^l}{u_c^l} = f_a - t\theta\dfrac{f_{ka}}{f_{kk}}$
$0 < \theta < 1/2$	$t = -kf_{kk} > 0$	$-\dfrac{u_a^n}{u_c^n} = -t\theta\dfrac{f_{ka}}{f_{kk}}$

tax-constrained case, for our Niskanen model with revenue maximization, and for our two cases involving mixed jurisdictions. The homogeneous case generates a socially optimal outcome, while the remaining cases do not.

The results of the analysis are admittedly somewhat mixed, but they do have some interesting implications. For instances of relatively homogeneous communities where the benefits and costs of public programs are clearly understood and where public decisions reflect the well-being of the jurisdiction's residents, the analysis indicates that outcomes will tend to be roughly efficient. Such communities will tend to select both incentives for new industry and standards for local environmental quality that are socially optimal. In this regard Fischel (1975) demonstrated some years ago that, in a simple framework in which firms pay communities an entrance fee in compensation for environmental damage, a socially efficient allocation of firms and environmental quality results. Our basic model in a sense replicates Fischel's results, although the mechanism for compensation in our model – a higher wage – is somewhat different from the direct payment in the Fischel model. Nevertheless, it achieves the same result. In our basic model, interjurisdictional competition is efficiency-enhancing.

As we have seen, however, there are three distinct sources of potential distortion in local decision-making. First, if the jurisdiction does not have access to efficient tax instruments – if, as in our analysis, it is constrained to tax capital – then distortions occur in both fiscal and environmental decisions. More specifically, communities, because of the fiscal effects associated with environmental decisions, will opt for a socially excessive level of pollution. Second, if public decisions deviate from the will of the electorate (as in our Niskanen model), then efficient outcomes, not surprisingly, are not to be expected. In particular, we found that (as in the tax-constrained case) revenue-maximizing behavior will lead to excessive taxation of capital and suboptimal environmental quality in the jurisdiction. And third, conflicts of interest within a heterogeneous community can also introduce distortions into public decisions. Depending on which group gets the upper hand, such conflict can result in either the taxation or the subsidization of capital with consequent inefficiencies in decisions on environmental amenities.

In concluding the paper, there are two further issues that we wish to raise. The first concerns the meaning of the term 'local' in the analysis. We have used this term in a rather imprecise way to refer to units for decentralized decision-making. But the question arises as to the sorts of units to which the analysis would presumably be applicable. We can offer a few observations on this. It is clear that the units cannot typically be the smallest units of local government such as municipalities within a metropolitan area. As we noted earlier, the jurisdictions in our model are sufficiently large that residents live and work within their boundaries and that pollution generated in the area does not spill across these boundaries. This would suggest that the units suitable for decentralized choice under this framework would have to be at least as large as metropolitan areas and perhaps, in some instances, larger – state boundaries might, for certain pollutants and commuting patterns, provide the best approximation. At any rate our analysis clearly does not refer to the standard Tiebout kind of community where individuals may work in a jurisdiction other than that in which they reside. What is involved here are larger jurisdictions: metropolitan areas or perhaps even states or regions.

Second, our colleague Peter Murrell has raised a troublesome issue that we have not attempted to incorporate into the formal analysis: the well-being of future generations. Certain dimensions of environmental quality, if degraded by current generations, are not easily restored later. The development of wilderness areas and the creation of certain forms of long-lived, hazardous wastes come quickly to mind. The issue here is that the concern for future generations is, in one important sense, more difficult to incorporate in local policy decisions than at the national level. In particular, the well-being of one's own progeny is unlikely to depend in important ways on environmental decisions within one's present locality. An individual's children and their offspring will probably live elsewhere so that their 'environmental heritage' under a system of local decision-making will be determined by others. This may well result in a form of myopia under local standard-setting that leads to socially suboptimal levels of environmental quality for one's descendants. In principal, at least, more centralized decision-making should serve to 'internalize' these concerns and provide better representation of the interests of those yet to come. This is, however, a complicated matter. As William Fischel and Bruce Hamilton have pointed out to us, in a setting of mobile individuals, the phenomenon of capitalization would provide some protection for the interests of future generations. Decisions that lead to degradation of the local environment at some later date will be reflected in reduced current property values. Capitalization of future streams of benefits and costs can thus compel even myopic decision-makers to take cognizance of the future.

Appendix

In this appendix we explicitly incorporate a local public good into our median-voter model. Let z be per-capita consumption of the public good which the community purchases at a price p, and continue to let c be a composite private good which serves as the numeraire. Suppose, initially, that the community can finance the local public good with a combination of head taxes and taxes on capital. The first-order conditions for a welfare maximum in this problem require: (i) the community must set the tax rate on capital equal to zero and thus finance the public good entirely through the head tax; (ii) the marginal rate of substitution between α and c must equal f_α; and (iii) the marginal rate of substitution between z and c must equal p. The first two of these conditions are consistent with the discussion in section 2 of the paper; the third is not surprising.

Now suppose that we rule out the use of the head tax and require that the public good be financed entirely by taxing capital; this is, we require:

$$pz = tk. \tag{A.1}$$

The problem then becomes: maximize $u(c, z, \alpha)$ subject to the private budget constraint, the government budget constraint in (A.1), and the rate of return constraint in (2). Let γ_1, γ_2 and γ_3 be the Lagrange multipliers associated with these constraints. Then the first-order conditions for this problem require:

$$u_c = \gamma_1, \tag{A.2}$$

$$u_z = \gamma_2 p, \tag{A.3}$$

$$\gamma_2 t = -f_{kk}[\gamma_3 - \gamma_1 k], \tag{A.4}$$

$$\gamma_3 - \gamma_2 k = 0, \tag{A.5}$$

$$u_\alpha = -\gamma_1 f_\alpha - f_{k\alpha}[\gamma_3 - \gamma_1 k]. \tag{A.6}$$

Assuming the community chooses a positive level of z, t must be positive. Given that t is positive and f_{kk} is negative, (A.4) implies that $(\gamma_3 - \gamma_1 k)$ must be positive. If $(\gamma_3 - \gamma_1 k)$ is positive, then (A.5) requires that γ_2 must be greater than γ_1; (A.2) and (A.3) then imply that the marginal rate of substitution between the private good will exceed the price of the public good, i.e. the public good will be underprovided. This result is consistent with those in the Wilson (1986), Zodrow and Mieszkowski (1986), and Wildasin (1986) papers.

Combining the first-order conditions shows that the community will choose a level of environmental quality such that:

$$-u_\alpha/u_c = f_\alpha - t(f_{k\alpha}/f_{kk})(u_z/u_c)/p. \tag{A.7}$$

The community's marginal willingness-to-pay for better environmental quality is greater than f_α, and therefore the community sets an inefficiently low environmental standard. As in the simpler model presented in the text, the source of the inefficiency is the fiscal effect of environmental policy, $-t(f_{k\alpha}/f_{kk})$; the community relaxes standards in pursuit of greater tax revenues as well as higher wages.

References

Advisory Commission on Intergovernmental Relations, 1981, Regional growth: Interstate tax competition (ACIR, Washington, DC).
Break, George F., 1967, Intergovernmental fiscal relations in the United States (The Brookings Institution, Washington, DC).
Brennan, Geoffrey and James Buchanan, 1980, The power to tax: Analytical foundations of a fiscal constitution (Cambridge University Press, Cambridge and New York).
Cumberland, John H., 1979, Interregional pollution spillovers and consistency of environmental policy, in: H. Siebert, et al., eds., Regional environmental policy: The economic issues (New York University Press, New York) 255–281.
Cumberland, John H., 1981, Efficiency and equity in interregional environmental management, Review of Regional Studies, No. 2, 1–9.
Deacon, Robert and Perry Shapiro, 1975, Private preference for collective goods revealed through voting on referenda, American Economic Review 65, 943–955.
Fischel, William A., 1975, Fiscal and environmental considerations in the location of firms in suburban communities, in: E. Mills and W. Oates, eds., Fiscal zoning and land use controls (D.C. Heath, Lexington, MA) 119–174.
Fischel, William A., 1979, Determinants of voting on environmental quality: A study of a New Hampshire pulp mill referendum, Journal of Environmental Economics and Management 6, 107–118.
Gordon, Roger, 1983, An optimal taxation approach to fiscal federalism, Quarterly Journal of Economics 97, 567–586.
Mintz, Jack and Henry Tulkens, 1986, Commodity tax competition between member states of a federation: Equilibrium and efficiency, Journal of Public Economics 29, 133–172.
Niskanen, Jr., William, 1977, Bureaucracy and representative government (Aldine, Chicago).
Oates, Wallace E., 1972, Fiscal federalism (Harcourt Brace Jovanovich, New York).
Oates, Wallace E. and Robert M. Schwab, 1987, Pricing instruments for environmental protection: The problems of cross-media pollution, interjurisdictional competition and intergenerational effects, Unpublished paper (University of Maryland, College Park).

Stigler, George, 1957, The tenable range of functions of local government, in: Joint Economic Committee, U.S. Congress, Federal Expenditure Policy for Economic Growth and Stability (U.S. Government Printing Office, Washington, DC) 213–219.

Tiebout, Charles M., 1956, A pure theory of local expenditures, Journal of Political Economy 64, 416–424.

Wildasin, David E., 1986, Interjurisdictional capital mobility: Fiscal externality and a corrective subsidy, Unpublished paper (University of Indiana, Bloomington, Indiana).

Wilson, John D., 1985, Optimal property taxation in the presence of interregional capital mobility, Journal of Urban Economics 17, 73–89.

Wilson, John D., 1986, A theory of interregional tax competition, Journal of Urban Economics 19, 356–370.

Zodrow, George R. and Peter Mieszkowski, 1983, The incidence of the property tax: The benefit view versus the new view, in: G. Zodrow, ed., Local provision of public services: The Tiebout model after twenty-five years (Academic Press, New York) 109–129.

Zodrow, George R. and Peter Mieszkowski, 1986, Pigou, Tiebout, property taxation and the under-provision of local public goods, Journal of Urban Economics 19, 296–315.

The Theory of Regulatory Federalism: The Case of Environmental Management

Wallace E. Oates and Robert M. Schwab*

I. Introduction

In the design of public regulatory programs, the appropriate locus of authority is a fundamental issue. Should the central government establish regulations applicable to all areas in the nation or should regulatory measures be tailored to fit the particular circumstances of individual local jurisdictions? Public policy often reveals considerable ambivalence on this matter. In the United States, for example, the U.S. Congress under the Clean Air Act Amendments in 1970 directed the Environmental Protection Agency to set uniform national standards for air quality – maximum permissible concentrations of air pollutants applicable to all jurisdictions. But two years later, under the Clean Water Act, the Congress decided to let individual states determine their own standards for water quality. Which approach – the centralized determination of uniform national standards or decentralized standard setting – is the appropriate one?

In this paper, we address this issue of regulatory federalism in the context of environmental standard setting. But as the discussion will make clear, the analysis is applicable to the more general issue of the decentralization of regulatory authority. Environmental decision-making is an interesting and important case, one that is convenient for purposes of framing the analysis.

The basic tension that exists between centralized and decentralized regulatory activity is widely recognized. On the one hand, there is a strong argument for decentralizing regulatory management to account for 'local circumstances'. In the case of setting standards for environmental quality, for example, the marginal benefits of a cleaner environment and the marginal abatement costs are likely to vary (and vary quite significantly) across regions or localities. This suggests that the optimal level of environmental quality – the level for which marginal benefits equal marginal abatement cost – will in general differ from one jurisdiction to another [Peltzman and Tideman (1972)]. The setting of a single uniform standard with which all localities must comply will thus entail welfare losses relative to the first-best optimum in which each jurisdiction attains its own best outcome.

Although there is a persuasive case for tailoring environmental programs to local conditions, there is, on the other hand, a widespread concern that local decision-making on environmental matters is likely to be subject to 'destructive interjurisdictional competition' [Cumberland (1979, 1981)]. The fear is that, in their eagerness to attract new business and jobs, local officials will compete with one another in the relaxation of environmental standards, resulting in excessive levels of environmental degradation. In the next section we address this matter in terms of a model of interjurisdictional competition for a mobile stock of national capital. Building on some earlier work [Oates and Schwab (1988)], this model suggests that incentives for the local use of pricing instruments, like a tax on waste emissions, can lead to efficient outcomes. Interjurisdictional competition in this model does *not* result in excessive pollution: local government employs the tax as a Pigouvian levy equal to marginal social damage. This is an encouraging finding, for it suggests that local decision-making on environmental matters may be able to realize the potential welfare gains from environmental policies that are adapted to local conditions.

This result, however, is critically dependent upon our characterization of a 'local' jurisdiction. We find (not surprisingly) that decentralized regulatory authority leads to efficient outcomes only if the structure of governments is such that the jurisdiction that sets regulations includes precisely the set of individuals who bear all of the benefits and all of the costs of those regulations.[1] This suggests that in the design of a system of decentralized regulatory activity, it is of central importance to assign regulatory authority to jurisdictions of (approximately) optimal size.

Finally, the paper looks at a related question: if we vest local governments with the authority to set regulatory policy, will they properly take into account the interests of future generations? In the context of environmental policy, there exists the concern that communities will be inclined to follow policies which yield benefits now (e.g., more jobs) but substantial damages in the future (e.g., increased exposure to long-lived pollutants such as hazardous wastes). Such problems would seem to be more acute at the local than at the central level. We would presumably all want the central government to take into account the interests of our children since it is likely that they will live somewhere in this country. Since, however, an individual's children and their offspring will probably reside in a community elsewhere, their 'environmental heritage' will depend upon the decisions of others. This could well result in a kind of myopia of local decisions with the consequence of suboptimal environmental quality for future generations.

In the third section, we address this issue by incorporating into our model of interjurisdictional competition a pollutant whose effects are felt in future time periods. In this model, we find that current residents cannot escape the costs of future pollution. Such costs inevitably become capitalized into local property values so that the future effects of current decisions must figure into the current decision calculus. This result, incidentally, provides a further argument for local decision-making on environmental issues. Local officials *may* have stronger incentives to consider the well-being of future generations than do national officials.

II. Decentralized environmental policy

In this section of the paper we set forth a simple model which allows us to look at some of the important issues in environmental federalism. In this model, jurisdictions may lower environmental standards in order to attract capital. In return for an increased capital stock, residents receive higher wages. The community must, however, weigh the benefits of higher wages against the cost of lower environmental quality.

The definition of community boundaries is a key issue in this analysis. We begin by assuming that each of the N communities in this society is sufficiently large that (i) individuals live and work in the same jurisdiction, and (ii) pollution generated in one jurisdiction does not spill over into another. The first part of the assumption implies that voters must bear the cost of a strict environmental policy; it rules out, for example, the possibility that people can realize the benefits from living in a community with a very strict environmental policy and still earn high wages by working in a nearby community where policy is lax. The second part of this assumption means that the residents of a community realize all of the benefits from a strict environmental policy in their community.

Clearly these are strong assumptions, but they provide a very useful benchmark. They allow us to ask if local standard setting can lead to efficient outcomes under 'ideal' circumstances. In addition since, at the most general level, the jurisdiction or level of government to exercise regulatory authority is a choice variable, it is valuable to determine the properties of a jurisdiction that are compatible with the potential for efficient regulatory decisions. It may well be that, although the smallest units of local government are inappropriate levels for certain regulatory functions, somewhat larger units, encompassing for example metropolitan areas or regions, may well have sufficient 'extent' to satisfy the conditions for an optimal-size regulatory jurisdiction.

Each jurisdiction in the model produces a private good Q which is sold in a national market. Production requires capital K, labor L, and a single pollutant X.[2] The production function for the private good F(K, L, X) exhibits constant returns to scale.

We incorporate three assumptions about labor markets in our model: (i) the aggregate stock of labor for this society is fixed, (ii) the 'size' of each community is fixed (i.e., the quantity of labor in each community is given), and (iii) labor is perfectly mobile. Since labor is free to choose among communities, when all of the N labor markets in this society clear, workers must be indifferent among the communities.

It is helpful to take advantage of our assumptions about the technology and the fixed supply of labor and write the production function in a community as

(1) $Q = F(K, L, X)$

$\quad\quad = Lf(k, x)$

where k and x are the capital–labor and emissions–labor ratio respectively. We let Q be the numeraire. Thus if labor receives the value of its marginal product, then (1) implies that the wage w in each community will equal $(f - kf_k - xf_x)$.

We assume that each community sets a unit tax on waste emissions τ. Given τ, firms choose a level of emissions which equates the tax to the value of the marginal product of pollution; therefore

(2) $\tau = f_x$.

The revenues from this tax are distributed equally among the residents of the community.[3]

The aggregate stock of capital is also fixed in our model. Capital, at least in the long run, is perfectly mobile. This implies that the return to capital will be equated across jurisdictions, since the owners of capital would move their capital to a community which offered an above-normal return. All of the communities are small in the sense that they treat this rate of return as a parameter. Capital receives its marginal product; therefore, if capital can earn a payment c in other jurisdictions, then the stock of capital in a community must adjust so that

(3) $c = f_k$.

Each of the individual residents receives utility from consumption of the private good z and from the level of environmental quality Lx. This implies that we can then write a resident's utility function as

(4) $u = u(z, Lx)$.

Note that pollution is a pure public good in our model and that each individual 'consumes' the total emissions generated in his or her community. Thus one person's consumption of pollution does not diminish that of anyone else.

As we noted above, since workers are identical, mobility implies that workers must receive the same level of utility in all communities. We could incorporate a housing market in our model and allow house prices to adjust so that, in equilibrium, utility is the same everywhere. But we can make our basic point more simply. Suppose each community charges an 'annual' admission fee T. Then this fee will serve the same role as property values; in particular, individuals will bid up the price of admission into a specific community until the marginal entrant is indifferent between residing there or in the next best alternative. As a result, differences in T will offset the incentive for labor to migrate to high-wage and low-pollution communities.[4]

The budget constraint for an individual requires that the sum of exogenous income m, wages $f - kf_k - xf_x$, and revenues from the tax on emissions equal expenditures on the composite good z and the cost of admission to the community T:

(5) $m + (f - kf_k - xf_x) + \tau x = z + T$.

Environmental policy

Local government in this model must set the tax rate τ on emissions. Adopting the widely used median-voter model as a collective choice rule and noting that all individuals are identical, we can simply assume that public decisions are made 'as if' a representative individual were allowed to set policy so as to maximize his utility function in (4) subject to the budget constraint in (5) and the factor demands in (2) and (3). The first-order conditions emerging from this maximization problem are

(6) $u_z = \lambda_1$

$$Lu_x = -\lambda_1[-kf_{kx} - xf_{xx} + \tau_x] - \lambda_2 f_{kx} + \lambda_3 f_{xx}$$

$$\lambda_1[kf_{kk} + xf_{kx}] = \lambda_2 f_{kk} + \lambda_3 f_{kx}$$

$$\lambda_1 x = \lambda_3$$

where λ_1, λ_2 and λ_3 are the Lagrange multipliers associated with the three constraints discussed above. Combining these first-order conditions, we find that local decision-makers should set the level of the emissions tax such that

(7) $-L(u_x / u_z) = \tau$

$$= f_x.$$

The left side of (7) measures the benefit to the residents of a community of reducing emissions as measured by their aggregate marginal willingness to pay. The right side of (7) measures the cost to the community of improving environmental quality as measured by foregone revenue from the emissions tax. The community thus equates marginal gains and losses from abatement when setting policy.

Efficiency in the interjurisdictional competition model
Clearly, this outcome is efficient. We argued above that $-L(u_x / u_z)$ represents marginal private benefit from environmental improvement. But given our assumption that all pollution generated in a community affects only the residents of that community, it must also represent marginal social benefit. We also argued that τ represented marginal private abatement cost. But since τ must equal the marginal product of emissions, it also represents marginal abatement cost from society's perspective as measured by foregone production. Thus our basic result is that a tax on waste emissions is an effective tool in the hands of local governments: local decision-makers employ the tax as a Pigouvian levy equal to marginal social damages, leading to a socially efficient level of environmental quality.[5]

The fear of 'destructive interjurisdictional competition' is thus misplaced in this framework. Local residents surely wish to attract more capital to increase local wage income, but the relaxation of environmental standards to achieve this end comes at a cost to the community – namely local environmental deterioration. In our model, the tradeoff between wage income and the disutility of pollution incorporates the proper incentives so that residents select the socially optimal level of environmental quality. Any attempt to increase income further by reducing the tax on waste emissions would result in increments to pollution that residents find more costly than the associated rise in income.

The transboundary problem
It should also be clear that the efficiency properties of local Pigouvian taxes hinge crucially on the appropriate definition of community boundaries. In particular, our

conclusion that social and private benefits from abatement are equal requires the assumption that the pollution generated in one community never harms the residents of other communities. If pollution generated in one community crosses political boundaries, then this equivalence between private and social benefit will be broken and local policy setting will no longer lead to an efficient outcome. In this case we would expect to find that communities set an environmental policy which is too lax, since they ignore the impact of pollution emitted in their community on others.

We can incorporate this transboundary problem in our model in the following way. Let d^{ij} be a transfer coefficient which equals the proportion of a unit of pollution emitted in jurisdiction i which falls in jurisdiction j. Suppose the residents of community i take emissions in all communities other than their own as given when setting environmental policy (the Cournot assumption). Then it is not difficult to show that community i will set policy so that

$$(8) \quad -L^i d^{ii} (u^i_x / u^i_z) = \tau^i$$

$$= f^i_x.$$

Efficiency, on the other hand, requires that emissions in community i be set at a level such that

$$(9) \quad -\sum_j d^{ij} L^j (u^j_x / u^j_z) = f^i_x.$$

Equations (8) and (9) make the transboundary problem clear. (9) states that efficiency requires us to reduce pollution in a community to the point that the marginal social benefit from abatement, as measured by marginal willingness to pay aggregated over all of the communities into which emissions fall, must equal marginal social abatement cost. (8) states that communities will only consider the impact of pollution on the residents of the community where it is emitted. (8) and (9) are equivalent only if d^{ij} equals 0 for all i not equal to j; i.e., if all pollution remains in the community where it is generated, thus bringing us back to the model we looked at initially. If some pollution does fall on other communities (if at least one of the d^{ij} other than d^{ii} is positive), then (8) and (9) together show that communities will set environmental policy which is too lax: the marginal social benefit from abatement will exceed marginal abatement cost.

III.   Long-lived pollution
We have shown in the confines of our model that if local governments set taxes on waste emissions and if all of the damages from pollution are borne by the current residents of a community, the outcome is efficient. In this section we show that this result holds even if some of the damage from emissions is borne by future residents.

An intertemporal extension of the basic model
To address this issue, we incorporate the framework we presented above in a simple overlapping generations model. In this extended model, consumers live two

periods. Each member of the generation born at time t purchases admission into the community of his choice for the first period of his life where he works and where he consumes y^t. At the end of the first period, he sells his place in this community and 'retires' to a retirement community where all residents pay a fixed admission fee which, for simplicity, we take to be zero. There is no pollution in the retirement community. During this second period, our 'retiree' consumes z^t.[6]

During the first period, he receives disutility from environmental degradation in the community as measured by the *stock* of pollutants x^t. While the stock of pollution enters consumers' utility functions, the *flow* of emissions c^t into the stock enters firms' production functions. This treatment is consistent, for example, with the hazardous waste problem. Consumers are harmed by the stock of hazardous wastes in their community. Firms, on the other hand, gain from being able to dispose of their emissions (i.e. from the flow into the stock).[7] We assume that the stock decays at the rate δ; therefore, stock and flow are related by the perpetual inventory equation

$$(10) \quad x^t = e^t + (1-\delta)x^{t-1}.$$

The market solution
Moving to an intertemporal framework requires us to make two changes in the consumer's budget constraint. First, we need to consider carefully the price people pay for the right to live in a community. This we can think of somewhat loosely as the price of property. The price a member of generation t pays to live in a particular community, namely $T(x^{t-1})$, is a function of the quality of its environment. Similarly, the price at which he can sell that right, $T(x^t)$, depends on the quality of the environment that remains for residents of the community in the next period. Changes in x^t, and therefore changes in $T(x^t)$, are controlled by current residents who must therefore take into account the impact of environmental policy on property values.

Second, we need to incorporate savings in the model. Suppose a consumer can spend c^{t+1} dollars in the second period of his life for each dollar he saves during the first period.[8] Then the analog to the problem we considered in the second section of the paper can be written[9]

$$(11) \quad \max \ u(y^t, z^t, Lx^t)$$

subject to

$$(12) \quad m^t + [f^t - k^t f_k^t - e^t f_e^t] + \tau^t e^t - c^t T(x^{t-1}) - y^t$$

$$+ T(x^t) - (z^t / c^{t+1})$$

$$= 0$$

$$f_k^t - c^t = 0$$

$$f_e^t - \tau^t = 0$$

and the constraint which defines the stock of pollutants next period in (10).[10] The solution to this problem requires

(13a) $u_y^t / u_z^t = c^{t+1}$

(13b) $-L(u_x^t / u_y^t) = f_e^t + T_x$

where T_x is the derivative of the sales price with respect to the stock of the pollutants in the community in the next period. The right side of (13b) tells us that the community's cost of improving the environment equals foregone income from the emissions tax less the increase in property values.

In the Appendix, we show that

(14) $T_x = -(1-\delta)(f_e^{t+1}) / c^{t+1}$

which has the following interpretation. If current residents increase emissions by one unit, then the stock of pollutants will be $(1 - \delta)$ units higher next period. Residents next period would have to reduce emissions by that amount in order to restore the environment to its original quality, and would therefore lose $(1-\delta)f_e^{t+1}$ in income as a result. The price they pay for the right to live in this community must fall by that amount if they are to remain willing to live in this community.

We can therefore write the utility maximizing condition for the community as

(13b') $-L(u_x^t / u_y^t) = f_e^t - [(1-\delta)(f_e^{t+1} / c^{t+1})]$.

Efficiency in the overlapping-generations model
In the Appendix, we show that efficiency requires that

(15a) $u_y^{i,t} / u_z^{i,t} = f_k^{t+1}$ $i = 1, ..., N$

(15b) $-L(u_x^{i,t} / u_y^{i,t}) =$

          $f_e^{i,t} - (1-\delta)(f_e^{i,t+1} / f_k^{t+1})$ $i = 1, ..., N$

(15c) $f_k^{i,t} = f_k^{j,t} = f_k^t$ $i, j = 1, ..., N$

where the superscripts i and j refer to communities. Equation (15c) tells us that the aggregate stock of capital should be distributed across communities so that the marginal product of capital is everywhere identical; the same result emerged in our static model. Equation (15a) says that the marginal rate of substitution between current and future consumption should always equal the marginal product of capital.

Equation (15b) characterizes optimal environmental policy. Two comments are in order. First, the rule for optimal policy in our static model can be seen as a special case of (15b). If pollution dissipates entirely within one period, so that all damages from pollution are borne at the time it is emitted, then δ equals 1. But if δ

is 1, then (15b) states that the marginal product of pollution in the current period should equal current period residents' marginal rate of substitution between pollution and consumption, which is the conclusion we reached in our static model.

Second, we can offer the following interpretation of (15b). Suppose we were to consider allowing firms in a community to emit one more unit of pollution. If the extra output they could produce as a result, $f_e^{i,t}$, were sufficient to compensate current and future generations, then efficiency would require us to follow this policy. The required compensation for current period residents equals their aggregate willingness to pay, $L^i(u_x^{i,t} / u_y^{i,t})$.

Now consider compensation for future residents. As a result of the additional pollution at time t, the stock of pollutants at time t+1 is greater by $(1 - \delta)$ units. We could compensate future residents by simultaneously reducing emissions at time t+1 by enough to restore the environment to its original condition and increasing the capital stock by an amount which would leave production unchanged. The required increase in capital would equal the product of the reduction in emissions and the marginal rate of technical substitution between capital and emissions, $(1-\delta)(f_e^{i,t+1} / f_k^{t+1})$. The rule for efficiency in (15b) thus tells us to continue to emit pollution until the consequent increases in output just equal the required compensation (i.e. until marginal abatement cost equals marginal social damage).

It is not difficult to see that the market outcome in this model is efficient. As we have argued, firms will hire capital until its marginal product equals its price; therefore f_k^t equals c^t and f_k^{t+1} equals c^{t+1}. The utility maximizing conditions in (13a) and (13b') are therefore equivalent to the efficiency conditions in (15a) and (15b). Thus a decentralized system of local emissions taxes leads to an efficient outcome in our model, even if the damages from pollution are long-lived.

IV.   Some concluding remarks

The analysis in this paper makes the case for 'environmental federalism' in which the determination of environmental standards is undertaken in a decentralized setting. So long as the effects of the pollutants under consideration are confined within the borders of the relevant jurisdictions, we have found that there exist incentives for 'local' authorities to make socially optimal decisions on levels of environmental quality.[11] This is important, for there is some emerging empirical work in environmental economics suggesting that optimal pollution levels often vary widely among jurisdictions and that the enforcement of uniform national standards may impose heavy losses in welfare as compared to the optimal decentralized set of standards. If local decision-making on environmental matters does not diverge too far from optimal outcomes, then the case for environmental federalism is a forceful one.

We found, moreover, that our results apply both to single- and overlapping-generation models. The capitalization of any changes in the values of local amenities into local property values provides a powerful incentive for current residents of a jurisdiction to take into account the effects of their decisions on future residents. The disciplinary force provided by such capitalization is absent at the national level, for its source is the mobility of individuals across jurisdictions. It is thus quite possible that decentralized decision-making on certain environmental issues provides more protection for the interests of future generations than does a more centralized system. From both static and overlapping-generations perspectives, environmental federalism offers some important advantages relative to a wholly centralized form of environmental policy.

These results apply only in a setting in which jurisdictions are sufficiently large to encompass all (or nearly all) the effects of the polluting activities within their boundaries. Our use of the term 'local' must be understood in this sense. Where pollution from one region of the country has important effects elsewhere, there is clearly an important regulatory role for the central government. But where it is possible to assign regulatory authority to a decentralized level of government that can internalize the relevant effects, the analysis suggests that there is a strong case for doing so. Competition among jurisdictions for economic activity need not be 'destructive'. As the analysis suggests, such competition (much like its role in the private sector) can encourage efficient decisions in the local public sector.

Appendix

The first objective of this Appendix is to derive equation (14) in the text. Define $V(x^t, T(x^t))$ as the maximum utility a resident of a community at time $t+1$ can realize, given that he inherits a stock of pollutants x^t and must pay $T(x^t)$ for the right to live in the community. Therefore

$$(1A) \quad V(x^t, T(x^t)) = \max \; u(y^{t+1}, z^{t+1}, Lx^{t+1})$$

s.t.

$$m^{t+1} + [f^{t+1} - k^{t+1}f_k^{t+1} -$$

$$e^{t+1}f_e^{t+1}] + \tau^{t+1}e^{t+1} - c^{t+1}T(x^t) -$$

$$y^{t+1} + T(x^{t+1}) - (z^{t+1}/c^{t+2})$$

$$= 0$$

$$f_k^{t+1} - c^{t+1} = 0$$

$$f_e^{t+1} - \tau^{t+1} = 0$$

$$x^{t+1} = e^{t+1} + (1-\delta)x^t.$$

The envelope theorem states that the derivative of an indirect objective function with respect to a parameter equals the derivative of the associated Lagrangian evaluated at the optimal quantities. Therefore

$$(2A) \quad V_x = -(1-\delta)\lambda_4$$

(3A) $V_T T_x = -\lambda_1 T_x c^{t+1}$

where λ_4 and λ_1 are the Lagrange multipliers associated with the perpetual inventory equation and the budget constraint.

If consumers are mobile, then in equilibrium they must be able to realize the same level of utility in all communities. This implies that if generation t residents change x^t, then $T(x^t)$ must adjust so that $V(x^t, T(x^t))$ remains unchanged. In light of (2A) and (3A), this implies that

(4A) $c^{t+1} T_x = -(V_x / V_T)$

$$= -(1-\delta)(\lambda_4 / \lambda_1).$$

The first order conditions for generation t+1 require that (λ_4 / λ_1) equals the Pigouvian tax, and therefore the marginal product of emissions, at time t+1. Equation (14) in the text follows directly.

The second purpose of the Appendix is to state the intertemporal efficiency problem for society more formally. We can frame the efficiency problem as one of maximizing the welfare of the residents of community 1 at time 1, subject to constraints on production, on the welfare of residents of other communities, and on the welfare of future generations. Production at time t uses the capital stock at time t, labor, and emissions to produce a homogeneous good. Aggregate production of this homogeneous good is then divided between (i) second period consumption by people born at time $t-1$, (ii) first period consumption by people born at time t, and (iii) the capital stock at time t+1. Let s^i equal community i's share of the total labor force and let t' be society's planning horizon. Then the aggregate consumption constraint for this society requires

(5A) $\sum s^i [f^i(k^{i,t}, x^{i,t}) - z^{i,t-1} - y^{i,t} - k^{i,t+1}]$

$$= 0 \qquad t = 1, \dots t'.$$

This specification of technology implicitly assumes that it is always possible to consume part of society's capital stock.

We can then state the efficiency problem as

(6A) $\max u(y^{1,1}, z^{1,1}, L^1 x^{1,1})$

s.t.

$u(y^{i,1}, z^{i,1}, L^i x^{i,1})$

$= u(y^{1,1}, z^{1,1}, L^1 x^{1,1}) \quad i = 2, \dots N$

$u(y^{i,t}, z^{i,t}, L^i x^{i,t}) = \bar{u}^t \quad i = 2, \dots N \quad t = 2, \dots t'$

$$k^l = \sum k^{i,l}$$

$$x^t = e^t + (1-\delta)x^{t-l} \quad t = 1, \ldots t'$$

and the aggregate production constraint in (5A) for a given initial aggregate stock of capital k^l, $z^{0,i}$ and $x^{0,i}$. Note that (6A) requires that all consumers in a given generation reach the same level of utility regardless of their community. We impose this restriction so that we can compare market and efficient outcomes; if people are perfectly mobile, then migration will lead to equal utility for identical people in different communities.

Notes

*   Department of Economics and Bureau of Business and Economic Research, University of Maryland and Department of Economics, University of Maryland. Schwab was a Gilbert White Fellow at Resources for the Future during the writing of the first draft of this paper, and Oates is a University Fellow there. We thank Ralph Braid for first raising the issue of local Pigouvian taxes with us and Paul Portney and David Wildasin for some helpful comments on an earlier draft. We are grateful to the National Science Foundation and Resources for the Future for their support of this research.

1.   This condition is the analog in regulatory federalism to a 'perfect correspondence' [Oates (1972)] and the 'principle of fiscal equivalence' [Olson (1969)] in the fiscal federalism literature.

2.   In order to simplify the notation, we will not index the variables and functions by jurisdiction, although it is to be understood that we are examining one of the N jurisdictions and that the functions are jurisdiction-specific.

3.   In Oates and Schwab (1988), communities choose a tax on capital. We show there that it is optimal for each community to set a tax rate of zero. We therefore restrict our attention in this paper to the emissions tax. Local authorities, incidentally, could just as well set the efficient quantity of emissions directly and allow market forces to allocate these emissions (through a system of transferable permits) among polluters. We assume further that local governments provide efficient quantities of local public goods which they finance by imposing lump-sum taxes on citizens.

4.   We shall develop more carefully the role and properties of T in the next section where we consider the many period case. As David Wildasin has pointed out to us, we can take T to represent land rents without any essential changes to the results. For now we simply assume that the revenues from these 'fees' go into a general economy-wide fund and are returned as exogenous income to the individuals in the system. Any individual's level of exogenous income [m in equation (5)] is taken to be independent of his or her admission fee.

5.   Efficiency also requires that society's capital stock be distributed among the communities so that the marginal product of capital is the same everywhere; if this were not true, then it would be possible to move capital from a community where its marginal product was low to one where it was high and thus increase society's aggregate output. This second efficiency condition will be satisfied since the return to capital must be the same in all communities given the perfect mobility of capital.

6.   Here again, even though we have not indexed variables by community, it is to be understood that we are looking at consumers who live in a particular jurisdiction. Note that the superscript t does not refer to time period t but to an individual born at t.

7.   Our formulation of the problem is similar to that in Plourde (1972) and Forster (1973).

8.   We can think of c^{t+1} as 1 plus the interest rate next period.

9.   We have incorporated the following assumptions about the timing of income and expenditures in this model. Consumers pay for housing at the beginning of the first period of their lives. At the end of that period, they pay for first period consumption of the composite good and receive their wage income, non-labor income, proceeds from the Pigouvian tax, and the proceeds from the sale of their home. They pay for second period consumption of the composite good at the end of the second period.

10. m^t may be thought of as the present discounted value of exogenous income over both periods of the individual's life. We have not explicitly incorporated any bequests in the model, but these could be treated as part of z^t.

11. We have obtained this result in a model in which the populations of jurisdictions are homogeneous. Where there are groups in a single jurisdiction with conflicting interests or where the local authority pursues its own objectives (e.g. revenue-maximization), then (not surprisingly) outcomes will, in general, no longer be optimal. For a more extended treatment of this matter, see Oates and Schwab (1988).

References

Cumberland, John H. (1979) 'Interregional Pollution Spillovers and Consistency of Environmental Policy' in H. Siebert et al. (eds), *Regional Environmental Policy: The Economic Issues* (New York: New York University Press), 255–81.

Cumberland, John H. (1981) 'Efficiency and Equity in Interregional Environmental Management', *Review of Regional Studies* 2, 1–9.

Forster, B.A. (1973) 'Optimal Capital Accumulation in a Polluted Environment', *Southern Economic Journal* 39, 544–7.

Oates, Wallace E. (1972) *Fiscal Federalism* (New York: Harcourt Brace Jovanovich, Inc.).

Oates, Wallace E. and Robert M. Schwab (1988) 'Economic Competition Among Jurisdictions: Efficiency Enhancing or Distortion Inducing?', *Journal of Public Economics* 35, 333–54.

Olson, Mancur (1969) 'The Principle of "Fiscal Equivalence": The Division of Responsibilities Among Different Levels of Government', *American Economic Review* 59, 479–87.

Peltzman, Sam and Nicholaus Tideman (1972) 'Local versus National Pollution Control: Note', *American Economic Review* 62, 959–63.

Plourde, C.G. (1972) 'A Model of Waste Accumulation and Disposal', *Canadian Journal of Economics* 5, 119–25.

The Management of the Chesapeake Bay: Alternative Structures for Decision-Making

Dennis C. Mueller and Wallace E. Oates

Both theoretical analysis and historical experience suggest that the management of resources whose geography cuts across existing jurisdictional boundaries poses particularly difficult problems. In such instances, the record typically indicates considerable rhetoric among the interested parties, but often reveals very little in the way of effective measures to remedy the basic ills. Perhaps the most dramatic case in the recent news involves the problem of acid rain. In spite of the documentation and publicity given to the damaging airborne flows of sulfur and nitrous oxides across national boundaries in Europe and North America, not much of a truly substantive nature has yet been accomplished to regulate these flows. Other examples come quickly to mind, including the polluting in one jurisdiction of stretches of river just before they flow into another and the disposal of toxic wastes. In short, it has proven very hard for decision-makers in different jurisdictions to combine forces in effective ways to protect environmental quality.

From a public-choice perspective, this experience is, at least under certain circumstances, not very surprising. To take a particularly simple case (but one that makes the point clearly), consider an instance of 'unidirectional' pollution between jurisdictions – acid rain deposition in which the polluting emissions from tall stacks in one area lead to serious accumulations of pollutants in distant locations falling within a different political jurisdiction. In terms of standard microeconomics, this represents a familiar case of an externality in which the polluting activities of one group of agents impose external costs on others. The textbook solution to this problem is the imposition of a Pigouvian tax on the sources of the emissions. While the logic of the analysis may be impeccable, a public-choice approach suggests immediately that such a corrective measure will not be politically acceptable in an interjurisdictional setting. The polluting jurisdiction, in our case of unidirectional pollution, can only lose from such a policy decision; this jurisdiction is being asked to bear the full costs of pollution control while the benefits from these abatement activities accrue to the other (or 'downstream') jurisdiction. Such a measure can hardly command mutual agreement in the political arena.

Yet, as the literature has made clear (Coase, 1960), the resulting distortions in activity levels from such externalities create the opportunity for mutual gains from trade among the concerned parties. There exists, in short, a real incentive for the polluters and their victims to get together and work out some mutually beneficial reduction in levels of emissions. Often, however, this doesn't seem to happen. We will have more to say about this later, but one basic point can be made here.

332

Voluntary agreements among economic agents must typically promise gains to the various parties. As we have just seen in our unidirectional model, there are no direct gains to the polluting jurisdiction from abatement activities. It follows that if mutually advantageous bargains are to be struck, the victims must effectively bribe the sources to reduce their levels of polluting activities.

The trouble with this approach is that it entails an implicit assignment of property rights to polluters which is often unacceptable. Victims (with a certain moral justification) generally seem unwilling to buy off their tormentors. Their response, instead, is to appeal to a standard of social justice that would require the sources of the pollution to mend their ways by undertaking the requisite control measures. Put in these terms, it is not hard to understand why trans-jurisdictional pollution has generated heated debate but why real problems often remain unresolved.

The Chesapeake Bay, while representing a case that is considerably more complex than our instance of unidirectional pollution, nevertheless is subject to these same obstacles to the formulation and introduction of effective policy measures. The management of the Chesapeake Bay presents some difficult and complicated issues in collective decision-making. From one perspective, the Bay and its resources constitute a public good that is shared by the members of several different political jurisdictions. At the same time, there are activities taking place in these (and other) jurisdictions that impinge on the quality of the services provided by the Bay. These activities generate wastes that pollute the Bay and degrade the services that it provides to its users. This raises the important question of how we can best integrate the interests of the different parties to the Bay in terms of decision-making institutions that can effectively control those activities that pollute the Bay and regulate the use of the recreational and other services that the Bay's resources provide to consumers. There are presently some eight interstate institutions that bear responsibility for activities influencing the resources and quality of the Chesapeake Bay.[1] It is a complicated institutional network with overlapping memberships and responsibility for coordinating interstate action on a wide range of management issues.

Our purpose in this paper is not to review in detail this existing structure of collective decision-making. Rather, we wish to step back and consider in a somewhat more general way the issues posed in making collective decisions in a setting like that of the Chesapeake Bay. In particular, we shall set forth a conceptual framework involving the joint use of a public good in which participants relate to the good in quite different ways. Some jurisdictions are both users and polluters of the public good (as, for example, are Maryland and Virginia with respect to the Bay); others do not make direct use of the services of the Bay but do engage in activities that degrade the public good (as does Pennsylvania through wastes emitted into the Susquehanna River Basin).

In the context of this model, we shall explore the issue of what might be called the 'optimal jurisdiction' for the management of the Bay. We consider three 'pure' alternatives. The first simply takes the existing structure of jurisdictions as given and relies on Coasian types of agreements among the interested parties to produce a set of agencies and decisions for the regulation of the Bay. The second alternative is a more radical one: the formation of a new polity – a Chesapeake Bay political jurisdiction – to manage the Bay. We devote much of our analysis to the second alternative. We recognize that the introduction of a new polity is, politically, the least feasible of the three alternatives. But it is the most intriguing and perhaps the most promising in terms of its potential for effectively coming to grips with the real issues. Moreover, it is the least familiar of the various approaches. For these reasons, we take this opportunity to explore a number of facets of such a new polity. For one, it provides an opportunity to investigate a new proposal for collective decision-making – a voting rule recently proposed by Hylland and Zeckhauser (1979) that possesses some appealing properties. While we are not seriously proposing this approach as viable, we would suggest that the material in the section on a new Chesapeake polity represents a fresh perspective on the Bay that, at least at a conceptual level, deserves a hearing. The third alternative invokes a larger jurisdiction, namely the nation with the federal government, which can 'internalize' all the benefits and costs of decisions affecting the Chesapeake Bay. This third approach, however, loses the focus on 'local' activities that characterizes the other alternatives.

1. The analytical framework

The model that we present in this section is a fairly general representation of the use of a public good. But as we shall try to make clear, we were guided in its construction by the characteristics of the Bay management problem. We have thus tried to capture in the model what we see as some of the important features of the Bay and its use.

We begin by distinguishing between two classes of jurisdictions that relate to the public good in quite different ways. We shall simplify matters in this regard by treating a 'representative citizen' for each of the jurisdictions under consideration. We describe the utility function for a representative individual from the first class of jurisdictions as follows:

$$(1) \quad U_i\{Y_i[Q(\textstyle\sum X), X_i], Q(\textstyle\sum X)\} \qquad\qquad i = 1,\dots,k,$$

where the subscripts refer to jurisdictions. We use Y_i to denote the private income (spent on a numeraire good) of the representative person from jurisdiction i, where that income depends positively on Q, the level (or quality) of the collective good, and on X_i, the level of 'waste emissions' in jurisdiction i. Increased waste emissions by a producer make a direct contribution to his level of output, since it is less expensive to discharge wastes into the environment than to undertake costly abatement activities; thus, $\partial Y_i / \partial X_i$ in (1) is positive.[2] However, in the aggregate, waste emissions serve to degrade or reduce the level of Q; this is indicated in equation (1) by the dependence of Q on the total level of waste emissions across all jurisdictions. Higher levels of X thus result in lower levels of Q, which reduces output and private income. The level of Q also enters in its own right as the second argument in the utility function, where the partial derivative U_Q is assumed to be positive; this indicates the enhancement of consumption activities resulting from improved environmental quality. Thinking in terms of the Bay, what we have in mind in equation (1) is a representative citizen of, say, Maryland or Virginia whose level of private income depends, for example, on the quality of commercial fishing in the Bay, but whose agricultural pursuits generate runoff that reduces the ability of the Bay to support fish life. In addition, such an individual derives utility directly from the Bay in terms of various recreational uses such as swimming and boating.

The second class of jurisdiction involves those whose citizens do not make direct use of the public good, but whose activities reduce the services it provides. For a representative citizen from this class of jurisdiction, we can simply write a utility function of the form

(2) $U_j[Y_j(X_j)]$ $\hspace{6cm}$ $j = k + 1,...,m.$

In this instance, the individual derives no gain in either private income or consumption from an increased output of the public good. His activities, however, do impinge unfavorably on Q. What we have in mind here is the case of a jurisdiction like Pennsylvania which does not directly border on the Bay, but whose waste emissions into the Susquehanna River Basin find their way into the Bay, with detrimental effects on water quality.

The choice variables in this model are the levels of polluting activities, the X_i, in each of the m jurisdictions. To determine the socially efficient levels of emissions, we form the Lagrangian:

(3) $L = U_1\{Y_1[Q(\sum X), X_1], Q(\sum X)\}$

$\hspace{1cm} + \sum \lambda_i (U_i\{Y_i[Q(\sum X), X_i], Q(\sum X)\} - U_i^0)$

$\hspace{1cm} + \sum \lambda_j \{U_j[Y_j(X_j)] - U_j^0\}.$

Maximizing the utility of the representative citizen from jurisdiction 1, while holding constant the levels of utility of the other representative citizens, give us the first-order conditions for an efficient pattern of waste emissions. The conditions are notationally cumbersome but quite straightforward in interpretation. We can summarize them as follows:

(4) $G_i - \sum C_j = 0,$ $\hspace{4cm}$ $i = 1,...,m$ and $j = 1,...,k$ with $i \neq j.$

G_i here indicates the marginal private gain to representative citizen i from another unit of waste emissions, while $\sum C_j$ are the external costs that marginal emissions impose on other users of the public good. For individuals from the first class of jurisdictions, G_i is composed of three terms that reflect the increase in private income attributable to the emissions minus the loss in income to i from the deterioration in the public good and the loss in consumption from this deterioration. Thus, G_i denotes the net private benefits to representative individual i. The external costs are those associated with reduced private income from production and the reduced consumption of other users of the public good. For individuals from the second class of jurisdictions, there are fewer terms, since they are not users of the public good. For these representative persons, G_i is simply the increment to private income afforded by another unit of waste discharges.

Seen in this way, the problem of the efficient management of the public good is basically a standard case of an externality. Individuals in the various jurisdictions need the proper incentive to take into account the costs that their 'waste emissions' impose on others. The standard response to such a problem in the economics literature is to recommend the adoption of a Pigouvian tax on waste emissions so as to internalize the social costs. In terms of equation (4), we must confront each actor with a levy on his waste emissions equal to ΣC_j. There is, however, a serious problem with this policy prescription in our setting. In particular, we are dealing with a set of jurisdictions, each of which must presumably agree to a program for the regulation of waste emissions. But as noted earlier, a program of Pigouvian fees imposes costs but offers no benefits to jurisdictions of the second class. Since they are not users of the public good, they have no reason to shoulder any costs necessary to increase the level of the good. If we are looking for policy instruments that promise welfare gains to all the jurisdictions involved, we must find something other than Pigouvian fees.[3] With this in mind, we turn in the next section to an exploration at the more fundamental constitutional level of the kinds of collective institutions that offer some promise for the joint management of such a public good.

2. The Coasian solution

A classic solution to a public good-externality problem is to rely upon the self-interest of the affected parties to negotiate an agreement which leaves all better off. Coase (1960) first proposed this method for resolving externality issues. With a series of bilateral-externality examples, he demonstrated that solutions to externality problems would be reached which were both Pareto optimal and independent of the prior assignment of property rights. If the law favored the polluter, the party injured by the pollution would approach the polluter and offer payment in return for curtailing the pollution-creating activity. Pareto optimality would require that the marginal cost to the polluter from reducing the quantity of pollutants released just equals the amount of gain to the injured party from this reduction in pollution activity. If the latter is willing to make this offer to curtail pollution, the Pareto optimal level of pollution activity should be reached.

To see how the Coasian solution would work, consider first the case where there are only jurisdictions of type 1, jurisdictions which both benefit from reducing pollution through the impact of improved quality, Q, on income and utility directly, but which sacrifice income when the level of waste emissions, X_i, is curtailed. The algebra is simplified slightly if we assume that income is not affected by environmental quality. The utility function of the representative individual in the ith jurisdiction then becomes

$$(5)   U_i[Y_i(X_i), Q(\textstyle\sum X)].$$

The Pareto optimal levels of pollution for each jurisdiction can be found by maximizing the utility level for the representative person in one jurisdiction, while holding those of all other jurisdictions constant:

(6) $\quad \text{Max } L = U_1[Y_1(X_1), Q(\sum X)] + \sum_{j=2}^{k} \lambda_j \{U_j[Y_j(X_j), Q(\sum X)] - \overline{U}_j\}$

where the $\overline{U}_j$s are constants. Maximizing (6) with respect to the individual levels of pollution, X_i, yields the following optimality condition:

(7) $\quad \sum_{i=1}^{k} \frac{\partial U_i / \partial Q}{(\partial U_i / \partial Y_i) \cdot Y_i'} = \frac{-1}{Q'}.$

This is a form of the familiar Samuelson-Buchanan-Stubblebine condition for Pareto optimality in the presence of a public good-externality. The sum of the marginal rates of substitution of environmental quality for income (where the marginal utility of income is weighted by the marginal rate of transformation of pollutant into income, $Y_i' > 0$) equals the marginal cost of environmental quality. In contrast, if each jurisdiction chooses an optimal level of waste emissions, ignoring the interdependence of their activities, each simply equates its marginal rate of substitution to the marginal rate of transformation:

(8) $\quad \frac{\partial U_i / \partial Q}{\partial U_i / \partial Y_i} = -\frac{Y_i'}{Q'}, \quad i = 1, \dots, k.$

The set of equations (8) will result in excessive levels of waste emissions relative to the Pareto optimal levels implied by (7). In effect, we have a Prisoners' dilemma for the k jurisdictions in which each community can be made better off if an agreement is reached for each to reduce its waste emissions, X_i, in exchange for the other $k - 1$ communities also curtailing their discharges in accordance with the levels dictated by (7). The Coase theorem presumes that such mutually beneficial trades are reached wherever they exist.

Setting aside the transaction costs of reaching agreement, it is reasonable to assume that agreements satisfying (7) could be reached among communities of type 1. Although each suffers some loss of income by curtailing X, each gains from the increased environmental quality ensuing from the reduction in aggregate waste discharges. Thus, each has an incentive to cooperate through abatement efforts: all are made better off by the collectively imposed costs of reducing waste emissions.

But consider now the problem when one jurisdiction of type 2 exists whose income rises with the level of waste emissions, but where individual utility is not affected by the level of environmental quality. For a community of type 2, $\partial U / \partial Q$ is zero for all levels of Q, and thus there is no gain to this jurisdiction from curtailing waste emissions. Its optimal level of emissions occurs when either $\partial Y / \partial X_i$ or $\partial U / \partial Y$ equals zero. To induce a jurisdiction of type 2 to reduce its level of emissions, the jurisdictions of type 1 must offer it a bribe. An optimal outcome requires that each jurisdiction of type 2 reduce its waste discharges to the point at which marginal abatement cost equals the sum of the benefits to the type 1 jurisdictions. The optimal bribe (at the margin) will thus be:

(9) $\sum_{i=1}^{k} \dfrac{-\partial U_i \, / \, \partial Q}{\partial U_i \, / \, \partial Y_i} \cdot Q'.$

Jurisdictions of type 2 will increase their abatement efforts so long as their marginal abatement cost is less than (9).

Thus, the Coasian solution to the Chesapeake Bay pollution problem can be thought of as arising from a two-step negotiation process. First, the benefiting jurisdictions, Maryland and Virginia, agree to curtail their levels of waste emission. Second, they agree to offer a bribe to Pennsylvania if it will do likewise.

3.   Reducing Coasian transaction costs: A new polity

We have proceeded thus far as if there were but three parties concerned with the Chesapeake: Maryland, Virginia and Pennsylvania. Bilateral and even trilateral negotiations are sufficiently straightforward to give one reason to hope that the parties in question might be capable of reaching an agreement where all could hope to benefit. However, we have vastly simplified matters. There are, as we know, other states involved as well as the District of Columbia. But even more basic, the various states are themselves composed of differing jurisdictions of types 1 and 2, representing interests which stand to gain in varying degrees from the control of waste emissions. To rely entirely on Coasian agreements to resolve the Chesapeake Bay pollution problem would require at least three sets of negotiations: one within each state, a second between the states benefiting from quality improvements, and a third between the beneficiaries of improved quality and those who benefit entirely from emitting wastes at no charge. A moment's reflection indicates that this additional layer of Coasian negotiation significantly raises the transactions costs of achieving a Pareto optimal solution. Within the states of Virginia and Maryland, the beneficiaries from improved water quality differ greatly. Those residing in the western parts of each state benefit much less than those residing near the Chesapeake. Similarly, residents of Western Pennsylvania contribute little to the pollution of the Chesapeake. Thus, within each state a non-trivial Coasian negotiation problem would have to be addressed before one could begin to rely on a Coasian agreement among the states and the District to resolve the issues surrounding the quality of the Chesapeake Bay.

As the number of participants increases, the transaction costs of relying upon bilateral agreements to achieve Pareto optimality rise exponentially. There is thus a need to find some alternative characterized by lower transaction costs to achieve Pareto optimality in the presence of externalities. The polity is one such transaction costs saving institution (Dahlman, 1979). In terms of the Chesapeake, one might consider forming a special polity – a new and autonomous governmental unit – for dealing with problems of the Bay.[4]

The formation of a new polity involves two basic issues: the geographical delineation of the new jurisdiction and the establishment of a set of constitutional rules that specifies how decisions are to be made. A cursory inspection suggests that the first of these issues is not simple since existing state boundaries do not correspond very exactly with the constituency directly concerned with the quality of the Chesapeake Bay. For example, residents of the western sections of Maryland

and Virginia generally have little interest in the Bay and its resources. This suggests that a new polity formed by merging certain states is likely to deviate significantly from the 'optimal' jurisdiction. It might make more sense to define the Chesapeake polity along the boundaries of existing counties. The polity would then consist of those counties that border on the Bay. We touch upon this point again below.

The second issue involves the classic problem in public choice of the selection of a voting rule (Buchanan and Tullock, 1962). Majority rule is an attractive choice only when one can reasonably assume that constituents have more or less equal intensities of preferences on the various issues to be resolved (Buchanan and Tullock, 1962, ch. 9; Rae, 1969). Such an assumption, however, seems inappropriate with respect to the Bay, for individuals and their activities relate to the Bay in very different ways. A community characterized by widespread fishing activity will have quite different preferences regarding the Bay than a nearby farming community. A voting rule which allows for differing intensities across voters seems in order.

Several new voting procedures have appeared in recent years, some of which take into account differing intensities of preferences across voters. The most famous among them is the class of demand-revealing processes developed by Clarke (1971) and Groves and Ledyard (1977); see also Tideman and Tullock (1976). There is, however, an alternative and simpler procedure proposed by Hylland and Zeckhauser (1979) that we wish to explore here.

In terms of applying the Hylland-Zeckhauser procedure, one can think of an m-dimensional issue set, with each dimension d referring to an activity that impinges on the Bay – a quantity of waste to be emitted into the Bay or a level of fish to be taken out. The issues which a Bay-area polity would need to resolve are then the levels of the m activities making up the issue set. The procedure is iterative. The voters are first presented with a status-quo vector of activity levels

$$(X_1^0, X_2^0, \ldots, X_d^0, \ldots, X_m^0).$$

Each voter is given a stock of vote points, A_i, to be allocated across the m activity levels. A voter wishing an increase in activity d allocates a positive number of points to d; a voter wishing a contraction assigns negative points. Each voter's assignment of points satisfies the budget constraint

$$(10) \quad A_i = \sum_{d=1}^{m} |a_{id}|.$$

A new vector of activity levels is determined by the following rule

$$(11) \quad X_d' = X_d^0 + \sum_i b_{id}$$

where $b_{id} = f(a_{id})$, and b_{id} and a_{id} have the same sign. Voters are then given the new vector of activity levels $(X_1', X_2', \ldots, X_d', \ldots, X_m')$ and asked to make a new assignment of vote-points. The procedure is continued until, for some round z, $\Sigma b_{id} = 0$ for all d. Hylland and Zeckhauser make a plausible argument suggesting that the procedure does in fact converge. In addition, they show that the function required to induce an optimal allocation of vote-points is simply the square root formula; under this formula, the 'diminishing productivity' of vote-points on a particular issue leads each voter to allocate his points in a manner that equates the marginal value of a vote across all activities. Thus, $f(a_{id}) = \sqrt{|a_{id}|}$ with sign of a_{id}, where the stocks of vote-points are chosen to ensure that

$$(12) \quad 2\mu_i = 1/\lambda_i.$$

Here λ_i is the weight given to the ith voter in the social welfare function

$$(13) \quad W = \sum_i \lambda_i U_i$$

and μ_i is the marginal utility of a vote-point. If all voters receive equal weights in the social welfare function – that is, if $\lambda_i = \lambda$ for all i – then satisfying (12) requires providing those voters who feel more intensely about the issues with a larger stock of vote-points.

As Hylland and Zeckhauser show, this decision rule possesses some important and appealing properties. First, the incentives under this procedure are such as to induce a truthful revelation of preferences. And, second, if marginal tax shares correspond (approximately) to marginal benefit shares, then the outcome of the process is (approximately) Pareto optimal. The Hylland-Zeckhauser procedure could, in principle, be used to reveal preferences for the various issues that arise with respect to the Bay. If one were to take the county as the basic unit of analysis, then a polity could be made up with, say, one representative from each county in the polity. The initial constitution would assign stocks of vote-points to each representative based on his jurisdiction's proximity to the Bay and perhaps other criteria related to intensity of preferences. Thus, all interested parties could participate in the polity to determine Bay management, but influence on collective decisions would vary with degree of interest in the Bay's environment.

The Hylland and Zeckhauser point-voting scheme, like the demand revelation process, is a procedure for revealing preferences for public goods. It is effective only where the public good in question benefits all participants. Thus, one could envisage forming a new polity to manage the Bay with respect only to those counties that are likely to be net beneficiaries of improved Bay quality. Only such net beneficiaries would be willing to join a new polity to improve Bay quality by restricting waste emissions and perhaps other activities like fishing. Were such a polity formed, it would only eliminate the Coasian negotiations among potential gainers from Bay management programs. Counties in Pennsylvania, for example, would have nothing to gain by joining such a polity, since many outcomes would involve reductions in the incomes of Pennsylvania residents, with no offsetting gains from water quality improvement. The new Chesapeake Bay polity would still have to negotiate with Pennsylvania à la Coase and induce Pennsylvanians to reduce their levels of emissions into the Susquehanna River Basin which feeds into the Bay.

4. The centralized solution: Federal intervention

Maryland, Virginia and Pennsylvania are, of course, already members of a polity, the nation of the United States. Rather than engage in multilateral Coasian bargaining or form a new polity, the lowest transaction cost strategy for resolving Bay issues might be to make use of the existing polity to which all concerned members already belong: to enlist the assistance of the federal government.

One objection to the application of the Coase theorem to environmental problems is that existing property rights often favor polluters. Although the outcomes from Coasian bargaining may be independent of the assignment of property rights in terms of their efficiency effects, they have obvious and potentially significant differences in terms of their distributional consequences. Those injured by pollution often seem to be forced to make payments to those causing injury to achieve Pareto optimality, as in the example described where Maryland and Virginia pay Pennsylvania to reduce waste emissions. Were the auspices of the federal government used to resolve Chesapeake Bay environmental issues, the distributional implications of the Coase theorem could be obviated. While Pennsylvania can refuse to participate in, or to abide by, the outcomes emanating from a newly formed Chesapeake Bay polity, it cannot escape the dictates of the federal polity.

Despite these advantages of using the federal government to manage the Bay, there are significant disadvantages and transaction costs from resorting to this institutional solution. The Senators from Maryland, Virginia and Pennsylvania make up only six percent of the Senate, while the Representatives from the districts most affected comprise an even smaller percentage of the House. Thus, their ability to introduce and pass legislation affecting the Bay must be limited. Moreover, such legislation as they might be able to effectuate would most likely come about as part of a logrolling environmental package. The three affected states and congressional districts would thus have to 'trade away' revenue or other potential benefits from federal policies to solve Bay problems. The Senators, Congressmen and their staffs are burdened by so many issues that it is unlikely that they could spend sufficient time in drafting legislation that would deal adequately with the range of Bay problems, even if they could push through all the legislation that they wished.

A similar problem arises in relying on a federal-level regulatory solution, as through the Environmental Protection Agency. This and other federal agencies are responsible for a wide range of regulatory issues of which the problems of the Bay would be but a small set. Lacking time and resources, federal regulatory agencies are unlikely to devote sufficient attention to Bay problems to resolve them to the satisfaction of the interested parties. Nor are existing regulatory legislation and interpretations thereof by the federal regulatory agencies likely to be sufficiently 'fine tuned' to the problems of Bay management to make theirs a first-best solution.

5. Other approaches

In the preceding sections, we have explored in a fairly general way three alternative decision-making structures for the management of the Chesapeake Bay. While each has its appeal, all three are subject to serious objections. The complex interplay among the large number of parties with interests in the Bay suggests that voluntary negotiations of the sort envisioned by Coase are likely to be difficult; moreover, the potentially high transaction costs and inducements for various forms of strategic behavior are likely to bedevil Coasian attempts at effective management of the Bay. The centralized solution involving turning to the federal government has the virtue, in principle at least, of internalizing the costs associated with individual decisions. The federal 'jurisdiction' does at least encompass the entire Bay. But, as we have argued, it encompasses so much more than the Bay that federal agencies may have neither the interest nor the resources available to attend properly to its needs.

Our third alternative is the formation of a new 'polity' for management of the Chesapeake Bay. This is attractive in that it creates a jurisdiction whose boundaries encompass the area to be managed. There would, in principle, be no external effects; also the jurisdiction would not be so large for problems at hand to be lost among other issues (as might happen under the centralized approach). To create such a new polity is obviously a complicated matter. At the 'constitutional' level, there is the issue of establishing a structure integrating the various constituencies and of formulating a set of effective decision-making 'rules.' One possibility along these lines would be to elect representatives to this new polity by county. These representatives could be chosen either by a direct vote of the citizens in each county or by a vote of the existing 'legislature' (or representative body) of the county. To take into account the differing intensities of interest of each county in the various issues arising, a procedure like the voting scheme of Hylland and Zeckhauser described above could be used. Differences in the total stakes of each county regarding outcomes in the Bay would be allowed for at the constitutional level by assigning different stocks of vote-points to the representative from each county based upon that county's total stake in the outcomes. The costs of running the polity would be shared in the same proportions. Agreement on these vote-point and tax-share allocations would have to be reached prior to the formation of the polity at the constitutional stage. Since membership in the polity would be voluntary, agreement at the constitutional stage would need to be unanimous. While this requirement might seem to impose a heavy burden on those writing the constitution, if improved Bay management is indeed a public good, all those counties which stand to gain from improved management would have an incentive to join. By matching share of tax payments to voice in outcomes as measured by A_i, voluntary membership in the polity by potential beneficiaries should be possible.[5] We are uneasy about imposing on the American system yet another set of political institutions, with their bureaucracies and associated political activities. However, for a matter of such importance as the management of the Bay, such a set of institutions may well be worth their cost.

In addition to these 'pure' approaches, there are others that represent a kind of amalgam of them. Much has been made in recent times of so-called 'cooperative federalism.' Under this approach, representatives from all the interested jurisdictions join together in some kind of decision-making entity. Just this kind of approach was embodied in the Delaware River Basin Commission, created in 1961 to manage the Delaware River. The DRBC was a new 'model regional agency' endowed with broad decision-making powers. It was composed of representatives from the concerned states and the federal government, including as voting members the Governors of Delaware, New Jersey, New York and Pennsylvania as well as the Secretary of the Interior. In a fascinating interdisciplinary study, Ackerman et al. (1974) have provided a rather discouraging assessment of the Delaware experience with the DRBC. In particular, they conclude that the various members of the Commission tended to pursue their own narrow political interests and that a truly regional orientation to the Delaware and its problems never emerged. If there is any lesson in this, it would seem to be that such regional agencies are not a real substitute for the formation of an actual polity to address major issues.

Our discussion does not lead to any neat set of conclusions concerning an optimal decision-making structure for the Bay. As we noted at the outset of this paper, both analysis and historical experience indicate deep-seated problems in the management of resources that stretch across jurisdictional boundaries. There is no easy solution. Various forms of cooperative measures are probably the likely political outcome. But they may not, in the end, provide the focus of interest on the problems of the Bay that could emerge within a polity formed specifically for this purpose.

Notes

1. For a concise and useful description of these eight interstate institutions, see U.S. Environmental Protection Agency (September 1983).
2. Introducing waste emissions into the production function as a 'productive input' is a standard way of incorporating these emissions into economic models (e.g., see Baumol and Oates, 1975, ch. 4).
3. Alternatively, we might consider a system of marketable pollution permits; such a permit system possesses, in principle, the same desirable economic properties as a fee system. However, by a suitable initial distribution of the permits, it may be possible to make all parties better off.
4. We prefer to remain somewhat vague about the meaning of the term 'polity' here. There are obviously a host of very complicated constitutional and political issues surrounding the formation of a new jurisdiction of the sort we are discussing. To avoid becoming embroiled in all this, we shall simply use the term polity to refer to an autonomous political jurisdiction that is vested with responsibility for a particular range of decisions – in this instance on programs to regulate the environment and use of the Bay.
5. As Hylland and Zeckhauser point out, their voting proposal in a sense formalizes existing and more informal decision processes in which the primary beneficiaries of a particular measure typically agree to bear a relatively large share of the costs.

References

Ackerman, Bruce A. et al., *The Uncertain Search for Environmental Quality* (New York: Free Press, 1974).

Baumol, William J. and Oates, Wallace E., *The Theory of Environmental Policy* (Englewood Cliffs, New Jersey: Prentice-Hall, 1975).

Buchanan, James M. and Tullock, Gordon, *The Calculus of Consent* (Ann Arbor, Michigan: University of Michigan Press, 1962).

Clarke, Edward H., 'Multipart Pricing of Public Goods', *Public Choice* 11 (Fall 1971), pp. 17–33.

Coase, Ronald H., 'The Problem of Social Cost', *Journal of Law and Economics* 3 (October 1960), pp. 1–44.

Dahlman, Carl J., 'The Problem of Externality', *Journal of Law and Economics* 22 (April 1979), pp. 141–62.

Groves, Theodore and Ledyard, John, 'Optimal Allocation of Public Goods: A Solution to the "Free Rider" Problem', *Econometrica* 45 (May 1977), pp. 783–809.

Hylland, Aanund and Zeckhauser, Richard, 'A Mechanism for Selecting Public Goods When Preferences Must Be Elicited', Kennedy School of Government Discussion Paper 70D (August 1979).

Rae, Douglas W., 'Decision-Rules and Individual Values in Constitutional Choice', *American Political Science Review* 63 (March 1969), pp. 40–56.

Tideman, T. Nicolaus and Tullock, Gordon, 'A New and Superior Process for Making Social Choices', *Journal of Political Economy* **84** (December 1976), pp. 1145–60.

U.S. Environmental Protection Agency, *Chesapeake Bay: A Framework for Action*, Appendix G 'Existing Interstate Institutional Arrangements' (Washington, D.C.: U.S. E.P.A., September 1983).

PART VI

OPEN ECONOMY ENVIRONMENTAL ECONOMICS

347-63
[1992]

waking paper
Q20 Q28

Wallace E. Oates*

University of Maryland

Global Environmental Management: towards an Open Economy Environmental Economics

Environmental pollutants display a troublesome tendency to spill over jurisdictional boundaries. This proclivity, operating from the regional to the global scale, is making it increasingly clear that strictly nationally oriented environmental measures are inadequate to cope with the world's environmental problems. We need to develop an international perspective on environmental phenomena to address in a meaningful way some of the most threatening of the global prospects for environmental degradation.

This point is obviously not new. The Oecd, for example, has been exploring the problem of transnational pollution for over two decades. But in recent years, the concern with CFCs, and now with global warming, is pressing home in an even more urgent way the need for a global perspective on the environment. Many environmental economists are directing their efforts to extending the existing body of economic analysis of environmental problems from a domestic perspective to one that incorporates explicitly the issues arising in an international economy linked by trade, financial, and environmental flows. The movements of pollutants across national borders, either unintentionally or as the result of agreements for the disposal of wastes, as well as the impact of environmental policy decisions on trade flows, suggest that these international links must become an integral part of environmental economic analysis.

My purpose in this paper is to join this ongoing effort of the development of what might be called "open economy environmental economics". In the first section, I

* The author is also a University Fellow at Resources for the Future. He is grateful for helpful comments and assistance from Alan Krupnick, Karen Palmer and Paul Portney.

144

present a simple "model" of global environmental flows. I stress that this is not intended in any serious sense as a real theoretical exercise. It is simply a means of providing a perspective on open economy environmental economics around which I can organize the treatment of some specific issues. The model makes clear that there are potential "gains-from-trade" from international dealings in "pollution". The subsequent sections of the paper explore some of the different forms that these gains-from-trade may take. My interest here is less in providing answers to specific questions than in outlining a kind of research agenda for needed work in open economy environmental economics.

The general approach and selection of issues in this paper are founded on three "stylized facts" concerning the global environmental setting and some of the most pressing problems:

1. Several of the most troubling of the world's environmental issues (such as global warming) suggest not only potential damages of huge magnitude but imply preventive or corrective policy measures of enormous cost. William Nordhaus (1990), for example, estimates that the cost of reducing greenhouse gas emissions could easily run in excess of one per cent of world output. In our search for appropriate policy instruments, we must, therefore, place a high premium on economic efficiency. We need to identify instruments that can achieve our policy objectives both effectively and at the least cost if we are to avoid a huge waste of the world's resources.

2. The positions of different countries both with respect to their vulnerability to global "pollution" and their willingness-to-pay to avoid environmental degradation differ dramatically. While presenting opportunities for gains-from-trade in, for example, waste-disposal services, these differences in position pose major obstacles to attaining the sorts of international co-operation that will be needed for effective policies to protect the global environment.

3. The nature of many of these global problems (like global warming) is such that widespread and coordinated action across countries is essential for effective global policies. The issue of global warming is one for which it will be quite difficult for a single country or even a substantial set of countries to "go it alone". Individual efforts will be swamped in terms of any meaningful effects in the absence of truly global participation.

With these considerations in mind, I turn to a conceptual framework around which to organize the treatment of global environmental issues.

1. A Conceptual Framework

Let us assume that the world consists of two kinds of countries: relatively wealthy, industrialized (or I-) countries and poorer, developing (or D-) countries. To make the basic points, I shall assume that countries within each of the two classes are identical and will simply use a representative country from each group for purposes of the analysis.

Each country produces outputs using a production function where one of the inputs is waste emissions:

(1) $\quad Q_i = F_i(L_i, E_i) \quad i = I, D$

where Q_i is output, L_i is a vector of inputs, and E_i is the level of waste emissions. Input proportions are variable such that the same level of output can be produced with a reduced level of emissions and more of other inputs (i.e., with these additional inputs devoted to abatement activities).

In the first version of the model, I take global environmental quality to be a pure public good whose level is determined by the aggregate level of waste emissions from all countries:

(2) $\quad G = G(\Sigma E_i)$

Individual households have utility functions that contain as arguments the consumption of private goods (Q) and the level of global environmental quality (G):

(3) $\quad U_{ij} = U_{ij}(C_{ij}, G)$

where the subscripts refer to the jth person in country i.

Figure 1 depicts the key relationships. The aggregate marginal benefit curve (MB_w) is simply (*à la* Samuelson) the vertical summation of the benefit curves over the individuals in the two countries (where MB_I and MB_D are the aggregate benefit curves for the individual countries). The shape of the curves is uncertain — I shall simply give them the conventional downward slope. The global marginal abatement cost curve (MAC_w) is the horizontal summation of individual abatement cost curves. There is good evidence to suggest that this has an upward slope and a positive second derivative. The Pareto efficient level of emissions reductions in this highly simplified setting is OA where $MB_w = MAC_w$. A first-best policy response would be a global effluent charge equal to OB.

The problem is that (at least in the existing international setting) there is no global agency to introduce and enforce such a world-wide policy measure. Of course, we

Ambiente etica economia e istituzioni

Figure 1

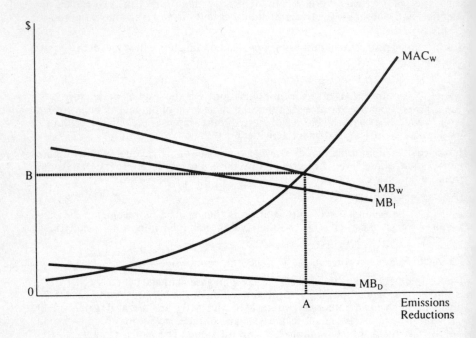

might look to some kind of an international alliance or treaty to create an agency to carry out such policies, much like the Montreal Protocol to limit production and use of chlorofluorocarbons (CFCs). The difficulty here is that certain countries

Figure 2

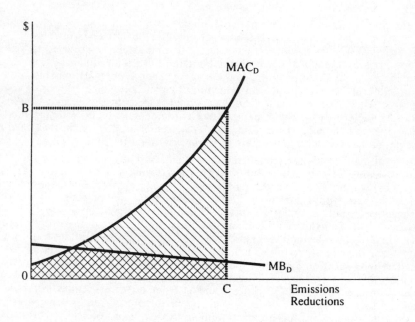

could easily be made worse off by a global measure consisting, say, of a worldwide effluent fee. Figure 2 depicts such a case where the control costs for the developing country (the area under the MAC_D curve) exceed the benefits (the area under the MB_D curve). The citizens of Country I receive substantial benefits (as measured by their willingness-to-pay) from improved environmental quality. But individuals in the poorer Country D have (by assumption) a much lower willingness-to-pay for reduced levels of pollution; for them, the problem of degradation of the global commons is a relatively unimportant one. A treaty to improve global environmental quality is likely to be a difficult undertaking in such a setting because of the sharply differing perspectives of the two countries.

In the absence of such an international alliance, we might look for some kind of non-cooperative equilibrium (perhaps of the Nash-Cournot form). As is well known, such an "independent-adjustment" outcome could be expected to yield a suboptimal level of global environmental quality. In such an equilibrium, we might anticipate the wealthier Country I to engage in a more energetic pursuit of environmental quality through the introduction of significantly higher levels of abatement activities than in Country D. This would lead us to expect that Country I (with its higher MB for any given level of environmental quality) will push its control activities to a point where $MAC_I > MAC_D$ so that the costs at the margin of reducing waste emissions will be less in Country D than in Country I.

The resulting level of environmental quality could thus be achieved at lower cost by shifting some of the abatement activity from Country I to Country D. This obviously will not happen under purely independent behavior. But there are some obvious "gains-from-trade" here. Country I, in effect, can "buy" emissions reductions more cheaply in Country D than it can at home. [It may, for example, be less expensive for the industrialized countries to increase the size of the world's forests to absorb CO_2 by paying the opportunity costs of conservation of the tropical forests in the developing countries than by planting more trees within their own borders]. There exists an incentive, therefore, for Country I to approach Country D and to offer to pay D to reduce its polluting waste emissions. There are potential gains-from-trade to both Countries I and D from such transactions in providing "environmental services". Indeed, such payments are currently being made by Sweden to Poland to reduce Polish point-source emissions of acidic substances.

The first version of our simple model envisions global environmental quality as a pure public good: G is a function solely of aggregate world emissions and enters into the utility functions of all individuals with no distinctions between these individuals or where they reside. Such a framework may be a resonable one for thinking about issues like global warming.

This appears to involve the case of "perfect mixing" in which a unit of carbon emissions from one place on the planet is a perfect substitute in terms of its effects on world climate for emissions from any other location in the world.

International pollutants need not, however, take the form of a pure public good. Source location may matter, as in the case of acid rain. Or waste emissions may be generated as a byproduct of production in one area, but be transportable to other locations for purposes of disposal with the damages to the environment being localized in the "region" of disposal. In this spirit of the latter example, we can construct a second version of our open economy model in which we distinguish between the country that generates the emissions and the country that provides for their disposal. The pollutant in this setting takes what Baumol and Oates (1988, pp. 19-21) have described as the "depletable" form. Disposal of such a pollutant in one country implies that other countries are free from its degrading effects on their environments.

In this modified model, equation (1) describing the generation of pollutants remains unchanged. But we replace equation (2) with a country-specific measure of environmental quality:

(4) $G_i = G_i(Z_i)$

where Z_i indicates the quantity of wastes that are disposed of in country i. We must also introduce an identity between the quantity of wastes generated on a global scale and the aggregate level of disposal across countries:

(5) $\Sigma E_i = \Sigma Z_i$

The utility of individuals will now depend not on a global measure of environmental quality but on the amount of the pollutant absorbed in their own country:

(6) $U_{ij} = U_{ij}(C_{ij}, G_i)$

where G_i is the level of pollution in Country i. Like the first version of the model, it is clear that the second version also presents opportunities for gains-from-trade in the pollutant. In this model of a depletable pollutant, such gains take a somewhat different form. They involve the actual transport of the pollutant from nations with a high demand for environmental quality to those with less aversion to pollution. The former will pay the latter to undertake the disposal of the pollutant.

The remaining sections of the paper explore the nature of these international environmental linkages and examine the potential gains-from-trade that they imply. On a purely descriptive level, this will provide insights into the motivation and forms of "environmental trading" between countries that we observe. In addition, it will suggest the ways in which such trading (or its absence) falls short of generating an efficient and equitable pattern of global environmental protection.

2. The International Transport and Disposal of Hazardous Pollutants

The first issue draws on the second (or depletable-pollutant) version of the model: direct trade in units of the pollutant for purposes of disposal. There is widespread concern on a global level with the substantial and growing shipment of hazardous wastes across national boundaries to their disposal destination. This concern has manifested itself in the U.N. supported Basel Convention (1989), already signed by over thirty countries. The Convention contains 29 articles that govern the international transport and disposal of hazardous wastes.

Such shipments represent an obvious case of direct gains-from-trade, typically of a bilateral form, in which the country generating the wastes pays someone else to dispose of them. It is straightforward to develop a simple model in the spirit of our version 2 to describe an efficient outcome for such a trading process. In such a model, different countries around the world would have varying reservation prices at which they would be willing to accept wastes from outside their borders for disposal. These reservation prices would presumably depend upon such things as the quantity of waste to be processed, its relative toxicity, the assimilative capacities of the environment in the respective countries, and their levels of demand for a clean environment. There would thus exist a global supply curve of disposal sites. Countries generating wastes could then determine whether it was cheaper to dispose of these wastes at home or to ship them to another country for disposal. Free trade in such a setting would encourage both the generation of efficient quantities of wastes and an efficient global pattern of disposal.

If this were all there were to the story, it would not be of much interest. Moreover, we might wonder at the level of international concern over such disposal practices. Some of the concern has its source in equity issues. A positive income elasticity of demand for environmental quality and risk reduction suggests that hazardous wastes are likely to be shipped from high income to low income countries. And one line of ethical argument suggests that the limited nature of the options for these latter countries may call into question the interpretation of their acceptance of such wastes as "consent" (MacLean, 1990).

But even apart from such ethical concerns, there are some important issues of economic efficiency here that elude the simple model. For free trade in wastes to be economically efficient, there are several important conditions that must be satisfied:

1. The transactions must take place in a setting of full information. In particular,

the supplier of disposal services must be fully informed of the contents of the waste that he is accepting and of the risks associated with these wastes.

2. The reservation price for waste disposal must incorporate the full social costs of disposal, not just the opportunity costs of the land and any other physical resources devoted to the disposal process.

3. Transport costs of the wastes must also reflect the full social costs, including any risks associated with the movement of the wastes to their point of disposal.

4. There must be no "illegal dumping" of wastes that creates substantial social costs.

The explicit recognition of the full range of conditions required for free trade in hazardous wastes to be economically efficient opens up a number of important and interesting questions. The information requirements for the assessment of risks and for the effective and safe disposal of hazardous wastes involves some basic issues of technology transfer and the associated ability of receiving nations to employ appropriate disposal techniques. The Basel Convention, for instance, requires exporters of hazardous wastes to ensure that importing countries have the facilities with which to dispose of the wastes in an environmentally sound manner. Such assurances are important, for there exist cultural and other barriers to the transfer of technology, particularly in the form of human capital, that present real obstacles to efficiency-enhancing trade in waste disposal services.

Condition (2) is also fundamental and points to some troubling possibilities. An implicit assumption in the free-trade argument is that the price structure in both the exporting and importing countries reflects accurately true social costs (a theme to which we shall return in later sections). Suppose, however, that disposal in Country A is expensive because existing environmental policies have effectively internalized the social costs of waste disposal. Sources of wastes in Country A thus face a relatively high price for disposal. In Country B, in contrast, environmental legislation is not well developed — and agents (be they private firms or government units) are free to engage in disposal activities at low cost to themselves but not to society. We would then expect to see a shipment of wastes from A to B, even though such transport of wastes may not be justified by a full accounting of the social costs. In view of the wide variation around the globe in the development of environmental regulations, this issue may be a very basic one in assessing the welfare implications of existing trade in hazardous wastes.

This general view of trade in hazardous wastes carries with it some implications for patterns of trade that, it seems to me, could be the subject of some interesting and useful empirical work. We might expect (for the reasons discussed) to observe shipments of wastes from high income to low income countries. Perhaps less obvious, we might expect such flows of wastes to reflect governmental structure. In line with the argument above, other things equal, countries with governments that are more sensitive and responsive to the wishes of the electorate might be expected to have higher reservation prices for wastes than governments (say dictators) who can turn a quick profit from accepting wastes and ignore the external costs that disposal imposes on their citizens. At the same time, we should recognize that some shipments of wastes will be motivated by genuine differences in the full social costs of disposal; they will represent real gains-from-trade from a welfare perspective. Interestingly in this respect, the great bulk (estimates run at around 80%) of cross-boundary hazardous waste shipments are from one developed country to another. From this perspective, we might (as a testable hypothesis) expect to observe flows of wastes for disposal from densely populated nations to less heavily populated countries.

What this suggests is the value of efforts to pull together a systematic inventory of international trade flows in hazardous pollutants and to use these data to "test" the hypothesis flowing from a model of the sort described in this section. Some careful case studies of flow of specific pollutants would also be useful to determine the extent to which trade in hazardous wastes reflects the full social costs in the exporting and importing countries (including the costs and risks associated with the transport of the pollutant).

3. Developing Countries and the Global Environment

A fundamental challenge to effective global environmental management has its source in the strikingly different perspectives of countries around the world. The developing countries, in particular, tend to place much less importance on the global environment in light of the formidable pressures for sustained economic growth. And yet their participation in efforts to control, for example, planetary carbon emissions is essential if global objectives are to be achieved.

The design and implementation of effective global policies must, therefore, integrate the functioning of both the industrialized and the developing economies. But this requires that we take into account the special concerns and circumstances of the developing countries. In particular, the economies of these countries are typically characterized by basic and important distortions in prices and resource allocation [Pearce and Turner (1990, ch. 22)]. And these distortions have some fundamental implications for the "gains-from-trade" in environmental services and for the design of policy.

Such distortions often exist in the energy sector where prices are frequently maintained well below free-market levels. Kosmo (1989) cites pretroleum and natural gas prices in Egypt of, respectively, one-third and from 10 to 20% of world levels. In the electric-power industry in Turkey, lignite prices (in 1983) were held to only 68% of the coal-equivalent border prices. In China, a two-tiered structure of prices for coal exists: "in plan" coal in Beijing was selling for about $50 per ton in the late 1980's while the "out-plan", or negotiated, coal price was over double this figure (Wang, 1988). These distortions in prices result in excessive use of energy inputs and, on the supply side, in inadequate investment both in the development of energy resources and in pollution-control efforts. More generally, the developing countries tend to place a heavier reliance on a variety of excise taxes and subsidies on particular goods resulting in distorted prices across wide ranges of commodities.

The existence of such price distortions raises some fundamental issues for the potential gains-from-trade in environmental resources. We addressed this problem in the specific context of trade in hazardous wastes in the preceding section with reference to countries that ignore the full social costs of waste disposal. But the issue is a broader one. What happens to the welfare-enhancing "gains-from-trade" when trade takes place in the context of varying distortions in relative prices across countries?

This issue has received some attention in the literature on international economics. Bhagwati (1971) and Eaton and Panigariya (1979), for example, have looked at gains-from-trade where price distortions are present. And this literature provides a useful point of departure for the analysis of open economy environmental issues.

In the context of version one of the simple model, we noted that the efficient control of a global pollutant requires the equalization of marginal abatement cost across all countries. And that such an outcome could, in principle, be achieved by a uniform global effluent charge. But this result depends, of course, on cost-minimizing behavior of polluting units in the context of prices that reflect the true opportunity costs of environmental resources. With significant distortions in prices of, say, energy inputs across countries, a uniform effluent charge will no longer produce a least-cost outcome for the management of global environmental quality. It is important to develop both theoretical models and associated empirical estimates to get some clearer sense of the implications of allocative distortions in the developing countries for the design of efficient global measures for environmental management (a theme to which I shall return shortly).

Research on developing countries will need to address a further and more institutional issue relating to policy design: the "administrative capacity" of the developing countries for the implementation of environmental measures. There is widespread discussion in the policy arena of a global system of effluent charges, or, as an alternative, a system of transferable emissions permits. But such policy regimes require a significant degree of regulatory sophistication and management. To implement such measures, the regulatory authority in each country must be able to monitor emissions and to enforce the regulations. There are real questions concerning the capacities of some countries to employ such policy instruments. And the answers to these questions are obviously critical to the realistic consideration of policy alternatives for global management.

This suggests the need for careful investigation of the administrative capacity of the developing countries for the management of environmental regulation. This shoud begin with an examination of existing environmental management structures. One should not assume, incidentally, that these structures are absent in developing nations. China, for example, has an extensive and sophisticated structure for administering its environmental laws (even including economic-incentive mechanisms). In addition, we may be able to get some sense of potential administrative capacity for environmental measures by examining other forms of regulations in developing countries. For instance, most (if not all) developing countries have administrative structures for regulating (or providing directly) electricity, local bus services, trash collection, and other infrastructure services. Analyses of successes and failures in these areas may suggest models for the design of environmental policy that optimize the mix of efficiency and administrative burden. Finally, it will be worth considering the efficiency and administrative consequences of a variety of more "blunt" instruments, such as taxes or direct controls on energy, that could be used to control pollution with lower levels of enforcement and monitoring costs.

4. Policy Instruments for Global Environmental Management

There are already moves in several countries to introduce "Green Taxes" and discussion of other policy instruments to control emissions of greenhouse gases. The analysis of global policy instruments will obviously be a central issue in open economy environmental economics.

As we noted in the introduction, containment efforts for global carbon emissions are likely to be enormously expensive, and there is a large premium attached to finding efficient policy measures that can achieve the objective of reduced emissions at relatively low cost. This suggests immediately a serious consideration of systems of economic incentives for pollution control. A central theme of the existing literature in environmental economics [see, for example, Baumol and Oates (1988)] is the great cost-saving potential of policy measures embodying economic incentives relative to their command-and-control (CAC) counterparts. In a static framework, it can be shown that fees or systems of transferable permits can, in principle, attain any proposed level of emissions reductions at the least cost to society. Moreover, from a dynamic perspective, such systems of economic incentives provide powerful incentives for research and development of more effective and less costly abatement technology.

The two major instruments to be considered here are systems of effluent charges and systems of transferable permits. There has been some experience with both of these policy instruments in a handful of countries. In addition, there exists a large literature in environmental economics that has analyzed in great detail the properties of these policy instruments in a regional or national context [see Cropper and Oates (1990) for a recent survey]. And this literature serves as a useful point of departure for the examination of their potential in a global setting. But it is clear that the employment of fees or transferable permits on a worldwide scale introduces a number of new and difficult issues [Bohm (1991b)]. There are the makings of a heated and important international debate over which of these two instruments would most effectively address global environmental and economic concerns [see Gaskins and Stram (1990) and Grubb (1990) for the cases for effluent taxes and marketable permits, respectively].

Oates and Portney (1990), in a recent and informal paper have undertaken a preliminary investigation of some of these issues — in part simply to enumerate the matters about which we must learn more if we are to make informed choices among policy alternatives in a global setting. There are some important questions concerning how these measures would be introduced and function in a global context. Under a system of effluent charges, where would the taxes be levied — in energy-producing countries or in energy-consuming countries? The answer to this question has momentous consequences for the international incidence of such a system of taxes. Likewise, how would the system of taxes be managed in a world of floating exchange rates? If, instead, we were to opt for a system of transferable permits, how would the initial allocation of permits be determined [Bohm (1991a)]? And what conditions would govern trades?

The choice between the fee and permit approaches in a global setting raises some fascinating and challenging issues. In a setting of uncertainty, Weitzman (1974) has shown that the expected welfare gains from the two policy instruments depend upon the relative slopes of the marginal benefit and marginal cost functions. But what are the relative slopes of these functions for global warming? Are there important threshold effects or rapidly increasing marginal control costs that point to the use of one of these instruments rather than the other? There are some of the important issues that must be addressed in the debate over "instrument choice" for global change.

These issues concerning global policy measures intersect the problems addressed in the preceding sections of the paper. First, the efficiency properties of uniform global measures depend in basic ways on an absence of major price distortions across countries. But, as we have discussed, there are compelling reasons for believing that such distortions, in all likelihood, are present. And, second, there may exist real administrative constraints on the range of feasible policy instruments in the developing countries.

These two considerations suggest an important and quite challenging problem for the design and implementation of global policy: the issue of the optimal mix of policies for the containment of global waste emissions. This will be a formidable second-best kind of problem that requires the explicit introduction as constraints both of existing distortions and administrative limitations in some countries. There are some challanging opportunities here for the development of economic models with which to explore the optimal policy mix. Such a mix, for instance, might well involve the introduction of economic incentives in the industrialized countries alongside the use of more "blunt" CAC measures in developing countries. Analytical efforts can help to clarify the kinds of tradeoffs that are involved in a world of diverse policy regimes.

A second set of issues for international environmental policy involves the potential role for the use of trade measures such as tariffs or quotas against countries that refuse to participate in global efforts at environmental management. Economists somewhat naturally approach this topic "gingerly" in the light of the general economic case for free trade. However, there may well be instances in a setting of price distortions where discrimination against certain goods produced in countries using environmentally damaging technologies can be welfare-enhancing from a global perspective. This, I suspect, is an issue that will get real consideration in the policy arena — it seems likely that "green tariffs" or import restrictions on goods from "dirty" countries will be seriously debated in the international forum within this decade.

There is some literature on this topic that can serve as a point of departure for a richer analysis of the problem. Baumol and Oates (1988, ch. 16), for example, have explored the case of an importing country that suffers from pollution created in the production of the traded good by the exporter. In the absence of a truly global Pigouvian tax on production in the exporting country and where the importing nation is of sufficient economic size to have a discernible impact on the world price of the traded good, they show that a second-best optimum will not involve a zero tariff by the importing country. In addition, they prove that the "optimal tariff" for the importing nation will be higher than that in the absence of the detrimental externality. The analysis is thus suggestive in that it points to a role for trade restrictions in such a second-best setting.

However, it is difficult in such a general framework to get much sense of the appropriate magnitude of such tariffs and their potential effects. This may well be an issue for which some computable general-equilibrium (CGE) analysis could prove illuminating. John Merrifield (1988) has, in fact, used a CGE model to explore the effects of alternative abatement strategies on transnational pollution. His analysis is limited to the effects of domestic measures for pollution control on transnational pollution flows. But there is real potential for an expansion on this approach to explore the workings and likely effects of such trade measures when employed either singly by one nation of jointly by a whole set of importing countries. CGE simulations could give us some sense of the capacity of countries working in concert in "trade alliances" to put economic "pressure" on uncooperative, global polluters.

5. Concluding Remarks

International economic linkages in environmental "services", like for other commodities, involve potential gains-from-trade. But what I have tried to suggest in this paper is that the realization of these gains-from-trade may not come easily. Large price distortions, especially in the developing countries, and various public-goods problems make it difficult for normal, decentralized decisions by "trading agents" to result in unambiguously welfare-enhancing international transactions.

In consequence, open economy environmental economics will have to address a series of complicated issues both in terms of understanding the full nature of these linkages and in the design of policy measures to achieve our global environmental objectives. This will, I believe, inevitably lead us into some challenging, second-best analysis of the optimal policy mix across countries with widely different priorities and economic conditions. Sets of policies may vary in basic ways across countries — and we will need to explore the resulting interaction of such policies in a global setting.

Bibliography

W.J. BAUMOL, and W.E. OATES, *The Theory of Environmental Policy*, Second Edition, Cambridge University Press, 1988.

J. BHAGWATI, *The Generalized Theory of Distortions and Welfare*, in J. BHAGWATI *et al.*, (eds.), *Trade, Balance of Payments, and Growth*, North - Holland, Amsterdam 1971.

P. BOHM, *Distributional Implications of Allowing International Trade in CO_2 Emission Quotas*, unpublished paper, January 1991a.

P. BOHM, *Incomplete International Cooperation to Reduce CO_2 Emissions: Alternative Policies*, unpublished paper, January 1991b.

M.L. CROPPER and W.E. OATES, *Environmental Economics: A Survey*, Resources for the Future Discussion Paper QE90-12, Washington D.C. 1990.

J. EATON and A. PANAGARIYA, *Gains from Trade Under Variable Returns to Scale, Commodity Taxation, Tariffs and Factor Market Distortions*, in "Journal of International Economics", 9, 1979, pp. 481-501.

D. GASKINS and B. STRAM, *A Meta Plan: A Policy Response to Global Warming*, Vienna Workshop for Cooperative Research on Climate Change, unpublished paper, 1990.

M. GRUBB, *The Greenhouse Effect: Negotiating Targets*, Royal Institute of International Affairs, London 1990.

M. KOSMO, *Economic Incentives and Industrial Pollution in Developing Countries*, Policy and Research Division Working Paper, 2, 1989, Environmental Department, The World Bank, Washington D.C. 1989.

D. MACLEAN, *Equity Task Report: Some Normative Dimensions*, Report of the Equity Task Force of the Research Nuclear Waste Project Office, 1989.

J.D. MERRIFIELD, *The Impact of Selected Abatement Strategies on Transnational Pollution, the Terms*

Global Environmental Management: towards an Open Economy Environmental Economics

of Trade, and Factor Rewards: A General Equilibrium Approach, in "Journal of Environmental Economics and Management", 15, 1988, pp. 259-84.

W.D. NORDHAUS, *Global Warming: Slowing the Greenhouse Express*, in H. AARON, eds., *Setting National Priorities: Policy for the Nineties*, The Brookings Institution, Washington D.C. 1990, pp. 185-212.

W. OATES and P. PORTNEY, *Policies for the Regulation of Global Carbon Emissions*, unpublished paper, 1990.

D.W. PEARCE, and R.K. TURNER, *Economics of Natural Resources and the Environment*, Johns Hopkins University Press, Baltimore 1990.

Y. WANG, *Coal Prices in Beijing*, unpublished paper, The World Bank, Washington D.C. 1988.

M. WEITZMAN, *Prices vs. Quantities*, in "Review of Economic Studies", 41, 1974, pp. 477-91.

ECONOMIC INCENTIVES AND THE CONTAINMENT
OF GLOBAL WARMING

Wallace E. Oates
University of Maryland
and
Resources for the Future

Q28

and

Paul R. Portney
Resources for the Future

INTRODUCTION

It is hard to imagine a policy problem more daunting than global warming. To begin with, we are not sure what we are up against. The problem is shrouded in uncertainties of the most difficult sort. Actions today to reduce emissions of greenhouse gases will have their effects on global climate many years down the road, and the magnitude and timing of these effects are the subject of much dispute. Point estimates of possible changes in temperature, rainfall, and other dimensions of global climate come with large confidence intervals, and the estimates are themselves often based on relatively simplistic extrapolations that do not allow for potentially frightening changes in climate should we set off some nonlinear, self-reinforcing processes of which we are currently unaware. Our imperfect knowledge has led to sharply contrasting policy positions: at one extreme are those suggesting that we wait until we have a firmer understanding of the global warming process before adopting costly preventive measures; at the other are those urging rapid action to forestall some possibly catastrophic outcomes.

But uncertainty is not the only aspect of global warming that makes it so difficult to address in the policy arena. Effective policies to reduce emissions of greenhouse gases are likely to be very expensive. William Nordhaus [1991], for example, estimates that the cost of cutting greenhouse gas emissions in half, *if* done efficiently on a worldwide scale, would be on the order of 1 percent of world output, and could easily cost more. We could find ourselves in the United States spending as much on such policies as we spend on all other efforts to control pollution combined! Broad support for such costly policies will be hard to find.[1]

Moreover, global warming is an international public good. Emissions from one country are essentially a perfect substitute for emissions elsewhere. The issue then is one of total planetary emissions of these gases. And no one country is of sufficient size to "go it alone." It has been estimated, for example, that even if the OECD countries (the source of most of the world's *current* emissions of greenhouse gases) were to eliminate all such discharges over the next 15 years, the effect would be insufficient to obtain a 20 percent reduction in total world emissions by 2005 if the USSR and Eastern Europe only stabilize their emissions at current levels and if the developing countries undertake no measures to control their emissions of these gases. Effective policies to address global warming will have to be international in scope--they must enlist widespread participa-

Eastern Economic Journal, Vol. 18, No. 1, Winter 1992

tion if there is to be any hope of success. We are all-too-familiar with the various public-goods or free-rider problems that put obstacles in the path of such cooperation.

These obstacles might not seem so formidable if we could assume a broad similarity in the positions and views of different countries. But this is emphatically not the case. Global warming is projected to have dramatically different effects on the well-being of populations in different areas. Some countries are likely to be net beneficiaries from global warming, as their present cold climates become milder. Others will suffer from changes that promise agricultural ruin. In addition to differences in projected effects, there are widely differing *perceptions* of the seriousness of the problem. There are important North-South differences here. The push for policies to contain global climate change is coming largely from the wealthier, industrialized countries. Many developing countries, in contrast, have what they see as more pressing issues of economic growth. They are slow, quite understandably, to consider seriously policies that would impede development efforts. It thus appears that the industrialized countries are going to be asked to *assist* the developing countries with programs to control emissions of green-house gases if their participation is to be expected. A consensus on global policy is not going to come easily!

Our purpose in this paper is not to present a blueprint for policy, or even to advocate a general policy approach. Indeed, the issues here are so formidable and complicated that we are far from clear in our own minds about the appropriate policy response. But a wide ranging and heated debate is underway. More than this, some countries are taking the lead in introducing policy measures unilaterally as a spur to more widespread participation. Sweden, Finland, and the Netherlands, for example, have already intro-duced "Green Taxes" to reduce emissions of carbon dioxide.

Our more modest aim is to try to sort out some of the policy issues in a systematic way. We begin in the early sections of the paper by returning to the basic literature in environmental economics and reviewing what we have learned about the properties and use of various policy instruments in a domestic context. With this as background, we then venture into a global setting and explore how we must restructure the analysis to incorporate the additional complexities that "openness" introduces for the design and implementation of effective policy. Our primary objective is to provide an overview of the policy debate that will help both to channel the debate in constructive directions and to suggest a research agenda that poses the questions that we must answer to make sensible policy decisions.[2]

A REVIEW OF POLICY INSTRUMENTS

The literature in environmental economics has drawn a sharp distinction between the so-called "command-and-control" (CAC) approach to environmental regulation and the use of economic incentives, or incentive-based (IB) approaches, to pollution control. Under the CAC rubric are policies where the environmental authority specifies, often in great detail, the regulations for each of a very large number of sources or group of sources. These regulations typically go well beyond establishing discharge limits for individual sources: they often specify the form of pollution-control technology that the source must employ, the pollutant content of the fuels to be used, certain features of the products to be produced, and so on. Such measures are characterized by their inflexibil-ity: they typically allow little latitude for innovative responses on the part of sources.

Incentive-based approaches, in contrast, establish a set of penalties for emissions (or rewards for reductions in discharges) but allow the source wide scope for choosing both the form and magnitude of its response. A central theme in this literature is the large cost-saving potential of IB as compared to CAC. At a theoretical level, it is straightforward to show that various economic-incentive instruments have the capacity to achieve *any* desired level of environmental quality at the least cost to society [Baumol and Oates, 1971]. Moreover, there now exists a substantial body of empirical work that produces estimates of the magnitude of these cost-savings, estimates that range from roughly 50 to over 90 percent relative to CAC outcomes.[3]

In addition to these potentially large savings based on the more efficient deployment of existing control technologies in the short run, the literature emphasizes the longer-term savings that IB approaches provide through continued research and development of new control technologies. In short, environmental economists have established a powerful case for the use of economic incentives to achieve our environmental objectives at much lower cost than the more widely used CAC measures.

From the perspective of the containment of global warming, the cost-saving properties of the IB approach to environmental regulation take on real significance, for (as we noted in the introductory section) it could be a very expensive enterprise. With this in mind, we turn first to a consideration of the two major economic instruments emerging from the literature on environmental regulation: emissions taxes and systems of transferable emissions permits.

Emissions Taxes

Under the tax approach, the environmental authority would levy a fee on each pound of carbon (or other greenhouse gas) discharged, and the source would have a tax liability equal to the fee times the number of pounds of carbon that it chooses to emit. Since carbon emissions are equally damaging irrespective of the particular place where they are emitted, there is no need to tailor the tax rate geographically. A single tax rate applicable to all sources is what is needed. And, if the environmental authority is committed to the attainment of some target level of aggregate reductions in carbon discharges, it can adjust the tax rate until this target is achieved. Cost-minimizing behavior by individual sources will ensure that marginal abatement cost is equated across all sources so that the aggregate reduction is achieved at minimum overall cost. Decentralized decisions in the presence of the tax lead to the least-cost outcome.[4]

Transferable Emission Permits

The basic alternative to the tax approach is a system of transferable emissions permits. In a simplified setting, it is easy to show that the two are, in a fundamental sense, equivalent. Under the tax approach, the environmental authority raises the tax to the level needed to achieve the target level of emissions reductions. Under the permit approach, the agency simply issues permits that, in total, equal the target level of emissions. Sources are then free to buy and sell these permits. In the first case, the authority sets "price" and the sources respond by choosing quantities of emissions; in the second case, the agency sets quantity directly and sources bid the price of permits up to their market-clearing level.

While this basic equivalence exists in principle, these two approaches have some important differences in a policy setting. Three of these differences appear to have disposed regulators in the United States to the permit, rather than the fee, approach. They explain to some extent why regulators in the U.S. have chosen the transferable-permit approach under the Emissions Trading Program rather than a system of effluent charges, and also why the 1991 Clean Air Act Amendments included such a permit system to achieve the mandated reductions in national sulfur-dioxide emissions to address the acid-rain problem.

First, the permit approach gives the environmental regulator direct control over the quantity of emissions. This is a very important advantage since environmental goals are typically formulated in quantity terms, e.g., in terms of specified levels of emissions or pollutant concentrations. The new amendments to the Clean Air Act, for example, call for a 10 million ton (roughly a 50 percent) reduction in annual sulfur emissions by the end of the next decade. A regulator will thus prefer having direct control over the quantity of emissions through the issue of permits, rather than indirect (and uncertain) control through the manipulation of the tax rate. In contrast, and especially in a changing world, a regulator would find it necessary periodically to adjust the rate of an effluent tax to prevent emissions of pollutants from rising with a growing economy. No such problem of adjustment exists under permits in the sense that quantity will remain fixed. The price of permits will simply rise to clear the market in the face of increased demand from new sources wishing to discharge the pollutant.

Second, the permit approach offers a way around some of the political opposition that has blocked the introduction of emissions taxes. It is true, of course, that permits *could* be issued through an auction so that sources would have to pay directly for all their emissions, much as they do under a system of effluent charges. But there is another way to set a permit system in motion. The regulator can simply distribute the permits free of charge to existing sources who can then trade among themselves or sell them to new sources. The granting of a valuable asset will obviously encounter much less resistance from polluting firms than will the levying of a tax. This is, in fact, what has been done under the Emissions Trading Program in the United States for the control of air pollution.

And third, the permit approach promises much more ready acceptance simply on the grounds of familiarity. Regulators have experience and are comfortable with the permit instrument. It seems a much less radical move to make permits transferable than to replace an existing permit system with a scheme of emission taxes.

Transferable permits, for all these reasons, have real appeal. They appear to share all the desirable properties of a system of effluent fees, but to avoid certain administrative and distributive problems that have made fee systems unattractive to environmental regulators. The experience over the past decade with Emissions Trading does, however, raise one potentially serious problem with the permit approach: the operation of permit markets. As we have indicated, it is easy to show in theory that a competitive equilibrium in the permit market has all the nice economic properties, including aggregate cost minimization, that we wish for our system of emissions control. The difficulty is that, in practice, markets for air pollution permits haven't worked as smoothly as envisioned. In particular, these markets have been quite thin, especially on the supply side. Robert Hahn [1989] contends that this has been largely the result of unfortunate restrictions on trading that have clouded definitions of property rights and raised serious uncertainties about the ability to obtain these rights in the marketplace when needed. Even so, the number of potential participants in these markets is often small with certain large sources in a position to exercise monopolistic price-setting powers [Hahn, 1984]. The thinness of these markets and infrequency of transactions suggest that sources may not observe a clear, well defined price signal to indicate the opportunity cost of their emissions. The absence of such a clear price signal is likely to impair the functioning of the permit system, unlike a regime of emission taxes where the tax itself gives a clear and clean measure of the cost of emissions.

While market thinness has been a real problem under Emissions Trading, it seems unlikely that this would be a significant problem in a market for carbon emissions. The markets for Emissions Trading relate to specific air pollutants in particular areas. The markets are highly localized, and this limits the number of potential participants. In contrast, the market for carbon emissions would presumably be national or international in scope. In such a setting, there should be plenty of active buyers and sellers so that competitive conditions would prevail.

POLICY CHOICE IN AN UNCERTAIN WORLD

The formal equivalence of systems of emission taxes and transferable permits exists in a world of perfect information. We find in the more realistic setting of imperfect knowledge that there are some important asymmetries between these two policy instruments. If we are uncertain about the benefits and costs of emission control, then, in hindsight we will tend to make errors in our choices of values for tax rates or quantities of permits. And, as Martin Weitzman [1974] and others have shown, the errors can be of very different magnitude depending on the policy instrument in use. If we are going to make mistakes (and we surely will), we want these mistakes to involve as little damage as possible.

The Weitzman theorem shows that it is the *relative* steepness of the marginal benefit and marginal abatement cost curves that determines which of the two policy instruments, pollution taxes or a system of transferable permits, promises the larger expected welfare gain. The basic idea is straightforward. Suppose that the marginal benefit curve associated with pollution control is quite steep while marginal abatement costs are relatively constant over the relevant range. This would represent a case where the benefits from changes in environmental quality vary dramatically with changes in pollution levels. Such a case might involve crucial threshold effects, where, if pollutant concentrations exceed some critical level, disastrous consequences take place. Under these circumstances, we want to be sure that we have reliable and precise control over the quantity of polluting waste emissions. It is clear that in a setting of uncertainty concerning true levels of abatement costs and, perhaps, benefits, we would use the tax instrument at our peril. If the environmental authority were to set the tax too low (which could easily happen where we are uncertain of the response of sources to a particular level of the tax rate), then emissions would turn out to be higher than planned. Were they to exceed the critical level, an environmental catastrophe would result. It is best in such instances to employ a permit system under which the regulator has direct control over the quantity of emissions and can avoid the threat associated with too low a tax rate. In Weitzman's words, "Our intuitive feeling, which is confirmed by the formal analysis, is that it doesn't pay to 'fool around' with prices in such situations" [1974, 489].

In contrast, under other circumstances, the marginal damages from additional polluting emissions may not vary significantly. The effects from more emissions will, in such cases, be fairly constant. There will not exist any serious threshold effects over the relevant range of emissions. However, it may be that the marginal costs of control vary dramatically. There exist, in fact, many careful estimates of the marginal costs of emission control which indicate that, after a relatively constant range, marginal costs begin to increase sharply. In this setting, the more pressing danger from a policy-making perspective is one of excessive costs. If, for example, the regulator were to set too tough a standard for emissions reductions, he might impose enormous costs on sources. The danger in this case is greater under the permit instrument, for if the supply of permits is set too low, excessive control costs will be forced upon sources. Under a fee regime, this danger is avoided, since sources can always opt to pay the fee and avoid the more costly control activities.

Uncertainty and imperfect information thus introduce another set of quite important considerations in the selection of the preferred policy instrument. In which direction is this argument likely to cut in the case of carbon emissions and the problem of global warming? The answer is not entirely clear, but it is worth some thought.

Is the problem of global warming characterized by critical threshold concentrations of greenhouse gases, the violation of which sets off a catastrophic reaction? Most projections of the process of global warming involve a gradual, continuous process, but this is because that is the way in which the problem has been modelled. There are fears that significant *non-linearities* might be present in the processes of global change - that at some point the process of global warming could suddenly become self-reinforcing and take off [Peck and Teisberg, 1991; Chao, 1991]. But, at this point, such fears are no more than conjectures about the range of possible courses that global warming might conceivably take. In truth, we don't know if there are significant threshold effects, and, if there are, we don't know what the critical levels of carbon-dioxide concentrations are. We are thus not in a position to build our policies around avoiding certain critical concentrations of atmospheric greenhouse gases.

On the cost side, there are good reasons to believe that the costs of additional increments of emissions reductions will rise, and probably quite rapidly, after some point. There are certain measures that can be undertaken relatively inexpensively to reduce carbon emissions. After these measures are taken, we will have to turn to more expensive options. *If* existing studies of abatement cost functions are a guide, we should expect these rising costs to set in quite sharply as we attempt to decrease carbon emissions yet more dramatically [Jorgenson and Wilcoxen, forthcoming; Nordhaus, 1991, forthcoming]. This suggests that there is a real danger in setting purely quantitative targets for emissions reductions; such targets could involve enormous costs, much higher than those envisioned at the outset.

This danger could be avoided by selecting a price rather than a quantity instrument, that is, by using emissions taxes instead of a system of transferable permits. Taxes could be set at the level which will call forth those control activities that we can *reasonably afford*. Note that such a policy choice implies uncertainty as to just how much emission reductions we would get. But in return for this uncertainty, we would protect ourselves against the potentially large costs that could be incurred to get some (perhaps quite small) additional reductions in carbon discharges.

For the case of global warming, the uncertainty argument would thus seem to favor the use of emissions taxes over transferable permits. But there are some important qualifications. First, if, as our scientific knowledge concerning global warming expands, we find that there are, in fact, some critical threshold values of carbon concentrations that we must not violate, then the case would swing back to support the policy instrument that gives us a firmer control over levels of emissions, namely, a permit system. Second, the force of this particular argument for taxes should be seen in the proper perspective. In the use of a permit system, if it were found that the supply of permits had been restricted to excessively stringent levels with unjustifiable cost implications, adjustments could be made over time to increase the supply of permits and alleviate somewhat the cost pressures. However, such adjustments take time, are not always accommodated easily in a regulatory system, and involve other costs of their own. But it is important to recognize that these policy instruments, be they transferable permits or tax rates on carbon emissions, can be adjusted over time to produce more satisfactory results. There is, in short, some room for the correction of "mistakes." But we would do well to try to avoid the larger mistakes at the outset.

POLICY DESIGN IN A GLOBAL SETTING

Although we have examined briefly certain general aspects of the major policy instruments for the control of global carbon emissions, we turn now explicitly to the issue of policy choice and design in a global environment. The existing literature on environmental regulation presumes that there is a central environmental authority that is empowered to introduce and enforce policy measures. In a global setting, things become more complicated. Most important, there typically does not exist an international agency with the authority to introduce and ensure compliance with global policies. Such an agency can only come into being upon the agreement of all the countries involved, and even then its powers are likely to be significantly more circumscribed than those of a national or regional authority.[5]

As we discussed earlier, problems of international coordination loom large for the containment of global warming because of the widely differing positions and perspectives of various countries. The examination of policy alternatives must be seen in this context.

Economic Incentives for the Containment of Global Warming

The discussion in this paper has focused on two primary incentive-based policy measures: emission taxes and transferable permits. In view of their tremendous cost-saving potential, they are strong candidates to play a central role in containing global warming and deserve careful consideration.

The debate over the relative merits of these two policy instruments for the control of carbon emissions is already underway. Several thoughtful studies have addressed the issue and, interestingly, reach quite different conclusions. Darius Gaskins and Bruce Stram [1990], for example, contend that carbon taxes are the more promising approach, while Michael Grubb [1989] and Joshua Epstein and Raj Gupta [1990] opt for systems of transferable permits.

The central issues in this choice do not revolve around the basic economic properties of the two policy instruments, but around their feasibility and effectiveness in the existing international setting. In order to achieve the least-cost allocation of abatement efforts under the tax approach, cost-minimizing sources must all face a *single* tax rate per unit of carbon emissions. This will result in the requisite equating of marginal abatement cost across all sources. This would require, in a strict sense, that every source of carbon emissions on the planet face the *same* tax per unit of emissions.

Designing, instituting, and managing such a regime is a tall order to put it mildly. The problems of determining the rate and administering the tax are formidable. Would a single international agency manage the system and collect the revenues? This would seem highly unlikely: the potential revenues from such taxes are enormous, and as Thomas Schelling has observed [1991], no country is likely to give over control of such a major revenue source to an international agency. Moreover, there are other tricky issues to be resolved: How would tax rates be adjusted over time in response to changing exchange rates? Should the taxes be levied at the point of production or consumption of fossil fuels? Do all countries have the "administrative capacity" to operate such a tax system effectively? Finally, there is the troublesome issue of widespread distortions in existing price structures in many countries, notably the developing countries, such that a single, uniform carbon tax would not, in fact, result in equating the true marginal abatement costs across nations. We will return to these last two issues shortly.

The obstacles to the introduction of a "pure" global emissions tax may well be insurmountable. But this certainly does not mean that the tax approach should be abandoned at this point. There are various compromises that deserve careful study. The use of carbon taxes that are designed and administered by each of many countries (perhaps with some coordination) has real appeal. While such a system admittedly would forgo some of the cost-saving potential of the tax approach in terms of intercountry pollution "quotas," it would promote a cost-effective pattern of abatement within individual countries and would provide a powerful incentive for R&D efforts to find new ways to reduce carbon discharges. As James Poterba [1991] finds, such taxes are likely to be regressive in their pattern of incidence, but this regressivity can, if desired, be offset by adjustments in the rest of the tax system and/or with transfers. We need to investigate carefully the ways in which such taxes could be introduced on a national scale with, perhaps, some degree of coordination across countries. Such studies are already underway in many countries, e.g., for the United States, the study by the Congressional Budget Office [1990].

One potential peril in the design of such tax measures and their management concerns their enormous revenue potential. Not only can they be a source of considerable macroeconomic disturbance [Jorgenson and Wilcoxen, 1990; Poterba, 1991], but it will be easy to lose sight of their primary objective of environmental regulation: as they become a significant element in the revenue system, there will be pressures to use them for other purposes such as reducing the federal deficit. Interestingly, it is unclear whether an attempt to maximize revenues from this source would involve higher or lower tax rates than would be appropriate for purposes of environmental management. This depends on the elasticity of the carbon tax base [Oates, 1991]. But what is clear is that the attempt to achieve two objectives - regulating carbon emissions and raising additional tax revenues - with a single policy instrument can pose conflicts. The revenues from carbon taxes can provide a welcome addition to the public treasury, one that can be used to replace revenues from other distorting taxes that impair the functioning of the economy [Terkla, 1984]. But these revenues are best regarded as a kind of *bonus,* a serendipitous inflow into the treasury, whose level is determined independently by the need to control emissions of greenhouse gases.[6]

The use of transferable permits for the containment of global warming must also involve compromises relative to a *pure* system that would have sources around the globe trading entitlements to carbon emissions in a single international market. There are various ways that this could work [Grubb, 1989; Epstein and Gupta, 1990]. At one level, permits could be used basically as a mechanism to allocate entitlements across countries with trading limited to transactions between national governments. Countries which found abatement (at the margin) especially difficult and expensive could then negotiate for purchases of permits from other countries for whom abatement efforts come more easily and cheaply. Within each country, national authorities would institute systems to keep carbon emissions within the national allowance. Such national systems could make use of transferable permits but need not.

Instituting a transferable permit system requires agreement on an initial allocation of permits among countries, potentially a very contentious matter. Grubb [1989] and Epstein and Gupta [1990] suggest that some kind of per-capita allocation (perhaps modified by population age structure) could serve as a reasonable and acceptable basis for this allocation. With the initial allocation in place, countries could proceed with trading.

Epstein and Gupta regard the explicit quantity restriction associated with a permit system as a compelling advantage over a tax regime; taxes, they fear, could have little effect on levels of emissions, resulting in "toying with basic parameters of a complex system whose sensitivities are not fully understood" [1991, 17]. While this is a danger, we remain uneasy with the potential cost "errors" under a permit system. Jorgenson and Wilcoxen [forthcoming], along with others, find that, after some point, marginal abatement costs for controlling carbon emissions rise quite rapidly. This makes the selection of a particular quantity target a delicate matter. Too stringent a target could prove very costly and disruptive.

Gaskins and Stram [1990] raise important issues related to the visibility and flexibility of the regulatory instrument. They contend that the tax approach has important advantages on these counts. Once permits are issued and traded, they argue, the cost of curtailing carbon emissions becomes hidden in product prices and is less apparent to the public and its representatives than a tax that is paid over and over again. Moreover, entitlements tend to create vested interests, making adjustments in the supply of permits difficult to bring about. For example, if after some time we learned that the atmosphere could accommodate significantly more greenhouse gases than earlier had been believed, we would want to increase the number of permits. But existing permit holders (like those owning taxi medallions in New York City) would object since this would devalue their permits for which they may have paid a sizeable sum. For these reasons, Gaskins and Stram contend that "political-economy" considerations favor the tax regime. While there may well be some force to their contention, we point out that it is not always that easy to change tax rates either!

Abatement Versus Adaptation

The literature in environmental economics demonstrates that the optimal response to a "detrimental externality" is a unit tax on the source of the externality, equal to marginal social damage, accompanied by *no* payments (compensation) to victims of the damaging activity [Baumol and Oates, 1988, chs. 3 and 4]. The latter part of this prescription addresses the need for appropriate levels of *defensive activities*. Victims of pollution often have at their disposal various kinds of defensive measures through which they can alleviate to some degree the damages they suffer. They may, for example, be able to locate away from the sources of the pollution or alter their daily pattern of activities to avoid harm. If, however, victims are compensated for whatever damages they absorb, they will not have the proper inducement to engage in such defensive activities. Compensation of victims thus results in distortions: too little in the way of defensive activities by victims and too much in the way of abatement by sources. This analysis, we stress, assumes that all defensive activities are private in nature. They provide benefits only to the individual that undertakes them. In such a setting the damages that victims experience provide precisely the correct incentive to engage in defensive activities. No additional incentives in the form of payments or taxes are appropriate.

It is important in finding the least-cost response to environmental externalities to get the appropriate balance of abatement and defensive efforts. In the context of global warming, these defensive efforts, or "adaptation" as they are called in the emerging literature, are likely to play an important role in addressing the global warming problem [Rosenberg et al., 1989]. Many forms of adaptive response are private in nature, involving relocation decisions or changing patterns of tillage, irrigation, and crop selection. For them, we can presumably rely on individual decisions over time to make the appropriate adjustments.

But there are potential forms of adaptation to global warming that do not involve purely private benefits. To cite only a few:

1) The construction of sea walls to prevent inundation with rising levels of the sea;
2) The protection of natural ecosystems;
3) Agricultural research to identify, for instance, new plant cultivars suitable for expected alterations in climate.

Adaptation to global warming thus involves some important activities that have dimensions of *publicness* and will presumably require public programs. It is important that such forms of adaptation be identified and provided for.

Administrative Capacity and Distorted Prices

The cost-saving properties of the two IB policy measures considered above depend in fundamental ways on the presence of two conditions: the "administrative capacity" of governments to introduce and manage these policy measures effectively, and the operation of reasonably competitive markets that are not characterized by serious price distortions. If the latter condition is not satisfied, then existing prices obviously will not provide accurate signals to users of the true opportunity costs of resources.

While the assumption of *roughly* efficient markets may be a reasonable one for the advanced industrialized economies, it is far from clear that it is legitimate for many of the developing countries. Quite pervasive and sizeable price distortions appear to exist in many developing economies, and they are frequently present in the energy sector where prices are often maintained at well below free-market levels. Kosmo [1989], for example, cites petroleum and natural gas prices in Egypt of, respectively, one-third and from ten to twenty percent of world levels. In China, a two-tiered structure of prices for coal exists with "in-plan" coal in Beijing selling for about $50 per ton in the late 1980s, while the "out-plan," or negotiated, coal price was over double this figure [Wang, 1988]. More generally, the developing countries tend to make much wider use of excise taxes and subsidies that distort prices across broad classes of commodities.

Even if price distortions were not such a widespread phenomenon, it is not clear that the administrative capacity always exists in the developing countries to operate a system of effluent taxes or transferable permits. Such policy regimes require a substantial level of regulatory sophistication and experience. (Of course, most forms of CAC regulation also require some administrative sophistication for both their design and effective enforcement.) Our concern here is that certain *institutional* realities must be faced up to in the design of global policy measures. And the problems of price distortions and administrative capacity are important ones that will require careful study in the analysis of the international response to global warming.[7]

Recognition of these kinds of constraints on feasible policy suggests a somewhat broader frame of reference in terms of the most effective *mix* of policies on a global scale. This is admittedly a formidable problem of the "second-best." But it may well be that the most effective global policy strategy will be one that involves the introduction of some fairly sophisticated IB policies in the industrialized countries alongside the use of various more *blunt* measures in some of the developing countries.

This leads to one further observation. We noted in the introduction the sharp distinction that the environmental economics literature makes between economic incentives and CAC policies. While useful, perhaps, for certain pedagogical purposes, this lumping of all "other" policies into the CAC class is quite misleading. In fact, it is sometimes unclear just where this dividing line is. A program under which the regulator specifies precisely what treatment technology is to be used clearly falls in the CAC class. But what about a program under which the regulator assigns an overall emissions limitation, but leaves the source to find the most effective method of compliance? Such flexibility clearly allows some scope for cost-saving efforts on the part of the polluter. Moreover, some studies have found that cost-sensitive CAC measures can stack up reasonably well relative to their IB counterparts [Oates, Portney, and McGartland, 1989].

This is not to suggest that IB policies will not have a central role to play in an efficient system for the containment of global warming. They surely will. But at the same time, we must be sensitive to the wide array of potential policy instruments and the existing constraints on their use if we are to fashion a policy *mix* that addresses the problem in an effective way.

On the Need for Global Participation

We stressed in the introduction the need for widespread participation in global efforts to reduce emissions of greenhouse gases. This reflects largely the simple fact that in the future no country (or even select group of countries) will account for the vast bulk of carbon emissions. Nations in all parts of the world and in varying stages of development must become partners in this effort if we are to have any realistic hope of effectively controlling emissions of these gases.

Grubb [1989] and others have argued that in the absence of an effective global agreement, much can still be done through regional or select group (e.g., OECD) agreements, or even through unilateral action. Such efforts can provide leadership, create a co-operative environment conducive to broader participation at a later time, and set in motion efforts to develop substitute technologies. While there is surely some merit to these arguments, it is important to recognize their limitations. One especially serious issue arises. Suppose, for example, that the OECD countries were to form an effective alliance to reduce carbon emissions. One result of such an effort is likely to be a dramatic decrease in the world demand for fossil fuels with a consequent fall in fuel prices. This fall in price would *encourage* other countries to increase their consumption of fossil fuels. To some extent, then, the efforts of the co-operating countries would be offset by natural market responses elsewhere. The extent of this "displacement" would depend on the relative price elasticities of demand, but it could be a substantial offsetting effect. This is a troublesome obstacle to effective action by a limited number of countries. And how to avoid it is not entirely clear. Perhaps the co-operating countries could use some of the revenues from their emission taxes to bolster the demand for fossil fuels and simply build up reserves of these fuels. This issue requires further attention [Bohm, 1991].

A COMPREHENSIVE APPROACH TO REGULATION OF GREENHOUSE GASES

The discussion throughout the paper has run primarily in terms of the control of carbon emissions. Carbon dioxide, however, is but one, albeit the most important, of several greenhouse gases. Others include chlorofluorocarbons (CFCs), methane, nitrous oxides, and ozone. The control of carbon dioxide will likely be the centerpiece of any policy to regulate greenhouse gas emissions, but the other gases are far from insignificant. As Richard Stewart and Jonathan Wiener [1990] emphasize, a comprehensive program to address global warming must incorporate the whole class of greenhouse gases.

The extension of the basic IB instruments to encompass these other gases does not, *in principle*, create any serious problems [Morgenstern, 1991]. The contribution to global warming of the different greenhouse gases varies quite dramatically. Methane, for example, is estimated to have twenty-one times the "radiative-forcing" effect (i.e., capacity to trap heat in the atmosphere) of an equivalent amount of carbon dioxide. The Intergovernmental Panel on Climate Change [1990] has estimated the global warming potential for numerous gases, and from these estimates we can express the warming effects of different gases in terms of a common metric: "carbon equivalents."

Systems of effluent taxes or transferable permits can address this issue by tailoring tax rates or trading ratios to reflect the carbon equivalents of the various gases. The tax, for instance, per unit of methane emissions would, under this approach, be twenty-one times that on discharges of carbon dioxide. This is admittedly a further complication in such systems, but it will be important to build these distinctions into any IB policy measures.

To conclude, we return to the theme of identifying regulatory instruments that can achieve our global environmental objectives in a cost-effective way. To this end, we should look to policies that allow wide flexibility on the part of sources to seek out and adopt the most inexpensive means of reducing their greenhouse gas emissions. Incentive-based measures are obviously strong candidates, and ways of structuring them to function effectively in the global arena rank high on the policy-research agenda. But where we find it necessary to turn to the command-and-control class of policy instruments, it is essential to keep this theme before us. As we emphasized, there exists a wide range of CAC approaches to regulation, and some are much superior to others. In particular, regulatory approaches that involve government officials specifying the precise ways in which sources are to comply with emissions limitations are likely to be extremely inefficient. They provide no flexibility in the short run to adopt less expensive means of compliance and little incentive over the longer haul for research and development activities for new and less costly technologies. A sensible mix of policies should allow wide flexibility in the response of sources and provide incentives for the development of improved methods for controlling emissions.

We are grateful to Lee Friedman, James Kahn, and Jonathan Wiener for helpful comments on earlier drafts of the paper and to the National Science Foundation for its support of this work.

NOTES

1. There is, incidentally, some controversy over the likely costs of reducing emissions of greenhouse gases. Some studies find that the costs cited above are greatly exaggerated. For an excellent survey and assessment of these cost studies, see Joel Darmstadter [1991].

2. For a useful treatment of greenhouse warming, including both a description of the process and its effects and analyses of the various economic aspects of the problem, see Rosenberg et al. [1989].

3. See Tietenberg [1985, ch. 3] for a useful survey of these empirical studies.

4. The literature has also explored unit subsidies for emissions reductions as an alternative to taxes. While such subsidies can establish the same incentives for pollution control by individual sources as unit taxes, they have the serious problem of encouraging entry into polluting industries by making these industries more, rather than less, profitable. Subsidies thus distort the entry-exit decisions of polluting firms. On this, see, for example, Baumol and Oates [1988, ch. 14].

5. The United Nations occasionally tries to play this role, and did so with some success for the Protocol leading to the phasing-out of CFC use among the signatories. Likewise, the European Community has some powers to enforce environmental and other agreements in the member countries. But the many-nation character of these programs makes them much more complex and delicate than national measures for environmental management.

6. In principle, under an optimal-taxation approach, we can determine a second-best tax rate on waste emissions that optimizes the tradeoff between environmental gains and the gains from an improved tax system that places reduced reliance on distorting taxes [Lee and Misiolek, 1986]. While such a result may be unimpeachable in principle, it makes enormous demands in terms of information *and* in terms of institutions. It would require a public decision-maker who is not only informed but is in a position to transcend competing environmental and revenue needs and reach the proper compromise. The dangers here, since there are many other tax bases available, would seem to lie largely on the side of reduced effectiveness in environmental regulation. For this reason, it seems to us that the determination and management of taxes on polluting waste emissions should fall under the aegis of an environmental regulator, rather than the tax authority [Oates, 1991].

7. We do not mean to imply that regulatory structures for environmental management are absent in developing countries. China, for example, has an extensive and fairly sophisticated system for administering its environmental laws (even including economic incentive mechanisms).

REFERENCES

Baumol, W. J., and Oates W. E. The Use of Standards and Prices for Protection of the Environment. *Swedish Journal of Economics*, March 1971, 42-54.

———. *The Theory of Environmental Policy*, 2nd ed. Cambridge: Cambridge University Press, 1988.

Bohm, P. Incomplete International Cooperation to Reduce CO_2 Emissions: Alternative Policies, unpublished paper, 1991.

Chao, H. Managing the Risk of Global Climate Change. Electric Power Research Institute, unpublished paper, 1991.

Darmstadter, J. The Economic Cost of CO_2 Mitigation: A Review of Estimates for Selected World Regions. *Resources for the Future Discussion Paper ENR91-06*, 1991.

Epstein, J. M., and Gupta, R. Controlling the Greenhouse Effect:Five Global Regimes Compared. *Brookings Occasional Papers.* Washington: The Brookings Institution, 1990.

Gaskins, D., and Stram, B. A Meta Plan: A Policy Response to Global Warming. Vienna Workshop for Cooperative Research on Climate Change, unpublished paper, 1990.

Grubb, M. *The Greenhouse Effect: Negotiating Targets.* London: Royal Institute of International Affairs, 1989.

Hahn, R. Market Power and Transferable Property Rights. *Quarterly Journal of Economics,* November 1984, 753-65.

_____. Economic Prescriptions for Environmental Problems: How the Patient Followed the Doctor's Orders. *Journal of Economic Perspectives,* Spring 1989, 95-114.

Intergovernmental Panel on Climate Change. *Climate Change: The IPCC Scientific Assessment.* Cambridge: Cambridge University Press, 1990.

Jorgenson, D. W., and Wilcoxen, P. J. Global Change, Energy Prices, and U.S. Economic Growth. *Harvard Institute of Economic Research Discussion Paper No. 1511,* August 1990.

_____. Reducing U.S. Carbon Dioxide Emissions: The Cost of Different Goals, in *Advances in the Economics of Energy and Natural Resources,* edited by J. R. Moroney. Greenwich, CT: JAI Press, forthcoming.

Kosmo, M. Economic Incentives and Industrial Pollution in Developing Countries. *Policy and Research Division Working Paper #1989-2,* Washington: Environmental Department, The World Bank, 1989.

Lee, D. R., and Misiolek, W. S. Substituting Pollution Taxation for General Taxation: Some Implications for Efficiency in Pollution Taxation. *Journal of Environmental Economics and Management,* December 1986, 338-47.

Morgenstern, R. D. Towards a Comprehensive Approach to Global Climate Change Mitigation. *American Economic Review,* May 1991, 140-45.

Nordhaus, W. D. A Sketch of the Economics of the Greenhouse Effect. *American Economic Review,* May 1991, 146-50.

_____. The Cost of Slowing Climate Change: A Survey. *The Energy Journal,* forthcoming.

Oates, W. E. Pollution Charges as a Source of Public Revenues, unpublished paper, 1991.

Oates, W.E., Portney, P. R., and McGartland, A. M. The *Net* Benefits of Incentive-Based Regulation: A Case Study of Environmental Standard Setting. *American Economic Review,* December 1989, 1233-42.

Peck, S., and Teisberg, T. Exploring Optimal Intertemporal CO_2 Control Paths. Electric Power Research Institute, unpublished paper, 1991.

Poterba, J. M. Tax Policy to Combat Global Warming: On Designing a Carbon Tax. *National Bureau of Economic Research Working Paper No. 3649,* 1991.

Rosenberg, N. J., et al., eds. *Greenhouse Warming: Abatement and Adaptation.* Washington: Resources for the Future, 1989.

Schelling, T. C. Economic Responses to Global Warming: Prospects for Comparative Approaches, in *Global Warming: Economic Policy Responses,* edited by R. Dornbusch and J. Poterba. Cambridge: MIT Press, 1991, 197-221.

Stewart, R. B., and Wiener, J. B. A Comprehensive Approach to Climate Change. *The American Enterprise,* November/December 1990, 75-80.

Tietenberg, T. H. *Emissions Trading: An Exercise in Reforming Pollution Policy.* Washington: Resources for the Future, 1985.

Terkla, D. The Efficiency Value of Effluent Tax Revenues. *Journal of Environmental Economics and Management,* June 1984, 107-23.

U.S. Congressional Budget Office. *Carbon Charges as a Response to Global Warming: The Effects of Taxing Fossil Fuels.* Washington: Congressional Budget Office, 1990.

Wang, Y. Coal Prices in Beijing, unpublished paper. Washington: The World Bank, 1988.

Weitzman, M. Prices vs. Quantities. *Review of Economic Studies,* October 1974, 477-91.

PART VII

A SURVEY OF ENVIRONMENTAL ECONOMICS

[22]

Journal of Economic Literature
Vol. XXX (June 1992), pp. 675–740

Environmental Economics: A Survey

By MAUREEN L. CROPPER AND WALLACE E. OATES

University of Maryland and Resources for the Future

Both authors are members of the Department of Economics, University of Maryland, and are Fellows at Resources for the Future. We are grateful for many valuable comments on earlier drafts of this paper to a host of economists: Nancy Bockstael, Gardner Brown, Richard Carson, John Cumberland, Diane DeWitt, Anthony Fisher, A. Myrick Freeman, Tom Grigalunas, Winston Harrington, Robert Hahn, Charles Howe, Dale Jorgenson, Charles Kolstad, Ray Kopp, Allen Kneese, Alan Krupnick, Randolph Lyon, Ted McConnell, Albert McGartland, Robert Mitchell, Arun Malik, Roger Noll, Raymond Palmquist, John Pezzey, Paul Portney, V. Kerry Smith, Tom Tietenberg, and James Tobey. Finally, we want to thank Jonathan Dunn, Joy Hall, Dan Mussatti, and Rene Worley for their assistance in the preparation of the manuscript.

I. Introduction

WHEN THE ENVIRONMENTAL revolution arrived in the late 1960s, the economics profession was ready and waiting. Economists had what they saw as a coherent and compelling view of the nature of pollution with a straightforward set of policy implications. The problem of externalities and the associated market failure had long been a part of microeconomic theory and was embedded in a number of standard texts. Economists saw pollution as the consequence of an absence of prices for certain scarce environmental resources (such as clean air and water), and they prescribed the introduction of surrogate prices in the form of unit taxes or "effluent fees" to provide the needed signals to economize on the use of these resources. While much of the analysis was of a fairly general character, there was at least some careful research underway exploring the application of economic solutions to certain pressing environmental problems (e.g., Allen Kneese and Blair Bower 1968).

The economist's view had—to the dismay of the profession—little impact on the initial surge of legislation for the control of pollution. In fact, the cornerstones of federal environmental policy in the United States, the Amendments to the Clean Air Act in 1970 and to the Clean Water Act in 1972, *explicitly* prohibited the weighing of benefits against costs in the setting of environmental standards. The former directed the Environmental Protection Agency to set maximum limitations on pollutant concentrations in the atmosphere "to protect the public health"; the latter set as an objective the

675

"elimination of the discharge of *all* [our emphasis] pollutants into the navigable waters by 1985."[1]

The evolution of environmental policy, both in the U.S. and elsewhere, has inevitably brought economic issues to the fore; environmental regulation has necessarily involved costs—and the question of how far and how fast to push for pollution control in light of these costs has entered into the public debate. Under Executive Order 12291 issued in 1981, many proposed environmental measures have been subjected to a benefit-cost test. In addition, some more recent pieces of environmental legislation, notably the Toxic Substances Control Act (TSCA) and the Federal Insecticide, Fungicide, and Rodenticide Act (FIFRA), call for weighing benefits against costs in the setting of standards. At the same time, economic incentives for the containment of waste discharges have crept into selected regulatory measures. In the United States, for example, the 1977 Amendments to the Clean Air Act introduced a provision for "emission offsets" that has evolved into the Emissions Trading Program under which sources are allowed to trade "rights" to emit air pollutants. And outside the United States, there have been some interesting uses of effluent fees for pollution control.

This is a most exciting time—and perhaps a critical juncture—in the evolution of economic incentives for environmental protection. The Bush Administration proposed, and the Congress has introduced, a measure for the trading of sulfur emissions for the control of acid rain under the new 1990 Amendments to the Clean Air Act. More broadly, an innovative report from within the U.S. Congress sponsored by Senators Timothy Wirth and John Heinz, *Project 88: Harnessing Market Forces to Protect Our Environment* (Robert Stavins 1988) explores a lengthy list of potential applications of economic incentives for environmental management. Likewise, there is widespread, ongoing discussion in Europe of the role of economic measures for pollution control. Most recently in January of 1991, the Council of the Organization for Economic Cooperation and Development (OECD) has gone on record urging member countries to "make a greater and more consistent use of economic instruments" for environmental management. Of particular note is the emerging international concern with global environmental issues, especially with planetary warming; the enormous challenge and awesome costs of policies to address this issue have focused interest on proposals for "Green Taxes" and systems of tradable permits to contain global emissions of greenhouse gases. In short, this seems to be a time when there is a real opportunity for environmental economists to make some valuable contributions in the policy arena—if, as we shall argue, they are willing to move from "purist" solutions to a realistic consideration of the design and implementation of policy measures.

Our survey of environmental economics is structured with an eye toward its policy potential. The theoretical foundations for the field are found in the theory of externalities. And so we begin in Section II with a review of the theory of environmental regulation in which we explore recent theoretical results regarding the choice among the key policy instruments for the control of externalities: effluent fees, subsidies, and marketable emission permits. Section III takes us

[1] Although standards were to be set solely on the basis of health criteria, the 1970 Amendments to the Clean Air Act did include economic feasibility among its guidelines for setting source-specific standards. Roger Noll has suggested that the later 1977 Amendments were, in fact, more "anti-economic" than any that went before. See Matthew McCubbins, Roger Noll, and Barry Weingast (1989) for a careful analysis of this legislation.

from the theory of externalities to policy applications with a focus on the structuring and implementation of realistic measures for environmental management. This section reviews the work of environmental economists in trying to move from formal theorems to measures that address the variety of issues confronting an environmental regulator. We describe and evaluate briefly, as part of this treatment, the U.S. and European experiences with economic incentives for pollution control. In addition, we explore a series of regulatory issues—centralization versus decentralization of regulatory authority, international effects of domestic environmental policies, and enforcement—matters on which environmental economists have had something to say.

In Section IV, we turn to the measurement of the benefits and costs of environmental programs. This has been a particularly troublesome area for at least two reasons. First, many of the benefits and costs of these programs involve elements for which we do not have ready market measures: health benefits and aesthetic improvements. Second, policy makers, perhaps understandably, have proved reluctant to employ monetary measures of such things as "the value of human life" in the calculus of environmental policy. Environmental economists have, however, made some important strides in the valuation of "nonmarket" environmental services and have shown themselves able to introduce discussion of these measures in more effective ways in the policy arena.

In a survey in this *Journal* some fifteen years ago, Anthony Fisher and Frederick Peterson (1976) justifiably contended that techniques for measuring the benefits of pollution control are "to be taken with a grain of salt" (p. 24). There has been considerable progress on two distinct fronts since this earlier survey. First, environmental (and other) economists have shown considerable ingenuity in the development of techniques—known as indirect market methods—that exploit the relationships between environmental quality and various marketed goods. These methods allow us to infer the value of improved environmental amenities from the prices of the market goods to which they are, in various ways, related. Second, environmental economists have turned to an approach regarded historically with suspicion in our profession: the direct questioning of individuals about their valuation of environmental goods. Developing with considerable sophistication the so-called "contingent valuation" approach, they have been able to elicit apparently reliable answers to questions involving the valuation of an improved environment. In Section IV, we explore these various methods for the valuation of the benefits and costs of environmental programs and present some empirical findings.

In Section V, we try to pull together our treatment of measuring benefits and costs with a review of cases where benefit-cost analyses have actually been used in the setting of environmental standards. This provides an opportunity for an overall assessment of this experience and also for some thoughts on where such analyses are most needed. We conclude our survey in Section VI with some reflections on the state of environmental economics and its potential contribution to the formulation of public policy.

Before turning to substantive matters, we need to explain briefly how we have defined the boundaries for this survey. For this purpose, we have tried to distinguish between "environmental economics" and "natural resource economics." The distinguishing characteristic of the latter field is its concern with the intertemporal allocation of renewable and nonrenewable resources. With its origins in the seminal paper by Harold Hotelling

(1931), the theory of natural resource economics typically applies dynamic control methods of analysis to problems of intertemporal resource usage. This has led to a vast literature on such topics as the management of fisheries, forests, minerals, energy resources, the extinction of species, and the irreversibility of development over time. This body of work is excluded from our survey. The precise dividing line between environmental economics and natural resource economics is admittedly a little fuzzy, but in order to keep our task a manageable one, we have restricted our survey to what we see as the two major issues in environmental economics: the regulation of polluting activities and the valuation of environmental amenities.

II. *The Normative Theory of Environmental Regulation*

The source of the basic economic principles of environmental policy is to be found in the theory of externalities. The literature on this subject is enormous; it encompasses hundreds of books and papers. An attempt to provide a comprehensive and detailed description of the literature on externalities theory reaches beyond the scope of this survey. Instead, we shall attempt in this section to sketch an outline of what we see as the central results from this literature, with an emphasis on their implications for the design of environmental policy. We shall not address a number of formal matters (e.g., problems of existence) that, although important in their own right, have little to say about the structure of policy measures for protection of the environment.

A. *The Basic Theory of Environmental Policy*[2]

The standard approach in the environmental economics literature charac-

terizes pollution as a public "bad" that results from "waste discharges" associated with the production of private goods. The basic relationships can be expressed in abbreviated form as:

$$U = U(X,Q) \qquad (1)$$
$$X = X(L,E,Q) \qquad (2)$$
$$Q = Q(E) \qquad (3)$$

where the assumed signs of the partial derivatives are $U_X > 0$, $U_Q < 0$, $X_L > 0$, $X_E > 0$, $X_Q < 0$, and $Q_E > 0$. The utility of a representative consumer in equation (1) depends upon a vector of goods consumed (X) and upon the level of pollution (Q). Pollution results from waste emissions (E) in the production of X, as indicated in (2). Note that the production function in (2) is taken to include as inputs a vector of conventional inputs (L), like labor and capital, the quantity of waste discharges (E), and the level of pollution (Q). In this formulation, waste emissions are treated simply as another factor of production; this seems reasonable since attempts, for example, to cut back on waste discharges will involve the diversion of other inputs to abatement activities—thereby reducing the availability of these other inputs for the production of goods. Reductions in E, in short, result in reduced output. Moreover, given the reasonable assumption of rising marginal abatement costs, it makes sense to assume the usual curvature properties so that we can legitimately draw isoquants in L and E space and treat them in the usual way.

---

[2] For comprehensive and rigorous treatments of the general ideas presented in this section, see, for example, William Baumol (1972), Baumol and Wallace Oates (1988), Paul Burrows (1979), and Richard Cornes and Todd Sandler (1986). We have not included in this survey a literature on conservation and development that has considered issues of irreversibility in the time of development for which the seminal papers are John Krutilla (1967), and Kenneth Arrow and Anthony Fisher (1974). This literature is treated in the Anthony Fisher and Peterson survey (1976) and, more recently, in Anthony Fisher (1981, ch. 5).

The production function also includes as an argument the level of pollution (Q), since pollution may have detrimental effects on production (such as soiling the output of the proverbial laundry or reducing agricultural output) as well as producing disutility to consumers. The level of pollution is itself some function of the vector of emissions (E) of all the producing units. In the very simplest case, Q might be taken to equal the sum of the emissions over all producers.[3]

One extension of the model involves the explicit introduction of "defensive" activities on the part of "victims." We might, for example, amend the utility function:

$$U = U[X, F(L, Q)] \qquad (4)$$

to indicate that individuals can employ a vector of inputs (L) to lessen, in some sense, their exposure to pollution. The level of pollution to which the individual is actually exposed (F) would then depend upon the extent of pollution (Q) and upon the employment of inputs in defensive activities (L). We could obviously introduce such defensive activities for producers as well. We thus have a set of equations which, with appropriate subscripts, would describe the behavior of the many individual households and firms that comprise the system.

It is a straightforward exercise to maximize the utility of our representative individual (or group of individuals) subject to (2) and (3) as constraints along with a further constraint on resource availabil-

ity. This exercise produces a set of first-order conditions for a Pareto-efficient outcome; of interest here is the condition taking the form:

$$\frac{\partial X}{\partial E} = -\left[\sum \left(\frac{\partial U}{\partial Q} \frac{\partial Q}{\partial E} \right) \bigg/ \frac{\partial U}{\partial X} \right.$$
$$\left. + \sum' \left(\frac{\partial X}{\partial Q} \frac{\partial Q}{\partial E} \right) \right] \qquad (5)$$

Equation (5) indicates that polluting firms should extend their waste discharges to the point at which the marginal product of these emissions equals the sum of the marginal damages that they impose on consumers [the first summation in (5)] and on producers [the second summation in (5)]. Or, put slightly differently, (5) says that pollution-control measures should be pursued by each polluting agent to the point at which the marginal benefits from reduced pollution (summed over all individuals and all firms) equal marginal abatement cost.

Another of the resulting first-order conditions relates to the efficient level of defensive activities:

$$\frac{\partial U}{\partial F} \frac{\partial F}{\partial L} = \frac{\partial U}{\partial X} \frac{\partial X}{\partial L} \qquad (6)$$

which says simply that the marginal value of each input should be equated in its use in production and defensive activities.

The next step is to derive the first-order conditions characterizing a competitive market equilibrium, where we find that competitive firms with free access to environmental resources will continue to engage in polluting activities until the marginal return is zero, that is, until $\partial X/\partial E = 0$. We thus obtain the familiar result that because of their disregard for the external costs that they impose on others, polluting agents will engage in socially excessive levels of polluting activities.

The policy implication of this result is

[3] This highly simplifed model, although useful for our analytical purposes, admittedly fails to encompass the complexity of the natural environment. There is an important literature in environmental economics that develops the "materials-balance" approach to environmental analysis (see Kneese, Robert Ayres, and Ralph d'Arge 1970; Karl-Göran Mäler 1974, 1985). This approach introduces explicitly the flows of environmental resources and the physical laws to which they are subject. Some of these matters will figure in the discussion that follows.

clear. Polluting agents need to be confronted with a "price" equal to the marginal external cost of their polluting activities to induce them to internalize at the margin the full social costs of their pursuits. Such a price incentive can take the form of the familiar "Pigouvian tax," a levy on the polluting agent equal to marginal social damage. In the preceding formulation, the tax would be set equal to the expression in equation (5). Note further that the unit tax (or "effluent fee") must be attached *directly* to the polluting activity, not to some related output or input. Assuming some substitution among inputs in production, the Pigouvian tax would take the form of a levy per unit of waste emissions into the environment—not a tax on units of the firm's output or an input (e.g., fossil fuel associated with pollution).[4]

The derivation of the first-order conditions characterizing utility-maximizing behavior by individuals yields a second result of interest. Inasmuch as defensive activities in the model provide only private benefits, we find that individual maximizing behavior will satisfy the first-order conditions for Pareto efficiency for such activities. Since they are confronted with a given price for each input, individuals will allocate their spending so that a marginal dollar yields the same increment to utility whether it is spent on consumption goods or defensive activities. There is no need for any extra inducement to achieve efficient levels of defensive activities.

Although this is quite straightforward, there are a couple of matters requiring further comment. First, the Pigouvian solution to the problem of externalities has been the subject of repeated attack along Coasian lines. The Ronald Coase

(1960) argument is that in the absence of transactions costs and strategic behavior, the distortions associated with externalities will be resolved through voluntary bargains struck among the interested parties. No further inducements (such as a Pigouvian tax) are needed in this setting to achieve an efficient outcome. In fact, as Ralph Turvey (1963) showed, the introduction of a Pigouvian tax in a Coasian setting will itself be the source of distortions. Our sense, however, is that the Coasian criticism is of limited relevance to most of the major pollution problems. Since most cases of air and water pollution, for example, involve a large number of polluting agents and/or victims, the likelihood of a negotiated resolution of the problem is small—transactions costs are simply too large to permit a Coasian resolution of most major environmental problems. It thus seems to us that a Nash or "independent adjustment" equilibrium is, for most environmental issues, the appropriate analytical framework. In this setting, the Pigouvian cure for the externality malady is a valid one.[5]

Second, there has been no mention of any compensation to the victims of externalities. This is an important point—and a source of some confusion in the literature—for Coase and others have suggested that in certain circumstances compensation of victims for damages by polluting agents is necessary for an efficient outcome. As the mathematics makes clear, this is not the case for our model above. In fact, the result is even stronger: compensation of victims is not permissible (except through lump-sum transfers). Where victims have the opportunity to engage in defensive (or "averting") activities to mitigate the effects of the pollution from which they

---

[4] Where it is not feasible to monitor emissions directly, the alternative may be to tax an input or output that is closely related to emissions of the pollutant. This gives rise to a standard sort of second-best problem in taxation.

[5] For comparative analyses of the bargaining and tax approaches to the control of externalities, see Daniel Bromley (1986), and Jonathan Hamilton, Eytan Sheshinski, and Steven Slutsky (1989).

suffer, compensation cannot be allowed. For if victims are compensated for the damages they suffer, they will no longer have the incentive to undertake efficient levels of defensive measures (e.g., to locate away from polluting factories or employ various sorts of cleansing devices). As is clear in the preceding formulation, the benefits from defensive activities are private in nature (they accrue solely to the victim that undertakes them) and, as a result, economic efficiency requires no incentives other than the benefits they confer on the victim.[6]

The basic theoretical result then (subject to some qualifications to be discussed later) is that the efficient resolution of environmental externalities calls for polluting agents to face a cost at the margin for their polluting activities equal to the value of the damages they produce and for victims to select their own levels of defensive activities with no compensation from polluters. We consider next some policy alternatives for achieving this result.

B. *The Choice Among Policy Instruments*[7]

The analysis in the preceding section has run in terms of a unit tax on polluting

[6] There may, of course, exist cases where defensive activities have "publicness" properties—where the actions of one victim to defend himself against pollution also provide defense for others. In such cases, there is clearly an externality present so that individual maximizing behavior will not yield the efficient levels of defensive activities. For a careful and thorough examination of defensive activities, see Richard Butler and Michael Maher (1986). Incidentally, the general issue of compensation of victims from pollution obviously has much in common with the moral hazard problem in insurance.

[7] A further policy instrument not discussed in this section but with some potentially useful applications in environmental policy is deposit-refund systems (Peter Bohm 1981). Such systems can shift some of the responsibility for monitoring and effectively place the burden of proof on the source. For under this approach, the source, to recoup its deposit, must demonstrate that its activities have not damaged the environment. See Robert Costanza and Charles Perrings (1990) for a policy proposal under this rubric.

activities. There are, however, other approaches to establishing the proper economic incentives for abatement activities. Two alternative policy instruments have received extensive attention in the literature: unit subsidies and marketable emission permits.

It was recognized early on that a subsidy per unit of emissions reduction could establish the same incentive for abatement activity as a tax of the same magnitude per unit of waste discharges: a subsidy of 10 cents per pound of sulfur emissions reductions creates the same opportunity cost for sulfur emissions as a tax of 10 cents per unit of sulfur discharges. From this perspective, the two policy instruments are equivalent: the regulator can use either the stick or the carrot to create the desired incentive for abatement efforts.

It soon became apparent that there are some important asymmetries between these two policy instruments (e.g., Morton Kamien, Nancy L. Schwartz, and F. Trenery Dolbear 1966; D. Bramhall and Edwin Mills 1966; Kneese and Bower 1968). In particular, they have quite different implications for the profitability of production in a polluting industry: subsidies increase profits, while taxes decrease them. The policy instruments thus have quite different implications for the long-run, entry-exit decisions of firms. The subsidy approach will shift the industry supply curve to the right and result in a larger number of firms and higher industry output, while the Pigouvian tax will shift the supply curve to the left with a consequent contraction in the size of the industry. It is even conceivable that the subsidy approach could result in an increase in the total amount of pollution (Baumol and Oates 1988, ch. 14; Stuart Mestelman 1982; Robert Kohn 1985).

The basic point is that there is a further condition, an entry-exit condition, that long-run equilibrium must satisfy for an efficient outcome (William Schulze and d'Arge 1974; Robert Collinge and Oates 1982; Daniel Spulber 1985). To obtain the correct number of firms in the long run, it is essential that firms pay not only the cost of the marginal damages of their emissions, but also the total cost arising from their waste emissions. Only if firms bear the total cost of their emissions will the prospective profitability of the enterprise reflect the true social net benefit of entry and exit into the industry.[8] In sum, unit subsidies are not a fully satisfactory alternative to Pigouvian taxes (Donald Dewees and W. A. Sims 1976).

In contrast, in a world of perfect knowledge, marketable emission permits are, in principle, a fully equivalent alternative to unit taxes. Instead of setting the proper Pigouvian tax and obtaining the efficient quantity of waste discharges as a result, the environmental authority could issue emission permits equal in the aggregate to the efficient quantity and allow firms to bid for them. It is not hard to show that the market-clearing price will produce an outcome that satisfies the first-order conditions both for efficiency in pollution abatement activities in the short run and for entry-exit decisions in the long run. The regulator can, in short,

set either "price" or "quantity" and achieve the desired result.[9]

This symmetry between the price and quantity approaches is, however, critically dependent upon the assumption of perfect knowledge. In a setting of imperfect information concerning the marginal benefit and cost functions, the outcomes under the two approaches can differ in important ways.

C. *Environment Policy Under Uncertainty*

In a seminal paper, Martin Weitzman (1974) explored this asymmetry between price and quantity instruments and produced a theorem with important policy implications. The theorem establishes the conditions under which the expected welfare gain under a unit tax exceeds, is equal to, or falls short of that under a system of marketable permits (quotas). In short, the theorem states that in the presence of uncertainty concerning the costs of pollution control, the preferred policy instrument depends on the *relative* steepness of the marginal benefit and cost curves.[10]

---

[8] In an intriguing qualification to this argument, Martin Bailey (1982) has shown that not only subsidies to polluters, but also compensation to victims, will result in no distortions in resource use where benefits and damages are capitalized into site rents. For a discussion of the Bailey argument, see Baumol and Oates (1988, pp. 230–34). In another interesting extension, Gene Mumy (1980) shows that a combined charges-subsidy scheme can be fully efficient. Under this approach, sources pay a unit tax for emissions above some specified baseline, but receive a unit subsidy for emissions reductions below the baseline. The key provision is that the right to subsidy payments is limited to existing firms (i.e., new sources have a baseline of zero) and that this right can either be sold or be exercised even if the firm chooses to exit the industry. For a useful development of Mumy's insight, see John Pezzey (1990).

[9] The discussion glosses over some quite troublesome matters of implementation. For example, the effects of the emissions of a particular pollutant on ambient air or water quality will often depend importantly on the location of the source. In such cases, the optimal fee must be tailored to the damages per unit of emissions source-by-source. Or, alternatively, in a market for emission permits, the rate at which permits are traded among any two sources will vary with the effects of their respective emissions. In such a setting, programs that treat all sources uniformly can forego significant efficiency gains (Eugene Seskin, Robert Anderson, and Robert Reid 1983; Charles Kolstad 1987). More on all this shortly.

[10] This result assumes linearity of the marginal benefit and cost functions over the relevant range and that the error term enters each function additively. Uncertainty in the benefits function, interestingly, is not enough in its own right to introduce any asymmetries; while it is the source of some expected welfare loss relative to the case of perfect information, there is no difference in this loss as between the two policy instruments. For useful diagrammatic treatments of the Weitzman analysis, see Zvi Adar and James Griffin (1976), Gideon Fishelson (1976), and Baumol and Oates (1988, ch. 5).

The intuition of the Weitzman proposition is straightforward. Consider, for example, the case where the marginal benefits curve is quite steep but marginal control costs are fairly constant over the relevant range. This could reflect some kind of environmental threshold effect where, if pollutant concentrations rise only slightly over some range, dire environmental consequences follow. In such a setting, it is clearly important that the environmental authority have a close control over the quantity of emissions. If, instead, a price instrument were employed and the authority were to underestimate the true costs of pollution control, emissions might exceed the critical range with a resulting environmental disaster. In such a case, the Weitzman theorem tells us, quite sensibly, that the regulator should choose the quantity instrument (because the marginal benefits curve has a greater absolute slope than the marginal cost curve).

Suppose, next, that it is the marginal abatement cost curve that is steep and that the marginal benefits from pollution control are relatively constant over the relevant range. The danger here is that because of imperfect information, the regulatory agency might, for example, select an overly stringent standard, thereby imposing large, excessive costs on polluters and society. Under these circumstances, the expected welfare gain is larger under the price instrument. Polluters will not get stuck with inordinately high control costs, since they always have the option of paying the unit tax on emissions rather than reducing their discharges further.

The Weitzman theorem thus suggests the conditions under which each of these two policy instruments is to be preferred to the other. Not surprisingly, an even better expected outcome can be obtained by using price and quantity instruments in tandem. As Marc Roberts and Michael

Spence (1976) have shown, the regulator can set the quantity of permits at the level that equates expected marginal benefits and costs and then offer a subsidy for emissions reductions in excess of those required by the permits and also a unit tax to provide a kind of "escape hatch" in case control costs turn out to be significantly higher than anticipated. In this way, a combination of price and quantity instruments can, in a setting of imperfect information, provide a larger expected welfare gain than an approach relying on either policy instrument alone (see also Weitzman 1978).[11]

D. Market Imperfections

The efficiency properties of the policy measures we have discussed depend for their validity upon a perfectly competitive equilibrium. This is a suspect assumption, particularly since many of the major polluters in the real world are large firms in heavily concentrated industries: oil refineries, chemical companies, and auto manufacturers. This raises the issue of the robustness of the results to the presence of large firms that are not price takers in their output markets.

James Buchanan (1969) called attention to this issue by showing that the imposition of a Pigouvian tax on a monopolist could conceivably reduce (rather than raise) social welfare. A monopolist restricts output below socially optimal levels, and a tax on waste emissions will lead to yet further contractions in output. The net effect is unclear. The welfare gains from reduced pollution must be offset against the losses from the reduced output of the monopolist.

The first-best response to this conun-

[11] Butler and Maher (1982) show that in a setting of economic growth, the shifts in the marginal damage and marginal control cost schedules are likely to be such as to increase substantially the welfare loss from a fixed fee system relative to that from a system of marketable permits.

drum is clear. The regulatory authority should introduce two policy measures: a Pigouvian tax on waste emissions plus a unit subsidy to output equal to the difference between marginal cost and marginal revenue at the socially optimal level of output. Since there are two distortions, two policy instruments are required for a full resolution of the problem. Environmental regulators, however, are unlikely to have the authority (or inclination) to subsidize the output of monopolists. In the absence of such subsidies, the agency might seek to determine the second-best tax on effluents. Dwight Lee (1975) and Andy Barnett (1980) have provided the solution to this problem by deriving formally the rule for the second-best tax on waste emissions. The rule calls for a unit tax on emissions that is somewhat less than the unit tax on a perfectly competitive polluter (to account for the output effect of the tax):

$$t^* = t_c - \left| (P - MC)\frac{dX}{dE} \right| \qquad (7)$$

Equation (7) indicates that the second-best tax per unit of waste emissions (t^*) equals the Pigouvian tax on a perfectly competitive firm (t_c) *minus* the welfare loss from the reduced output of the monopolist expressed as the difference between the value of a marginal unit of output and its cost times the reduction in output associated with a unit decrease in waste emissions. It can be shown by the appropriate manipulation of (7) that the second-best tax on the monopolist varies directly with the price elasticity of demand. The rationale is clear: where demand is more price elastic, the price distortion (i.e., the divergence between price and marginal cost) tends to be smaller so that the tax on effluent need not be reduced by so much as where demand is more price inelastic.

It seems unlikely, however, that the regulator will have either the information needed or the authority to determine and impose a set of taxes on waste emissions that is differentiated by the degree of monopoly power. Suppose that the environmental authority is constrained to levying a uniform tax on waste discharges and suppose that it determines this tax in a Pigouvian manner by setting it equal to marginal social damages from pollution, completely ignoring the issue of market imperfections. How badly are things likely to go wrong? Oates and Diana Strassmann (1984) have explored this question and, using some representative values for various parameters, conclude that the complications from monopoly and other noncompetitive elements are likely to be small in magnitude; the losses from reduced output will typically be "swamped" by the allocative gains from reduced pollution. They suggest that, based on their estimates, it is not unreasonable simply to ignore the matter of incremental output distortions from effluent fees.[12] Their analysis suggests further that the failure of polluting agents to minimize costs because of more complex objective functions (a la Williamson), public agencies of the Niskanan sort, or because of regulatory constraints on profits need not seriously undermine the case for pricing incentives for pollution control. This subject needs further study, especially since many of the principal participants in the permit market for trading sulfur allowances under the new Amendments to the Clean Air Act will be regulated firms.

E. On the Robustness of the Pigouvian Prescription: Some Further Matters

Although the literature has established certain basic properties of the Pi-

---

[12] For more on this issue, see Peter Asch and Joseph Seneca (1976), Walter Misiolek (1980), and Burrows (1981).

gouvian solution to the problem of externalities, there are some remaining troublesome matters. One concerns the information requirements needed to implement the approach. Developing reliable measures of the benefits and costs of environmental amenities is, as we shall see shortly, a difficult undertaking. To determine the appropriate Pigouvian levy, moreover, we not only need measures of existing damages and control costs, but we need to develop measures of the incremental costs and benefits over a substantial range. For the proper Pigouvian levy is not a tax equal to marginal social damages at the *existing* level of pollution; it is a tax equal to marginal damages *at the optimal outcome*. We must effectively solve for the optimal level of pollution to determine the level of the tax. As an alternative, we might set the tax equal to the existing level of damages and then adjust it as levels of pollution change in the expectation that such an iterative procedure will lead us to the socially optimal outcome. But even this is not guaranteed (Baumol and Oates 1988, ch. 7).

There is, moreover, a closely related problem. In the discussion thus far, we have examined solely the first-order conditions for efficient outcomes; we have not raised the issue of satisfying any second-order conditions. As Baumol and David Bradford (1972) have shown, this is a particularly dangerous omission in the presence of externalities.[13] In fact, they demonstrate that if a detrimental externality is of sufficient strength, it *must* result in a breakdown of the convexity-concavity conditions required for an optimal outcome. As a result, there may easily exist a multiplicity of local maxima from which to choose—with no simple rule to determine the first-best out-

come.[14] Under such circumstances, equilibrium prices may tell us nothing about the efficiency of current output or the direction in which to seek improvement.

There are thus reasons for some real reservations concerning the direct application of the Pigouvian analysis to the formulation of environmental policy. It is to this issue that we turn next.

III. *The Design and Implementation of Environmental Policy*

A. *Introduction: From Theory to Policy*

Problems of measurement and the breakdown of second-order conditions (among other things) constitute formidable obstacles to the determination of a truly first-best environmental policy. In response to these obstacles, the literature has explored some second-best approaches to policy design that have appealing properties. Moreover, they try to be more consistent with the procedures and spirit of decision making in the policy arena.

Under these approaches, the determination of environmental policy is taken to be a two-step process: first, standards or targets for environmental quality are set, and, second, a regulatory system is designed and put in place to achieve these standards. This is often the way environmental decision making proceeds. Under the Clean Air Act, for example, the first task of the EPA was to set standards in the form of maximum

---

[13] See also Richard Portes (1970), David Starrett (1972), J. R. Gould (1977), and Burrows (1986).

[14] This problem is further compounded by the presence of defensive activities among victims of pollution. The interaction among abatement measures by polluters and defensive activities by victims can be a further source of nonconvexities (Hirofumi Shibata and Steven Winrich 1983; Oates 1983). Yet another source of nonconvexities can be found in the structure of subsidy programs that offer payments for emissions reductions to firms in excess of some minimum size (Raymond Palmquist 1990).

permissible concentrations of the major air pollutants. The next step was to design a regulatory plan to attain these standards for air quality.

In such a setting, systems of economic incentives can come into play in the second stage as effective regulatory instruments for the achievement of the predetermined environmental standards. Baumol and Oates (1971) have described such a system employing effluent fees as the "charges and standards" approach. But marketable permit systems can also function in this setting—a so-called "permits and standards" approach (Baumol and Oates 1988, ch. 12).[15]

The chief appeal of economic incentives as the regulatory device for achieving environmental standards is the large potential cost-savings that they promise. There is now an extensive body of empirical studies that estimate the cost of achieving standards for environmental quality under existing command-and-control (CAC) regulatory programs (e.g., Scott Atkinson and Donald Lewis 1974; Seskin, Anderson, and Reid 1983; Alan Krupnick 1983; Adele Palmer et al. 1980; Albert McGartland 1984). These are typically programs under which the environmental authority prescribes (often in great detail) the treatment procedures that are to be adopted by each source. The studies compare costs under CAC programs with those under a more cost effective system of economic incentives. The results have been quite striking: they indicate that control costs under existing programs have often been several times

the least-cost levels. (See Thomas Tietenberg 1985, ch. 3, for a useful survey of these cost studies.)

The source of these large cost savings is the capacity of economic instruments to take advantage of the large differentials in abatement costs across polluters. The information problems confronting regulators under the more traditional CAC approaches are enormous—and they lead regulators to make only very rough and crude distinctions among sources (e.g., new versus old firms). In a setting of perfect information, such problems would, of course, disappear. But in the real world of imperfect information, economic instruments have the important advantage of economizing on the need for the environmental agency to acquire information on the abatement costs of individual sources. This is just another example of the more general principles concerning the capacity of markets to deal efficiently with information problems.[16]

The estimated cost savings in the studies cited above result from a more cost effective allocation of abatement efforts within the context of existing control technologies. From a more dynamic perspective, economic incentives promise additional gains in terms of encouraging the development of more effective and less costly abatement techniques. As John Wenders (1975) points out in this context, a system that puts a value on any discharges remaining after control (such as a system of fees or marketable permits) will provide a greater incentive to R&D efforts in control technology than will a regulation that specifies some given level of discharges (see also Wesley Magat 1978, and Scott Milliman and Raymond Prince 1989).

---

[15] This is admittedly a highly simplified view of the policy process. There is surely some interplay in debate and negotiations between the determination of standards and the choice of policy instruments. More broadly, there is an emerging literature on the political economy of environmental policy that seeks to provide a better understanding of the process of instrument choice—see, for example, McCubbins, Noll, and Weingast (1989), and Robert Hahn (1990).

[16] There is also an interesting literature on incentive-compatible mechanisms to obtain abatement cost information from polluters—see, for example, Evan Kwerel (1977).

B. *The Choice of Policy Instruments Again*[17]

Some interesting issues arise in the choice between systems of effluent fees and marketable emission permits in the policy arena (John H. Dales 1968; Dewees 1983; David Harrison 1983). There is, of course, a basic sense in which they are equivalent: the environmental authority can, in principle, set price (i.e., the level of the effluent charge) and then adjust it until emissions are reduced sufficiently to achieve the prescribed environmental standard, or, alternatively, issue the requisite number of permits directly and allow the bidding of polluters to determine the market-clearing price.

However, this basic equivalence obscures some crucial differences between the two approaches in a policy setting; they are by no means equivalent policy instruments from the perspective of a regulatory agency. A major advantage of the marketable permit approach is that it gives the environmental authority direct control over the quantity of emissions. Under the fee approach, the regulator must set a fee, and if, for example, the fee turns out to be too low, pollution will exceed permissible levels. The agency will find itself in the uncomfortable position of having to adjust and readjust the fee to ensure that the environmental standard is attained. Direct control over quantity is to be preferred since the standard itself is prescribed in quantity terms.

This consideration is particularly important over time in a world of growth and inflation. A nominal fee that is adequate to hold emissions to the requisite levels at one moment in time will fail to do so later in the presence of economic growth and a rising price level. The regulatory agency will have to enact periodic (and unpopular) increases in effluent fees. In contrast, a system of marketable permits automatically accommodates itself to growth and inflation. Since there can be no change in the aggregate quantity of emissions without some explicit action on the part of the agency, increased demand will simply translate itself into a higher market-clearing price for permits with no effects on levels of waste discharges.

Polluters (that is, *existing* polluters), as well as regulators, are likely to prefer the permit approach because it can involve lower levels of compliance costs. If the permits are auctioned off, then of course polluters must pay directly for the right to emit wastes as they would under a fee system. But rather than allocating the permits by auction, the environmental authority can initiate the system with a one-time distribution of permits to existing sources—free of charge. Some form of "grandfathering" can be used to allocate permits based on historical performance. Existing firms thus receive a marketable asset, which they can then use either to validate their own emissions or sell to another polluter.[18] And finally, the permit approach has some advantages in terms of familiarity. Regulators have long-standing experience with permits, and it is a much less radical change to make permits effectively transferable than to introduce a wholly new system of regulation based on effluent fees. Mar-

---

[17] For a useful, comprehensive survey of the strengths and weaknesses of alternative policy instruments for pollution control, see Bohm and Clifford Russell (1985).

[18] In an interesting simulation study, Randolph Lyon (1982) finds that the cost of permits to sources under an auction system can be quite high; for one of the auction simulations, he finds that aggregate payments for permits will exceed treatment costs. Lyon's results thus suggest potentially large gains to polluting firms from a free distribution of permits instead of their sale through an auction. These gains, of course, are limited to current sources. Polluting firms that arrive on the scene at a later date will have to purchase permits from existing dischargers.

ketable permits thus have some quite appealing features to a regulatory agency—features that no doubt explain to some degree the revealed preference for this approach (in the U.S. at least) over that of fees.

Effluent charges have their own appeal. They are sources of public revenue, and, in these days of large budget deficits, they promise a new revenue source to hard-pressed legislators. From an economic perspective, there is much to be said for the substitution of fees for other sources of revenues that carry sizable excess burdens (Lee and Misiolek 1986). In a study of effluent charges on emissions of particulates and sulfur oxides from stationary sources into the atmosphere. David Terkla (1984) estimates, based on assumed levels of tax rates, that revenues in 1982 dollars would range from $1.8 to $8.7 billion and would, in addition, provide substantial efficiency gains ($630 million to $3.05 billion) if substituted for revenues from either the federal individual income tax or corporation income tax.

Moreover, the charges approach does not depend for its effectiveness on the development of a smoothly functioning market in permits. Significant search costs, strategic behavior, and market imperfections can impede the workings of a permit market (Hahn 1984; Tietenberg 1985, ch. 6). In contrast, under a system of fees, no transfers of permits are needed—each polluter simply responds directly to the incentive provided by the existing fee. There may well be circumstances under which it is easier to realize a cost-effective pattern of abatement efforts through a visible set of fees than through the workings of a somewhat distorted permit market. And finally, there is an equity argument in favor of fees (instead of a free distribution of permits to sources). The Organization for Economic Cooperation and Development (OECD), for example, has adopted the "Polluter Pays Principle" on the grounds that those who use society's scarce environmental resources should compensate the public for their use.

There exists a large literature on the design of fee systems and permit markets to attain predetermined levels of environmental quality. This work addresses the difficult issues that arise in the design and functioning of systems of economic incentives—issues that receive little or only perfunctory attention in the purely theoretical literature but are of real concern in the operation of actual policy measures. For example, there is the tricky matter of spatial differentiation. For most pollutants, the effect of discharges on environmental quality typically has important spatial dimensions: the specific location of the source dictates the effects that its emissions will have on environmental quality at the various monitoring points. While, in principle, this simply calls for differentiating the effluent fee according to location, in practice this is not so easy. The regulatory agency often does not have the authority or inclination to levy differing tax rates on sources according to their location. Various compromises including the construction of zones with uniform fees have been investigated (Tietenberg 1978; Seskin, Anderson, and Reid 1983; Kolstad 1987).

Similarly, problems arise under systems of transferable permits where (as is often the case) the effects of the emissions of the partners to a trade are not the same. (The seminal theoretical paper is W. David Montgomery 1972.) Several alternatives have been proposed including zoned systems that allow trades only among polluters within the specified zones, ambient permit systems under which the terms of trade are determined by the relative effects of emissions at binding monitors, and the pollution-offset system under which trades are subject to the constraint of no violations of the prevailing standard at any point in the area (Atkinson and Tietenberg 1982; Atkinson and Lewis 1974; Hahn and Noll 1982; Krupnick, Oates, and Eric Van de Verg 1983; McGartland and Oates 1985; McGartland 1988; Tietenberg 1980, 1985, Walter Spofford 1984; Baumol and Oates 1988, ch. 12). For certain pollutants, these studies make clear that a substantial portion of the cost-savings from economic-incentive approaches will be lost if spatial differentiation is not, at least to some degree, built into the program (Robert Mendelsohn 1986).

The actual design of systems of economic incentives inevitably involves some basic compromises to accommodate the range of complications to the regulatory problem (Albert Nichols 1984). It is instructive to see how some of these issues have been dealt with in practice.

C. *Experience with Economic Incentives for Environmental Management*[19]

In the United States proposals for effluent fees have met with little success; however, there has been some limited experience with programs of marketable permits for the regulation of air and water quality. In Europe, the experience (at least until quite recently) has been the reverse: some modest use of effluent charges but no experience with transferable permits. We shall provide in this section a brief summary of these measures along with some remarks on their achievements and failures.

Largely for the reasons mentioned in the preceding section, policy makers in the U.S. have found marketable permits preferable to fees as a mechanism for providing economic incentives for pollution

control.[20] The major program of this genre is the EPA's Emission Trading Program for the regulation of air quality. But there are also three other programs worthy of note: the Wisconsin system of Transferable Discharge Permits (TDP) for the management of water quality, the lead trading program (known formally as "interrefinery averaging"), and a recent program for the trading of rights for phosphorus discharges into the Dillon Reservoir in Colorado.[21]

By far the most important of these programs in terms of scope and impact, Emissions Trading has undergone a fairly complicated evolution into a program that has several major components. Under the widely publicized "Bubble" provision, a plant with many sources of emissions of a particular air pollutant is subjected to an overall emissions limitation. Within this limit, the managers of the plant have the flexibility to select a set of controls consistent with the aggregate limit, rather than conforming to specified treatment procedures for each source of discharges with the plant. Under the "Netting" provision, firms can avoid stringent limitations on new sources

---

[20] One case in which there has been some use of fees in the U.S. is the levying of charges on industrial emissions into municipal waste treatment facilities. In some instances these charges have been based not only on the quantity but also on the strength or quality of the effluent. The charges are often related to "average" levels of discharges and have had as their primary objective the raising of funds to help finance the treatment plants. Their role as an economic incentive to regulate levels of emissions has apparently been minor (see James Boland 1986; Baumol and Oates 1979, pp. 258–63). There are also a variety of taxes on the disposal of hazardous wastes, including land disposal taxes in several states.

[21] Tietenberg's book (1985) is an excellent, comprehensive treatment of the Emissions Trading Program. Robert Hahn and Gordon Hester have provided a series of recent and very valuable descriptions and assessments of all four of these programs of marketable permits. See Hahn and Hester (1989a, 1989b), and Hahn (1989). For analyses of the Wisconsin TDP system, see William O'Neil (1983), and O'Neil et al. (1983).

---

[19] The OECD (1989) has recently provided a useful "catalog" and accompanying discussion of the use of economic incentives for environmental protection in the OECD countries.

of discharges by reducing emissions from other sources of the pollutant within the facility. Hahn and Hester (1989b) report that to date there have been over 100 approved Bubble transactions in the U.S. and a much larger number of Netting "trades" (somewhere between 5,000 and 12,000). The estimated cost savings from these trades have been quite substantial; although the estimates exhibit a very wide range, the cost savings probably amount to several billion dollars.

There are provisions under Emissions Trading for external trades across firms—mainly under the Offset provision which allows new sources in nonattainment areas to "offset" their new emissions with reductions in discharges by existing sources. Offsets can be obtained through either internal (within plant) or external trades. Hahn and Hester (1989b) indicate that there have been about 2,000 trades under the Offset policy; only about 10 percent of them have been external trades—the great bulk of offsets have been obtained within the plant or facility.

Emissions Trading, as a whole, receives mixed marks. It has significantly increased the flexibility with which sources can meet their discharge limitations—and this has been important for it has allowed substantial cost savings. The great majority of the trades, however, have been internal ones. A real and active market in emissions rights involving different firms has not developed under the program (in spite of the efforts of an active firm functioning as a broker in this market). This seems to be largely the result of an extensive and complicated set of procedures for external trades that have introduced substantial levels of transactions costs into the market and have created uncertainties concerning the nature of the property rights that are being acquired. In addition, the program has been grafted onto an elaborate set of command-and-control style

regulations which effectively prohibit certain kinds of trades. Many potentially profitable trades simply have not come to pass.[22]

Likewise, the experience under the Wisconsin TDP system has involved little external trading. The program establishes a framework under which the rights to BOD discharges can be traded among sources. Since the program's inception in 1981 on the Fox River, there has been only one trade: a paper mill which shifted its treatment activities to a municipal wastewater treatment plant transferred its rights to the municipal facility. The potential number of trades is limited since there are only about twenty major sources (paper mills and municipal waste treatment plants) along the banks of the river. But even so, preliminary studies (O'Neil 1983; O'Neil et al. 1983) indicated several potentially quite profitable trades involving large cost savings. A set of quite severe restrictions appears to have discouraged these transfers of permits. Trades must be justified on the basis of "need"—and this does not include reduced costs! Moreover, the traded rights are granted only for the term of the seller's discharge permit (a maximum period of five years) with no assurance that the rights will be renewed. The Wisconsin experience seems to be one in which the conditions needed for the emergence of a viable market in discharge permits have not been established.

In contrast, EPA's "interrefinery averaging" program for the trading of lead rights resulted in a very active market over the relatively short life of the program. Begun in 1982, the program allowed refiners to trade the severely lim-

[22] In an interesting analysis of the experience with Emissions Trading, Roger Raufer and Stephen Feldman (1987) argue that some of the obstacles to trading could be circumvented by allowing the leasing of rights.

ited rights to lead additives to gasoline. The program expired in 1986, although refiners were permitted to make a use of rights that were "banked" through 1987. Trading became brisk under the program: over the first half of 1987, for example, around 50 percent of all lead added to gasoline was obtained through trades of lead rights, with substantial cost savings reported from these trades. Although reliable estimates of cost-savings for the lead-trading program are not available, Hahn and Hester (1989b) surmise that these savings have run into the hundreds of millions of dollars. As they point out, the success of the program stemmed largely from the absence of a large body of restrictions on trades: refiners were essentially free to trade lead rights and needed only to submit a quarterly report to EPA on their gasoline production and lead usage. There were, moreover, already well established markets in refinery products (including a wide variety of fuel additives) so that refinery managers had plenty of experience in these kinds of transactions.[23]

Finally, there is an emerging program in Colorado for the trading of rights to phosphorous discharges into the Dillon Reservoir. This program is noteworthy in that among those that we have discussed, it is the only one to be designed and introduced by a local government. The plan embodies few encumbrances to trading; the one major restriction is a 2:1 trading ratio for point/nonpoint trading, introduced as a "margin of safety" because of uncertainties concerning the effectiveness of nonpoint source controls. The program is still in its early stages: although no trades have been approved, some have been requested.

The U.S. experience with marketable

permits is thus a limited one with quite mixed results. In the one case where the market was allowed to function free of heavy restrictions, vigorous trading resulted with apparently large cost savings. In contrast, under Emissions Trading and the Wisconsin TDP systems, stringent restrictions on the markets for trading emissions rights appear to have effectively increased transaction costs and introduced uncertainties, seriously impeding the ability of these markets to realize the potentially large cost savings from trading. Even so, the cost savings from Emissions Trading (primarily from the Netting and Bubble provisions) have run into several billion dollars. Finally, it is interesting that these programs seem not to have had any significant and adverse environmental effects; Hahn and Hester (1989a) suggest that their impact on environmental quality has been roughly "neutral."

In light of this experience, the prospects, we think, appear favorable for the functioning of the new market in sulfur allowances that is being created under the 1990 Amendments to the Clean Air Act. This measure, designed to address the acid rain problem by cutting back annual sulfur emissions by 10 million tons, will permit affected power plants to meet their emissions reduction quotas by whatever means they wish, including the purchase of "excess" emissions reductions from other sources. The market area for this program is the nation as a whole so that there should be a large number of potential participants in the market. At this juncture, plans for the structure and functioning of the market do not appear to contain major limitations that would impede trading in the sulfur allowances. There remains, however, the possibility that state governors or public utility commissions will introduce some restrictions. There is the further concern that regulated firms may not behave

[23] We should also note that various irregularities and illegal procedures were discovered in this market—perhaps because of lax oversight.

in a strictly cost-minimizing fashion, thereby compromising some of the cost-effectiveness properties of the trading scheme. But as we suggested earlier, this may not prove to be a serious distortion.

The use of effluent fees is more prevalent in Europe where they have been employed extensively in systems of water quality management and to a limited extent for noise abatement (Ralph Johnson and Gardner Brown, Jr. 1976; Bower et al. 1981; Brown and Hans Bressers 1986; Brown and Johnson 1984; Tietenberg 1990). There are few attempts to use them for the control of air pollution. France, Germany, and the Netherlands, for example, have imposed effluent fees on emissions of various water pollutants for over two decades. It should be stressed that these fee systems are not pure systems of economic incentives of the sort discussed in economics texts. Their primary intent has not been the regulation of discharges, but rather the raising of funds to finance projects for water quality management. As such, the fees have typically been low and have tended to apply to "average" or "expected" discharges rather than to provide a clear cost signal at the margin. Moreover, the charges are overlaid on an extensive command-and-control system of regulations that mute somewhat further their effects as economic incentives.

The Netherlands has one of the oldest and most effectively managed systems of charges—and also the one with relatively high levels of fees. There is some evidence suggesting that these fees have, in fact, had a measurable effect in reducing emissions. Some multiple regression work by Hans Bressers (1983) in the Netherlands and surveys of industrial polluters and water board officials by Brown and Bressers (1986) indicate that firms have responded to the charges with significant cutbacks in discharges of water borne pollutants.

In sum, although there is some experi-

ence with systems of fees for pollution control, mainly of water pollution, these systems have not, for the most part, been designed in the spirit of economic incentives for the regulation of water quality. Their role has been more that of a revenue device to finance programs for water quality management.

These systems, it is worth noting, have addressed almost exclusively so-called "point-source" polluters. Non-point source pollution (including agricultural and urban runoff into waterways) has proved much more difficult to encompass within systems of charges or permits. Winston Harrington, Krupnick, and Henry Peskin (1985) provide a useful overview of the potential role for economic incentives in the management of non-point sources. This becomes largely a matter of seeking out potentially effective second-best measures (e.g., fees on fertilizer use), since it is difficult to measure and monitor "discharges" of pollutants from these sources. Kathleen Segerson (1988) has advanced an ingenious proposal whereby such sources would be subject to a tax (or subsidy payment) based, not on their emissions, but on the observed level of environmental quality; although sources might find themselves with tax payments resulting from circumstances outside their control (e.g., adverse weather conditions), Segerson shows that such a scheme can induce efficient abatement and entry/exit behavior on the part of non-point sources.

D. *Legal Liability as an Economic Instrument for Environmental Protection*

An entirely different approach to regulating sources is to rely on legal liability for damages to the environment. Although we often do not include this approach under the heading of economic instruments, it is clear that a system of "strict liability," under which a source is financially responsible for damages, embodies important economic incentives.[24]The imposition of such liability effectively places an "expected price" on polluting activities. The ongoing suits, for example, following upon the massive Exxon-Valdez oil spill suggest that such penalties will surely exert pressures on potential polluters to engage in preventive measures.

Under this approach, the environmental authority, in a setting of uncertainty, need not set the values of any price or quantity instruments; it simply relies on the liability rule to discipline polluters. Two issues are of interest here. The first is the capacity, in principle, for strict liability to mimic the effects of a Pigouvian tax. And the second is the likely effectiveness, in practice, of strict liability as a substitute for other forms of economic incentives. There is a substantial literature in the economics of the law that addresses these general issues and a growing number of studies that explore this matter in the context of environmental management (see, for example, Steven Shavell 1984a, 1984b; Segerson 1990).

It is clear that strict liability can, in principle, provide the source of potential damages with the same incentive as a Pigouvian tax. If a polluter knows that he will be held financially accountable for any damages his activities create, then he will have the proper incentive to seek methods to avoid these damages. Strict liability serves to internalize the external costs—just as does an appropriate tax. Strict liability is unlike a tax, however, in that it provides compensation to victims. The Pigouvian tax possesses an important asymmetry in a market sense: it is a charge to the polluter—but not a payment to the victim. And, as noted

earlier, such payments to victims can result in inefficient levels of defensive activities. Strict liability thus does not get perfect marks on efficiency grounds, even in principle, for although it internalizes the social costs of the polluter, it can be a source of distortions in victims' behavior.

The more important concern, in practice, is the effectiveness of legal liability in disciplining polluter behavior. Even if the basic rule is an efficient one in terms of placing liability on the source of the environmental damage, the actual "price" paid by the source may be much less than actual damages because of imperfections in the legal system: failures to impose liability on responsible parties resulting from uncertainty over causation, statutes of limitation, or high costs of prosecution.[25] There is the further possibility of bankruptcy as a means of avoiding large payments for damages. The evidence on these matters is mixed (see Segerson 1990), but it seems to suggest that legal liability has functioned only very imperfectly.

An interesting area of application in the environmental arena involves various pieces of legislation that provide strict liability for damages from accidental spills of oil or leakage of hazardous wastes. The Comprehensive Environmental Responses, Compensation, and Liability Act (CERCLA) of 1980 and its later amendments (popularly known as "Superfund") are noteworthy for their broad potential applicability (Thomas Grigalunas and James Opaluch 1988). Such measures may well provide a useful framework for internalizing the external

[24] The major alternative to strict liability is a negligence rule under which a polluter is liable only if he has failed to comply with a "due standard of care" in the activity that caused the damages. Under strict liability, the party causing the damages is liable irrespective of the care exercised in the polluting activity.

[25] As one reviewer noted, in these times of heightened environmental sensitivity, liability determinations could easily exceed actual damages in some instances. However, this seems not to have happened in the recent Exxon-Valdez case. The case was settled out of court with Exxon agreeing to pay some $900 million over a period of several years. Some observers believe that this falls well short of the true damages from the Exxon-Valdez oil spill in Alaska.

costs of spills (Opaluch and Grigalunas 1984). In particular, the liability approach appears to have its greatest appeal in cases like those under Superfund where damages are infrequent events and for which monitoring the level of care a firm takes under conventional regulatory procedures would be difficult.[26]

E. Environmental Federalism

In addition to the choice of policy instrument, there is the important issue of the locus of regulatory authority. In the case of fees, for example, should a central environmental authority establish a uniform fee applicable to polluters in all parts of the nation or should decentralized agencies set fee levels appropriate to their own jurisdictions? U.S. environmental policy exhibits considerable ambivalence on this matter. Under the Clean Air Act in 1970, the U.S. Congress instructed the Environmental Protection Agency to set uniform national standards for air quality—maximum permissible concentrations of key air pollutants applicable to all areas in the country. But two years later under the Clean Water Act, the Congress decided to let the individual states determine their own standards (subject to EPA approval) for water quality. The basic question is "Which approach, centralized decision making or environmental federalism, is the more promising?"

Basic economic principles seem to suggest, on first glance, a straightforward answer to this question. Since the benefits and costs of reduced levels of most forms of pollution are likely to vary (and vary substantially) across different jurisdic-

tions, the optimal level of effluent fees (or quantities of marketable permits) will also vary (Sam Peltzman and T. Nicolaus Tideman 1972). The first-best outcome must therefore be one in which fees or quantities of permits are set in accord with local circumstances, suggesting that an optimal regulatory system for pollution control will be a form of environmental federalism.

Some environmental economists have raised an objection to this general presumption. John Cumberland (1981), among others, has expressed the concern that in their eagerness to attract new business and jobs, state or local officials will tend to set excessively lax environmental standards—fees that are too low or quantities of permits that are too high. The fear is that competition among decentralized jurisdictions for jobs and income will lead to excessive environmental degradation. This, incidentally, is a line of argument that has appeared elsewhere in the literature on fiscal federalism under the title of "tax competition." The difficulty in assessing this objection to decentralized policy making is that there exists little systematic evidence on the issue; most of the evidence is anecdotal in character, and, until quite recently, there has been little theoretical work addressing the phenomenon of interjurisdictional competition.[27]

In a pair of recent papers, Oates and Robert Schwab (1988a, 1988b) have set forth a model of such competition in which "local" jurisdictions compete for a mobile national stock of capital using both tax and environmental policy instruments. Since the production functions

---

[26] A more complicated and problematic issue relates to the permission of the courts to sue under Superfund for damages from toxic substances using "the joint and several liability doctrine." Under this provision, each defendant is potentially liable for an amount up to the entire damage, irrespective of his individual contribution. For an analysis of this doctrine in the Superfund setting, see Tietenberg (1989).

[27] Two recent studies, one by Virginia McConnell and Schwab (1990), and the other by Timothy Bartik (1988c), find little evidence of strong effects of existing environmental regulations on the location decisions of firms within the U.S. This, of course, does not preclude the possibility that state and local officials, in fear of such effects, will scale down standards for environmental quality.

are neoclassical in character, an increase in a jurisdiction's capital stock raises the level of wages through an associated increase in the capital-labor ratio. In the model, local officials simultaneously employ two policy tools to attract capital: a tax rate on capital itself which can be lowered or even set negative (a subsidy) to raise the return to capital in the jurisdiction, and a level of allowable pollutant emissions (or, alternatively, an effluent fee). By increasing the level of permissible waste discharges either directly or by lowering the fee on emissions, the local authority increases the marginal product of capital and thereby encourages a further inflow of capital. The model thus involves two straightforward tradeoffs: one between wage income and tax revenues, and the other between wage income and local environmental quality. The analysis reveals that in a setting of homogeneous worker-residents making choices by simple majority rule, jurisdictions select the socially optimal levels of these two policy instruments. The tax rate on capital is set equal to zero, and the level of environmental quality is chosen so that the willingness to pay for a cleaner environment is equal to marginal abatement cost. The analysis thus supports the case for environmental federalism: decentralized policy making is efficient in the model.[28]

In one sense, this is hardly a surprising result. Since local residents care about the level of environmental quality, we should not expect that they would wish to push levels of pollution into the range where the willingness to pay to avoid environmental damage exceeds the loss in wage income from a cleaner environment. At the same time, this result is not immune to various "imperfections." If, for example, local governments are constrained constitutionally to use taxes on capital to finance various local public goods, then it is easy to show that not only will the tax rate on capital be positive, but officials will select socially excessive levels of pollution. Likewise, if Niskanen bureaucrats run the local public sector, they will choose excessively lax environmental standards as a mechanism to attract capital so as to expand the local tax base and public revenues. Finally, there can easily be conflicts among local groups of residents with differing interests (e.g., workers vs. nonworkers) that can lead to distorted outcomes (although these distortions may involve too little or too much pollution).

The basic model does at least suggest that there are some fundamental forces promoting efficient decentralized environmental decisions. If the regions selected for environmental decision making are sufficiently large to internalize the polluting effects of waste discharges, the case for environmental federalism has some force. Exploration of this issue is admittedly in its infancy—in particular, there is a pressing need for some systematic empirical study of the effects of "local" competition on environmental choices.[29]

F. *Enforcement Issues*

The great bulk of the literature on the economics of environmental regulation simply assumes that polluters comply with existing directives: they either keep their discharges within the prescribed limitation or, under a fee scheme, report accurately their levels of emissions and pay the required fees.

---

[28] Using an alternative analytical framework in which local jurisdictions "bid" against one another for polluting firms in terms of entry fees, William Fischel (1975) likewise finds that local competition produces an efficient outcome.

[29] For some other recent theoretical studies of interjurisdictional fiscal competition, see Jack Mintz and Henry Tulkens (1986), John Wilson (1986), David Wildasin (1989), and George Zodrow and Peter Mieszkowski (1986).

Sources, in short, are assumed *both* to act in good faith and to have full control over their levels of discharges so that violations of prescribed behavior do not occur.

Taking its lead from the seminal paper by Gary Becker (1968) on the economics of crime and punishment, a recent literature has addressed enforcement issues as they apply to environmental regulations.[30] As this literature points out, violations of environmental regulations can have two sources: a polluter can willfully exceed his discharge limitation (or under-report his emissions under a fee system) to reduce compliance costs *or* a stochastic dimension to discharges may exist so that the polluter has only imperfect control over his levels of emissions. In such a setting, the regulatory problem becomes a more complicated one. Not only must the regulatory agency set the usual policy parameters (emissions limitations or fees), but it must also decide upon an enforcement policy which involves both monitoring procedures and levels of fines for violations.

The early literature explored these enforcement issues in a wholly static framework. The seminal papers, for example, by Paul Downing and William Watson (1974) and by Jon Harford (1978), established a number of interesting results. Downing and Watson show that the incorporation of enforcement costs into the analysis of environmental policy suggests that optimal levels of pollution control will be less than when these costs are ignored. Harford obtains the especially interesting result that under a system of effluent fees, the level of *actual* dis-

charges is independent both of the level of the fine for underreporting and of the probability of punishment (so long as the slope of the expected penalty function with respect to the size of the violation is increasing and the probability of punishment is greater than zero). The polluter sets the level of actual wastes such that marginal abatement cost equals the effluent fee—the efficient level! But he then, in general, underreports his discharges with the extent of underreporting varying inversely with the level of fines and the probability of punishment.

Arun Malik (1990) has extended this line of analysis to the functioning of systems of marketable permits. He establishes a result analogous to Harford's: under certain circumstances, noncompliant polluters will emit precisely the same level of wastes for a given permit price as that discharged by an otherwise identical compliant firm. The conditions, however, for this equivalence are fairly stringent ones. More generally, Malik shows that noncompliant behavior will have effects on the market-clearing price in the permit market—effects that will compromise to some extent the efficiency properties of the marketable permit system.

One implication of this body of work is the expectation of widespread noncompliance on the part of polluters. But as Harrington (1988) points out, this seems not to be the case. The evidence we have from various spot checks by EPA and GAO suggests that most industrial polluters seem to be in compliance most of the time.[31] Substantial compliance seems

---

[30] Russell, Harrington, and William Vaughan (1986, ch. 4) provide a useful survey of the enforcement literature in environmental economics up to 1985. Harrington (1988) presents a concise, excellent overview both of the more recent literature and of the "stylized facts" of actual compliance and enforcement behavior. See also Russell (1990).

[31] Interestingly, noncompliance seems to be more widespread among municipal waste treatment plants than among industrial sources! (Russell 1990, p. 256). Some of the most formidable enforcement problems involve federal agencies. The GAO (1988), for example, has found the Department of Energy's nuclear weapons facilities to be a source of major concern; the costs of dealing with environmental contamination associated with these facilities are estimated at more than $100 billion.

to exist in spite of modest enforcement efforts: relatively few "notices of violation" have been issued and far fewer polluters have actually been fined for their violations. Moreover, where such fines have been levied, they have typically been quite small. And yet in spite of such modest enforcement efforts, "cheating" is not ubiquitous—violations are certainly not infrequent, but they are far from universal.

This finding simply doesn't square at all well with the results from the static models of polluter behavior.[32] An alternative line of modeling (drawing on the tax-evasion literature) seems to provide a better description of polluter behavior; it also has some potentially instructive normative implications. This approach puts the problem in a dynamic game-theoretic framework. Both polluters and regulators react to the activities of one another in the previous period. In a provocative paper, Harrington (1988) models the enforcement process as a Markov decision problem. Polluters that are detected in violation in one period are moved to a separate group in the next period in which they are subject to more frequent inspection and higher fines. Polluting firms thus have an incentive to comply in order to avoid being moved into the second group (from which they can return to the original group only after a period during which no violations are detected). In such a framework, firms may be in compliance even though they would be subject to no fine for a violation. Following up on Russell's analysis (Russell, Harrington, and Vaughan 1986, pp. 199–216), Harrington finds that the addition of yet a third group, an absorbing state from which the polluter can never emerge, can result in a "spectacu-

lar reduction in the minimum resources required to achieve a given level of compliance" (p. 47). In sum, the dynamic game-theoretic approach can produce compliance in cases in which the expected penalty is insufficient to prevent violations in a purely static model. Moreover, it suggests some potentially valuable guidelines for the design of cost-effective enforcement procedures. Enforcement is an area where economic analysis may make some quite useful contributions.

G. *The Effects of Domestic Environmental Policy on Patterns of International Trade*

The introduction of policy measures to protect the environment has potential implications not only for the domestic economy but also for international trade. Proposed environmental regulations are, in fact, often opposed vigorously on the grounds that they will impair the "international competitiveness" of domestic industries. The increased costs associated with pollution control measures will, so the argument goes, result in a loss of export markets and increased imports of products of polluting industries.

These potential effects have been the subject of some study. It is clear, for example, that the adoption of costly control measures in certain countries will, in principle, alter the international structure of relative costs with potential effects on patterns of specialization and world trade. These trade effects have been explored in some detail, making use of standard models of international trade (Kazumi Asako 1979; Baumol and Oates 1988, ch. 16; Anthony Koo 1974; Martin McGuire 1982; John Merrifield 1988; Rüdiger Pethig 1976; Pethig et al. 1980; Horst Siebert 1974; James Tobey 1989; Ingo Walter 1975). In particular, there has been a concern that the less developed countries, with their emphasis on

---

[32] Perhaps public opprobrium is a stronger disciplinary force than economists are typically inclined to believe!

economic development rather than environmental protection, will tend over time to develop a comparative advantage in pollution-intensive industries. In consequence, they will become the "havens" for the world's dirty industries; this concern has become known as the "pollution-haven hypothesis" (Walter and Judith Ugelow 1979; Walter 1982).

Some early studies made use of existing macro-econometric models to assess the likely magnitudes of these effects. These studies used estimates of the costs of pollution control programs on an industry basis to get some sense of the effects of these programs on trade and payments flows. Generally, they found small, but measurable, effects (d'Arge and Kneese 1971; Walter 1974).

We are now in a position to examine historically what has, in fact, happened. To what extent have environmental measures influenced the pattern of world trade? Have the LDC's become the havens of the world's dirty industries? Two recent studies, quite different in character, have addressed this issue directly. H. Jeffrey Leonard (1988), in what is largely a case study of trade and foreign-investment flows for several key industries and countries, finds little evidence that pollution-control measures have exerted a systematic effect on international trade and investment. After examining some aggregate figures, the policy stances in several industrialized and developing countries, and the operations of multinational corporations, Leonard concludes that "the differentials in the costs of complying with environmental regulations and in the levels of environmental concern in industrialized and industrializing countries have not been strong enough to offset larger political and economic forces in shaping aggregate international comparative advantage" (p. 231).

Tobey (1989, 1990) has looked at the same issue in a large econometric study of international trade patterns in "pollution-intensive" goods. After controlling for the effects of relative factor abundance and other trade determinants, Tobey cannot find any effects of various measures of the stringency of domestic environmental policies. Tobey estimates two sets of equations that explain, respectively, patterns of trade in pollution-intensive goods and changes in trade patterns from 1970 to 1984. In neither set of equations do the variables measuring the stringency of domestic environmental policy have the predicted effect on trade patterns.

Why have domestic environmental measures not induced "industrial flight;" and the development of "pollution havens?" The primary reason seems to be that the costs of pollution control have not, in fact, loomed very large even in heavily polluting industries. Existing estimates suggest that control costs have run on the order of only 1 to 2½ percent of total costs in most pollution-intensive industries; H. David Robison (1985, p. 704), for example, reports that total abatement costs per dollar of output in 1977 were well under 3 percent in all industries with the sole exception of electric utilities where they were 5.4 percent. Such small increments to costs are likely to be swamped in their impact on international trade by the much larger effects of changing differentials in labor costs, swings in exchange rates, etc. Moreover, nearly all the industrialized countries have introduced environmental measures—and at roughly the same time—so that such measures have not been the source of significant cost differentials among major competitors. There seems not to have been a discernible movement in investment in these industries to the developing countries because major political and economic uncertainties have apparently loomed much larger in location decisions than have the modest savings from less stringent environmental controls.

In short, domestic environmental policies, at least to this point in time, do not appear to have had significant effects on patterns of international trade. From an environmental perspective, this is a comforting finding, for it means that there is little force to the argument that we need to relax environmental policies to preserve international competitiveness.

H. *Command-and-Control vs. Economic Incentives: Some Concluding Observations*

Much of the literature in environmental economics, both theoretical and empirical, contrasts in quite sharp and uncompromising terms the properties of systems of economic incentives with the inferior outcomes under existing systems of command-and-control regulations. In certain respects, this literature has been a bit misleading and, perhaps, unfair. The term command-and-control encompasses a very broad and diverse set of regulatory techniques—some admittedly quite crude and excessively costly. But others are far more sophisticated and cost sensitive. In fact, the dividing line between so-called CAC and incentive-based policies is not always so clear. A program under which the regulator specifies the exact treatment procedures to be followed by polluters obviously falls within the CAC class. But what about a policy that establishes a fixed emissions limitation for a particular source (with no trading possible) but allows the polluter to select the form of compliance? Such flexibility certainly allows the operation of economic incentives in terms of the search for the least-cost method of control.

The point here is that it can be quite misleading to lump together in a cavalier fashion "CAC" methods of regulatory control and to contrast them as a class with the least-cost outcomes typically associated with systems of economic incentives. In fact, the compromises and "imperfections" inherent in the design and implementation of incentive-based systems virtually guarantee that they also will be unable to realize the formal least-cost result.

Empirical studies contrasting the cost effectiveness of the two general approaches have typically examined the cost under each system of attaining a specified *standard* of environmental quality—which typically means ensuring that at no point in an area do pollutant concentrations exceed the maximum level permissible under the particular standard. As Atkinson and Tietenberg (1982) and others have noted, CAC systems typically result in substantial "over-control" relative to incentive-based systems. Since it effectively assigns a zero shadow price to any environmental improvements over and above the standard, the least-cost algorithm attempts to make use of any "excess" environmental capacity to increase emissions and thereby reduce control costs. The less cost-sensitive CAC approaches generally overly restrict emissions (relative to the least-cost solution) and thereby produce pollutant concentrations at nonbinding points that are less than those under the least-cost outcome. In sum, at most points in the area, environmental quality (although subject to the same overall standard) will be higher under a CAC system than under the least-cost solution. So long as there is some value to improved environmental quality beyond the standard, a proper comparison of benefits and costs should give the CAC system credit for this increment to environmental quality. One recent study (Oates, Paul Portney, and McGartland 1989) which does just this for a major air pollutant finds that a relatively sophisticated CAC approach produces results that compare reasonably well to the prospective outcome under a fully cost effective system of economic incentives.

Our intent is not to suggest that the economist's emphasis on systems of economic incentives has been misplaced, but rather to argue that policy structure and analysis is a good deal more complicated than the usual textbooks would suggest (Nichols 1984). The applicability of systems of economic incentives is to some extent limited by monitoring capabilities and spatial complications. In fact, in any meaningful sense the "optimal" structure of regulatory programs for the control of air and water pollution is going to involve a combination of policy instruments—some making use of economic incentives and others not. Careful economic analysis has, we believe, an important role to play in understanding the workings of these systems. But it can make its best contribution, not through a dogmatic commitment to economic incentives, but rather by the careful analysis of the whole range of policy instruments available, insuring that those CAC measures that are adopted are effective devices for controlling pollution at relatively modest cost (Kolstad 1986).

At the same time, it is our sense that incentive-based systems have much to contribute to environmental protection—and that they have been much neglected in part because of the (understandable) predisposition of regulators to more traditional policy instruments.[33] There are strong reasons for believing, with supporting evidence, that this neglect has seriously impaired our efforts both to realize our objectives for improved environmental quality and to do

so at the lowest cost. A general realization of this point seems to be emerging with a consequent renewed interest in many countries in the possibility of integrating incentive-based policies into environmental regulations—a matter to which we shall return in the concluding section.

IV. *Measuring the Benefits and Costs of Pollution Control*

As we suggested in the previous sections, effluent fees and transferable permits are capable, in principle, of achieving a given pollution standard at least cost. Eventually, however, economists must ask whether environmental standards have been set at appropriate levels: does the marginal cost of achieving the ozone standard in the Los Angeles basin exceed the marginal benefits? The answer to this question requires that we measure the benefits and costs of pollution control.

While the measurement of control costs is itself no simple task, environmental economists have turned most of their attention to the benefit side of the ledger. Of central concern has been the development of methodologies to measure the benefits of goods—such as clean air or water—that are not sold in markets. These techniques fall into two categories: indirect market methods, which attempt to infer from actual choices, such as choosing where to live, the value people place on environmental goods; and direct questioning approaches, which ask people to make tradeoffs between environmental and other goods in a survey context. We shall review both approaches, and then discuss the application of these methods to valuing the benefits of pollution control. In particular, we will try to highlight areas where benefits have been successfully measured, as well as areas where good benefit estimates are

---

[33] See Steven Kelman (1981) for a fascinating—if somewhat dismaying—study of the politics and ideology of economic incentives for environmental protection.

most needed. But first we must be clear about the valuation of changes in environmental quality.

A. Defining the Value of a Change in Environmental Quality

We noted at the beginning of this review that pollution may enter both consumers' utility functions and firms' production functions. (See equations (1) and (2).) To elaborate on how this might occur we introduce a *damage function* that links pollution, Q, to something people value, S,

$$S = S(Q). \tag{8}$$

For a consumer, S might be time spent ill or expected fish catch; for a firm it might be an input into production, such as the stock of halibut. We assume that S replaces Q in the utility and production functions (equations (1) and (2)).

There are two cases of interest here. First, if the consumer (or firm) views S as out of his control, we can define the value of a change in S (which may be easier to measure than the value of a change in Q), and then predict the change in S resulting from a change in Q. For example, if people view reductions in visibility associated with air pollution as beyond their control, one can predict the reduction in visibility from (8) and concentrate on valuing visibility. This is commonly known as the damage function approach to benefit estimation.

The second case is more complicated. It may sometimes be possible to mitigate the effects of pollution through the use of inputs, Z. For example, medicine may exist to alleviate respiratory symptoms associated with air pollution. In this instance, equation (8) must be modified to

$$S = S(Q,Z), \tag{9}$$

and it is Q rather than S that must be valued, because S is no longer exogenous.

For the case of a firm, the value of a change in Q (or S) is the change in the firm's profits when Q (or S) is altered. This amount is the same whether we are talking about the firm's willingness to pay (*WTP*) for an improvement in environmental quality or its willingness to accept (*WTA*) compensation for a reduction in environmental quality.

For a consumer, in contrast, the value of a change in Q (or S) depends on the initial assignment of property rights. If consumers are viewed as having to pay for an improvement in environmental quality, for example, from Q^0 to Q^1, the most they should be willing to pay for this change is the reduction in expenditure necessary to achieve their original utility level when Q improves. Formally, if $e(P,S(Q^0),U^0)$ denotes the minimum expenditure necessary to achieve pre-improvement utility U^0 at prices P and environmental quality Q^0, then the most people would be willing to pay (WTP) for the improvement in environmental quality to Q^1 is

$$WTP = e(P,S(Q^0),U^0) \\ - e(P,S(Q^1),U^0). \tag{10}$$

If, on the other hand, consumers are viewed as having rights to the higher level of environmental quality and must be compensated for a reduction in Q, then the smallest amount they would be willing to accept is the additional amount they must spend to achieve their original utility level when Q declines. Formally, willingness to accept (*WTA*) compensation for a reduction in Q from Q^1 to Q^0 is given by

$$WTA = e(P,S(Q^0),U^1) \\ - e(P,S(Q^1),U^1), \tag{11}$$

where U^1 is the utility level achieved at the higher level of environmental quality.

In general, willingness to accept compensation for a reduction in Q will be higher than willingness to pay for an increase in Q of the same magnitude. As W. Michael Hanemann (1991) has recently shown, the amount by which WTA exceeds WTP varies directly with the income elasticity of demand for S and inversely with the elasticity of substitution between S and private goods. If the income elasticity of demand for S is zero or if S is a perfect substitute for a private good, WTP should equal WTA. If, however, the elasticity of substitution between S and private goods is zero, the difference between WTA and WTP can be infinite. It is therefore important to determine which valuation concept, WTP or WTA, is appropriate for the problem at hand.

The preceding definitions of the value of a change in environmental quality do not by themselves characterize all of the welfare effects of environmental policies. Improvements in environmental quality may alter prices as well as air or water quality, and these price changes must be valued in addition to quality changes.

In contrast to valuing quality changes, valuing price changes is relatively straightforward. WTP for a reduction in price is just the reduction in expenditure necessary to achieve U^0 (the consumer's original utility level) when prices are reduced. As is well known, this is just the area to the left of the relevant compensated demand function (i.e., the one that holds utility at U^0) between the two prices. Willingness to accept compensation for a price increase is the increase in expenditure necessary to achieve U^1, the utility level enjoyed at the lower price, when price is increased.

Unlike the case of a quality change, WTA compensation for a price increase exceeds WTP for a price decrease only by the amount of an income effect. As long as expenditure on the good in question is a small fraction of total expenditure, the difference between the two welfare measures will be small. Moreover, approximating WTP or WTA by consumer surplus—the area to the left of the Marshallian demand function will produce an error of no more than 5 percent in most cases (Robert Willig 1976).[34]

One problem with the definitions of the value of a change in environmental quality (equations (10) and (11)) is that not all environmental benefits can be viewed as certain. Reducing exposure to a carcinogen, for example, alters the probability that persons in the exposed population will contract cancer, and it is this probability that must be valued.

To define the value of a quality change under uncertainty, suppose that the value of S associated with a given Q is uncertain. Specifically, suppose that two values of S are possible: S^0 and S^1. For example, S^0 might be 360 healthy days per year and S^1 no healthy days (death). Q no longer determines S directly, but affects π, the probability that S^0 occurs. If the individual is an expected utility maximizer and if $V(M,S^i)$, $i = 0,1$, denotes his expected utility in each state (M being income), willingness to pay for a change in Q from Q^0 to Q^1 is the most one can take away from the individual and leave him at his original expected utility level (Michael Jones-Lee 1974).

$$\pi(Q^0)V(M,S^0) + [1 - \pi(Q^0)]V(M,S^1)$$
$$= \pi(Q^1)V(M - WTP,S^0)$$
$$+ [1 - \pi(Q^1)]V(M - WTP,S^1). \qquad (12)$$

For a small change in Q, WTP is just the difference in utility between the two states, divided by the expected marginal utility of money,

---

[34] Sufficient conditions for this to hold are that (1) consumer surplus is no more than 90 percent of income; (2) the ratio of consumer surplus to income, multiplied by one-half the income elasticity of demand, is no more than 0.05.

$$WTP = \frac{[V(M,S^0) - V(M,S^1)]}{\pi V_M^0 + (1 - \pi)V_M^1}$$

$$\cdot \frac{\partial \pi}{\partial Q} \, dQ. \quad (13)$$

An important point to note here is that the value of the change in Q is an ex ante value: changes in Q are valued before the outcomes are known. For example, suppose that reducing exposure to an environmental carcinogen is expected to save two lives in a city of 1,000,000 persons. The ex ante approach views this as a 2-in-one-million reduction in the probability of death for each person in the population. The ex post approach, by contrast, would value the reduction in two lives with certainty.

We are now in a position to discuss the principal methods that have been used to value changes in pollution.

B. *Indirect Methods for Measuring the Benefits of Environmental Quality*

Economists have employed three approaches to valuing pollution that rely on observed choices: the averting behavior approach, the weak complementarity approach, and the hedonic price approach.

1. *The Averting Behavior Approach.* The averting behavior approach relies on the fact that in some cases purchased inputs can be used to mitigate the effects of pollution.[35] For example, farmers can increase the amount of land and other inputs to compensate for the fact that ozone reduces soybean yields. Or, for another, residents of smoggy areas can take medicine to relieve itchy eyes and runny noses.

As long as other inputs can be used to compensate for the effects of pollution,

the value of a small change in pollution can be measured by the value of the inputs used to compensate for the change in pollution. If, for example, a reduction in one-hour maximum ozone levels from 0.16 parts per million (ppm) to 0.11 ppm reduces the number of days of respiratory symptoms from 6 to 5, and if an expenditure on medication of $20 has the same effect, then the value of the ozone reduction is $20.

Somewhat more formally, if $S = S(Q,Z)$, willingness to pay for a marginal change in Q may be written as the marginal rate of substitution between an averting good and pollution, times the price of the averting good (Paul Courant and Richard Porter 1981).

$$WTP = -p_1 \frac{\partial S/\partial Q}{\partial S/\partial z_1}, \quad (14)$$

where z_1 is medication. Marginal WTP can thus be estimated from the production function alone.

To value a nonmarginal change in pollution, one must know both the cost function for the good affected by pollution and the marginal value function for that good. For example, in the case of health damages, a large improvement in air quality will shift the marginal cost of healthy days to the right (see Figure 1) and the value of the change is given by the area between the two marginal cost curves, bounded by the marginal value of healthy time. When the good in question is not sold in markets, as is the case for health, estimating the marginal value function is, however, difficult.[36]

---

[35] In terms of the notation above, either (9) applies, or other inputs can be substituted for S in production; see equation (2).

[36] If S were sold in markets, estimation of the marginal value function would be simple, assuming one could observe the price of S and assuming that the price was exogenous to any household. The problem is that, for a good produced by the household itself, one cannot observe the price (marginal cost) of the good—it must be estimated from the marginal cost function. Furthermore, the price is endogenous, since it depends on the level of S.

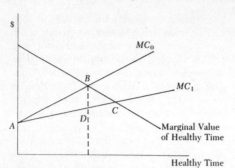

Figure 1. Morbidity Benefits of a Nonmarginal Pollution Reduction

An alternative approach, suggested by Bartik (1988a), is to use the change in the cost of producing the original level of S, i.e., the area between the marginal cost functions to the left of S^0 (area ABD in Figure 1), to approximate the value of the environmental quality change. For an improvement in Q, this understates the value of the change because it does not allow the individual to increase his chosen value of S. When the marginal cost of S increases, the relevant area will overstate the value of the welfare decrease. The advantage of this approximation is that it can be estimated from knowledge of the cost function alone.

The usefulness of the averting behavior approach is clearly limited to cases where other inputs can be substituted for pollution. Most pollution damages suffered by firms occur in agriculture, forestry, and fishing. In the case of agriculture, irrigation can compensate for the effects of global warming on crop yields. Likewise, capital (boats and gear) and labor can compensate for fish populations depleted as a result of water pollution.

In the case of pollution damages suffered by households, averting behavior has been used to value health damages and the soiling damages caused by air pollution. Households can avoid health damages either by avoiding exposure to

pollution in the first place, or by mitigating the effects of exposure once they occur. For example, the deleterious effects of water pollution can be avoided by purchasing bottled water (V. Kerry Smith and William Desvousges 1986b), and pollutants in outdoor air may be filtered by running an air-conditioner (Mark Dickie and Shelby Gerking 1991).

Two problems, however, arise in applying the averting behavior method in these cases. First, in computing the right-hand-side of (14), the researcher must know what the household imagined the benefit of purchasing water $(\partial S/\partial z_1)$ to be, since it is the *perceived* benefits of averting behavior that the household equates to the marginal cost of this behavior. Second, when the averting input produces joint products, as in the case of running an air-conditioner, the cost of the activity cannot be attributed solely to averting behavior. Inputs that mitigate the effects of pollution include medicine and doctors' visits (Gerking and Linda Stanley 1986); however, use of the latter often runs into the joint product problem—a doctor's visit may treat ailments unrelated to pollution, as well as pollution related illness.

2. *The Weak Complementarity Approach.* While the averting behavior approach exploits the substitutability between pollution and other inputs into production, the weak complementarity approach values changes in environmental quality by making use of the complementarity of environmental quality, e.g., cleaner water, with a purchased good, e.g., visits to a lake. Suppose that a specified improvement in water quality at a lake resort results in an increase in a household's demand for visits to the resort from *ED* to *AB* (see Figure 2). One can view the value of access to the lake at the original quality level Q^0 as the value of being able to visit the lake at a cost of *C* rather than at some cost *E*.

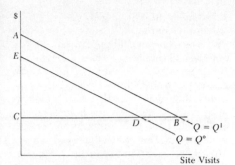

Figure 2. The Effect of a Change in Environmental Quality on the Demand for Visits to a Recreation Site

The value of access to the lake is thus the area EDC.[37] The increase in the value of access when Q changes (area $ABDE$) is the value of the water quality improvement.

For area $ABDE$ to measure the value of the water quality improvement, environmental quality must be weakly complementary to the good in question (Mäler 1974; Nancy Bockstael and Kenneth McConnell 1983). This means that (1) the marginal utility of environmental quality (water quality) must be zero if none of the good is purchased (no visits are made to the lake); (2) there is a price above which none of the good is purchased (no visits are made). If (1) did not hold, three would be additional benefits to a change in water quality not reflected in the demand for visits.

In practice, the weak complementarity approach has been used most often to value the attributes of recreation sites— either water quality, or a related attri-

bute, such as fish catch.[38] Although site visits do not have a market price, their cost can be measured by summing the cost of traveling to the site, including the time cost, as well as any entrance fees.

A problem in measuring the demand for site visits as a function of site quality is that there is no variation in site quality among persons who visit a site. A popular solution to this problem is the varying parameters model, which assumes that site quality enters recreation demand functions multiplied by travel cost or income, both of which vary across households.[39] In the first stage of the model, the demand for visits to site i is regressed on the cost of visiting the site and on income. In the second stage the coefficients from stage one are regressed on quality variables at site i. This is equivalent to estimating a set of demand functions in which visits to site i depend on the quality of the ith site, the cost of visiting the ith site, income, and interactions between travel cost and quality, and income and quality.

One drawback of this approach is that it allows visits to a given site to depend only on the cost of visiting that site— the cost of visiting substitute sites is not considered. This is equivalent to assuming that, except for the quality variables that enter the model in stage two, all sites are perfect substitutes. The varying parameters model may, therefore, give misleading results if one wishes to value quality changes at several sites.

A second approach to valuing quality changes is to use a discrete choice model. This approach examines the choice of

---

[37] Strictly speaking EDC should be measured using the consumer's compensated demand function. When measuring the value of access to a good, use of the Marshallian demand function may no longer provide a good approximation to the welfare triangle since the choke prices of the Marshallian and compensated demand functions may vary substantially. The Willig bounds do not apply in this case.

[38] Surveys of recreation demand models may be found in Mendelsohn (1987) and also in John Braden and Kolstad (1991). Bockstael, Hanemann, and Catherine Kling (1987) discuss their application to valuing environmental quality at recreation sites.

[39] This solution was first used by Vaughan and Russell (1982) and has also been used by V. Kerry Smith, Desvousges, and Matthew McGivney (1983), and V. Kerry Smith and Desvousges (1986a).

which site to visit on a given day as a function of the cost of visiting each site, and the quality of each site. If the choice of which site to visit on the first recreation day can be viewed as independent of which site to visit on the *i*th, a simple discrete choice model, such as the multinomial logit, can be applied to the choice of site, conditional on participation (Clark Binkley and Hanemann 1978; Daniel Feenberg and Mills 1980). The choice of whether to participate and, if so, on how many days, is made by comparing the maximum utility received from taking a trip with the utility of the best substitute activity on that day.[40]

The advantage of the discrete choice model is that the probability of visiting any one site depends on the costs of visiting all sites and the levels of quality at all sites. The drawback of the model is that the decision to take a trip or not and, if so, which site to visit, is made independently on each day of the season. The number of trips made to date influence neither which site the individual chooses to go to on a given day, nor whether he takes a trip at all.[41] Thus, these models must be combined with models that predict the total number of trips taken.

3. *Hedonic   Market   Methods.* The

---

[40] If one estimates a discrete choice model of recreation decisions, the value of a change in environmental quality at site *i* is no longer measured as indicated in Figure 2 (Hanemann 1984). Because utility is random from the viewpoint of the researcher, compensating variation for a change in quality at a recreation site on a given day equals the change in utility conditional on visiting the site times the probability that the site is visited, plus the change in probability of visiting the site times the utility received from the site.

[41] One solution to this problem, proposed by Edward Morey (1984), is to estimate a share model, which allocates the recreation budget for a season among different sites. The drawback of this model is that the share of the budget going to each site is assumed to be positive, whereas, in reality, a household may not visit all sites.

third method used by economists to value environmental quality, or a related output such as mortality risk, exploits the concept of hedonic prices—the notion that the price of a house or job can be decomposed into the prices of the attributes that make up the good, such as air quality in the case of a house (Ronald Ridker and John Henning 1967), or risk of death in the case of a job (Richard Thaler and Sherwin Rosen 1976). The hedonic price approach has been used primarily to value environmental disamenities in urban areas (air pollution, proximity to hazardous waste sites), which are reflected both in housing prices and in wages. It has also been used to value mortality risks by examining the compensation workers receive for voluntarily assuming job risks. Finally, the hedonic travel cost approach has been used to value recreation sites. We discuss each approach in turn.

Urban Amenities. Air quality and other environmental amenities can be valued in an urban setting by virtue of being tied to residential location: they are part of the bundle of amenities—public schools, police protection, proximity to parks—that a household purchases when buying a house.

The essence of the hedonic approach is to try to decompose the price of a house (or of residential land) into the prices of individual attributes, including air quality. This is done using an hedonic price function, which describes the equilibrium relationship between house price, p, and attributes, $A = (a_1, a_2, \ldots, a_n)$. The marginal price of an attribute in the market is simply the partial derivative of the hedonic price function with respect to that attribute. In selecting a house, consumers equate their marginal willingness to pay for each attribute to its marginal price (S. Rosen 1974; A. Myrick Freeman 1974). This implies that the gradient of the hedonic price function, evaluated at the chosen house, gives the buyer's marginal willingnesses to pay for each attribute.

Somewhat more formally, utility maximization in an hedonic market calls for the marginal price of an attribute to equal the household's marginal willingness to pay for the attribute,

$$\partial p / \partial a_i = \partial \theta / \partial a_i, \qquad (15)$$

where θ is the household's bid function, the most one can take away from the household in return for the collection of amenities, A, and keep its utility constant. Equation (15) implies that, in equilibrium, the marginal willingness to pay for an attribute can be measured by its marginal price, computed from the hedonic price function.

If a large improvement in environmental quality is contemplated in one section of a city—an improvement large enough to alter housing prices—the derivative of the hedonic price function no longer measures the value of the amenity change. In the short run, before households adjust to the amenity change and prices are altered, the value of the amenity change is the area under the household's marginal bid function—the right hand side of (15)—between the old and new levels of air quality. To value the amenity change in the long run, however, one must take into account the household's adjustment to the amenity change *and* to any price changes that may result. The area under the marginal bid function (the short-run welfare measure) is, however, a lower bound to the long-run benefits of the amenity change (Bartik 1988b).

Empirical applications of the hedonic approach have typically focused either on valuing marginal amenity changes, which requires estimating only the hedonic price function, or on computing the short-run benefits of nonmarginal amen-

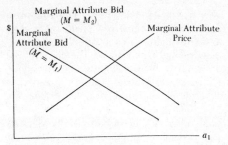

Figure 3. The Identification Problem in an Hedonic Market

ity changes, which requires estimating marginal bid functions. S. Rosen originally suggested that this be done by regressing marginal attribute price, computed from the gradient of the hedonic price function, on the arguments of the marginal bid function. This procedure, however, may encounter an identification problem which is caused by the fact that the arguments of the marginal attribute bid function determine marginal attribute price as well.

An example of the identification problem, provided by James Brown and Harvey Rosen (1982), occurs when the hedonic price function is quadratic and the marginal value functions are linear in attributes. In the case of a single amenity, a_1,

$$\partial p / \partial a_1 = \beta_0 + \beta_1 a_1 \qquad (16)$$
$$\partial \theta / \partial a_1 = b_0 + b_1 a_1 + b_2 M. \qquad (17)$$

In this case regressing $\beta_0 + \beta_1 a_1$ on a_1 and M will reproduce the parameters of the marginal price function, i.e., $\hat{b}_0 = \beta_0$, $\hat{b}_1 = \beta_1$ and $\hat{b}_2 = 0$. This is illustrated graphically in Figure 3. The problem is that the marginal price function does not shift independently of the marginal bid function. Shifts in the latter, due, say, to differences in income, thus trace out points on the marginal price function.

To achieve identification in this example, one can introduce functional form restrictions, such as adding a_1^2 to the marginal price function, but not to the marginal value function, which will cause $\partial p/\partial a_i$ to shift independently of $\partial\theta/\partial a_i$ (Mendelsohn 1984). Another solution is to estimate hedonic price functions for several markets, so that the coefficients of the marginal price function vary across cities (Palmquist 1984; Robert Ohsfeldt and Barton Smith 1985; Ohsfeldt 1988). For this to work, households in all cities must have identical preferences; however, the distribution of measured household characteristics and/or the supply of amenities must vary across cities so that the hedonic price function and its gradient vary from one city to another. In the case of several a_i's, one can impose exclusion restrictions on the a_i's that enter each marginal value function (Dennis Epple 1987) so that marginal prices vary independently of the variables that enter the marginal value function.

In view of the problems in estimating marginal attribute bid functions, it is important to note that an upper bound to the long-run benefits of an amenity improvement can be obtained from the hedonic price function alone. Yoshitsugu Kanemoto (1988) has shown that the change in prices in the improved area predicted by the hedonic price function is an upper bound to the long-run benefits of an amenity improvement. Thus, from knowledge of the hedonic price function alone one can obtain (1) the exact value of a marginal attribute change, and (2) an upper bound to the long-run value of an attribute change.

Wage-Amenity Studies. The analysis of hedonic housing markets, by focusing on housing market equilibrium within a city, implicitly ignores migration among cities. If one takes a long-run view and assumes that workers can move freely from one city to another, then data on compensating wage differentials across cities can be used to infer the value of environmental amenities (Glenn Blomquist, Mark Berger, and John Hoehn 1988; Maureen Cropper and Amalia Arriaga-Salinas 1980; V. Kerry Smith 1983). Intuitively, the value people attach to urban amenities should be reflected in the higher wages they require to live in less desirable cities.

When migration is possible, consumers choose the city in which they live to maximize utility; however, wage income, as well as amenities, vary from one city to another (S. Rosen 1979; Jennifer Roback 1982).[42] Household equilibrium requires that utility be identical in all cities. The fact that consumers in all cities must enjoy the same level of utility implies that wages and land rents must adjust to compensate for amenity differences. The marginal value of an amenity change to a consumer is thus the sum of the partial derivatives of an hedonic wage function and an hedonic property value function (Roback 1982).

Hedonic Labor Markets. The fact that risk of death is a job attribute traded in hedonic labor markets has provided economists with an alternative to the averting behavior approach as a means of valuing mortality risk (Thaler and S. Rosen 1976). The theory behind this approach is simple: other things equal, workers in riskier jobs must be compensated with higher wages for bearing this risk. As in the case of hedonic housing markets, the worker chooses his job by equating the marginal cost of working in a less risky job—the derivative of the hedonic price function—to the marginal benefit, the value (in dollars) of the resulting increase in life expectancy.

There are three problems in using the compensating wage approach. One is

---

[42] In most models wages, lot size, and amenities vary among, but not within, cities.

that compensating wage differentials exist only if workers are informed of job risks. Thus, the absence of compensating differentials need not mean that workers do not value reducing the risk of death. A second problem is that compensating differentials appear to exist only in unionized industries (William Dickens 1984; Douglas Gegax, Gerking, and Schulze 1985). This suggests that the wage differential approach may provide estimates of the value of a risk reduction only for certain segments of the population. This problem is compounded by the fact that the least risk averse individuals work in risky jobs. Third, if workers have biased estimates of job risks, or if the objective measures of job risk used in most wage studies over- or understate workers' risk perceptions, market wage premia will yield biased estimates of the value of a risk reduction.

The Hedonic Travel Cost Approach. Yet another area in which the hedonic approach has been applied is in valuing the attributes of recreation sites (G. Brown and Mendelsohn 1984). In valuing sites, the analog to the hedonic price function is obtained by regressing the cost of travelling to a recreation site on the attributes of the site, such as expected fish catch, clarity of water, and water color. However, because this relationship is not the result of market forces, there is nothing to guarantee that the marginal cost of an attribute is positive. More desirable sites may be located closer to population centers rather than farther away from them.[43] In this case, the individual's choice of site will not be described by (13), and care must be taken when inferring values from marginal attribute costs (V. Kerry Smith, Palmquist, and Paul Jakus 1990).

[43] The problem may be reduced by using only sites actually visited from a given origin in estimating the hedonic travel cost function.

C. *The Contingent Valuation Method*

While the indirect market approaches we have described above can be used to value many of the benefits of pollution reduction, there are important cases in which they cannot be used. When no appropriate averting or mitigating behavior exists, indirect methods cannot be used to estimate the morbidity benefits of reducing air pollution. Recreation benefits may be difficult to measure since there may not be enough variation in environmental quality across sites in a region to estimate the value of water quality using the travel cost approach.

There is, in addition, an entire category of benefits—*nonuse values*—which cannot even in principle be measured by indirect market methods. Nonuse values refer to the benefits received from knowing that a good exists, even though the individual may never experience the good directly. Examples include preserving an endangered species or improving visibility at the Grand Canyon for persons who never plan to visit the Grand Canyon.

This suggests that direct questioning can play a role in valuing the benefits of pollution control. Typically, direct questioning or contingent valuation studies ask respondents to value an output, such as a day spent hunting or fishing, rather than a change in pollution concentrations per se. Examples of commodities that have been valued using the contingent valuation method (CVM) include improvements in water quality to the point where the water is fishable or swimmable (Richard Carson and Robert Mitchell 1988), improvements in visibility resulting from decreased air pollution (Alan Randall, Berry Ives, and Clyde Eastman 1974; Schulze and David Brookshire 1983; Decision Focus 1990), the value of preserving endangered species (James Bowker and John Stoll 1988;

Kevin Boyle and Richard Bishop 1987), and days free of respiratory symptoms (George Tolley et al. 1986b; Dickie et al. 1987).

Any contingent valuation study must incorporate (1) a description of the commodity to be valued; (2) a method by which payment is to be made; and (3) a method of eliciting values. In studies that value recreation-related goods, hypothetical payment may take the form of a user fee or an increase in taxes; in the case of improved visibility, a charge on one's utility bill, since power plant pollution can contribute to air quality degradation. To determine the maximum a person is willing to pay for an improvement in environmental quality, the interviewer may simply ask what this amount is (an open-ended survey), or he may ask whether or not the respondent is willing to pay a stated amount (a closed-ended survey). The yes/no answer does not yield an estimate of each respondent's willingness to pay; however, the fraction of respondents willing to pay at least the stated amount gives a point on the cumulative distribution function of willingness to pay for the commodity (Trudy Cameron and Michelle James 1987).

There seems to be general agreement that closed-ended questions are easier for respondents to answer and therefore yield more reliable information than open-ended questions, especially when the commodity valued is not traded in conventional markets. Asking an open-ended question about a good that respondents have never been asked to value, such as improved visibility, often yields a distribution of responses that has a large number of zero values and a few very large ones. This may reflect the fact that respondents have nothing to which to anchor their responses, and are unwilling to go through the reasoning necessary to discover the value they place on the good. Answering a yes/no question is, by

contrast, a much easier task, and one that parallels decisions made when purchasing goods sold in conventional markets.

It must be acknowledged that, despite advances made in contingent valuation methodology during the last 15 years, many remain skeptical of the method. Perhaps the most serious criticism is that responses to contingent valuation questions are hypothetical—they represent professed, rather than actual, willingness to pay. This issue has been investigated in at least a dozen studies that compare responses to contingent valuation questions with actual payments for the same commodity.

How close hypothetical values are to actual ones depends on whether the commodity is a public or private good, on the elicitation technique used, and on whether it is willingness to pay (WTP) for the good or willingness to accept compensation (WTA) that is elicited. Most experiments comparing hypothetical and actual WTP for a private good (strawberries or hunting permits) have found no statistically significant difference between mean values of hypothetical and actual willingness to pay (Dickie, Ann Fisher, and Gerking 1987; Bishop and Thomas Heberlein 1979; Bishop, Heberlein, and Mary Jo Kealy 1983). Such is not the case when hypothetical and actual WTA are compared. In three experiments involving willingness to accept compensation for hunting permits, Bishop and Heberlein (1979) and Bishop, Heberlein, and Kealy (1983) found that actual WTA was statistically significantly lower than hypothetical WTA in two out of three cases. Hypothetical and actual WTP have also been found to differ when the commodity valued is a public good (Kealy, Jack Dovidio, and Mark L. Rockel 1987).

Other criticisms of the CVM have focused on: (1) the possibility that individuals may behave strategically in answering questions—either overstating WTP if this increases the likelihood that an improvement is made, or understating WTP if it reduces their share of the cost (the free-rider problem); (2) the fact that individuals may not be sufficiently familiar with the commodity to have a well-defined value for it; and (3) the fact that WTP for a commodity is often an order of magnitude less than willingness to accept (WTA) compensation for the loss of the commodity.

The possibility that respondents behave strategically has been tested in laboratory experiments by examining whether announced WTP for a public good varies with the method used to finance the public good. Studies by Bohm (1972), Bruce Scherr and Emerson Babb (1975), and Vernon Smith (1977, 1979) suggest that strategic behavior is not a problem, possibly because of the effort that effective strategic behavior requires.

If the commodity to be valued is not well understood, contingent valuation responses are likely to be unreliable: responses tend to exhibit wide variation, and respondents may even prefer less of a good to more! One interpretation of this result is that people really do not have values for the commodity in question—they are created by the researcher in the course of the survey (Thomas Brown and Paul Slovic 1988). This is a serious criticism: Do people really know enough about groundwater contamination or biodiversity to place a value on either good?

Fortunately, it is possible to defend against this criticism by seeing how responses vary with the amount of information that is provided about the commodity being valued. If values are well defined, they should not, on average, vary with small changes in the amount of information.

One of the most striking and challenging findings emerging from this work is

that willingness to pay for an environmental improvement is usually *many times lower* than willingness to accept compensation to forego the same improvement (Judd Hammack and G. Brown 1974; Bishop and Heberlein 1979; Robert Rowe, d'Arge, and Brookshire 1980; Jack Knetsch and J. A. Sinden 1984). This is sometimes interpreted as evidence that the method of eliciting responses is unsatisfactory; however, as we noted above, there is no reason why WTA for a quality (public good) decrease should not exceed WTP for an increase of the same magnitude, provided that there are few substitutes for the public good.[44] An alternative explanation for the WTA/WTP discrepancy that has been offered by some economists (Donald Coursey, John Hovis, and Schulze 1987; Brookshire and Coursey 1987) is that individuals are simply not as familiar with the sale of an item as with its purchase. These authors find that, in experiments where individuals were allowed to submit bids or offers for the same commodity, WTA approached WTP after several rounds of transactions.[45]

D. *Applications of Valuation Techniques*

Having described the main techniques used to value environmental amenities, we now wish to give the reader a feel for the way in which these

---

[44] The explanation of the discrepancy between WTA and WTP offered by psychologists—that monetary losses from some reference point are valued more highly than monetary gains (Daniel Kahneman and Amos Tversky 1979)—also suggests that this disparity has nothing to do with flaws in the contingent valuation method.

[45] None of these explanations, however, seems to account for results obtained by Kahneman, Knetsch, and Thaler (1990). They find that, even for common items such as coffee mugs and ballpoint pens, sellers have reservation prices that are higher, much higher on average, than buyers' bid prices. This disparity does not disappear after several rounds of trading. The initial distribution of property rights (the "endowment effect") may, therefore, matter, even for goods with many substitutes.

TABLE 1

TOTAL ANNUALIZED ENVIRONMENTAL COMPLIANCE COSTS, BY MEDIUM, 1990

(Millions of 1986 dollars)

Medium	Costs	Major Statutes
Air and Radiation, Total	28,029	
Air	27,588	Clean Air Act (CAA)
Radiation	441	Radon Pollution Control Act
Water, Total	42,410	
Water Quality	38,823	Clean Water Act (CWA)
Drinking Water	3,587	Safe Drinking Water Act
Land, Total	26,547	
RCRA	24,842	Resource Conservation and Recovery Act (RCRA)
Superfund	1,704	Comprehensive Environmental Response, Compensation and Liability Act (CERCLA)
Chemicals, Total	1,579	
Toxic Substances	600	Toxic Substances Control Act (TSCA)
Pesticides	979	Federal Insecticide, Fungicide and Rodenticide Act (FIFRA)
Total Costs	100,167	

Note: These represent the costs of complying with all federal pollution control laws, assuming full implementation of the law (USEPA 1990).

techniques have been used to value the benefits of pollution control. We shall begin with an overview of the types of benefits associated with the major pieces of environmental legislation. We then turn to a description and assessment of actual benefit estimation.

Table 1 lists the major pieces of environmental legislation in the U.S. and the estimated costs of complying with each statute in 1990. With the exception of the Clean Water Act, the primary goal of U.S. environmental legislation is to protect the health of the population. According to the Clean Air Act, ambient standards for the criteria air pollutants are to be set to protect the health of the most sensitive persons in the population.[46] The goal of the Safe Drink-

ing Water Act is, similarly, to provide a margin of safety in protecting the country's drinking water supplies from toxic substances, while the goal of the Federal Insecticide, Fungicide, and Rodenticide Act (FIFRA) is to prevent adverse effects to human health and to the environment from the use of pesticides.

Each of the statutes in Table 1 also results in certain nonhealth benefits. The Clean Air Act provides important aesthetic benefits in the form of increased visibility, and the 1990 Amendments to the Act, designed to reduce acid rain, may yield ecological and water quality benefits. The Clean Water Act—whose goal is to make all navigable water bodies fishable and swimmable—yields recreational and ecological benefits. Both Acts yield benefits to firms in agriculture, forestry, and commercial fishing. FIFRA, the primary law governing pesticide us-

[46] The criteria air pollutants are particulate matter, sulfur oxides, nitrogen oxides, carbon monoxide, lead, and ozone.

age, is designed to protect animal as well as human health.

In addition to the pollution problem addressed by the major environmental statutes, there is increasing concern about the effects of emissions of greenhouse gases, including carbon dioxide, chlorofluorocarbons (CFCs) and methane. Studies suggest that emissions of these gases may contribute to increases in mean temperature, especially in the Northern Hemisphere, changes in precipitation, and sea level rises that could average 65 cm by the end of the next century. The main effects of these changes are likely to be felt in agriculture, in animal habitat, and in human comfort.

In light of the preceding discussion, we review empirical work for four categories of nonmarket benefits: health, recreation, visibility, and ecological benefits. We also discuss the benefits of pollution control to agriculture.

1. *The Health Benefits of Pollution Control*. The statutes listed in Table 1 contribute to improved human health in several ways. By reducing exposure to carcinogens—in the air, in drinking water, and in food—environmental legislation reduces the probability of death at the end of a latency period—the time that it takes for cancerous cells to develop. Mortality benefits are also associated with control of noncarcinogenic air pollutants, which reduces mortality especially among sensitive persons in the population, e.g., angina sufferers or persons with chronic obstructive lung disease. Lessening children's exposure to lead in gasoline or drinking water avoids learning disabilities and other neurological problems associated with lead poisoning. Finally, controlling air pollution reduces illness—ranging from minor respiratory symptoms associated with smog (runny nose, itchy eyes) to more serious respiratory infections, such as pneumonia and influenza. Water borne disease (e.g.,

giardiasis) may also cause acute illness.

Reductions in risk of death have been valued using three methods: averting behavior, hedonic analysis, and contingent valuation. The most common approach to valuing changes in risk of death due to environmental causes is hedonic wage studies. The results of these studies are typically expressed in terms of the value per "statistical life" saved. If reducing exposure to some substance reduces current probability of death by 10^{-5} for each of 200,000 persons in a population, it will save two statistical lives ($10^{-5} \times$ 200,000). If each person is willing to pay \$20 for the 10^{-5} risk reduction, then the value of a statistical life is the sum of these willingnesses to pay (\$20 $\times$ 200,000), divided by the number of statistical lives saved, or \$2,000,000.

Recent compensating wage studies (Ann Fisher, Daniel Violette, and Lauraine Chestnut 1989) generate mean estimates of the value of a statistical life that fall within an order of magnitude of one another: \$1.6 million to \$9 million (\$1986), with most studies yielding mean estimates between \$1.6 million and \$4.0 million. Contingent valuation studies that value reductions in job-related risk of death (Gerking, Menno DeHaan, and Schulze 1988) or reductions in risk of auto death (Jones-Lee, M. Hammerton, and P. R. Philips 1985) fall in the same range.

Averting behavior studies—based on seat belt use (Blomquist 1979) or the use of smoke detectors (Rachel Dardis 1980)—yield estimates of the value of a statistical life that are an order of magnitude lower than the studies cited above. These studies, however, estimate the value of a risk reduction for the person who just finds it worthwhile to undertake the averting activity. This is because buckling a seat belt or purchasing a smoke detector are 0-1 activities. They are undertaken provided that their marginal benefit equals *or exceeds* their marginal cost, with equality of marginal benefit and marginal cost holding only for the marginal purchaser. If 80 percent of all persons use smoke detectors, the value of the risk reduction to the marginal purchaser may be considerably lower than the mean value.

There are, however, other problems in using the indirect market approaches we have reviewed here to value changes in environmental risks. One problem is that the risks valued in labor market and averting behavior studies are more voluntary than many environmental risks. Work by Slovic, Baruch Fischhoff, and Sarah Lichtenstein (1980, 1982) suggests that willingness to pay estimates obtained in one context may not be transferable to the other. Second, death due to an industrial accident is often instantaneous, whereas death resulting from environmental contaminants may come from cancer and involve a long latency period. Deaths due to cancer thus occur in the future and cause fewer years of life to be lost than deaths in industrial accidents. At the same time, however, cancer is one of the most feared causes of death.

In a study designed to value reductions in chemical contaminants (trihalomethanes) in drinking water, Mitchell and Carson (1986) found that the former effect seems to be important: the value of a statistical life associated with a reduction in risk of death 30 years hence was only $181,000 ($1986). This is lower than the value of a statistical life associated with current risk of death for two reasons: (1) the number of expected life years lost is smaller if the risk occurs 20 years hence, and (2) the individual may discount the value of future life years lost (Cropper and Frances Sussman 1990; Cropper and Paul Portney 1990).

In spite of these difficulties, valuing mortality risks is an area in which economists have made important contributions. The notion that, ex ante, individuals are willing to spend only a certain amount to reduce risks to life makes possible rational debate and analysis in the policy arena over tradeoffs in risk reduction. Moreover, estimates of the value of a statistical life are in sufficiently close agreement to permit their use in actual benefit-cost calculations (subject, perhaps, to some sensitivity analysis).

The valuation of morbidity has been less successful. Estimates of the value of reductions in respiratory symptoms come from two sources: averting behavior studies and contingent valuation studies. The averting behavior approach has been used to value illnesses associated with both water and air pollution. It has been more successful in the case of water pollution because an averting behavior exists (buying bottled water) that is closely linked to water pollution (Abdalla 1990; Harrington, Krupnick, and Walter Spofford 1989). By contrast, the averting behaviors used to value air pollution—running an air-conditioner in one's home or car—are in most cases not undertaken primarily because of pollution. The use of doctor visits (purpose unspecified) to mitigate the effects of air pollution suffers from a similar shortcoming.

Contingent valuation studies of respiratory symptoms (coughing, wheezing, sinus congestion) have encountered two problems. The first concerns what is to be valued. Ideally, one would like to value a change in air pollution which, after defensive behavior is undertaken, might cause a change in the level of the symptom experienced. The individual's willingness to pay for the pollution change includes the value of the change in illness after mitigating behavior is undertaken, plus the cost of the mitigating behavior. This suggests that a symptom day be valued after mitigating actions have been taken. A second problem is that the respondent must be encouraged to consider carefully his budget constraint. Failure to handle these problems has led to unbelievably high average values of a symptom day. In more careful studies, mean willingness to pay to eliminate one day of coughing range from $1.39 ($1984) (Dickie et al. 1987) to $42.00 ($1984) (Edna Loehmann et al. 1979); for a day of sinus congestion $1.88 (Dickie et al.) to $52.00 (Loehmann et al.).

An alternative approach to valuing morbidity is to use the cost of illness—the cost of medical treatment plus lost earnings—which, as Harrington and Portney (1976) have shown, is a lower bound to willingness to pay for the change in illness. Mean willingness to pay for symptom reduction is usually three to four times higher than the traditional cost of illness. Berger et al. (1987) report a mean *WTP* of $27 to eliminate a day of sinus congestion, compared with an averge cost of illness of $7. The corresponding figures for throat congestion are $44 and $14.

Studies of willingness to pay to reduce the risk of chronic disease are few (W. Kip Viscusi, Magat, and Joel Huber 1988, is a notable exception), and cost of illness estimates are more prevalent in valuing chronic illness (Ann Bartel and Paul Taubman 1979; Barbara Cooper and Dorothy Rice 1976). Viscusi, Magat, and Huber estimate the value of a statistical case of chronic bronchitis to be $883,000, approximately one-third of the value of a statistical life. This may be contrasted with cost of illness estimates of $200,000 per case of chronic lung disease (Cropper and Krupnick 1989).

As the preceding discussion indicates, more work is needed in the area of both morbidity and mortality valuation. Because of the difficulty in finding activities that mitigate the effects of air pollution, contingent valuation studies would seem to be a more promising approach to valuing morbidity. If new studies are done, they should value combinations of symptoms rather than individual symptoms, since pollution exposures often trigger

multiple symptoms, and since the value of jointly reducing several symptoms is generally less than the sum of the values of individual symptom reductions. In the case of mortality risks, more refined estimates are needed that take into account the timing of the risk, the degree of voluntariness, and the cause of death. The timing issue is especially crucial here: the benefits of environmental programs to reduce exposure to carcinogens, such as asbestos, are not realized until the end of a latency period—perhaps 40 years in the case of asbestos. Since the exposed population is 40 years older, fewer life-years are saved, compared with programs that save lives immediately.[47]

2. *The Recreation Benefits of Pollution Control.* Reductions in water pollution may enhance the quality of recreation experiences by allowing (or improving) swimming, boating, or fishing. Most studies of the recreation benefits of water pollution control have focused on fishing-related benefits, and it is on them that we concentrate our attention.

Travel cost studies have taken one of three approaches to valuing the fishing benefits of improved water quality. In some studies (V. Kerry Smith and Desvousges 1986a), measures of water quality such as dissolved oxygen are valued directly. That is, water quality variables directly enter equations that describe the choice of recreation site or demand functions for site visits.[48] This approach is clearly useful if one wishes to link the valuation study to pollution control poli-

---

[47] While some studies have attempted to take the latency period and number of life-years saved into account (Josephine Mauskopf 1987), this is not the general practice (Cropper and Portney 1990).

[48] This approach is also used when the recreation activity studied is swimming or viewing, activities where perceptions of water quality are likely to be linked to water clarity and odor. It has, for example, been applied in studies of beach visits in Boston (Bockstael, Hanemann, and Kling 1987) and lake visits in Wisconsin (George Parsons and Kealy 1990).

cies, such as policies to reduce biochemical oxygen demand (BOD), a measure of the oxygen required to neutralize organic waste. A second approach is to relate site visits (or choice of site) to fish catch. Fish catch is clearly more closely associated with motives for visiting a site than is dissolved oxygen; however, it must be linked to changes in the fish population, which must, in turn, be linked to changes in ambient water quality.

A third approach is to treat changes in water quality as effectively eliminating or creating recreation sites. This approach has been used in valuing the effects of acid rain on fishing in Adirondack lakes: reductions in pH below certain thresholds have been treated as eliminating acres of surface area for fishing of particular species (John Mullen and Frederic Menz 1985). It is also the approach used by Vaughan and Russell (1982) in valuing the benefits of the Clean Water Act. They treat the benefits of moving all point sources to the Best Practical Control Technology Currently Available (BPT) as an increase in the number of acres of surface water that support game fish (bass, trout) as opposed to rough fish (carp, catfish). The Clean Water Act is thus viewed as increasing the number of recreation sites, rather than raising fish catch at existing sites.

Regardless of the form of water recreation valued, an improvement in water quality has two effects: it increases the utility of people who currently use the resource, and it may increase participation rates (number of days spent fishing). Varying parameter models that value changes in water quality or fish catch using the shift in demand for site visits (see Figure 2) capture both effects. Discrete choice models measure the effect of a quality improvement on a given recreation day, but do not estimate the effect of quality changes on the total number of days spent fishing; however, these

models are typically used in conjunction with models that predict the total number of trips. Treating changes in water quality as altering the supply of available sites captures participation effects but not improvements in quality at existing sites.

In addition to travel cost models, contingent valuation studies have been used to value improvements in fish catch or water quality. Because it is difficult to ask consumers to value changes in dissolved oxygen levels or fecal coliform count—another measure of water quality—without linking these water quality measures to the type of activities they support, many CVM studies use the RFF Water Quality Ladder (Vaughan and Russell 1982), which relates a water quality index to the type of water use—boating, fishing (rough fish), fishing (game fish), swimming—that can be supported by various levels of the index. It is these activity levels that are valued by respondents. The water quality ladder has been used both to value water quality at specific sites (e.g., the Monongahela River, by V. Kerry Smith and Desvousges 1986a) and at all sites throughout the country (Carson and Mitchell 1988).

It is interesting to compare estimates of the value of water quality improvements obtained by the travel cost and contingent valuation approaches. Carson and Mitchell (1988) report that households are, on average, willing to pay $80 per year (in 1983 dollars) for an improvement in water quality throughout the U.S. from boatable to fishable (capable of supporting game fish). V. Kerry Smith and Desvousges (1986a) report a mean value of $25 per household for the same improvement in a five-county region in western Pennsylvania. The difference between these estimates reflects the fact that non-use values are important: households care about clean water in areas where they do not live. Even the $25 estimate for western Pennsylvania reflects nonuse values, since only one-third of the households surveyed engaged in some form of water based recreation.

Because they do not capture nonuse values, travel cost estimates of the value of improving water quality are not directly comparable with those obtained using the CVM. Using a varying parameter model, V. Kerry Smith and Desvousges (1986a) find the value of an improvement in water quality from boatable to fishable to be between $0.06 and $30.00 per person per day ($1983) for 30 Army Corps of Engineers sites. This value may be contrasted with estimates of $5 to $10 per person per day ($1983) obtained by Vaughan and Russell.

The preceding discussion suggests two problems that arise in valuing water quality benefits that do not arise in valuing health effects. The first is an aggregation problem. Suppose that one wishes to value the benefits of water quality improvements in a river basin, and suppose that the travel cost approach is used to measure use values associated with an improvement in dissolved oxygen or fish catch. The nonuse values associated with these improvements could be measured using a contingent valuation study. However, while the responses of nonusers could be added to values obtained from the travel cost approach, it would, in practice, be hard to separate use from nonuse values in the responses of fishermen.

The second problem is one of transferring results from a water quality study done in one geographic area to another area. While one can easily control for differences in willingness to pay in the two regions associated with differences in income and population, the value of water quality improvements is also likely to vary with the particular aesthetic and other characteristics of the region—and such characteristics are intrinsically hard to measure. Thus, whereas one can value

a day of coughing independently of location, it is harder to value a generic fishing day.

This raises important questions concerning priorities for research in the area of recreation benefits.[49] Future research can proceed using a contingent valuation approach in which use and nonuse values are elicited simultaneously for sites in the respondent's region. The problem here is to have the respondent value an improvement to recreation that is sufficiently specific that it can be related to changes in pH levels from acid rain or changes in levels of dissolved oxygen associated with the adoption of BPT. The advantage of this approach is that it would capture both use and nonuse values. The advantage of the travel cost approach is that it could use endpoints more closely related to pollution (such as dissolved oxygen); however, it would not yield estimates of nonuse values.

3. *The Visibility Benefits of Pollution Control.* Reductions in air pollution, by increasing visibility, may improve the quality of life in urban areas as well as at recreation sites. Since the number of persons affected by improvements in visibility is large—at least as great as the number of persons whose health is affected by air pollution—the potential value of such benefits is great.

One can view the results of hedonic property value studies performed in the 1970s and early 1980s as evidence that people value the visibility benefits of pollution control. In these studies housing prices were regressed on measures of ambient air quality such as particulates or sulfates, which are negatively correlated

---

[49] It should be emphasized that, while there exist several dozen studies of water quality benefits in a recreation context, many studies analyze the same data. Thus, empirical estimates of water quality benefits exist for only a few areas of the country—lakes in Wisconsin and the Adirondacks, beaches in Boston and on the Chesapeake Bay, recreation sites in western Pennsylvania.

with visibility. The studies, most of which found significant negative effects of air pollution on housing prices, thus provide indirect evidence that people are willing to pay for improved visibility.[50] For example, John Trijonis et al. (1984) estimated based on differences in housing prices that households in San Francisco were willing, on average, to pay $200 per year for a 10 percent improvement in visibility.

The difficulty in using these studies to estimate benefits, however, is that the coefficient of air pollution (or visibility) captures all reasons why households may prefer to live in nonpolluted areas—including both improved health and reduced soiling. Indeed, the reason why property value studies have become less popular as a method of valuing the benefits of pollution control is that it is difficult to know what the pollution coefficient captures and, therefore, difficult to aggregate benefit estimates obtained from these studies with those obtained from other approaches. Such aggregation is necessary because residential property value studies capture benefits only at home and not at the other locations the household frequents.

For these reasons contingent valuation seems the most promising method for valuing visibility. Because visibility benefits vary regionally, CVM studies can most usefully be classified according to whether they measure urban visibility benefits or benefits at recreation sites, and according to whether the locations studied are in the Eastern or in the Western United States. The former distinction is important because visibility benefits at recreation sites—especially national parks—are likely to have a substantial nonuse component; consequently, the relevant population for which benefits

are computed may be considerably larger than for urban visibility benefits. The East/West distinction is important both because of differences in baseline visibility and because of qualitative differences in the nature of visibility impairments, e.g., haze versus brown cloud.

There are two key problems in any contingent valuation study of visibility. One is presenting changes in visibility that are both meaningful to the respondent and that can be related to pollution control policies. The other is separating the respondent's valuation of health effects from his valuation of visibility changes.

Most CVM studies define increased visibility as an improvement in visual range—the distance at which a large, black object disappears from view. Visual range is both correlated with people's perceptions of visibility and with ambient concentrations of certain pollutants (fine nitrate and sulfate aerosols). Differences in visual range are presented in a series of pictures in which all other conditions—weather, brightness, the objects photographed—are, ideally, kept constant.

It has long been recognized (Brookshire et al. 1979) that, in responding to such pictures, people assume that the health effects of pollution diminish as visibility improves. Health effects are therefore inherently difficult to separate from visibility changes. The best way to handle this problem is to ask respondents what they assume health effects to be and then to control for these effects.

Unfortunately, existing CVM studies of visibility benefits—especially those for urban areas—have failed to treat the issues raised above in a satisfactory manner. With this limitation in mind, it is nonetheless of interest to contrast the magnitude of benefits associated with improvements in urban air quality with estimates obtained from hedonic property

---

[50] Freeman (1979a) provides an excellent summary of early studies.

value studies. Studies of visibility improvements in eastern U.S. cities (Tolley et al. 1986a; Douglas Rae 1984) have estimated that households would pay approximately $26 annually for a 10 percent improvement in visibility.[51] Loehmann Boldt, D., and Chaikin, K. (1981) reports an annual average willingness to pay per household of $101 for a 10 percent improvement in visibility in San Francisco. Both figures are considerably lower than estimates implied by property value studies.

Studies in recreation areas have focused on major national parks, including the Grand Canyon (Decision Focus 1990; Schulze and Brookshire 1983), because of the possibility of large nonuse values attached to visibility benefits at these sites Two conclusions emerge from these studies. First, nonuse values appear to be large relative to use values Use values associated with an improvement in visibility at the Grand Canyon from 70 to 100 miles are under $2.00 per visitor party per day ($1988) (Schulze and Brookshire 1983; K. K. MacFarland et al. 1983). By contrast, Schulze and Brookshire found that a random sample of households were willing to pay $95 per year ($1988) to prevent a deterioration in visibility at the Grand Canyon from the 50th percentile to the 25th percentile.

Second, the embedding, or superadditivity, problem is potentially quite serious. This refers to the fact that, in general, an individual's willingness to pay for simultaneous improvements in visibility at several sites should be less than the sum of his willingness to pay for isolated improvements at each site (Hoehn and Randall 1989). In a follow-up study to Schulze and Brookshire (1983), Tolley

et al. (1986a) found respondents were willing to pay only $22 annually for the same visibility improvement at the Grand Canyon when this was valued at the same time as visibility improvements in Chicago (the site of the interviews) and throughout the East coast.

4. *The Ecological Benefits of Pollution Control.*[52] By the ecological benefits of pollution control, we mean reduced pollution of animal and plant habitats, such as rivers, lakes, and wetlands. Because the benefits of clean water to recreational fisherman or larger populations of deer to hunters are captured in recreation studies, the benefits discussed in this section are the nonuse benefits associated with reduced pollution of ecosystems.

It should be clear to the reader that valuing this category of benefits poses serious conceptual problems. One is defining the commodity to be valued. Does one value reductions in pollution concentrations, increases in animal populations, or some more subtle index of the health of an ecosystem? Two approaches can be taken here. The "top down" approach asks the respondent to value the preservation of an ecosystem, such as 100 acres of wetland (John Whitehead and Blomquist 1991). The "bottom up" approach values the preservation of particular species inhabiting the wetland, such as geese and other birds.

Regardless of the approach taken, several problems must be faced. One difficulty is defining what substitutes are assumed to exist, whether for a particular species or for a wetland (Whitehead and Blomquist 1991). Presumably the value

---

[51] This figure, reported by Chestnut and Rowe (1989), is an average of mean willingness to pay for each city surveyed by Tolley and Rae, based on Chestnut and Rowe's reanalysis of the data.

[52] Outside environmental economics, there is a considerable literature in environmental ethics that explores the issue of nonhuman rights and their policy implications. From this perspective, the economist's benefit-cost calculation with its wholly anthropocentric orientation is an excessively narrow and illegitimate framework for analysis. Kneese and Schulze (1985) provide an excellent treatment of this set of issues.

placed on the preservation of 10,000 geese depends on the size of the goose population. A related problem arises when programs are valued one at a time; in general, the value attached to preserving several species at the same time is less than the sum of the values attached to preserving each species in isolation. This implies that the totality of what is to be preserved should be valued: one cannot compute this by summing the values attached to individual components.

To date, most studies of endangered species have valued individual species in isolation. For example, Bowker and Stoll (1988) estimate that households are, on average, willing to pay $22 per year ($1983) to preserve the whooping crane, while Boyle and Bishop (1987) find that non-eagle watchers are willing to spend $11 per year to preserve the bald eagle in the state of Wisconsin. These values are appropriate if one is considering a program to preserve either of these species in isolation; however, the values should not be added together if one is contemplating preserving both species.

Even if one decides to value a wetland (of given size) and defines the nature of substitutes, an important question remains: do people really have well-defined, or in the terminology of psychologists, "crystallized" values for these commodities? Since respondents in CVM studies are likely to be less familiar with ecological benefits than with health and recreation benefits, responses are likely to depend critically on the information given to respondents in the survey itself (Karl Samples, John Dixon, and Marcia Gown 1986). This problem, however, is widely recognized, and recent studies have taken pains to see how responses are influenced by the amount of information provided.

5. *The Agricultural Benefits of Pollution Control.* Although we have empha-

sized the nonmarket benefits of pollution control, some benefits accrue directly to firms, and can be measured by examining shifts in the supply curves for the affected outputs. The industries that are most subject to ambient air and water pollution are forestry, fishing, and agriculture. We focus on agriculture because it is the sector that is likely to experience the largest benefits from pollution control.

Reductions in ozone concentrations and, possibly, in acid rain, should increase the yields of field crops such as soybeans, corn, and wheat. In addition, reductions in greenhouse gases, to the extent that they prevent increases in temperature and decreases in precipitation in certain areas, should also increase crop yields.

In measuring the effects on agricultural output of changes in pollution concentrations or climate, two approaches can be taken. The damage function approach translates a change in environmental conditions into a yield change, assuming that farmers take no actions to mitigate the effects of the change. The yield change shifts the supply curve for the crop in question, and the corresponding changes in consumer and producer surpluses are calculated.[53] This is the predominant approach used thus far to analyze the effects of global climate change (Sally Kane, John Reilly, and Tobey 1991). It has also been used in some studies of the effects of ozone on field crops (Richard Adams, Thomas Crocker, and Richard Katz 1984; Raymond Kopp et al. 1985; Kopp and Krupnick 1987).

The averting behavior approach allows farmers to adjust to the change in pollution/climate by altering their input mix and/or by adjusting the number of acres

---

[53] In calculating the welfare effects of a shift in supply, one must be careful to take into account the effects of agricultural price support programs, which distort market prices. See Erik Lichtenberg and David Zilberman (1986).

planted. In some applications, a profit function is estimated in which the environmental pollutant enters as a parameter (James Mjelde et al. 1984; Philip Garcia et al. 1986). The value of the change in Q can then be computed directly from the profit function. If the resulting shift in supply is big enough to alter market price, the welfare effects of these price changes must also be computed.

A more common approach is to solve for the effect of the change in pollution on output using a mathematical programming model whose coefficients have not been econometrically estimated (Adams, Scott Hamilton, and Bruce McCarl 1986; Scott Hamilton, McCarl, and Adams 1985). The effect of output changes on price is then computed separately.

While benefit estimates that allow farmers to adjust to changes in pollution are clearly preferable on theoretical grounds to estimates that do not allow such adjustments, it is important to ask how much of a difference this is likely to make empirically, especially as the damage function approach is much easier to implement. For changes in temperature and precipitation, damages are likely to be greatly overstated if opportunities for mitigating behavior (e.g., irrigation) are ignored.[54] On the other hand, mitigating behavior does not seem to make a great deal of difference in the case of ozone damage (Scott Hamilton, McCarl, and Adams 1985).

Estimates of annual damage to field crops from a 25 percent increase in ozone are in the neighborhood of $2 billion ($1980)—not negligible, but small relative to estimates of health damages. It is also interesting to note that most of

these damages are borne by consumers. Producers in most cases gain from yield decreases due to the resulting increases in prices!

Kane, Reilly, and Tobey (1991) obtain similar results when estimating the welfare effects of global climate change on agriculture: reductions in the yields of field crops (wheat, corn, soybeans, and rice) in the U.S., Canada, China, and the USSR benefit producers worldwide due to increases in commodity prices. Consumers, however, lose. Thus, although the aggregate losses to producers and consumers worldwide are small (about one-half of one percent of world GDP), food-importing countries such as China suffer large welfare losses (equal to 5.5 percent of GDP) while food exporters such as Argentina enjoy welfare gains.

E. Measuring the Costs of Pollution Control

Table 1, which lists the costs of the major environmental statutes, may give the reader the impression that measuring the costs of pollution control is a straightforward matter. Such is not the case.

To begin with, the costs of pollution control must be measured using the same concepts that are used to measure the benefits of pollution control: the change in consumer and producer surpluses associated with the regulations and with any price and/or income changes that may result. The figures in Table 1 represent, for the most part, expenditures on cleaner fuels or abatement control equipment by firms. They do not represent the change in firms' profits, and thus ignore any adjustments firms may make to these expenditures. The figures also ignore the price and output effects associated with reducing emissions. At the very least, one would want to take into account the price changes likely to result within a sector because of environmental regulations—for example, one would

---

[54] We base this statement on the results of the RFF MINK project (Norman Rosenberg et al. 1990), which examines damages associated with climate change—specifically, a return to the climate of the dust bowl—in Missouri, Iowa, Nebraska, and Kentucky, under alternate adjustment scenarios.

want to measure the welfare effects of an increase in electricity prices resulting from the 10 million ton reduction in SO_2 emissions by electric utilities projected under the 1990 Amendments to the Clean Air Act.

We note that, at least in the short run, the effect of ignoring these adjustments is to overstate the cost of environmental regulations. Abatement expenditures overstate the loss in firms' profits if firms can pass on part of their cost increase to consumers. Consumers in turn can avoid some of the welfare effects of price increases of "dirty" goods by substituting "clean" goods for "dirty" ones.

When environmental regulations affect sectors, such as electricity production, that are important producers of intermediate goods, it may be important to measure the impacts that environmental regulations have throughout the economy. Computable general equilibrium models, preferably those in which supply and demand functions have been econometrically estimated, may be needed to measure correctly the social costs of environmental regulation.

Michael Hazilla and Kopp (1990) have used an econometrically estimated CGE model of the U.S. economy to compute the social costs of the Clean Air and Clean Water Acts, as implemented in 1981. The effects of these regulations on firms are modeled as an upward shift in firms' cost functions, to which firms can adjust by altering their choice of inputs and outputs. It is interesting to contrast the estimates of social costs obtained from this approach with EPA's estimates of compliance costs. The EPA estimated the costs of complying with the Clean Air and Clean Water Acts in 1981 to be $42.5 billion (1981 dollars). Hazilla and Kopp estimate the costs to be $28.3 billion; the lower figure reflects the substitution possibilities that the expenditure approach ignores.

In the long run, however, the social costs of the Clean Air and Clean Water Acts exceed simple expenditure estimates because of the effects of decreases in income on saving and investment. In their analysis of the effects of environmental regulation on U.S. economic growth, Dale Jorgenson and Peter Wilcoxen (1990a) measure this effect. Using a CGE model of the U.S. economy, they estimate that mandated pollution controls reduced the rate of GNP growth by .191 percentage points per annum over the period 1973–85.

V. *The Costs and Benefits of Environmental Programs*

The value of a symptom-day or a statistical life is, of course, only one component in evaluating a pollution control strategy. To translate unit benefit values into the benefits of an environmental program requires three steps: (1) the emissions reduction associated with the program must be related to changes in ambient air or water quality; (2) the change in ambient environmental quality must be related to health or other outcomes through a dose-response function; (3) the health or nonhealth outcomes must be valued. The information required for the first two tasks is considerable, especially if one wants to evaluate a major piece of legislation such as the Clean Air Act or Clean Water Act.

In this section we review attempts to estimate the benefits and costs of environmental programs. Of central interest are cases in which benefit-cost analyses have actually been used in setting environmental standards; in addition, we discuss instances in which such analyses have not been used but should be. This leads naturally to a discussion of priorities for research in the area of benefit and cost measurement.

A. *The Use of Benefit-Cost Analysis in Setting Environmental Standards*

Executive Order 12291, signed in 1981, requires that benefit-cost analyses be performed for all major regulations (defined as those having annual costs in excess of $100 million). Furthermore, the order requires, *to the extent permitted by law*, that regulations be undertaken only if the benefits to society exceed the costs.

One consequence of Executive Order 12291 is the undertaking of benefit-cost analyses for all major environmental regulations; however, the extent to which benefits and costs can be considered in making regulations is limited by the enabling statutes. Of the major environmental statutes only two, the Toxic Substances Control Act (TSCA) and the Federal Insecticide, Fungicide, and Rodenticide Act (FIFRA) explicitly require that benefits and costs be weighed in setting standards.[55] Some standards—specifically, those pertaining to new sources under the Clean Air Act and to the setting of effluent limitations under the Clean Water Act—allow costs to be taken into account, but do not suggest that benefits and costs be balanced at the margin. In contrast, the National Ambient Air Quality Standards and regulations for the disposal of hazardous waste under RCRA and CERCLA are to be made without regard to compliance costs.

In spite of these limitations, benefit-cost analyses have been used in EPA's rulemaking process since 1981. Between February of 1981 and February of 1986, EPA issued 18 major rules (USEPA 1987), including reviews of National Ambient Air Quality Standards for three pollutants—nitrogen dioxide, particulate

matter, and carbon monoxide—effluent standards for water pollutants in the iron and steel and chemicals and plastics industries, and regulations to ban lead in gasoline, as well as certain uses of asbestos.[56] Regulatory Impact Analyses (RIAs) were prepared for 15 of these rules.

In five of the RIAs, both benefits and costs were monetized; however, benefits could legally be compared with costs only in the case of lead in gasoline. In this case, the benefits in terms of engine maintenance alone were judged to exceed the costs by $6.7 billion over the period 1985–92, and the regulation was issued. In two other cases—the PM standard and effluent limitations for iron and steel plants—the benefits exceeded the costs of the proposed regulation and the regulation was implemented, although EPA denied that it weighed benefits against costs in reaching its decision. The remaining cases are more difficult to evaluate. The clean water benefits of proposed effluent guidelines for chemicals and plastics manufacturers were judged to exceed regulatory costs in some sections of the country but not in others. EPA recommended that these guidelines be implemented. Of several alternative standards for emissions of particulate matter by surface coal mines, only one was found to yield positive net benefits, and these were small ($300,000). Eventually, no regulation was issued by EPA.

The preceding review suggests that benefit-cost analysis has not entirely been ignored in setting environmental standards, but its use has been selective. In part, this is the result of law—EPA was allowed to weigh benefits against costs for only 5 of the 18 major regulations that it issued between 1981 and

[55] Some portions of the Clean Air Act, specifically, those pertaining to aircraft emissions, motor vehicle standards and fuel standards, also require that marginal benefits and costs be balanced.

[56] A complete listing of the regulations may be found in USEPA (1987). Also included were regulations governing the disposal of used oil, and standards regarding land disposal of hazardous waste.

1986.[57] One could argue that the government should not invest resources in a full blown benefit-cost analysis if the results of such an analysis cannot be used in regulating the polluting activity. But this would be a mistake. Even where the explicit use of a benefit-cost test is prohibited, such studies can be informative and useful. In their own way, they are likely to influence the views of legislators and regulators. In particular, the issue is often one of amending standards—either raising them or lowering them. Benefit-cost information on such adjustments, although not formally admissible, may well have some impact on decisions to revise standards. In addition, simply demonstrating the feasibility and potential application of such studies may lead to their explicit introduction into the policy process at a later time.

B. *The Need for Benefit-Cost Analyses of Environmental Standards*

We turn now to a set of priorities for benefit-cost analyses of environmental regulation: which of existing environmental programs require closest scrutiny and what benefit techniques must be developed in order to perform these analyses? We begin with an enumeration of these programs, as we see them, and then offer some thoughts on the analysis of each of them.

There are, broadly, two areas in which careful benefit-cost analyses are most needed. One is for statutes whose total costs are thought to exceed their total benefits. A widely cited example is the Clean Water Act (CWA), which will soon be up for renewal. Freeman (1982) sug-

gests that the recreational use values associated with the adoption of BPT are small, relative to the costs presented in Table 1. Justification for these standards must then rest on other grounds. A second example where costs may exceed benefits involves the extent of cleanup of Superfund sites under CERCLA. While the cost of cleaning up these sites is predicted to run into the hundreds of billions of dollars, the health benefits of these cleanups are thought by many to be modest (Curtis Travis and Carolyn Doty 1989). Current law does not require an explicit benefit-cost analysis of remedial alternatives at each Superfund site, but, in our view, it probably should.

The second general class of cases in which careful benefit-cost analyses are needed is where environmental standards are sufficiently stringent to push control efforts onto the steep portion of the marginal cost of abatement curve. Even though the total costs of these standards may exceed their total benefits (see Figure 4), society might experience a gain in welfare from relaxing the standard if the marginal benefits of abatement are considerably below the marginal costs at the level of the standard. In terms of Figure 4, we need to know whether the marginal benefit function is MB_2 or MB_1. There are several instances of actual policies that appear to fall within this class: (1) the ground-level ozone standard, in areas that are currently out of compliance with the standard; (2) certain provisions in RCRA for disposal of hazardous waste; and (3) the 1990 acid rain amendments to the Clean Air Act. In addition to these existing laws, proposals for significant reductions in CO_2 emissions may entail high marginal costs, suggesting a close scrutiny of benefits.

Turning first to the Clean Water Act, we note that evaluating the CWA will require computing the use (recreation) and nonuse (ecological) benefits of im-

---

[57] For the other four regulations where a comparison of costs and benefits was allowed—the three toxic substances (TSCA) regulations and the setting of emission standards for light duty trucks—benefits were quantified but not monetized. In the case of PCB's the cost per catastrophe avoided was computed; in the case of asbestos, the cost per life saved.

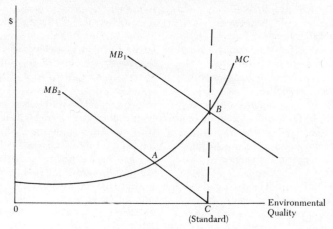

Figure 4. Welfare Loss from Setting Incorrect
Standards

proved water quality. As we noted above, one can either use a contingent valuation approach that captures both values, or one can attempt to capture use values using travel cost methods and measure nonuse values separately. Whichever approach is used, we emphasize the regional character of the costs and benefits of improved water quality; benefit estimates must, in consequence, be available at this level of disaggregation. The contingent valuation method avoids two problems inherent in the use of travel cost models. First, unless the transferability problem can be solved, travel cost models will have to be estimated for each river or lake throughout the U.S.! And, second, if a contingent valuation survey of nonuse values is to be added to travel cost measures of use values, it may be hard to get users to separate use from nonuse values.

A key issue in valuing the benefits of Superfund cleanups is how to value health risks—usually risks of cancer—that will not occur until the distant future. Many Superfund sites pose very low health risks today, primarily because

there is no current route of exposure to toxic waste. People could, however, be exposed to contaminated soils or groundwater if substances were to leak from storage containers in the future. This involves valuing future risks to persons currently alive as well as to persons yet unborn. While some research has been done in this area (Mauskopf 1987; Cropper and Portney 1990; Cropper and Sussman 1990), there are few empirical studies that examine either the value that people place on reducing future risks to themselves or the rate at which they discount lives saved in future generations. Estimates of these values are also crucial if one is to analyze regulations governing the current disposal of hazardous waste under RCRA, as well as other regulations that affect exposure to carcinogens (e.g., air toxics and pesticide regulations).

An additional problem is how to incorporate uncertainty regarding estimates of health risks into the analysis. While most valuation studies treat the probability of an adverse outcome as certain, in reality there is great uncertainty about health risks, especially the risk of contracting cancer from exposure to environmental carcinogens. This uncertainty has two sources: uncertainty about actual exposures received, and uncertainty about the effects of a given exposure.[58] The standard procedure in risk assessments is to "correct" for this uncertainty by presenting a point estimate based on very conservative assumptions (Nichols and Richard Zeckhauser 1986). It would, however, be more appropriate to incorporate the distribution of cancer risk into the analysis.

Existing estimates of the marginal costs and marginal benefits of achieving the one-hour ozone standard in areas that are currently out of attainment suggest that marginal costs exceed marginal benefits (Krupnick and Portney 1991). Estimates of the health benefits of ozone control have, however, focused on the value of reducing restricted-activity or symptom days. There is some evidence that ozone may exacerbate the rate at which lung tissue deteriorates, contributing to chronic obstructive lung disease (COPD). Since, for healthy individuals, the probability of contracting COPD is uncertain, what must be valued is a change in the risk of contracting chronic lung disease corresponding to a change in ozone concentrations.

The objective of the provisions of the 1990 Amendments to the Clean Air Act aimed at reducing SO_2 and NO_2 is to reduce acid rain, primarily in the Eastern U.S. and Canada. Although the 10-million-ton reduction in sulfur emissions specified in the amendments is likely to have some health benefits, most of the anticipated benefits are ecological or rec-

reational, resulting from an increase in the pH of lakes.[59] There are also likely to be visibility benefits (reduced haze) in the Eastern U.S. This underscores the need for better estimates of the value of improved visibility, especially in urban areas. It will also be necessary to measure the ecological benefits associated with reduced acid rain, especially as these are likely to differ qualitatively from the ecological benefits associated with the CWA.

Finally, we note that in the area of global climate change, considerable attention has been devoted to measuring the costs of reducing greenhouse gas emissions, especially through the use of a tax on the carbon content of fuels (Jorgenson and Wilcoxen 1990b). Little, however, is known about the benefits of reducing greenhouse gases, even if one assumes that the link between CO_2 and climate change is certain.[60]

The benefits of preventing these climate changes differ from the benefits associated with conventional air and water pollutants in two respects. First, many—though by no means all—of the effects of climate change are likely to occur through markets. These include effects on agriculture and forestry, as well as changes in heating and cooling costs. While this should make benefits easier to measure, the problem is that the effects of CO_2 emissions are not likely to be felt for decades. This implies that valuing such damages is difficult. A damage function approach, which ignores adaptation possibilities, is clearly inappropriate; however, predicting technological possibilities for adaptation is not easy.

Second, the benefits of reducing greenhouse gases will not be felt until the next century. The problem here is that, even at a discount rate of only 3

---

[58] Estimates of the effect of a given exposure usually come from rodent bioassays, which are used to estimate a dose-response function. In addition to uncertainty regarding the parameters of the dose-response function, there is uncertainty as to how these estimates should be extrapolated from rodents to man.

[59] For a dissenting view see Portney (1990).
[60] A useful beginning here is the work of William Nordhaus (1990).

percent, one dollar of benefits received 100 years from now is worth only 5 cents today. This problem has typically been addressed by suggesting that benefits should be discounted at a very low rate, if at all. An alternative approach is to make transfers to future generations to compensate them for our degradation of the environment, rather than to alter the discount rate.

C. *The Distribution of Costs and Benefits*

In addition to examining the costs and benefits of environmental legislation, it is of interest to know who pays for pollution abatement and who benefits from it. Typically, studies of the distributional effects of environmental programs emphasize the distribution of benefits and costs by income class.

To determine how the benefits of environmental programs are distributed across different income classes, we must measure how the programs alter the physical environments of different income groups. In one study of the distributional effects of programs aimed at raising the level of national air quality, Leonard Gianessi, Peskin, and Edward Wolff (1979) found striking locational differentials in benefits; not surprisingly, most of the benefits from efforts to improve air quality are concentrated in the more industrialized urban areas (largely the heavily industrialized cities of the East) with fewer benefits accruing to rural residents. Even within metropolitan areas, air quality may differ substantially. Since the poor often live in the most polluted parts of urban areas, they might be thought to be disproportionately large beneficiaries of programs that reduce air pollution—and there is evidence that this is, indeed, the case (Asch and Seneca 1978; Jeffrey Zupan 1973). While this may be true, certain indirect effects can follow that offset such benefits. For ex-

ample, cleaner air in what was a relatively dirty area may increase the demand for residences there and drive up rents, thereby displacing low-income renters. All in all, this is a complicated issue. At any rate, Gianessi, Peskin, and Wolff find that within urban areas the distribution of benefits may be slightly pro-poor, but, as we shall see next, this is likely to be offset (or more than offset) by a regressive pattern of the costs of these programs.[61]

We are on somewhat more solid ground on the distribution of the costs of environmental programs (G. B. Christainsen and Tietenberg 1985). There exist data on the costs of pollution control by industry with which one can estimate how costs have influenced the prices of various classes of products and how, in turn, these increased prices have reduced the real incomes of different income classes. In one early study of this kind, Gianessi, Peskin, and Wolff (1979) examined the distributive pattern of the costs of the Clean Air Act and found that lower-income groups bear costs that constitute a larger fraction of their income than do higher-income classes. (See also Nancy Dorfman and Arthur Snow 1975; Gianessi and Peskin 1980.) Three independent studies of automobile pollution control costs all reach similar findings of regressivity (Dorfman and Snow 1975; Harrison 1975; Freeman 1979b).

In a more recent study, Robison (1985) uses an input-output model to estimate the distribution of costs of industrial pollution abatement. Assuming that the costs of pollution control in each industry are passed on in the form of higher prices, Robison traces these price in-

---

[61] Moreover, there is some persuasive evidence from observed voting patterns on proposed environmental measures (Robert Deacon and Perry Shapiro 1975; Fischel 1979) indicating that higher income individuals are willing to pay more for a cleaner environment than those with lower incomes.

creases through the input-output matrix to determine their impact on the pattern of consumer prices. Robison's model divides individuals into twenty income classes. For each class, estimates are available of the pattern of consumption among product groups. This information, together with predictions of price increases for each product, is used to estimate the increase in the prices of goods consumed by each income group. Robison finds that the incidence of control costs is quite regressive. Costs as a fraction of income fall over the entire range of income classes; they vary from 0.76 percent of income for the lowest income class to 0.16 percent of income for the highest income class.

It is true that these studies relate to existing environmental programs and do not measure directly the potential distributional effects of a system of economic incentives such as effluent fees. But our sense is that the pattern of control costs across industries would be roughly similar under existing and incentive-based programs. It is the same industries under both regimes that will have to undertake the bulk of the abatement measures. Our conjecture thus is that the pattern of costs for our major environmental programs is likely to be distinctly regressive in its incidence, be they of the command-and-control or incentive-based variety.

While the distributional effects of environmental programs may not be altogether salutary, we do not wish to exaggerate their importance. We emphasize that the primary purpose of environmental programs is, in economic terms, an efficient allocation of resources. Environmental measures, as Freeman (1972) has stressed, are not very well suited to the achievement of redistributional objectives. But an improved environment provides important benefits for all income classes—and we will be doing no groups a favor by opposing environmental pro-

grams on distributional grounds. At the same time, there are opportunities to soften some of the more objectionable redistributive consequences of environmental policies through the use of measures like adjustment assistance for individuals displaced from jobs in heavily polluting industries and the reliance on the more progressive forms of taxation to finance public spending on pollution control programs.

VI. Environmental Economics and Environmental Policy: Some Reflections

As suggested by the lengthy (and only partial) list of references and citations in this survey, environmental economics has been a busy field over the past two decades. Environmental economists have reworked existing theory, making it more rigorous and clearing up a number of ambiguities; they have devised new methods for the valuation of benefits from improved environmental quality; and they have undertaken numerous empirical studies to measure the costs and benefits of actual or proposed environmental programs and to assess the relative efficiency of incentive-based and CAC policies. In short, the "intellectual structure" of environmental economics has been both broadened and strengthened since the last survey of the field by Fisher and Peterson in this *Journal* in 1976.

But what about the contribution of environmental economics to the design and implementation of environmental policy? This is not an easy question to answer. We have seen some actual programs of transferable emissions permits in the United States and some use of effluent charges in Europe. And with the enactment of the 1990 Amendments to the Clean Air Act, the U.S. has introduced a major program of tradable allowances to control sulfur emissions—moving this country squarely into the use of incentive-based approaches to regulation in at least one area of environmental policy.[62] But, at the same time, effluent charge and marketable permit programs are few in number and often bear only a modest resemblance to the pure programs of economic incentives supported by economists. As we noted in the introduction, certain major pieces of environmental legislation prohibit the use of economic tests for the setting of standards for environmental quality, while other directives require them! The record, in short, is a mixed and somewhat confusing one: it reveals a policy environment characterized by a real ambivalence (and, in some instances, an active hostility) to a central role for economics in environmental decision making.[63]

What is the potential and the likelihood of more attention to the use of eco-

nomic analysis and economic incentives in environmental management? It is easy to be pessimistic on this matter. There is still some aversion, both in the policy arena and across the general public, to the use of "market methods" for pollution control. While we were working on this survey, one of the leading news magazines in the U.S. ran a lengthy feature story entitled "The Environment: Cleaning Up Our Mess—What Works, What Doesn't, and What We Must Do to Reclaim our Air, Land, and Water" (Gregg Easterbrook 1989, in *Newsweek*). A central argument in the article is that the attempt to place environmental policy on a solid "scientific" footing has been a colossal error that has handcuffed efforts to get on with pollution control. Proceeding "on the assumption that environmental protection is a social good transcending cost-benefit calculations" (p. 42), Easterbrook argues that we should not place a high priority on scientific work on the complicated issues of measuring benefits and costs and of providing carefully designed systems of incentives, but should get on with enacting pollution control measures that are technologically feasible. In short, we should control what technology enables us to control without asking too many hard questions and holding up tougher legislation until we know all the answers.

Such a position has a certain pragmatic appeal. As we all know, our understanding of complicated ecological systems and the associated dose-response relationships is seriously incomplete. And as our survey has indicated, our ability to place dollar values on improvements in environmental quality is limited and imprecise. Nevertheless, we have some hard choices to make in the environmental arena—and whatever guidance we can obtain from a careful, if imprecise, consideration of benefits and costs should not be ignored.

[62] Under this provision, the U.S. will address the acid rain problem by cutbacks in sulfur emissions over the next decade of 10 million tons (about a 50 percent reduction). This is to be accomplished through a system of tradable allowances under which affected power plants will be allowed to meet their emissions reductions by whatever means they choose—including the purchase of "excess" emissions reductions from other sources that choose to cut back by more than their required quota. Also noteworthy is the U.S. procedure to implement reductions in chlorofluorocarbon emissions under the Montreal Protocol. Under this measure, EPA has effectively grandfathered the U.S. quota among existing producers and importers; from these baselines, firms are allowed to trade allowances (Hahn and McGartland 1989).

[63] Some recent studies of actual environmental decision making are consistent with this "mixed" view. Magat, Krupnick, and Harrington (1986), for example, in a study of EPA determination of effluent standards under the Clean Water Act Amendments of 1972, found that "simple rules based either on economic efficiency or the goal of distributional equity did not dominate the rulemaking process" (p. 154). Their analysis did find that standards across industry subcategories reflected to some extent differences in compliance costs among firms. In contrast, Cropper et al. (1992) find that EPA decisions on pesticide regulation have, in fact, reflected a systematic balancing of environmental risks and costs of control. Economic factors, it appears, have mattered in some classes of decisions and not in others.

We stress, moreover, that the role for economic analysis in environmental policy making is far more important now than in the earlier years of the "environmental revolution." When we set out initially to attack our major pollution problems, there were available a wide array of fairly direct and inexpensive measures for pollution control. We were, in short, operating on relatively low and flat segments of marginal abatement cost (MAC) curves. But things have changed. As nearly all the cost studies reveal, marginal abatement cost functions have the typical textbook shape. They are low and fairly flat over some range and then begin to rise, often quite rapidly. Both the first and second derivatives of these abatement cost functions are positive—and rapidly increasing marginal abatement costs often set in with a vengeance.

We now find ourselves operating, in most instances, along these rapidly rising portions of MAC functions so that decisions to cut pollution yet further are becoming more costly. In such a setting, it is crucial that we have a clear sense of the relative benefits and costs of alternative measures. It will be quite easy, for example, to enact new, more stringent regulations that impose large costs on society, well in excess of the benefits, health or otherwise, to the citizenry. As Portney (1990) has suggested, this may well be true of the new measures to control urban air pollution and hazardous air pollutants under the most recent Amendments to the Clean Air Act. Portney's admittedly rough estimates suggest that the likely range of benefits from these new provisions falls well short of the likely range of their cost.

Economic analysis can be quite helpful in getting at least a rough sense of the relative magnitudes at stake. This is not, we would add, a matter of sophisticated measures of "exact consumer surplus" but simply of measuring as best we can

the relevant areas under crude approximations to demand curves (compensated or otherwise). In addition to measurement issues, this new setting for environmental policy places a much greater premium on the use of cost-effective regulatory devices, for the wastes associated with the cruder forms of CAC policies will be much magnified.[64]

In spite of the mixed record, it is our sense that we are at a point in the evolution of environmental policy at which the economics profession is in a very favorable position to influence the course of policy. As we move into the 1990s, the general political and policy setting is one that is genuinely receptive to market approaches to solving our social problems. Not only in the United States but in other countries as well, the prevailing atmosphere is a conservative one with a strong disposition toward the use of market incentives, wherever possible, for the attainment of our social objectives. Moreover, as we have emphasized in this survey, we have learned a lot over the past twenty years about the properties of various policy instruments and how they work (or do not work) under different circumstances. Economists now know more about environmental policy and are in a position to offer better counsel on the design of measures for environmental management.

This, as we have stressed, takes us from the abstract world of pure systems of fees or marketable permits. Environmental economists must be (and, we be-

[64] Following our earlier discussion of the Weitzman theorem, we note its implication for the issue under discussion here: a preference for price over quantity instruments. So long as there is little evidence of any dramatic threshold effects or other sources of rapid changes in marginal benefits from pollution control, the steepness of the MAC function suggests that regulatory agencies can best protect against costly error by adopting effluent fees rather than marketable emission permits (Hadi Dowlatabadi and Harrington 1989; Oates, Portney, and McGartland 1989).

lieve, are) prepared to come to terms with detailed, but important, matters of implementation: the determination of fee schedules, issues of spatial and temporal variation in fees or allowable emissions under permits, the life of permits and their treatment for tax purposes, rules governing the transfer of pollution rights, procedures for the monitoring and enforcement of emissions limitations, and so on. In short, economists must be ready to "get their hands dirty."

But the contribution to be made by environmental economists can be a valuable one. And there are encouraging signs in the policy arena of a growing receptiveness to incentive-based approaches to environmental management. As we noted in the introduction, both in the United States and in the OECD countries more generally, there have been recent expressions of interest in the use of economic incentives for protection of the environment. As we were finishing the final draft of this survey, the Council of the OECD issued a strong and lengthy endorsement of incentive-based approaches, urging member countries to "make a greater and more consistent use of economic instruments" for environmental management (OECD 1991).

Finally, we note the growing awareness and concern with global environmental issues. Many pollutants display a troublesome tendency to spill over national boundaries. While this is surely not a new issue (e.g., transnational acid rain), the thinning of the ozone shield and the prospect of global warming are pressing home in a more urgent way the need for a global perspective on the environment. The potential benefits and costs of programs to address these issues, particularly global warming, are enormous—and they present a fundamental policy challenge. The design and implementation of workable and cost-effective measures on a global scale are formidable

problems, to put it mildly. And they call for an extension of existing work in the field to the development of an "open economy environmental economics" that incorporates explicitly the issues arising in an international economy linked by trade, financial, *and* environmental flows.[65]

REFERENCES

ABDALLA, CHARLES. "Measuring Economic Losses from Ground Water Contamination: An Investigation of Household Avoidance Cost," *Water Resources Bulletin,* June 1990, 26(3), pp. 451–63.

ADAMS, RICHARD M.; CROCKER, THOMAS D. AND KATZ, RICHARD W. "Assessing the Adequacy of Natural Science Information: A Bayesian Approach," *Rev. Econ. Statist.,* Nov. 1984, 66(4), pp. 568–75.

ADAMS, RICHARD M.; HAMILTON, SCOTT A. AND McCARL, BRUCE A. "The Benefits of Pollution Control: the Case of Ozone and U.S. Agriculture," *Amer. J. Agr. Econ.,* Nov. 1986, 68(4), pp. 886–93.

ADAR, ZVI AND GRIFFIN, JAMES M. "Uncertainty and the Choice of Pollution Control Instruments," *J. Environ. Econ. Manage.,* Oct. 1976, 3(3), pp. 178–88.

ARROW, KENNETH J. AND FISHER, ANTHONY C. "Environmental Preservation, Uncertainty, and Irreversibility," *Quart. J. Econ.,* May 1974, 88(2), pp. 312–19.

ASAKO, KAZUMI. "Environmental Pollution in an Open Economy," *Econ. Rec.,* Dec. 1979, 55(151), pp. 359–67.

ASCH, PETER AND SENECA, JOSEPH J. "Monopoly and External Cost: An Application of Second Best Theory to the Automobile Industry," *J. Environ. Econ. Manage.,* June 1976, 3(2), pp. 69–79.

———. "Some Evidence on the Distribution of Air Quality," *Land Econ.,* Aug. 1978, 54(3), pp. 278–97.

ATKINSON, SCOTT E. AND LEWIS, DONALD H. "A Cost-Effectiveness Analysis of Alternative Air Quality Control Strategies," *J. Environ. Econ. Manage.,* Nov. 1974, 1(3), pp. 237–50.

ATKINSON, SCOTT E. AND TIETENBERG, T.H. "The Empirical Properties of Two Classes of Designs for Transferable Discharge Permit Markets," *J. Environ. Econ. Manage.,* June 1982, 9(2), pp. 101–21.

BAILEY, MARTIN J. "Externalities, Rents, and Optimal Rules." Sloan Working Paper in Urban Public Eco-

---

[65] For a useful effort to develop a research perspective and agenda on the economic analysis of global change, see U.S. National Oceanic and Atmospheric Administration, National Science Foundation and National Aeronautics and Space Administration (1991).

nomics 16–82, Economics Dept., U. of Maryland, College Park, MA, 1982.

BARNETT, ANDY H. "The Pigouvian Tax Rule Under Monopoly," *Amer. Econ. Rev.*, Dec. 1980, *70*(5), pp. 1037–41.

BARTEL, ANN P. AND TAUBMAN, PAUL. "Health and Labor Market Success: The Role of Various Diseases," *Rev. Econ. Statist.*, Feb. 1979, *61*(1), pp. 1–8.

BARTIK, TIMOTHY J. "Evaluating the Benefits of Non-marginal Reductions in Pollution Using Information on Defensive Expenditures," *J. Environ. Econ. Manage.*, March 1988a, *15*(1), pp. 111–27.

––––––. "Measuring the Benefits of Amenity Improvements in Hedonic Price Models," *Land Econ.*, May 1988b, *64*(2), pp. 172–83.

––––––. "The Effects of Environmental Regulation on Business Location in the United States," *Growth Change*, Summer 1988c, *19*(3), pp. 22–44.

BAUMOL, WILLIAM J. "On Taxation and the Control of Externalities," *Amer. Econ. Rev.*, June 1972, *62*(3), pp. 307–22.

BAUMOL, WILLIAM J. AND BRADFORD, DAVID F. "Detrimental Externalities and Non-Convexity of the Production Set," *Economica*, May 1972, *39*(154), pp. 160–76.

BAUMOL, WILLIAM J. AND OATES, WALLACE E. "The Use of Standards and Prices for Protection of the Environment," *Swedish J. Econ.*, March 1971, *73*(1), pp. 42–54.

––––––. *Economics, environmental policy, and quality of life.* NY: Prentice-Hall, 1979.

––––––. *The theory of environmental policy*, Second Edition. Cambridge, England: Cambridge U. Press, 1988.

BECKER, GARY S. "Crime and Punishment: An Economic Approach," *J. Polit. Econ.*, Mar./Apr. 1968, *76*(2), pp. 169–217.

BERGER, MARK C. ET AL. "Valuing Changes in Health Risks: A Comparison of Alternative Measures," *Southern Econ. J.*, Apr. 1987, *53*(4), pp. 967–84.

BINKLEY, CLARK S. AND HANEMANN, W. MICHAEL. *The recreation benefits of water quality improvement: Analysis of day trips in an urban setting.* EPA-600/5-78-010. Washington, DC: U.S. Environmental Protection Agency, 1978.

BISHOP, RICHARD C. AND HEBERLEIN, THOMAS A. "Measuring Values of Extramarket Goods: Are Indirect Measures Biased?" *Amer. J. Agr. Econ.*, Dec. 1979, *61*(5), pp. 926–30.

BISHOP, RICHARD C.; HEBERLEIN, THOMAS A. AND KEALY, MARY JO. "Contingent Valuation of Environmental Assets: Comparisons with a Simulated Market," *Natural Res. J.*, 1983, *23*(3), pp. 619–34.

BLOMQUIST, GLENN C. "Value of Life Saving: Implications of Consumption Activity," *J. Polit. Econ.*, June 1979, *87*(3), pp. 540–58.

BLOMQUIST, GLENN C.; BERGER, MARK C. AND HOEHN, JOHN P. "New Estimates of Quality of Life in Urban Areas," *Amer. Econ. Rev.*, Mar. 1988, *78*(1), pp. 89–107.

BOCKSTAEL, NANCY E.; HANEMANN, W. MICHAEL AND

KLING, CATHERINE L. "Estimating the Value of Water Quality Improvements in a Recreational Demand Framework," *Water Resources Res.*, May 1987, *23*(5), pp. 951–60.

BOCKSTAEL, NANCY E. AND MCCONNELL, KENNETH E. "Welfare Measurement in the Household Production Framework," *Amer. Econ. Rev.*, Sept. 1983, *73*(4), pp. 806–14.

BOHM, PETER. "Estimating Demand for Public Goods: An Experiment," *European Econ. Rev.*, June 1972, *3*(2), pp. 111–30.

––––––. *Deposit-refund systems: Theory and applications to environmental, conservation, and consumer policy.* Washington, DC: Johns Hopkins U. Press for Resources for the Future, 1981.

BOHM, PETER AND RUSSELL, CLIFFORD F. "Comparative Analysis of Alternative Policy Instruments," in *Handbook of natural resource and energy economics.* Volume 1. Eds.: ALLEN V. KNEESE AND JAMES L. SWEENEY. Amsterdam: North-Holland, 1985, pp. 395–460.

BOLAND, JAMES "Economic Instruments for Environmental Protection in the United States," ENV/ ECO/86.14. Paris, France: Organisation for Economic Cooperation and Development. Sept. 11, 1986.

BOWER, BLAIR ET AL. *Incentives in water quality management: France and the Ruhr area.* Washington, DC: Resources for the Future, 1981.

BOWKER, JAMES AND STOLL, JOHN R. "Use of Dichotomous Choice Nonmarket Methods to Value the Whooping Crane Resource," *Amer. J. Agr. Econ.*, May 1988, *70*(2), pp. 372–81.

BOYLE, KEVIN J. AND BISHOP, RICHARD C. "Valuing Wildlife in Benefit-Cost Analyses: A Case Study Involving Endangered Species," *Water Resources Res.*, May 1987, *23*(5), pp. 943–50.

BRADEN, JOHN B. AND KOLSTAD, CHARLES D., EDS. *Measuring the demand for environmental quality.* Amsterdam, North Holland, 1991.

BRAMHALL, D. F. AND MILLS, EDWIN S. "A Note on the Asymmetry between Fees and Payments," *Water Resources Res.*, 1966, *2*(3), pp. 615–16.

BRESSERS, HANS. "The Effectiveness of Dutch Water Quality Policy." Mimeo. The Netherlands: Twente University of Technology, 1983.

BROMLEY, DANIEL W. "Markets and Externalities," in *Natural resource economics: Policy problems and contemporary analysis.* Ed.: DANIEL W. BROMLEY. Hingham, MA: Kluwer Nijhoff, 1986, pp. 37–68.

BROOKSHIRE, DAVID D. AND COURSEY, DON L. "Measuring the Value of a Public Good: An Empirical Comparison of Elicitation Procedures," *Amer. Econ. Rev.*, Sept. 1987, *77*(4), pp. 554–66.

BROOKSHIRE, D. S. ET AL. *Methods development for assessing air pollution control benefits.* Vol. 2: *Experiments in valuing non-market goods: A case study of alternative benefit measures of air pollution in the south coast air basin of Southern California.* Prepared for the U.S. Environmental Protection Agency, Washington, DC, 1979.

BROWN, GARDNER, JR. AND BRESSERS, HANS. "Evidence Supporting Effluent Charges." Mimeo. The Netherlands: Twente University of Technology, Sept. 1986.

BROWN, GARDNER, JR. AND JOHNSON, RALPH W. "Pollution Control by Effluent Charges: It Works in the Federal Republic of Germany, Why Not in the U.S.," *Natural Res. J.*, Oct. 1984, *24*(4), pp. 929–66.

BROWN, GARDNER, JR. AND MENDELSOHN, ROBERT "The Hedonic Travel Cost Method," *Rev. Econ. Statist.*, Aug. 1984, *66*(3), pp. 427–33.

BROWN, JAMES N. AND ROSEN, HARVEY S. "On the Estimation of Structural Hedonic Price Models," *Econometrica*, May 1982, *50*(3), pp. 765–68.

BROWN, THOMAS C. AND SLOVIC, PAUL. "Effects of Context on Economic Measures of Value," in *Amenity resource valuation: Integrating economics with other disciplines.* Eds.: G. PETERSON, B. DRIVER, AND R. GREGORY. State College, PA: Venture Publishing, Inc., 1988.

BUCHANAN, JAMES M. "External Diseconomies, Corrective Taxes, and Market Structure," *Amer. Econ. Rev.*, Mar. 1969, *59*(1), pp. 174–77.

BURROWS, PAUL. *The economic theory of pollution control.* Oxford: Martin Robertson, 1979.

BURROWS, PAUL. "Controlling the Monopolistic Polluter: Nihilism or Eclecticism?" *J. Environ. Econ. Manage.*, Dec. 1981, *8*(4), pp. 372–80.

BURROWS, PAUL. "Nonconvexity Induced by External Costs on Production: Theoretical Curio or Policy Dilemma?" *J. Environ. Econ. Manage.*, June 1986, *13*(2), pp. 101–28.

BUTLER, RICHARD V. AND MAHER, MICHAEL D. "The Control of Externalities in a Growing Urban Economy," *Econ. Inquiry*, Jan. 1982, *20*(1), pp. 155–63.

———. "The Control of Externalities: Abatement vs. Damage Prevention," *Southern Econ. J.*, Apr. 1986, *52*(4), pp. 1088–1102.

CAMERON, TRUDY ANN AND JAMES, MICHELLE D. "Efficient Estimation Methods for 'Closed-Ended' Contingent Valuation Surveys," *Rev. Econ. Statist.*, May 1987, *69*(2), pp. 269–76.

CARSON, RICHARD T. AND MITCHELL, ROBERT CAMERON. "The Value of Clean Water: The Public's Willingness to Pay for Boatable, Fishable, and Swimmable Quality Water." Discussion Paper 88-13. La Jolla, CA: U. of California at San Diego, 1988.

CHESTNUT, LAURAINE AND ROWE, ROBERT D. "Economic Valuation of Changes in Visibility: A State of the Science Assessment for NAPAP" in *Methods for valuing acidic deposition and air pollution effects.* Report 27, 1989, pp. 5-1–5-44.

CHRISTAINSEN, G. B. AND TIETENBERG, THOMAS H. "Distributional and Macroeconomic Aspects of Environmental Policy," in *Handbook of natural resource and energy economics.* Vol. 1. Eds.: ALLEN V. KNEESE AND JAMES L. SWEENEY. Amsterdam: North-Holland, 1985, pp. 345–93.

COASE, RONALD H. "The Problem of Social Cost," *J. Law Econ.*, Oct. 1960, *3*, pp. 1–44.

COLLINGE, ROBERT A. AND OATES, WALLACE E. "Efficiency in Pollution Control in the Short and Long Runs: A System of Rental Emission Permits," *Can. J. Econ.*, May 1982, *15*(2), pp. 347–54.

COOPER, BARBARA S. AND RICE, DOROTHY P. "The Economic Cost of Illness Revisited," *Soc. Sec. Bull.*, Feb. 1976, *39*(2), pp. 21–36.

CORNES, RICHARD AND SANDLER, TODD. *The theory of externalities, public goods, and club goods.* Cambridge, Eng.: Cambridge U. Press, 1986.

COSTANZA, ROBERT AND PERRINGS, CHARLES. "A Flexible Assurance Bonding System for Improved Environmental Management," *Ecological Economics*, Feb. 1990, *2*, pp. 57–75.

COURANT, PAUL N. AND PORTER, RICHARD. "Averting Expenditure and the Cost of Pollution," *J. Environ. Econ. Manage.*, Dec. 1981, *8*(4), pp. 321–29.

COURSEY, DONALD L.; HOVIS, JOHN L. AND SCHULZE, WILLIAM D. "The Disparity Between Willingness to Accept and Willingness to Pay Measures of Value," *Quart. J. Econ.*, Aug. 1987, *102*(3), pp. 679–90.

CROPPER, MAUREEN L. AND ARRIAGA-SALINAS, AMALIA. "Inter-city Wage Differentials and the Value of Air Quality," *J. Urban Econ.*, 1980, *8*(2), pp. 236–54.

CROPPER, MAUREEN L. ET AL. "The Determinants of Pesticide Regulation: A Statistical Analysis of EPA Decisionmaking," *J. Polit. Econ.*, Feb. 1992, *100*(1), pp. 175–97.

CROPPER, MAUREEN L. AND KRUPNICK, ALAN J. "The Social Costs of Chronic Heart and Lung Disease." Quality of the Environment Division Discussion Paper QE89-16. Washington, DC: Resources for the Future, 1989.

CROPPER, MAUREEN L. AND PORTNEY, PAUL R. "Discounting and the Evaluation of Lifesaving Programs," *J. Risk Uncertainty*, Dec. 1990, *3*(4), pp. 369–79.

CROPPER, MAUREEN L. AND SUSSMAN, FRANCES G. "Valuing Future Risks to Life," *J. Environ. Econ. Manage.*, Sept. 1990, *19*(2), pp. 160–74.

CUMBERLAND, JOHN H. "Efficiency and Equity in Interregional Environmental Management," *Rev. Reg. Stud.*, Fall 1981, *10*(2), pp. 1–9.

DALES, JOHN HARKNESS. *Pollution, property, and prices.* Toronto, Ont.: U. of Toronto Press, 1968.

DARDIS, RACHEL. "The Value of a Life: New Evidence from the Marketplace," *Amer. Econ. Rev.*, Dec. 1980, *70*(5), pp. 1077–82.

D'ARGE, RALPH C. AND KNEESE, ALLEN V. "International Trade, Domestic Income, and Environmental Controls: Some Empirical Estimates," in *Managing the environment: International economic cooperation for pollution control.* Eds.: ALLEN V. KNEESE, SIDNEY E. ROLFE, AND JOSEPH W. HARNED. NY: Praeger, 1971, pp. 289–315.

DEACON, ROBERT T. AND SHAPIRO, PERRY. "Private Preference for Collective Goods Revealed Through Voting on Referenda," *Amer. Econ. Rev.*, Dec. 1975, *65*(5), pp. 943–55.

DECISION FOCUS INCORPORATED. *Development and design of a contingent value survey for measuring the public's value for visibility improvements at* the Grand Canyon National Park. Revised Draft Report, Los Altos, CA, Sept. 1990.

DEWEES, DONALD N. "Instrument Choice in Environmental Policy," *Econ. Inquiry*, Jan. 1983, *21*(1), pp. 53–71.

DEWEES, DONALD N. AND SIMS, W. A. "The Symmetry of Effluent Charges and Subsidies for Pollution Control," *Can. J. Econ.*, May 1976, *9*(2), pp. 323–31.

DICKENS, WILLIAM T. "Differences Between Risk Premiums in Union and Nonunion Wages and the Case for Occupational Safety Regulation," *Amer. Econ. Rev.*, May 1984, *74*(2), pp. 320–23.

DICKIE, MARK T. ET AL. "Reconciling Averting Behavior and Contingent Valuation Benefit Estimates of Reducing Symptoms of Ozone Exposure (draft)," in *Improving accuracy and reducing costs of environmental benefit assessments*. Washington, DC: U.S. Environmental Protection Agency, 1987.

DICKIE, MARK; FISHER, ANN AND GERKING, SHELBY. "Market Transactions and Hypothetical Demand Data: A Comparative Study," *J. Amer. Stat. Assoc.*, Mar. 1987, *82*(397), pp. 69–75.

DICKIE, MARK AND GERKING, SHELBY. "Willingness to Pay for Ozone Control: Inferences From the Demand for Medical Care," *J. Urban Econ.*, forthcoming.

DORFMAN, NANCY S., ASSISTED BY SNOW, ARTHUR. "Who Will Pay for Pollution Control?—The Distribution by Income of the Burden of the National Environmental Protection Program," *Nat. Tax J.*, Mar. 1975, *28*(1), pp. 101–15.

DOWLATABADI, HADI AND HARRINGTON, WINSTON. "The Effects of Uncertainty on Policy Instruments: The Case of Electricity Supply and Environmental Regulations." Quality of the Environment Division Discussion Paper QE89-20. Washington, DC: Resources for the Future, 1989.

DOWNING, PAUL B. AND WATSON, WILLIAM D., JR. "The Economics of Enforcing Air Pollution Controls," *J. Environ. Econ. Manage.*, Nov. 1974, *1*(3), pp. 219–36.

EASTERBROOK, GREGG. "Cleaning Up," *Newsweek*, July 24, 1989, *114*, pp. 26–42.

EPPLE, DENNIS. "Hedonic Prices and Implicit Markets: Estimating Demand and Supply Functions for Differentiated Products," *J. Polit. Econ.*, Feb. 1987, *95*(1), pp. 59–80.

FEENBERG, DANIEL AND MILLS, EDWIN S. *Measuring the benefits of water pollution abatement*. NY: Academic Press. 1980.

FISCHEL, WILLIAM A. "Fiscal and Environmental Considerations in the Location of Firms in Suburban Communities," in *Fiscal zoning and land use controls*. Eds.: EDWIN S. MILLS AND WALLACE E. OATES. Lexington, MA: Heath, 1975, pp. 119–73.

———. "Determinants of Voting on Environmental Quality: A Study of a New Hampshire Pulp Mill Referendum," *J. Environ. Econ. Manage.*, June 1979, *6*(2), pp. 107–18.

FISHELSON, GIDEON. "Emission Control Policies Under Uncertainty," *J. Environ. Econ. Manage.*, Oct. 1976, *3*, pp. 189–97.

FISHER, ANN; VIOLETTE, DAN AND CHESTNUT, LAU-

RAINE. "The Value of Reducing Risks of Death: A Note on New Evidence," *J. Policy Anal. Manage.*, Winter 1989, *8*(1), pp. 88–100.

FISHER, ANTHONY C. *Resource and environmental economics*. Cambridge, Eng.: Cambridge U. Press, 1981.

FISHER, ANTHONY C. AND PETERSON, FREDERICK M. "The Environment in Economics: A Survey," *J. Econ. Lit.*, Mar. 1976, *14*(1), pp. 1–33.

FREEMAN, A. MYRICK, III. "Distribution of Environmental Quality," in *Environmental quality analysis: Theory and method in the social sciences*. Eds.: ALLEN V. KNEESE AND BLAIR BOWER. Baltimore, MD: Johns Hopkins University Press for Resources for the Future, 1972, pp. 243–78.

———. "On Estimating Air Pollution Control Benefits from Land Value Studies," *J. Environ. Econ. Manage.*, May 1974, *1*(1), pp. 74–83.

———. *The benefits of environmental improvement*. Baltimore, MD: Johns Hopkins U. Press for Resources for the Future, Inc., 1979a, p. 63.

———. "The Incidence of the Cost of Controlling Automobile Air Pollution," in *The distribution of economic well-being*. Ed.: F. THOMAS JUSTER. Cambridge, MA: Ballinger, 1979b.

———. *Air and water pollution control: A benefit-cost assessment*. NY: John Wiley, 1982.

GARCIA, PHILIP ET AL. "Measuring the Benefits of Environmental Change Using a Duality Approach: The Case of Ozone and Illinois Cash Grain Farms," *J. Environ. Econ. Manage.*, Mar. 1986, *13*(1), pp. 69–80.

GEGAX, DOUGLAS; GERKING, SHELBY AND SCHULZE, WILLIAM. "Perceived Risk and the Marginal Value of Safety." Working paper prepared for the U.S. Environmental Protection Agency, Aug. 1985.

GERKING, SHELBY; DEHAAN, MENNO AND SCHULZE, WILLIAM. "The Marginal Value of Job Safety: A Contingent Valuation Study," *J. Risk Uncertainty*, June 1988, *1*(2), pp. 185–99.

GERKING, SHELBY AND STANLEY, LINDA R. "An Economic Analysis of Air Pollution and Health: The Case of St. Louis," *Rev. Econ. Statist.*, Feb. 1986, *68*(1), pp. 115–21.

GIANESSI, LEONARD P.; PESKIN, HENRY M. AND WOLFF, EDWARD N. "The Distributional Effects of Uniform Air Pollution Policy in the United States," *Quart. J. Econ.*, May 1979, *93*(2), pp. 281–301.

GIANESSI, LEONARD P. AND PESKIN, HENRY M. "The Distribution of the Costs of Federal Water Pollution Control Policy," *Land Econ.*, Feb. 1980, *56*(1), pp. 85–102.

GOULD, J. R. "Total Conditions in the Analysis of External Effects," *Econ. J.*, Sept. 1977, *87*(347), pp. 558–64.

GRIGALUNAS, THOMAS A. AND OPALUCH, JAMES J. "Assessing Liability for Damages Under CERCLA: A New Approach for Providing Incentives for Pollution Avoidance?" *Natural Res. J.*, Summer 1988, *28*(3), pp. 509–33.

HAHN, ROBERT W. "Market Power and Transferable Property Rights," *Quart. J. Econ.*, Nov. 1984, *99*(4), pp. 753–65.

_____. "Economic Prescriptions for Environmental Problems: How the Patient Followed the Doctor's Orders," *J. Econ. Perspectives,* Spring 1989, *3*(2), pp. 95–114.

_____. "The Political Economy of Environmental Regulation: Towards a Unifying Framework," *Public Choice,* Apr. 1990, *65*(1), pp. 21–47.

HAHN, ROBERT W. AND HESTER, GORDON L. "Marketable Permits: Lessons for Theory and Practice," *Ecology Law Quarterly,* 1989a, *16*(2), pp. 361–406.

_____. "Where Did All the Markets Go? An Analysis of EPA's Emissions Trading Program," *Yale J. Regul.,* Winter 1989b, *6*(1), pp. 109–53.

HAHN, ROBERT W. AND MCGARTLAND, ALBERT M. "The Political Economy of Instrument Choice: An Examination of the U.S. Role in Implementing the Montreal Protocol," *Northwestern U. Law Rev.,* Spring 1989, *83*(3), pp. 592–611.

HAHN, ROBERT W. AND NOLL, ROGER G. "Designing a Market for Tradable Emission Permits," in *Reform of environmental regulation.* Ed.: WESLEY MAGAT. Cambridge, MA. Ballinger, 1982, pp. 119–46.

HAMILTON, JONATHAN H.; SHESHINSKI, EYTAN AND SLUTSKY, STEVEN M. "Production Externalities and Long-Run Equilibria: Bargaining and Pigovian Taxation," *Econ. Inquiry,* July 1989, *27*(3), pp. 453–71.

HAMILTON, SCOTT A.; MCCARL, BRUCE A. AND ADAMS, RICHARD M. "The Effect of Aggregate Response Assumptions on Environmental Impact Analyses," *Amer. J. Agr. Econ.,* May 1985, *67*(2), pp. 407–13.

HAMMACK, JUDD AND BROWN, GARDNER M., JR. *Waterfowl and wetlands: Toward bioeconomic analysis.* Baltimore, MD: Johns Hopkins U. Press for Resources for the Future, 1974.

HANEMANN, W. MICHAEL. "Discrete/Continuous Models of Consumer Demand," *Econometrica,* May 1984, *52*(3), pp. 541–61.

HANEMANN, W. MICHAEL. "Willingness to Pay and Willingness to Accept: How Much Can They Differ?" *Amer. Econ. Rev.,* June 1991, *81*(3), pp. 635–47.

HARFORD, JON D. "Firm Behavior Under Imperfectly Enforceable Pollution Standards and Taxes," *J. Environ. Econ. Manage.,* Mar. 1978, *5*(1), pp. 26–43.

HARRINGTON, WINSTON. "Enforcement Leverage When Penalties Are Restricted," *J. Public Econ.,* Oct. 1988, *37*(1), pp. 29–53.

HARRINGTON, WINSTON; KRUPNICK, ALAN J. AND PESKIN, HENRY M. "Policies for Nonpoint-Source Water Pollution Control," *J. Soil and Water Conservation,* Jan.–Feb. 1985, *40*, pp. 27–32.

HARRINGTON, WINSTON; KRUPNICK, ALAN J. AND SPOFFORD, WALTER O., JR. "The Economic Losses of a Waterborne Disease Outbreak," *J. Urban Econ.,* Jan. 1989, *25*(1), pp. 116–37.

HARRINGTON, WINSTON AND PORTNEY, PAUL R. "Valuing the Benefits of Health and Safety Regulations," *J. Urban Econ.,* July 1987, *22*(1), pp. 101–12.

HARRISON, DAVID, JR. *Who pays for clean air: The cost and benefit distribution of federal automobile emissions standards.* Cambridge, MA: Ballinger, 1975.

HARRISON, DAVID H. "The Regulation of Aircraft Noise," in *Incentives for environmental protection.* Ed.: THOMAS C. SCHELLING. Cambridge, MA: MIT Press, 1983, pp. 41–143.

HAZILLA, MICHAEL AND KOPP, RAYMOND J. "Social Cost of Environmental Quality Regulations: A General Equilibrium Analysis," *J. Polit. Econ.,* Aug. 1990, *98*(4), pp. 853–73.

HOEHN, JOHN P. AND RANDALL, ALAN. "Too Many Proposals Pass the Benefit Cost Test," *Amer. Econ. Rev.,* 1989, *789*(3), pp. 544–51.

HOTELLING, HAROLD. "The Economics of Exhaustible Resources," *J. Polit. Econ.,* Apr. 1931, *39*(2), pp. 137–75.

JOHNSON, RALPH W. AND BROWN, GARDNER M., JR. *Cleaning up Europe's waters.* NY: Praeger, 1976.

JONES-LEE, MICHAEL W. "The Value of Changes in the Probability of Death or Injury," *J. Polit. Econ.,* July/Aug. 1974, *82*(4), pp. 835–49.

JONES-LEE, MICHAEL W.; HAMMERTON, M. AND PHILIPS, P. R. "The Value of Safety: Results of a National Sample Survey," *Econ. J.,* Mar. 1985, *95*(377), pp. 49–72.

JORGENSON, DALE W. AND WILCOXEN, PETER J. "Environmental Regulation and U.S. Economic Growth," *Rand J. Econ.,* Summer 1990a, *21*(2), pp. 314–40.

_____. "Reducing U.S. Carbon Dioxide Emissions: The Cost of Different Goals." Harvard U., 1990b.

KAHNEMAN, DANIEL; KNETSCH, JACK L. AND THALER, RICHARD H. "Experimental Tests of the Endowment Effect and the Coase Theorem," *J. Polit. Econ.,* Dec. 1990, *98*(6), pp. 1325–48.

KAHNEMAN, DANIEL AND TVERSKY, AMOS. "Prospect Theory: An Analysis of Decisions Under Risk," *Econometrica,* Mar. 1979, *47*(2), pp. 263–91.

KAMIEN, MORTON I.; SCHWARTZ, NANCY L. AND DOLBEAR, F. T. "Asymmetry between Bribes and Charges," *Water Resources Res.,* 1966, *2*(1), pp. 147–57.

KANE, SALLY; REILLY, JOHN AND TOBEY, JAMES. "An Empirical Study of the Economic Effects of Climate Change on World Agriculture." Mimeo USDA Report, Jan. 1991.

KANEMOTO, YOSHITSUGU. "Hedonic Prices and the Benefits of Public Prices," *Econometrica,* July 1988, *56*(4), pp. 981–90.

KEALY, MARY JO; DOVIDIO, JACK AND ROCKEL, MARK L. "Willingness to Pay to Prevent Additional Damages to the Adirondacks from Acid Rain," *Reg. Sci. Rev.,* 1987, *15*, pp. 118–41.

KELMAN, STEVEN J. *What price incentives? Economists and the environment.* Boston, MA: Auburn House, 1981.

KNEESE, ALLEN V.; AYRES, ROBERT V. AND D'ARGE, RALPH C. *Economics and the environment: A materials balance approach.* Washington, DC: Resources for the Future, 1970.

KNEESE, ALLEN V. AND BOWER, BLAIR T. *Managing water quality: Economics, technology, institutions.* Baltimore, MD: Johns Hopkins University Press for Resources for the Future, 1968.

KNEESE, ALLEN V. AND SCHULZE, WILLIAM D. "Ethics and Environmental Economics," in *Handbook of natural resource and energy economics*. Vol. 1. Eds.: ALLEN V. KNEESE AND JAMES L. SWEENEY. Amsterdam: North-Holland, 1985, pp. 191–220.

KNETSCH, JACK L. AND SINDEN, J. A. "Willingness to Pay and Compensation Demanded: Experimental Evidence of an Unexpected Disparity in Measures of Value," *Quart J. Econ.*, Aug. 1984, 99(3), pp. 507–21.

KOHN, ROBERT E. "A General Equilibrium Analysis of the Optimal Number of Firms in a Polluting Industry," *Can. J. Econ.*, May 1985, 18(2), pp. 347–54.

KOLSTAD, CHARLES D. "Empirical Properties of Economic Incentives and Command-and-Control Regulations for Air Pollution Control," *Land Econ.*, Aug. 1986, 62(3), pp. 250–68.

———. "Uniformity versus Differentiation in Regulating Externalities," *J. Environ. Econ. Manage.*, Dec. 1987, 14(4), pp. 386–99.

KOO, ANTHONY Y. C. "Environmental Repercussions and Trade Theory," *Rev. Econ. Statist.*, May 1974, 56(2), pp. 235–44.

KOPP, RAYMOND J. AND KRUPNICK, ALAN J. "Agricultural Policy and the Benefits of Ozone Control," *Amer. J. Agr. Econ.*, Dec. 1987, 69(5), pp. 956–62.

KOPP, RAYMOND J. ET AL. "Implications of Environmental Policy for U.S. Agriculture: The Case of Ambient Ozone Standards," *J. Environ. Manag.*, June 1985, 20(4), pp. 321–31.

KRUPNICK, ALAN J. "Costs of Alternative Policies for the Control of NO₂ in the Baltimore Region." Unpub. working paper. Washington, DC: Resources for the Future, 1983.

KRUPNICK, ALAN J.; OATES, WALLACE E. AND VAN DE VERG, ERIC. "On Marketable Air-Pollution Permits: The Case for a System of Pollution Offsets," *J. Environ. Econ. Manage.*, Sept. 1983, 10(3), pp. 233–47.

KRUPNICK, ALAN J. AND PORTNEY, PAUL R. "Controlling Urban Air Pollution: A Benefit-Cost Assessment," *Science*, Apr. 26, 1991, 252, pp. 522–28.

KRUTILLA, JOHN V. "Conservation Reconsidered," *Amer. Econ. Rev.*, Sept. 1967, 57(4), pp. 777–86.

KWEREL, EVAN R. "To Tell the Truth: Imperfect Information and Optimal Pollution Control," *Rev. Econ. Stud.*, Oct. 1977, 44(3), pp. 595–601.

LEE, DWIGHT R. "Efficiency of Pollution Taxation and Market Structure," *J. Environ. Econ. Manage.*, Sept. 1975, 2(1), pp. 69–72.

LEE, DWIGHT R. AND MISIOLEK, WALTER S. "Substituting Pollution Taxation for General Taxation: Some Implications for Efficiency in Pollution Taxation," *J. Environ. Econ. Manage.*, Dec. 1986, 13(4), pp. 338–47.

LEONARD, H. JEFFREY. *Pollution and the struggle for the world product*. Cambridge, Eng. Cambridge U. Press, 1988.

LICHTENBERG, ERIK AND ZILBERMAN, DAVID. "The Welfare Economics of Price Supports in U.S. Agriculture," *Amer. Econ. Rev.*, Dec. 1986, 76(5), pp. 1135–41.

LOEHMAN, EDNA T. ET AL. "Distributional Analysis of Regional Benefits and Cost of Air Quality Control," *J. Environ. Econ. Manage.*, Sept. 1979, 6(3), pp. 222–43.

LOEHMAN, EDNA; BOLDT, D. AND CHAIKIN, K. "Measuring the Benefits of Air Quality Improvements in the San Francisco Bay Area." Prepared for the U.S. Environmental Protection Agency by SRI International, Menlo Park, CA, 1981.

LYON, RANDOLPH M. "Auctions and Alternative Procedures for Allocating Pollution Rights," *Land Econ.*, Feb. 1982, 58(1), pp. 16–32.

MACFARLAND, K. K. ET AL. "An Examination of Methodologies and Social Indicators for Assessing the Value of Visibility," in *Managing air quality and scenic resources at national parks and wilderness areas*. Eds.: ROBERT D. ROWE AND LAURAINE G. CHESTNUT. Boulder, CO: Westview Press, 1983.

MAGAT, WESLEY A. "Pollution Control and Technological Advance: A Dynamic Model of the Firm," *J. Environ. Econ. Manage.*, Mar. 1978, 5(1), pp. 1–25.

MAGAT, WESLEY A.; KRUPNICK, ALAN J. AND HARRINGTON, WINSTON. *Rules in the making: A statistical analysis of regulatory agency behavior*. Washington, DC: Resources for the Future, 1986.

MÄLER, KARL-GÖRAN. *Environmental economics: A theoretical inquiry*. Baltimore, MD: Johns Hopkins U. Press for Resources for the Future, 1974.

———. "Welfare Economics and the Environment," in *Handbook of natural resource and energy economics*. Vol. 1. Eds.: ALLEN KNEESE AND JAMES SWEENEY. Amsterdam: North-Holland, 1985, pp. 3–60.

MALIK, ARUN. "Markets for Pollution Control When Firms Are Noncompliant," *J. Environ. Econ. Manage.*, Mar. 1990, 18(2, Part 1), pp. 97–106.

MAUSKOPF, JOSEPHINE A. "Projections of Cancer Risks Attributable to Future Exposure to Asbestos," *Risk Analysis*, 1987, 7(4), pp. 477–86.

McCONNELL, VIRGINIA D. AND SCHWAB, ROBERT M. "The Impact of Environmental Regulation in Industry Location Decisions: The Motor Vehicle Industry," *Land Econ.*, Feb. 1990, 66, pp. 67–81.

McCUBBINS, MATTHEW D.; NOLL, ROGER G. AND WEINGAST, BARRY R. "Structure and Process, Politics and Policy: Administrative Arrangements and the Political Control of Agencies," *Virginia Law Rev.*, Mar. 1989, 75(2), pp. 431–82.

McGARTLAND, ALBERT M. *Marketable permit systems for air pollution control: An empirical study*. Ph.D. Dissertation, U. of Maryland, College Park, MD, 1984.

———. "A Comparison of Two Marketable Discharge Permits Systems," *J. Environ. Econ. Manage.*, Mar. 1988, 15(1), pp. 35–44.

McGARTLAND, ALBERT M. AND OATES, WALLACE E. "Marketable Permits for the Prevention of Environmental Deterioration," *J. Environ. Econ. Manage.*, Sept. 1985, 12(3), pp. 207–28.

McGUIRE, MARTIN. "Regulation, Factor Rewards, and International Trade," *J. Public Econ.*, Apr. 1982, 17(3), pp. 335–54.

MENDELSOHN, ROBERT. "Estimating the Structural Equations of Implicit Markets and Household Production Functions," *Rev. Econ. Statist.*, Nov. 1984, 66(4), pp. 673–77.

———. "Regulating Heterogeneous Emissions," *J. Environ. Econ. Manage.*, Dec. 1986, 13(4), pp. 301–12.

———. "Modeling the Demand for Outdoor Recreation," *Water Resources Res.*, May 1987, 23(5), pp. 961–67.

MERRIFIELD, JOHN D. "The Impact of Selected Abatement Strategies on Transnational Pollution, the Terms of Trade, and Factor Rewards: A General Equilibrium Approach," *J. Environ. Econ. Manage.*, Sept. 1988, 15(3), pp. 259–84.

MESTELMAN, STUART. "Production Externalities and Corrective Subsidies: A General Equilibrium Analysis," *J. Environ. Econ. Manage.*, June 1982, 9(2), pp. 186–93.

MILLIMAN, SCOTT R. AND PRINCE, RAYMOND. "Firm Incentives to Promote Technological Change in Pollution Control," *J. Environ. Econ. Manage.*, Nov. 1989, 17(3), pp. 247–65.

MINTZ, JACK M. AND TULKENS, HENRY. "Commodity Tax Competition between Member States of a Federation: Equilibrium and Efficiency," *J. Public Econ.*, Mar. 1986, 29(2), pp. 133–72.

MISIOLEK, WALTER S. "Effluent Taxation in Monopoly Markets," *J. Environ. Econ. Manage.*, June 1980, 7(2), pp. 103–07.

MITCHELL, ROBERT C. AND CARSON, RICHARD T. "Valuing Drinking Water Risk Reductions Using the Contingent Valuation Methods: A Methodological Study of Risks from THM and Giardia." Paper prepared for Resources for the Future, Washington, DC, 1986.

———. *Using surveys to value public goods: The contingent valuation method.* Washington, DC: Resources for the Future, 1989.

MJELDE, JAMES W. ET AL. "Using Farmers' Actions to Measure Crop Loss Due to Air Pollution," *J. Air Pollution Control Association*, Apr. 1984, 34(4), pp. 360–64.

MONTGOMERY, W. DAVID. "Markets in Licenses and Efficient Pollution Control Programs," *J. Econ. Theory*, Dec. 1972, 5(3), pp. 395–418.

MOREY, EDWARD R. "The Choice of Ski Areas: A Generalized CES Preference Ordering with Characteristics," *Rev. Econ. Statist.*, Nov. 1984, 66(4), pp. 584–90.

MULLEN, JOHN K. AND MENZ, FREDRIC C. "The Effect of Acidification Damages on the Economic Value of the Adirondack Fishery to New York Anglers," *Amer. J. Agr. Econ.*, Feb. 1985, 67(1), pp. 112–19.

MUMY, GENE E. "Long-Run Efficiency and Property Rights Sharing for Pollution Control," *Public Choice*, 1980, 35(1), pp. 59–74.

NICHOLS, ALBERT L. *Targeting economic incentives for environmental protection.* Cambridge, MA: MIT Press, 1984.

NICHOLS, ALBERT L. AND ZECKHAUSER, RICHARD J. "The Perils of Prudence," *Regulation*, Nov./Dec. 1986, 10(2), pp. 13–24.

NORDHAUS, WILLIAM D. "To Slow or Not to Slow: The Economics of the Greenhouse Effect." Cowles Foundation Discussion Paper, 1990.

OATES, WALLACE E. "The Regulation of Externalities: Efficient Behavior by Sources and Victims," *Public Finance*, 1983, 38(3), pp. 362–75.

OATES, WALLACE E.; PORTNEY, PAUL R. AND McGARTLAND, ALBERT M. "The *Net* Benefits of Incentive-based Regulation: A Case Study of Environmental Standard Setting," *Amer. Econ. Rev.*, Dec. 1989, 79(5), pp. 1233–42.

OATES, WALLACE E. AND SCHWAB, ROBERT M. "Economic Competition Among Jurisdictions: Efficiency Enhancing or Distortion Inducting?" *J. Public Econ.*, Apr. 1988a. 35(3), pp. 333–54.

OATES, WALLACE E. AND SCHWAB, ROBERT M. "The Theory of Regulatory Federalism: The Case of Environmental Management." Working Paper No. 88–26, Dept. of Economics. U. of Maryland, 1988b.

OATES, WALLACE E. AND STRASSMAN N., DIANA L. "Effluent Fees and Market Structure," *J. Public Econ.*, June 1984, 24(1), pp. 29–46.

OHSFELDT, ROBERT L. "Assessing the Accuracy of Structural Parameter Estimates in Analyses of Implicit Markets," *Land Econ.*, May 1988, 64(2), pp. 135–46.

OHSFELDT, ROBERT L. AND SMITH, BARTON A. Estimating the Demand for Heterogeneous Goods," *Rev. Econ. Statist.*, Feb. 1985, 67(1), pp. 165–71.

O'NEIL, WILLIAM B. "The Regulation of Water Pollution Permit Trading Under Conditions of Varying Streamflow and Temperature," in *Buying a better environment: Cost-effective regulation through permit trading.* Eds. ERHARD F. JOERES AND MARTIN H. DAVID. Madison, WI: U. of Wisconsin Press, 1983, pp. 219–31.

O'NEIL, WILLIAM ET AL. "Transferable Discharge Permits and Economic Efficiency: The Fox River," *J. Environ. Econ. Manage.*, Dec. 1983, 10(94), pp. 346–55.

OPALUCH, JAMES J. AND GRIGALUNAS, THOMAS A. "Controlling Stochastic Pollution Events through Liability Rules: Some Evidence from OCS Leasing," *Rand J. Econ.*, Spring 1984, 15(1), pp. 142–51.

ORGANIZATION FOR ECONOMIC COOPERATION AND DEVELOPMENT. *The application of economic instruments for environmental protection.* Paris: O.E.C.D., 1989.

———. *Recommendation of the council on the use of economic instruments in environmental policy.* Paris: O.E.C.D, Jan. 1991.

PALMER, ADELE R. ET AL. "Economic Implications of Regulating Chlorofluorocarbon Emissions from Nonaerosol Applications." Report R-2524-EPA. Santa Monica, CA: Rand Corp., 1980.

PALMQUIST, RAYMOND B. "Estimating the Demand for the Characteristics of Housing," *Rev. Econ. Statist.*, Aug. 1984, 66(3), pp. 394–404.

———. "Pollution Subsidies and Multiple Local Optima," *Land Econ.*, Nov. 1990, 66, pp. 394–401.

PARSONS, GEORGE R. AND KEALY, MARY JO. "Measuring Water Quality Benefits Using a Random Utility Model of Lake Recreation in Wisconsin." Working Paper No. 90–14, Dept. of Economics, U. of Delaware, 1990.

PELTZMAN, SAM AND TIDEMAN, T. NICOLAUS. "Local versus National Pollution Control: Note," *Amer. Econ. Rev.*, Dec. 1972, *62*(5), pp. 959–63.

PETHIG, RÜDIGER. "Pollution, Welfare, and Environmental Policy in the Theory of Comparative Advantage," *J. Environ. Econ. Manage.*, Feb. 1976, *2*(3), pp. 160–69.

PETHIG, RÜDIGER ET AL. *Trade and Environment: A Theoretical Inquiry*. Amsterdam: Elsevier, 1980.

PEZZEY, JOHN. "Changes versus Subsidies versus Marketable Permits as Efficient and Acceptable Methods of Effluent Controls: A Property Rights Analysis." Unpub. paper, 1990.

PORTES, RICHARD D. "The Search for Efficiency in the Presence of Externalities," in *Unfashionable economics: Essays in honor of Lord Balogh*. Ed.: PAUL STREETEN. London: Weidenfeld and Nicholson, 1970, pp. 348–61.

PORTNEY, PAUL R. "Policy Watch: Economics and the Clean Air Act," *J. Econ. Perspectives*, Fall 1990, *4*(4), pp. 173–81.

RAE, DOUGLAS A. "Benefits of Visual Air Quality in Cincinnati: Results of a Contingent Ranking Survey." RP-1742, final report prepared by Charles River Associates for Electric Power Research Institute, Palo Alto, CA, 1984..

RANDALL, ALAN; IVES, BERRY AND EASTMAN, CLYDE. "Bidding Games for Valuation of Aesthetic Environmental Improvements," *J. Environ. Econ. Manage.*, Aug. 1974, *1*(2), pp. 132–49.

RAUFER, ROGER K. AND FELDMAN, STEPHEN L. *Acid rain and emissions trading*. Totowa, NJ: Rowman & Littlefield, 1987.

RIDKER, RONALD G. AND HENNING, JOHN A. "The Determinants of Residential Property Values with Special Reference to Air Pollution," *Rev. Econ. Statist.*, May 1967, *49*(2), pp. 246–57

ROBACK, JENNIFER. "Wages, Rents, and the Quality of Life," *J. Polit. Econ.*, Dec. 1982, *90*(6), pp. 1257–78.

ROBERTS, MARC J. AND SPENCE, MICHAEL. "Effluent Charges and Licenses Under Uncertainty," *J. Public Econ.*, Apr./May 1976, *5*(3)(4), pp. 193–208.

ROBISON, H. DAVID. "Who Pays for Industrial Pollution Abatement?" *Rev. Econ. Statist.*, Nov. 1985, *67*(4), pp. 702–06.

ROSEN, SHERWIN. "Hedonic Prices and Implicit Markets: Product Differentiation in Pure Competition," *J. Polit. Econ.*, Jan./Feb. 1974, *82*(1), pp. 34–55.

ROSEN, SHERWIN. "Wage-Based Indexes of Urban Quality of Life," in *Current issues in urban economics*. Eds.: PETER MIESZKOWSKI AND MAHLON STRASZHEIM. Baltimore, MD: Johns Hopkins U. Press for Resources for the Future, 1979, pp. 74–104.

ROSENBERG, NORMAN J. ET AL. "Processes for Identifying Regional Influences of and Responses to Increasing Atmospheric CO_2 and Climate Change—The MINK Project." Prepared by Resources for the Future for Pacific Northwest Laboratory, Oct. 1990.

ROWE, ROBERT D.; D'ARGE, RALPH C. AND BROOKSHIRE, DAVID S. "An Experiment on Economic Value of Visibility," *J. Environ. Econ. Manage.*, Mar. 1980, *7*(1), pp. 1–9.

RUSSELL, CLIFFORD S. "Monitoring and Enforcement," in *Public policies for environmental protection*. Ed.: PAUL PORTNEY. Washington, DC: Resources for the Future, 1990, pp. 243–74.

RUSSELL, CLIFFORD S.; HARRINGTON: WINSTON AND VAUGHAN, WILLIAM J. *Enforcing pollution control laws*. Washington DC: Resources for the Future, 1986

SAMPLES, KARL C.; DIXON, JOHN A. AND GOWEN, MARCIA M. "Information Disclosure and Endangered Species Valuation," *Land Econ.*, Aug. 1986, *62*(3), pp. 306–12.

SCHERR, BRUCE A. AND BABB, EMERSON M. "Pricing Public Goods: An Experiment with Two Proposed Pricing Systems," *Public Choice*, Fall 1975, *23*(3), pp. 35–48.

SCHULZE, WILLIAM D. AND BROOKSHIRE, DAVID S. "The Economic Benefits of Preserving Visibility in the National Parklands of the Southwest," *Natural Res. J.*, Jan. 1983, *23*(1), pp. 149–73.

SCHULZE, WILLIAM D. AND D'ARGE, RALPH C. "The Coase Proposition, Information Constraints, and Long-Run Equilibrium," *Amer. Econ. Rev.*, Sept. 1974, *64*(4), pp. 763–72.

SEGERSON, KATHLEEN. "Uncertainty and Incentives for Nonpoint Pollution Control," *J. Environ. Econ. Manage.*, Mar. 1988, *15*(1), pp. 87–98.

_____ . "Institutional 'Markets': The Role of Liability in Allocating Environmental Resources," in *Proceedings of AERE workshop on natural resource market mechanisms*. Association of Environmental and Resource Economists, June 1990.

SESKIN, EUGENE P.; ANDERSON, ROBERT J., JR. AND REID, ROBERT O. "An Empirical Analysis of Economic Strategies for Controlling Air Pollution," *J. Environ. Econ. Manage.*, June 1983, *10*(2), pp. 112–24.

SHAVELL, STEVEN. "A Model of the Optimal Use of Liability and Safety Regulations," *Rand J. Econ.*, Summer 1984a, *15*(2), pp. 271–80.

_____ . "Liability for Harm versus Regulation of Safety," *J. Legal Stud.*, 1984b, *13*(2), pp. 357–74.

SHIBATA, HIROFUMI AND WINRICH, J. STEVEN. "Control of Pollution When the Offended Defend Themselves," *Economica*, Nov. 1983, *50*(200), pp. 425–37.

SIEBERT HORST. "Environmental Protection and International Specialization," *Weltwirtsch. Arch.*, 1974, *110*(3), pp. 494–508.

SLOVIC, PAUL; FISCHHOFF, BARUCH AND LICHTENSTEIN, SARAH. "Facts Versus Fears: Understanding Perceived Risk," in *Social risk assessment: How safe is enough*. Ed. WALTER A. ALBERS. NY: Plenum, 1980.

_____ . "Response Mode, Framing, and Information-Processing Effects in Risk Assessment," in *Question framing and response consistency*. Ed.:

ROBIN M. HOGARTH. San Francisco, CA: Jossey-Bass, 1982.

SMITH, V. KERRY. "The Role of Site and Job Characteristics in Hedonic Wage Models," *J. Urban Econ.*, May 1983, *13*(3), pp. 296–321.

SMITH, V. KERRY AND DESVOUSGES, WILLIAM H. "The Generalized Travel Cost Model and Water Quality Benefits: A Reconsideration," *Southern Econ. J.*, Oct. 1985, *52*(2), pp. 371–81.

_____. *Measuring water quality benefits.* Norwell, MA: Kluwer-Nijhoff, 1986a.

_____. "Averting Behavior: Does It Exist?" *Economics Letters*, 1986b, *20*(3), pp. 291–96.

SMITH, V. KERRY; DESVOUSGES, WILLIAM H. AND McGIVNEY, MATTHEW P. "Estimating Water Quality Benefits: An Econometric Analysis," *Land Econ.*, Aug. 1983, *59*(3), pp. 259–78.

SMITH, V. KERRY; PALMQUIST, RAYMOND B. AND JAKUS, PAUL. "Combining Farrell Frontier and Hedonic Travel Cost Models for Valuing Estuarine Quality." Nov. 15, 1990, second revision.

SMITH, VERNON L. "The Principle of Unanimity and Voluntary Consent in Social Choice," *J. Polit. Econ.*, Dec. 1977, *85*(6), pp. 1125–39.

_____. "Incentive Compatible Experimental Processes for the Provision of Public Goods," in *Research in experimental economics.* Ed.: VERNON L. SMITH. Greenwich, CT: JAI Press, 1979.

SPOFFORD, WALTER O., JR. "Efficiency Properties of Alternative Control Policies for Meeting Ambient Air Quality Standards: An Empirical Application to the Lower Delaware Valley." Discussion Paper D-118. Washington, DC: Resources for the Future, Feb. 1984.

SPULBER, DANIEL F. "Effluent Regulation and Long-Run Optimality," *J. Environ. Econ. Manage.*, June 1985, *12*(2), pp. 103–16.

STARRETT, DAVID A. "Fundemantal Nonconvexities in the Theory of Externalities," *J. Econ. Theory*, Apr. 1972, *4*(2), pp. 180–99.

STAVINS, ROBERT N., ed. *Project 88—Harnessing market forces to protect our environment: Initiatives for the new president.* A Public Policy Study Sponsored by Senator Timothy E. Wirth, Colorado, and Senator John Heinz, Pennsylvania. Washington, DC, Dec. 1988.

TERKLA, DAVID. "The Efficiency Value of Effluent Tax Revenues," *J. Environ. Econ. Manage.*, June 1984, *11*(2), pp. 107–23.

THALER, RICHARD AND ROSEN, SHERWIN. "The Value of Life Savings," in *Household production and consumption.* Ed.: NESTER TERLECKYJ. NY: Columbia U. Press, 1976.

TIETENBERG, THOMAS H. "Spatially Differentiated Air Pollutant Emission Charges: An Economic and Legal Analysis," *Land Econ.*, Aug. 1978, *54*93), pp. 265–77.

_____. "Transferable Discharge Permits and the Control of Stationary Source Air Pollution: A Survey and Synthesis," *Land Econ.*, Nov. 1980, *56*(4), pp. 391–416.

_____. *Emissions trading: An exercise in reforming pollution policy.* Washington, DC: Resources for the Future, 1985.

_____. "Indivisible Toxic Torts: The Economics of Joint and Several Liability," *Land Econ.*, Nov. 1989, *65*, pp. 305–19.

_____. "Economic Instruments for Environmental Regulation," *Oxford Rev. Econ. Policy*, Mar. 1990, *6*.

TOBEY, JAMES A. "The Impact of Domestic Environmental Policies on International Trade." Ph.D. Dissertation, Dept. of Economics, U. of Maryland, College Park, 1989.

_____. "The Effects of Domestic Environmental Policies on Patterns of World Trade: An Empirical Test," *Kyklos*, 1990, Fasc. 2.

TOLLEY, GEORGE ET AL. "Establishing and Valuing the Effects of Improved Visibility in Eastern United States." Prepared for the U.S. Environmental Protection Agency, Washington, DC, 1986a.

_____. *Valuation of reductions in human health symptoms and risks.* Final Report for the U.S. Environmental Protection Agency. U. of Chicago, 1986b.

TRAVIS, CURTIS AND DOTY, CAROLYN. "Superfund: A Program Without Priorities," *Environmental Science and Technology*, 1989, *23*(11), pp. 1333–34.

TRIJONIS, J. ET AL. "Air Quality Benefits for Los Angeles and San Francisco Based on Housing Values and Visibility." Final Report for California Air Resources Board, Sacramento, CA, 1984.

TURVEY, RALPH. "On Divergences between Social Cost and Private Cost," *Economica*, Aug. 1963, *30*(119), pp. 309–13.

U.S. ENVIRONMENTAL PROECTION AGENCY. "EPA's Use of Benefit-Cost Analysis: 1981–1986." Aug. 1987, EPA Report 230–05–87–028.

_____. "Environmental Investments: The Cost of a Clean Environment." Dec. 1990, EPA Report 230–12–90–084.

U.S. GENERAL ACCOUNTING OFFICE. *Energy issues.* Washington, DC, Nov. 1988.

U.S. NATIONAL OCEANIC AND ATMOSPHERIC ADMINISTRATION, NATIONAL SCIENCE FOUNDATION, AND NATIONAL AERONAUTICS AND SPACE ADMINISTRATION. *Economic and global change, New Haven Workshop, May 1990.* Washington, DC, Jan. 1991.

VAUGHAN, WILLIAM J. AND RUSSELL, CLIFFORD S. "Valuing a Fishing Day: An Application of a Systematic Varying Parameter Model," *Land Econ.*, Nov. 1982, *58*(4), pp. 450–63.

VISCUSI, W. KIP; MAGAT, WESLEY A. AND HUBERT, JOEL. "Pricing Environmental Health Risks: Survey Assessments of Risk-Risk and Risk-Dollar Tradeoffs," in *AERE workshop proceedings: Estimating and valuing morbidity in a policy context*, 1988.

WALTER, INGO. "Pollution and Protection: U.S. Environmental Controls as Competitive Distortions," *Weltwirtsch. Arch.*, 1974, *110*(1), pp. 104–13.

_____. "Trade, Environment and Comparative Advantage," in *International economics of pollution.* Ed.: INGO WALTER. NY: Wiley, 1975, pp. 77–93.

_____. "Environmentally Induced Industrial Relocation in Developing Countries," in *Environment and trade.* Eds.: SEYMOUR J. RUBIN AND THOMAS R. GRAHAM. Totowa, NJ: Allanheld, Osmun, and

Co., 1982, pp. 67–101.

WALTER, INGO AND UGELOW, JUDITH. "Environmental Policies in Developing Countries," *Ambio*, 1979, *8*(2,3), pp. 102–09.

WEITZMAN, MARTIN L. "Prices vs. Quantities," *Rev. Econ. Stud.*, Oct. 1974, *41*(4), pp. 477–91.

————. "Optimal Rewards for Economic Regulation," *Amer. Econ. Rev.*, Sept. 1978, *68*(4), pp. 683–91.

WENDERS, JOHN T. "Methods of Pollution Control and the Rate of Change in Pollution Abatement Technology," *Water Resources Res.*, 1975, *11*(3), pp. 393–96.

WHITEHEAD, JOHN C. AND BLOMQUIST, GLENN C. "Measuring Contingent Values for Wetlands: Effects of Information About Related Environmental Goods," *Water Resources Research*, Oct. 1991, 27(10). pp. 2523–31.

WILDASIN, DAVID E. "Interjurisdictional Capital Mobility: Fiscal Externality and a Corrective Subsidy," *J. Urban Econ.*, Mar. 1989, 25(2), pp. 193–212.

WILLIG, ROBERT D. "Consumer's Surplus Without Apology," *Amer. Econ. Rev.*, Sept. 1976, *66*(4), pp. 589–97.

WILSON, JOHN D. "A Theory of Interregional Tax Competition," *J. Urban Econ.*, May 1086, *19*(3), pp. 296–315.

ZODROW, GEORGE R. AND MIESZKOWSKI, PETER. "Pigou, Tiebout, Property Taxation and the Under-Provision of Local Public Goods," *J. Urban Econ.*, May 1986, *19*(3), pp. 356–70.

ZUPAN, JEFFREY. *The distribution of air quality in the New York region.* Washington, DC: Resources for the Future, 1973.

Author index

Economists of the Twentieth Century

Monetarism and Macroeconomic
Policy
Thomas Mayer

Studies in Fiscal Federalism
Wallace E. Oates

The World Economy in Perspective
Essays in International Trade and European
Integration
Herbert Giersch

Towards a New Economics
Critical Essays on Ecology, Distribution and
Other Themes
Kenneth E. Boulding

Studies in Positive and Normative
Economics
Martin J. Bailey

The Collected Essays of Richard E.
Quandt (2 volumes)
Richard E. Quandt

International Trade Theory and Policy
Selected Essays of W. Max Corden
W. Max Corden

Organization and Technology in Capitalist
Development
William Lazonick

Studies in Human Capital
Collected Essays of Jacob Mincer, Volume 1
Jacob Mincer

Studies in Labor Supply
Collected Essays of Jacob Mincer, Volume 2
Jacob Mincer

Macroeconomics and Economic Policy
The Selected Essays of Assar Lindbeck,
Volume I
Assar Lindbeck

The Welfare State
The Selected Essays of Assar Lindbeck,
Volume II
Assar Lindbeck

Classical Economics, Public Expenditure
and Growth
Walter Eltis

Money, Interest Rates and Inflation
Frederic S. Mishkin

The Public Choice Approach to Politics
Dennis C. Mueller

The Liberal Economic Order
Volume I Essays on International Economics
Volume II Money, Cycles and Related Themes
Gottfried Haberler
Edited by Anthony Y.C. Koo

Economic Growth and Business Cycles
Prices and the Process of Cyclical Development
Paolo Sylos Labini

International Adjustment, Money and
Trade
Theory and Measurement for Economic Policy,
Volume I
Herbert G. Grubel

International Capital and Service Flows
Theory and Measurement for Economic Policy,
Volume II
Herbert G. Grubel

Unintended Effects of Government
Policies
Theory and Measurement for Economic Policy,
Volume III
Herbert G. Grubel

The Economics of Competitive Enterprise
Selected Essays of P.W.S. Andrews
*Edited by Frederic S. Lee
and Peter E. Earl*

The Repressed Economy
Causes, Consequences, Reform
Deepak Lal

Economic Theory and Market Socialism
Selected Essays of Oskar Lange
Edited by Tadeusz Kowalik

Trade, Development and Political
Economy
Selected Essays of Ronald Findlay
Ronald Findlay

General Equilibrium Theory
The Collected Essays of Takashi Negishi,
Volume I
Takashi Negishi

The History of Economics
The Collected Essays of Takashi Negishi,
Volume II
Takashi Negishi

Studies in Econometric Theory
The Collected Essays of Takeshi Amemiya
Takeshi Amemiya

Exchange Rates and the Monetary System
Selected Essays of Peter B. Kenen
Peter B. Kenen

Econometric Methods and Applications
(2 volumes)
G.S. Maddala

National Accounting and Economic
Theory
The Collected Papers of Dan Usher, Volume I
Dan Usher

Welfare Economics and Public Finance
The Collected Papers of Dan Usher, Volume II
Dan Usher

Economic Theory and Capitalist Society
The Selected Essays of Shigeto Tsuru, Volume I
Shigeto Tsuru

Methodology, Money and the Firm
The Collected Essays of D.P. O'Brien
(2 volumes)
D.P. O'Brien

Economic Theory and Financial Policy
The Selected Essays of Jacques J. Polak
(2 volumes)
Jacques J. Polak

Sturdy Econometrics
Edward E. Leamer

The Emergence of Economic Ideas
Essays in the History of Economics
Nathan Rosenberg

Productivity Change, Public Goods and
Transaction Costs
Essays at the Boundaries of Microeconomics
Yoram Barzel

Reflections on Economic Development
The Selected Essays of Michael P. Todaro
Michael P. Todaro

The Economic Development of Modern
Japan
The Selected Essays of Shigeto Tsuru,
Volume II
Shigeto Tsuru

Money, Credit and Policy
Allan H. Meltzer

Macroeconomics and Monetary Theory
The Selected Essays of Meghnad Desai,
Volume I
Meghnad Desai

Poverty, Famine and Economic
Development
The Selected Essays of Meghnad Desai,
Volume II
Meghnad Desai

Explaining the Economic Performance of Natio
Essays in Time and Space
Angus Maddison

Economic Doctrine and Method
Selected Papers of R.W. Clower
Robert W. Clower

Economic Theory and Reality
Selected Essays on their Disparities and
Reconciliation
Tibor Scitovsky

Doing Economic Research
Essays on the Applied Methodology of
Economics
Thomas Mayer

Institutions and Development Strategies
The Selected Essays of Irma Adelman,
Volume I
Irma Adelman

Dynamics and Income Distribution
The Selected Essays of Irma Adelman,
Volume II
Irma Adelman

The Economics of Growth and
Development
Selected Essays of A.P. Thirlwall
A.P. Thirlwall

Theoretical and Applied Econometrics
The Selected Papers of Phoebus J. Dhrymes
Phoebus J. Dhrymes

Innovation, Technology and the Economy
The Selected Essays of Edwin Mansfield
(2 volumes)
Edwin Mansfield

Economic Theory and Policy in Context
The Selected Essays of R.D. Collison Black
R.D. Collison Black

Location Economics
Theoretical Underpinnings and Applications
Melvin L. Greenhut

Spatial Microeconomics
Theoretical Underpinnings and Applications
Melvin L. Greenhut

Capitalism, Socialism and Post-
Keynesianism
Selected Essays of G.C. Harcourt
G.C. Harcourt

Time Series Analysis and
Macroeconometric Modelling
The Collected Papers of Kenneth F. Wallis
Kenneth F. Wallis

Foundations of Modern Econometrics
The Selected Essays of Ragnar Frisch
(2 volumes)
Edited by Olav Bjerkholt

Growth, the Environment and the
Distribution of Incomes
Essays by a Sceptical Optimist
Wilfred Beckerman

The Economics of Environmental
Regulation
Wallace E. Oates

Econometrics, Macroeconomics and
Economic Policy
Selected Papers of Carl F. Christ
Carl F. Christ

Economic Analysis and Political Ideology
The Selected Essays of Karl Brunner,
Volume One
Edited by Thomas Lys